American Government

A Comparative Approach

CHARLES W. DUNN
MARTIN W. SLANN

Clemson University

 HarperCollins*CollegePublishers*

To Carol and Ruth

Acquisitions Editor: Maria Hartwell
Development Editor: Jinny Joyner
Project Editor: David Nickol
Design Supervisor/Text Design: Heather A. Ziegler
Cover Design: Heather A. Ziegler
Cover Photo: Comstock Inc.
Photo Researcher: Leslie Coopersmith
Production Manager/Assistant: Willie Lane/Sunaina Sehwani
Compositor: Ruttle, Shaw & Wetherill, Inc.
Printer and Binder: R. R. Donnelley & Sons Company
Cover Printer: The Lehigh Press, Inc.

For permission to use copyrighted material, grateful acknowledgement is made to the copyright holders on pp. C-1, which is hereby made part of this copyright page.

American Government: A Comparative Approach

Library of Congress Cataloging-in-Publication Data

Dunn, Charles W.
    American government : a comparative approach / Charles Wythe Dunn, Martin Slann.
      p. cm.
    ISBN 0-06-041812-5
    1. United States—Politics and government.   2. Comparative government.   I. Slann, Martin W.   II. Title.
JK274.D83   1994
320.973—dc20   93-25484
                                                           CIP

98 99 00 01 9 8 7 6 5 4

CONTENTS

reference

CHAPTER EIGHT   ★ POLITICAL PARTIES   249

- reference

CHAPTER NINE   ★ VOTING, CAMPAIGNS,
AND ELECTIONS   291

CHAPTER FIFTEEN   ★   THE POLITICS OF THE POLICY PROCESS   557

PREFACE

OBJECTIVES

The primary purpose of this text is to teach students how their government works. Thus, the book covers all the traditional American government topics in a brief but comprehensible way. But we have a secondary—and no less important—purpose in writing this book: we also want students to *think* about how government works. That is why we have incorporated the following in each chapter: (1) an extensive section that analyzes the pros and cons of controversial issues in American political life and (2) a section that makes direct comparisons with the political systems of other nations.

Critical thinking, a topic of much concern today, is a prime goal of the "Issues to Analyze" section. Students learn that politics and government necessarily involve choices, and they also learn that many problems have no easy solutions. It is our hope that students will read and think critically, not passively. Teachers can use these issues to stimulate class discussion and to reinforce the students' understanding of the fundamentals of American government.

The comparative perspective has not been a traditional element in the American government course. Yet how else is the student to learn what makes the American system of government unique? Or why it has endured for more than 200 years, longer than that of any other country? We want our readers to grasp the common features of democratic governments that distinguish them from totalitarian and authoritarian systems. We also want them to be aware of how a presidential system differs from a parliamentary form of government, a bicameral legislature from a unicameral one, a federal government from a centralized system, a single member district from proportional representation, the two-party system from a multiparty system, and so on. They should have not only an awareness of these differences but also an understanding of their consequences in how government functions.

An appreciation of the uniqueness of the American form of governing is not the only goal of the comparative approach. There is another reason to look at the way other nations govern themselves: The United States is no longer an isolated world power. What our country does in its national political life continues to have impact beyond its borders, but the same is now true for the actions of other nations. The Muslim fundamentalist movement, for example, is driving the forms of government and governing philosophies in many Middle Eastern nations. The struggles for democratization in formerly communist countries have changed the balances of power in the world. Just one nation's trade policy, such as Japan's, can have a global economic effect. Sharpened ethnic identification is wreaking havoc in many parts of the world. Unless Americans understand these processes and these changes, they won't be able to function effectively in the international arena.

The comparative approach, then, actually helps clarify the subject of American government by putting it in context and pinpointing its distinguishing features. It also enriches the student's knowledge and enhances his or her appreciation for the way government works.

In these times of global change, America is increasingly defined by what is going on elsewhere. Yet the course about the government most responsible for, and influenced by, changes in the world has been sadly silent on the subject. By rights, the American government course should be in the *vanguard* of curriculum internationalization. This book is intended to respond to that urgent need.

Gaining geographic literacy is yet another important byproduct of the comparative approach. Geographic illiteracy, of course, is frequently cited as a serious problem among America's college students. To combat this critical problem, *American Government: A Comparative Approach* naturally makes extensive use of maps, tables, charts, and diagrams with geographic and demographic data.

ORGANIZATION

One overriding concern in preparing this book was to make it easy for professors to teach and for students to learn. The first chapter introduces the comparative approach by describing in general terms the democratic, totalitarian, and authoritarian governmental systems and focusing on distinguishing features of the American style of government.

The fourteen chapters that follow cover traditional topics in a standard sequence, but every chapter reflects a uniform format to aid students in conceptually integrating the subject. This streamlined format keeps the reader focused and alert to what is coming next in the chapter:

- The first section discusses the fundamentals of American government.
- The second section presents in a debate format issues to analyze about American government.
- The third section provides comparisons with other nations, based on loose categorizations of democratic, totalitarian, and authoritarian systems.

Of moderate length, *American Government: A Comparative Approach* is designed for a one-semester or one-quarter American government course. The format is flexible, so that a teacher can take up chapters in a different order to adapt the text to his or her own style.

PEDAGOGICAL AIDS

The "Issues to Analyze" sections, as noted above, provide ready-made discussions to encourage critical thinking. Many professors require a supplementary text to accomplish this, but our text is self-contained, providing a savings bonus for students. There are, in addition, numerous pedagogical aids throughout the book:

- Boxes entitled "A View from the States" and "A View from Abroad" present the political observations of American and foreign journalists and officials.
- Pertinent tables, maps, and graphs are used throughout the book. Many are of a comparative nature.
- Chapter outlines, summaries, key terms, and suggested readings are found in each chapter.
- The backmatter includes a glossary, the U.S. Constitution, and the Declaration of Independence.

SUPPLEMENTS

The following supplements are also available from HarperCollins:

- *Instructor's Manual* by the authors, Charles Dunn and Martin Slann.
- *Study Guide* by Joseph Bristow of County College of Morris.
- *Test Bank* (paper version, and computerized *TestMaster* for IBM and compatibles) by Jacqueline Vaughn Switzer of Southern Oregon State University.
- *Democracy in Action: American Government Computer Simulations* (IBM and compatibles and MacIntosh versions).

ACKNOWLEDGMENTS

The authors would like to thank the following political scientists for reviewing the manuscript of *American Government: A Comparative Approach.* Their help was invaluable in preparing the final product. Our thanks go to

Peter Bergerson, Southeastern Missouri State University

Joseph Bristow, County College of Morris

Charlie Burke, Baldwin-Wallace College

William Carroll, Sam Houston State University

Shirley Chapman, East Tennessee State University

Suzan Cheek, Methodist College

John Csomor, North Georgia College

Gerald De Maio, Baruch College

Jane Elza, Valdosta State University

Dennis Goldford, Drake University

Gregory Goodwin, Bakersfield College

George Gordon, Illinois State University

Roger Govea, Cleveland State University

Forrest Grieves, University of Montana

Michael Johnston, Colgate University

Margaret Langford, El Paso Community College

Judith Mack, Columbia University

Carroll McKibbin, California Polytechnic State University

James S. Magee, Eastern Michigan University

Curtis Reithel, University of Wisconsin-La Crosse

J. L. Renneker, Francis Marion University

James R. Soles, University of Delaware

Jackie Switzer, Southern Oregon State College

David Warren, University of Rhode Island

Jonathan West, University of Miami

Several persons and organizations have made invaluable contributions to *American Government: A Comparative Approach*. First, no publishing house has ever been more professional and helpful to us on any of our books than HarperCollins has been on this one. Among the staff who have contributed so much to the book's development are Acquisitions Editor Maria Hartwell, Director of Development Art Pomponio, Project Editor David Nickol, Marketing Manager Suzanne Daghlian, Photo Researcher Leslie Coopersmith, Editorial Assistant Ashley Chase, and former Executive Editor Lauren Silverman. We would especially single out here for her crucial contribution to the quality of the manuscript Developmental Editor Jinny Joyner, who provided heartfelt inspiration, keen intellect, and hard work. Second, the ideas and inspiration of Professors William Lasser and Dave Woodard, and the encouragement of our Department Head Tim O'Rourke are deeply appreciated. Third, the Earhart Foundation provided timely assistance during a crucial stage of the book's development. Fourth, three secretaries merit special mention for their invaluable assistance, Kim Gibby, Angie Newell, and Sharon Fletcher.

Many have helped give birth to this book. Now it must stand on its own as a comprehensive approach to American government in an increasingly integrated global society.

Charles W. Dunn
Martin W. Slann

American Government

CHAPTER ★ ONE

AN INTRODUCTION TO THE COMPARATIVE APPROACH

Government's ancestry can be traced back about 8000 years to the beginnings of written history. The institution of government coincided with the development of agriculture and the establishment of permanent settlements that eventually became cities. Since this first appearance of government its goal has been clear: to achieve a rational degree of order for society's members to enjoy a maximum degree of physical security. This is not easily accomplished. American society in this sense is not different from any other. During the debate over the ratification of the new constitution in 1787 Alexander Hamilton noted "that it seems to have reserved to the people of this country to decide the important question, whether societies . . . are really capable or not of establishing good government from reflection and choice, or whether they are forever destined to depend for their constitutions on accident and force."[1]

Government, good or otherwise, is the result of politics. A large proportion of people who think about politics at all come to the hasty and dismal conclusion that it is a corrupting, hypocritical, and debasing business. They are right. But they are wrong if that is *all* they believe politics is. Politics is not inevitably any of those things. Rather, politics is a common feature of all human society that "arises from accepting the fact of the simultaneous existence of different groups, hence different interests and different traditions within a territory ruled."[2]

Politics may be defined in a variety of ways. One of the most famous and widely accepted definitions is that offered by the distinguished political scientist Harold Lasswell, who succinctly declared politics to be the activity of deciding "who gets what, when, and how." More recently, another respected political scientist, David Easton, defined politics as "the authoritative allocation of values." In its current manifestations, politics has been an important vehicle for determining nonmaterial and at times very intimate personal values as well. Whether to insist on prayers in public schools, whether English should be the official language, and whether to forbid homosexuals from serving in the military are all dilemmas that have been turned over to the political process for evaluation and resolution. More and more aspects of our lives have become political issues.

What both Lasswell and Easton were getting at was that **politics** is the method by which societies decide how to allocate values and distribute valued resources that are usually in short supply. When we view politics this way, we can see that it is not an isolated activity that occurs only in national capitals such as London, Washington, Moscow, or Tokyo. Politics is a common feature of daily human existence that occurs wherever and whenever decisions are made about "who shall get what, when, and how." Politics may take a variety of forms, some of which may be familiar and desirable to us and others of which may not.

The American governmental system and the play of politics within it are important to us not only for how they affect our nation but also for their effect on other nations. Most of the rest of the world watches the dynamics of American politics almost as eagerly as they consume American-style food, listen to American rock music, and wear American designer jeans. Within days after the 1992 presidential election, President-elect Bill Clinton was receiving phone calls from a variety of foreign leaders. Western Europeans wanted to talk to him about tariffs, Russian President Yeltsin about possible loans for economic development, and Arab and Israeli leaders about their stalled peace talks. In a global economy in which the United States plays a vital part we must constantly deal with other nations, including many whose political and social values are markedly different from our own. The tremendous and unprecedented political changes that recently took place in the former Soviet Union and Eastern Europe, for example, depended to a substantial degree on how we viewed and supported them.

If we as a nation are to prosper in the twenty-first century we will have to learn to cope with fundamental global changes already well under way. Some people find these changes threatening. They worry that the United States is becoming an economic colony. To an extent they have a point: Other countries, led by the United Kingdom, the Netherlands, and Japan, have heavily invested in the American economy. During the 1980s foreign investment in the United States increased from $90 billion to $304 billion. Hondas and Toyotas seem to outnumber Fords and Chevrolets on our highways. But what does this really portend? We can answer such a question only after we learn more about those countries whose governments and corporations are becoming a steadily increasing part of their own economy.

In short, what other societies are like and what their governments do are also important to us. It is impractical even to try to escape economic, political, and techno-

The United States is linked to other parts of the world today through treaties, trade, multinational corporations, as well as the minutiae of everyday life, like the kinds of clothes we wear. The American passion for jeans, for example, is matched by the Japanese.

logical interaction with other countries. It is also naive, especially for Americans. After all, we belong to a small (and still endangered) political species: We are only one of 30 or so full-fledged democracies, outnumbered by about 130 dissimilar and occasionally maniacal regimes. But whether other nations have democratic systems, are developing them, or remain firmly undemocratic, we share the same planet and at least some of the same problems on the planet.

This chapter attempts to set the tone for the remainder of the text by suggesting that the American political system can be fully understood only when placed in the context of our own and others' political experience. As our world opens up through a global economy, technology, and politics, it no longer makes much sense to try to understand the workings of American government without also understanding what is going on elsewhere.

WHAT IS GOVERNMENT?

Although often mentioned in one breath, politics and government are not the same thing. Politics, as we have defined it above, can and does occur outside of government. Similarly, politics may (and usually does) involve nongovernmental as well as governmental actors. For instance, the head of government in the United States (the president) will normally consult with staff and cabinet officials before making a political decision, but may just as easily consult with old friends, political allies and even former political foes, and family members who don't have official status or are not well known to the public. Jimmy Carter's administration (1977–1981), for example, became known as a "Mom and Pop" presidency since his closest and most trusted political advisor seemed to be Mrs. Carter. President Bush (1989–1993) and his successor, Bill Clinton, both regarded their wives as important political assets. Hillary Clinton, in fact, played a significant role in domestic policymaking in her husband's administration even before he was inaugurated, since she actively participated in the selection of important government appointments during the transition process between the election and the inauguration.[3] President John F. Kennedy (1961–1963) relied heavily on his brother, Attorney General Robert Kennedy, who was also his longtime campaign manager.

Most of us, though, don't much care how policy is made as long as it is done in a rational and humane fashion. **Government**, then, may be defined simply as the formal social instrument through which conflicts that arise among individuals or groups are partially or wholly resolved. The primary purpose of the ideal government is to manage and resolve conflict, providing security and continuance for both society and its members, and to generally improve our collective existence. In great part this is done through politics. Thus, politics is the activity of making allocation decisions, while government is generally the structure through which these decisions are made, implemented, and enforced.

Of course, governments differ in the *methods* they employ to manage conflict. Ideally, those methods will be based on some popularly approved and universally applicable set of principles. While it is true that there must be politicians for there to be politics, it is also true that there must be rules to guide the one and monitor the other. **Laws** are the basis of politics. There can be no legitimate politics without freedom and there is no freedom without laws that allow for no exceptions. The importance of laws was recognized (reluctantly) by the Greek philosopher Plato (427–347 B.C.), even though he preferred governance by all-knowing, all-wise philosopher-kings whose native genius required no laws to reach important decisions. As Plato gradually understood, true philosopher-kings are in short supply. This is a pity, but their absence forces on us a dire responsibility: the establishment and maintenance of lawful government.

Government, then, is a creation of necessity. We are simply better off with it than without it. Government exists because we understandably desire the protection and services it promises to provide. Even as the American system of government was being formulated, James Madison argued in *Federalist Paper 51* that "in framing a government which is to be administered by men over men, the great difficulty lies in this: you must first enable the government to control the governed; and in the next place to oblige it to control itself." Ideally, both are achieved through a political process that is open and competitive, in which the citizenry clearly recognizes its political obligations.

WHAT GOVERNMENTS DO

Allocating Scarce Values: The Decision-Making Process

Consider a brief fantasy: We enjoy the good fortune of living in a veritable Garden of Eden, in which government is unnecessary since everybody has everything he or she wants. End of fantasy.

Government is involved in the distribution of resources, but it doesn't always work out in an even-handed way. At a campaign speech in the 1992 primary, this New Hampshire resident let President George Bush know how his state was faring.

The reality is that most of what we want has the disconcerting habit of being in short supply or expensive or in dispute, or all three. It has fallen to government to serve the often thankless task of allocating or distributing resources we all want and of which there are never enough. For example, health care is an increasingly expensive service that a growing number of societies can't afford and that is only unevenly available in many developing countries.

The problem is that governments, even relatively good ones, do not always distribute resources in a completely fair or even-handed way. The extent to which they do or do not allocate resources equally to all members of society is one of the significant ways in which governments differ. Regardless of the outcome of their efforts, however, all governments are necessarily involved in the distribution of resources. It is one of their basic functions.

Managing Social Conflict

A second major function of government is to manage social conflict. The English political philosopher Thomas Hobbes (1588–1679) saw government's primary task as that of preventing the "war of all against all," which he believed to be the natural state of affairs in the absence of government. Under such circumstances, life could only be "nasty, brutish, and short."

Avoiding such a scenario, Hobbes argued, was so important that it more than justified the inevitable trade-offs associated with the existence of government, particularly the limitation of individual freedoms. In Hobbes's view, for example, it was not wise for governments to allow too much dissent. He believed very strongly that expressing opinions is not always a good idea. Too many ignorant people have them, Hobbes argued. And it is certainly stupid to quarrel about uninformed opinions. As Hobbes knew firsthand, strongly held and expressed opinions that come in the guise of extreme religious or political convictions can destroy a society. This almost happened in Hobbes's England in the 1640s and in the United States in the 1860s. It did happen in Lebanon after 1975 and in Yugoslavia in the early 1990s.

How extensive should the limits be that governments place on their citizens? The issue is an endlessly debated one. Governments cannot be completely blamed for acting in their own interest. However, from the American point of view a government should be (and in democracies is constitutionally obligated to be) sensitive to at least the basic needs of the individual citizen. Remember, too, that some conflicts are probably incapable of being resolved (religious differences in Northern Ireland provide an all too obvious example). "Lebanonization"—fragmentation along the ethnic and religious lines suffered by Lebanon—is a distinct possibility for a large number of societies that suffer from ethnic or religious divisions that are too deep to heal effectively or permanently.

Democratic government must necessarily be vigilant about protecting every individual's essential freedoms, such as freedom of speech and assembly. In the United States the Constitution insists on this. Government must also enforce the law. This is often easier said than done. "States cannot choose their citizens," one scholar has written, "and, in the nature of things, all states will have to deal with a percentage of criminally inclined, unreasonable and selfish members of the population."[4] This is the reason most of us prefer government to exist even with its flaws.

Enhancing the Citizenry's Quality of Life

A third function of government is to enhance the lives of its citizens. Successful societies like to boast about low infant mortality rates, high literacy levels, extended life spans, and the like. They are also fond of making encouraging and often optimistic projections. When governmental agencies do this, of course, it often takes the form of self-congratulations. By 2035, for example, the United States and other Western societies expect their community of octogenarians to triple, making people over 80 the largest-growing demographic age group. Governments like to take credit (sometimes deserved) for this sort of thing.

They also receive (usually deserved) the blame when something goes wrong. One reason the Soviet Union became obsessed with self-examination in the mid-1980s is that its quality of life had steadily deteriorated over the previous two decades. It was the only modern industrialized society in the world, for instance, that had experienced a *decline* in average life expectancy. To a Soviet citizen standing in line for hours at a time to purchase a loaf of bread, it was little comfort to be told that the Soviet military was achieving parity with that of the United States. Of more immediate interest was whether meat, bread, and milk would be available when the person reached the head of the line.

Throughout the twentieth century government has taken on an ever increasing amount of responsibilities for at least two reasons: (1) we want government to do more and more for us (even though we are reluctant to pay for additional services through

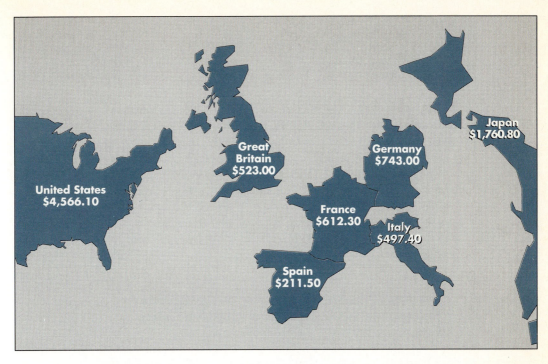

Figure 1.1 REDRAWING THE MAP: ECONOMICALLY PROSPEROUS NATIONS. The relative sizes of various nations are based on the sizes of their economies. The number below each country name is the level of its gross domestic product for 1991, in billions of constant dollars. Source: "Redrawing the Map," from *The New York Times,* September 8, 1992. Copyright © 1992 The New York Times Company. Reprinted by permission.

increased taxation), and (2) government is able to do more because of modern technology and increased (if unevenly distributed) economic prosperity.

    With some exceptions, governments are evaluated by the citizenry on the basis of how well their lives are enhanced by comfort and security. When living standards deteriorate, so does confidence in government. Economic downturns in the United States ensured the denial of a second term for Presidents Jimmy Carter and George Bush. By the 1990s the three dozen or so nations of North America, non-Communist East Asia, and Western Europe accounted for more than three-quarters of the world's gross national product, even though their populations totaled less than one-fifth of the people on this planet (see Figure 1.1). That left the large majority of the world's people in poorer circumstances and no doubt unhappy with their governments.

    And, as the box suggests, it left them unhappy with the cost of living. It's a lot cheaper for a citizen to purchase a hamburger in Chicago, Toronto, Tokyo, Paris, or London (all major cities in prosperous countries) than in Mexico City, Bombay, Lagos, and Kuala Lumpur (all major cities in relatively unprosperous countries).

    Most Western countries are established or at least fledgling democracies. They are allies of and trading partners with the United States. They are also among the most stable political societies in the world. Their citizenries generally support their govern-

A VIEW FROM ABROAD
The Cost of a Big Mac: Relative Earnings

The Economist's "Big Mac Index" is a useful guide to real exchange rates. Now the Union Bank of Switzerland has used the McDonald's burger to compare earnings around the world. The bank used a weighted average of earnings in 12 jobs—ranging from machinist to department manager—to calculate how long it takes the average worker to earn the price of a Big Mac and large french fries. By this measure, the best-paid workers are in Chicago, where it takes only 18 minutes to earn a Big Mac. Compare that with Mexico City, where workers have to labor for almost four hours to earn their bite. Union Bank does not include Moscow where, says our correspondent, a Big Mac costs locals almost two days' pay.

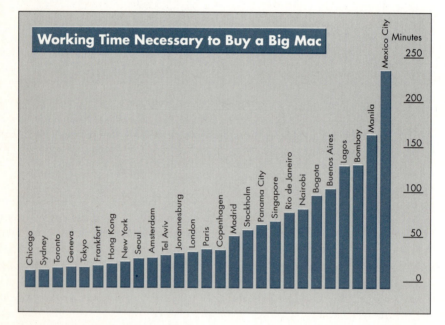

Working Time Necessary to Buy a Big Mac

Source: Union Bank of Switzerland.

ments, mostly because of the extent to which the governments have fostered prosperity. Of course, material well-being is not the only criterion for evaluating governmental performance. It is, however, a good indicator of how much confidence governments place in their citizenries. A government that does not encourage access to economic resources will not be inclined to encourage access to political resources.

SOME COMMON FORMS OF GOVERNMENT

Now that we have an idea of what government is or does, we can take a look at the various forms a government can take. Probably the earliest systematic scheme for categorizing government was devised by Aristotle (384–322 B.C.). He correctly assumed that those regimes that rule on behalf of the entire citizenry are doing their job and deserve to endure; those that don't are not doing their job and deserve to fail. Thus, he classified each of six forms of government as either "pure" or "corrupt" (Table 1.1). This scheme summarizes Aristotle's study of 150 Greek city-state constitutions. (He didn't bother about non-Greek ones since he considered them barbaric and therefore unworthy of inclusion.) The pure regimes always rule for the entire citizenry's benefit; the corrupt ones (mis)rule on behalf of the interests of one, a few, or a mob.

Like Aristotle, we will find it convenient to divide current political regimes into three general but descriptive categories: (1) modern democracy, (2) totalitarian regimes, and (3) authoritarian regimes

Modern Democracy

For most of us, democracy is the type of government with which we are most familiar. Because of this, we tend to view it as normal, not to mention highly desirable. It is well to realize, however, that not everyone would agree with that assessment today.

This was even more true in the past. Plato, for example, believed in the desirability of a "just" government, but he did not favor democracy. Plato had his reasons. In his best and most memorable work, *The Republic*, Plato indicates his dislike and distrust of democracy's permissiveness:

> It exhibits a fine lack of concern for all the requirements we so painstakingly set forth when founding our city. It scorns our judgment that in the absence of transcendent gifts no man can become a good man unless from childhood on his play and all his activities are guided by what is fair and good. All these things are trampled underfoot; the democratic city cares nothing for the past behavior of the man who enters public life. He need only proclaim himself a friend of the people, and he will be honored.[5]

Plato's views notwithstanding, democracy has endured. Its history extends back for two and a half millennia, beginning with some Greek city-states. Early democracies,

TABLE 1.1 Aristotelian Forms of Government		
Number of Rulers	Pure	Corrupt
One	King	Tyrant
Few	Aristocracy	Oligarchy
Many	Democracy	Mobocracy

like contemporary ones, were imperfect. One scholar, for example, has documented that in Athens, the most successful of the ancient Greek experiments in democracy, fewer than one in five of the city's population enjoyed full political participation.[6] But imperfections are really democratic virtues. It is only through trial and error that democracy has advanced to its present state. In our society civil liberties are legally denied only to convicted felons. When politics is played out in democracies, the scene often appears to be chaotic, yet order usually results from this apparent chaos. Our experience with democracy provides some basic ingredients for a definition: **Democracy** is a form of government that is created by and is responsible to the people it serves and that ensures, among other things, that civil liberties are equally applied, laws are adhered to by all of society's members, and political leaders are chosen through regularly scheduled and competitive elections in which all adult citizens may participate.

It is important to keep in mind that democracies are neither created nor sustained in the same way, nor do they have identical political practices. While all democracies are strongly and legally committed to guaranteeing and protecting individual rights, some inconsistencies exist among the forms this takes. The death penalty, for example, has been abolished by all democracies except one—the United States. And as of 1992, the United States was the only industrialized democracy to lack a comprehensive national health insurance program. While all democracies are quite protective of religious freedom (with understandable constitutional curtailment of fire worshipers, snake handlers, and polygamists), a formal and tax-supported state church exists in the United Kingdom and the Scandinavian countries.

Neither the process nor the term *democratization* is neatly defined. We know that countries having little or no experience with democracy can apparently adapt easily to it. The Germans and Japanese did this after 1945 (with both assistance and insistence from the United States). Their enforced adoption of democracy occurred even in the face of strong traditions of autocracy and militarism. Most modern democracies, though, are the product of a gradual evolutionary process. The roots of British parliamentary democracy, for instance, can, with little exaggeration, be traced back nearly a millennium. The United States and other democracies have progressed dramatically over two centuries by gradually extending the franchise to adult citizens regardless of their religion, economic standing, gender, or race. While democratic societies have democratized, however imperfectly, at different rates over time, all such societies are readily identifiable.

How to Distinguish a Democratic Regime. Watch how civilians react when they see soldiers or police on the street. If there is no reaction, the civilians live in a democracy. However, if they trip over themselves to move to the side of the street or quickly go inside their homes, they probably do not.

Democratic regimes tend to be more self-assured than nondemocratic ones. In other words, they don't worry about coups or mass uprisings. It is interesting to note that democratic regimes rarely succumb to the lures of extremist politics. In fact, none have done so in at least a half-century. As the following list of characteristics suggests, democratic regimes are fairly easy to spot:

1. Civil liberties are widely enjoyed and constitutionally protected. Political issues often revolve around where civil liberties begin and end. The liberties themselves are not in question, only their boundaries.

One sign of a democratic regime is that citizens have access to the political decision makers. This New York City schoolteacher is one of thousands of New Yorkers who showed up at City Hall on a day that Mayor David Dinkins set aside to solicit citizen opinion and advice.

2. No ideology or theology is constitutionally endorsed over any other. There is, for example, widespread religious freedom in both the United Kingdom and the United States, even though the former does have a state church. Many Americans consider capitalism and individualism to be ideologies that compete with ideologies such as socialism or communism.

3. Regular elections, occasional turnover in government, and a general acceptance of the rules of the political game, including a willingness to accept both electoral victories and defeats gracefully, are recognized practices and standards.

4. There is an awareness that government neither is perfect nor claims to be. Thus, public inquiries into the activities of governmental agencies or personnel may result in an admission of mistakes or (more likely) a resignation from office. Both appointed and elected personnel usually find it necessary to tolerate close public scrutiny of both their public and private lives.

5. Citizens enjoy widespread access to the political decision-making process. Citizens can join political parties and interest groups (or start their own), write letters to editors, and even confront their elected representatives.

6. The law is applied as equally as circumstances allow to every citizen, including those who hold political office.

7. Strict control over the military is exercised by the civilian government. In

the United States, for instance, the president, a civilian, is the commander in chief of the armed forces.

Totalitarian Regimes

Governments that seek control over their citizens that is so extensive as to be nearly total are known as **totalitarian** systems. The best example of this type of government is the communist system. Historically, communist systems have sought (and, where possible, practiced) far more control over the lives of their citizens than either democratic or authoritarian systems. **Communism** may be defined as an economic and political system in which the entire society is coordinated and monitored by a government whose actions are both authorized and justified by a party that views itself as the only legitimate guarantor of the welfare of the working class.

Events in the late 1980s and early 1990s confirmed the economic and political shortcomings of communism, but the ideology has left its imprint and remains a still viable governmental form in several countries even today. The first communist state was established in 1917 in the country then known as Russia, and for the next 74 years as the Union of Soviet Socialist Republics (USSR), or Soviet Union. Proponents of communism have long insisted that communism is really the highest form of democracy. They maintain that only a communist society truly represents the interests of the working class—the only class that matters, according to communist doctrine. Typically, such a system is known as a **party state**: It is dominated by a single and unopposed Communist party on the grounds that other political movements are false and wasteful.

The chief characteristic shared by all communist regimes was their at least nominal acceptance of Marxist-Leninist ideology. This doctrine included a program of political and social revolution designed to establish a new society in which only the workers—the producers of wealth—would receive the benefits of their labor. The only employer would be the state. The Communist party invariably determines the political structure and practice of communist regimes.

By the late 1980s, however, many communist systems were in the midst of rapid, unprecedented, and occasionally fatal change. In several Eastern European countries it became embarrassing to be known as a member of the Communist party since the party had become correctly associated with economic incompetence, political ineptitude, and overall corruption. By 1989 the Poles and by 1990 the Czechoslovaks and Hungarians had elected noncommunist parliaments. From being the most politically rigid region in the world, Eastern Europe had within a period of several months become perhaps the least predictable.

We now understand that communism was neither monolithic (that is, uniform) nor very durable as a political system; its staying power in the twentieth century apparently is less than that of either authoritarianism or democracy. Much, of course, depends on the extent and nature of reform in the Commonwealth of Independent States (CIS), the successor to the Soviet Union. Before the three-day coup by communist hardliners in August 1991, the Soviet elite was divided into orthodox communists who thought reform was unnecessary or undesirable, moderates who seemed to be in at least temporary control, and intense reformers who believed that the Soviet economy and the communist system would be in serious jeopardy if wholesale administrative and political changes were not made quickly. Many of the latter, including Russian president Boris Yeltsin, had quit the

Communist party even before the coup, believing it to be hopelessly incapable of any meaningful reform. Orthodox communists were discredited after the coup, but there is still a debate within the CIS as to how and at what pace economic and political reform should proceed.

Totalitarian regimes have left an imprint on our century in great part because rapid technological advancements in communication and transportation made them possible. The National Socialist (Nazi) regime in Germany (1933–1945) and the Fascist regime in Italy (1922–1945) took full advantage of radio and film to attract and impress tens of millions of followers. During the 1930s the National Socialist leader, Adolf Hitler, was the first German politician to make extensive use of the airplane. Electronic and other technical devices enabled totalitarian governments to exert unprecedented control over the daily lives of their citizens.

How to Distinguish a Totalitarian Communist Regime. It is becoming difficult to find communist regimes, much less describe their characteristics with great accuracy, since the remaining ones are entering an unstable era. By the early 1990s a number of these totalitarian regimes had succumbed to demands for economic and/or political reforms that made them distinctly less communist. The United States became the acknowledged winner of the Cold War that pitted the Soviet Union against the Western World, but this acknowledgment may be slightly premature. Communist regimes, after all, still exist in the People's Republic of China, Cuba, and North Korea.

As the following list of characteristics suggests, totalitarian communist systems are highly organized:

为全面开创社会主义现代化建设的新局面而努力奋斗！

Citizens of China are constantly reminded of the authority and doctrine of their founding communist leader, Mao Tse-tung. The communist ideology permeates their entire life-style.

1. They all profess adherence to Marxist-Leninist doctrine, which in turn provides a basis for the regime's legitimacy. Often the doctrine is reinterpreted or revised by a founding communist leader. Stalin (1924–1953) in the Soviet Union, Mao Tse-tung (1949–1976) in China, Enver Hoxha (1945–1987) in Albania, and Ceausescu (1966–1989) in Romania are examples of Communist party general secretaries who enjoyed putting an "ism" after their names.

2. Communist party cadres are present at every level of political life. Insofar as is practical, most communist systems exclude other influences, such as church or civic groups.

3. An overwhelming bureaucracy oversees nearly every aspect of economic development. The bureaucracy itself is far from efficient and tends to be both competitive and duplicative since both state and party have their own apparatus.

4. The secret police are technologically sophisticated and ideologically motivated. In the early years of the regime the police are given wide powers since there is fear of counterrevolution (fear that is often well founded). The police can become even more important later on, as an aging general secretary becomes increasingly paranoid, although by then most of his real enemies are already dead. Only Stalin's death in 1953 saved the party from a purge similar to that in the late 1930s, which wiped out a third of its membership.

5. The people are indoctrinated into an entire life-style based on Marxist-Leninist ideology, which permeates every educational level and continues throughout one's career. Citizens are continuously extolled to be productive for the sake of building communism.

6. The citizen's first and ultimate loyalty is to the state as coordinated by the Communist party.

Authoritarian Regimes

A majority of governments today fall into the oldest category—authoritarian regimes. An authoritarian regime is less interested than a totalitarian one in controlling the daily lives of its citizens. Most authoritarian dictators are more concerned with personal enrichment, finding jobs for their relatives, and catering to those forces in the country that enable them to stay in power, such as the army or landed nobility. More than a hundred of these regimes are to be found in developing areas in Asia, Sub-Saharan Africa, the Middle East, and Latin America. Most, although certainly not all, govern poor countries. A small political elite dominates authoritarian regimes. Usually the leadership is unwilling to hold regular and fairly conducted elections, let alone accede to their outcome. We can define **authoritarianism** as an essentially pyramidal structure in which power filters down from and is ultimately monopolized by a small and privileged elite that permits no challenge to its political position, while allowing a degree of individual freedom in nonpolitical activities.

Although many authoritarian regimes do not place a high priority on serving their citizens, not all are malicious, or at least not intentionally so. Furthermore, not all despots are disliked. Some have the good fortune to die before they become unpopular. Gamal Abdul Nasser, who ruled Egypt from 1952 to 1970, probably could have won a free election if he had held one. Others, like Alfredo Stroessner (Paraguay's dictator between 1954 and 1989), neither die in timely fashion nor are measurably popular at any stage in their careers. Perhaps they last for seemingly interminable periods of time because, like Stroessner, they simply enjoy military parades that also serve the purpose of intimidating people with an unsubtle hint of violence. Generally, though, thugs like Stroessner leave people alone as long as they remain politically quiet.

A few dictators can become genuinely liked and respected. Kemal Ataturk took control of Turkey in the early 1920s and, until his death in 1938, insisted on secularizing and westernizing the country. And dictators may actually perform beneficial services for their country, but these services tend to be both temporary and intangible . Nasser, for instance, made Egyptians feel good about themselves (they considered him to be the first native Egyptian leader since Cleopatra), even while their already miserable standard of living deteriorated further. Ironically, a few dictators can actually create thriving economies and still be detested. Augusto Pinochet accomplished this double distinction in Chile between 1973 and 1989 after coming to power in a bloody coup.

The degree of authoritarianism will vary from one regime to another. In countries such as Brunei and Kuwait, which became extremely wealthy from oil export revenues, the royal families ensure both their own wealth and their political continuance by distributing a good part of their wealth to the rank-and-file citizenry. They often literally own the countries they rule. Before Iraq's invasion of Kuwait in 1990, for example, Kuwait's citizens generally received what amounted to free health care, housing, and education. When the royal family returned to Kuwait after Iraqi soldiers were driven out, it distributed money to Kuwaiti families to rebuild their looted and destroyed homes. The Kuwaitis thus have good reason to support a monarchical regime that had used its impressive financial resources to eliminate most poverty from the country. In other systems, such as Haiti, an insensitive and factionalized elite spent its time and the country's meager resources in often futile political maneuvers to stay in power, further impoverishing an already poor economy by completely ignoring the basic needs of the population.

How to distinguish an authoritarian regime. If you walk down the main avenue of a city and are greeted everywhere you look with huge portraits of a genial-looking father-figure, chances are you have stumbled into an authoritarian regime. In general, authoritarian governments base their legitimation on the personal qualities of a national leader or upon the simple and direct monopoly of political power. In authoritarian regimes elections are irregular, if they are even held at all; the political party system is either noncompetitive or nonexistent; and the press is generally censored. Here are some other characteristics of authoritarian regimes:

1. They are among the most unstable in the world; they are often succeeded by either a communist or democratic government. In 1986 the Marcos dictatorship was removed from the Philippines and replaced by a democratically elected government; in 1979 leftist rebels dislodged the Samoza regime in Nicaragua and replaced it with a Marxist-dominated government. In turn, it was replaced by a democratic government in 1990.

2. The military exerts a strong presence. Even a nominally civilian regime

Murals throughout Iraq extol the personal virtues of its dictator- president, Saddam Hussein. This mural in Baghdad depicts Hussein as the guardian of Iraq's military, industrial, and energy strengths.

can be installed by a clique of generals or colonels. This was certainly true in Panama, where General Manuel Noriega manufactured at least three different presidencies for his country before being removed from the country in 1989.

3.   They experience rampant corruption, which rarely brings down the government but contributes to a lack of public confidence. A high level of nepotism and corruption did lead to the demise of the Iranian monarchy in 1979.

4. They lack the level of institutionalization of authority usually found in communist and democratic societies. But the removal of an authoritarian government does not by itself ensure that the political system will become any more stable. If the removal is violent or sudden, instability may actually accelerate. This was the case in 1955 in Argentina after the departure of Juan Peron.

5. The presence of a secret police can make the regime brutal. The excesses of the police, often carried out with the military's help, undermine a regime's credibility, as with the right-wing death squads in El Salvador.

Authoritarian systems are less organized than democratic or communist governments, and they tend to come and go on an irregular basis. One can find many former dictators living comfortably in Europe and Florida on money stolen from their countries. (Dictators are often kleptomaniacs who think big.) Authoritarian governments can generally be divided into three types: military, theocratic, and traditional monarchical. Cases in point are fascism in Chile (1973–1989), religious fanaticism in Iran (since 1979), and the monarchy in Jordan (at least since the 1950s).

It is important to emphasize the great diversity of authoritarianism. Not all these regimes are harsh and corrupt. Some moderate authoritarian systems even have strong elements of democracy lurking within them. Since the late 1980s, for example, Mexico has begun to move slowly away from what amounts to one-party governments. But only infrequently does an authoritarian regime reveal signs of cultivating democratic practices. Most such governments are preoccupied with retaining political power. Others, such as South Korea and Taiwan, begin democratic reforms after their economies industrialize and the overall standard of living is raised. Usually, though, these reforms tend to come from those who have previously been excluded from the political process.

Table 1.2 summarizes the characteristics of the three types of regimes described above. It is also interesting to note that the three kinds of government tend to cluster in certain specific regions of the world. Most fully established democracies are geographically contiguous with one another: Democracy's heartland is in North America and Western Europe. The majority of current and former communist systems are located in Eastern Europe and Asia. Authoritarian systems are found in large numbers in Africa, the Middle East, and parts of Latin America and South Asia. But as Figure 1.2 shows, democracy is spreading.

It is more than coincidence that the most democratic societies in the world tend also to be the more innovative and technologically advanced, as Figure 1.3 shows. Of the top 15 countries with the most patents—an indication of technological strength—14 are democratic. The former Soviet Union, which ranked thirteenth, had fewer patents than Taiwan, a country with less than a tenth of the Soviet population. The map in Figure 1.3 also reveals that the greatest technological (and, therefore, economic) competition in the world is between democracies. Authoritarian and communist systems have never come close. Also, Japan is beginning to overtake the United States as the world leader in patents. With half the population, the Japanese have three-fourths the patents Americans have: in 1989 Fuji Film had 26 "influential patents" compared with Kodak's 15 and Hitachi had 35 compared with IBM's 21. The Japanese have long since ceased being imitators of American products.

TABLE 1.2 CHARACTERISTICS OF THREE FORMS OF GOVERNMENT

	Democratic Regimes	Totalitarian Regimes	Authoritarian Regimes
Political Party System	Two or more parties that accept electoral outcomes peacefully.	Dominated by a single party whose control and influence extend to social and cultural arenas.	One or none; an officially sanctioned party may revolve around a (living or dead) charismatic personality.
Elections or Referenda	Held regularly at constitutionally prescribed intervals.	Held at regular intervals to emphasize the legitimacy of the regime; elections are noncompetitive.	Ignored or fixed.
Media Control	Minimal or nonexistent; self-restraint usually prevails.	Dominance of the media by the government and/or party with heavy usage of propaganda techniques.	Varying degrees of tolerance with careful monitoring.
Public Policymaking	Elected rulers are sensitive to and interested in placating public opinion, especially at election time.	Rank-and-file input at lower levels; tendency for the elite to be isolated from public opinion.	Lack of interest in and/or knowledge of public opinion among policymakers.
Political Legitimacy	Temporary electoral mandate that may be renewed or withdrawn at the next election.	Derived from a comprehensive ideology (Marxist-Leninist in communist regimes).	Personal appeal of, or effective monopolization of, political power by a self-appointed or hereditary national leader.
Civil Liberties	Government is charged with scrupulous protection of individual rights.	Generally far more extensive in theory than practice; constitutional guarantees are often extensive, but largely ignored, as in the case of conflict between individual rights and party interests.	Generally allowed to the extent that they do not conflict with the regime's continued control over the political process.

Figure 1.2 THE MAP OF FREEDOM, 1981 AND 1991. Is democracy spreading? These two maps suggest that it is. The collapse of communism in Eastern Europe and the former Soviet Union and the collapse of authoritarianism in many Latin American countries are responsible for the greatest democratic inroads. These maps are based on data developed by Freedom House's *Comparative Survey of Freedom*. The survey analyzes such factors as the degree to which fair and competitive elections occur, individual and group freedoms are guaranteed in practice, and press freedom exists. In some countries, the category reflects active citizen opposition rather than political rights granted by a government. Source: "The Map of Freedom, 1981 and 1991"; *Freedom Review*, Vol. 22, No. 1, pp. 32–33, Freedom House, New York, NY 10005.

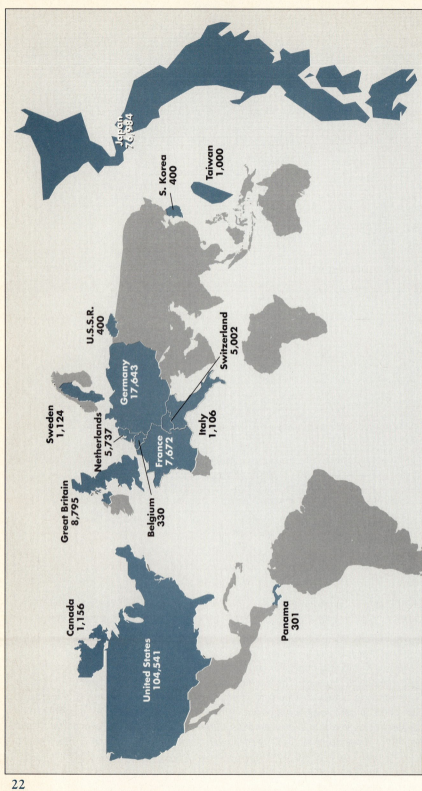

Figure 1.3 THE NEW WORLD ORDER, BASED ON SHARE OF LEADING PATENTS. A nation's size on the map corresponds to its technical strength, as measured by an index based on the number of influential patents it holds. The index number is given below the country name. Only the top 15 countries (in color) are ranked. Others would mostly be of negligible size on the same scale and are shown for context. Scores for Taiwan, South Korea, and the former Soviet Union are estimated. Source: "The New World Order, Based on Share of Leading Patents," from *The New York Times*, May 28, 1991. Copyright © 1991 The New York Times Company. Reprinted by permission.

DISTINCTIVE FEATURES OF AMERICAN GOVERNMENT AND POLITICS

The American political system offers an example of a political process that is at once a presidential democracy with viable legislative and judicial branches of government; a two party system that is unusually undisciplined; a religiously, ethnically, and even linguistically heterogeneous society that is cohesive in great part because it is modernized and technologically advanced; and a political tradition that has evolved (not always peacefully or evenly) through two centuries of democratization. This is not to say that the United States is a model that every other political society should emulate, but its distinctive qualities are relevant to the study of modern government and politics.

The Senior Democracy

The United States is the world's oldest democracy, and the American Constitution is the oldest written constitution still in effect. At the time of its adoption in 1789, the Constitution was a precedent-setting document, widely hailed and often condemned as a revolutionary innovation in government. But, in fact, the United States did not appear in 1789 as a complete or mature democracy. Two centuries later it is still evolving, as are most democratic societies. It is safe to say that the United States has experienced a substantial amount of democratization. There is an old adage that change is inevitable, whether or not it is always desirable. The American system has shown its ability to survive and even prosper by monitoring and adjusting to social and technological change.

Our political stability is perhaps a more notable achievement than the venerable age of our Constitution. This stability has enabled Americans to ride out some near-catastrophic interruptions, such as the Civil War and the Great Depression of the 1930s. It has also helped the country to assimilate wave after wave of immigrants from distant and different societies. As the immigrants were incorporated into a political culture characterized by innovation and opportunity, they voluntarily adopted a political process unfamiliar to most immigrants then and now: political democracy.

A Distinctive Society

The distinctive nature of the American political system reflects the distinctive nature of American society. In comparison with other democracies, the United States is a larger, wealthier, and more recently established nation, and has a more heterogeneous population, greater social mobility, a larger middle class, and an unusual stress on individualism. These characteristics together provide the United States with a unique socioeconomic profile.

Not the least of these characteristics is wealth. To be sure, national wealth is not as equitably distributed here as it is in some other industrialized democracies. Table 1.3 suggests that wealth in the United States is more heavily concentrated in the upper fifth of the population than is the case in other Western democracies. The fluidity of the class structure, which enables persons of lower-class status to move up through educational and economic attainment, makes the middle class the largest of all classes in America. But the size of the middle class is not its greatest significance. Compared with most other societies, including democratic ones, entrance into the middle class is relatively easy in the United States.

TABLE 1.3	DISTRIBUTION OF INCOME IN SELECTED COUNTRIES IN THE LATE 1980S

Country	National Income Held by the Wealthiest 20% of Families
United States	50%
France	46%
Germany	40%
United Kingdom	38%

Source: Congressional Budget Office, *The Changing Distribution of Federal Taxes: 1975–1990* (Washington, D.C.: U.S. Government Printing Office, 1987), p. 70.

Moreover, it is cheaper and easier to be middle class in the United States. One simply does not have to work as hard here as in other industrialized democracies to get what one wants. America is still a wealthy nation without precedent or equal. Without the daily and inexcusable reminder of homeless people, some of whom sleep on grates a few blocks away from the White House, and perhaps as many as 35 million other poor people who are not as visible because they are usually segregated in urban ghettos or reservations, it might be possible to get away with the commercialized image of the United States as thoroughly middle class. But the middle class is large enough to do what Aristotle suggested it is supposed to do—to help ensure political stability.

Other countries with middle-class societies became politically independent decades, sometimes generations, after the United States. They are also considerably smaller, ranging in size from 3.5 million people in New Zealand to 27 million in Canada. Contemporary observers have subscribed to the theory that middle-class societies are inherently stable politically and democratically disposed. Some evidence suggests that this assumption has a substantial basis. In Taiwan and South Korea, for example, a growing middle class in the late 1980s began with some success to push their relatively authoritarian governments toward democratization.

Class identity is less noticeable in the United States than in Europe. In great part this is because class membership in the United States tends to be based on income rather than ancestry. While there are families in Britain fond of tracing their ancestry back to companions of William the Conqueror, Americans are more concerned with one's current status. We are more interested in income brackets than in whose ancestors arrived on the Mayflower. The United States, however, is not devoid of an authentic class structure. We do have extremely rich people and many more tragically poor people. But our society is dominated by middle-class values and culture, which leads many of us to think of ourselves as classless. The general acceptance of these values and culture expedites forming an overall political consensus.

The term *Americanization*, which has been circulating for a few decades, refers most tangibly to an almost classless situation in which common values (extending to food, education, and even housing choices) have become predominant. They overshadow

A VIEW FROM ABROAD
Money and Class in Britain: Are Times Changing?

Britain's ambivalence towards money could not have been better illustrated yesterday. *The Sunday Times* published its league table of the country's 300 wealthiest people, a list that people pore over with a mixture of fascination and distaste. Meanwhile, the Archbishop of Canterbury, Dr George Carey, was preaching that it was wrong "to make money for its own sake. . . ."

There may indeed be a difference between respecting capitalism and worshipping it. In America, the rich are widely admired for their success. There, people are open about their incomes and their social status is usually determined by their wealth. The British are coyer but less judgmental. People who lose their money are not dropped by their friends. Yet the British display an often unseemly streak of envy and resentment.

. . . But "earning" rather than inheriting wealth is clearly increasing. The story of Paul McCartney, who came 19th on the list with assets of 390m [British pounds], proves that even in class-conscious Britain people from a humble background can make vast sums of money. Only a half of the 300 inherited most of their money and aristocrats make up a mere sixth. Many of those are second-or-third generation descendants of men who made their own fortune and were subsequently ennobled. . . .

Britain is far from being classless. But a good idea and a penchant for hard work can still propel people from any background to great wealth. Who would have thought that Anita Roddick's dream of natural cosmetics in no-frills plastic bottles would have made her the 48th richest person in the country? It still helps to inherit money, and starting with 900,000 [pounds] may be the quickest way to make a million. But it is no longer the only way.

Source: "The Eye of a Needle," *The Times* (London), May 11, 1992, p. 13. Copyright © Times Newspapers Ltd 1992. Used by permission.

the tremendous ethnic, religious, and even linguistic diversity for which American society is so well known. This homogenization of class in the United States has been criticized as being conducive to rootlessness, a loss of ethnic identity. Maybe. But it has also resulted in a highly flexible class structure envied and imitated elsewhere.

The American Political Party System: Institutionalized Chaos?

One of the more obvious features of the American political scene is the so-called party system. We say "so-called" since *system* implies a degree of organization, and that is precisely what seems to be lacking in both major parties. Will Rogers's famous quote—"I don't belong to any organized political party, I'm a Democrat"—is only a modest exaggeration, and applies equally to Republicans. It is difficult to find another party system that has as little party discipline.

Can anyone name the leader for the party currently out of power? Probably not and certainly not without some disagreement. Is this because there may not be one? Quite possibly. We have a somewhat easier time when a party controls the presidency. In 1993 Bill Clinton was clearly the Democratic party leader. But even here problems arise. All presidents face some opposition from their own party in Congress or from state governors over legislative issues. Jimmy Carter was regularly criticized by his Democratic congressional colleagues or, as happened on occasion, ignored by them. George Bush was forced on the presidential campaign trail early in 1992 by the unexpectedly strong primary showings of Republican challenger Patrick Buchanan.

Both parties have very loose organizational structures. Whereas the British parties hold annual party conferences, their American counterparts have held only quadrennial ones (to nominate presidential and vice presidential candidates) for most of their history. This is unlikely to change. In a real way, the exceptionally loose (dis)organization of the American parties reflects the overall dislike and distrust Americans have traditionally demonstrated toward politics and government in general (a matter we will discuss shortly). Indeed, the American federal system itself is a manifestation of the historical and deeply rooted distrust of centralization in any form and purposely divides power between a central and state governments.

While American parties tend to be unorganized, individual candidates often thrive amidst the chaos. This is particularly true of those who have the money and resources to conduct campaigns that emphasize their own qualifications rather than their party backgrounds. Individual candidates can and often do make names for themselves in Europe, but most candidacies are grounded in one's party affiliation. Once elected, a member of the British parliament who hopes to continue in politics is usually unwise to vote against the wishes of the party leadership.

No other democratic or nondemocratic society with a party system is likely to have one as undisciplined as ours. American voters are usually more loyal to their representatives than to their representative's political party. During the 1980s up to 98 percent of incumbents running for reelection were returned to the House of Representatives, a tradition somewhat interrupted in 1992, when a record number of incumbents chose not to run for reelection: Still, of those who did, about 93 percent were reelected.

In most other democracies both the executive and legislative branches are consistently controlled by the same party or coalition of parties. Europeans are amazed at and frequently confused by the lack of coherence in our party system (as will be analyzed in the chapter on political parties).

Deliberate Constitutional Complexity

Perhaps the most distinctive feature of American government is its deliberate complexity. The federal government was *designed* to make it exceedingly difficult for any single agency or individual to abuse political power. The Founders devised a central government consisting of three co-equal branches (the doctrine of **separation of powers**) that are at all times watchful of one another's political and constitutional prerogatives (the idea of **checks and balances**). This cross-checking arrangement among the legislative, executive, and judicial branches has ensured the full play of politics in the United States.

The two principles of separation of powers and checks and balances make it difficult for one branch of government to dominate the others. The Constitution ensures that personnel as well as activities are different from branch to branch. As the following list suggests, the legislative branch, Congress, is designed to debate legislation and (sometimes) to pass bills into laws that the executive branch may or may not have recommended. The president can veto legislation he prefers not to see as law. Congress can decide to override a veto with a two-thirds majority. Finally, the federal court system, at the apex of which stands the United States Supreme Court, has the power to interpret and review the constitutionality of legislative acts.

THE TENUOUS PROGRESS OF A LAW IN THE AMERICAN FEDERAL SYSTEM

Congress: Passes a law of its own accord or on the recommendation of the President; the law is then sent to the president who . . .

President: Either signs legislation into law or vetoes it. If the president signs or if Congress overrides a veto, the law may have its constitutionality tested should private groups or individuals succeed in bringing it to the attention of the federal court system. Ultimately, it may be taken to the Supreme Court, which . . .

Supreme Court: Reviews laws and decides their constitutionality.

The principles of separation of powers and checks and balances create a dramatic distinction between the American and other established democracies. Only a few countries, mostly in Latin America, have constructed democracies that resemble the American one. In most European countries (France being a notable and qualified exception) the executive is *recruited from* the legislature rather than being separate from it, a form of government known as the **parliamentary system**. In such a system there is no separation of powers. The executive is selected from the leadership of the majority party (or coalition of parties) that controls the legislature, and the individuals thus recruited retain their parliamentary seats even while functioning as cabinet ministers.

This system usually requires that the prime minister (sometimes referred to as *premier*) and other senior cabinet members be exposed daily to questions and criticisms from the parliamentary opposition (usually referred to respectfully as the **loyal opposition**), a phenomenon that has been traditionally avoided like the plague in the United States. American presidents appear before Congress only on special and well planned occasions, such as the annual State of the Union address. Separation of powers may have some advantages, but it also helps explain why our system has a harder time than parliamentary systems passing legislation.

Even more striking is the unusual constitutional authority of the federal court system in the United States. Very few political systems even come close to allowing courts the independence and prerogatives enjoyed by the Supreme Court of the United States. This is particularly evident in the practice of **judicial review**, in which the Supreme Court can decide whether laws passed by Congress or actions taken by the executive branch are constitutional. Most other democracies leave it up to the legislature to decide whether the government is acting constitutionally.

A Tradition of Distrust of Government

Do Americans distrust government more than other democratic societies do? There is enough evidence to suggest that they do. In the late 1950s a classic study, *The Civic Culture*, revealed that Americans had lower expectations of fair treatment by government bureaucrats than citizens in two other established democracies, Britain and West Germany.[7] American dislike for bureaucrats and their forms was revealed again during the 1990 census when a third of American households did not return census forms by the due date.

The federal Constitution itself is in some ways an expression of distrust of government. The **Bill of Rights**, the first ten amendments to the Constitution, is an explicit list of protections accorded the individual citizen against government abuse. Carefully constructed wording that prescribes elections at specific intervals is another example. And of all the established democracies we are nearly alone in limiting the number of years and terms the head of government can serve. Parliamentary systems impose no legal limit on executive tenure. (Former British Prime Minister Margaret Thatcher once threatened to remain in office until the next millennium.) Even in France's presidential system there is more confidence in the top executive, whose term of office is seven years with no limit on the number of terms. Only a few Latin American democracies and Switzerland place more severe term limitations on the executive than the United States.

Interestingly, though, we place fewer limits on the terms of officials whom we perceive to be closer to us. Members of city councils and the Congress occasionally serve for so long that holding public office becomes a permanent career. But even here there are telling exceptions. Many states limit the number of terms governors can serve. Some big cities, notably Atlanta, limit the number of consecutive terms a mayor can serve. As the 1990s began several states were seriously considering imposed terms limitations on the legislative branch and even on their representatives in the federal Congress. Perhaps we distrust those who govern more than we distrust the principle of government.

If so, this isn't a recent development. A prevailing notion in the Republic's early history was that government service should be a part-time job of brief duration. Citizens are supposed to have better things to do than constantly run for and serve in public office. If they don't, an unconscionable love of power is suggested. From the beginning there was enthusiasm for the Jeffersonian adage that "government that governs least governs best."

Unlike most democracies, the United States was created under circumstances that were essentially hostile or indifferent to the concept of government in the first place. Early settlers, mainly from the islands of Britain and Ireland, came to New England in large part to escape persecution at home, often but not exclusively for dissident religious or political views. One of America's greatest attractions was its lack of comprehensive government. After all, colonial jurisdictions extended rather haphazardly only along the eastern seaboard.

In contrast, older political systems such as the British had over the centuries created a central government that became a prevalent feature in nearly everyone's life. Religious conflicts and competition between the landed aristocracy and a rising entrepreneurial middle class were gradually resolved, but the notion of social class rank remains a characteristic of British political life today. Well into the twentieth century it was comforting for rank-and-file Britons to accept the idea of government by one's economic and social "betters." However undemocratic this sentiment sounds today, it was readily accepted at the time. Affluent and well-educated members of the aristocracy were expected to apply their leisure time usefully, and governing tended to occupy a segment of this elite. Right into the 1970s it was a rare Conservative party prime minister, for example, who was not educated at either Cambridge or Oxford, the two most prestigious and selective universities in England.

The Germans and Japanese also have tended to place great and sometimes unquestioned confidence in their political leaders. During the first half of the twentieth century their confidence was overdone, resulting in disastrous world wars. Yet, even today, they remain more trusting of their leaders than Americans. The reasons may have changed, though. Each country has been able to produce a first-rate industrialized economy. The government claims and usually receives credit for this.

Americans have not developed this habit of gratitude. Even when economic times are good, Americans seem to think they have achieved prosperity in spite of government rather than because of it. In the 1992 election voting turnout picked up, but, generally speaking, in bad or good times voting turnout is low compared with that in other democracies. And the fact that term limitations were endorsed in all fourteen states where they appeared on the ballot suggests a continuing distrust of politicians.

A WORD ABOUT THIS BOOK

The Uses of the Comparative Perspective

American government does not operate in a vacuum. That is why the authors of this book have determined to analyze it by making frequent and occasionally extensive references to other governments and other governmental forms. We believe the following list includes some good reasons for doing this:

1. The apparently sudden appearance of democratization has become notice-able not only in much of Eastern Europe but even in some areas that have been traditionally hostile toward and distrustful of political democracy. Examples of democratic seedlings taking root (while still in need of sub-stantial nurturing) include Kuwait and Jordan in the Middle East and Guatemala and Nicaragua in Central America.

2. The established democracies of France, Germany, Japan, and the United Kingdom are political allies as well as intense economic and technological competitors. Their political economies influence our own more than ever. Their policymaking apparatus is therefore of more than passing concern to Americans.

3. The events in Eastern Europe since 1989 represent both risks and oppor-tunities for the United States. The former Soviet Union, in particular, is of paramount importance to us not because of its economic competitiveness (there isn't any), but because of the potential for political instability that is not conducive to American interests or even national security.

4. The developing world is already in the throes of political instability. But its potential for economic growth remains impressive. This factor is partic-ularly true of large regional powers such as Mexico (the third-largest coun-try in the Western hemisphere) and Nigeria (the largest country on the African continent). How the United States deals with them and how their political systems develop will provide insight into the American relation-ship with and standing among the developing countries in the decades ahead.

5. Finally, we cannot neglect the American relationship with China and the more prosperous East Asian societies, as well as Japan. The dynamic quality of the economies of these countries and their political development is crucial to American interests abroad.

The above-named countries represent most members of the human race and the overwhelming proportion of productive economies. In this text we will make frequent reference to the following countries: France, Germany, Japan, the United Kingdom, and the former Soviet Union, as well as to several countries in the Third World. These references will at times be less extensive than others. Not all the political systems will be referred to all the time, since there may be no compelling reason to do so. We will not force comparisons where none are viable.

Several chapters will be laced with maps and comparative demographic and economic data. These are intended to assist in comprehending the text's emphases, but, what is more important, they are there to provide some basic knowledge of societies that are crucial to and often dependent on both American domestic and foreign policies.

To varying extents, all these countries also send immigrants to the United States every year. Despite a low birth rate, our population is increasing because of the annual

TABLE 1.4 FOREIGN STUDENTS IN AMERICA, 1988–1989

WHO THEY ARE

Rank	Country of Origin	Student Immigrants
1	China	29,040
2	Taiwan	28,760
3	Japan	24,000
4	India	23,350
5	South Korea	20,610
6	Malaysia	16,170
7	Canada	16,030
8	Hong Kong	10,560
9	Iran	8,950
10	Indonesia	8,720

WHERE THEY GO

Rank	Institution	Foreign Enrollment
1	Miami-Dade Community College	5,080
2	University of Southern California	3,486
3	University of Texas at Austin	3,385
4	Boston University	2,940
5	University of Wisconsin, Madison	2,919
6	University of California at Los Angeles	2,859
7	Ohio State University	2,790
8	Columbia University	2,673
9	University of Pennsylvania	2,654
10	University of Illinois, Urbana	2,569

Source: "Foreign Students in America: Where They Come From—Where They Go," from *The New York Times*, November 29, 1989. Copyright © 1989 The New York Times Company. Reprinted by permission.

addition of a million immigrants. Most of them are either Hispanic or Asian, and an increasing number come from Africa, the majority Nigerian. These facts should neither shock nor alarm. Most immigrants arrive and remain quite legally, often with more capital and better educations than some Americans who complain about them. But there is no doubt that recent and current immigrants are changing the demographic and cultural fabric of American society. In 1990, for example, one out of four first-year students entering the University of California in Los Angeles claimed East or Southeast Asian heritage. Table 1.4 comments on the current influx of students from abroad.

Finally, for better or worse, the Americanization of the planet that got under way in earnest a half-century ago continues unabated. The opening of a Moscow McDonald's in 1990 demonstrated that even the Soviet Union was vulnerable. The biggest Kentucky Fried Chicken franchise is in Beijing, the capital city of China. Not everyone welcomes Americanization. Many openly resent it. But the democratic ideals that the United States has long proclaimed are also being emulated. Both economically and politically we are being carried deep into the social currents that are so evident in the 1990s.

Asians are swelling student populations on campuses across America. This East Asian Studies Theme House is found at Stanford University.

Some Assumptions, Biases, and Points of View

It isn't possible for anyone of reasonable intelligence, even textbook authors, to study and teach about a subject like American politics for a quarter of a century without coming to some opinions about it. We could try to conceal our views, but that could be described as "dirty pool." We could attempt to avoid any and all statements of belief in the hope of writing a so-called objective text, but this strategy, even if successfully employed, makes for dull reading. Given these alternatives it's probably best and only fair to divulge our opinions to the reader.

You are certainly encouraged to formulate your own opinions or intelligently change some you may already have. In the meantime, here are some of our beliefs (which do tend to be widely shared) that have played a role in shaping this text:

1. Politics arises inevitably out of human diversity, requires choosing among imperfect alternatives, and cannot be substituted for **political ideology,** *or a set of comprehensive beliefs about what government should do.*

Politics admits no set of beliefs as necessarily superior to others (while also allowing that one might be), but allows advocates of competing and conflicting values to make free appeals in the open marketplace of ideas. To a large extent, the art of politics is the art of selecting the best possible choice from a set of imperfect alternatives. In making such choices it is easier to be an ideologue than a democrat, because the ideologue knows all the answers and therefore doesn't feel compelled to ask questions. It is as dangerous as it is irresponsible to embrace ideology as a substitute for politics. Ideology should be viewed as a guide to but not the governor of politics and society. That is, ideology at its best should provide taste and flavor to politics, but like any seasoning, too much of it spoils the product.

2. We employ government to help us live better and more productive lives as members of the human community.

Not all governments do this. Most fail dreadfully. When they fail it is generally because those who control the processes of government don't understand or don't care about its purposes. Despite its imperfections, democratic government has demonstrated the greatest understanding of its purpose, communist government the least. The latter has assumed that adherence to an ideology would result in a better society. That seems benign enough. The corollary, unfortunately, seems to be an insistence on the right to rule without allowance for dissent or political alternatives.

With the exception of theocracies such as Iran, authoritarian systems tend to be nonideological, having defined no substantial set of values, and nonpolitical, since they are intolerant of any doctrine that has the potential to restrain expressions of power. Unlike democracies, authoritarians regard dissent as dangerous; unlike communists, they rarely offer, even polemically, a vision of change for a better future.

3. Political stability is enhanced when as much of the citizenry as possible have legitimate and guaranteed access to government.

The most significant revolutions in modern history—the English in 1688, ours in the 1770s, the French in the 1790s, the Russian and Chinese in our own century—were both political and social. Their consequences are still with us; in some cases they are still inspirational. They were political in the sense that old regimes were replaced by newer ones that promised (but not always delivered) a more open political process. They were social in that new economic and politically astute classes were substantially responsible for the displacement of the old regimes.

All these revolutions insisted that the individual mattered for something. In both the Soviet Union and China this principle soon collapsed, but only in practice. In the realm of ideology and constitutional theory, communism continued to maintain that government should be responsible to the governed. It is perhaps ironic that such a principle was not put into political practice in many communist countries until the late 1980s.

4. Economic prosperity can most easily result from a relatively decentralized marketplace and an open political process.

The global political economy became distinctively internationalized during the third quarter of the twentieth century. The accumulation of capital and material wealth by Western Europe, North America, and East Asia has induced others to emulate them. Thus, the economy and the politics of very tightly controlled societies, including China, are opening up. There is no guarantee that the process will continue, but the point has been made that the freer the society, the more interested its citizens are in both participating in and contributing to its maintenance.

5. Political democracy has staying power.

In light of the recent events in Eastern Europe some people are tempted to indulge in unabashed democratic chauvinism. This is understandable. Having access to the political process—that is, being able to participate in one way or another in a decision-making process—is the least risky way of avoiding stagnation or tyranny. It is also the most challenging. Since we all live in a time of rapid technological change and most likely will continue to do so, it is natural to grasp for some sort of an ideology in order to make sense of our existence.

Hindsight allows us to appreciate the fact that totalitarian regimes, the most sophisticated and dangerous dictatorships in history, either are violently destroyed because of the threat they pose to other nations, as were the Nazis in Germany by 1945, or are forced to mellow, as several communist regimes did in the late 1980s. Our early political thinker Aristotle could have warned them. Those whose governing makes miserable the lives of a certain group of people or an entire nation miss the whole point of politics. The political process must work on behalf of everyone in the society (or at least genuinely try to), regardless of who is governing. It is pleasant and, one hopes not inaccurate to believe that democratic government comes closest to achieving this goal.

Taking the long view, the democracies do have staying power. They managed to survive and eventually eliminate the nightmare of nazism and successfully compete against communism, while consistently upgrading most citizens' standard of living during the last half-century. Those who benefit from society's economic and political arrangements tend to support its institutions. But what about those who don't benefit? Some members of society feel, often with reason, that they are more deprived than they deserve to be. They have less motivation to be politically supportive than those who feel quite satisfied with the rewards they receive from the political system. In one sense it may not matter: Government can survive and even prosper without the active support of these segments of the population that have little or no influence on the political decision-making process.

But that is precisely democracy's imperfection. In the United States, for example, we cannot take pride in this disturbing statistic: Between 1966 and 1987 the percentage of children growing up in poverty increased from 17.6 to 20.6.[8] And these children are disproportionately African-American or Hispanic. Here are some other disturbing statistics:

More than 7 million children have no health insurance.

Any given night in the year, 100,000 children are homeless.

At the current rate, it will be 2090 before universal prenatal care is achieved.[9]

In a society as conspicuously wealthy as the United States, these statistics are a national disgrace, even if they aren't enough of a tragedy to destroy overall confidence in the government.

6. Given such imperfections, we must ask ourselves whether we are entitled to judge nondemocratic societies.

Yes, seems to be the answer. If we acknowledge our own mistakes and shortcomings (and there are many), other governments ought to acknowledge theirs.

This may be happening. The former Soviet Union presents a sterling example of how a deteriorating economy can provide a strong stimulus for candor. Ironically, Soviet citizens had one of the highest savings rates in the world, but this was mainly because they had little to spend money on. While preaching equality the Soviet government actually created elitism in the form of the Communist party. The fairest distribution of resources is an obligation of the political system. Maldistribution is perhaps the greatest cause of political instability. The democracies have managed to avoid the worst extremes of wealth and poverty by creating a large and innovative middle class. Neither communist nor authoritarian systems have done this.

7. We should avoid becoming democratic chauvinists. Or maybe not.

It is difficult to avoid chauvinism because of a relentless need to simply defend our political system. Both democracy and general political participation end when civil liberties are suspended, elections postponed (often indefinitely), and rule by decree becomes commonplace. Yet nondemocratic regimes, to one degree or another, accept these restrictions on politics as both necessary and justified. Governments shouldn't make people disappear in the middle of the night. Governments should busy themselves instead with more mundane tasks such as ensuring safe drinking water and dependable garbage collections. A democratic government acknowledges that unlimited power cannot be a part of the process of governing.

Summary

1. Government and politics are not the same, but they are inseparable from one another. Politics precedes and results in government and is the driving mechanism of government.

2. We have government because we are much better off with it than without it. We depend on government to allocate and equitably distribute resources that are almost never present in sufficient supply.

3. A perennial dilemma for government is what limitations should be placed on it and to what extent individual freedoms need to be curtailed.

4. Aristotle devised a formulation for different kinds of government—rule by one, a few, or many—that is still useful today. Modern categories of government include democracy, totalitarianism, and authoritarianism.

5. Government that is chosen by and responsible to the citizenry is democratic. Individual rights take precedence over and are considered superior to the prerogatives of government.

6. Totalitarianism, made possible by twentieth-century technology, is a form of government intent on exercising maximum control of the daily lives of its citizens. It considers the state as superior to the individual and is normally legitimated by an all-encompassing ideology that tolerates no competing political principles.

7. Authoritarianism is government in the hands of a political elite that excludes popular participation, discourages political dissent, and ignores the rights of the individual.

8. The political system in the United States can be distinguished from other political systems by (1) the length of time it has been democratized, (2) the heterogeneous and heavily middle-class nature of its society, (3) its loosely organized party system, (4) the deliberate complexity of its constitutional framework, and (5) the tradition of distrust of government among its citizens.

9. The comparative perspective is useful because the United States plays an important role in the global community and because the policies of other countries, especially the developed nations, affect the welfare of our nation. These interrelationships make it extremely important for Americans to understand the workings of other political societies.

10. Throughout this textbook, the authors will not try to hide their prejudice on behalf of democratic government and politics.

Terms to Define

Authoritarianism	Loyal opposition
Bill of Rights	Parliamentary system
Checks and balances	Party state
Communism	Politics
Democracy	Political ideology
Government	Separation of powers
Judicial review	Totalitarian
Laws	

Suggested Readings

Bernard Crick. *In Defense of Politics*. Baltimore: Penguin Books, 1964. An excellent and very readable introduction to politics, why politics is necessary, what sorts of people are unfriendly to politics, and why politics will continue anyway.

William Ebenstein and Alan O. Ebenstein, eds. *Introduction to Political Thinkers*. Fort Worth: Harcourt Brace Jovanovich, 1992. In addition to providing primary sources, this reader is a useful primer on the more important political philosophers in history, beginning with Plato and Aristotle.

Eric Hoffer. *The True Believer*. New York: Harper & Row, 1951. A classic and easily understood treatment of one of the lower forms of political life—the political fanatic.

Donald Kagan. *Pericles of Athens and the Birth of Democracy*. New York: Free Press, 1991. The ingredients of both political stability and responsible political institutions are thoroughly explored in an excellent essay that reveals the personalities intimately involved in the creation of the world's first democracy.

Paul Wilkinson. *Terrorism and the Liberal State*, 2nd ed. New York: New York University Press, 1986. While terrorism is the focal point of this treatment, there is valuable material on how well a democracy can cope with and protect itself against the relentless violence that normally surrounds and is always eager to attack it.

Notes

1. *Federalist Papers*, No. 51.
2. Bernard Crick, *In Defense of Politics* (Baltimore: Penquin Books, 1964), p. 18.
3. "Morning Edition," National Public Radio, December 2, 1992.
4. Paul Wilkinson, *Terrorism and the Liberal State*, 2nd ed. (New York: New York University Press, 1986), p. 20.
5. *The Republic* (New York: Norton, 1985), p. 249.
6. For an excellent analysis of this time and place, see R. K. Sinclair, *Democracy and Participation in Athens* (Cambridge: Cambridge University Press, 1988) and Donald Kagan, *Pericles and Athenian Democracy* (Glencoe, Ill.: Free Press, 1990).
7. Gabriel A. Almond and Sidney Verba, *The Civic Culture* (Princeton: Princeton University Press, 1963).
8. *The New York Times*, May 6, 1992.
9. "Rich land, poor kids," *The Economist*, January 7, 1989, pp. 25-26.

CHAPTER ★ TWO

THE DYNAMICS OF DEMOCRACY

Democracy is a versatile word. It is used even by dictators and totalitarian leaders to describe their nations and governments. For example, before the fall of communism in Eastern Europe, East Germany was known as the German Democratic Republic; today, North Korea, and Vietnam are called the Democratic People's Republic of Korea, and the Democratic Republic of Vietnam. Are these communist regimes democracies as well as the United States?

Communist countries would argue that they are *economic* democracies, in which the government's primary concern is the economic well-being of the people. An **economic democracy** emphasizes collective or governmental ownership of the means of production and distribution of goods and services. The state or government ends up being considered more important than the individual. Western nations, such as the United States, profess to be *political* democracies, in which the individual counts for more than the state or government. In a **political democracy**, the government's primary objective is to ensure the political freedom of individuals through such guarantees as the freedoms of religion, speech, press, and assembly, and the right to vote.

An economic democracy gives the government the right to make the best decision for the individual, while a political democracy protects the right of the individual to influence the government. In the typical communist nation claiming to be an economic democracy there is only one political party, while in a political democracy, such as the United Kingdom or Germany, there are two or more political parties.

Which correctly represents democratic history and tradition: economic or political democracy? Only in a political democracy does a government manifest the characteristics of democratic regimes discussed in Chapter 1: two or more political parties, regularly scheduled elections, uncensored media, sensitivity of political leaders to public opinion, temporary but renewable electoral mandates, and protection of individual rights.

Our focus in this chapter will, therefore, be on political democracy. First we will look more closely at the meaning of democracy and its ingredients. Then we will examine several important issues concerning the founding and practice of democracy in America. In the final section we place the American system in the world setting and make some comparisons.

★ THE INGREDIENTS OF DEMOCRACY

The word **democracy** comes from two Greek words—*demos*, meaning "people," and *kratos*, meaning "rule." Thus, the term indicates that governmental authority in a democracy resides in the people; it is a form of government in which power is exercised by the people. The Greeks, especially the Athenians, distinguished among government by the many (democracy), government by the few (oligarchy), and government by one person (monarchy). Pericles (495–429 B.C.) declared in his famous "Funeral Oration" that "our constitution is named a democracy, because it is in the hands not of the few, but of the many." The first thorough discussion of democracy occurred in the writings of Aristotle, who spoke favorably about what we call today **constitutional democracy**: a system in which basic laws allow majority rule while protecting minority rights and individual freedoms and promoting the general public interest.

There are two major types of political democracy. In a **direct democracy** (or pure democracy), all citizens participate equally in decision making; this occurs, for example, in a New England town meeting. In a **representative democracy** (also known as indirect democracy), people elect representatives to make their decisions. This form of government, sometimes called a **republic**, is the American system.

DEMOCRATIC PRINCIPLES AND PROCEDURES

Both types of political democracy recognize certain basic democratic *principles*. One of these is **majority rule**, wherein the people make their decisions (on their own or through representatives) based on the wishes of the majority or plurality. But **minority rights** are also of absolute importance for democracy. For example, even though a minority loses to the majority in the selection of representatives, the minority still retains the right to exist, to express its points of view, and to challenge (and become) the majority when the people next decide who their leaders will be. In general, the principle of majority rule demands that (1) public officials be chosen by majority rule and that (2) every citizen have the right to influence government policy. At the same time, the minority should be free to criticize majority decisions, and the people in the minority should be free to try to win majority support for their opinions. Other basic principles that should be nurtured in a democracy are freedom and equality.

Democratic principles are reflected in democratic *procedures*, such as the competitive elections through which people choose their leaders. For example, freedoms of

Direct democracy at work: a town meeting in Stratford, Vermont, where all the town's citizens can participate in decision making.

speech and press enable voters to make informed decisions in voting. Majority rule and minority rights allow the majority or plurality to elect its representatives while protecting the right of the minority. Although Adolf Hitler came to power in Germany through democratic procedures, one could hardly look upon his government as a democracy, because he did not respect the minority rights of German citizens who were Jewish, gypsies, or politically opposed to his policies.

The individual in a democracy has rights that governmental procedures should not ignore. As noted by political scientist Carl Becker, democracy's fundamental "assumption is the worth and dignity of the individual."[1] Procedures that respect both the rights of individuals and the desire of the majority should be the means of achieving democratic principles.

CHARACTERISTICS OF DEMOCRACIES

Democracy thrives in some settings and not in others. Why, for example, has democracy flourished with relative ease in North America and yet been established with reluctance in much of Latin America? Latin America has traditionally lacked six characteristics that North America possesses:

1. A well-educated citizenry,
2. A large and accessible middle class,
3. Substantial national wealth that is fairly widespread among the people,

4. A general desire of the people to organize into groups to seek common goals and to influence the government's policies,

5. General pursuit of the goals of liberty and equality, and

6. An open class system that allows and encourages people to improve their lives economically, socially, educationally, and politically.

These characteristics are important because they help people cope with the substantial demands that democracy makes. Citizens must be both able and willing to participate in politics. Minorities must be willing to accept defeat on an issue and not react with violence or revolution. The majority must be willing to allow minorities to challenge its position. The government must respond to numerous and conflicting group demands. At the same time it must allow full and vigorous debate and dissent on issues, and show respect and tolerance for the individuals and groups that differ. And while fulfilling all these demands in a democracy, the government must still function in a reasonably efficient manner. No wonder British Prime Minister Winston Churchill observed that democracy is "the worst form of government except all those other forms that have been tried from time to time."[2]

The dynamics of American democracy best reveal the advantages and disadvantages of that form of government. Critics offer persuasive reasons why American democracy fails to live up to its promises, while supporters set forth equally compelling reasons why it succeeds. By looking at both interpretations in regard to certain key issues, we will learn about the failures and accomplishments of democracy as well as about important concepts, such as elitism and pluralism. Another goal, of course, is to be able to compare American democracy with other forms of democracy.

? ISSUES TO ANALYZE

Sometimes the best way to learn about a subject is to listen attentively to both sides of a debate. Then you can utilize the best arguments to form your own opinion. That is essentially what we will be doing as we examine the key issues in this section as well as in other chapters. Each side of the debate is presented from an advocate's point of view (but, remember, not necessarily the point of view of the authors). A concluding section highlights the most compelling arguments, but you should reach your own conclusions in each case. The issues under consideration in this chapter are whether the Founders intended to establish democracy, whether our system is sufficiently democratic, whether democratic values are eroding, and whether elitism or pluralism best characterizes our democratic system.

ISSUE 1   WERE THE FOUNDERS DEMOCRATS?

REASONS WHY THE FOUNDERS WERE NOT DEMOCRATS

Did the Founders intend to establish a democracy? Far from believing in the principle of government by the people, many of those who wrote our Constitution disliked and distrusted the principle of majority rule. Some of them, notably Alexander Hamilton, almost equated democracy with mobocracy—rule of the mob. As a result, the Constitution of the United States was designed to restrain the majority of the people or even prevent them from acting. Ironically, the Founders believed in the ultimate authority of the people, but feared an unrestrained majority.

The idea of a *direct* democracy had few advocates at the Constitutional Convention. At most, the Founders had in mind a republic, or a representative democracy, with a complicated set of restraints on the majority. Among these restraints are (1) the division of governmental power between the national and state governments, and (2) the separation of power among the three branches of the national government—legislative, executive, and judicial. The people (in reality, the small portion of the people then qualified to vote) had direct influence only in the selection of members of the House of Representatives. Members of the Senate were to be chosen by state legislatures; the president, by the electoral college; and judges, by presidential nomination and senatorial confirmation. Could a government be called democratic when only some of the people could vote directly for only one of the four major units of the national government?

These restraints on popular participation in government indicated the Founders' basic distrust of popular majorities, a conclusion for which there is substantial support. In No. 10 of *The Federalist Papers*, James Madison wrote: "Complaints are everywhere heard from our most considerate and virtuous citizens . . . that our governments are too unstable, and that measures are too often decided, not according to rules and justice and the right of the minor party, but by the superior force of an interested and overbearing majority." The 85 essays of *The Federalist Papers*, authored by Alexander Hamilton, James Madison, and John Jay, were influential in the adoption of the Constitution and in shaping later interpretations of it.

The Founders reflected a belief in the Judeo-Christian assessment of human nature that people are capable of both good and evil. Madison argued that if men were angels, government wouldn't be necessary. But they aren't angels. The Founders considered restraints and restrictions necessary to prevent the abuse of governmental power by a majority (or mob) that might trample on the rights of others as well as by a minority that might impose its views from a position of power.

The real irony of American democracy is that full democracy was never intended. One might argue that we have *become* a democracy, but one cannot say that the purpose of our Constitution was to establish a republic that reflected genuine majority rule.

REASONS WHY THE FOUNDERS WERE DEMOCRATS

To fully understand the democratic principles and procedures established by the Founders one needs to take into account other important documents of the time besides the Constitution itself. The principles and procedures outlined in the Declaration of Independence, the Constitution, and the Bill of Rights represented at the time of their adoption an unprecedented advancement in the implementation of democratic ideals. No other nation had anything comparable. The Founders extended the principles and procedures of democracy further than any other nation had ever dared or desired to. With late-twentieth-century hindsight, we might be critical of the accomplishment of the Founders, but not if we apply a late-eighteenth-century perspective.

A fundamental concern of the Founders was the dignity of the individual—the right to be free to pursue one's own best interest on an equal footing with others. The individual rather than the state was the central measure of value in their thinking. This

According to English philosopher John Locke, the natural rights of the individual took precedence over the state. Locke emphasized both the liberty and the equality of individuals.

concern reflected the writings of theorists and philosophers of the Enlightenment, or Age of Reason in eighteenth-century Europe. These writers condemned earlier political views that emphasized the state over the individual. For example, English philosopher John Locke, whose writings greatly influenced the Founders, wrote:

> To understand political power aright, and derive it from its original, we must consider what state all men are naturally in, and that is a state of perfect freedom to order their actions and dispose of their possessions and person as they think fit, within the bounds of the law of nature, without asking leave, or depending upon the will of any other man. A state also of equality, wherein all the power and jurisdiction is reciprocal, no one having more than another.[3]

The Declaration of Independence, of course, exemplifies this emphasis on individual liberty and equality by stating that "all men are created equal, that they are endowed by their Creator with certain inalienable Rights, that among these, are Life, Liberty, and the pursuit of Happiness."

Central to liberty is the right to self-determination; central to equality is the right to have a fair chance, given one's abilities, to compete with everyone else. The Founders, recognizing the dangers of a supreme state, felt that a limited government would best enhance the liberty of the individual and protect the rights of each person to equal opportunity. Therefore, the government was not to be all-powerful, but was to have sufficient power to protect the individual's rights.

The Founders were both procedural and principle democrats. In general, their procedures were enunciated in the Constitution, their principles in the Declaration of

Independence, and both principles and procedures in the Bill of Rights. They knew that democratic procedures without adequate guarantees of democratic principles would be a hollow shell, as would a declaration of democratic principles without an institution of democratic procedures.

The Declaration of Independence provides evidence that the Founders were democrats, especially in the political aims of their own time:

> *That to secure these rights, Governments are instituted among Men, deriving their just powers from the consent of the governed. That whenever any Form of Government becomes destructive of these ends, it is the Right of the People to alter or to abolish it, and to institute new Government, laying its foundation on such principles and organizing its powers in such form, as to them shall seem most likely to effect their Safety and happiness.*

Clearly, the people and their interests were at the heart of the Founders' concern in breaking away from British rule and establishing the new government for the United States.

While the Founders held the individual to be more important than the state, they wisely avoided deifying human beings. James Madison referred to the "degree of depravity in mankind which requires a certain degree of circumspection and distrust,"[4] "the caprice and wickedness of man,"[5] and the "infirmities and depravities of the human character."[6] Alexander Hamilton was no more optimistic when he spoke of the "folly and wickedness of mankind,"[7] while John Jay regarded the individual as governed by "dictates of personal interest."[8] Even Thomas Jefferson said, "Free government is founded on jealousy, not on confidence; it is jealousy and not confidence which prescribes limited constitutions, to bind those we are obligated to trust with power. In questions of power, let no more be heard of confidence in man but bind him down from mischief by the chains of the constitution."[9]

This view of the nature of those who govern us influenced the *type* of democratic government the Founders established: one limited by checks and balances of power among the several branches of the government, and protection of the individual from the capricious exercise of governmental power through a Bill of Rights.

ISSUE 1: Summary ★ *Were the Founders Democrats?*

The Founders did not believe in a democracy in the strict sense nor in the way democracy has developed in America. Their substantial distrust of popular government led them to allow a restricted electorate to elect directly only the members of the U.S. House of Representatives, denying direct popular election of the president, members of the Senate, and members of the Supreme Court.

At the same time, the Founders were clearly more democratic in their beliefs and in the structure of government they devised than any other people or government up until then. They believed that ultimate governmental power should reside with the people. They established a representative or republican democracy. They were strong advocates of the two most fundamental concepts undergirding democracy: liberty and equality. They devised a government that had the *potential* of becoming more democratic. ■

ISSUE 2   *IS AMERICA SUFFICIENTLY DEMOCRATIC?*

REASONS WHY AMERICA IS NOT SUFFICIENTLY DEMOCRATIC

Several rhetorical questions provide examples of the inadequacy of democratic procedures in American government. Should the United States be called democratic when the following are true?

1. Many major businesses and industries with incomes totaling billions of dollars pay little or no federal income taxes.

2. In 1984, 36.57 million voters elected just 182 Republicans to the House of Representatives while 36.61 million voters elected 253 Democrats. (Fair and equitable representation would have divided the 435 seats almost equally at 217 or 218 for each.) This inequitable representation occurred because state legislatures draw Congressional district boundaries. Since a majority of state legislatures are controlled by Democrats, they were able to draw districts favoring Democratic candidates.

3. Women constitute over 50 percent of the population, but make up only about 10 percent of the membership of the U.S. House of Representatives.

4. African-Americans constitute nearly 13 percent of the population, but make up only 9 percent of the U.S. House of Representatives.

5. Hispanics account for 9 percent of the population, but only 4 percent of the U.S. House of Representatives.

6. Its citizens do not have the right to directly elect their highest government official, the president. The American chief executive is elected not by popular majority vote, but rather by the cumbersome electoral college. In this system voters in each state select a slate of electors, who then vote for the president. On three occasions (1824, 1876, and 1888), this procedure has given us a president who did not win the national popular vote. H. Ross Perot's independent candidacy in 1992 threatened a similar occurrence.

These practices, together with the constitutional restraints previously discussed, are examples of undemocratic procedures in what is commonly called a democratic nation. Two political scientists, Harold Lasswell and Daniel Lerner, summed it up this way: "Government is always government by the few, whether in the name of the few, the one, or the many."[10] The heart of the argument is that the procedures of American democracy have an undemocratic bias, favoring the few over the many.

REASONS WHY AMERICA IS SUFFICIENTLY DEMOCRATIC

Critics suggest that legislative representation and government leadership should generally mirror characteristics of the population, such as age, sex, education, and so on. But a representative need not be of a particular sex or age or race to represent those interests effectively. To illustrate, the Nineteenth Amendment, granting suffrage to women, and the Twenty-sixth Amendment, granting suffrage to 18- through

When Professor Anita Hill testified before the all-male, all-white Senate Judiciary Committee in late 1991, many Amerians asked themselves just how representative their representative body was. Well aware of how the committee appeared to the millions of viewers of the televised hearings, the chairman made a point of placing two newly elected female senators (one African-American) on the committee in 1993.

20-year-olds, were adopted primarily by men well over 21 years of age. The Civil Rights Act of 1964 and the Voting Rights Act of 1965 were enacted primarily by white males. Some suggest that failure to ratify the Equal Rights Amendment, a priority plank in the feminist platform during the 1970s and 1980s, was undemocratic. Despite the inability of advocates to obtain timely ratification, however, many women's rights issues have received favorable treatment in the courts.

Concerning charges of economic inequality, no society as large and as complex as ours has ever had such a relatively equal distribution of economic resources. Economic resources are better distributed in America than in most other societies today. Most Americans are in the middle class, where resources are more evenly distributed; the upper and lower classes in the United States are much smaller than those in other nations.

Over time, democracy has been extended in the United States by granting the right to vote to non-property-owners, women, and African-Americans; by equalizing legislative representation among urban, suburban, and rural populations; and by extending to minority groups the right to serve on juries.

Let us consider one of the most crucial indictments of American democracy, namely, that it perpetuates bias and prejudice against racial minorities, particularly African-Americans. Yet African-Americans today can vote throughout the country; can be served in hotels, motels, and restaurants; and can enjoy the facilities of all public establishments. That could not have been said of them earlier in this century. They are also being elected to office in rapidly increasing numbers, entering colleges and universities in large numbers, obtaining more lucrative jobs, and appearing regularly on television programs and in advertisements. Moreover, they have been the beneficiaries of affirmative action programs designed to provide greater opportunities in education and employment. These programs illustrate the American emphasis on equality of opportunity rather than the guarantee of equality.

As long ago as 1976, African-American activist Eldridge Cleaver remarked that African-American people are now inside the system, with the same equal rights under the Constitution as Ford or Rockefeller: "I believe this will call for a tremendous shift of energy—that black people need to focus their energies on improving the system, as opposed to banging on the door to get in, or to tearing it down because they are not let in."[11]

ISSUE 2:   Summary   ★   *Is America Sufficiently Democratic?*

Historically, there is evidence that America was not sufficiently democratic, particularly regarding such issues as the denial of voting rights for African-Americans and women. However, during the 200 years since the founding of American democracy, most of the flagrant undemocratic procedures have been abolished and others are now being remedied. Thus, we can say that the dynamics of democracy in America have allowed the democratic process to be used to correct undemocratic procedures. ■

ISSUE 3   *ARE DEMOCRATIC VALUES ERODING?*

REASONS WHY DEMOCRATIC VALUES ARE ERODING

The philosopher Sidney Hook has said that democracy is simply a system of rules for playing the game, rules that allow some measure of mass participation and government accountability, and that the Constitution is the rule book.[12] This definition of democracy is based on procedures, but what of principles? Here we come up against a key obstacle to understanding American democracy: To say that a nation is democratic because it holds elections begs the question. For 70 years the Soviet Union held elections, but was it a democracy? Democracy without certain principles is hollow. There are, therefore, what we might call "procedural democrats" and "principle democrats."

Concerning the principles of democracy, especially those of liberty and equality, we must ask searching questions. For example, can the United States be called a democracy when the intelligence agencies, such as the Central Intelligence Agency and the Federal Bureau of Investigation, have abused their power and illegally spied on Americans, and when the court system prosecutes and penalizes poor and minority offenders more severely than it does the rich? These examples illustrate abuses of liberty and equality. Citizens who are illegally spied upon lose a basic human right to be free from invasion of privacy, and unequal court sentences point to a glaring inequality between the rich and the poor. For a nation to be a democracy, there should be widespread respect for the liberty of all citizens and adequate provision for their equality.

A worse charge, according to some, is that the United States has practiced actual repression. For years Americans have been taught that only other countries practice repression, particularly dictatorships like Hitler's Germany, Mussolini's Italy, and Stalin's Soviet Union. A new breed of American scholars, however, contests this conclusion: "The U.S. government has hassled workers, Indians, African-Americans, women, left-wingers, right-wingers, immigrants. In this century alone there have been two Red scares, concentration camps, guilt by association, deportation, preventive detention, political espionage—all carried out by a government supposedly dedicated to freedom."[13]

Watergate, a phenomenon of the Vietnam era, demonstrates how repression can be used to silence critics. A break-in at the Democratic party headquarters in the Watergate building during the 1972 presidential campaign was eventually traced to the Republican headquarters. President Nixon and his advisors subsequently went to great lengths to "cover up" the administration's involvement in the break-in. The Watergate affair involved the use of intimidation by the Internal Revenue Service, the Federal Bureau of Investigation, the Central Intelligence Agency, and the White House staff. The episode suggests that in periods of mass unrest, as occurred in reaction to the war in Vietnam in 1972, elites may convince themselves that repression is necessary to preserve the political system. During the presidencies of both Lyndon Johnson (1963–1969) and Richard Nixon

Democracies, unfortunately, are not exempt from conducting an occasional repression. During World War II, Americans of Japanese descent were rounded up, taken from their homes, and relocated in internment camps under armed guard for the duration of the war. This flagrant violation of lawful procedures and rights was excused on the grounds that the Japanese-Americans posed a threat to a nation at war with Japan.

(1969–1974), the Internal Revenue Service subjected many political opponents to special tax investigations.

American philosopher John Dewey wrote that "the keynote of democracy as a way of life may be expressed as the necessity for the participation of every mature human being in the formation of the values that regulate the living of men together."[14] But the American scene shows a gross disparity between promise and performance in this goal. For example, television has enormous influence over the development of American values, yet the producers of American television programs differ dramatically from rank-and-file Americans in their ideological, political, and theological positions.

75 percent classify themselves as political liberals.

44 percent say they have no religion.

Only 7 percent attend religious services regularly.

A majority take liberal political and theological stands on specific economic, political, and social issues.

An average of only 19.25 percent voted for Republican candidates from 1968 through 1980, a time when Republican candidates won three of the four elections.[15]

Intellectuals can also exercise undue influence over American society's values. For example, University of Chicago sociologist James Coleman was the principal intellectual architect and proponent of school busing to achieve racial balance in the 1960s. Then, busing's principal advocate reversed himself during the 1970s, calling his theory incorrect. For about a decade this nation agonized over school busing. The policy was implemented by judicial decisions and administrative edicts, not by the popularly elected legislative branch.

Clearly, ordinary citizens are having less and less influence in determining America's values. To the extent that this is happening, democracy in the United States is being challenged.

Even those who favor a greater role for the federal government acknowledge that the increasing emphasis on governmental action and regulation is contrary to the intentions of the Founders, who believed in a limited government. Rexford Guy Tugwell, himself an architect of increased federal regulation as an advisor to President Franklin D. Roosevelt, wrote of the Constitution:

> Above all, men were to be free to do as they like, and since the government was likely to intervene, and because prosperity was to be found in the free management of their affairs, a constitution was needed to prevent such intervention. . . . The law would maintain order, but not touch the individual who behaved reasonably. He must pay taxes to support a smallish government, and he must not interfere with commerce; but otherwise laws would do him neither good nor ill. The government of the Constitution was this kind of government.[16]

According to Tugwell, the changes that enhanced the federal power, though designed to broaden democracy, were made "irregularly and according to doctrines the framers would have rejected."[17] Tugwell felt that the Constitution had been altered more through judicial interpretation than through such popular measures as constitutional amendments. The Supreme Court, of course, is an appointed, not a democratically elected, body.

Regardless of how changes were made, there is little doubt that they increased the size and regulatory power of the government, sometimes at the expense of individual liberty. Some argue that American government has moved along the road toward totalitarianism, with governmental power becoming more important than personal freedom. It is difficult to think of any area of American life in which the federal government does not exercise at least some regulatory power. The American system has clearly moved since its founding toward a more powerful government.

Still another voice arguing in yet another way that traditional democratic values have been lost is Russian exile Aleksandr Solzhenitsyn, whose views are supported by conservatives holding to traditional religious and social values. In his Harvard University commencement address of 1978, Solzhenitsyn concluded that unrestrained freedom has led to a decline of traditional values and that Americans have abandoned their religious value foundation. Instead of bolstering values to stem the tide of decay, reformers have focused on changes in economic, political, and social structures. In essence, he is saying that we are treating the symptoms of the disease rather than the disease itself.[18]

Solzhenitsyn is not the first thinker to identify American democracy with a value base. President Woodrow Wilson said: "A nation which does not remember what it was yesterday, does not know what it is today, nor what it is trying to do. We are trying to do a futile thing if we do not know where we came from or what we have been about."[19] Thomas Jefferson asked: "Can the liberties of a nation be thought secure, when we have removed their only firm basis, a conviction in the minds of the people that these liberties are the gift of God."[20] Also echoing the same theme, historian Samuel Eliot Morison said there is a strong relationship between American democracy and its value foundation:

> *Puritanism was a cutting edge which hewed liberty, democracy, humanitarianism, and universal education out of the black forest of feudal Europe and the American wilderness.*
>
> *Puritan doctrine taught each person to consider himself a significant if sinful unit to whom God had given a particular place and duty, and that he must help his fellow men.*
>
> *Puritanism was an American heritage to be grateful for and not to be sneered at because it required everyone to attend divine worship and maintained a strict code of moral ethics.*[21]

Individualism can be an asset for American democracy but too much of it poses a serious liability. Alexis de Tocqueville warned in his classic work *Democracy in America* (1835) that rampant individualism could ruin American democracy by causing an authoritarian government to be established to control the overly self-centered society. Tocqueville argued that family, friends, neighborhoods, and churches are needed to preserve American democracy, because they help reduce the tendency toward excessive individualism and selfishness. Today we see the ascendance of self-centered "yuppyism" (the "greed is good" syndrome) in the 1980s apparently giving way in the early 1990s to at least a partial restoration of traditional values, with their emphasis on Tocqueville's community ideals.

No other nation elects more public officials than the United States nor allows more disputes to be settled through the political process. One person has even sued his parents for malpractice in parenting, contending that his parents failed to rear him properly. His bringing of the case certainly proves the point. Excessive politicization due to excessive individualism is more a threat to democracy now than too little politics. The politicizing of all of society has historically been a prelude to a totalitarian society, as was emphatically demonstrated in Hitler's Germany.

REASONS WHY DEMOCRATIC VALUES ARE NOT ERODING

The very fact that American government can be criticized reveals its democratic character. Criticism is not only allowed, it is protected under the guarantees of freedom of speech and of the press. Critics, or course, provide the public at large with a diversity of viewpoints that enable us to make better judgments about the performance of our government. Both leaders and followers benefit. With more information and alternatives, they can make better decisions. And if the government makes a poor decision, critics can develop support for changing it. By contrast, during seven decades of Marxist rule in the Soviet Union, hundreds of thousands of Soviet citizens were imprisoned and exiled, many even murdered for their criticisms.

Leading students of democracy have recognized that the existence of democracy does not necessarily depend on the public's belief in democratic principles. J. Roland Pennock has noted that democracy can tolerate disagreement on principles if people are willing to compromise and to follow established rules and procedures, and Carl J. Freidrich has concluded that democracy depends on habitual patterns of behavior rather than on conscious agreement about "democratic" principles.[22] Thus, even though some surveys show that Americans do not generally believe in democratic principles, it does not matter so long as the public settles its differences and adheres to accepted democratic procedures.

Some critics point to government's increasing power as an example of how democratic values, especially as envisioned by the Founders, are eroding. But what should be the proper role of government in ensuring democratic principles? The men who wrote the Constitution certainly saw the role of government as limited, but that idea became

---

A VIEW FROM THE STATES
Where Democracy Begins

Strange as it may seem to an era governed by mass-market politics, democracy begins in human conversation. The simplest, least threatening investment any citizen may make in democratic renewal is to begin talking with other people about these questions, as though the answers matter to them.

Harmless talk around a kitchen table or in a church basement will not affect anyone but themselves, unless they decide that it ought to. When the circle is enlarged to include others, they will be embarking on the fertile terrain of politics that now seem so barren.

Source: The Christian Science Monitor, July 8, 1992, p. 19. Excerpted from William Greider, Who Will Tell the People: The Betrayal of American Democracy. New York: Simon & Schuster, 1992.

less relevant in the twentieth century. In 1931 Charles Beard attacked the principle that the government that governs least governs best:

> The cold truth is that the individualist creed of everybody for himself and the devil take the hindmost is principally responsible for the distress in which Western civilization finds itself— with investment racketeering at one end and labor racketeering at the other. Whatever merits the creed may have had in days of primitive agriculture and industry, it is not applicable in an age of technology, science, and rationalized economy. Once useful, it has become a danger to society.[23]

Beard's prescription to counteract rampant individualism is stronger government control, not reliance on traditional values to rein in our worst instincts. Thirty years later, Arthur Schlesinger, Jr., noted the changing definition of liberalism between the nineteenth and twentieth centuries:

> Jefferson had dreamed of a nation of small freeholders and virtuous artisans, united by a sturdy independence, mutual respect and the ownership of property. . . . But the industrial revolution changed all that.
>
> The state consequently had to expand its authority in order to preserve the ties which hold society together. The history of governmental intervention has been the history of the growing ineffectiveness of the private conscience as a means of social control. The only alternative is the growth of the public conscience, whose natural expression is the democratic government.[24]

The dominant and controlling view changed from one favoring a limited government to one favoring a less limited government that acted, for example, to enforce voting rights or to provide for equal employment opportunity. The new idea was to strengthen government to compete more effectively with other centers of power, such as big business. Government's role became one of representing the public interest against competing private interests.

The principles of liberty and equality were once generally considered to be separate and distinct. It was also felt that the more government, the less liberty, and vice versa. Many twentieth-century thinkers believe that absence of government does *not* guarantee liberty. When the government did not act to prevent lynching, its inaction ensured the liberty of the mob, but not that of the individual at the other end of the rope.

Moreover, most people today recognize a link between the principles of liberty and equality. If all people can act freely, disregarding the rights of others, then the armed assailant makes a mockery of the victim's equality of opportunity. But if all people must remain on an equal plane, with no one allowed to get ahead of anyone else, then liberty to pursue one's own goals cannot be said to exist.

The twentieth century has witnessed a dynamic tension between liberty and equality. Roosevelt's New Deal, Kennedy's New Frontier, and Johnson's Great Society defined equality in specific ways—economic, political, legal, and social. The government's role shifted to being the guarantor of equality of opportunity in all these areas. The Voting Rights Act of 1965, for example, allowed African-Americans to compete on a more equal plane with whites in the political process. Such actions enabled more citizens to become better participants in their respective communities.

In sum, the role of government expanded to ensure that democratic procedures promoted democratic principles. In both areas, the goal was the enhancement of individual dignity. At the same time, America remains a deeply religious country with a strong value base. Both Ronald Reagan and George Bush demonstrated this by appealing to the values of religion, family, and community.

ISSUE 3: Summary ★ *Are Democratic Values Eroding?*

Both liberty and equality have been denied on numerous occasions by means of governmental acts, toleration of economic inequality, the undue influence of elite groups in the determination of American values, the adoption of social reforms that make the cure worse than the disease, the encroachment of government into so many areas of private life that it has reduced the freedom of Americans, and the loss of the underlying value base of American democracy.

On the other hand, the freedoms of religion, speech, press, and assembly, greater than those permitted in most other nations, make a strong case that democratic principles are widespread. Also, the government has taken on a larger and more positive role in assisting the less fortunate in society and enabling them to become full participants in their communities. At the same time traditional values have not been neglected. The United States remains perhaps the most religious nation among the Western democracies, making it crucial for politicians to respect religious convictions or at least to tread carefully when considering religious issues. ■

ISSUE 4   *ELITISM VERSUS PLURALISM*

REASONS WHY ELITISM BEST EXPLAINS AMERICAN GOVERNMENT

Various theories have been devised to explain how American government functions. Two of the best known are elitism and pluralism. Proponents of **elitism** argue that to know who actually makes the decisions in American government, we must know who the economic, social, media, and intellectuals elites are. Theorists of **pluralism** contend that public policy results from compromises made between and among competing groups of people; thus, to know how democracy actually works, we must look at what the competing groups are.

Several factors point to the idea that American democracy is a system of elitism. The elites—the few who govern—are unlike the many who are governed. The United States may have a representative democracy, but the representatives do not reflect the essential characteristics of the represented. First, the representatives have substantially greater resources. These include status, leadership skill, information, power, education, wealth, understanding of government and politics, and the skills of communication and organization.[25]

Second, the representatives are much more likely to come from socially prominent and economically affluent groups than from the rank and file of society. Studies of the leaders in American government show that they are not typical of the American public in educational background, socioeconomic status, and other characteristics. And for a long time they could get away with more questionable activities than the rest of us. Then came the check-writing scandal. In September 1991, *Roll Call*, the Capitol Hill newspaper

> *revealed that members of the House of Representatives had written 8,331 bad checks on their own bank in one year. In vain did Tom Foley, the Speaker, rebuke his colleagues; in vain did the House vote overwhelmingly to shut down the bank. The damage was done, and revelation followed revelation: bills in the dining room left unpaid, special perks and expense accounts. Plus embarrassing rehashing of an old scandal: the way Congress routinely excludes its own operations from many employment-protection laws.*[26]

Commenting on the key ingredients of democratic elitism, the Italian political scientist Gaetano Mosca said: "In all societies . . . two classes of people appear—a class that rules and a class that is ruled. The first class, always the less numerous, performs all of the political functions, monopolizes the power, and enjoys the advantages that power brings, whereas the second, the more numerous class, is directed and controlled by the first."[27]

In the United States, as elsewhere, race and class have long been interrelated and often serve as the basis of elitism. As Figure 2.1 suggests, it is better to be white than African-American in the United States if you want to live a longer and healthier life. Democracy is never a smooth process. Inequities are apparent in most democracies and gains toward ending them are rarely shared equally.

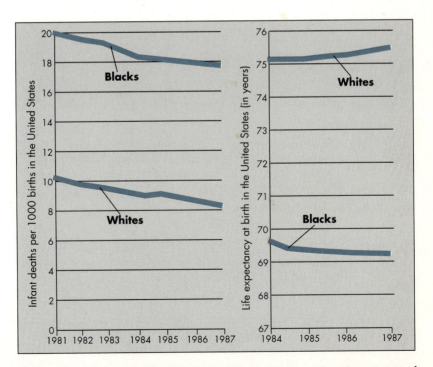

Figure 2.1 TWO BAROMETERS OF HEALTH. Source: "Two Barometers of Health," from *The New York Times*, March 23, 1990. Copyright © 1990 The New York Times Company. Reprinted by permission.

Another powerful force is the bureaucracy and the technological-managerial elite that often makes decisions behind the scenes without adequate public influence. This elite operates in a way that raises serious questions about democracy. Few Americans know about, much less try to influence, the federal regulatory commissions such as the Federal Trade Commission and the Nuclear Regulatory Commission. Dwight D. Eisenhower touched on this issue when he left the presidency in 1961, noting that, although we should hold "scientific research and discovery in respect . . . we must also be alert to the equal and opposite danger that public policy could itself become the captive of a scientific-technological elite."[28]

Certainly, elite groups such as intellectuals, bureaucrats, and media managers occupy an important role in determining values for American society as well as in proposing and implementing public policies. Some might ask: Would we want it any other way? If anything, it could be argued that American society does not utilize its leaders enough. Regardless of the level of elite influence on American society, however, Americans may and sometimes do reject that influence.

REASONS WHY PLURALISM BEST EXPLAINS AMERICAN GOVERNMENT

Certain fundamental democratic procedures and principles operating in the United States offer ample reason to conclude that the nation is in fact a pluralist democracy:

1. *Voting power*. Each adult citizen, with relatively few exceptions, has the right to vote. Each vote is counted as one vote, and each person may cast only one vote. Through voting, the people can change their government's leadership.

2. *Access to information*. Individuals have access to facts and are free to criticize. Given access to information, people can develop alternatives to government policies.

3. *Political organization*. Citizens are generally free to organize for political purposes, as long as they do not abridge the constitutional rights of others. Political organizations, of course, help people to change governmental leadership if they so desire.

4. *Majority rule*. Elections are decided by a majority or plurality: The candidate with the most votes wins.

5. *Minority rights*. The minority has the right to compete to become a majority. The ability of the minority to challenge the majority is always a threat to the majority's leadership and policies.

Each of these procedures and principles allows the people to limit governmental power by giving them the ability to change the government.

Democracy is maintained by the equilibrium of group interaction. A center of power never becomes so powerful that it has no competition or allows for none. Pluralism pits labor against management, teachers against administrators, and producers against consumers. All may compete with one another in influencing government policy. Out of

MADD (Mothers Against Drunk Driving), an interest group composed of ordinary citizens, has been very successful in challenging the liquor industry. This wall of photos of victims of drunk drivers was displayed on the steps of the Capitol.

this competition decisions are made and public policy emerges. In the words of political scientist Aaron Wildavsky, public policy is made by "different small groups of interested and active citizens in different issue areas with some overlap, if any, by public officials, and occasional intervention by a larger number of people at the polls."[29]

Did the beer, wine, and liquor industry want the drinking age increased from 18 to 19, 20, or 21 years of age, as occurred in most states during the 1980s? The organization MADD (Mothers Against Drunk Driving), formed in the early 1980s by an ordinary California woman whose child was killed by a drunk driver, helps to prove that in American pluralism major businesses and industries can be challenged by an aroused citizenry that organizes itself into an interest group. Democracy, after all, does not mean that an individual's rights cannot be abridged in order to safeguard the rights of others. The right to drink is quite sensibly limited by the more important right to live.

ISSUE 4: Summary ★ *Elitism Versus Pluralism*

Elitism offers a persuasive explanation of how elite groups with superior resources have greater opportunity to influence American politics and public policy. Pluralism, on the other hand, offers an excellent analysis of the struggle between and among interest groups vying to influence American politics and public policy. The former, therefore, focuses on leadership while the latter looks at groups influencing policy. While there are leading political scientists on both sides of this question, most are pluralists. However, a reasonable political scientist, whether pluralist or elitist, must necessarily agree that *both* elitism and pluralism are to be found in varying degrees in American constitutional democracy. ■

 ## COMPARISONS WITH OTHER NATIONS

When we look at certain obvious features of the world's political democracies there is a danger of being oversimplistic. Most of us are trained, almost programmed, to look at the bottom line. When we do so, it is easy to see that, overall, the quality of life is better in democracies than nearly everywhere else. Consider, for example, the United Nations publication of *Human Development Report 1990*. The report provides a list of 130 countries (leaving out about 30 small countries with populations under 1 million) and ranks them according to a "human development index" (HDI). The HDI considers such variables as purchasing power, life expectancy, and literacy. The top 21 countries on the list are all political democracies (Table 2.1). Eighteen of these have a higher (but statistically insignificant) ranking than the United States, in great part because our literacy and infant mortality rates lag behind theirs.[30]

TABLE 2.1 SAMPLE HUMAN DEVELOPMENT INDEX*

Democracies		Communist		Selected Authoritarian	
Japan	99.6	North Korea	78.9	Iraq	75.9
Sweden	98.7	Mongolia	73.7	Iran	66.0
Switzerland	98.6	China	71.6	Haiti	35.6
Netherlands	98.4	Vietnam	60.8	Chad	15.7
Canada	98.3	Laos	50.6		
Norway	98.3	Cambodia	47.1		
Australia	97.8				
France	97.4				
Denmark	97.1				
United Kingdom	97.0				
(West) Germany	96.7				
Finland	96.7				
Belgium	96.6				
Italy	96.6				
New Zealand	96.6				
Spain	96.5				
Austria	96.1				
Ireland	96.1				
United States	**96.1**				
Greece	94.9				
Portugal	89.9				

* Key: Less than 50—low human development; 50–80—medium; above 80—high.
Source: From *The Economist Book of Vital World Statistics* by Economist Books Ltd. Copyright © 1990 by Economist Books Ltd. Reprinted by permission of Times Books, a division of Random House, Inc.

Interestingly, democracy also correlates in an inverse manner with the ratio of soldiers to teachers in a country. Britain, for example, has 62 soldiers per 100 teachers; the United States has about an even amount in each category. On the other hand, Syria, a thoroughgoing dictatorship, has 320 soldiers for every 100 teachers. This disproportionate emphasis affects the literacy rate. While the United States and Britain have literacy rates of 96 percent and 99 percent, respectively, Syria's is only 60 percent. Costa Rica, the only authentic democracy in Central America, boasts the region's highest literacy rate, 93 percent. It abolished its army in 1948 and retains only a small national police force.[31]

As noted earlier, democracies tend to be economically prosperous. Even during hard times democracies usually retain a relatively dynamic and innovative economic environment. This is nowhere more apparent than in the purchasing power of the individual consumer. Explore, for example, the information in Table 2.2. Overall, the greatest purchasing power of individuals, as expressed in the per capita share of the country's gross domestic product (GDP), is to be found in democracies. Of the top 25 countries ranked by consumer buying power, 22 are democratic. Despite serious economic problems and unprecedented federal deficits, Americans still have the greatest purchasing power of any nation. It is still less expensive, for example, to own a car, purchase groceries, buy a home, or be entertained here than anywhere else.

It is also important to note that while the United States has long been applauded for its emphasis on political democracy, it provides for few economic guarantees. As we saw in Chapter 1, the United States was the only industrialized democracy without a comprehensive national health insurance program in the early 1990s. This is not a problem for those Americans who can afford private health care. But many members of the minority communities can't afford such care. That helps to explain why African-Americans, for example, have infant mortality and stroke rates more than twice those of whites.[32] Such a large gap between segments of other democratic societies is difficult to find because their governments usually play a heavy role in health-care delivery.

DIFFERENCES AND SIMILARITIES IN DEMOCRATIC STYLES

Political democracies tend to develop in their own time and in their own ways. This is because no standard or universal political doctrine, or ideology, applies across the board. It is just as well, since each country's particular history, geography, and overall culture distinguish its **political culture**—that is, its shared ways of thinking about how political life should function.

The United States is no exception. The American political experience evidences a popular distrust of government emulated by few other countries. We have seen, for instance, that the United States is one of only a handful of established democracies (and the only large one) that limits the terms of its chief executive. And, in the 1992 elections, as we will see in future chapters, voters in 14 states approved term limitations for their senators and representatives. Few democracies have seen fit to opt for limitations for either branch.

Certainly none of the parliamentary systems have. A **parliamentary system** is a democratic form of government that chooses its legislators through national elections but does not popularly elect its chief executive. Instead the executive (prime minister) is

TABLE 2.2   TOP 25 NATIONS RANKED BY BUYING POWER, 1990

Country*	Per Capita GDP
United States	$17,615
Canada	$16,375
Norway	$15,940
Switzerland	$15,403
Luxembourg	$15,247
Denmark	$15,119
West Germany	$14,730
France	$13,961
Hong Kong	$13,906
Kuwait†	$13,843
Sweden	$13,780
Iceland	$13,324
Belgium	$13,140
Japan	$13,135
Finland	$12,795
Singapore	$12,790
Netherlands	$12,661
Austria	$12,386
Britain	$12,270
United Arab Emirates	$12,191
Australia	$11,782
Bahrain	$11,142
Italy	$10,682
New Zealand	$10,541
Israel	$9,182

* Democratic countries in bold.
† Figure precedes Iraqi occupation on August 2, 1990.
Source: Reprinted by permission from *Fortune* magazine; © 1990 Time Inc. All rights reserved.

chosen by the party members with a majority of seats in parliament. The prime minister is not disadvantaged by any term limitation other than the ballot box. Unlike American presidents, prime ministers also make political comebacks: Their party may lose its majority in a national election, but win it back in the next election. Even the French presidential system, which has some similarities to the American one, allows its chief executive to serve as many terms as he or she can get elected to.

Another difference is that most other democracies have large and competitive social democratic parties that occasionally win national elections, and several have communist parties (or former communist parties now operating under a new name) that receive a significant amount of electoral support. The United States has neither. Most democracies still retain a distinct social class system, especially noticeable in Western Europe, whereas the United States is one of a few democratic societies that enjoys a high degree of social mobility. Finally, democracies are usually found in relatively homogeneous societies, such as Australia and Sweden, in which the overwhelming majority of the population belongs to a single ethnic, religious, and linguistic community; the United States, in contrast, is a heterogeneous society, increasingly composed of a variety of ethnic, religious, and language groups.

Still, a great deal more binds democracies than distinguishes them from one another. It would be difficult to locate a political democracy that lacked many of the following characteristics:

Protection of individual rights. In the United States the Bill of Rights has guaranteed individual rights since 1791. Few democracies go farther back: Britain, for example, slowly enacted individual guarantees after 1688, but this process only picked up steam after 1832. The French revolutionary government in 1789 declared the Rights of Man.

Separation of church and state. The American Constitution stipulates this all-important principle in the First Amendment. Other democracies have found other means to accomplish the same guarantee. Interestingly, separation does not formally exist in Britain, where the Church of England is state-supported and the monarch is head of both state and church—but full religious freedom exists anyway. Israel was established as a Jewish state, but legally provides religious freedom to non-Jewish minorities. The opposite extreme is found in France: Article 2 of the French constitution specifically declares the republic to be secular.

Majority government. Democratic political systems depend on a consensual majority of some sort. That is, the American president must be elected by a majority of the electoral college; parliamentary governments like Britain's must control a majority of seats in the national legislature to take and remain in political power; and popularly elected presidents, as in France, must secure an absolute majority of the voting electorate.

Loyal opposition. The losing party must be confident that it will have another opportunity to transform itself into the government and in the meantime feel comfortable being critical of the government. Guaranteeing that another election will be held in a constitutionally prescribed time period normally guarantees the opposition's loyalty to the political system. In presidential elections in the United States this custom came to be very special for the consistently losing Democratic party (until its victory in 1992).

Political consensus. Democracies are fragile affairs and have to count on a broad consensus on political values and norms. This consensus is usually developed over time and in a fairly voluntary fashion.

CONDITIONS FOR DEMOCRATIZATION

It is not always clear when a society becomes a political democracy. The process of **democratization**—the establishment of a democratic political culture—can be a long one.

Older democracies took their time about maturing. Political institutions in Britain began slowly to assume democratic characteristics as far back as 1215, when King John signed the Magna Charta. After 1789 the French experimented with different forms of government that included five republics, three constitutional monarchies, and two emperorships. Sometimes the process of democratization is a tortured one. Democracy in several countries seemed to gain impetus only after serious civil conflict. As Table 2.3 indicates, democracies can have their times of trouble.

Sometimes a country sprouts a full-blown democracy almost overnight. This is known as an **instantaneous democracy**. Japan and Germany were allowed to regain their national sovereignty after losing World War II only by agreeing to become democratic. Israel, a newly formed state in 1948, deliberately started off as a democracy and has remained that way. Other instantaneous democracies may have begun to appear among the Eastern European countries in the early 1990s.

Why doesn't every country take the opportunity to become democratic? Answering that question could take the rest of this book. Suffice it to say, though, that democracies in their late-twentieth-century guise usually require a number of socioeconomic and technological conditions, along with the political ones, to be successful. The following list is not all-inclusive and surely needs to allow for exceptions, but the conditions for democratization itemized below are fairly commonplace.

A broad, large, and accessible middle class. Nearly 2500 years ago Aristotle strongly urged basing political stability in great part on the reduction of extremes of wealth and poverty. The United States and other established democracies are far from being Aristotle's ideal, but the numbers of people within their middle-class system are overwhelming. Exceptions among democratic countries include Costa Rica, in which poverty is more evenly distributed.

Literacy. Although American high schools (and some universities) regularly graduate a great many functionally illiterate students, a literate population does exist and in large enough numbers to safely refer to the United States as a literate society. (Americans, however, are literate without necessarily being literary. In 1990, when Supreme Court nominee David Souter was discovered to be an avid reader of serious literature, it made the news.) But literacy does not by itself promote democracy. Germany, a very literate and cultured society, produced the

TABLE 2.3 CIVIL CONFLICT IN SELECTED POLITICAL DEMOCRACIES	
Country	Time of Conflict
Britain	1640s*
Switzerland	1840s*
United States	1861–1865
Spain	1936–1939
* Conflict was sporadic throughout the period indicated.	

Nazis, and the Russians, whose reading habits tend to be more sophisticated than those of Americans, took 70 years to get out from under the communist yoke.

Health. Sick and malnourished people have neither the leisure nor the inclination to care about government. For example, until most of the population of Africa, the poorest continent in the world and the fount of such terrifying diseases as AIDS, reaches a certain level of physical health there is little hope for a political evolution in the direction of democracy. Africa is the only region in the world that still experiences major periodic famines. In many authoritarian countries, it is the army that is the best-fed social unit. Its officers often control the government, usually in a fairly brutal fashion.

Modern technology. A number of nondemocratic societies possess state-of-the-art technologies of communication and transportation. However, it is mostly the democratic ones that are willing and able to share this technology with their citizens in the form of personal computers, telephone answering machines, microwave ovens, and affordable modes of mass transport.

Of course, the qualities of political democracies can remain elusive. For example, how many consecutive free elections must occur before they are accepted by both winners

Sometimes the qualities of a political democracy can be elusive. In 1992, when Peru was unsettled by internal conflicts, its president abruptly suspended the constitution and instituted martial law. The protesting legislators shown here were trying to get to the National Congress but were turned back by the soldiers.

and losers? How assured can a nation be that the military will not stage a coup and oust an elected civilian government? And at what point can people go to sleep at night confident that its government will not suspend constitutionally protected rights before they wake up in the morning?

The answers to such questions will differ somewhat from democracy to democracy. There is little doubt that Japan could be considered a slightly less developed democracy than the United States because of its emphasis on male prerogatives. Few Americans think anything, for instance, of female golfers. Until the late 1980s, though, a female golfer was nearly unheard of in Japan. By 1989 younger women were teeing off anyway (with designer golf balls, no less). Even in conservative Japan some traditions are breaking down.[33] As they do, the society tends to adopt increasingly democratic values that gradually (but rarely entirely) dissolve distinctions between social classes, genders, and even age groups.

A revealing demographic study suggests that democracy could come last of all to most of the women of the world. In nondemocratic societies many women tend to "disappear." "If sex discrimination in the West means office harassment or fewer good jobs for women, in the Third World it often means death. A traditional preference for boys translates quickly—in China, India, and many other developing countries—into neglect and death for girls. This phenomenon usually takes the form of abortion or infanticide. Table 2.4 indicates the frightening statistics.

IS DEMOCRACY INEVITABLE?

It would be foolish to assume that democracy is inevitable. The "tide" of democracy is neither inevitable nor completely practical in a number of countries. Many countries are

TABLE 2.4 MISSING WOMEN IN POPULATIONS OF SELECTED AREAS

	China	India	Pakistan	Bangladesh	Nepal	West Asia	Egypt
Census date	1990	1991	1981	1981	1981	1985	1986
Actual ratio of males to females	1.066	1.077	1.105	1.064	1.050	1.060	1.047
Expected ratio	1.010	1.020	1.025	1.025	1.025	1.030	1.020
Number of females (millions)	548.7	406.3	40.0	42.2	7.3	55.0	23.5
Number of missing females (millions)	**30.5**	**22.8**	**3.1**	**1.6**	**0.2**	**1.7**	**0.6**

Data from *Population and Development Review*.
Source: "Missing Women in Populations of Selected Areas," from "Stark Data on Women: 100 Million Are Missing," *The New York Times*, November 5, 1991. Copyright © 1991 The New York Times Company. Reprinted by permission.

A VIEW FROM THE STATES
"Democracy" in Kuwait

Kuwait on Monday [October 5, 1992] holds its first national election since the Persian Gulf war, reopening a 30-year-old battle between the political opposition and the emirate's ruling family over how democratic the nation will be.

The United States and other nations that sent forces to drive Iraqi troops out of Kuwait last year have pressed the ruling family to establish a more representative system. They are uneasy that Western troops spilled their blood to reinstate a government perceived as cavalier about democracy.

But the election for the 50-seat Parliament is hardly democratic in the Western sense. Women are denied the vote. And only men aged 21 or over whose families have been in the emirate since before 1921—81,400 of Kuwait's 606,000 nationals—can cast ballots for the 278 candidates.

Election campaigning, although directed only at the 13 percent of the populace that can vote, is a costly and elaborate business. . . .

Western diplomats and opposition candidates contend that many Government-backed candidates simply dole out money and favors for votes, a charge the Government denies.

. . . [T]he ruling family, in power in the emirate for over two centuries, has always been reluctant to give up the iron grip it has on everything from the public purse to foreign policy. Over the last decade it has become more insular, increasingly filling major posts with family members and shunning the participation of outsiders.

Source: "Democracy in Kuwait," from "Kuwait Today Reopens Democracy Fight," by Chris Hedges. *The New York Times,* October 5, 1992. Copyright © 1992 The New York Times Company. Reprinted by permission.

as far away from either developing or welcoming democratic institutions as they were generations ago. And as Tocqueville observed in the 1830s, democracy (and American democracy in particular) has its own flaws. The problem is that majoritarianism is often equated with democratic governance. Tocqueville wrote, "I know no country in which, speaking generally, there is less independence of mind and true freedom of discussion than in America."[34]

Tocqueville feared the danger of tyranny of the majority. He was right to do so. Many despotic governments insist that they are democratic, and that if 99 percent of the electorate agree with the government's policies, that proves the point that there is something wrong with the individuals who disagree. The remaining 1 percent are simply permanent malcontents. Such governments are personal regimes, in which political megalomaniacs convince themselves that their presence is essential for both the present and future well-being of their country.

It is the institutional framework that guarantees, sustains, and promotes democratic government. And institutions are remarkably versatile. For example, in the United

Kingdom, a thoroughly democratic society, at least two of its foremost and oldest political institutions are the inherited monarchy and the unelected House of Lords. Neither of these had democratic origins and both at one point exercised considerable power. Over several generations they gradually (and sometimes painfully) relinquished their power to the lower house, the popularly elected House of Commons.

But no political process will always be smooth or peaceful. The democratization of the United Kingdom succeeded in great part because incumbent elites understood that their survival required them to yield power to other political forces, which grew out of the social and economic changes of the industrial revolution. The British were able to do this better than most. Other entrenched elites, such as Russia's in 1917, had to be forcibly removed through rather brutal revolutions. Political reforms made at the top tend to produce democratization much more efficiently, in less time, and usually with less violence than revolutions from below.

The apparent demise of communism may provide some local impetus to democracy. But, in the global demographic context, even the addition of Eastern Europe to the politically democratic "column" will not change things very much. Eastern Europe and the republics of the former Soviet Union, the next logical area for democracy to take root, account for a total of 8 percent of the world's population. Even when combined with the West's 15 percent, less than one-fourth of the globe's people will be living under democratic regimes.[35] Because of the rapid population growth of the developing countries of the Third World, that proportion will sink to only one-fifth by 2010.

Democracy's challenge is thus perhaps best understood in the context of a global underclass. Not only is population growing considerably faster than the ability of governments to provide minimal food, shelter, and jobs, but the leisure required to induce people to carefully consider their political destinies is lacking. Between 1990 and 2005 the Third World work force will have increased by 700 million, the numerical equivalent of the work force in both democratic and formerly communist industrialized societies in 1985. It is unlikely that jobs will be created for a large part of that 700 million. And if they aren't, the world's political stability is obviously at risk.[36]

It is likely that many of the Third World workers will be looking to the democratic nations (or First World) for employment. Millions already have. Table 2.5 suggests where some of the immigrants are coming from and where they are going. The United States shares with several other Western industrialized democracies a common challenge: how to integrate a substantial influx of unskilled and often illiterate workers and their families not only into a national economy but also into a totally alien political culture.

TABLE 2.5 A BRIEF LIST OF MIGRATORY PATTERNS

From	To
Algeria and Tunisia	France
Turkey, several Eastern European countries	Germany
South Asia (India, Pakistan, Sri Lanka), West Indies	United Kingdom
Mexico, Central America, Cuba, Haiti, East Asia	United States

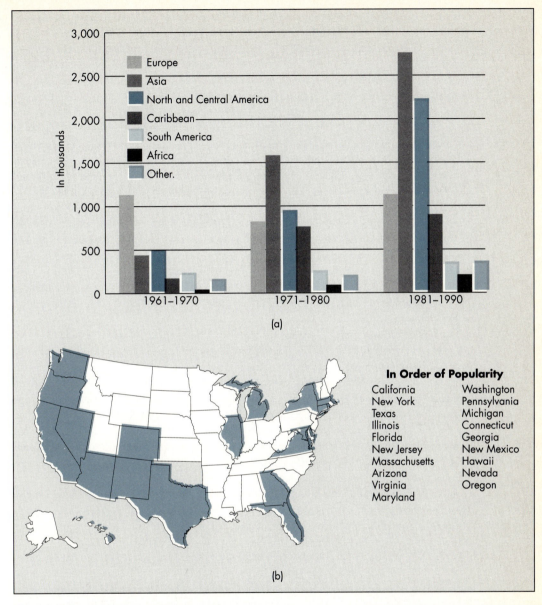

Figure 2.2 PATTERNS OF IMMIGRATION. (a) U.S. Immigration by Country 1961–1990. (b) Preferred States in Which to Settle in 1990. Source: "U.S. Immigration by Country 1961–1990" by Shirley Horn, *The Christian Science Monitor,* June 17, 1992; © 1992 Christian Science Publishing Society.

And, to complicate matters, Third World immigrants may be competing with other immigrants from former communist countries where economic conditions have deteriorated.

The United States is still the immigrant destination of choice. During the 1980s more immigrants entered the United States than in any other previous decade. They were setting records for another reason as well: In 1965 only one in ten immigrants were non-European; by 1985 nine in ten were.[37] (See Figure 2.2.)

The most serious obstacle to the integration of immigrants and to the progress of political democracy may very well be extremist organizations whose advocacy of racism already had an established electoral appeal by the early 1990s. The movement over the last several years of North Africans to France and Italy, and Eastern and southeastern Europeans to Germany—accelerated by the departure of thousands of Bosnians and Croatians from the former Yugoslavia, where they encountered millions of Turks in already established neighborhoods of German cities—has put unprecedented pressures on job markets, school systems, and social welfare agencies. Many Germans, French, and Italians are fearful that, unless the number of immigrants is reduced or at least contained, their relatively prosperous economic status as well as the indigenous culture will be overtaken. Some have turned to extremist political parties that have succeeded in winning local legislative seats and even seats in the national parliament. Some extremists have also taken to beating up those they regard as foreigners in order to encourage them to leave. The danger (and, for democracies, the embarrassment) is certainly apparent: "Neo-nazis in Germany; anti-Semitism in Poland; anti-immigrant parties surging in Austria and Switzerland; a former imperial grand wizard of the Ku Klux Klan running as a Republican for the governorship of Louisiana: from the Urals to the Ozarks, it seems, the scum is rising."[38]

The process of democratization has a long and probably hard road left to travel. Democracy is still far from fully established in Eastern Europe. Old and entrenched elites are understandably reluctant to democratize if it means a lessening of their political power (and it always does). The elite, however, may not be the only or even the most formidable obstacle to democratization. Table 2.6 outlines other possibilities, including ethno-nationalist political movements, religious authorities, and the military.

To be sure, many Western societies labored under similar difficulties. Very few observers believed half a century ago that Germany or Japan would be sterling examples of democracy in the 1990s. Some even believed that such countries had cultures completely alien to the democratic process.

Nations that firmly establish democracies are unlikely to destroy them. One or two free elections does not a democracy make, of course. But it is obvious that some countries adjust more readily to democratic processes than others. The opportunities may

TABLE 2.6 OBSTACLES TO DEMOCRATIZATION

Region	Obstacles
Eastern Europe and the former Soviet Union	Residues of Communist party apparatus; ethno-nationalist political movements
Middle East	Traditional monarchies; intolerant religious agendas; radical nationalist regimes
Africa	Strong military influence on government or actual control; tribal loyalties

be greater than ever before. Democracy has become the political system of choice for those societies that have a choice about their politics. Its association with economic prosperity along with the convenient collapse of communism have produced an appeal that is unlikely to be challenged.

Summary

1. There are important differences between economic and political democracies. The latter dominate Western society while the former were emphasized in communist societies.

2. *Democracy* itself is a term and a political activity first defined and created in Greece. From its beginnings 2500 years ago, democracy has come to mean rule by the people or their elected representatives, and includes both principles (such as majority rule and respect for minority rights) and procedures (such as regularly scheduled competitive elections).

3. Representative government—government by elected representatives—is commonplace because of the great numbers of people to be governed. Direct democracy—decision making by citizens themselves—is a thing of the past except for local and town meetings.

4. Several features characterize democracy, including a large and well-educated middle class, a relatively equitable distribution of national wealth, and opportunities for individual improvement and development.

5. Were the Founders democrats? The founders of the United States may not have produced a democracy in the strict sense, in large part because of their distrust of majority rule, but they did create a government that had the potential of becoming more democratic. The Bill of Rights guaranteed the implementation of democratic ideals, particularly safeguards for individual rights.

6. Is America sufficiently democratic? Democracies are imperfect political systems. The United States has some inadequate procedures, such as inequitable distribution of resources and inequitable representation of groups. But over time a great deal of progress has been made to include all people in the democratic process. African-Americans, for example, have more opportunities and greater potential today than at any time in the past.

7. Are democratic values eroding? Those who think they are point to various governmental abuses, the undue influence of elite groups, the growth of government that has threatened individual liberty, and excessive individualism. Yet the dilemma of maximizing democracy in America or anywhere else has to do with the contradictory emphases on liberty and equality. The government has taken on a larger role in order to help those who are not full participants in our society. In any society a balance is required between the extremes of too little or too much individualism.

8. Elitism and pluralism are two concepts utilized to examine democracy and political society in general. Proponents of elitism believe that the important decisions in

government are made by economic, social, media, and intellectual elites. Pluralists contend that public policy results from the interaction of competing groups.

9. Political democracies tend to be stable, literate, and prosperous. While their ideologies and political cultures may differ in significant ways, there are many similarities as well, including generally accepted respect for individual rights, separation of church and state, and majority government.

10. The process of democratization requires certain socioeconomic conditions if it is to be successful: a large middle class, literacy, health, and widespread technology.

11. Democracy today applies to only a small percentage of the world's population. Obstacles to democracy come from authoritarian tendencies in many societies, the growing Third World work force, and resentment stirred by migratory patterns of several Third World communities.

Terms to Define

Constitutional democracy

Democracy

Democratization

Direct democracy

Economic democracy

Elitism

Instantaneous democracy

Majority rule

Minority rights

Parliamentary system

Pluralism

Political culture

Political democracy

Representative democracy

Republic

Suggested Readings

"Black Americans: Still Trailing Behind," *The Economist*, March 3, 1990, pp. 17–19. A timely comparison of the white and black communities in the United States. The evidence is overwhelming that the American democracy is still an incomplete dream for African-Americans.

Brown, Bernard. *Protest in Paris: Anatomy of a Revolt* (Morristown, N.J.: General Learning Press, 1974). This very readable essay concentrates on the Paris revolt led by university students in the spring of 1968 (just before final examinations). The revolt was a remarkable test of traditional democratic institutions and their ability to be resilient during a time of great social change.

Ellul, Jacques. *The Political Illusion*. Trans. Konrad Keller (New York: Vintage, 1967). The author offers a depressing but impressive argument that democracy is not always a reality. Elites do rule and, worse, manipulate the rest of us.

Ladd, Everett C. "The Prejudices of a Tolerant Society," *Public Opinion*, July/August 1987, pp. 2–3 and 56. The American democracy, as this essay suggests, is not as tolerant as it could or should be, nor is prejudice restricted to extremist organizations such as the Ku Klux Klan. Economic adversity tends to bring out the bigot in a lot of otherwise decent people.

Plato. *The Republic*. Trans. Richard W. Sterling and William C. Scott (New York and London: Norton, 1985). This earliest statement of Western political philosophy is hostile to both politics and to democracy. The reasons are frighteningly convincing.

Notes

1. Carl Becker, *Modern Democracy* (New Haven: Yale University Press, 1941), p. 26.
2. *Parliamentary Debates*, House of Commons, 5th Series, Vol. 444 (London: His Majesty's Stationery Office, 1947), pp. 206–207.
3. John Locke, "An Essay Concerning the True Origin, Extent and End of Civil Government," in Edwin A. Burtt, ed., *The English Philosophers from Bacon to Mill* (New York: Modern Library, 1939), p. 404.
4. *The Federalist*, 55, p. 346 (Rossiter edition).
5. Ibid., p. 353.
6. Ibid., 37, p. 231.
7. Ibid., 48, p. 471.
8. Ibid., 2, p. 40.
9. Thomas Jefferson, *"Resolution Relative to the Alien and Sedition Laws"* 1978 in Philip S. Faver (ed.), *Basic Writings of Thomas Jefferson* (New York: John Wiley, 1944), p. 330.
10. *The Comparative Study of Elites* (Stanford: Stanford University Press, 1952), p. 7.
11. Laile E. Barlett, "The Education of Eldridge Cleaver," *Reader's Digest*, September 1976, pp. 71, 72.
12. Sidney Hook, *Political Power and Personal Freedom* (New York: Criterion, 1959), pp. 19–28.
13. Alan Wolfe, *The Seamy Side of Democracy* (New York: David McKay, 1973), p. 4.
14. John Dewey, "Democracy and Education Administration," *School and Society* 45 (April 3, 1937): 457.
15. Linda Lichter et al., "Hollywood and America: The Odd Couple," *Public Opinion*, December/January 1983, pp. 54–59.
16. Rexford Guy Tugwell, "Rewriting the Constitution," *The Center Magazine*, March 1968, pp. 18-25.
17. Ibid.
18. Aleksandr I. Solzhenitsyn, *A World Split Apart* (New York: Harper & Row, 1979).
19. As quoted in Charles L. Wallis, ed., *Our American Heritage* (New York: Harper & Row, 1970), p. 19.
20. Ibid., p. 52.
21. Ibid., p. 26.
22. James W. Protho and Charles M. Grigg, "Fundamental Principles of Democracy," *The Journal of Politics* 22 (1960): 294.
23. Quoted in Howard Zinn, ed., *New Deal Thought* (Indianapolis: Bobbs-Merrill, 1966), p. 10.
24. Arthur Schlesinger, Jr., *The Vital Center* (Boston: Houghton Mifflin, 1962), p. 176.
25. Donald R. Mathews, *The Social Background of Political Decision-makers* (New York: Doubleday, 1954); and David T. Stanley, Dean E. Mann and Jameson W. Doieg, *Men Who Govern* (Washington, D.C.: The Brookings Institution, 1967).
26. "Something Awful Has Happened," *The Economist*, October 19, 1991, p. 25.
27. *The Ruling Class* (New York: McGraw-Hill, 1939), p. 50.
28. "Farewell Address," *The New York Times*, January 18, 1961, p. A1.
29. Aaron Wildavsky, *Leadership in a Small Town* (Totowa, N. J.: Bedminster Press, 1964), p. 20.
30. *The Economist*, May 26, 1990, pp. 80–81.
31. Ibid.
32. *The New York Times*, March 22, 1990, p. A8.
33. *The Wall Street Journal*, July 27, 1990, pp. A1 and A8.
34. Alexis de Tocqueville, *Democracy in America*, trans. George Lawrence, ed. J. P. Mayer (Garden City, N.Y.: Doubleday, 1969), pp. 252–255.
35. R. Scott Fosler, William Alonso, Jack A. Meyer, and Rosemary Kem, *Demographic Change and the American Future* (Pittsburgh: University of Pittsburgh Press, 1990), p. 11.
36. *The Economist*, March 16, 1991, p. 42.
37. Ibid.
38. "Racism's Back," *The Economist*, November 16, 1991, p. 15.

THE CONSTITUTION

The oldest written national constitution is the Constitution of the United States. Only four nations—Norway, Argentina, Luxembourg, and Colombia—have constitutions that were written prior to 1900, and only 15 contemporary national constitutions existed before World War II. About 75 of the national constitutions now in effect were written after 1970, in great part because most of the countries they govern did not exist before then. Remarkably, only five nations—the United Kingdom, New Zealand, Israel, Saudi Arabia, and Oman—do not have written constitutions.

The United States Constitution is both revered and repudiated. Some scholars regard it as one of the greatest democratic documents in all history. They see it as a major milestone in the evolution of democracy, ranking it in importance with Britain's Magna Charta, the English Bill of Rights of 1689, and the Declaration of Independence.

A second view, however, holds that the Constitution has outlived whatever usefulness it once had. Those who adhere to this view believe the document is irrelevant to the needs and problems of the last quarter of the twentieth century. They contend that mass communication and advanced technology, together with the crisis atmosphere in which we live, necessitate a government that can act quickly. Yet the structure set up by the American Constitution is slow and cumbersome. It divides power between the national and state governments and disperses national authority among the legislative, executive, and judicial branches.

A third view is that, although the Constitution was an imposing document when it was drafted, its basic concepts have been corrupted. Those holding this attitude are especially concerned by such developments as the centralization of power in the national government and extensive federal regulation of American society. They maintain that the intentions of the Founders was to limit the scope and power of the government.

According to a fourth view, the American Constitution was not very democratic when drafted, but became more so with changes over the years. As evidence, those holding this view point to constitutional amendments that extend the rights of African-Americans, broaden the suffrage, and provide for a graduated income tax, popular election of senators, and abolition of the poll tax.

A fifth view, held mostly by radical and revolutionary persons, contends that the Constitution was drafted and ratified to protect the interests of elite groups and that it has continued to do so. In other words, it was undemocratic when drafted and remains so today.

In this chapter we will examine the strengths and weaknesses of these differing views and interpretations of the Constitution and compare our Constitution to others in the world. But first it is necessary to understand how our Constitution came about and what its main features are.

★ INTRODUCTION TO THE AMERICAN CONSTITUTION

HISTORICAL BACKGROUND

From their earliest days in America, the colonists gave ample indication of their belief in law and representative government. The Mayflower Compact (1620), drafted and signed by the Pilgrims before they landed at Plymouth, declared that "we . . . do by Presents, solemnly and mutually in the Presence of God and one another, covenant and combine ourselves together into a civil Body Politick." This document is important as a covenant establishing civil government by common consent. In 1619 settlers at Jamestown created the first representative assembly in America, the Virginia House of Burgesses. In 1639 New England Puritans drafted America's first written constitution, the Fundamental Orders of Connecticut. Another early document, the Massachusetts Body of Liberties (1641), guaranteed such rights as trial by jury and due process of law.

An additional factor in the democratic development of the Constitution was colonial government. Although the 13 colonies were set up and ruled in various ways, they had certain elements in common. Each had a written charter, which established the form of government and the rights of the colonists. Each colonial government had executive, legislative and judicial branches. Decisions of colonial courts could generally be appealed to the Privy Council in London. Also, several colonies had bicameral legislatures, elections of legislators, and bills of rights to protect their citizens. At least six characteristics of colonial government, then, were subsequently incorporated into the United States Constitution:

1. The idea of a written document spelling out government functions and citizens' rights,
2. Separation of powers,
3. A bicameral legislature,
4. Elections,
5. Judicial appeal, and
6. A bill of rights.

The paradox of the American Revolution is that the colonists rebelled because they felt that their rights as English subjects were being denied. Yet, to support their contention, they turned to such British legal landmarks as the Magna Charta, the Habeas Corpus Act of 1679, and the Bill of Rights of 1689. Numerous ideas in the American Declaration of Independence, the Constitution, and the Bill of Rights had their origin in English history. Of course, the whole English common law system—the cumulative body of law as expressed in judicial decisions and custom—influenced Americans, especially as it was conceived as a limitation on the power of the king.

Another important influence was the political theory of John Locke, which emphasized natural rights. These rights, Locke argued, are more basic and fundamental than government itself and indeed existed before the government did. All people are free, equal, and independent, according to Locke, and cannot be governed by others, unless they give their consent.[1] Locke thus conceived of government as limited, an institution created by people who agreed through what he called a "social contract" (which the Constitution was).

Locke also advocated a separation or balancing of powers, with authority divided among different branches of government. The French philosopher the Baron de Montesquieu, who had substantial influence among the men who drafted the Constitution, also advanced this idea.

The drafting of the Constitution itself was prompted by dissatisfaction with the Articles of Confederation, which had established the structure of the first national government from 1781 to 1789. The Articles originated with a proposal placed before the Continental Congress that a plan for "perpetual union" be created. Following the adoption of the Declaration of Independence in 1776, Congress appointed a committee to draw up a plan of confederation. After Congress approved the committee's work in 1777, four years passed before all the states finally ratified the Articles and they went into effect.

The United States achieved some successes under the Articles of Confederation. The country won the American Revolution and ratified a peace treaty, it established important allies in the international community, and it created a postal service and a national bureaucracy. But the "perpetual union" that the Articles created was more an alliance of 13 independent states than a union of the people. The few powers that the national government had were all in the hands of Congress. Neither an executive nor a judicial branch existed except as Congress created them. Committees of Congress addressed governmental affairs. This legislative focus, of course, reflected popular discontent with the centralized executive authority of the English Crown. But in their determination to avoid a strong central government, the drafters of the Articles built in certain structural deficiencies:

1. The national government could not levy taxes without the consent of the states (which the states were reluctant to provide). Without taxing power, the government could not pay its debts. And this angered the Americans who had lent money to the government during the Revolution but had no way to regain their investments after the war.

2. The national government could not regulate commerce among the states or with foreign governments. Commercial and shipping interests were at the mercy of the individual states, which set their own tariffs and thus impaired the flow of interstate and foreign commerce.

3. The national government could not coin money. The states printed cheap paper bills with which debtors paid their creditors. Thus, lenders received payments in money worth substantially less than their original loans.

4. Because the government had to have unanimity among the states to levy taxes and to amend the Articles, it lacked sufficient power to govern. Moreover, Congress often had second-rate delegates because well-qualified persons refused to serve in such a weak institution.

In addition to these structural deficiencies, the national government under the Articles failed to cope with some specific problems. One was local uprisings. In 1786 farmers, artisans, and laborers—angry because their property had been seized to satisfy their debts—joined to capture courthouses in several Massachusetts towns. Only a mercenary army paid for by propertied citizens quelled this uprising, known as Shays' Rebellion.

Another problem was that the government could not oust the British from their forts in the Northwest Territory. Consequently, its ability to protect settlers and foster the economic growth of inland America seemed limited. Finally, the national goverment enjoyed little prestige or power in foreign affairs. At a time when a strong sense of nationalism was developing, Americans felt frustrated by their poor showing on the international stage.

The Articles of Confederation, it might be noted, were not a total waste. They contributed several features to the Constitution of the United States. Under the Articles the national government had the power to declare war, send and receive ambassadors, make treaties, fix standards of weights and measures, regulate the value of coins, manage Indian affairs, establish post offices, borrow money, and build and equip an army and navy. These powers were retained under the Constitution. Under both systems each state was required to give "full faith and credit" to the records, acts, and judicial proceedings of every other state, and citizens of each state had the "privileges and immunities" of citizens in other states.

By 1785, there was a good deal of concern about economic problems in the new nation. During a conference between Virginia and Maryland called to settle differences about commerce and navigation, delegates suggested calling a general economic conference of all the states. This meeting, held in Annapolis the following year, focused on the weaknesses of the Articles of Confederation. Just after this convention met, Shays' Rebellion dramatically reinforced the arguments of those opposed to the Articles.

In February 1787, Congress issued a call for a convention to meet in Philadelphia "for the sole and express purpose of revising the Articles of Confederation and reporting to Congress and the several legislatures such alterations and provisions therein as shall, when agreed to in Congress and confirmed by the states, render the federal Constitution adequate to the exigencies of government and the preservation of the union."

CONVENTION COMPROMISES

At the Constitutional Convention, which convened in May 1787, it soon became apparent that "revising" the Articles would not be sufficient. An entirely new document would have to be created. Differences among the 13 states led to critical conflicts that frequently seemed insoluble. There was tension between the more populous and less

"Washington Addressing the Constitutional Convention" by Junius Brutus Stearns. Washington had his hands full that summer of 1787 managing the competing claims of large and small states, slave and free states, and commercial and agricultural states.

populous states, between the nonslave and the slave states, and between the somewhat commercial and the largely agricultural states. The Constitution that evolved over the long hot Philadelphia summer embodied numerous compromises among these varying interests.

Large Versus Small States

The delegates spent a good deal of time debating two alternative ways of setting up the government—the Virginia Plan and the New Jersey Plan. Both advocated separation of powers among legislative, executive, and judicial branches of the national government, but they differed in modes of representation.

The Virginia Plan, introduced by Governor Edmund Randolph of Virginia, contained these provisions, among others: (1) a **bicameral** (two-house) legislature in which the lower house would be chosen by the people and the upper house chosen by the lower; representation in the lower house would be proportionate to population; (2) a "national executive" (its precise makeup not spelled out) to be elected by the legislature; (3) a national judiciary to be chosen by the legislature.

The New Jersey Plan, introduced by William Paterson of that state, was basically a continuation of the Articles of Confederation. It included these stipulations: (1) a **unicameral** (one-house) legislature, with each state having one vote; (2) Congress to choose an executive consisting of more than one person; and (3) the executive to appoint justices to a Supreme Court.

Clearly, the Virginia Plan, with its call for proportionate representation in Congress, favored the more populous states, while the New Jersey Plan favored the smaller ones by specifying one vote for each state. The Convention finally adopted what came to be called the "Great Compromise" (sometimes called the "Connecticut Compromise" because it was proposed by Roger Sherman of Connecticut). It set up a bicameral legislature. The lower house—the House of Representatives—would be apportioned according to population. The upper house—the Senate—would consist of two members from each state, elected by the state legislatures. The large states obtained the advantage in the House of Representatives, where population determined the number of representatives. The small states had the advantage in the Senate, since each state, regardless of its population, had two senators. The "Great Compromise" also resolved several other disputes including the issues of slavery and taxation.

Slavery and Taxation

The southern states wanted to count their slaves as part of their population for the purpose of increasing their representation in the House of Representatives; the northern states held that slaves should be regarded solely as property. To resolve this dispute, the Convention agreed on the "three-fifths compromise": three-fifths of all slaves would be counted in apportioning members of the House of Representatives and also for tax purposes.

While there was substantial antislavery sentiment among the delegates, they agreed only that the slave trade itself could be abolished after 1808. The statements of two delegates illustrate the conflicting feelings on this issue. Charles Pinckney of South

Carolina declared that his state would not ratify the Constitution if the slave trade were abolished, while George Mason of Virginia, even though slavery was a thriving institution in his state, predicted that slavery would "bring the judgment of heaven" on the nation.[2]

Another element of the compromise concerning slavery and taxation dealt with commerce. Since the South exported almost all its agricultural products, it feared that export taxes would make its products noncompetitive in the international market. As a concession to the South, the Constitution specified that the United States could not levy export taxes. It is one of few nations denied this right.

Out of these compromises emerged a document that has now lasted more than two hundred years. Many of its provisions were then and still are controversial.

STRUCTURE OF THE CONSTITUTION

The U.S. Constitution—approximately 7,500 words long—is brief when compared with today's state constitutions (some well over 100,000 words) and with most constitutions of other democracies. The Founders seemingly tried to write a document embodying general principles that could be adapted to succeeding generations, rather than drafting a series of specific and precise provisions.

The Constitution created three branches of government: legislative—the Congress; executive—the president; and judicial—the courts. The first three articles, in particular, enumerate the powers of the three branches.

Article I specifies the structure of Congress (House and Senate), qualifications and method of election of members, and powers of the legislature. Of special importance are the powers to regulate commerce, coin money, and declare war. Taxes and appropriations can be increased or decreased only through congressional action, with the House, the body more directly representative of the people, initiating all revenue bills. Article I, section 8, not only lists those powers specifically delegated to the national government, but it also contains a clause giving Congress the power "to make all Laws which shall be necessary and proper for carrying into Execution the foregoing Powers." This has been called the **elastic clause** because the phrase "necessary and proper" can be interpreted to "stretch" national powers. Article I also includes some restrictions on federal power in order to preserve the rights of the people (restrictions that were emulated later by newer democracies, as we shall see):

- The **writ of habeas corpus**, which requires that an officer show adequate grounds for jailing or imprisoning a person, cannot be suspended under normal circumstances.

- **Bills of attainder**, which are legislative acts punishing persons without a trial, are forbidden.

- **Ex post facto laws**, which punish acts that were legal when committed, are declared unconstitutional.

The presidency and vice presidency, the qualifications and manner of election of the two offices, and the powers of the executive branch are the subjects of Article II.

Unlike senators and representatives, the president and vice president must be native-born citizens, at least 35 years old. An electoral college is provided for selection. One of four sections of Article II is devoted to how to get rid of a president through impeachment. This section highlights the entrenched distrust of executive power that was learned through hard experience during colonial times. The president is commander in chief of the armed forces, can make treaties subject to the advice and consent of the Senate, and appoints ambassadors, judges, and other high officials.

Article III discusses the Supreme Court, such lesser federal courts as Congress may establish, and their jurisdictions. **Jurisdiction** refers to the types of cases that a court may decide. Except as limited by the Constitution, Congress has the power to determine jurisdiction of the courts. Article III also provides another important right of the people, trial by jury, except in cases of impeachment.

Article IV establishes rules that govern relationships among the states and between the states and the national government. Each state shall respect the laws and judicial proceedings of other states, grant citizens from other states the same "privileges and immunities" enjoyed by its own citizens, and extradite fugitives from the law of other states. New states can be admitted to the Union but not if they are carved out of the jurisdiction of already existing states without the consent of the states involved. The national government guarantees every state a republican form of government and will protect the states from invasion and, on request, from domestic violence.

Article V describes how to amend the Constitution. The framers devised an amendment process consisting of two ways to propose and two ways to ratify an amendment (described in the next section).

Article VI incorporates the **supremacy clause:** "This Constitution, and the laws of the United States which shall be made in Pursuance thereof; and all Treaties made, or which shall be made, under the Authority of the United States, shall be the supreme Law of the Land; and the Judges in every State shall be bound thereby, any Thing in the Constitution or Laws of any State to the Contrary notwithstanding." In other words, this clause declares that the Constitution and the laws and the treaties adopted pursuant to it are the "supreme law of the land," taking precedence over state laws.

Article VII establishes how the Constitution was to be ratified: by state conventions in at least 9 of the 13 states.

THE CONSTITUTION'S AMENDMENTS

The addition of only 27 amendments to the Constitution in more than two hundred years is a tribute to its flexibility and versatility. It is also a reflection of how difficult the Founders made the procedure for amending the Constitution. Article V provides two ways to propose an amendment:

1. Two-thirds of the membership of both the House of Representatives (at least 290 out of 435) and the Senate (67 out of 100) can propose an amendment; or

2. Two-thirds of the state legislatures (34 out of 50) can call for a national convention for the purpose of proposing an amendment.

Only the first method has ever been used and only infrequently, given the difficulty of getting two-thirds of Congress to agree on anything.

Ratification is even more difficult:

1. Three-fourths of the state legislatures (38 out of 50) must approve by a simple majority, or

2. Approval must come from three-fourths of special state conventions called for the purpose of ratifying the amendments.

The second method of ratification has been used in only one instance—to ratify the Twenty-first Amendment (1933), which repealed the prohibition of alcohol established by the Eighteenth Amendment. This was the only time an amendment has ever been repealed.

The most recent proposed amendment to be denied ratification was the Equal Rights Amendment (ERA). The ERA received ratification in 35 states (four of which later rescinded) and got no further before the time for ratification by the states ran out on June 30, 1982.

The amendments to the Constitution can be divided into three chronological groups: early remedial amendments, Civil War amendments, and twentieth-century amendments.

Early Remedial Amendments

Soon after the Constitutional Convention ended, it became evident that a bill of rights had to be added, or at least promised, in order to obtain the necessary support for ratification. The first ten amendments—the Bill of Rights—are thus considered *remedial*; that is, they were designed to remedy deficiencies in the original document.

The Bill of Rights, ratified in 1791, was devised to protect American citizens against the power of the national government. It guaranteed, among other things, freedom of speech, religion, the press, and assembly; protection against "unreasonable searches and seizures"; and the right not to be deprived of life, liberty, or property "without due process of law." (See Table 3.1.)

Two other remedial amendments were ratified soon after the Bill of Rights. The Eleventh (1798) declared it illegal for a state to be sued in the federal courts by a citizen of another state or foreign nation. The Twelfth Amendment (1804) provided that presidential electors vote for president and vice president separately. Prior to 1804, the person receiving the second-highest number of votes for president became vice president. In the disputed election of 1800, the House of Representatives had to choose between Thomas Jefferson and Aaron Burr, who had received the same number of electoral votes for president. This changed the nature of elections within the electoral college. Now each party has a candidate for president and vice president.

Civil War Amendments

After the Civil War, three amendments protected the rights of the newly freed slaves. The Thirteenth Amendment (1865) forbade slavery in the United States and its terri-

TABLE 3.1 THE BILL OF RIGHTS BY CATEGORY	
Guarantee, Right, Protection	Amendment
Religious beliefs	
No establishment of religion	1
Free exercise of religion	1
Personal expression	
Freedom of speech and press	1
Right to peaceable assembly	1
Right to petition government for redress of grievances	1
Personal privacy	
Right to keep and bear arms	2
Owner's consent required to house troops in peacetime; may be prescribed by law in wartime	3
Protection against unreasonable searches and seizures; warrants to search require probable cause	4
Freedom from self-incrimination (i.e., testifying against oneself)	5
Government encroachment	
Indictment by grand jury required in serious cases; no double jeopardy, i.e., being tried twice for the same crime; due process of law required in cases of life, liberty, or property; just compensation required for government confiscation of property	5
Right to a speedy and public trial by an impartial jury of local citizens; habeas corpus (i.e., knowing why you are being held); right to confront witnesses against you; right to acquire favorable witnesses; right to legal counsel	6
Trial by jury in civil suits if the issue surpasses $20; juries have right to obtain facts in a case	7
No excessive bail, excessive fines, or cruel and unusual punishment	8
Unspecified guarantees, rights, protections	
Rights specifically stated do not deny or disparage unspecified rights	9
Reserved powers—those not specifically delegated to the national government or specifically denied to the states—belong to the states or to the people	10

tories. The Fourteenth Amendment (1868) made the former slaves citizens. It contained two clauses—relating to "due process" of law and "equal protection" of laws—that were to have far-reaching effects in the field of civil liberties. The Fifteenth Amendment (1870) precluded the federal and state governments from denying anyone the right to vote "on account of race, color, or previous condition of servitude."

Twentieth-Century Amendments

Three types of amendments have been ratified in the twentieth century: (1) those relating to public policy, of which the Eighteenth and Twenty-first, enacting and repealing prohibition, are most famous; (2) those extending democratic procedures, such as the Nineteenth, which gave women the right to vote; and (3) those that refined the structure of the Constitution, such as the Twenty-second, which limited the president to two terms or a maximum of ten years in office. (See Table 3.2 for a description of Amendments 11 through 27 by category.)

These amendments, relatively few in number, have generally broadened democracy. They have demonstrated the Constitution's adaptability to a changing society—from rural to urban, from agricultural to industrial, and from a government dominated by the legislature to one dominated by the executive.

THE CONSTITUTION'S SILENCES

The Constitution is cleverly silent on several important issues. Provisions dealing with these issues, if written into the document, might have damaged it irreparably, either in the process of obtaining ratification or in adapting to changes in later years. Many state constitutions that did just that had to be revised or replaced. Omission of some of these issues represented a conscious decision by the Founders. They knew they could not predict the future. They knew that issues would arise that an overly precise constitution could not anticipate. They wisely decided to leave future problems to future generations and provided them with as much flexibility as possible without jeopardizing the essential integrity of the document.

The Constitution, for example, says nothing about political parties. This silence might be considered serious in view of the important role later played by parties, but this neglect allowed the parties to develop and change without undue constitutional restrictions. Several of the framers were ill disposed anyway toward what they called factions. Given this attitude, constitutional regulation of parties might have made their survival exceedingly difficult. It is hard to imagine our nation without parties today (although H. Ross Perot demonstrated in 1992 that it was possible to be a serious presidential candidate without one, providing the alternative of having $60 million to spend on the campaign was available). In many respects, the parties are the glue that holds the constitutional framework together.

Another political institution not specifically established in the Constitution is the Cabinet. The Cabinet and the executive departments have grown as new problems and new interest groups emerged in American society. For example, no one in 1787 could have foreseen the need for a Department of Housing and Urban Development, a Department of Transportation, or a Department of Energy. By the last decades of the twentieth century, however, urban problems, traffic congestion, and the energy shortage became critical issues, and incorporation of these departments into the Cabinet made sense.

Critics have leveled volleys of disapproval at the Founders for their silence on slavery. The Constitution merely forbade Congress to abolish the slave trade until 1808. As a matter of human rights, their action was clearly wrong. In the interest of creating a nation and adopting a constitution, however, their action was clearly right. To have taken a position against slavery would have ensured opposition to the proposed document in the six southern states—enough to defeat ratification of the Constitution. Although many delegates (including a few southern ones) wanted to abolish slavery, they opted in

TABLE 3.2 CONSTITUTIONAL AMENDMENTS 11–27 BY CATEGORY

Category/Amendment	Subject	Ratification Time
Structural corrections		
11	Prevents a person from suing a state in a federal court without the state's consent	1794–1795
12	Mandates that the electoral college vote separately for president and vice president	1803–1804
20	Moves presidential inauguration from March 4 to January 20, and opening of Congress to January 3	1932–1933
22	Limits presidential terms to two or no more than a total of ten years	1947–1951
25	Establishes presidential succession in cases of death, removal from office, incapacity, or resignation of the president or vice president	1965–1967
Public policy initiatives		
18	Prohibits making and selling of intoxicating liquors	1917–1919
21	Repeals Prohibition (Eighteenth Amendment)	1933
Equality amendments		
13	Abolishes slavery	1865
14	Grants citizenship to all persons born or naturalized in the United States; provides citizens with "due process of law" and "equal protection of the laws" in their relationships with states	1866–1868
15	Provides that voting cannot be denied "on account of race, color, or previous condition of servitude"	1869–1870
17	Provides for popular election of U.S. senators	1912–1913
19	Grants women's suffrage	1920
23	Grants District of Columbia suffrage in presidential elections	1960–1961
26	Lowers voting age to 18 years	1971
27	Prohibits members of Congress from voting for their own pay raise	1992

favor of political practicality and again assigned to later generations the task of dealing with this injustice.

The Constitution did not clearly define the scope of the national government's power. As a result, central authority has grown with changing circumstances, especially during times of national and international crises. During the Great Depression of the 1930s and also in wartime, presidential powers have been enlarged. President Franklin D. Roosevelt was given extraordinary powers by Congress to deal with the Depression and to conduct World War II. Successor presidents such as Harry S. Truman, John F. Kennedy, Lyndon B. Johnson, and Richard M. Nixon have either exercised or sought to expand these powers.

The Founders wisely did not attempt to define the Supreme Court's precise limits, but left it to history, circumstance, and, in effect, the Court itself, to determine. As it turned out, John Marshall, as Chief Justice, quickly extended the scope of the highest court's authority. As early as 1803, he exercised the concept of judicial review when he said: "It is emphatically the province and duty of the judicial department to say what the law is. . . . A law repugnant to the Constitution is void."[3] The principle of judicial review, as we shall see in a later chapter, was first established in the United States. Even in the late twentieth century it has been adopted elsewhere only reluctantly.

All these instances show how valuable it is to be governed by a document of general principles. With the passage of time, the Constitution has adapted to a changing nation without encountering severe problems. The Constitution provided a framework; time and circumstance have filled in the details.

Nevertheless, after two hundred years, there are still questions about whether the U.S. Constitution is a document sufficient to guide the governance of modern America. Critics set forth several disadvantages and liabilities of the Constitution while defenders are at least equally strong in their views of the document's advantages. During the past decade or two in particular, there has been a debate about whether a constitutional convention should be called and, if so, whether it should be limited to certain subjects or allowed to review and propose an entirely new constitution if necessary. We will take a look now at some of the most contentious issues surrounding the Constitution.

? ISSUES TO ANALYZE

ISSUE 1   *IS THE CONSTITUTION AN ELITIST DOCUMENT?*

REASONS WHY THE CONSTITUTION IS AN ELITIST DOCUMENT

Who were the 55 men who drafted the Constitution? Most of them were well-to-do, with interests in real estate, banking, manufacturing, shipping, and large-scale agriculture. They were men of extraordinary prestige and reputation. Many were personal friends. They had received excellent educations and typically had had some experience in governing. To be more specific:

- Over half the delegates held degrees from Princeton, Yale, Harvard, Columbia, University of Pennsylvania, William and Mary, or English universities.

- Twenty-four delegates were involved in moneylending and investments; 14 speculated in land; 15 owned plantations; and all 55 held bonds or other public securities.

- At the time of the Convention, more than 40 delegates held important positions in state government, including three governorships; over 40 had served in the Continental Congress.

These men were hardly representative of the general population. In 1787 a minuscule middle class was composed primarily of shopkeepers, artisans, and successful farmers. Exclusive of the native Americans, a large proportion of the total population consisted of frontier settlers and debt-ridden farmers. Below them on the social scale were tenant farmers and indentured servants, both male and female, constituting perhaps 20 percent of the population. Below them were all slaves, constituting another 20 percent. Eight of ten Americans made their living through farming; one in ten earned a living in fishing or lumbering; and most of the rest were involved in commerce as merchants, lawyers, dockhands, or sailors. Interest and participation in political affairs were left mainly to the upper class, with a very modest level of participation among the small but emerging middle class.

Undemocratic Provisions. As noted by historian Charles A. Beard in his *Economic Interpretation of the Constitution*, the Constitution was "an economic document drawn with superb skill by men whose property interests were immediately at stake."[4] It was fitting that the men who drafted the Constitution were from the upper classes because they stood to benefit most from it. The deficiencies of the Articles of Confederation posed a threat to the propertied class. The national government's inability to levy taxes, regulate commerce, print money, and impose tariffs harmed people of wealth more than citizens of ordinary means. These same affluent Americans worried most about debtor unrest, limitations to westward expansion, and international respectability.

The governmental structure and procedures embodied in the Constitution reflected the interests of the delegates. They benefited from many of the powers granted to the national government:

1. The power to levy taxes and thus produce revenue would protect the investments of those who had helped to finance the government during the Revolution. The restriction against direct taxation was interpreted as a prohibition of a graduated income tax, further protecting the financial interests of the upper class. (This restriction was subsequently overturned by the Sixteenth Amendment in 1913.)

2. The power to regulate interstate commerce would protect trading and commercial interests.

3. The power to protect money and property through the supervision of weights and measures, roads, copyrights, and patents also protected mercantile interests.

4. The sole power to mint money, previously enjoyed by the states as well, shut off a source of cheap currency that benefited the debtor classes.

Were the delegates to the Constitutional convention representative of the general population? Most of the delegates came from the same stratum of society as the Ramsey-Polk family of Carpenter's Point, Maryland, depicted here in a painting by James Peale around 1793. Most Americans, however, were more typical of the other family shown on the right; they farmed small plots, cooked simple meals, and spun their own cloth while eking out a far more marginal existence.

5. The power to establish a permanent military could be used to quell such disturbances such as Shays' Rebellion, which threatened the upper classes.

These specific grants of power enhanced the interests of the elite groups, a small minority of Americans. So did the composition of the three branches of the national government. The Constitution provided that the people (which then meant white male property owners) would have a direct voice in electing only one governmental body, the House of Representatives. Senators were to be elected by state legislatures; the selection of the president was to be protected from the (often fickle) will of the masses by the device of the electoral college.

The original draft of the Constitution lacked a bill of rights that would give people important guarantees and protections from a powerful government. Because certain states, such as New York, insisted on a bill of rights before they would ratify the document, the Founders proposed the first ten amendments to the Constitution, known collectively as the Bill of Rights. But the Constitution did nothing to abolish slavery; in fact, it guaranteed that the slave trade could continue until 1808. Also it did not grant women the full rights of citizenship. Liberty was emphasized more than equality. Democracy was neither the motif of the day nor the motive of the Founders.

In effect, the Constitution took power from the states, where the middle and lower classes had more influence, and shifted it to the national government, where the upper class was dominant. Article VI, the so-called supremacy clause making the Constitution and federal laws "supreme in the land," highlighted this basic shift.

Nothing in the Constitution drafted at Philadelphia might be construed as opposing the interests of the upper class. Instead, the Constitution consolidated the economic and social gains the upper class had achieved through the American Revolution. A strong national authority would protect and increase their position, which would be perpetuated by limited popular participation in government.

Arbitrary Procedures. The Convention delegates acted arbitrarily from the very beginning. When they first met—in secret—they violated the stated purpose of the convention by not considering *revisions* of the Articles of Confederation, as they had been mandated to do. Rather, they focused on the Virginia Plan, which aimed to create a totally new governmental structure.

After they had created this new government, the delegates violated the ratification procedure specified by the Articles of Confederation. Instead of referring the new document to the state legislatures, they provided for special state constitutional conventions; approval by 9 of these (out of 13) would establish the new government. It should be noted that the only state whose legislature was controlled by the debtor classes—Rhode Island—did not send delegates to the Constitutional Convention. Rhode Island was also the last to ratify the new Constitution, and it did so by the narrowest margin (two votes) of any state.

Only an estimated 160,000 of 4 million citizens were eligible to vote on the new charter. This was less than one-twentieth of the total population. Two leading speakers for the middle class, Richard Henry Lee and Patrick Henry, opposed ratification because they felt that the Constitution disregarded middle- and lower-class interests. From this evidence, one might conclude that the American Constitution was not adopted by what we would call democratic procedures in which the majority of citizens participated.

REASONS WHY THE CONSTITUTION IS NOT AN ELITIST DOCUMENT

The motives of the Founders really are not relevant to the 1990s. Even if their motives were elitist and even if they acted to protect class interests, many of the Constitution's provisions have since been used to protect the interests of the middle and lower classes. For example, the very fact that the Constitution forbade the abolition of slavery until after 1808 was an implied invitation to abolish the slave trade and probably served to encourage the abolitionist forces after that date.

The national supremacy clause in Article VI and the elastic clause in Article I have since been used to help the national government to act in preventing racial abuses, in providing financial aid to underprivileged school children, and in many other similar ways. Since the Constitution and the laws and treaties made pursuant to it are the supreme law of the land, actions of the national government have precedence over actions of state and local governments. Similarly, since Congress can "make all Laws which shall be necessary and proper for carrying into Execution" its powers, the national government has very wide latitude in determining the issues and problems it can address. For example, in forbidding racial discrimination in interstate transportation, the national government relied on the "necessary and proper" clause to execute its specific power of regulating interstate commerce.

But *did* the Founders represent only elite interests? According to constitutional scholar Forrest McDonald, of the 55 delegates, no more than a dozen "clearly acted according to the dictates of their personal economic interest." McDonald concluded that Charles Beard's thesis is "impossible to justify."[5] Another constitutional scholar, Robert E. Brown, declared that "we would be doing a grave injustice to the political sagacity of the Founding Fathers if we assumed that property or personal gain was their only motive."[6] For example, George Mason—a wealthy Virginian who might have been expected to support a strong central government—opposed such a government. Conversely, Alexander Hamilton, who was far from wealthy, fervently supported powerful national authority.

Was the Constitution undemocratic because it was drafted in secrecy? Public meetings are not necessarily more democratic than secret ones. At any rate, the emphasis on open meetings,which has attracted attention since the 1960s, did not characterize the formative period of American government. Moreover, the delegates did debate at length and did vote on what the new government should be like.

Did the Founders violate their expressed mandate to revise the Articles of Confederation? Yes, but certainly the result was preferable to the Articles.

Did the Founders violate the requirements of the Articles of Confederation by not submitting the proposed document to the state legislatures for ratification? Yes, but the state legislatures were likely to have opposed the new document because it took power away from them. State ratifying conventions gave the new Constitution greater legitimacy because the delegates were chosen expressly to consider the proposed document. The conventions established a broad popular base of support for the Constitution.

Were the masses prevented from voting to choose delegates to these state ratifying conventions? Hardly! According to Robert E. Brown, property qualifications kept barely 5 percent of the adult white male population from voting. By Brown's analysis, most adult white males were farmers who owned land and were therefore eligible to vote. Although voter turnout was light, indicating that "the Constitution was adopted with a great show of indifference,"[7] small farmers had the numerical strength to defeat the document. Their failure to vote may be interpreted as passive support rather than active opposition.

In order to properly judge the motives and actions of the Founders it is necessary to put their accomplishment in historical perspective. Standing as a landmark in the growth of democracy, the U.S. Constitution embodies principles strikingly at variance with those animating most European governments of the late eighteenth century. As Table 3.3 shows, government and society in the United States had made significant advances. Thus, far from emulating the undemocratic systems of continental Europe (in the 1780s only the British and the Dutch maintained any semblance of political democracy), the framers consciously made use of their English heritage and colonial experiences to create a different and more democratic form of government: a republic.

Certainly, democracy as we know it today did not exist in colonial America. But compared with other governments of the eighteenth century, the one established by the U.S. Constitution was democratic.

Did the Founders allocate power through the Constitution to benefit only those

TABLE 3.3   GOVERNMENT AND SOCIETY IN THE LATE EIGHTEENTH CENTURY

	Type of Government	Basis of Governmental Authority	Social Structure
United States	Republic	Consent of the governed	Fluid: Belief in equality of citizens who possessed "certain inalienable rights"
Continental Europe	Hereditary monarchy with a privileged nobility	Consensus of aristocratic political elite	Fixed: Rigid class system

of wealth and substance? Far from it. The Constitution utilizes both the concepts of **division of power**—creating the federal system, in which power is divided between the national and state governments—and **separation of powers**—creating three branches of the national government that check and balance one another. In reality, the term **shared powers** is more accurate: power is neither completely divided nor completely separated. The national and state governments have some powers in common, such as taxation, road construction, and education. Within the national government, overlap exists among the executive, legislative, and judicial branches, even though they are independent of one another. For example, Congress has the power to declare war, but the president is the commander in chief.

The average American benefits from these many centers of governmental power because they provide **multiple access points** to government. That is, a citizen may work to influence government or redress grievances through national, state, or local governments and through the executive, legislative or judicial branches. To illustrate, the National Association for the Advancement of Colored People (NAACP) has worked through every access point. Its earliest successes were in the national judicial branch before the U.S. Supreme Court (see Chapter 14 for a discussion), but more recently it has been successful at a number of other points of access.

ISSUE 1:   Summary   ★   *Is the Constitution an Elitist Document?*

In the narrow economic view of Charles A. Beard, the Constitution is an elitist document that men protecting their economic interests drafted both in secrecy and in violation of the Convention's purpose to simply revise the Articles of Confederation. A broader examination of the Founders by Forrest McDonald and Robert E. Brown reveals that their decisions did not reflect strictly their own economic interests. Even if all of the critics' charges are accepted as valid, it is still true that that same elitist document has been used to extend more democratic rights to more people than any other constitution.

While both critics and defenders of the Constitution make valid points, it is important to put the Constitution in historical perspective rather than to try to impose late-twentieth-century standards on a late-eighteenth-century document. For its time, our

Constitution was democratically advanced. Moreover, it has adapted to changing times and circumstances. ■

ISSUE 2   *IS THE CONSTITUTION AN IMPEDIMENT TO PROGRESS?*

REASONS WHY THE CONSTITUTION IS AN IMPEDIMENT TO PROGRESS

In 1790, the 13 states had a population of 3,929,214, but by 1991, the population of the 50 states exceeded 252,000,000. More people today live in Philadelphia alone than there were in the entire United States in 1790. Population per square mile in 1790 was 4.5; in 1986 it was over 60. From 3 small departments in 1790, the executive branch of the national government has increased to 14 departments and numerous agencies and commissions. For the much smaller and less sophisticated society of the late eighteenth and early nineteenth centuries, the American Constitution might have been excellent. But now, in a time of complex social and economic problems and international crises as well as a much more heterogeneous population, the government set up by the Constitution impedes progress. And the large majorities needed to propose and ratify amendments often thwart public opinion on an issue and impair effective action in a crisis. The result is that action is frequently accomplished through judicial interpretation, a decidedly undemocratic process that may or may not take into account the will of the people.

Delay and confusion. The separation of powers between the president and Congress is just one factor that slows down and often prevents implementation of necessary reforms. Public policy becomes the product of dispute and delay rather than the timely result of efficient planning. During the Carter and Reagan administrations (1977–1989), dispute and delay occurred even though Carter's party controlled both houses of Congress and Reagan's party controlled one house (the Senate) for six years of an eight-year administration. The Democratic Congress constantly fought President Carter's initiatives, especially on urgent energy legislation. Although President Reagan had some successes with Congress, he had to expend extraordinary effort on public relations campaigns and press conferences to rally public opinion to move a recalcitrant Congress. President Bush complained of "gridlock" throughout his administration and blamed a Democratic-controlled Congress for lack of progress in passing economic programs to end the longest recession in more than half a century.

Another difficulty is the existence of 82,000 units of government throughout the United States—state, county, and municipal. Developing a solution to a major national domestic problem typically requires coordination with many units of government, and this is frequently difficult to achieve.

An inefficient American government cannot take proper advantage of modern technology. For example, the efficiency and technology of space exploration have not been applied to railroad transportation, the postal service, and public housing. Citizens suffer from train delays, inadequate mail service, and unfinished public housing projects. The national government finds it ever more difficult to act swiftly and efficiently to solve these and other serious problems.

Unresolved Issues. The nature of our present constitutional structure often prevents final decisions on issues of importance to large parts of the population. There

The Equal Rights Amendment (ERA) remains an unresolved issue on the American constitutional agenda. One of the key states that failed to ratify the amendment was Illinois, despite rallies by thousands of supporters and marches like this one in Chicago in 1980.

are three types of unresolved issues: proposed constitutional amendments, changes in the structure and scope of the federal government that have not followed established constitutional procedures, and controversial U.S. Supreme Court decisions.

In the past two hundred years more than nine thousand amendments have been proposed, but only 27 have made their way into the Constitution. Substantial portions of the populace support amendments against legalized abortion, school busing, and flag burning, and in favor of a balanced budget and a national initiative, yet the necessary two-thirds vote of both houses of Congress to propose these amendments cannot be obtained. These proposals have been left "hanging on the vine," without adequate public debate and clear resolution.

The Equal Rights Amendment suffered another fate and raised a number of constitutional issues. Proposed overwhelmingly by Congress in the early 1970s and ratified very quickly thereafter by a substantial majority of the states, it languished without ratification by the required three-fourths (38) of states, even after a three-year extension granted by Congress. Then 4 of the 35 states that had ratified the amendment rescinded their approval. Should that be allowed? Congress provided that no state could rescind or withdraw its ratification—but is that Congress's decision to make? And can Congress extend the period of ratification? The states of Idaho and Arizona plus four Washington state legislators brought suit challenging the constitutionality of the extension. Legal scholars disagree on all these issues.

Because the Constitution makes change so difficult to accomplish, it often gets done in ways the Founders never anticipated. For instance, during the crisis of the Great Depression of the 1930s the scope of the federal government was greatly enlarged mainly through the decisions of judges loosely interpreting the Constitution. In 1936, for example, the Supreme Court declared that the clause in Article I, section 8, giving Congress the power "to provide for . . . the general welfare of the United States" permitted Congress to authorize expenditure of public money for just about any purpose it chose. Whether one likes the Constitution as now interpreted and the national government's powers as expanded is not the issue. The issue is that the basic document of government should be altered through the people's action, not through judicial fiat. But the Constitution itself impedes popular action.

Another problem is that the U.S. Supreme Court, especially from the early 1950s through the late 1960s, has handed down some controversial decisions opposed by substantial portions of the electorate. For example, its decisions declaring school prayer unconstitutional would most likely have been reversed if the public had been allowed to vote on them. The meaning of separation of church and state as well as definitions of other individual rights guaranteed by the Constitution might best be resolved by the public through the forum of a constitutional convention. Citizens could then decide to abide by the Court's decisions or to adhere to the intentions of the Founders, who did not explicitly encourage or exclude prayer and Bible reading in the schools.

REASONS WHY THE CONSTITUTION IS NOT AN IMPEDIMENT TO PROGRESS

The preeminent virtue of the Constitution is its creation of a framework through which democracy could grow and mature. The Constitution did not straitjacket history by imposing the governmental and social forms of the late eighteenth century on the decades to come. Writing in 1819, Chief Justice John Marshall stated that the Constitution was "intended to endure for ages to come and, consequently, to be adapted to the various crises of human affairs."[8] It seems perfectly sensible, then, to admire the virtue of a constitutional system that changes slowly on purpose. The Founders understood that change was inevitable and relentless, and fashioned a document to ensure that change would come about only after careful deliberation.

Considering that the Constitution has withstood a civil war, two world wars, and a host of political, economic, and social changes, it has more than proved its worth as an effective instrument of government. The key is stability through flexibility—the ability to adapt to changing circumstances. Flexibility has been achieved partly through outright silences in the Constitution and, even more importantly, through amendment and judicial interpretation of the Constitution.

The critics point to the lack of success of several amendment proposals and petitions for constitutional conventions as reasons why the Constitution is an impediment to progress, but we must ask ourselves whether the subjects of these proposals properly belong in the Constitution:

Since the Fourteenth Amendment provides for "equal protection of the laws" and the Civil Rights Act of 1964 prohibits sexual discrimination, is there any overriding reason to add the Equal Rights Amendment to the Constitution?

Would it be wise to straitjacket the U.S. government with a balanced budget amendment for all time? Shouldn't Congress and the president be trusted to respond to public opinion and the needs of the time in developing an annual budget?

Would an amendment to ban flag burning pose a threat to freedom of speech under the First Amendment?

Would an amendment to abolish school busing have the same continuing constitutional and historical significance as such important guarantees as due process of law and freedom of religion? School busing is most likely a passing issue that should not be resolved in the Constitution, which is supposed to provide general principles for resolving specific issues.

ISSUE 2: Summary ★ *Is the Constitution an Impediment to Progress?*

The continuing struggles over public policy between the president and Congress indicate to some that structures specified by the Constitution are impediments to change. They believe that in a space-age society our government should be able to make and implement new policies at a pace faster than in a horse-and-buggy society.

Defenders perceive the impediments of separation of powers and division of power as assets rather than liabilities: They cause changes to be generally well considered before being approved and implemented. Supporters argue that the Constitution's flexibility has allowed necessary changes and prevented unnecessary changes.

In a society accustomed to a daily diet of public opinion polls, a simple response to the question is "yes," because whatever inhibits the will of the majority can easily be construed as undemocratic. A more sober analysis reveals that proposed constitutional amendments and convention calls (as shown below) have influenced government actions even when the proposals have been unsuccessful; that is, they have had an *indirect* effect. Moreover, it can be argued that public officials in a republican or representative democracy are not elected merely to rubber-stamp public opinion, but rather to consider conscience and evidence as well as public opinion before making decisions. ■

ISSUE 3 *SHOULD A CONSTITUTIONAL CONVENTION BE CALLED?*

REASONS WHY A CONSTITUTIONAL CONVENTION SHOULD BE CALLED

In 1787 the Founders intended to use the Constitutional Convention as a tool to circumvent an unwilling Confederation Congress. The United States Congress has received about 400 petitions calling for a convention, most of them since 1900 and most of them to consider one specific issue or amendment. It has never acted favorably on any of them. The chairman of the House Judiciary's Committee on Civil and Constitutional Rights, Don Edwards (D-Calif.), said: "There is no assurance that [a constitutional convention] would not be a runaway. We've had only one constitutional convention and it tore up the Articles of Confederation."[9] On the other hand, the American Bar Association said: "The charge of radicalism [in calling for a convention] does a disservice to the ability of the states and people to act responsibly when dealing with the Constitution."[10]

The House of Representatives has never even passed legislation providing for convention procedures. One of its members said: "We have never felt it was significant enough to hold hearings."[11] But the Senate has shown that it believes a convention could be called and conducted properly. It has passed simple and straightforward convention procedures, including how delegates are to be chosen.[12] Another support for the practicality of a convention is that many states, including large states like Michigan, New York, and Illinois, have successfully held constitutional conventions since 1960. Voters in Michigan and Illinois ratified the results of their conventions while New York voters rejected their convention's proposed constitution.

A convention would be both practical and useful because contemporary Americans could determine whether they wish to be governed by a document two hundred years old. They could also consider proposed controversial constitutional amendments that Congress has not acted on, such as antiabortion, school prayer, flag-burning and anti–school busing amendments. Among the virtues of a convention would be a fresh and complete review of the Constitution to determine whether and how it should be modernized, the opportunity to resolve some very controversial issues.

REASONS WHY A CONSTITUTIONAL CONVENTION SHOULD NOT BE CALLED

Although conventions may not have been held, the calls themselves have often been instrumental in bringing about change. The balanced budget amendment proposal of the late 1970s caused Congress to police itself in proposing budgetary expenditures. One of the most influential convention calls was the one for direct election of senators in the early 1900s. Some observers believe that the submission of convention petitions by two-thirds of the states led directly to the congressional proposal of the Seventeenth Amendment.

James Madison said he had no objection to a constitutional convention call to amend or to write a new constitution "except only that difficulties might arise as to the form, the quorum etc. which in constitutional regulations ought to be as much as possible avoided."[13] Madison's reservations are well founded. On several crucial questions, neither the Constitution nor statutory law provides definite answers:

> What constitutes a valid call? Do the petitions from the various states have to be identically worded? Do both houses of the state legislature have to approve a petition? Can the governor exercise a veto over the legislature's petition for a convention?

> Can Congress limit the scope of the call for a convention?

> How long do the states have to submit petitions? Although the U.S. Supreme Court has said Congress may limit the time states have to ratify amendments, there is no such limit on petitioning for a convention.

> Is Congress *obligated* to call a convention if two-thirds of the states petition for one?

Successful state constitutional conventions do not mean that a national convention will succeed. After all, the nation is far larger and more complex than the individual states.

The Constitution has demonstrated its relevance through adapting to economic and social changes. Before calling a constitutional convention to replace the Constitution, there should be evidence that the existing Constitution inhibits or precludes meaningful changes, especially those that broaden democracy.

ISSUE 3: **Summary** ★ *Should a Constitutional Convention Be Called?*

Fundamentally, those who oppose a constitutional convention do so for one or both of two reasons: (1) distrust of the people's ability to call and conduct a convention, and (2) fear that the convention would undermine major democratic gains made over the last two hundred years under the existing Constitution. Much of the support for a constitutional convention comes from conservative groups who want certain policy goals, such as a balanced budget and school prayer, written into a new constitution. A more conservative Senate Judiciary Committee in 1984 approved procedures for calling and conducting a convention, while the more liberal House Judiciary Committee has failed to act on such procedures.

 # COMPARISONS WITH OTHER NATIONS

CONSTITUTIONS IN DEMOCRACIES

The United States Constitution is the oldest written constitution still in force (Table 3.4). It is also one of the most emulated. Many contemporary constitutions have been partially modeled on the American constitution and/or have been formulated with the assistance of American legal experts who created a sort of constitutional cottage industry.[14] When Japan and the Federal Republic of Germany regained sovereignty in 1947 and 1949, respectively, after World War II, it was under the auspices of constitutions written in part and approved by American occupation forces. The enthusiasm for political democracy in the 1990s is contributing to our Constitution's continuing popularity.

Constitutions influenced by the American experience tend to be more detailed (and therefore longer) than our own. They also have provisions that reflect the political culture of the societies they govern. For example, in Japan academic freedom is consti-

TABLE 3.4 CONSTITUTIONS OF SELECTED DEMOCRACIES AND YEAR OF RATIFICATION	
Country	Ratification Year
Spain	1978
France	1958
Germany	1949
Italy	1948
Japan	1947
United States	**1788**

Japan's prime minister and members of the legislature bow to Emperor Hirohito (on upper dais) after his proclamation of the sovereignty of the Japanese people with the promulgation of Japan's new constitution in 1946. American occupation forces in Japan helped write the constitution.

tutionally guaranteed whereas it is not even mentioned in any article or amendment of the American Constitution. The intense social discipline of Japan necessitates spelling out individual freedoms. The same is true of Germany. The German constitution prohibits political parties that advocate undemocratic or antidemocratic positions. The internal organization of German political parties "must conform to democratic principles."[15] It would be quite unconstitutional to try to enforce a code of behavior for political parties in the United States. But given the German experience with political extremism of the right and left (the Nazis governed all of Germany between 1933 and 1945, and the communists governed East Germany between 1945 and 1990), it is understandable that there is a generally accepted desire to avoid the twin plagues of naziism and communism. And the Japanese generally have no desire to return to the militaristic style of politics that brought their country to ruin.

Some countries have constitutionally accepted norms without written constitutions. The United Kingdom has functioned for hundreds of years without a written constitution (although there has recently been some talk of the need for one). An unwritten constitution differs from a written one in several important ways:

1. There is no precise time or date that indicates when the unwritten constitution originated. The British, for example, trace their constitutional prerogatives back nearly a millenium to at least the Magna Charta in 1215.

2. The content of the unwritten constitution may not always be explicit. This can cause some confusion. While the federal judiciary in the United States is relied upon to interpret what the U.S. Constitution may say about a particular issue, there is no final interpreter in Britain. It is often the

A VIEW FROM THE STATES

Britain's Constitutional Question

Britain has long taken pride in the fact that its constitution, unlike those of most other democracies, is unwritten. But pride is giving way to doubt, and pressure is building for a fresh look at ways of securing the rights of British citizens. Anthony Barnett, an advocate of a written constitution and a bill of rights, says he thinks that relying on Magna Charta, signed by England's King John at Runnymede in 1215, is an insufficient basis for ensuring that the rule of law prevails. . . .

He notes that Britain is the only member of the 12-nation European Community and its 25-nation sister body, the Council of Europe, without a written constitution.

"The result is that Britain is now regularly facing constitutional issues it is ill-equipped to handle," Barnett says.

King John's "great charter" was imposed on him by rebel barons who saw it as a barrier against the monarch's arbitrary actions. It remains the basis of Britain's common-law system and such institutions as the right of trial by jury and habeas corpus.

But growing numbers of British political observers and groups say its rambling provisions do not fit with modern times. . . .

Prominent members of Britain's political and legal establishment are now counted among those who demand that the country should have a bill of rights.

Lord Scarman, a former judge of the Court of Appeal, has been campaigning for a written constitution for decades, arguing that allowing Parliament to pass laws without regard to a framework of citizens' rights is a recipe for unfairness.

Source: Alexander Macleod, "Britain's Constitutional Question," *The Christian Science Monitor*, March 3, 1992, p. 12. Reprinted by permission of *The Christian Science Monitor.* © 1992 The Christian Science Publishing Society. All rights reserved.

legislature itself that decides whether it is passing constitutional legislation, although it may refer to legalists when an issue is sufficiently complicated.

3. Nations with unresolved societal concerns may find an unwritten constitution useful and any attempt to formulate a written one liable to seriously divide its polity on fundamental issues. Israel, for example, has not yet resolved the difficult area of the relationship between church and state. Israel is officially a "Jewish state" as well as a parliamentary democracy. What does this mean for non-Jews and nonpracticing Jews? There are occasions when the less said the better. For the time being Israel gets along without a written constitution.

The United States Constitution may well be the shortest written constitution in the world. It is intended to structure a limited government, and it does so with great elegance and economy of language. Given the constitution's effectiveness there is a lot to say on behalf of brevity. For example, the United States is a democracy, but the term *democracy* appears nowhere in the Constitution (whereas it is rather emphatically stated in the constitutions of France and Germany). It was the evolution of the American constitution that eventually created the thorough democracy in place today.

The more a constitution says the more problems in governance may incur. Yet one important reason for detailed constitutions, in both democratic and nondemocratic systems, is the intense desire to do all that is practical to preserve the current political institutions. To this end the constitution is generally tied into a judicial apparatus that is far from being as independent, neutral, and objective as the federal Supreme Court in the United States. In France, Italy, and Spain, the highest judicial authority is called the Constitutional Council, reflecting the fact that such an authority is geared primarily to protect the integrity of the government. In Germany, the Federal Constitutional Court is charged with overseeing and resolving disputes between various levels of government.

Arriving at an acceptable and durable constitution is difficult. The United States made it look easy in great part because the activities and obligations of our political institutions were only vaguely defined once the basics were stated. Other societies, however, have tried to do either too much or too little. Even the more established democracies have not escaped the necessity of scrapping old constitutions and writing completely new ones.

Constitutions can even be self-contradictory. The French kept insisting over several regimes that each citizen should be guaranteed both liberty and equality. The two aren't really compatible. Enforced equality produces something resembling a totalitarian system, while unfettered liberty often produces chaos. The trick, apparently, is to guarantee enough of each without trying to remake human nature.

France experimented with seemingly every known kind of political regime before hitting on what may be a lasting and successful formula for durability, in 1958 (see Table 3.5). What was the problem? France had difficulty developing a **political consensus:** a national agreement on the kind of political institutions it should have. Throughout its history the French have been divided into those who wanted a workers' society dominated by the working class, a republic dominated by the middle class, a monarchy ruled by an upper class (the monarchists were themselves divided into Bourbonists and Bonapartists), and an imitation of British parliamentarianism.

But the French are not alone. In less than a century, for example, the Germans actually have gone through five distinct political regimes. Their empire lasted from 1871 to 1918, a catastrophic attempt at democracy floundered between 1919 and 1933, the Nazis practically destroyed the country between 1933 and 1945, military occupation ensued from 1945 to 1949, and the federal republic has existed since 1949. In 1990 it was enlarged to accommodate five additional states from East Germany.

Many important differences show up in democratic constitutions. Democracy is probably as apparent in Western Europe as it is in the United States. An American student or tourist would not notice any more restriction on freedoms in most other democracies. Taking a close look at the national government, however, might produce some confusion. The concept and practice of the constitutional separation of powers, so familiar in the United States, is definitely missing in most of these countries. (In this respect, probably Germany comes closest to emulating the American model.)

TABLE 3.5   FRANCE'S POLITICAL REGIMES

Regime	Years
Constitutional Monarchy	1791–1793
First Republic	1793–1799
Consulate	1799–1804
First Empire	1804–1814
Restoration of Bourbon Monarch	1814–1830
Orleanist Monarch	1830–1848
Second Republic	1848–1852
Second Empire	1852–1870*
Third Republic	1875–1940†
Fourth Republic	1946–1958
Fifth Republic	1958–Present

* Between 1870 and 1875 France's political development and sovereignty were interrupted by war and a long debate as to where to go next.
† From 1940 to 1944 France was occupied by the Germans; between 1944 and 1946 a national debate ensued before a new constitution was adopted, which for the next 12 years satisfied practically no one.

After all, Americans are politically characterized by a lack of trust in government that is nearly as pronounced as their lack of interest in it. The Constitution was so formulated that it would be difficult to accumulate power in any office. Parliamentary systems, which evolved slowly over long centuries in Europe, saw nothing wrong with simply recruiting the executive from the legislative branch. This practice was not considered so much an accumulation of power as a responsible application of it: The party that controlled a majority of parliamentary seats furnished the cabinet ministers.

While a number of countries in Eastern Europe may eventually construct a separation of powers arrangement, its absence from most of Western Europe appears permanent. Despite its lack of a formal existence, though, government powers are generally separate and do display checks on one another.

The United States Constitution differs in other substantial ways from most other political democracies. The more important differences are summarized in Table 3.6. What these differences reveal is that democracy is not the result of a single formula, but most often the result of national history. For example, many early colonists arrived in America to escape religious persecution or, at least, the violence that accompanied religious disputes. The First Amendment later confirmed the principle that the easiest way to avoid conflict over theological arguments was to avoid a linkup between any particular religion and the state. But this isn't a problem in the United Kingdom (with the notable exception of Northern Ireland), Israel, or the Scandinavian democracies. For varying cultural and

TABLE 3.6 CONSTITUTIONAL PREROGATIVES IN SELECTED COUNTRIES THAT ARE UNCONSTITUTIONAL IN THE UNITED STATES	
Prerogative	Country
Hereditary titles	Germany and United Kingdom
Banning of undemocratic political parties	Germany
Ability to delay or postpone legislative elections	United Kingdom
President can exercise emergency powers at her or his discretion	France
State-supported church	United Kingdom, Israel, and Scandinavian countries
Head of government can dissolve the national legislature before the normal expiration of term	All parliamentary regimes
No limit on number of terms or years head of government can serve	All parliamentary regimes
No one can be head of government without majority support of the legislature	All parliamentary regimes and most presidential ones

historical reasons, these countries all have officially endorsed religions, yet have guaranteed to all their citizens complete religious freedom. Indeed, Israel was established as a "Jewish state," but fully ensures to the sixth of its population that isn't Jewish complete toleration of their religious practices and observance of religious holidays.

Despite these differences, there is still a running debate as to whether the United States is more or less of a political democracy than its counterparts, nor can we be confident that one democracy runs more smoothly than others. What is sure, however, is that democracies are not uniform, and there is little reason for them to be.

CONSTITUTIONS IN TOTALITARIAN SYSTEMS

While the drafters of the United States Constitution could not, of course, anticipate the tremendous diversity of the American population in the late twentieth century, even during their own lifetimes they could easily recognize a variety of religious and political points of view. The Constitution was geared to protect and enhance individual rights. The document is clearly a political one.

But it is important to remember that in totalitarian societies the regime has a different set of priorities and quite different agendas. Two examples are important to mention here. Constitutions inspired by communist ideology tend to offer guarantees for both political *and* economic rights. In the Soviet Constitution, economic rights were listed as follows:

Although Israel was established as a "Jewish state" and without a written constitution, it guarantees freedom of religious practice to the sixth of the population that is not Jewish. For example, a secular law requires every business to close for one day a week, but that day is the choice of the business establishment. Thus, Muslims would close on Fridays, Jews on Saturdays, and Christians (as represented here by the Armenian quarter in Jerusalem) on Sundays.

Article 10:   Denies right to be selfish.

Article 13:   Property owned or used by citizens shall not serve as a means of deriving unearned income.

Article 14:   The citizen is enjoined to do "socially useful work."

Article 23:   "The state pursues a steady policy of raising people's pay levels and real incomes through increase in productivity."

Before the Soviet Union was dissolved, the Soviet Constitution of 1977 could have been interpreted as one of the most democratic ever written, except for at least two things: the special role guaranteed for the Communist party, and the fact that many democratic provisions were never put into effect. The Soviet Constitution was basically a propaganda statement praising the role of Marxist-Leninist teaching. Several articles in the Constitution were also devoted to the Soviet economic system, even to the point of stipulating that "No one has the right to use socialist property for purposes of personal gain or for other selfish purposes."

Such statements suggest some of the crucial differences between the American system and former Soviet system (and help to explain how the Soviets developed a stagnant economy). In the Soviet Constitution the role of the state was maximized, whereas in the United States the government's activities, though massive, are constitutionally contained. The following list reveals constitutionally prescribed activities in the Soviet state that are generally expressed only in the private sector in the United States.

Development of mass physical culture and sports

Spiritual development of young people

Moral and aesthetic education of the Soviet people

Organization and introduction of inventions and proposals in the economy

No American government at any level could try any of these activities without violating the Constitution. But the state had such an all-encompassing role in the Soviet Union that very little was left to individual initiative.

The Soviet Union's constitution was quite deliberate in its quest to have the economy, like the government and even like the culture, controlled by and directed from a central agency. As we now know, the Soviet constitution achieved its desired result only too well. Most other constitutions in communist societies were modeled at least in part on the Soviet one, with much the same results: an uninnovative citizenry devoid of individual rights living in a destroyed economy. North Korea went even further: It incorporated its long-time leader, Kim Il Sung, into its entire legal system, basically producing a legal and constitutional system that was simply what the leader said it was. One individual's pronouncements either became law or had the force of law.

A communist constitution also tends to create a special class of citizenry. In the Soviet and other similar constitutions during the communist era in Eastern Europe a special status was reserved for the Communist party. Not only was it the only legal party, but it was also the "keeper of the faith." Actually, the communist constitution became a legitimater for political corruption. Party members, particularly the party hierarchy, were constitutionally placed above the law since they were the ones responsible for the proper interpretation of communist ideology. Eventually, their privileged constitutional status became a rationale for a blatantly higher standard of living than was enjoyed by the rest of the citizenry, including lavish homes, private hospitals, and foodstuffs (imported from Western Europe and the United States) that were unaffordable for the average Soviet citizen, even if he or she could locate them.

The communist regime in China has at least been more democratic about distributing poverty. Except in selected "special economic zones," where modified forms of capitalism are allowed to function, China's economy is still a long way from the level enjoyed by the East Asian democracies. This is in part because the regime is still intent on retaining political control of the country (thus avoiding the deterioration that characterized the last years of communism in the Soviet Union).

Many of the products China exports are the result of forced prison labor.[16]

A VIEW FROM THE STATES

Writing a New Constitution in Russia: Not an Easy Task

When it came time to adopt a new constitution, legislators at the Russian Congress of People's Deputies resorted to the old practice of putting off the toughest decisions until a later date. . . .

The Congress' decision is seen as a minor victory by some advocates of radical reform in parliament because it keeps alive the chances for passing a new constitution this year. The new document would replace the 1977 Constitution, a legacy of the communist era that must be discarded if Russia hopes to make a successful transition to a market economy, radical reformers say.

But in failing to adopt a specific constitutional framework, the lawmakers avoided confronting perhaps the biggest problem facing Russia's young democracy: how to divide power among the different branches of government. Until the legislative and executive branches can precisely determine their responsibilities, the long-term picture for reforms remains cloudy, say some deputies. . . .

"It's bad when all power is in the hands of the president, or Cabinet, [Sergei Shakhrai] told fellow lawmakers, "but it's also bad when all power is in the hands of the legislature. We need balance. . . ."

The jockeying between the legislative and executive branches is not the only factor holding up passage of the new constitution. . . . [A]nother big obstacle [is] the struggle between the old communist order and the new democratic order. . . .

Whatever the reasons for the delay in adopting a new constitution, some argue that the Congress' bloated size makes it impossible for the body to find a solution that would set Russia on firm ground for the future.

Source: Justin Burke, "Russia Defers Constitution Debate," *The Christian Science Monitor,* April 20, 1992, p. 3. Reprinted by permission from *The Christian Science Monitor.* © 1992 The Christian Science Publishing Society. All rights reserved.

Obviously, this sort of production strategy results in substantial profit *because* human rights are denied.[17] Individual rights, therefore, are not considered a politically affordable luxury and are constitutionally guaranteed on paper only.

If communist societies are almost totally monitored by an ideology with a materialist emphasis, there are also countries whose focus is a spiritual totality. In other words, a constitution can become a device to evaluate every aspect of an individual's life and life-style. Iran is an example of an authoritarian society with a constitutional framework that is in effect a moral prescription. Iran's constitution is based on Islamic law. This constitution is not simply a body of rules to guide the governing process, but a holy writ that insists on the conformity of every member of society to a single religious ideal.

Iran's constitution is very prescriptive: it requires that Islamic women be fully clothed in public at all times.

The constitution provides for a Council of Constitutional Guardians consisting of six specialists on Islamic law; places ultimate political power in the hands of religious authorities; and includes as capital offenses adultery (by women), alcohol consumption, women not wearing the chador (veil) in public, and prostitution.

Does this sound like a formula for male chauvinism? It is. But Iranian constitutional theory and law are based on the Islamic Koran, the scriptural value system for any practicing Muslim. There is no pretense of separation of church and state, as in most democratic societies, and certainly no hint of tolerated or even official atheism, as in communist ones. Instead, Iran compels the behavior of its 53 million citizens (some of whom are not Muslim or do not belong to the main Islamic sect in Iran, Shi'ite). Neither individual nor minority rights have any place in Iran: It is the orderliness of the greater community that is stressed.

CONSTITUTIONS IN AUTHORITARIAN SYSTEMS

Most autocratic regimes don't bother about constitutional niceties. Many even have rather democratic-sounding constitutions that are consistently ignored. In such cases governments behave in brutal and extraconstitutional ways. For example, in some Central American societies, such as El Salvador and Guatemala, death squads, frequently composed of moonlighting murderers from the armed services, kidnap or kill citizens who take their country's constitutional guarantees too seriously and oppose or criticize the regime[18] or are even suspected of being likely to do so at some time. People are sometimes killed simply because they are related to an individual who has defied the government. In some extreme cases, where government sponsors actual genocide, the regime may simply choose to ignore a constitution that gives lip service to individual rights in order to physically eliminate a minority it considers undesirable. The Iraqi government under Saddam Hussein has been doing this to the Kurds in the northern part of the country and to the Shi'ites in the southern half for years.

For authoritarian governments that actually acknowledge their constitution there remains the option of simply suspending it, often under the guise of martial law. This frequently occurs when governments feel themselves to be under siege. Latin American and African governments were doing this sort of thing regularly in the 1970s and 1980s. Several of these governments were under siege in part because of their violations of human rights.

Authoritarian regimes only want to stay in power and enrich themselves. They are usually uninterested in perpetuating an ideological message. The constitution in such political systems therefore is really no more than a scrap of paper.

The distinction between a democratic constitution and an undemocratic one, then, is usually based on whether a government actually practices what its constitution preaches. Dictators normally either ignore their own constitutions or, if they worry about appearing hypocritical, find a rationale to "temporarily" suspend them. In the American and nearly all European constitutions, in contrast, safeguards for guaranteeing individual rights are practically the cornerstones of the documents.

Summary

1. The U.S. Constitution is the oldest working written constitution in the world. This is both its greatest asset and its most severe criticism, since its provisions may no longer be fully applicable in a world much changed from 1789.

2. The Constitution became necessary as the Articles of Confederation proved to be deficient. Under the Articles the central government was extremely weak and mostly ineffective. Nor could the Articles enable the government to cope with domestic disturbances or conduct foreign policy in any meaningful way.

3. Compromise was essential for a successful Constitutional Convention in 1787 because of the problems of big versus small states, slavery, and taxation.

4. The Constitution outlines the structure and powers of the three branches of government as well as the overall rules governing relationships between levels of government and the (difficult) process of amending the Constitution.

5. The Constitution allows two ways of proposing and two ways of ratifying an amendment. Early amendments were remedial in the sense that citizens were guaranteed their rights against the power of the national government; the Civil War amendments extended this process; twentieth-century amendments continued to broaden democracy in the United States.

6. The Constitution's silences have permitted needed institutions to develop, such as political parties and the Cabinet.

7. The suggestion that the Constitution is an elitist document is based on the educational, social, and professional backgrounds of the 55 delegates. They were responsible for the constitutional provisions that seem to protect property and moneyed interests. Moreover, the delegates met in secret and formulated a document that some would argue they were not empowered to write. But one can also argue that the delegates acted for the most part to create legitimate political institutions that eventually proved beneficial for the entire society.

8. The argument that the Constitution is an impediment to progress is based on the notion that separation of powers slows the process of government, that the amendment process is so complicated it often defeats the public will, and that judges must often make the decisions to resolve social problems. On the other hand, the Constitution offers a basic framework in which democracy has consistently grown. The amending process has worked when it needed to.

9. Some people want to call a new constitutional convention in order to update the Constitution. This call has produced a debate between those who want a more streamlined government and those who are concerned that a new convention could actually destroy the familiar and time-tested political process.

10. Most democratic constitutions do not bother to separate the various branches of government as the United States does. And some democratic constitutions actually allow for actions that are considered unconstitutional in the United States.

11. Constitutions may be written for different purposes and with different agendas in mind. In the Soviet Union the 1977 Constitution emphasized the protection of both economic and political rights.

12. Other constitutions defeat the purpose of democracy by emphasizing and enforcing a moral code, sometimes based on religious dicta, while other authoritarian systems systematically violate individual rights through kidnapping and murdering citizens by unofficial government agents or even resorting to genocidal activities.

Terms to Define

Bicameral

Bills of attainder

Division of power

Elastic clause

Ex post facto laws

Jurisdiction

Multiple access points

Political consensus

Separation of powers

Shared powers

Supremacy clause

Unicameral

Writ of habeas corpus

Suggested Readings

Bailyn, Bernard. *The Ideological Origins of the American Revolution.* Cambridge: Harvard University Press, 1967. Excellent analysis of the justification of independence.

Beard, Charles A. *Economic Interpretation of the Constitution of the United States.* New York: MacMillan, 1913. Beard's thesis is that the drafters of the Constitution were driven more by economic self-interest than by noble ideals.

Becker, Carl L. *The Declaration of Independence.* New York: Vintage, 1942. The leading assessment of the meaning of the Declaration.

Farrand, Max. *The Framing of the Constitution of the United States.* New Haven: Yale University Press, 1913. The best brief analysis of the Constitutional Convention of 1787.

Goldwin, Robert A., and William Schambra, eds. *How Democratic Is the Constitution?* Wathington, D.C.: American Enterprise Institute, 1980. This relentless inquiry is responded to by examining the different views on the political intent and meaning of the Constitution.

Hamilton, Alexander, James Madison, and John Jay. *Federalist Papers.* Many editions available, but Jacob E. Cooke's published by Wesleyan University Press (Middletown, Conn., 1961) is perhaps the best.

Kurland, Philip B., and Ralph Lerner, eds. *The Founders' Constitution* (5 vols.). Chicago: University of Chicago Press, 1987. Collection of primary sources to explain the Constitution.

McDonald, Forrest. *Ordo Seclorum.* Lawrence: University of Kansas Press, 1985. Leading scholar offers an excellent study of the intellectual origins of the Constitution.

Robinson, Donald L., ed. *Reforming American Government.* Boulder, Colo.: Westview Press, 1985. Series of essays advocating constitutional reform.

Storing, Herbert J. *What the Anti-Federalists Were For.* Chicago: University of Chicago Press, 1981. Cogent study of the views and arguments of those opposed to Constitutional ratification.

Wills, Garry. *Inventing America.* Garden City, N.Y.: Doubleday, 1978. A significant effort to disprove Becker's interpretation of the Declaration.

Wood, Gordon S. *The Creation of the American Republic.* Chapel Hill: University of North Carolina Press, 1969. Thorough analysis of American political thought preceding the Constitutional Convention.

Notes

1. Peter Laslett, ed., *Locke's Two Treatises of Government* (New York: Cambridge University Press, 1960), p. 348.
2. Carl Van Doren, *The Great Rehearsal* (New York: Viking Press, 1948), p. 153.
3. *Marbury v. Madison* (1803).
4. Charles A. Beard, *An Economic Interpretation of the Constitution of the United States* (New York: Macmillan, 1960), p. 188.
5. Forrest McDonald, *We the People* (Chicago: University of Chicago Press, 1958), pp. vii, 350, 415.
6. Robert E. Brown, *Charles Beard and the Constitution* (Princeton: Princeton University Press, 1956), p. 198.
7. Ibid., pp. 170, 197.
8. *McCulloch v. Maryland* (1819).
9. *Congressional Quarterly*, February 17, 1979, p. 273.
10. Ibid.
11. Ibid.
12. *Washington Post*, September 17, 1984, p. 6.
13. *Congressional Quarterly*, February 17, 1979, p. 273.
14. *The New York Times*, February 2, 1990, p. B11.
15. Article 21. The previous article insists that Germany "is a democratic and social federal state" (Article 20, section (1)). No chances are being taken that would allow Germany to become a totalitarian state through "legal" means, as it did in 1933.

16. See, for example, the "60 Minutes," of July 26, 1992.
17. See Hongda Harry Wu, *Laogai: The Chinese Gulag* (Boulder, Colo.: Westview Press, 1992). The author spent nearly 20 years in labor camps in China doing what he describes in his book.
18. See, for instance, Martin McReynolds, "El Salvador Rights Record Challenged," *The Miami Herald*, May 22, 1990 and Lindsey Gruson, "Political Violence on the Rise Again in Guatemala, Tarnishing Civilian Rule," *The New York Times*, June 28, 1990.

CHAPTER FOUR

FEDERALISM

THE AMERICAN BRAND OF
  FEDERALISM

  Powers and Obligations
  Evolution of Federalism

ISSUES TO ANALYZE

  1. Is Federalism Inefficient?
  2. Are State Governments an
     Anachronism?

COMPARISONS WITH OTHER NATIONS

  Federalism in Democracies
  Federalism in Totalitarian Systems
  Federalism in Authoritarian Systems

Every nation must decide how it is going to divide power among its constituent governmental units. Some countries place all power in a central government, and any subordinate units have only as much power as the central government allows. This **unitary** form of government is used by such nations as the United Kingdom, France, Israel, and the Philippines. The relationship between American states and their local governments, such as cities and counties, is also unitary. A contrasting way to divide power is to form a **confederation**, such as existed in America between 1777 and 1787 under the Articles of Confederation and in the South during the Civil War (1861–1865). In this case, the central government exists only at the sufferance of the constituent governments, and its powers are limited by the confederated states.

The founders knew from experience that a confederation didn't work in America, and they had lived long enough under British rule to shy away from a unitary form of government, which was then equated with authoritarianism. They turned to a form of dividing powers that numerous Indian tribes in the Iroquois Federation had already found successful: **federalism**, division of powers between a central government and constituent governments in a manner that provides each with substantial power and functions. Canada, Mexico, India, Germany, and Australia are some other countries that have adopted federalism.

Federalism can take many forms. Today at least 18 countries, both democratic and nondemocratic, have some variant of federalism.[1] The United States developed its own unique brand. In fact, the distinctiveness of the American system has led political scientist Samuel Beer to state that "at Philadelphia in 1787, it is generally recognized, the Americans invented federalism."[2] Well, almost. The Greeks two thousand years earlier had experimented with federations, as had native Americans. Certainly, the American arrangement along with the one practiced in Switzerland were the earliest modern formulations of federalism.

In what follows we will take a close look at our style of federalism. Then we will examine some controversies concerning the efficiency and workability of our brand of federalism. Finally we'll compare our federal system with those in other nations.

★ THE AMERICAN BRAND OF FEDERALISM

POWERS AND OBLIGATIONS

The first three articles of the United States Constitution grant power exclusively to the national government. Many of these are **express powers**, specifically enumerated as belonging to the national government (minting money, for example). In addition, **implied powers** are inferred from the "elastic" clause of Article I, section 8, which (as we saw in Chapter 2) gives Congress the right "to make all Laws which shall be *necessary and proper* for carrying into Execution the foregoing Powers, and all other Powers vested . . . in the Government of the United States" (italics added). A third category is **inherent powers:** certain powers the national government may exercise by virtue of its position. For example, the national government has powers inherent in guiding the country's foreign policy and international relations. The states are not in a position to establish a foreign policy for the entire country.

Some powers belong to *both* the national and state governments. These **concurrent powers** include the right to levy taxes and to borrow money. States may exercise these powers as long as no conflict with the national law occurs. To the states alone belong **reserved powers**. These include the right to regulate local governments and to maintain the public health, welfare, safety, and morals. Such powers, however, cannot be used to frustrate or impede legitimate national government policies.

Over time the national government has increased the scope of its powers. The constitutional basis for growth of central authority rests primarily on three provisions: the war power, the power to regulate interstate and foreign commerce, and the power to tax and spend for the general welfare. (State governments have also increased in power through the exercise of concurrent and reserved powers.)

The war power is very different from what it was in 1787, which is only to be expected in a world where total war and total destruction are now possible. All manner of things, from the study of chemistry to the building of highways, may have a direct relationship to warfare. The national government has funded college scholarships through the National Defense Education Act and developed the interstate highway system through the National Defense Highway Act.

The regulation of interstate and foreign commerce is a power with enormous implications in conflicts between the national and state governments. The Supreme Court has used this power as the basis for declaring constitutional a wide range of laws, including regulation of farmers' corn or wheat crops. Even though the farmers may grow these crops only to feed their own families, the Court allowed for regulation because growing and using such products affects the price of these commodities in interstate commerce.[3] In another case, the Supreme Court upheld a law forbidding discrimination in hotel or motel accommodations, because such discrimination affects the flow of interstate commerce.[4]

The power to tax and spend for the public welfare has been used, especially since the New Deal era, to uphold a variety of national government programs ranging from local airports, hospitals, and sewage disposal facilities to employment services, slum control, and urban renewal projects. Each program contains controls or guidelines that the states must follow if they wish to use federal revenues. States, of course, also have significant powers in this area.

Constitutional safeguards of civil liberties and individual rights guaranteed in the Bill of Rights and by the Thirteenth, Fourteenth, Fifteenth, Nineteenth, and Twenty-sixth Amendments generally apply with some exceptions to both national and state governments. For example, the Fourteenth Amendment applies principally to the states: The states are required to guarantee "due process of law" *and* "equal protection of the laws" to all citizens.

The national government has certain constitutional obligations to the states:

1. It must guarantee each of them a republican form of government. Although the meaning of this constitutional provision is unclear, the framers probably meant a form distinguished from a monarchy on the one hand and a pure democracy on the other. Congress enforces the provision when it allows a state's representatives to take their seats in Congress.

2. It must protect the states against invasion and domestic violence. At various times, Congress, upon the request of proper state authorities, has delegated to the president the power to send federal troops to quell violence in a state. For example, in 1957 President Eisenhower sent troops to Little Rock, Arkansas, to enforce a school desegregation order at Central High School. In 1992 national guard troops were federalized during the Los Angeles riots.

As for the states, each has three obligations to the others:

1. Under the "full faith and credit" clause (Article IV, section 1), each state shall enforce the civil judgments of other states and accept their records and acts as valid.

2. Article IV, section 2, guarantees "all privileges and immunities" to citizens of one state who find themselves in another state. This clause means that

Federal troops may be sent into a state to keep the peace. When Little Rock Central High School was first integrated in 1957, the threat of violence led President Dwight Eisenhower to dispatch troops to Arkansas. In this photo, white students look on as the African-American students, under military escort, start up the steps (bottom left).

a state shall not deny to a citizen of another state the full protection of its law, the right to engage in a peaceful occupation, or access to its courts. Nor may it tax citizens of other states at a discriminatory rate or otherwise arbitrarily interfere with their property.

3. The third obligation is extradition. The Constitution provides that a state shall deliver anyone charged with a crime to the state making the accusation, when requested to do so by the latter's governor.

Since the Civil War, states have not settled their differences by force. Disputes are to be settled by the Supreme Court or through an **interstate compact**, an agreement through which two or more states with a common interest or problem establish a legally binding solution. Before an interstate compact becomes effective, it must be approved by Congress; its terms are then enforceable by the Supreme Court.

EVOLUTION OF FEDERALISM

Of the ten presidents from Franklin Roosevelt through George Bush perhaps only one (Harry Truman) has not tried to promote his own style of "federalism." Yet with all the fanfare about "new federalism," the product remains much the same. The appearance of automobiles may change, but they still have four wheels, an engine, a body, and seats. The look of federalism, like the automobile, has changed over the years, but its basic structure has remained the same.

The evolution of American federalism has taken it through five distinct stages: (1) competitive federalism, (2) dual federalism, (3) picket-fence federalism, (4) cooperative federalism, and (5) the "new federalism" of the 1980s.

Competitive Federalism

Political scientists describe our federal system from its founding to the Civil War as **competitive federalism**, in which the states and the federal government competed for power. Three Supreme Court cases during this period illustrate the competitive nature of American federalism.

Chisholm v. *Georgia* (1793) determined that states could be sued in the federal courts, thereby diminishing state sovereignty. Later, the Eleventh Amendment (1798) forbade suing states in the federal courts. *McCulloch* v. *Maryland* (1819) upheld the national government's creation of a national bank based on the "necessary and proper" clause of Article 1, section 8. Finally *Gibbons* v. *Ogden* (1824) ruled in favor of the national government's regulation of interstate commerce based on the commerce clause of Article I, section 8.

During this period, most cases and issues were decided in favor of the national government, but the states put up a fight. Three doctrines, in particular, were tested—nullification, interposition, and secession—although none of these prevailed.

Nullification occurs when a state disregards (declares null and void) a federal law within its boundaries. The Virginia and Kentucky Resolutions of 1798 and 1799, nullifying the passage of the Alien and Sedition Acts, contended that such a course was the "rightful remedy" for states to follow when the national government overstepped its bounds. As it turned out, the judiciary, not the states, was to determine whether this had happened.

Interposition occurs when a state tries to impede a federal law by interposing its own authority, as was advocated by South Carolina's John C. Calhoun in opposing the national tariff of 1828. When South Carolina tried to put the doctrine into practice in the 1830s, President Andrew Jackson forced it to back down.

Conflicts of this nature reached their climax with **secession**, when the Confed-

In the aftermath of the Civil War, much of the South lay in ruins. The cities of Atlanta, Columbia, and Richmond were gutted by fire. Shown here is the Canal Basin of Richmond, Virginia.

erate states declared that they had left (seceded from) the Union. Northern victory in the Civil War determined that this doctrine could not be regarded as a valid solution to nation-state conflicts.

Dual Federalism

Chief Justice Roger Taney laid the foundation for dual federalism prior to the Civil War in *Dred Scott* v. *Sandford* (1857), which held that slaves were not citizens and therefore were not protected by the Constitution. This decision developed the concept of "dual sovereignty": the Court ruled that national legislation prohibiting slavery in northern territories deprived people of property without due process of law, a decision that essentially left the issue of slavery in the hands of the states. Ultimately "dual sovereignty" became **dual federalism** as defined in an 1859 Supreme Court decision: "The powers of the General Government, and of the State, although both exist and are exercised within the same territorial limits, are separate and distinct sovereignties, acting separately and independently of each other, within their respective spheres."[5] Dual federalism is generally considered dominant from the Civil War to 1937: Each level of government was sovereign in certain policy areas, and neither could expand beyond its jurisdictional boundaries. Over time, however, the forces of urbanization and industrialization, depressions, wars, and social mobility led to greater growth in the power of the national government.

Picket-Fence Federalism

As national, state, and local bureaucracies grew during the New Deal period of the 1930s, administrators of government programs at these levels began to perceive that their com-

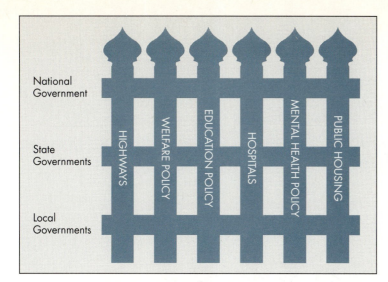

Figure 4.1 PICKET-FENCE FEDERALISM. Source; Picket-fence federalism: A schematic representation (Deil S. Wright, "A New Phase of IGR," in *Intergovernmental Relations in the 1980s,* edited by Richard H. Leach, Figure 1. Marcel Dekker, Inc., N.Y., 1983). Reprinted by courtesy of Marcel Dekker, Inc.

mon interests often differed from the interests of elected officials. Welfare bureaucrats, highway bureaucrats, and others, regardless of level of government, pursued their respective common interests so that ultimately the title "picket-fence federalism" was applied. Each picket represented a government policy in a particular area, such as welfare or highways. The pickets overlapped the respective spheres of national, state, and local government (see Figure 4.1).

Cooperative Federalism

The seeds of cooperative federalism lay in picket fence federalism, but it bloomed in the 1960s and 1970s, when the number of federal grant programs increased from 71 in 1950 to more than 490 in 1980, and their value rose from $7 billion in 1960 to $90 billion in 1980. The national government gave grants to state and local governments, for example, to fund hospitals and sewage treatment facilities so states could improve the standards of health. Under **cooperative federalism**, then, funding and regulations were the domain of the national government, while execution and administration were in the hands of state and local government. (See Figures 4.2 and 4.3.)

This type of federalism enables one unit of government to utilize the strength of others. State governments benefit from the revenue resources of the national government through federal aid. As needs have changed, so too have the methods for distributing federal revenue. Until the late 1960s, most grants, called **conditional** or **matching grants**, were earmarked for a specific purpose, and the state government had to match certain portions of the national grant. For example, federal funds might be set aside for a specific highway construction project; the state would supply a certain percentage of the money needed. If the federal government provided 90 percent of the funds, the matching percentage from the state would be 10 percent. (Matching grants have also been called **categorical grants**, because they are available for only one category or type of project.) Whatever the name, this type of grant entails a contract between two governments.

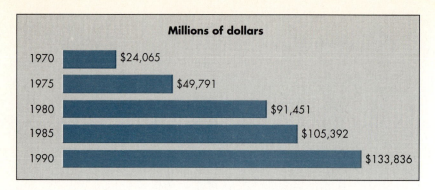

Figure 4.2 FEDERAL AID TO STATE AND LOCAL GOVERNMENTS, 1970 TO 1990. Source: *U.S. Statistical Abstract, 1992*, p. 282.

Beginning in the 1960s, **project grants** came into use. With these, the national government decides where money is needed; it can then bypass state governments and place funds directly on the target with local government, or even with private groups or individuals.

In the late 1960s two other forms of federal aid were developed to counteract the inflexibility of grants that required money be spent on specific projects. In one form, **block grants**, the recipient government may use the money for any of a variety of purposes that fall under a general heading.

The second innovation to increase flexibility was **revenue sharing**, which provides that a portion of national government revenue will be returned to state and local governments to be used at their discretion. These funds have just a few strings attached: They cannot be used to support programs that discriminate against any person because of race, national origin, or sex; and the funds must be spent on generally defined goals outlined by the federal government, such as public safety, environmental protection, transportation, and social services for the poor or aged. Revenue sharing was abolished in 1986.

Federalism in the 1980s

Between the early 1930s and the Reagan administration of the 1980s, the role of the national government in the federal system continued to increase. But declining national resources and a shift in political philosophy concerning the role of the national government dictated a slow retreat from this type of federalism. President Ronald Reagan's "new federalism" in the 1980s proposed to give both administrative and financial responsibility for government programs to state and local governments. This form of federalism might also be described as a do-it-yourself fiscal federalism.

The results of the "new federalism" were mixed. As state and local governments saw their own resources decline, most were forced to cut back on the delivery of public services. The economic slowdown of the early 1990s did not help. However, many states and local jurisdictions attempted with some success to find alternative ways of funding their activities. New York City, for example, has, for all its problems, remained a thriving

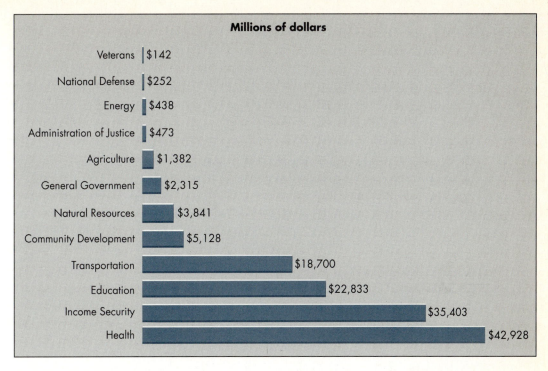

Figure 4.3 FEDERAL AID TO STATE AND LOCAL GOVERNMENTS BY CATEGORY, 1990. Source: *U.S. Statistical Abstract*, 1992, p. 282.

financial and cultural center and can reasonably expect to exceed its own record high population of 8 million by 2000. The reason is the growth of the middle class among minority communities. Much the same is true in other urban areas.[6] As immigrants from Third World countries move to American urban areas, a larger and more diverse middle class is growing and forming what eventually will be a solid local tax base.

One characteristic of American federalism that is becoming increasingly evident is its competitive nature. The 50 states are obligated to cooperate with one another in a variety of circumstances, but they are also rivals in a relentless race for economic prosperity. When President Clinton became governor of Arkansas in 1980, for example, his priority was to get more jobs into his state to lower an unacceptably high 13 percent unemployment rate.[7] To do so, though, he needed to entice businesses, with the lure of lower taxes, away from other states. Most governors feel the need to do the same thing, to the point that states are prone to try to "steal" jobs away from other states.[8]

The complex and diffused system of government provided by American federalism has led to several interpretations of its value. Its uniquely American origin and survival in various forms for about two hundred years put history and tradition on its side, but its intricate, ambiguous nature sometimes causes confusion in government. We can gain a better picture of its strengths and weaknesses by examining these differing interpretations of the value of federalism.

? ISSUES TO ANALYZE

ISSUE 1   IS FEDERALISM INEFFICIENT?

REASONS WHY FEDERALISM IS INEFFICIENT

Because of federalism, the American system is susceptible to numerous damaging conflicts between the national government and the state governments, between and among state governments, between those holding differing philosophical views, and among interest groups with special ties to one level of government or another. These conflicts make the workings of federalism inefficient.

States' Rightists Versus Nationalists. One important conflict is between those who favor a strong national government and those who want more power given to the states. This conflict actually harks back to the beginning of our nation, when Federalists lined up against Anti-Federalists in the battle for ratification of the Constitution. Advocates of **states' rights**, going back to Thomas Jefferson and John C. Calhoun, contend that the Constitution is like a treaty the states have made among themselves that gives the national government specific and very limited authority. States' rightists believe that the powers of the national government—a government they view as heavy-handed and bureaucratic—should be narrowly construed in order to protect the federal system. In conflicts between the national and state government, doubts should be resolved in favor of the latter. In the twentieth century, Senator Barry Goldwater (R-Ariz.), the Republican party's presidential candidate in 1964, and President Ronald Reagan have espoused the states' rights position.

States' rights advocates advance two main arguments in their cause. One rests on the Tenth Amendment, which reserves to the states those powers not delegated to the national government. The other argument holds that state government is closer to the people and can more accurately reflect their wishes and desires.

The nationalists, represented historically by John Marshall, Abraham Lincoln, Theodore Roosevelt, and Franklin Roosevelt, as well as by many liberal politicians today, reject the idea that the Constitution is a compact among states. They contend that it is a compact among *people*, who drew up the Constitution and established the national government as their agent. Nationalists hold that the people intended the national government's powers to be broadly construed and not to be denied unless specifically prohibited by the Constitution.

The nationalist cause has been aided by several Supreme Court decisions, one of the most important of which was a case mentioned earlier, *McCulloch v. Maryland* (1819). Maryland levied a tax against a branch of the Bank of the United States, and the bank's cashier refused to pay it. Two questions were to be resolved: (1) Did Congress have the right to incorporate a national bank? (2) Did Maryland have the right to tax it?

As we have seen, the Court ruled that the national bank was constitutional. The Constitution gives Congress the right to pass laws "which shall be necessary and proper" to carry out powers expressly delegated to it. A bank is an appropriate, convenient, and useful way to exercise the express powers of collecting taxes, borrowing money, and caring for the property of the United States. As for Maryland's taxing of the bank, Chief Justice John Marshall stated that "the power to tax involves the power to destroy" and declared the state's action unconstitutional.

The nationalist position suffered a setback in 1976, however, when the Supreme Court held that Congress cannot tell states and cities how much they must pay their employees. Justice William H. Rehnquist said in the majority opinion that "if Congress may withdraw from the states the authority to make those fundamental employment decisions upon which their systems for performance of these functions must rest, we think there would be little left of the states' separate and independent existence."[9]

Within ten years, however, the Court reversed itself,[10] forcing San Antonio, Texas, to abide by federal wage and hour laws. In this decision the Court declared Congress free of specific constitutional limits in its regulation of commerce, even when that regulation curtails the power of the states. In another case, in 1987, the Supreme Court ruled that Congress could require states to adopt a 21-year-old drinking age under penalty of losing a portion of their highway funds.[11] In an unexpected departure from tradition, the Court's majority closed the doors of federal courthouses to states and cities challenging acts of Congress. Instead of filing suit, states and cities must invoke the political process to find a remedy. But this decision is also susceptible to reversal as the composition of the Court changes. Thus, the federal system contributes to a yo-yo effect in the administration of law as states' rights advocates battle nationalists.

Financial "Yo-yo." Another kind of yo-yo effect involves federal aid to the states. During the 1960s, grants and revenue sharing from the national to state and local governments increased because the latter were hard pressed financially. By the end of 1970s, however, states had developed new revenue sources such as the income tax, and were running surpluses, while the national government had substantial deficits and severe financial problems. By the beginning of the 1990s all levels of government were running deficits and some states were so deeply in the red that their deficit amounts were almost as much as the gross national product of several small countries. California, for example, in 1993 groaned under the weight of a $14 billion deficit, the highest in the nation. The financial "yo-yo" effect suggests that federalism prevents a uniform and consistent solution to governmental fiscal strains and, indeed, exacerbates them.

Interstate Competition. Many states, as well as municipalities, compete for business and industry by manipulating their tax structures to keep taxes low. But states with lower taxes generally can provide fewer services for their people. States with higher taxes tend to be located in the North and East. While they provide more services for their residents, they are at the same time more likely to lose business and industry to low-tax states in the South and West. This ultimately results in deteriorating services because the exodus of industry lowers the tax base.

Federal legislation may be used as a weapon in this warfare between states. For example, one of the reasons for passage of the first minimum wage law in 1938 was to keep the wages of textile workers in the South as high as those in New England, so that northern industry would not be tempted to relocate.

Interstate Confusion. Although the Constitution clearly states that each state shall observe the obligations of full faith and credit, privileges and immunities, and extradition, each of these issues has led to substantial confusion. Concerning full faith and credit, for example, a state is not obliged to recognize a divorce granted in another state if one spouse has established residence there in order to obtain the divorce and has then returned to the state where the couple previously lived.

One example will serve to illustrate the violation of privileges and immunities: A state does not have to admit students from other states to its public colleges or universities at the same rate of tuition as its own students. Regarding extradition, a state (that is, its governor) does not have to return an accused person to the state where the crime was allegedly committed, even if the governor of the latter state has requested extradition. The word "shall" in Article IV, sections 1 and 2, has been interpreted in practice to allow states discretion in whether they adhere to these obligations.

Unitary systems, such as those in France and the United Kingdom, face no such problem. Regardless of what part of the country a crime is committed in, the ultimate jurisdiction applies and that is the one of the central government. For example, the governor of New York may refuse to extradite an individual accused of murder in South Carolina because South Carolina occasionally applies the death penalty for murder, whereas New York doesn't. No matter where one commits a crime in France, however, the punishment is nationally consistent.

Confusion also is raised by outmoded state lines and overlapping jurisdiction among states, both of which impede regional and national solutions to problems. States' boundaries are unnatural, the offspring of historical circumstance. They are also administratively inefficient because many problems do not stop at state boundary lines. Air pollution in the huge megalopolitan complexes stretching from Boston to Washington, D.C., and from Pittsburgh to Chicago illustrates this problem. A steel mill in Gary, Indiana, produces air pollution in Chicago, Illinois. Parts of Canada are victimized by pollution produced in the United States. As trade barriers come down between the United States and Mexico, much the same point applies. In their desire to economically develop their country the Mexican government may authorize the introduction of industries that produce air pollution, a major concern for the four southwestern states that border Mexico.

Influence of Local Governments. Local government proliferation also contributes to the inefficiency of the federal system. More than 82,000 separate units of government exist in the United States. Los Angeles County alone includes some 520 separate governmental units—77 cities, 100 school districts, and almost 350 special districts. The New York City metropolitan area has some 1,500 distinct governmental units. There are 228 major metropolitan areas in the United States, each with an average of 91 different governments. The problem is even worse when one considers the 38,000 counties, municipalities, and townships in the United States. Fewer than 1 percent of these have over 100,000 inhabitants; fewer than 10 percent have over 10,000 people. Their governments are often too small to provide adequate and proper public services.

In recent decades, needy local governments have begun to bypass stingy or impoverished state governments and look to the federal government. By turning to Washington, however, local governments confuse the basic outline of federalism in the United States. Under our federal form of government, both the national and state governments have a certain degree of independence from one another based on the division of powers between them. The relationship between state and local governments, however, is unitary, and the latter have only such powers as the states give them. Theoretically, states could abolish any or all local governments. The intrusion of financial assistance given by the federal government directly to local governments has damaged this unitary relationship between states and their local governments.

Some social problems are not meeting with an adequate response at any governmental level. For example, federal arrangements formulated two centuries ago and updated as needed may not be keeping pace with important demographic changes in the United States. During the 1980s, it became evident that young people as a group are getting poorer while older people are getting richer. Only one in eight elderly persons is considered to be living in poverty, but one in five youths is,

> *a situation without precedent in American history. . . . An alarming number of children commit suicide. Others kill themselves more slowly with drugs or risky sex. More and more overeat; the proportion who are grossly fat has risen from 6% (in the early 1960s) to 12%. School test scores have dropped with a thud since the early 1960s. Not all the decline is due to a widening spectrum of children taking the test; rich, white boys are stupider too.*[12]

Which level of government will (or can) address this problem?

Business Versus Labor. Another type of conflict arising out of the federal system—especially since the advent of cooperative federalism—has been that between

Deteriorating inner cities, as reflected by this tenement in Boston's Roxbury section, are frequently the result of neglect by state governments. More and more urban areas are looking to the federal government for aid.

business and labor. Business has tended to ally itself with the states; labor, with the national government. Business recognized that states gave them greater protection because states were less likely to engage actively in business regulation. Indeed, states shaped their actions to *entice* industry to locate in them. Labor found that the national government was more likely to pursue its interests.

Beginning in the late 1960s, however, some business organizations began to recognize that, on some issues at least, their interests would be better served at the national level. California, for example, has in some cases adopted more stringent pollution control laws, particularly when it comes to auto emissions, than has the federal government.

Symmetry Versus Asymmetry. To some extent this conflict could be titled the rich versus the poor, the large versus the small, or the populous versus the less populous states. The political scientist Charles Tarlton uses the terms *symmetrical* and *asymmetrical* to describe the relationship between the national government and these two types of states. The more a state is unlike the national norm, the more likely its policies are to conflict (or to be asymmetrical) with national government policies. A relatively poor, small, or sparsely populated state like Alabama or South Dakota is more likely to have policies conflicting with those of the national government than are Michigan, Illinois, or California, where the populations are more nearly representative of (or symmetrical to) the national population.[13] A classic case in point developed in the 1960s, when civil rights legislation was applied in the then still very rural and segregated South. The legislation had the support of most of Congress. Southerners, on the other hand, often saw race relations differently and accused much of the non-South of moral hypocrisy because of the de facto segregation in housing and public education facilities in many northern cities.

REASONS WHY FEDERALISM IS NOT INEFFICIENT

A nation of continental proportions, the United States has a wide variety of sections and groups that would not be eliminated by simply abolishing federalism. There would remain North and South, East and West, rich and poor, integrationists and segregationists, executives and wage earners. The framers of the Constitution in their foresight provided a federal system of government well before the United States became either fully democratic or industrialized. They devised an efficient federalism by virtue of what was omitted from the Constitution. Instead of trying to foresee the problems of the future, the framers wisely installed a flexibility in the Constitution that would allow future generations to resolve future problems.

Harmony Through Flexibility. We have been able to alter our political system without enduring the trials of changing our basic governmental structure because federalism has been adaptable to changing times and circumstances. For example, dual federalism prevailed in a simpler era, whereas cooperative federalism characterized a more complex and sophisticated age, yet each system has existed within precisely the same constitutional structure.

One of the first American statesmen to argue in favor of the flexibility of the federal system was Alexander Hamilton, who in 1787 sought to persuade the states to ratify the constitution. He aimed to obtain the support of both states' rightists and nationalists. In No. 16 of *The Federalist*, Hamilton stated that the national government would have only limited powers; it would be foolish, he wrote, to imagine a time when

Alexander Hamilton was one of the first to point out the flexibility of the federal system established by the Constitution. The central government could not dominate the states, he argued, but it could regulate the mutual concerns of states.

the central authority could dominate the states. The only way the national government could attain this kind of power, Hamilton believed, was through recruiting and maintaining a national army.

Some Americans felt that there was not enough centralized authority in the proposed Constitution. Hamilton, recognizing this, pointed out that the central government could regulate the mutual concerns of the states. The central government, in his words, "must itself be empowered to employ the arm of the ordinary magistrate [law officer] to execute its own resolutions." From this premise, Hamilton argued that the states could not evade federal laws. What point would there be to a central government whose laws could be violated by state governments? Hamilton believed that nullification of federal law by individual states could not take place "without an open and violent exertion of an unconstitutional power."[14] Thus, the flexibility of federalism allowed Hamilton to argue for both decentralization and centralization.

Balancing Concurrent Powers.   The flexible framework of federalism has permitted the relative strengths of national and state governments to shift as time and circumstance indicated. One area in which these shifts have occurred is the concurrent powers of the two levels of government. The controlling doctrine is **national preemption:** that is, national action is presumed to preclude state action. A relevant case is *Pennsylvania v. Nelson* (1956).[15] At issue was whether Steve Nelson, an acknowledged member of the Communist party, had violated a Pennsylvania statute by threatening to overthrow the federal government. The Supreme Court ruled that sedition was the province of the national government. Any state laws relating to sedition are superseded by federal laws, regardless of whether the state law is intended to supplement the federal statute.

But the Court has also recognized that there are times when *both* national and state action should be valid under their concurrent powers. In *Colorado Anti-Discrimination Commission v. Continental Airlines* (1963),[16] the court upheld a state antidiscrimination statute even though there were national laws on the subject. The Court reasoned that since the power of Congress is not always clearly defined, the judiciary must weigh each case on its merits before denying a state its traditional powers.

Another example of balancing concurrent powers is state power over intrastate commerce and national power over interstate commerce. For instance, states may set meat and poultry inspection standards for what is raised and sold within the state, while the national government may do the same for meat and poultry shipped across state lines.

Sometimes the balance of state authority against national authority serves to protect people and the environment. After the Three Mile Island nuclear accident in Pennsylvania, the governors of Washington, Nevada, and South Carolina threatened a moratorium on nuclear waste disposal in their states until a national solution could be obtained. In a far-reaching decision upholding a California law, the U.S. Supreme Court said a state can impose a moratorium on new nuclear plants until state officials are satisfied that there is a way to dispose of radioactive wastes.[17]

One way of resolving the impasse is through interstate compacts. For example, some states have used their position in Congress to bring pressure on other states to form interstate compacts that would provide for regional dumping sites for nuclear waste material. In congressional testimony,[18] South Carolina's senior senator, Strom Thurmond, had this exchange with a Massachusetts official in charge of environmental affairs, Alan S. Johnson:

THURMOND: What would happen if South Carolina, Washington and Nevada close their disposal sites?

JOHNSON: It would be an economic and environmental disaster for Massachusetts and the rest of the country.

THURMOND: What would your state do?

JOHNSON: We have no answer.

THURMOND: All right now, you're on notice. We do not intend to continue taking the waste from the whole nation. We mean business.

Throughout most of American history, the flexibility of federalism has encouraged the national and state governments to find peaceful solutions to their conflicts. When the national government has had to act, as in the examples just cited, there were simply no viable constitutional obstacles in the way of doing so.

Unity Amid Diversity. The flexibility of the federal system provides for unity amid diversity. Given the differences among the 50 states, it is obviously necessary to allow for diverse approaches in attacking state and regional problems. At the same time there is a need for unity, especially in foreign policy. In this area it is imperative that the entire country speak with one voice to the greatest extent possible.

The dominant role in education, health, and voting belongs to the states, which have the primary responsibility for financing and determining standards in each of these areas. States provide most of the funding for schools, set teacher certification standards, license doctors, and establish voting procedures. Federalism thus permits states to tailor solutions to their own needs rather than forcing them to accept a uniform national solution that might not fit their situations. States regularly vote on initiatives and referenda pertaining to taxes, civil liberties, crime, environment, gambling, health costs, labor, and other matters. Voters in adjacent states may decide the same matter in a different way.

At the same time, national organizations have helped states develop similar approaches to common problems. The Advisory Commission on Intergovernmental Relations (ACIR), created in the 1950s, helps all levels of government address federalism; the Council of State Governments provides states with model legislation on problem areas; the Citizens Conference on State Legislatures assists legislatures in becoming more efficient and effective; and the Education Compact of the States gives assistance to states in this area. To illustrate, since 1970 most states have taken steps to equalize school district spending per child. Local fiscal support for education has dropped to under 50 percent while state fiscal aid now accounts for more than 50 percent.

Several Supreme Court decisions have helped clarify the role of the national government in foreign affairs. In 1920, the Court declared that laws passed in accordance with the obligations of a national treaty take precedence over state law.[19] Pursuant to a treaty with Canada negotiated in 1918, Congress had passed a law to enforce strict standards for the protection of birds migrating between the United States and Canada. Missouri contended that this law interfered with reserved powers of the state in going beyond the express powers of Congress. The Court, noting that Article VI grants treaties the same legal status as the Constitution itself, ruled that any law passed in pursuance of a valid treaty would also be valid.

In 1942 the Supreme Court declared that national government action in the form of an executive agreement with another nation took precedence over state action.[20] An executive agreement has the same legal status as a treaty, but does not have to be ratified by the Senate. After the United States recognized the Soviet Union in 1933 through an executive agreement, the federal government claimed the assets of a Russian insurance company's New York branch. When New York disputed this claim, the Supreme Court ruled that the national government, even when it has acted through an executive agreement, is supreme over a state government.

ISSUE 1: Summary ★ *Is Federalism Inefficient?*

Without question many conflicts exist within the federal system. Indeed, the system itself was *designed* to produce conflict. Had conflict not been allowed, there probably would have been no Constitution. Both states' rightists and nationalists can point to portions of the Constitution that they contend favor their side. States' rightists and nationalists at the founding could not agree on the precise distribution of power between the national and state governments, nor have they been able to agree since then. In a narrow sense, the conflicts are a liability in that they produce competition and confusion between and among more than 82,000 units of government. However, no governmental system, especially a democratic system covering the land mass of the United States, could be free of conflicts. The benefits of federalism center around the maintenance of national unity on crucial matters of national interest while allowing local, state, and regional diversity on matters not of national interest.

Additionally, American federalism is sufficiently flexible to allow adaptation to changing times and circumstances without having to alter the basic governmental structure. The nationalists and the states rightists have both had their day over the course of two hundred years. Most of the time the nationalists have been more persuasive. Since the 1980s, however, there has been at least a brief period of states' rightist success. ■

ISSUE 2   ARE STATE GOVERNMENTS AN ANACHRONISM?

REASONS WHY STATE GOVERNMENTS ARE AN ANACHRONISM

Limits of state governments. The states within the federal system are unable to solve problems within their boundaries. This can be demonstrated on at least seven counts. First, unlike the national government, most states have lengthy and very specific constitutions that curtail their flexibility in solving problems. Moreover, the highly fractured executive branch typically established by state constitutions, with as many as ten statewide elected executive officials, inhibits coordinated and unified action in solving problems.

Second, states have been slow to use fiscal and other resources innovatively in developing needed programs. Proponents of federalism often argue that states are like laboratories for experimentation in devising programs. But experimentation needs money. Several states are therefore trying to entice industries seeking to transfer plants and factories. They are doing so with the promise of low taxes and in the hope that the investment of new plants and the payrolls they generate will gradually provide the resources necessary for state and local government agencies to meet their responsibilities. Obviously, though, shuffling industries from one state to another benefits one state at the expense of another.

Third, for decades state governments have been slow to deal with urban problems because of the control of state legislatures by rural and suburban forces. Despite legislative redistricting designed to give more representation to urban areas, these forces often retain enough influence to deny cities the funding they need to help solve problems created by high crime rates, breakdowns in educational infrastructures, unemployment, and, in some locales, the devastation caused by the AIDS epidemic. The occasional tension between New York City and the state of New York is an obvious example. Apathy on the state level has caused urban areas, especially the big cities, to turn increasingly to the more responsive federal government to obtain needed financial assistance.

Fourth, poorer states can afford fewer services for their citizens than richer states, perhaps most noticeably in the area of education. Federalism is a natural breeding ground for such inequities.

Fifth, many problems are regional, national, and global, thereby diminishing the effectiveness of the states in solving them.

Sixth, while state governments are free to create interstate compacts to solve regional problems, they are slow to do so. It is a time-consuming process. Legislatures and governors in each state affected, as well as Congress, must approve a compact. Then, each state in the compact must have representation on the compact's governing body, and individual members may tend to look out for state rather than regional interests.

Seventh, sometimes states may unwisely follow the lead of other states. California's famous Proposition 13, designed to bring tax relief by limiting government spending, carried with it unforeseen problems. What was promoted as tax relief for home owners, according to critics, was actually of more help to large corporations and large land owners. Also, in limiting what local governments could spend, Proposition 13 created the prospect of decreasing local responsibility in solving local problems. As other states tried to get on the bandwagon of Proposition 13, they faced some of the same problems as California.

Influence of Elites. The fragmentation of authority in the federal system has allowed powerful pressure groups to gain tremendous influence in certain states, such as the Du Pont interest in Delaware, the textile industry in several southern states (such as South Carolina), oil concerns in Texas and Oklahoma, and the Anaconda Company in Montana. Under federalism, public power is dispersed among so many units of government that concentrated private interests can more easily gain authority: as the old adage has it, "divide and conquer."

What are the consequences of the influence of these private elite groups? Consider the case of the textile industry in the South. Many of the states that have "right-to-work" laws, which prohibit making union membership a condition for employment, are in the South. Textile industry executives have vigorously encouraged adoption of right-to-work laws because they make union organization more difficult.

Inadequacies and Inequities of National Aid. The national government has tried to compensate for the weaknesses of state governments with monetary grants to state and local governments. In spite of all this aid, however, states have occasionally used the grants for inefficient, duplicative, or allegedly corrupt purposes. Some grants have helped pay for golf courses, and some have benefited local political organizations. Sometimes they have paid for projects for which local citizens were unwilling to tax themselves, such as pothole repair, museum aid, runaway youth, snow removal, and rural fire protection.

National grants have not eliminated one of the major problems of state and local government: inefficient and outmoded governmental structures. On the contrary, federal aid has tended to prop up these structures by not requiring adoption of administrative and fiscal reforms as a precondition for receiving funds.

A new war between the states has resulted from the competition for federal aid programs. Southern and western states tend to receive more aid than the northern industrialized states. Although such a regional war might still be waged under another form of government, the federal system, with its states' rights emphasis, encourages legislators in the Congress to organize to represent state and regional needs.

An Outdated Survival. Federalism was once considered by many scholars analogous to a layer cake, with its relatively clear lines of demarcation between national and state governments. But in this century federalism has become more like a marble cake, with confusing and indistinct lines of authority between the two levels of government.[21] Federalism has evolved into a form only faintly resembling what the Founders envisioned, even if they knew what they had in mind (which is open to question). The Founders were more concerned with creating a national government than they were with outlining a theory of federalism. What they did draft, however, has become tradition.

The test now is whether this tradition will collapse under the enormous pressures to make government more responsive, efficient, and economical in an era of scarce resources. Actually, we have gone a long way toward a unitary system of government in response to these pressures. History shows us generally moving from decentralization to centralization, except for some of President Reagan's decentralization. But even if it is decentralization we want, the national government can achieve it under a unitary system just as effectively. For example, the national government in Great Britain allocates a great deal of authority to the local governments. Certainly, creating a unitary system would be less hypocritical than keeping our federal system. What if we could do it all over again? Should not a country that is essentially a national state by almost any measure—economic, cultural, educational, and linguistic—have a unitary government? Federalism no longer fits the national character of the United States.

David Walker of the Advisory Commission on Intergovernmental Relations said that since the late 1960s, " We've emerged from a relatively simple governmental system to one that is more costly, more inefficient, more ineffective, and above all, less account- able than it has ever been." He likened American federalism to "a gelatinous mass, oozing, slithering, squishing."[22]

REASONS WHY STATE GOVERNMENTS ARE NOT AN ANACHRONISM

Many criticisms of federalism are poorly founded. To say that federalism allows elite interests to capture control of state government is spurious argument. The same interests would still exist under any form of democracy that retained an economic structure like that of the United States. Moreover, there is ample evidence to demonstrate that economic elites have not had the control some theorists claim. For example, even though the Du Pont interests have opposed reciprocal trade agreements, Delaware's congressional delegation has favored them. Indeed, some politicians have made their political careers by running *against* established interests in their constituencies.

Critics have overlooked the fact that federalism of state and national govern- ments has been an ideal system for the United States. It represents a middle ground between centralized and decentralized systems. When the Constitution was drafted, public opinion would not have permitted the adoption of a unitary form of government, and a confederation had already demonstrated its weaknesses. Federalism has been adaptable to changing conditions in the United States and has proved an essential tool for nation building. Without it, a people opposed to centralization and disenchanted with decen- tralization might have dismembered a nation of states into a collection of small nations.

Federalism and Democracy. Not only is federalism innocent of many of the sins of which it has been accused, but more importantly, it enhances democracy in a number of ways. Perhaps the most vital is that it inhibits the rise of dictatorships by dividing and diffusing power, thereby making it more difficult for one person or a small group to seize control. James Madison took note of this in No. 10 of *The Federalist:*

> *The influence of factious leaders may kindle a flame within their particular States, but will be unable to spread a general conflagration through the other States . . . A rage for paper money, for an abolition of debts, for an equal division of property, or for any other im- proper or wicked project, will be less apt to pervade the whole body of the Union than a particular member of it.*[23]

Federalism not only guards against a minority takeover; it also protects Americans against tyranny by the majority, according to the federalism authority Richard H. Leach: "A happy result of the federal system is that it prevents a majority from fully exercising its power arbitrarily and thereby reserves for the individual the possibility of a greater degree of self-government."[24]

Federalism also offers distinct advantages for the individual citizen. It enhances what might be called "preparatory democracy" by providing a training ground for public officials. After serving at state and local levels, they may then move up the ladder to national government offices. Many members of Congress previously served in state legislatures or on city councils.

Federalism promotes participatory democracy because over 82,000 units of government in the United States, need to be filled with officials. Citizens have the opportunity to participate in the democratic process at all levels, whether on a park commission or school board, in a city council, state legislature, or the United States Congress.

Another advantage of federalism is that the many units of government give the individual citizen many points of access to influence government. The multiple access points help to broaden the base of democracy. In an era of "bigness," when Americans are increasingly troubled by depersonalization, local governmental jurisdictions offer people a way to identify with and take pride in their own municipality, county, and state. Federalism allows individual citizens to have a greater sense of control over their own destinies.

State and Local Successes. In 1965, Senator Everett McKinley Dirksen (R-Ill.) warned that the time was not far off when " the only people interested in state boundaries will be Rand-McNally." Rather than withering on the vine, however, state governments updated their constitutions, improved their judicial branches, and staffed their legislatures adequately.

State and local governments have developed many innovative programs and policies. In some cases state action has *preceded* national action. A few examples will suffice:

States such as Minnesota and Wisconsin are striving to improve the public schools by making them more responsive to parental interests through the voucher system. A voucher pays for school expenses and can be redeemed at the school of the parent's choice.

Georgia pioneered in giving 18-year-olds the right to vote. (Kentucky and Alaska also lowered the voting ages before the national government did so.)

California imposed stricter air pollution control programs than those mandated by federal law.

New York, Massachusetts, Oregon, and Wisconsin were some of the states initiating fair employment practices legislation before the federal government did.

The Twenty-fourth Amendment, prohibiting a poll tax as a qualification for voting in federal elections, merely ratified what most states had already done.

Wyoming, followed by several other western states, provided for women's suffrage long before the federal government did.

Local government in action: A parent addresses the Austin (Texas) Independent School District board to protest budget cuts. With more than 82,000 units of government in the federal system, there are many opportunities for people to seek office as well as to have access to government.

Several states have advanced beyond federal job training programs. Small Delaware and large California have created innovative programs to train workers in electronics, computers, and machinery repair. Delaware gives insurance vouchers to those who are unemployed.

Innovative state programs have paved the way not only for the national government but also for other states. California, for example, is noted among other states for its system of higher education. South Carolina is known for its vocational and technical education and for its educational television. New York and California have provided their legislative branches with scientific and technical personnel.

States have also succeeded in making interstate compacts, aimed at achieving common solutions to regional problems. The Southern Regional Education Compact, for example, has allowed several southern states to pool education resources on behalf of the whole region. A South Carolina student may now attend the University of Georgia veterinary school without paying out-of-state tuition, since South Carolina does not have a veterinary school. Other subjects of compacts in various parts of the nation include water pollution, flood control, port operations, recreation and parks, and oil conservation.

The Multistate Tax Commission, a compact created in 1967 and now involving more than 30 participating states, has helped states collect taxes from multistate and multinational corporations. This compact requires a "unitary" accounting method that apportions a corporation's taxes among all the states in which it does business. Thus, companies cannot switch income earned in one state or county to another with lower tax rates or no income tax at all.

It is generally conceded that federal aid programs have stimulated improved performance among state and local governments, have increased citizen participation, and have made the states more innovative and responsive to the public interest.[25] Recognizing the new capabilities of state and local governments, a leading student of federalism, Daniel J. Elazar, said they are just as able to do the job as the federal government.[26] State and local governments have been included in problem solving through grant-in-aid programs. These are payments of the federal government to the states for general purpose or block-grant programs, such as education. The federal government has thus contributed to a sense of responsibility among those governments.

Although the national government has had superior taxing ability to finance its aid programs, especially through the income tax, the states have substantially improved their fiscal position during the past decades. Since 1960 the number of states with both the general sales tax and the income tax has increased from 19 to about 40. Since these taxes respond directly to economic growth and inflation, state governments greatly enlarged their revenues during the prosperous 1980s. During the decades of the 1970s and 1980s state government spending as a percentage of gross national product increased substantially, even as efforts were being made to contain federal government spending. In addition to the slow growth of the federal government's spending, the rate of growth in federal aid to state and local governments has declined.

ISSUE 2: Summary ★ *Are State Governments an Anachronism?*

States have not always been showcases of progressive government. Their constitutions have been outmoded, they have been slow to meet pressing problems, and they have often been dominated by elite groups. Regional problems make state boundaries seem obsolete. But in the past few decades, state governments have in many ways been more innovative than the national government. And there is no guarantee that another form of government would be better. A confederation would be more inefficient than a unitary government. Unitary government would still have to deal with the same problems without the advantages federalism gives to democratic representation of popular interests in states and regions. Federalism is useful because it meets the political needs of the United States.

COMPARISONS WITH OTHER NATIONS

FEDERALISM IN DEMOCRACIES

Federalism did not originate with the United States, but actually has a long history. More than two millennia ago the Greek city-states created a league that could reasonably be considered a very loose federal structure. Nations tend to create federal structures for the simple reason of heterogeneity, or diversity of culture. The central government is usually very strong, but residues of political authority remain with constituent parts of the federation.

TABLE 4–1   FOUR FEDERAL SYSTEMS: AN IMPRESSIONISTIC EVALUATION

Selected Indicators	Australia	Canada	United States	Germany
National unity	Strong	Fairly strong	Strong	Strong
State influence on federal policy-makers	Fairly strong	Strong	Fairly weak	Strong
State government constitutional status	Strong	Fairly strong de jure; very strong de facto	Fairly weak	Strong
Actual state control	Strong	Strong	Varies from fairly strong to fairly weak	Strong
Range of local government responsibilities	Limited	Fairly extensive	Fairly extensive	Limited
Local government influence on state policy	Weak	Fairly strong	Fairly strong	Weak
Local government influence on federal policy	Weak	Weak	Fairly strong	Weak

Source: Advisory Commission on Intergovernmental Relationships.

Federal systems are far from equal when it comes to distributing political power, and there is no reason for them to be. A successful federal system is based on considerations of the peculiar history and political culture of that country. Table 4.1 provides a summary of the more successful federal systems and differences among them. Some federal systems have better- (and sometimes longer-) established central authorities than others. Several have found it difficult to define what level of government has ultimate sovereign power.

Table 4.2 provides several examples of federal systems that have been or are in serious trouble. These systems have been so racked by divisions that their central governments could collapse altogether or already have.

Why do some federal systems survive and even prosper, and others totter or collapse? Are there some places where federations would not work? To suggest answers to these questions we might begin by again referring to James Madison. While affectionately referred to as the "Father of the Constitution," Madison might just as accurately be titled the Father of Modern Federalism. He designed our federal government to ensure

TABLE 4.2   THREATS TO FEDERAL SYSTEMS

Federal System	Source of Trouble	Time of Trouble
United States	States' rights	1861–1865
Canada	Quebec separatism	Current
India	Religious separatism	Current
Yugoslavia	Ethnic and religious conflict	Current
Czechoslovakia	Ethnic conflict	Early 1990s

Federalism probably could not work in Lebanon, which has a political culture split between two distinct and hostile communities. This woman is fleeing across the Green Line in Beirut, the line that marks the partition between the Christian and Moslem sections of the city.

that competing and narrow-minded factions would not destroy the political system. But in some societies it is actually possible to have too *few* rather than too many factions. Cyprus, Israel, Lebanon, and Sri Lanka, for example, have political and overall cultures that are dichotomized between two distinct (and often mutually hostile) communities.

These are all small countries with populations that number from under one million to no more than 16 million. None of these countries have federal structures, and it is unlikely that federalism could work there under any guise. Instead, there may be a resort to simple **partition**, in which the country is divided up territorially, often to no one's satisfaction. This has already happened in Cyprus, Lebanon, and Sri Lanka. Usually each side feels cheated in such an arrangement, and the hostility and distrust between them generally continue and even increase.

Federal systems differ in the forms, functions, and powers of their constituent parts. The *lander* (or states) of Germany, provinces of Canada, and cantons of Switzerland have neither the same meaning or function of the 50 American states (Table 4.3). Every federal system has evolved according to the peculiarities of the overall political culture. For example, there is no question that states within the American union are permanent members (the issue having been decided once and for all in 1865), but secession is still a very real possibility among the Canadian provinces.

Federalism is a relatively dynamic political arrangement, in the process of being transformed today in many respects. For example, economic cooperation among countries in one region can initiate closer political ties as well. The most successful and influential example is Western Europe. The **European Economic Community** (EEC) was created in

TABLE 4–3 SELECTED FEDERAL SYSTEMS AND THEIR UNITS

Country	Units	Degree of Authority
United States	States	Control various activities, such as education
Germany	Lander	Have direct parliamentary representation
Canada	Provinces	Have possible right of secession
Switzerland	Cantons	Mostly control justice system

Source: From *The Economist Book of Vital World Statistics* by Economist Books Ltd. Copyright © 1990 by Economist Books Ltd. Reprinted by permission of Times Books, a division of Random House, Inc.

1956 to ease trade restrictions among member nations. It gradually grew to include all of the major Western European countries and most of the smaller ones (Figure 4.4). Several years ago, the European Parliament was established in part to help shape and monitor the activities of the EEC. Another milestone was the elimination of most economic trade barriers (customs and tariffs) that have existed since 1945. Even a common currency, the ECU, is more and more of a possibility.

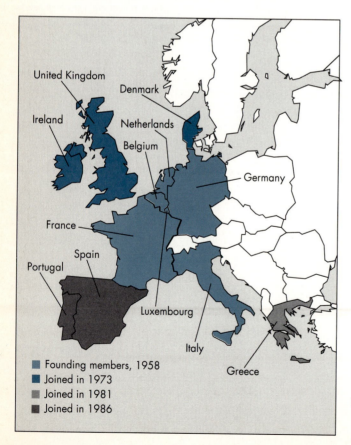

Founding members, 1958
Joined in 1973
Joined in 1981
Joined in 1986

Figure 4.4 MAP OF EUROPEAN ECONOMIC COMMUNITY.

TABLE 4.4 RESOURCES OF THE UNITED STATES AND (THE POTENTIAL) EUROPEAN FEDERATION (1990)		
	United States	Western Europe
Population	250 million	325 million
GNP	$5.3 trillion	$4.7 trillion
Per capita income	$17,615	$15,600

Source: From *The Economist Book of Vital World Statistics* by Economist Books Ltd. Copyright © 1990 by Economist Books Ltd. Reprinted by permission of Times Books, a division of Random House, Inc.

Integration within Europe is also proceeding geographically. A tunnel under the English Channel is expected to be operational by 1994. Affectionately known as the chunnel, this facility will literally link the United Kingdom with the continent. Some observers anticipate that the EEC has the potential to become a political as well as an economic rival of the United States. Table 4.4 suggests the viability of each region's resources.

Federations are becoming concoctions of political economy rather than simply political systems. Other smaller federations have also been proposed for the Central American countries as well for the Persian Gulf states. Generally speaking, we may find new federations emphasizing economic considerations rather than the more traditional ethnic and religious ones. Western Europe, for instance, is certainly one of the most heterogeneous regions in the world, with a long history of conflict, but the mutual economic advantages of federation overwhelm the differences.

In any federal system some units are clearly more politically influential than others. In the democracies this phenomenon occurs primarily as the result of demographic considerations. In the United States, for example, nearly one American in eight lives (and votes) in the country's biggest state, California. This proportion provides one state with the largest congressional delegation in history, 54, and the focus of every presidential campaign. It is possible for just three states—California, New York, and Texas—to decide the outcomes of presidential elections since they have a combined electoral college vote of 119, more than two-fifths of the total needed to win, 270.

If the largest states are deciding the outcome of presidential elections, they are also deciding the presidential candidates. In the eight presidential elections between 1964 and 1992, six were won by Californians and Texans. In this respect, the United States is actually a typical federal system. In Canada and Germany similar situations prevail. The Canadian federation includes ten provinces, but just two of them—Quebec and Ontario—account for nearly half of the country's total population. The situation in Germany is less lopsided, but even here only 3 states out of 15 account for nearly half of the total population.

From the time of the debate over the Constitution, Americans have been concerned with the principle of equal representation and how to implement it. So have other countries. Germany, for instance, is one of the few democratic federal systems that has an upper legislative body (the Bundesrat) composed of members based at least somewhat on population from each of the 15 states. In that sense this house is more democratically selected than the upper house in the United States, with two senators from each state, regardless of the size of the population. As a result, in the United States one senator can represent as few as 300,000 people or as many as 15 million. In Germany the spread is narrower: one Bundesrat deputy can represent as few as 250,000 or as many as 3.2 million.

Federalism is not always conducive to democracy. It isn't intended to be. Wherever it is functioning, a federal arrangement is geared in part to protect the interests of its constituent units. The American Senate and the German Bundesrat are among the few viable upper chambers in Western polities. Technically and, to a very real extent, practically, their primary function is to look after their respective states' interests. In such situations, the majority doesn't necessarily rule. After all, Delaware and California have the same number of senators. In Germany, the city-state of Bremen has three deputies in the Bundesrat, but Bavaria has five deputies, despite a population ten times that of Bremen. "One person, one vote" is not a mandatory rule in some federal systems.

The federated arrangements in the democracies are overwhelmingly voluntary. They evolved when the constituent parts decided to create a central authority. The American federal system grew from 13 to 50 states as the result of territories requesting permission to enter the union. The record of this growth was not always peaceful (e.g.,

---

A VIEW FROM ABROAD
Federalism or Secession in Canada?

In 1992 Canada voted "No" on an agreement worked out by provincial leaders that would have kept Quebec in a loose federal arrangement with the other provinces of Canada. Now the likelihood of Quebec's secession from Canada is greater. Here is what some writers in Canadian newspapers had to say about the vote:

Canadians have put an end to constitution-making by the politicians. Two years of politics built the Charlottetown agreement [to reform Canada's constitution], and six weeks of populism killed it. The national referendum on the constitutional accord quickly became a verdict on Canada's elected class. . . . Quebec's refusal sealed the fate of the accord.

—Susan Delacourt, *Globe and Mail* (Toronto)

The losers are easy to identify: the political leaders of Canada as a whole, as well as the business establishment and union leadership, who, in every province except Quebec, unanimously said "yes." . . . The winners? That is less clear, because the victory of the "no" is a victory divided among people with little in common.

—Lysiane Gagnon, *La Presse* (Montreal)

Senate reform and aboriginal self-government have been put on the shelf, where they will gather dust for decades. . . . As for Quebec, it. . . . will have to decide, on its own, if it wants to remain in Canada.

—*Calgary Herald* (Calgary)

Source: World Press Review, December 1992, p. 9.

native Americans were frequently and often forcibly removed from their ancestral homes, and a war was fought with Mexico for what became the southwestern part of the United States), but the formation of the Union was basically a voluntary enterprise. Not since 1865 in the United States has any state or region seriously contemplated leaving the Union, if only because there is no advantage in doing so. The situation is the same in Germany today. In 1990 the five states in East Germany eagerly joined the Federal Republic of Germany.

For large diverse societies federalism appears to be a practical political structure. For large diverse democracies federalism is mandatory. In fact, there is no large democracy that isn't federal. Even in some unitary systems, such as the United Kingdom, consideration is occasionally given to transforming the country into a federation. England, Scotland, Wales, and Northern Ireland are distinct regions, but the English are so predominant in population (they are five of every six Britons) and culture that a federal system might not be any more satisfactory than a unitary one. Federalism remains a very viable system of government, but not everywhere.

FEDERALISM IN TOTALITARIAN SYSTEMS

Federal arrangements in totalitarian systems are rarely genuine. Such systems are in fact antithetical to federalism. By definition they can't be federalist in any meaningful fashion since all political power must emanate from the central authority. Even those systems that do create at least a facade of federalism operate without a hint of decentralization, if only because the federation itself is often a forced one. The Soviet federalist system, for example, was throughout its history a predominantly *involuntary* one. None of its republics were provided an opportunity to freely enter the union. Nearly all of them had a politically autonomous past. The Soviet Union simply inherited most of the old Russian Empire, which for centuries had annexed outlying areas in a relentless expansion toward warm-water ports (Figure 4.5). The absorption of nations totally alien to Russia in religion, language, and ethnicity created a huge, unviable system that could be maintained only with difficulty and often by coercion. Non-Russians in the empire became virtually second-class (or worse) citizens, distrusted and exploited by what was then a Russian majority. Their experiences did not significantly change with the federation of the USSR. The absorption of these totally unwilling and alien cultures helps to explain the breakup of the Soviet federation in 1990–1991.

Much the same could be said for Yugoslavia. A federal system of six republics, Yugoslavia held together for 35 years under the charismatic leadership of Marshal Tito. After Tito died in 1980 the federation began to unravel, as ancient ethnic and religious hatreds surfaced among the various nationalities, particularly the Serbs, Croatians, and Muslims, culminating in a vicious civil war that left tens of thousands dead and produced as many as two million refugees. Yugoslavia was a forced federation that could not survive its founder nor overcome nationalist animosities that were centuries old.

China currently has a potential problem that thus far has been successfully contained. It forcibly incorporated non-Chinese areas such as Inner Mongolia and Tibet. But China remains a country dominated by a Communist party elite that has not relaxed its political control over any part of the country.

Communist societies are therefore in practice always unitary. Only the Soviet

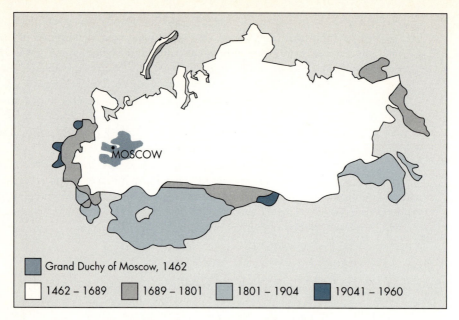

Grand Duchy of Moscow, 1462

1462 – 1689   1689 – 1801   1801 – 1904   19041 – 1960

Figure 4.5 FIVE HUNDRED YEARS OF RUSSIAN EXPANSION. Source: John T. Rourke, *International Politics on the World Stage,* Third Edition. Copyright © 1991, The Dushkin Publishing Group, Inc., Guilford, CT. All rights reserved. Reprinted by permission.

Union, China, and Czechoslovakia (which was divided into three small regions—Czech lands, Bohemia, and Slovakia) ever organized their political system even nominally along federalist lines.* Other communist societies tended to be small enough to allow communists simply to take over a unitary system already in place.

Earlier in this chapter an explanation was provided of how the United States was transformed from a confederation to a federal system. The former Soviet Union has recently undergone the reverse process: Its federal system has been transformed into a confederation (the Confederation of Independent States). Sovereign authority would be in the hands of, say, a dozen separate republics, but they would exercise a substantial degree of cooperation on defense and economic matters for mutual convenience. All of this assumes the republics would not be in conflict with one another. Some republics have established their sovereignty in possession of nuclear weapons while others feel nervous about not having any.

FEDERALISM IN AUTHORITARIAN SYSTEMS

Like communist polities, authoritarian states are almost completely unitary arrangements in practice and most often in theory. In other words, a federal authoritarian system is a contradiction in terms. But many authoritarian systems ought to be federal. For example,

---

* In 1993 Czechoslovakia peacefully split into two nations: the Czech Republic and Slovakia.

A VIEW FROM THE STATES
Yugoslavia: The Unraveling of a Nation

New York Times correspondent John F. Burns spent a New Year's lunch in 1993 with a family in the Yugoslavian province of Bosnia. Their views on the civil war indicate the depth of ethnic feeling in the formerly unified nation.

Except for two visitors, all at the lunch called themselves Yugoslavs before the war. More than citizenship, this was an idea, that all people of South Slavic origin, Serbs, Muslims, Croats and others, could belong together, and mix un-self-consciously, in the same nation.

Now, in a war that gave the world the term "ethnic cleansing," the Serbian nationalist practice of attacking Muslim and Croatian communities across Bosnia and driving survivors out as refugees, families like the Corovics and the Kenovics speak of themselves as they hardly ever did, as Muslims. Over lunch, there was laughter at the hosts' unfamiliarity with matters devout Muslims might be expected to know. . . .

"I'm sorry, we're not very good Muslims, from that point of view," Mr. Corovic said. "There are more Bibles in this house than Korans."

More than anything, what seemed to transfix those gathered around the fire was the motivation of the Serbian nationalists, who are believed to have left more than 130,000 Muslims dead or missing and more than a million others homeless. . . .

"I will never accept that a whole people, or even 50 percent of a people, can be inherently evil, and I don't believe that most Serbs are," Mr. Kenovic said. "I believe, I have to believe, that what happened here began with a small group of evil men, who spread this epidemic of hatred to others who were otherwise perfectly moral people."

Mr. Corovic, his son-in-law, who is 51, saw matters differently. Like many Muslims here, he recalled that many of his friends and fellow workers before the war were Serbs. . . . "When I think of those who went to the other side, I am deeply hurt, because it seems to me they were looking at me through two different prisms," he said.

"Through one, they saw me as a friend, as a competent businessman, as somebody to have a coffee or a brandy with," he said. "Through the other, and without ever giving me any hint of it, they saw me as a Muslim, as a living symbol of the 500-year Turkish occupation of Serbia, and thus as an enemy. It is this that really hurts me."

the Saddam Hussein regime in Iraq is particularly brutal toward large segments of its own population out of a fear (a well-founded one) that the country could disintegrate into at least three distinct parts because of a desire for political autonomy on the part of the Kurds in the north and the Shia Muslims in the south. (Together they represent half the Iraqi population of around 17 million.)

Furthermore, Iraq isn't an isolated situation. It is common to find authoritarian regimes persecuting an ethnic or religious minority in great part to forestall a separatist movement. Most of these regimes are located in the developing world. At any time there are perhaps a half-dozen civil conflicts or full-scale rebellions going on (in Ethiopia, Somalia, Indonesia, and the Philippines, just to name a few), usually over the issue of how much political autonomy a region or tribal group ought to have over its own affairs and distinct from the central government.

The collapse of the Soviet Union may have inadvertently signaled a new wave of desire for a more federal and less centralized political arrangement in dozens of countries. The fact that there are more than 5000 distinct ethnic groups in the world (only 3 percent of which have their own states)[27] suggests that federalism may still be in the process of developing and may be a much-needed remedy to political conflicts. It may very well be that as democracy takes root in previously hostile soils, federalism may become the political structure of choice as a means of keeping nations together, while allowing constituent parts to enjoy a substantial degree of local autonomy.

Summary

1. Federalism is distinguishable from unitary government and confederation. While unitary systems place all governmental power in the central government, and confederations have very weak central governments, federalism divides political power between the national government and governments of constituent units.

2. American federalism provides for express and inherent powers at the national level and reserved powers at the state levels. Some powers are concurrent, shared at both levels.

3. Federalism in the United States evolved with important judicial decisions such as *McCulloch v. Maryland* (1819). It proceeded through five distinct phases: competitive federalism, dual federalism, picket-fence federalism, cooperative federalism, and the "new federalism" of the 1980s.

4. The argument that federalism may be inefficient is based on the observation that too many levels of government exist and compete with or duplicate one another's constitutional assignments. As the United States became a more urbanized society, numerous and sometimes overlapping jurisdictions developed: Within one metropolitan area there might be dozens or even hundreds of governmental units.

5. Advocates of federalism argue that the United States is too large and complicated a society to have any other form of government. Besides, the central government from the beginning has had only limited powers, enabling various and diverse regions to develop and carefully tailor their own responses to local problems.

6. Are states an anachronism today? Many modern problems are regional rather than simply statewide and require coordination among several state governments.
At the same time, federalism no longer resembles a layer cake, with distinct divisions of national and state responsibilities, but is more analogous to a marble cake; it is increasingly difficult to determine what is a state and what is a federal responsibility.

7. The other side of the argument is that states enhance democracy by diffusing power and providing more access points for citizens. Moreover, states individually or together can provide innovative services and/or change laws that precede and inspire eventual national action.

8. Federalism has been suggested as a governmental form suited for large diverse societies as well as for smaller societies divided by a variety of social and cultural forces. However, it is unlikely that federalism can work in societies with just a few factions that are extremely divisive. Partition seems a more likely arrangement in those instances.

9. Federalism may assume different and perhaps bigger forms in democracies in the future. Western Europe may lead the way with its European Community and European Parliament.

10. Federalism may allow big units to politically dominate smaller ones, as can be seen in the United States as well as in other federal systems, such as Canada and Germany.

11. In totalitarian and authoritarian systems, federal arrangements are rarely genuine, since all power emanates from a central authority. Maintaining this power may require suppressing dissident ethnic or religious minorities.

12. Involuntary federations are inherently unstable since their great diversity and resistance to central authority tend to become unmanageable.

Terms to Define

Block grants	Interposition
Categorical grants	Interstate compact
Competitive federalism	Matching grants
Concurrent powers	National preemption
Conditional grants	Nullification
Confederation	Partition
Cooperative federalism	Project grants
Dual federalism	Reserved powers
European Economic Community	Revenue sharing
Express powers	Secession
Federalism	States' rights
Implied powers	Unitary
Inherent powers	

Selected Readings

Agranoff, Robert. "Approaches to the Comparative Analysis of Intergovernmental Relations." Paper presented at the 87th Annual Meeting of the American Political Science Association, August 29–September 1, 1991, Washington, D.C. A primer for basic understanding of other federal systems.

Beer, Samuel H. "The Modernization of American Federalism," *Publius* 3 (Fall 1973): 49–65. An excellent suggestion that the American federal system is an evolving one and is in near-constant change.

Conlin, Timothy. *New Federalism: Intergovernmental Reform from Nixon to Reagan.* Washington, D.C.: Brookings, 1985. An analysis of the effort and the degree of success under Republican presidents to return governmental authority from the federal to state and local jurisdictions.

Diamond, Martin. "The Federalist's View of Federalism." In George C. F. Benson, ed., *Essays in Federalism.* Claremont, Calif.: Institute for Studies in Federalism of Claremont Men's College, 1961, pp. 21-64. An interpretation of what the original Federalists (and drafters of the Constitution) thought of federalism.

Gunlicks, Arthur B. "Some Thoughts on Federalism and the Federal Republic." *German Politics and Society* (October 1988), pp. 1–7. Some current and useful comparisons of the federal systems of the United States and Germany on the eve of German reunification.

MacManus, Susan A. "Federalism and Intergovernmental Relations: The Centralization Versus Decentralization Debate Continues." In William Crotty, ed., *Political Science: Looking to the Future.* Vol. 4: *American Institutions.* Evanston, Ill.: Northwestern University Press, 1991, pp. 203–254. An excellent introduction to the complexity of the American federal system, with a comprehensive bibliography for further research.

Monkkonen, Eric. H. *America Becomes Urban: The Development of U.S. Cities and Towns, 1780–1980.* Berkeley: University of California Press, 1988. The United States has gone from a very rural society to an increasingly urban one in two centuries. The federal system outlined in 1787 must keep pace with some remarkable social, economic, and technological changes.

Notes

1. Daniel J. Elazar, "State Constitutional Design in the United States and Other Federal Systems," *Publius* 12 (Winter 1982): 8.
2. Samuel H. Beer, "Federalism, Nationalism and Democracy in America," *American Political Science Review* 72 (1987): 11.
3. *Wickard* v. *Filburn,* 317 U.S. 111 (1942).
4. *Heart of Atlanta Motel* v. *U.S.,* 379 U.S. 421 (1964).
5. *Abelman* v. *Booth,* 62 U.S. (21 How) 506 (1859).
6. On this point see Joel Garreau, *Edge City: Life on the New Frontier* (New York: Doubleday, 1991) and David Rieff, *Los Angeles: Capital of the Third World* (New York: Simon & Schuster, 1991).
7. "Searching for New Jobs, Many States Steal Them," *The New York Times,* November 25, 1992, pp. A1 and A9.
8. Ibid.
9. *National League of Cities* v. *Usery, California,* 426 U.S. 833 (1976).
10. *Garcia* v. *San Antonio Metropolitan Authority,* 469 U.S. 528 (1985).
11. *South Dakota* v. *Dole,* 483 U.S. 203 (1987).
12. "Beware of Imitations," *The Economist,* July 6, 1991, p. 25.
13. Charles D. Tarlton, "Symmetry and Asymmetry as Elements of Federalism," *Journal of Politics* 27 (November 1965): 871.
14. *The Federalist,* 16.
15. *Pennsylvania* v. *Nelson,* (1956)
16. *Colorado Anti-Discrimination Commission* v. *Continental Airlines* (1963).
17. *Pacific Gas & Electric* v. *State of California* 461 U.S. 190 (1983).

18. *Congressional Record*, March 16, 1985, p. 485.
19. *Missouri v. Holland*, 252 U.S. 416 (1920).
20. *United States v. Pink*, 315 U.S. 203 (1942).
21. Morton Grodzins, *The American System* (Chicago: Rand McNally, 1966).
22. *Today*, November 30, 1979, p. 6.
23. Henry C. Lodge, *The Federalist* (New York: G.P. Putnam, 1902), pp. 59–60.
24. Richard H. Leach, *American Federalism* (New York: Norton, 1970), p. 240.
25. Morton Grodzins, "The Federal System," in Aaron Wildavsky, ed., *American Federalism in Perspective* (Boston: Little, Brown, 1967), p. 275.
26. Daniel J. Elazar, "The New Federalism," *Public Interest* 34–37 (1974): 102.
27. Bernard Neitschmann, "The Miskito Indians," in Bernard Schechterman and Martin Slann, eds., *The Ethnic-Nationalist Dimension in International Relations* (New York: Praeger, 1993).

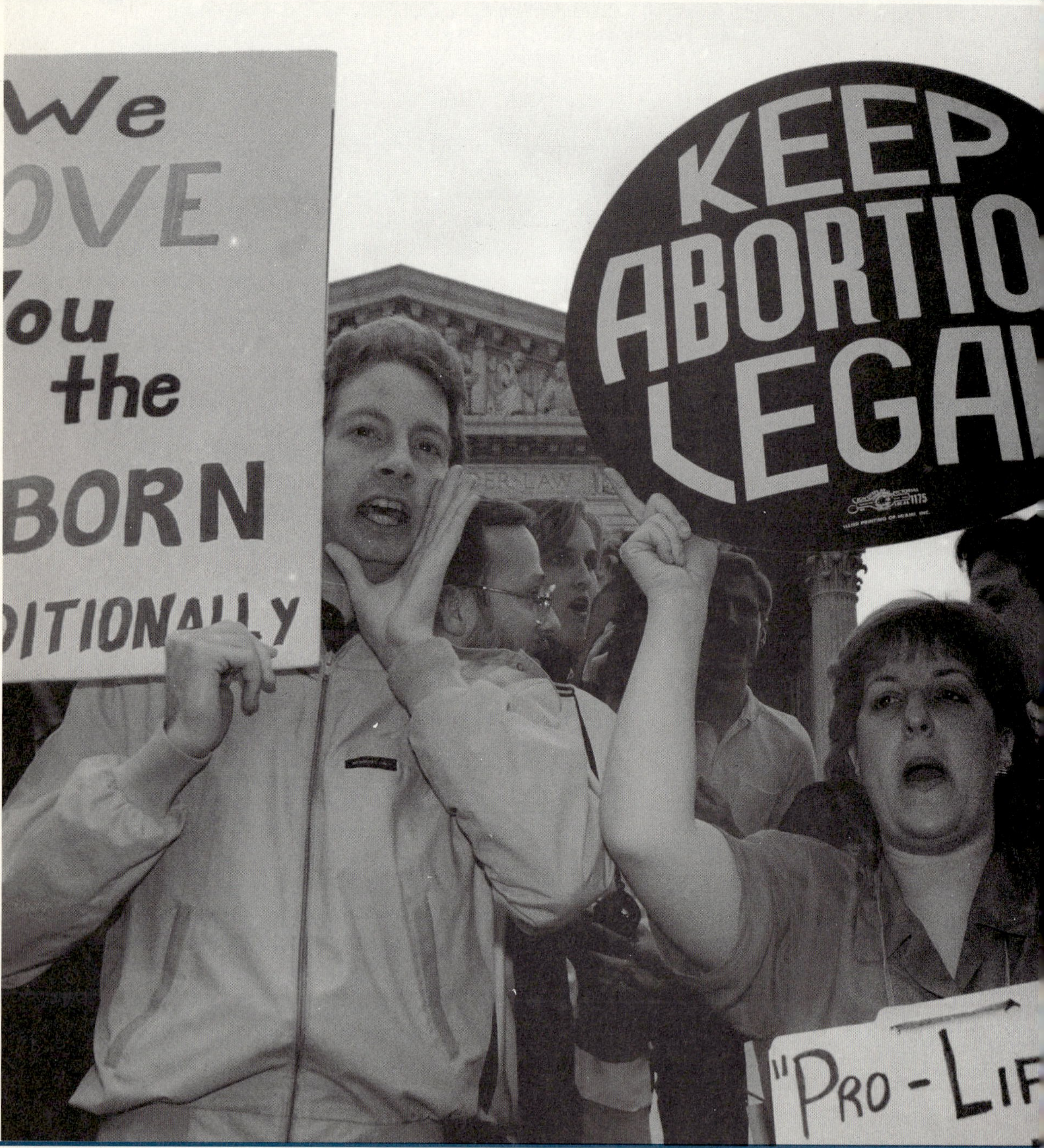
We
OVE
You
the
BORN
DITIONALLY
KEEP
ABORTIO
LEGA
"PRO - LIF

POLITICAL CULTURE AND IDEOLOGY

Most people would concur that there is something different ideologically between political leaders Jesse Jackson and Ronald Reagan, columnists Anthony Lewis and William F. Buckley, and Senators Ted Kennedy and Strom Thurmond. Those differences, whatever they are, are what we usually and loosely call the differences between liberalism and conservatism. A person on the street may not be able to explain those differences, but the terms *conservative* and *liberal* provide a convenient way for acknowledging that these differences exist. Yet, these same conservatives and liberals hold many ideas in common about American government and politics.

They share certain values and beliefs about the importance of such things as the two-party system; freedom of speech and competition of ideas; campaigning for office and acceptance of defeat; respecting the opinions of others; using established structures like the Congress, the courts, and the executive branch; and allowing interest groups to organize and represent segments of public opinion. These common beliefs are embodied by the American political culture.

Political culture refers to shared ideas about how government and politics should function, while **political ideology** refers more to various ideas as to what the political process should accomplish or do. The difference between political culture and political ideology is primarily between *how* and *what*.

American conservatives and liberals generally adhere to the same political culture, but differ in their ideology. A conservative like George Bush tends to accept and believe in the same ideas about how American government and politics should function as did his more liberal 1992 opponent Bill Clinton. But they may differ fundamentally on what should be accomplished by the political process. Their respective goals and desired results may cause the one to want to ban abortion and the other to support it, the one to oppose passage of the Equal Rights Amendment and the other to desire adoption, the one to resist school busing and the other to support it.

Put still another way, political culture is the general agreement on the means to achieve ends while ideology is the reflection of differences on the ends to be achieved. Both conservatives and liberals will use the institutions of American government and the procedures and principles guaranteed by the Constitution, but they will use them to achieve different results.

In what follows we will first examine further the nature of political culture and ideology in America. We then consider whether it is harmful for a country's ideological mind to be divided. Finally, we will compare our culture and ideology with those in other political societies.

UNDERSTANDING AMERICAN POLITICAL CULTURE AND IDEOLOGY

AMERICAN POLITICAL CULTURE

The peculiarities of the American political culture have fascinated people at home and abroad. Among the classic works on this subject are the Frenchman Alexis de Tocqueville's *Democracy in America*, a product of the early 1800s; the Englishman Lord James Bryce's *American Commonwealth*, produced around the turn of the century; and Max Lerner's *America as a Civilization*, published in the 1950s. Two recent efforts by Americans to define the American political culture are Daniel Boorstein's *American Experience* and Russell Kirk's *Roots of the American Order*.

While there are differences among these and the many other interpretations of American political culture, certain basic characteristics stand out in their analyses. The eight areas of common agreement are

> **Liberty**—the belief that Americans should be as free as possible from restraint, especially that imposed by government, to seek "life, liberty and the pursuit of happiness."
>
> **Equality**—allowing each American to compete for jobs, income, status, education, and other objectives on an equal basis with others, that is, guaranteeing equal opportunity to compete while not guaranteeing equality of results.

Property—granting individuals the right to own private property, recognizing that this is the primary means for them to find their place in society and to determine what they want to do with their lives (often called "democratic capitalism").

Merit—sometimes called "rugged individualism," referring to rewarding personal effort and achievement rather than a person's social class, family standing, or some other arbitrary privilege that has not been personally earned.

Civic duty—expecting Americans to fulfill their civic duty or obligation to participate in politics and community affairs by such means as voting, and also to be tolerant of opposing views.

Democracy—often called "rule of law," meaning that governmental power is to be exercised in a manner consistent with public opinion and constitutional limitations ("limited government").

Secularism—commonly called "civil religion," meaning that the pluralistic nature of American society and religion necessitates that there be no established or official religion. Thus, politicians may make references to deity and ask for prayer, but they will not specify a particular denominational context.

Efficacy—basically the belief that each individual has the power to influence the political system and American society.

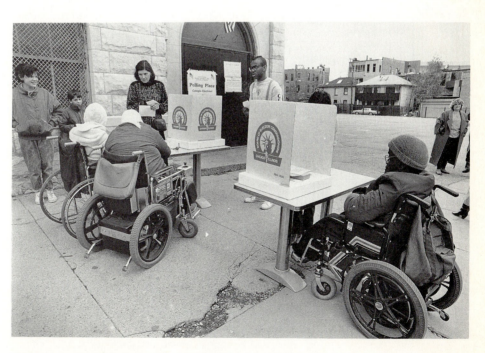

Voting as a civic duty is strongly ingrained in our political culture. When these handicapped citizens showed up to vote at their precinct in Chicago, they were prevented from entering the polling place by a set of steep steps. Election judges then set up voting booths on the sidewalk.

A VIEW FROM ABROAD
The Japanese View of Work and Fun

A society's political culture is at all times dominated by the overall culture. This is why the Japanese form of democracy may have less appeal for us than the American form.

A recent article in Tokyo's *Area* news magazine described the enviable life-style of a retired American couple in Lincoln, Nebraska. Wallace Peterson, who used to teach at the University of Nebraska, and his wife, Bonny. They own two cars; they also own a cottage on a nearby lake, a 25-foot boat, and a private plane—a Piper Cub, which they keep at a grass airstrip just five miles from their home. Only in America!

By working hard and saving money, we thought, we, too, could live like Americans. That was our goal, and we reached it in 1985, the year Japan overtook the United States in per-capita national income. But those who think we have caught up with the West simply because we have refrigerators, color television sets, and private cars should wake up. How many retired couples in Japan can afford to fly around in private planes, and how many middle-class people own sailboats? The high incomes we worked so hard to achieve are only the first step to true affluence. We have learned to produce wealth, but we do not yet know how to enjoy it.

Middle-class people in really affluent countries can indulge their aspirations in ways that are impossible in Japan. Prime Minister Kiichi Miyazawa says he wants to make the quality of life in Japan second to none, but his vision stops at shorter work hours and increased home ownership. The real goal for the government and citizens should be to make life more fun.

Source: "Sankei Shimbun" (Tokyo), quoted in *World Press Review*, December 1992, p. 20.

These basic characteristics of American political culture tend to blend together. They are like a formula in the sense that if one part is missing, the result will not be the same. The type of liberty that Americans have requires property, while the type of equality they have requires merit. These shared values, sometimes called "the national character," are bonded together and dependent on one another.

AMERICAN POLITICAL IDEOLOGY

American ideology tends to reflect two opposing views of America's past, present, and future. For example, the person who wants to reduce the power of the federal government has a particular interpretation of America's governmental foundations that says, "I believe that the Founders did not want a strong central government." On the other hand, the person who believes in increasing the power of the federal government naturally says the opposite: "I believe that the Founders did not intend to limit the power of the national government, and even if they did, that is immaterial, because we live in a different age that demands a strong central government to solve our problems." Generally speaking, these two views can be described as "conservative" and "liberal."

A **liberal** will tend to favor a strong and active government and place a high value on equality, whereas a **conservative** will tend to favor a more limited government and place a high value on liberty. These opposing traditions and interpretations of American political ideology compete in three areas: ideologically, historically, and constitutionally. These areas reinforce one another, since persons on one side of the ideological debate generally associate with those persons on the same side of the historical and constitutional conflicts. Let's look now at the competing traditions and interpretations.

Ideological Tradition and Interpretation

American liberalism and conservatism can trace their roots to the writings of the Frenchman Jean-Jacques Rousseau and the Englishman Edmund Burke, respectively. These two had differing views about the source of truth and the nature of God and man. Rousseau's view was that truth is to be derived from human reason, while Burke's position was that truth's ultimate source is twofold: in Holy Scripture and in nature. These differing roots led to different views of the role of government and of the position of America in the world. Table 5.1 presents a paradigm, or model, of liberal and conservative thought based on their respective origins and developments.

While liberalism and conservatism are fundamentally different, it does not follow that all liberals are alike, nor that all conservatives are alike. There are actually several types of liberalism and conservatism—authoritarian, economic, religious, political, and social. And each of these types has a different fundamental emphasis. Thus, an economic liberal is not necessarily a religious liberal, nor is an economic conservative necessarily a religious conservative. To illustrate this, Figure 5.1 shows that someone like George Bush or Senator Bob Dole (R-Kans.) may be conservative politically but liberal theologically, or Senator Mark Hatfield (R-Oreg.) and Representative Richard Gephart (D-Mo.) may be conservative theologically but liberal politically.

Each of these types of liberalism and conservatism has contributed to American politics and society in profound ways. For example, Thomas Paine's writings emphasized authoritarian liberalism: He wanted to eliminate class distinctions and prevent developing an aristocratic or elitist class. Alexander Hamilton, on the other hand, advocated authoritarian conservatism: He envisioned a society and government ruled principally by an elite or aristocratic class. He believed in preserving class distinctions as natural and necessary for the proper functioning of society. Both egalitarianism, with its emphasis on the elimination of rigid class lines, and elitism, with emphasis on leadership by well-trained public officials, have played important parts in American history.

Economic liberalism emphasizes social welfarism, which has helped to bring into American life such ideas and policies as social security, Medicare, and Medicaid. Economic conservatism, on the other hand, emphasizes private property and the profit motive as part of "democratic capitalism."

Political liberalism emphasizes the concept of equality, but not to the negation of liberty; it has played a part in such movements as the abolitionist movement prior to the Civil War and the contemporary civil rights movement. Political conservatism with its emphasis on liberty, but again not at the negation of equality, emphasizes the freedom

TABLE 5.1 CONSERVATISM AND LIBERALISM COMPARED

	TENDENCY OF BELIEF	
Topic	Liberal	Conservative
1. Government		
Primary focus	Individual	Community
Preferred government	National	State and local
Direction of sentiment	Internationalist	Nationalist
Method of government influence	Direct	Indirect
Accountability of government	To man	To God
Rate/type of change	Faster, utopian	Slower, prescriptive
Relative importance	Equality	Liberty
Primary citizen duty	Reform	Duty
Justice achieved by	Governmental reform	Spiritual regeneration
2. Economy		
Source of authority	Central government	Markets
Growth sector	Public	Private
Government function	Regulation	Competition
Tendency	Socialism	Capitalism
3. Cultural and religious values		
Ultimate source of knowledge	Human reason	Nature, Bible
Biblical interpretation	More symbolic	More literal
Moral standards	Relative/situational	Absolute/orthodox
Relative emphasis	Man	God
Moral emphasis	Social	Personal
Relative importance to man	Rights	Responsibilities
Origin of evil	Unjust social systems	Original sin

Source: From *American Conservatism* by Charles W. Dunn and J. David Woodard. Copyright © 1991 by Charles W. Dunn and J. David Woodard. By permission of Madison Books.

of each citizen to pursue his or her ambition with as little restraint as possible, especially from the government.

In some ways, the differences between social liberalism and conservatism can be illustrated with the racial issue in American history: Social conservatives, particularly in the South, generally desired to retain the existing order between the races, and social liberals desired to change the existing order. Thus, continuity or order has historically been the dominant characteristic of social conservatism while change has been the principal trait of social liberalism.

Three other ideologies are worth defining and distinguishing: libertarianism, populism, and neoconservatism. Superficially, libertarianism appears to be an offshoot of conservatism, and populism and neoconservatism offshoots of liberalism.

Libertarianism believes strongly in the autonomy of the individual and as small a role as possible for the government. Libertarians think that individuals should be free from governmental restraint in both economic and noneconomic areas. For example, a

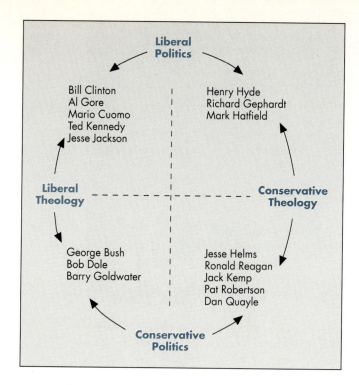

Figure 5.1 IDEOLOGICAL RELATIONSHIPS. There are various types of conservatism and liberalism, and one person can vary along several dimensions. For example, Senator Bob Dole can be classified as a theological liberal but a political conservative. Source: From *American Conservatism* by Charles W. Dunn and J. David Woodard. Copyright © 1991 by Charles W. Dunn and J. David Woodard. By permission of Madison Books.

libertarian would say that the government has no business regulating abortion since that is a personal matter. The heart of libertarian belief is the freedom of the individual. The Libertarian party's 1992 presidential candidate, André Maurass (who, like George Bush, is a Texan), argued for a wholesale dismantling of governmental activities.[1] By contrast, historic conservatism with its religious underpinnings holds that there are public policies that a government *should* implement since some values, like religious values, are superior to some individual rights and freedoms. Conservatives attack libertarianism for being radical and not properly considering the preservation of the values of a society.

Populism until recently was thought to be an offshoot of liberalism, but during the last decade, there has been talk of conservative populism. Regardless of its origin, the idea behind populism is that government has become unresponsive to average citizens, who must be aroused to fight for changes in public policies. Populism is typically concerned about big corporations and other institutions, including big government, that seem to be unresponsive to the needs of ordinary Americans. Among the best-known populists have been the turn-of-the-century politician William Jennings Bryan, Alabama's Democratic Governor George Wallace, and 1992 independent candidate H. Ross Perot.

Neoconservatism grew out of some Democrats' disenchantment with their party's emphasis on reducing the size of America's military and its support for such domestic policies as affirmative action. Neoconservatives may be distinguished from other conservatives principally on the issues of the size and purpose of government domestic policymaking. Neoconservatives would still generally hold to the social welfare policies of Democratic administrations since Franklin D. Roosevelt, while conservatives would be

Populists try to arouse their fellow citizens to fight for changes in public policies. One of the most famous populists was William Jennings Bryan, who spoke out at the turn of the century on behalf of rural America and against big business interests.

more likely to raise questions about these policies. Neoconservatives and conservatives find common ground in their opposition to communism, their belief in the need for a strong military, and their opposition to excessive emphasis on equal rights, such as affirmative action plans and quotas for admission to educational institutions and other purposes.

Historical Tradition and Interpretation

Another area in which ideologies compete has to do with how one interprets events in our country's past. For example, many people heatedly discuss the question of whether America was established as a Christian nation or a secular state. Generally, with some exceptions, conservatives argue for the former while liberals argue for the latter. Should conservatives be right, then we have displaced important precedents of the founding and allowed government to evolve in contradiction to the Founder's intentions. But should liberals be correct, then our history reveals that undue deference has been given to religious causes and issues.[2]

Those who argue that America was created as a secular state believe that at least four facts support their conclusion. First, the primary explanation of American government, *The Federalist Papers*, makes no references to God or to the Bible. Second, the designers of American government, such as James Madison and Thomas Jefferson, customarily did not invoke the Bible in their writings. Third, the Declaration of Independence contains only a few references to deity and the U.S. Constitution contains none.

Fourth, the Founders emphasized **natural law** rather than **divine law**. That is, they believed that humans have rights just because they are human and not because they are creatures of God.

Conservatives argue for Christian origins of America's government by pointing out, first, that delegates to the Constitutional Convention were generally of conservative Christian theological convictions. Second, one of the three authors of *The Federalist Papers*, John Jay, had ardent conservative Christian convictions, and other prominent Founders, such as James Madison, were educated in theologically conservative schools that influenced what the Founders perceived to be the role of government. Third, "law of nature" as used by Thomas Jefferson in the Declaration of Independence refers to "divine law," since the term was taken from William Blackstone's *Commentaries on the Laws of England*, in which the two terms were used synonymously. Fourth, scholars in the last century, such as Alexis de Tocqueville, generally viewed America's founding from a conservative Christian perspective. Fifth, the dominant conservative Christian influences of the founding era significantly influenced leading deists of the day, such as Thomas Jefferson and Benjamin Franklin. (Deists believe that God, the creator of the universe, lost interest in and subsequently abandoned control over life and natural phenomena.)

While these are two polar positions on this historical issue, there are at least two middle-of-the-road positions (in themselves contradictory). One is that the Declaration of Independence reflects more of a secular state or non-Christian origin since deists like Thomas Jefferson, Samuel Adams, and Thomas Paine greatly influenced the shape of that document, but the U.S. Constitution reflects more of a Christian origin since the framers were preponderantly of that persuasion. A second middle-of-the-road position is that the Declaration of Independence, with several references to deity, confirms a conservative Christian heritage, but the U.S. Constitution, with no references to deity, confirms a secular heritage.

Interestingly, and perhaps significantly, the Declaration of Independence and the U.S. Constitution were framed in Pennsylvania, a state that was hospitable to many different religions and sects. If the pluralist religious environment in Pennsylvania signifies anything about the founding, it most likely means that the United States was not founded as a secular state, but as a nation committed to the encouragement of a diversity of religious persuasions. Indeed, it can be argued that the "no establishment of religion" clause of the First Amendment of the Constitution simply means that no *one* religious group was to be preferred above any other and that "freedom of religion" means that the government is not to interfere in the practice of religion.

Constitutional Tradition and Interpretation

Is the American Constitution a static or dynamic document? Should it be interpreted in the light of what its authors presumably intended or what contemporary experience and necessity dictate?

In a now-famous debate carried out via the media in 1985, President Reagan's Attorney General Edwin Meese argued that judges and courts should be constrained to interpret the Constitution in the light of the Founders' views, while former Supreme Court Justice William Brennan argued that contemporary experience and needs should dictate constitutional interpretation.

Meese asserted:

> A constitution that is viewed as only what the judges say it is, is no longer a constitution in the true sense. Those who framed the Constitution chose their words carefully; they debated at great length most of the points. The language they chose meant something. It is incumbent upon the Court to determine what that meaning was. . . . Any other standard suffers the defect of pouring new meaning into old words, thus creating new powers and new rights totally at odds with the logic of our Constitution and its commitment to the rule of law.

Brennan retorted: "The genius of the Constitution rests not in any static meaning it might have had in a world that is dead and gone, but in the adaptability of its great principles to cope with current problems and current needs."[3]

Significantly, persons of liberal persuasions, whether authoritarian, economic, religious, political, or social, almost always take Justice Brennan's position, while conservatives regardless of type almost always take Meese's position. As Supreme Court nominees, Robert Bork and Clarence Thomas faced sharp questioning from liberal Senators opposed to the positions articulated by Meese.

? ISSUE TO ANALYZE

ISSUE 1   *ARE IDEOLOGICAL DIVISIONS HARMFUL?*

REASONS WHY IDEOLOGICAL DIVISIONS ARE HARMFUL

Abraham Lincoln on the eve of the Civil War reminded Americans that "A house divided against itself cannot stand." When a nation is deeply divided ideologically, as America was in the 1960s and 1970s over the Vietnam War, there are serious problems, including

Lack of clarity and unity regarding our nation's goals,

Deterioration in the institutions supporting American society, and

A tendency to be intolerant of the views of others.

Lack of Clarity and Unity on National Goals. Examination of America's ideological mind reveals sharp and heated differences on such issues as abortion, homosexuality, public school prayer, and capital punishment. This ideological division over issues that defy compromise has made it more difficult for America's leaders to develop policies that will capture the support of a large cross section of Americans.

Deterioration in Supporting Institutions. According to sociologist Robert Nisbet, disintegration and fragmentation of major socializing institutions like the family, church, and community have led to the disunity and lack of clarity on national purpose.[4] By fostering common bonds of both political culture and ideology these institutions have in many ways been like the glue holding society together in the past. But the weakening of the traditional American family, the increased divisions in America's churches, and the growing impersonal nature of American communities have weakened fundamental ties among Americans and made it more difficult to define what we mean by the American experience and the American dream.

Intolerance of Opposing Views. During various periods of American history, ideological divisions have become so pronounced that violence and bloodshed ensued, particularly in the Civil War. More recently, we have seen intolerance in the extreme ideological left in organizations like the Weathermen, who practiced violence in trying to overthrow American government in the 1970s, as well as in the ideological right among white supremacists who have been linked to physical attacks on their opponents and the anti-abortionists who have stormed abortion centers, sometimes using violent techniques. What this illustrates about American society is that when extreme ideological viewpoints get out of hand, violence erupts and society's stability is threatened. When ideological divisions lead to ideological intolerance, the result can be and often has been murderous.

REASONS WHY IDEOLOGICAL DIVISIONS ARE NOT HARMFUL

It is true that conservative and liberal ideological tensions have existed throughout American history and may be more divisive now than at some other times in history. But these arguments need to be offset by a more balanced understanding of American political ideology. This understanding sets forth arguments that

> The ideological center dominates the American mind and diffuses the negative excesses of conservatism and liberalism.
>
> American history reveals a cyclical change between the dominance of conservatism and liberalism.
>
> Comparison with other nations shows that America is generally more stable ideologically.

American society and government have survived the worst ideological tensions, including a civil war. Ultimately a bond of unity has been restored, which cannot be said about many other nations. The 1990s are revealing that national unity is very precarious elsewhere, as we have seen in Yugoslavia, the former Soviet Union, and even democracies, such as Canada.

Dominance of the Ideological Center. Although many Americans have shifted from the center to the left or right since the mid-1960s, the ideological center still dominates the thinking of most Americans. The **ideological center**, or moderate point of view, is not only where most Americans find themselves on an ideological scale, but it also serves as a buffer zone between the ideological extremes and as a magnet to pull the extremes toward the center. For example, Presidents Reagan and Bush ran for president on conservative platforms, but they moderated their positions during office. As will be shown in the chapters on political parties and voting, the ideological center tends to force the major parties to take generally moderate positions or to temper excessive liberal or conservative tendencies within their parties. Historically, when an extreme ideological

This cartoon takes note of the fact that President Bill Clinton immediately put his own ideological stamp on the office. The "religious right," with their conservative agenda, would no longer have the influence they wielded in the Reagan and Bush administrations.

point of view has captured a major party, such as the Republican Party in 1964 and the Democratic Party in 1972, the general populace has overwhelmingly and convincingly rejected that party.

Cyclical Nature of Ideology. Throughout American history there has been an ebb and flow between the dominance of conservatism and liberalism. During this century, for example, the conservatism of President William Howard Taft was followed by the liberalism of President Woodrow Wilson, which was followed by the conservatism of Presidents Warren Harding, Calvin Coolidge, and Herbert Hoover, which was followed by the liberalism of Presidents Franklin Roosevelt and Harry Truman, which was followed by the conservatism of President Dwight D. Eisenhower, and so forth (Figure 5.2). In no case, however, did any one of these presidents pursue an extreme ideological point of view. Thus, conservatism and liberalism have periods when one dominates the other, but the ideological center moderates their excessive tendencies.

Built into the system is a kind of self-correction over time. The conservatism of the Eisenhower presidency brought the administrations of Presidents John Kennedy and Lyndon Johnson to provide a liberal correction to our public policy course. Many of the public policy approaches taken since then, especially by the administration of President Ronald Reagan, have aimed to "correct" the liberal actions of the Kennedy and Johnson administrations. Ideological influence in the making of American public policy tends, therefore, not to get out of balance because cyclical correction is built into the system.

The ideological center also often benefits from new ideas generated by more conservative and liberal elements. Liberal populist ideas of the 1800s actually were

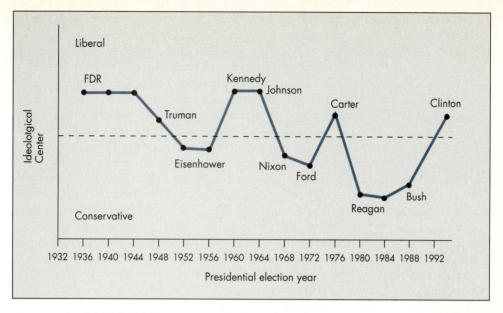

Figure 5.2 IDEOLOGICAL CYCLE IN AMERICAN PRESIDENCIES, 1937 TO PRESENT.

adopted into law during the early 1900s while the conservative populist ideas of people like George Wallace have had a profound effect on both major political parties.

ISSUE 1:   Summary   ★   *Are Ideological Divisions Harmful?*

A divided American ideological mind creates tensions that in the short run may be harmful, but in the long run have added a dynamic, healthy quality to American society and politics. We must acknowledge the current problems, such as a lack of clarity and unity on national goals, the deterioration of the supporting institutions of American society, and a tendency to be intolerant of opposing views, but we must hasten to mention the antidotes, such as the dominance of the ideological center and the cyclical change between conservatism and liberalism from generation to generation. Also, in comparison with other nations, as we will see below, the American ideological mind is generally more stable and less susceptible to extreme variations than the ideological mind in other countries. Moreover, America has survived the worst of its ideological tensions, including the Civil War. ■

 ## COMPARISONS WITH OTHER NATIONS

POLITICAL CULTURE AND IDEOLOGY IN DEMOCRACIES

A country's political culture and any of its ideological components are often reflected in its constitution. For example, in the democracy of France the president can, under certain critical circumstances, assume "emergency powers" that would be impeachable offenses for an American president.[5] The French political culture makes this device possible. The French were trying to escape a long tradition of political turmoil, but avoid a dictatorship (something they had been trying to do with uneven success since 1789) and establish a viable democracy when they created the Fifth Republic under the firm leadership of Charles de Gaulle in 1958. The de Gaulle-inspired constitution of that year produced a strong executive in the presidency to reassure those conservative-minded French who felt there is such a thing as too much democracy, but made the presidency popularly elected with a majority of votes cast to guarantee an undisputed mandate from the people.

Political cultures often receive a severe and occasionally violent jolt that results in a definitive change. The consequences of such a jolt are difficult to evaluate, but there is little doubt that a serious national crisis can produce a very substantial change in the political perspectives of an entire nation. As Table 5.2 suggests, neither democracies nor nondemocracies are immune from this phenomenon. The American political system, for example, remained intact during and after the Great Depression, but the role of the federal government in monitoring (some would say, interfering with) the economy grew to unprecedented proportions and has not significantly retreated from them in nearly two-thirds of a century. Our political culture has largely accepted the expanded role as a given. Other countries have endured even more emphatic changes.

After World War II, the losing powers had their political cultures in effect revised. The German constitution in 1949 included a provision to outlaw political parties that, in the opinion of the federal courts, advocate un- or antidemocratic programs. The Japanese constitution of 1947 banned the use of the military for offensive purposes. In both instances these measures were taken to placate victims of their aggression as well as internal critics of the dangers of an imperialist and militarist past.

TABLE 5.2   POLITICAL CULTURE AND POLITICAL TRAUMA

Country	Trauma	Result
United States	Great Depression (1930s)	Unprecedented government regulation of the economy
Soviet Union	World War II invasion; economic collapse and hardline coup, August 1991	Distrust of West; Breakup of USSR and democratization
Germany	Military occupation (World War II)	Democratization
Japan	Nuclear bombing and military occupation (World War II)	Democratization
France	Collapse of colonial empire, near civil war (1946–1958)	Strengthened executive
United Kingdom	Declining economic and political power (about 1945–1970)	Acceptance of United States as replacement as world power
Canada	Bifurcation into two national communities, English and French (ongoing)	As yet undetermined: possible separatism

The intolerance of neo-Nazi skinheads toward immigrants in Germany today is reminiscent of an earlier political culture—the Nazi regime. But the majority of German people back their constitution, which guarantees civil rights.

The political cultures of those countries whose immigration policies are fairly lenient face a new challenge. The demographic mosaics of their societies are changing, particularly those of the United States and Western Europe. The United States is now the fourth-largest Spanish-speaking country in the world; Germany's capital, Berlin, is the second-biggest Turkish city in the world; and one out of every five police officers in London is from Africa or the West Indies.[6] Most of the reaction to the newest immigrants has been positive (or at least noncommittal), but some of the reaction (neo-Nazi skinheads in Germany beating up immigrant workers, for example) has been unpleasant and probably will continue to be until the political culture can adjust.

Democracy is, of course, government by the governed—or, at least, it is supposed to be. But democracy is not itself an expression of ideology. As an earlier section of this chapter suggests, the American democracy is actually a marketplace of competing ideologies whose advocates take their chances with the voters at regular intervals.

And ideology is a fairly simple matter in the United States. We tend to label candidates for political office (or they label one another) as conservative or liberal, sometimes intending the label to be a political insult. In other democracies this dichotomy either doesn't exist or has assumed different (but usually respectable) meanings, as will be demonstrated in the chapters on political parties and interest groups.

The terms *left* and *right* have connotations that are at once both distinct and confusing. They have been in use for two centuries, apparently first used during the French Revolution when the more radical elements in the National Assembly sat on the left side of the chamber while the more conservative ones placed themselves on the right side. In the United States most Americans tend to think of liberals as being to the left of center while conservatives are found to the right. This is an efficient way of looking at American ideology, even if it is occasionally simplistic. In any case, the lack of a major socialist party in the United States has helped to prevent the sort of polarized politics that characterized several Western European countries during the first three-quarters of this century.

Throughout most of the twentieth century ideology was taken more seriously in Western Europe and in other parliamentary democracies. This focus existed in great part because extremist ideologies such as communism and fascism tended to participate in the activities of political democracy even while condemning and attacking them. A typical parliamentary democracy might have a political continuum that would roughly resemble this:

Left		Center		Right	
Communist	Socialist	Liberal	Conservative	Monarchist	Fascist

Political parties in most European countries reflect this sort of continuum. Throughout their modern history Americans have preferred to avoid consideration of extremist ideologies altogether. Europeans have increasingly adopted this habit by voting more and more for political parties that, regardless of their ideological traditions, were trying to place themselves in the political center. For example, the French Socialist party was kept out of power for the first 23 years of the Fifth Republic (1958–1981) because its policies were considered to be "economically incompetent."[7] Under Socialist leadership over the decade of the 1980s, however, the French achieved an economic growth rate higher than that of either of the other major economies in Europe, Western Germany and Britain.[8] The French socialists simply stopped being doctrinaire and quietly encouraged the free market, thereby demonstrating that they weren't incompetent after all.

Conservative and socialist political parties are both in hot pursuit of a mainstream vote. In most national elections over the last half-century the moderately left- or right-of-center parties in the larger democracies and most of the smaller ones have secured an overwhelming proportion of the total vote, as Table 5.3 suggests.

Before moving on to some mention of ideologies in totalitarian systems it is important to point out that totalitarian ideologies exist even in democratic societies. In

A VIEW FROM THE STATES

The End of Ideology in Britain?

Thirty years ago Daniel Bell, the Harvard sociologist, published his book "The End of Ideology." It is time for a new edition with Britain as a striking example.

Through this century the Labor Party has brought a heavy element of ideology to British politics. Labor based itself on egalitarian Socialist principles. In office, it nationalized leading industries, built massive public housing and established the National Health Service.

In recent years the Labor leader, Neil Kinnock, has worked hard to strip the party of ideological anachronisms. Little remained of the Socialist ideal except a commitment to spend more on public services such as health.

Even so, Labor lost the election three weeks ago [April 1992]—lost in the middle of a bad recession, after 13 years of Conservative Government. And one of the main reasons for its defeat was a campaign promise to raise tax rates on higher incomes.

The defeat has persuaded many in the party that it must shed the last remnants of ideology, recognizing that Britain is now a country of would-be capitalists. The next step will probably be for Labor to cut its links to the trade unions. It will try to make itself a mildly reformist middle-class party, perhaps under a new name.

The Conservatives, meanwhile, are happily discarding the ideological tone that lately marked their party. That was the strident voice of Margaret Thatcher.

With her message of unbridled free enterprise, Mrs. Thatcher had a profound effect on British attitudes in her 11 years as Prime Minister. But by the end of her reign she had worn out her welcome. . . .

In fact, the Conservatives won this election because they made the extraordinary decision in 1990 to ditch Mrs. Thatcher and then chose the bland Mr. Major as leader. He is the very model of a non-ideological politician, offending practically no one.

Source: Anthony Lewis, "The End of Ideology," *The New York Times*, May 6, 1992.

Western European countries the Communist party has served as a respectable leftist party that appealed to a basically working-class vote. While Communists had almost no chance to win a national election, they could and did win local elections and even on occasion got to participate in national governments as part of a coalition of several political parties. As recently as a decade ago Italy's Communists became the second-biggest party by polling close to a third of votes cast. But communism is gradually losing its appeal. Over the last three or four national elections in France, for example, Communists have barely been able to draw a tenth of the total vote, compared with nearly a fourth a few decades ago. In the English-speaking nations and in Germany, communism has never had much electoral appeal. In great part, this is because the political culture of these countries has regarded communism as a political pariah and a sure-fire formula for economic misery.

TABLE 5.3	PERCENTAGE OF VOTE FOR IDEOLOGICALLY CENTRIST POLITICAL PARTIES	
Country	Centrist Parties	National Vote
United States	Democrat	
	Republican	81% (1992)
West Germany*	Christian Democrats	
	Free Democrats	
	Social Democrats	95% (1991)
France*	Rally for the Republic	
	Socialist Party	
	Union for French Democracy	74% (1993)
Japan	Liberal Democrats	
	Socialist Party	78% (1992)
United Kingdom*	Conservative	
	Labor	
	Liberal	95% (1992)

* Includes recent elections to the European Parliament.
Source: Various analyses in *The New York Times*.

Often the question comes up: Can or should a basically democratic political culture tolerate a nondemocratic movement or political party in its midst? The answer has to be yes, since nearly any definition of democracy includes the concept of tolerance.

POLITICAL CULTURE AND IDEOLOGY IN TOTALITARIAN SYSTEMS

In totalitarian systems ideology often becomes identified with founding ideologues: Marxist-Leninism in the Soviet Union and Maoism in China are classic examples. Examples also abound of brute force and **political megalomania** (a form of psychotic madness characterized by a dictator whose word is law and whose wisdom is infallible). (Well, yes, these can be found in democracies as well, but at least they are limited by constitutional restraints.) For example, Kim Il Sung, the communist leader of North Korea since 1945, has had a statue built in his likeness larger than any building in the country. Communist leaders in the former Soviet Union justified all kinds of crimes by claiming that everything possible needed to be done to usher in a time of permanent peace and prosperity for workers.

All of this, of course, provides an excellent rationale for communist leaders. As the supreme guardians of the true faith, they cannot be expected to consider such vagaries as public opinion. They alone know what to do because they alone understand and can properly interpret the ideology that guides social development. **Political self-righteousness** is a useful term to describe those regimes that refuse to submit their programs to either criticism or a meaningful election. The government purports to know what is best for people without asking them and rules over them without their consent.

Ideology has great potential for danger to the individual because ideologues, whether communists, fascists, or religious fanatics, firmly adhere to the notion "that everything is relevant to government and that the task of government is to reconstruct society utterly according to the goals of an ideology."[9] It is easy to see where this can lead. Totalitarian ideology is all-pervasive, leaving to the individual little, if any, control over daily activities. The totalitarian nightmare envisioned in *1984* by George Orwell may be a worst-case scenario. In this maximization of misery no member of society has even a modicum of privacy: Television screens watch instead of being watched and civil servants keep busy by rewriting history according to a perpetually changing official version.

Self-righteousness is in ample supply in almost any political setting, but is especially characteristic of a political environment driven by ideology. Keepers of the faith assume that they monopolize truth. Ideologues in totalitarian systems are notorious for pursuing their political agenda without feeling the need for compromise or admitting that they might actually be wrong about something. They have little if any tolerance for those who dissent or question. The content of some ideologies simply doesn't permit compromise or flexibility. This is because much of their political program is concerned with the complete destruction or removal of those they consider to be political foes or enemies. (Such ideologies can be found in the democracies as well as in nondemocratic systems.)

In most instances these organizations and the political ideals they espouse are completely incompatible with democracy. With occasional exceptions they usually don't compete in free elections, although this does not mean they are incapable of doing so. But even in what we might call "recovering totalitarian systems," one totalitarian ideology may be discredited only to be replaced by another. Indeed, in the emerging democracies of Eastern Europe as well as in the established democracies of the West, communist movements are being replaced at least in small part by the opposite political extreme: fascism or **ethno-nationalism** (the expression of a nationalist identity by a subgroup in an overall political society, such as Serbs in Yugoslavia). Table 5.4 suggests several examples of this phenomenon, which take an antidemocratic or at least nondemocratic form.

TABLE 5.4   EXAMPLES OF CONTEMPORARY NON- OR ANTIDEMOCRATIC MOVEMENTS

Country	Political Movement	Characteristics
France	National Front	Anti-foreign (hostile to French-speaking Africans and Arabs who have migrated to France for better jobs) and anti-Semitic
Germany	Neo-Nazis	Inspired by Nazi ideals; hostile to non-German residents (particularly Turkish workers) and anti-Semitic
Republic of Russia	Pamyat	Politically reactionary, with expressed desire to restore the primacy of the Russian Orthodox Church and restore the monarchy; anti-Semitic
United States	Aryan Nation	Racist and anti-Semitic

When Communist hard-liners attempted a coup to regain the reins of government in the Soviet Union in August 1991, Boris Yeltsin led the reformers in resisting the coup. He is shown here (with paper in hand) standing on a tank outside a Soviet ministry building.

Are some societies predisposed by their political cultures to totalitarianism? There is no simple answer. However, we do know that totalitarian systems such as Nazi Germany or Stalinist Russia flourished at least in part because each appeared in a society that had little experience in political democracy. We may be consoled by the knowledge that, historically speaking, established and mature democracies do not lapse into some form of totalitarianism.

The former Soviet Union is currently in the midst of significant change in both its economic structure and political culture. The severity of this change was highlighted by the failed hard-line coup in August 1991. Perpetrated by Communists tied to the past (and politically dependent on it), the coup represented a possible last gasp on the part of those who viewed the direction of change in the Soviet Union to be both disastrous and traumatic. But the reforms had gone too far to be turned back by discredited Communist bureaucrats totally out of touch with events. Political culture in what was the Soviet Union will change more still in the years ahead. (For example, get used to learning a revised geography: Leningrad is once again St. Petersburg.)

It may be too optimistic to hope that all of the change will be peaceful. The American experience itself suggests that traumatic change in political culture rarely occurs without some severe and often violent social alterations. Our political culture changed drastically and relatively suddenly in the years 1861 to 1865, when the issue of national sovereignty was settled once and for all in the most violent conflict our nation has ever experienced.

POLITICAL CULTURE AND IDEOLOGY IN AUTHORITARIAN SYSTEMS

Developing a consensual political culture is a long and occasionally tortuous process for most political societies. Some countries in fact function for generations without achieving a political culture that satisfies the needs or gains the acceptance of the general citizenry. For a society to be divided over its political culture is a much more serious matter than to be split ideologically over a particular issue. Americans, for example, are deeply divided over abortion and the death penalty. Usually, however, all sides have found the political and legal process within the political culture as generally acceptable to work through.

In other words, we accept the institution of government as legitimate (if imperfect) and work from there. In many societies, **legitimacy** itself—conferred by a widely accepted procedure for selecting political leaders, generally through free elections—is a serious problem. Dictatorships often have a difficult time with this question. If a government doesn't rely on or take its chances with free elections, it usually still wants something to at least provide a pretense of legitimacy. There are several methods to achieve this, as Table 5.5 suggests. These include raising fears of "enemies," claiming moral superiority, and glorifying ancestry.

Most authoritarian systems are devoid of any discernible ideology, but some are eager to legitimate their existence with nationalism or myths or a combination. For example, the Shah Reza Pahlavi of Iran (1954–1979) in 1971 proclaimed the 25 hundredth anniversary of the founding of the Persian Empire by Cyrus the Great. It was an attempt to link Iran to its Persian history and the Shah with one of the greatest empire-builders in history.

Some of the more sophisticated authoritarian dictators at least take on the trappings of ideological finesse. The regime of Gamal Abdul Nasser in Egypt (1952–1970), for example, attempted to export "Nasserism," a hodgepodge of imported European socialism and Arab nationalism. Like most ideologies that have economic implications, Nasserism was less than a success.[10] However, Nasser was admired by Egyptians for being the first native ruler of Egypt since Cleopatra; the national pride his subjects felt guaranteed Nasser genuine popularity. In the 1960s and 1970s clever Latin American dictators tended to be "anticommunist" to both placate the United States and gain support. This was a sort of negative ideology that worked successfully as long as there were communists to worry about.

In many instances, when an authoritarian regime makes anything resembling an ideological commitment, it is frequently one Westerners would prefer not to hear about. For example, in the former federation of Yugoslavia, the term *ethnic cleansing* is applied with frightening accuracy. The government of Croatia is determined to rid its territory of Serbs, while Serbia wants to get rid of its Croats. Both are interested in frightening Muslims and each other out of the lands each claims in the region of Bosnia-Herzegovina.[11] Actually, this example is an expression of extreme ethno-nationalism, in that it seeks a homogeneous ethnic, religious, linguistic, and cultural society.

Some authoritarian ideologies escalate into totalitarianism. Cuban-manufactured and communist-inspired "Castroism" is an example. Today there is concern about fundamentalism, especially of the Islamic variety, sweeping a good part of the Middle East. Thus far, fundamentalism has been contained, but it has made inroads in Iran and North Africa. Westerners are apprehensive about this movement because its ideological appeal

TABLE 5.5 POLITICAL LEGITIMATION IN NONDEMOCRATIC REGIMES		
Type of Regime	Regime Characteristics	Examples
Military dictatorship	Few if any ideological justifications; harsh military rule offered as necessary until real or imagined enemies are eliminated	Chile (1973–1989); Iraq, Thailand
Ideological state	An all-pervasive polity that excludes and actively persecutes dissent while dominating every aspect of political as well as social behavior through a sophisticated system of communications and police apparatus	Soviet Union, 1917–late 1980s; most of Eastern Europe until 1989; China
Theocracy	Exclusive religious doctrine that mandates government by clergy who relentlessly eliminate distinctions between church and state and insist that state law be a perfect reflection of prescribed religious principles	Iran
Traditional monarchy	One politically dominant family and its retainers attempt to personify the history and the destiny of the nation through successive generations	Saudi Arabia

Source: Various analyses in *The New York Times*.

is both political and religious as well as anti-Western.[12] But these are exceptions to the general rule of authoritarian regimes. Many quite frankly lack any significant ideological character. Dictators generally don't see the point of going to the trouble of formulating their political thoughts since they are simply interested in staying in power. The opposite extreme is the case of Saddam Hussein who, during the Persian Gulf conflict, employed any ideology he considered useful for his purposes. He was at different times a believer in and self-proclaimed leader of the cause of Arab pan-nationalism, Islamic fundamentalism, Iraqi nationalism, and national self-determination.

But ideologies should not be confused with political goals for the enhancement of political power. Few authoritarian systems actually have, let alone practice, an ideology. Saddam Hussein, for example, doesn't really possess an ideology: He is bent on a genocidal and ecocidal program, usually directed against his own population. Eradicating any possible opposition is his first priority. His victims perish not as the result of a sophisticated ideology (as in Stalin's Soviet Union), but because of a relentless and brutal pursuit of power. It isn't necessary to be a political ideologue to be a menace.

Finally, authoritarian political cultures are inherently unstable. That can be good or bad news. A half-century of authoritarian governance in Cuba was succeeded by communism—hardly an improvement. On the other hand, many authoritarian regimes in Latin America and parts of Africa are at least in the process of being democratized. The next couple of decades may well reveal whether democracy has become an easily learned political habit.

Summary

1. Political culture refers to widely held values and beliefs about political institutions and practices; political ideology refers to various notions about what these institutions should accomplish.

2. Eight basic characteristics associated with the American political culture are liberty, equality, property, merit, civic duty, democracy, secularism, and efficacy.

3. The American political ideology reveals itself in three areas: ideological tradition, historical tradition, and constitutional tradition. Americans tend to divide along conservative and liberal lines.

4. Ideological divisions may be considered harmful in our society because they are associated with a lack of clarity and unity about national goals, fragmented support from key social institutions such as the family, and an intolerance for opposing views.

5. Those who do not consider such divisions harmful point to a healthy dominance by the ideological center that diffuses negative excesses, cyclical change between dominating conservative and liberal points of view, and a relative ideological stability compared with other countries.

6. Political legitimacy in nondemocratic regimes is usually more fragile than in democratic ones because ideology replaces the free play of politics.

7. Changes in political culture itself may be sudden. Two classic examples were Japan and Germany following their defeat in World War II. Both their political culture and political institutions were partially imposed by the victors in the war. Tremendous economic or social upheaval can also result in changes in political culture in both democratic and nondemocratic societies.

8. Most democracies, including those with substantial ideological political parties (such as the Communists in France and Italy), have been moving away from extremes toward a more pragmatic political center.

9. Totalitarian ideologies are all-encompassing and desire to control the activities, including the nonpolitical ones, of every citizen.

10. Strongly held ideologies can be dangerously violent because by their nature they allow for little or no compromise or dissent. Both democratic and nondemocratic societies have examples of intolerant ideologues. Ethnic and nationalist movements can also inspire ideological intolerance.

11. Authoritarian regimes often have no ideology beyond retaining political power. But some ideologies, like those relating to fundamentalism, border on totalitarianism.

Terms to Define

Conservative
Divine law
Ethno-nationalism
Ideological center
Legitimacy
Liberal
Libertarianism

Natural law
Neoconservativism
Political culture
Political ideology
Political megalomania
Political self-righteousness
Populism

Suggested Readings

Almond, Gabriel, and Verba, Sidney. *The Civic Culture*. Princeton: Princeton University Press, 1963. Based on five national samples in the United States, (then-West) Germany, the United Kingdom, Italy, and Mexico queried in the late 1950s, this study has now become a classic. While all five countries are democratic, there are some startling differences in how those samples perceived their respective governments.

Dunn, Charles W., and J. David Woodard. *American Conservatism from Burke to Bush: An Introduction*. Lanham, New York, and London: Madison Books, 1991. An up-to-date analysis of American political conservatism, including useful comparisons with the liberal tradition.

Hartz, Louis. *The Liberal Tradition in America*. New York: Harcourt Brace Jovanovich, 1955. An excellent interpretation of the American culture from the point of view of liberalism.

Hoffer, Eric. *The True Believer*. New York: Harper & Row, 1951. A readable classic on the sort of individual who is attracted to an ideology, becomes totally addicted to it, and then makes life miserable for everyone else who isn't a true believer.

McClosky, Herbert, and Alida, Brill. *Dimensions of Tolerance: What Americans Believe About Civil Liberties*. New York: Russell Sage Foundation, 1983. Disconcertingly, some Americans are less tolerant than the First Amendment suggests they ought to be.

Murray, Charles. *Losing Ground: American Social Policy, 1950–1980*. New York: Basic Books, 1984. A point of view and explanation of how well-intended government programs may be self-defeating when it comes to assisting the less advantaged citizens in American society.

Tocqueville, Alexis de. *Democracy in America*. Edited by Phillips Bradley. New York: Knopf, 1944. This particular classic is an easy one to read. De Tocqueville's notes were made in the late 1830s as he toured the United States. He suggests the good and less favorable elements of what was then the only popular democracy in the world.

Tuchman, Barbara. *The March of Folly: From Troy to Vietnam*. New York: Random House, 1983. A compelling and frightening explanation of how governments, with the assistance of the political culture they help manufacture, may lead a country into national disaster.

Notes

1. C-SPAN, July 1992.
2. See Charles W. Dunn, *American Political Theology* (New York: Praeger, 1984), for a fuller discussion of ideas presented here.
3. *Today*, November 15, 1985, pp. 6, 7.
4. Robert Nisbet, *The Quest for Community* (New York: Oxford University Press, 1953).
5. The French Constitution of 1958, Article 16.
6. David C. Gordon, *Images of the West: Third World Perspectives* (London and New York: Rowman & Littlefield Publishers, 1989), pp. 40–41.
7. "Brilliant, But for One Thing," *The Economist*, November 21, 1992, p. 61.
8. Ibid.
9. Bernard Crick, *In Defense of Politics* (Baltimore, Md.: Penguin Books, 1962), p. 34.
10. "Killing the Dinosaur," *The Economist*, July 25, 1992, pp. 42–43.
11. "A Setback," *The Economist*, July 25, 1992, pp. 48–49.
12. See, for example, the study by Barry Rubin, *Islamic Fundamentalism in Egyptian Politics* (New York: St. Martin's Press, 1990).

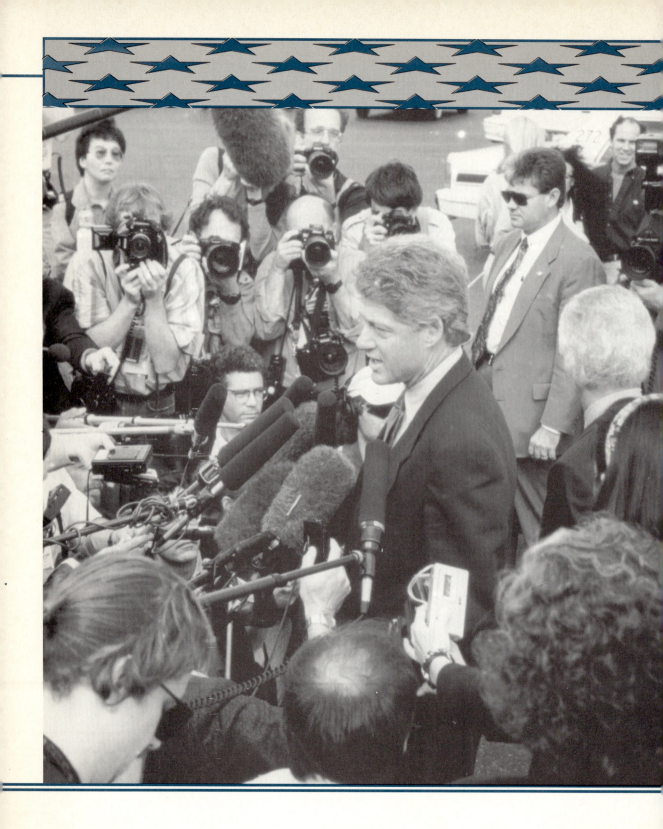

CHAPTER ★ SIX

PUBLIC OPINION AND THE MASS MEDIA

Public opinion has been defined in many different ways. The political scientist V. O. Key wrote that it consists of "those opinions held by private persons which governments find it prudent to heed."[1] His definition limits the concept to those opinions that influence governments. Thus, private opinion becomes public opinion when it relates to government and politics; another term for it might be *political* opinion. An opinion on the proper roles in marriage would most likely be a private opinion, whereas an opinion on the government's welfare policy would be a public, or political opinion. By referring to political opinion, we can distinguish between public opinion on detergents and on defense policy.

Not everyone has an opinion on every political question. Thus, each person is concerned with areas of his or her own interest. Labor union members, for example, may be interested in collective bargaining but not in farm subsidies. Publishers may be interested in copyright law but not in judicial reform. For this reason political scientists have devised the concept of **special publics.** Key described them as "those segments of the public with views about particular issues, problems, or other questions of public concern."[2]

People need information in order to form opinions. Some of that information comes from newspapers, magazines, radio, and television—collectively known as the mass media. The **mass media** are all the forms of communication that bring messages to the public. In the political arena the media both report on and interpret governmental actions as well as the public's responses to those actions.

Public opinion may be as unsettling as a roller-coaster ride or as stable as the Rock of Gibraltar. Buoyed by the unparalleled popularity common among presidents in their first year in office, President George Bush agreed to a tax increase, despite having pledged not to raise taxes with his famous "read my lips" pledge during the 1988 campaign. His popularity plummeted, damaging Republican prospects in the 1990 midterm elections. Then, rising like a sphinx out of the ashes of the Persian Gulf War, his popularity reached new highs in early 1991 only to come crashing on the rocks of a stagnant economy. Probably no president's popularity has ever produced such a turbulent roller-coaster ride. President Dwight D. Eisenhower, by contrast, enjoyed eight years in office in the 1950s with little change in the public's favorable opinion of this genial leader.

Public opinion can have a dramatic effect on the workings of government. Take the examples of some recent Supreme Court nominations. Robert Bork and Clarence Thomas, two nominees with similar judicial philosophies, were handed two different fates by the U.S. Senate on their confirmation votes. Despite being significantly better qualified on the basis of his judicial and scholarly background, Bork lost while Thomas won, not just in the Senate confirmation votes, but more importantly at the bar of public opinion. Before the Senate Judiciary Committee, Judge Bork openly discussed his conservative judicial philosophy, whereas Judge Thomas's evasiveness under questioning kept those doors closed. The public felt uncomfortable with Bork's blunt views but did not know enough about Thomas's views to form an unfavorable opinion.

Then at the last minute of the Judiciary Committee deliberations, Anita Hill alleged that Judge Thomas had sexually harassed her; some thought that her allegations might tip the scales against him. What they failed to foresee, however, was how adroitly Judge Thomas would cultivate public opinion before a prime-time television audience and how Anita Hill's story, which seemed to change as it was unveiled (and, to some extent, leaked to the media), would lose the luster of credibility. Thomas, portraying himself as a little David against the giant Goliath, charged his political opponents with a mass-media lynching. By frontally challenging the Judiciary Committee and the mass media, he turned the developing tide of opposition. While Thomas won the battle at the general bar of public opinion, Hill won the hearts of a special public.

President Bill Clinton had not been in office one day before he felt the full brunt of public opinion. His choice for Attorney General, Zoë Baird, came under fire for having hired illegal aliens for child care. Public outcry over this violation of the immigration law forced her to withdraw her nomination.

As we shall see in this chapter, public opinion is a dynamic entity—by turns fluid or stable, latent or manifest. Its changing quality makes it difficult to measure and to pin down. The media's role in forming—some might say creating—public opinion is a controversial one. Some countries, however, resort to more forceful means to manipulate opinion, as the comparative section will show.

THE STRUCTURE OF PUBLIC OPINION

Political scientists who specialize in the study of public opinion generally identify five characteristics: salience, stability, fluidity, intensity, latency, and distribution.[3]

Salience. The quality of standing out, of being important, is the characteristic that determines which special publics develop around an issue. For each public a certain issue or subject is "at the focus of attention, crowding out other items, a pivot for organizing one's thoughts and acts."[4]

Stability and **Fluidity.** Opinion on some issues is very stable (see Table 6.1, p. 177); on others, very fluid. For example, most people do not change their political party preferences quickly or often. But opinions on issues not necessarily related to party preference, such as the performance of a president, war, or inflation, may change rapidly. Perhaps no president, for example, suffered as severe a jolt in public opinion as Lyndon Johnson did on the issue of the Vietnam conflict. Entering that war with overwhelming public and congressional support, Johnson within four years (1965 through 1968) lost his reputation as the grand master of Congress and declined to seek his party's nomination for reelection. Johnson's humiliating departure from office was rivaled only by Richard Nixon's after the Watergate debacle. Both Johnson and Nixon had enjoyed landslide electoral victories only to watch a huge public endorsement of their policies gradually evaporate. President Bush enjoyed an 89 percent approval rating among the public after the Persian Gulf War in 1991, only to see his support vanish by the time of the 1992 presidential election.

Intensity. The public reacts to issues with varying degrees of intensity. People directly affected by a problem usually feel more strongly about it than those who are unaffected. Thus, parents of soldiers fighting in the Persian Gulf War no doubt had more intense opinions about the war than most other Americans.

Latency. During ordinary times, public opinion on a given issue may well be unexpressed, or latent; but if a crisis occurs, people's latent attitudes become focused and active. For example, a community may exhibit no visible opposition to school busing, but become aroused when a court orders it. Both Presidents Ronald Reagan and George Bush tapped latent public sentiment on issues raised by pro-life and anticrime groups. President Clinton aroused latent opinions about homosexual men and women in the military when he proposed lifting the ban on their military service, in the first week of his administration.

Distribution. How widely is an opinion held among various divisions of the public, such as racial, geographic, age, sex, and occupational categories? Answers to questions involving distribution are important to political candidates, who seek to build winning coalitions by taking positions that will appeal to certain groups. National parties have traditionally tried to balance their presidential

Public opinion can be characterized by its degree of intensity. People with a stake in an issue generally feel more intensely about it, as is the case of this man who intercepted Bill Clinton on a morning jog soon after the presidential election. His sign reads: "I have AIDS and would like to speak with you for 3 minutes . . . PLEASE!"

tickets by accounting for such variables as geography, ideology, age, and religion in their presidential and vice presidential candidates.

TYPES OF PUBLIC OPINION

How much freedom do public officials have in regard to public opinion? When can they ignore it? When must they yield to it? These questions lead us to examine briefly four types of public opinion: permissive, directive, supportive, and divisive.

Permissive public opinion occurs when there is a high degree of latency. An unaroused public allows public officials wide latitude in making decisions. In most cases involving foreign affairs, the public does not know enough about the issue, is not interested enough to put pressure on the government, or simply trusts Washington to do what is right and best. During the Persian Gulf War, decision making generally occurred in a permissive stage of public opinion: Only a few questioned presidential leadership .

Directive public opinion plays a much greater role in the decisions of public

TABLE 6.1	THE STABILITY OF PUBLIC OPINION ON GUN CONTROL LAWS, 1975–1991			
Year	More Strict	Less Strict	Kept as Are	No Opinion
1975	69%	3%	24%	4%
1980	59%	6%	29%	6%
1981	65%	3%	30%	2%
1983	59%	4%	31%	6%
1986	60%	8%	30%	2%
1990	78%	2%	17%	3%
1991	68%	5%	25%	2%

Note: Question: "In general, do you feel that the laws covering the sale of firearms should be made more strict, less strict, or kept as they are now?
Source: *The Gallup Poll News Service,* March 28, 1991, p. 1.

officials. Had the Persian Gulf War not been successfully and quickly concluded, criticism would likely have increased, as it did during the Vietnam War. At that time opposition mounted to the point that demands were made to withdraw American troops. This directive type of public opinion probably led to the troop withdrawal program initiated by President Nixon prior to his campaign for reelection in 1972. Directive public opinion can be a consensus in favor of or opposed to an action of government.

As the term suggests, **supportive public opinion** serves to uphold officials or decisions. When Nixon mounted the troop withdrawal program in 1972, supportive public opinion approved his decision and helped him win reelection. Supportive public opinion differs from permissive public opinion, in that it is active rather than latent or passive.

Divisive public opinion occurs when the public is sharply divided on what should be done, often leading to public demonstrations by both sides, as in the case of the abortion issue. Usually only a small portion of the populace is undecided when public opinion is sharply split on an issue. In these circumstances public officials have greater difficulty in deciding what to do, because they lack a clear popular mandate. Public opinion polling on such issues is sometimes suspect since the phrasing of a question can easily alter the results. Both pro-life and pro-choice groups have criticized various public opinion polls for this reason.

THE SHAPING OF PUBLIC OPINION

Some observers believe that the mass media exert too much influence on public opinion. They tend to see the public as an empty vessel waiting to be filled with the pronouncements of print and broadcast journalism. In that case, it would be natural to assume that most Americans would hold the same opinions, regardless of class, race, or ethnicity and other factors. This is simply not true. The mass communications do have a powerful

Children learn patriotism and other civic virtues early in life, both at home and in the classroom, through a process called political socialization.

effect, but they are by no means the sole determinants of public opinion. Its shaping is much more sophisticated and complex than media critics indicate.

Family and School

Scholars point out that a person's opinion on political subjects begins very early in life, when the child's awareness and knowledge of mass media are quite limited.[5] The two principal sources of public opinion formation in this early period of life are the family and the school. Through a process known as **political socialization** these sources teach children about the political culture and instill fundamental civic virtues.

In the family a child is inculcated with basic attitudes that will later shape his or her specific political opinions. One study reported a high correlation between political party identification of parents and that of their 12th-grade children; this correlation tends to exist throughout an individual's life.[6] Other research showed that children tend to identify most closely with the political views of the parent with whom they have a closer relationship.[7]

Some scholars believe that the school may be even more important than the family in developing political attitudes.[8] The principal role of elementary and secondary schools, they argue, has been to strengthen and reinforce faith in American government.[9] Stories about the honesty of George Washington and Abraham Lincoln, for example, also extol presidential character traits.

As children become older, they are more subject to mass media and government influences, such as presidential decisions, congressional actions, and court opinions, in forming their political perspectives. Even so, their attitudes toward these influences have been conditioned (probably throughout life) by family and educational experiences.

Other Factors

Along with family and school, several other factors help determine public opinion. One is social class. On an issue such as whether or not to cut capital gains taxes (taxes made on profits from investments), a blue collar worker who owns no stocks may well think it's a good idea not to cut in the belief that these tax cuts only benefit the wealthy; however, affluent people who risk money investing think that cutting capital gains taxes is a great way to stimulate further investment.[10] Religious affiliation, gender, and ethnic factors may also influence public opinion. For example, exit polls taken during the 1992 presidential election showed that women favored Bill Clinton by a margin of 6 percent; he won 47 percent of the female vote and 41 percent of the male vote.[11]

Finally, the public, far from being an "empty vessel to be filled at will by government and the media," engages in **selective perception**. In other words, people tend to listen to those speeches and read those newspapers that agree with already formed conceptions. The fact that people have been exposed to a particular point of view in the media does not mean that they accept it.[12]

MEASURING PUBLIC OPINION

Both scholars and public officials are interested (often for different reasons) in knowing the public's opinions on political issues. Experts have developed reliable ways for determining public opinion, using a sequence of steps. We see their results in the surveys of public opinion known as **polls.**

Suppose you wanted to determine accurately and fairly public opinion on the hotly contested issue of abortion. The first step in creating a reliable poll is to determine whose opinion on an issue is desired. This group is known as our **universe**. On the abortion issue the universe is all adult Americans, but on other issues the universe could be much smaller—say, senior Americans' opinions on social security cuts. Since in our example it is impossible to interview some 200 million Americans, pollsters work with a **random sample** of the universe. "Random" simply means that each person in the population has a roughly equal chance of being interviewed. It's a little like playing the lottery but with somewhat better odds. One main task of the pollsters is to ensure that their sample is *representative* of the population from which they are drawn (age, gender, education, ethnic, religious, and income levels are among the variables normally considered). That means they would not interview only urban residents or just use voting rolls to pick their sample. They must use methods that will allow all variables to be represented in the sample.

How can we be sure that a sample is sufficiently representative to be reliable? The mathematical law of probability provides the answer. Suppose you are bored and decide to toss a coin in the air 1000 times. Theoretically, the coin should come up heads about one-half of the time. When a sample is large enough and properly selected, this law of probability operates. National polling organizations, such as Gallup and Harris, may use a sample of 1000 to 1500 persons to represent the entire American population. The result obtained is customarily accurate to within a 4 percent margin of error; that is, the same survey conducted again would produce results not more than 4 percent different from the first results.

"PUT ME DOWN FOR 'NO COMMENT' ON THAT ONE... I REALLY HAVEN'T READ ENOUGH POLLS ON THE SUBJECT TO FORM AN OPINION!"

Generally, the larger the sample and the larger the margin separating two sets of opinions, the more accurate the results. If our sampling error is 4 percent and our percentage results are 65 for to 35 against abortion, we would have a high degree of confidence in our results. But if the results were 51 to 49, then our 4 percent sampling error would mean that another randomly chosen sample might produce a result of 48 for and 52 against. Mathematical formulae (which, rest assured, won't be quoted here) are used to compute sampling error.

Persons chosen in the random sample must be asked the same questions about abortion in the same way and even in the same tone of voice (avoiding an undue emphasis of one word over another). The questions cannot be "loaded" to bias a result. For example, if respondents are asked, "Do you favor the wanton murder of unborn and defenseless infants?" the percentage responding "no" would be very high. But if we were to ask, "Do you believe women should be forced to carry an unwanted pregnancy to term?" a high negative response would also be elicited, but with a different meaning than the result obtained with our first question. Thus, we need to have neutral questions, which would not unfairly tilt the response. Both pro-choice and pro-life language would bias our result and make it invalid.

Of course, the question posed must be easily understood by the persons interviewed. To ask a complicated question about the biological aspects of the fetus and whether life begins at conception or at birth (or somewhere in between) would confuse a great many respondents. The question must be simple and straightforward: "Should a woman be able to terminate her pregnancy through the first trimester?"

For both candidates and elected officials, public opinion polls provide critical information on how the public perceives them and how the public feels about particular issues. Recognizing the importance of conservative patriotic and religious symbols in wooing the electorate, Bill Clinton and Al Gore (the 1992 Democratic presidential and vice presidential candidates) wrapped themselves in the flag and quoted scripture during the campaign bus ride they took together right after the convention. During the 1993 presidential inauguration, Bill Clinton took the oath of office while holding his hand on a King James Version of the Bible that had been given to him by his grandmother, and the popular evangelist Billy Graham delivered the benediction. They thus projected an image very distinct from several previous Democratic tickets. Bill Clinton's position on abortion—personally opposed but supportive of the pro-choice position—enabled him to appeal to both pro-life and pro-choice voters.

When the results of opinion polls are reported to the public, they often help shape subsequent public opinion, particularly in the course of election races. For instance, polls taken early in the presidential campaign establish "front-runners" whose candidacies then take on new life. Bill Clinton was the beneficiary of such polls well before the first primaries in 1992. In most cases it is the mass media that conduct and publicize these polls.

INFLUENCE OF THE MASS MEDIA

As American society and technology have changed over the years, so too have the American media. In some ways the media have helped bring about changes in society and technology, while in other ways societal and technological changes have altered American media. Without the mass media, the civil rights movement of the 1960s that brought major social and political changes to America probably either would not have occurred or would have been substantially limited in its impact. On the other hand, to have this impact, the media depended on technological advances in communications and transportation to report extensively on the civil rights movement.

Four distinct periods of American media influences can be identified: (1) the partisan political press, (2) the popular press, (3) the reform press, and (4) the electronic media. Each has made distinct contributions to American politics and society.

Partisan Political Press. Early American newspapers were established and controlled by political groups, and they generally circulated to a select constituency who could afford to buy them. Without the mass advertising we have today, these newspapers depended on political parties and factions and sometimes the government for subsidies to operate. The two best-known early newspapers were the *Gazette of the United States*, the mouthpiece of the Federalist Party, and the *National Gazette*, the voice of the Jeffersonian-Republicans. These and other newspapers like them were intensely partisan in both news and editorial columns.

Popular Press. Technological advances in printing and the advent of the telegraph led to the rise of the financially self-supporting mass-readership newspapers of the 1800s. These papers, while not controlled by political parties, were often owned by people who used their newspaper empires to push pet positions on issues. For instance, publisher William Randolph Hearst used his papers to promote the Spanish-American War in the 1890s.

Reform Press. These publications exposed political corruption in the late 1800s and early 1900s and advocated reforms on specific political and social issues, such as trustbusting, municipal reform, and adoption of civil service. The often zealous investigation of these issues came to be known as **muckraking**. Influential writers like Lincoln

Steffens and Ida Tarbell gained fame for writing in such reformist and issue-oriented magazines as *Nation, Atlantic, Harper's, McClure's,* and *Scribner's.* Aided by major advertisers, these publications were financially able to reach a national audience and become a formidable force in American politics.

Electronic Media. With the arrival of the radio in the 1920s and of television in the 1940s, politicians gradually learned that they could go directly to the people with their messages. President Franklin D. Roosevelt made extraordinary use of the radio in his famous "Fireside Chats." The 1960 presidential campaign probably turned on the televised debates. In the first debate, John F. Kennedy's healthy image, contrasted with Nixon's sallow complexion and five-o'clock shadow, gave Kennedy the "look" of a winner. Ironically, people listening by radio thought Richard Nixon had won the debate. With his weekly radio programs on key issues and his mastery of television, President Ronald Reagan used both media better than any previous president. In 1988 President George Bush utilized some of the most effective political television commercials ever produced to portray his opponent, Michael Dukakis, as soft on crime. In the 1992 presidential campaign Bush, Clinton, and Ross Perot all found that appearances on non-news talk shows were an especially effective way to reach the voters directly.

Television has become the primary source of news for Americans, as well as the most believable source (Table 6.2). Unfortunately, television's tendency to sensationalize and condense news may not make it the most reliable or instructive source. A somewhat more alarming development is that children are the most affected (infected) by television. One study reveals that one-third of American children are in danger of flunking kindergarten in great part because "by the time the child has set foot in a kindergarten classroom, he or she is likely to have spent more than 4,000 hours in front of this electronic teacher."[13] Often this time is spent at the expense of reading or interactive play.

The mass media influence people's attitudes in a variety of ways. They may do so directly in such forms as newspaper editorials. They may do so more subtly through placement of a story in a newspaper (on page 1 versus page 15) or emphasis on television (3-minute versus 30-second coverage). One particularly powerful media technique is one of the simplest—to ignore an issue. To illustrate: Where were the mass media when the public needed to be alerted to the potential insolvency of the savings and loan industry in the late 1980s? Or why were they laggards in alerting the public to the impending AIDS epidemic and its implications for America and the world?[14] In each of these cases it might be argued that the media initially interfered with the public's need and right to know. During Bill Clinton's campaign for the Democratic party's 1992 presidential nomination, the press was, in contrast, overly eager to reveal rumors about his alleged adultery.[15]

Many people tend to give too much credence to what they learn through the media, or, conversely, distrust what they are told, simply because they do not understand how the media function. Journalist David Broder noted that the media should convey to the public an understanding of the pressures of time and space that govern journalists' work and often result in error. Broder concludes:

> Instead of promising "All the News That's Fit to Print" [the slogan of The New York Times], I would like to see us say—over and over, until the point has been made—that the newspaper that drops on your doorstep is a partial, hasty, incomplete and inevitably somewhat flawed and inaccurate rendering of some of the things we have heard about in the past 24 hours—distorted, despite our best efforts to eliminate gross bias, by the very process of

A VIEW FROM THE STATES
New Ways of Politicking in the Media

America's news media were driven to the edge of a breakdown in 1992, when the press found itself sharing Presidential campaign coverage with rap singers, cable channels, sitcoms, talk shows and televised town meetings.

Everybody seemed to like it but reporters, who saw their monopoly on political coverage shattered by the very culture we have been told for years is rotting our brains and eroding our civic consciousness.

Bill Moyers worried in this space about the new news, fearing that our "public discourse has become the verbal equivalent of mud wrestling." Last week, *The New Yorker* urged Bill Clinton to break his pledge to appear on "Larry King Live" while he is in the White House. "The dignity of the Presidency is at stake here," warned the magazine.

Mr. Clinton has said he will continue to communicate with the public through these new, increasingly diverse media. "Of course I'll continue it," he told a CNN reporter. Given his campaign's success, he would be foolish not to. If he sticks to his word, Mr. Clinton could radically alter the nation's political communications.

For much of this century, journalists decided which issues to press Presidents on. They also relayed most of the communications between the politicians and the public.

Ross Perot and Bill Clinton upended that for good. In May, George Bush scoffed at the "weird media" on which his opponents were taking calls and playing saxophones. But by the campaign's end, Mr. Bush had abandoned concerns about looking "Presidential" and was hopping from one talk show to another.

. . . Any information medium has the potential to be abused. But the 1992 election showed the promise of these technologies: the political process was reinvigorated. Ross Perot got 19 percent of the vote. MTV registered more than a million new voters and for the first time in decades the number of Americans who voted rose by millions to 55 percent.

Where will these changes take us next?

Network news will continue its withdrawal from covering breaking news. Unable to compete with cable, it will retreat further into quasi-journalistic broadcasts that are like news magazines. When CBS aired the baseball playoffs instead of the first Presidential debate, the era in which networks hosted Presidential campaigns officially ended. Similarly, newspapers will have to reinvent their missions, abandoning the pretense that they are bringing news to readers first, and turn more to commentary, distinctive writing and analysis.

The new information culture doesn't mean the death of news. In fact, it signals its rebirth—more information, greater diversity. Some critics fret that such interaction and informal conversation is undignified, unseemly behavior for a President. But it isn't all that new an idea. They used to call it democracy.

TABLE 6.2 USE AND TRUSTWORTHINESS OF MEDIA, 1959–1988				
	1959	1968	1978	1988
(1) Source of most news				
Television	51%	59%	67%	65%
Newspapers	57%	49%	49%	42%
Radio	34%	25%	20%	14%
Magazines	8%	7%	5%	4%
People	4%	5%	5%	5%
(2) Most believable				
Television	29%	44%	47%	49%
Newspapers	32%	21%	23%	26%
Radio	12%	8%	9%	7%
Magazines	10%	11%	9%	5%
Don't know/no answer	17%	16%	12%	13%

Questions: (1) "First, I'd like to ask you where you usually get most of your news about what's going on in the world today—from the newspapers or radio or television or magazines or talking to people or where?" (more than one answer permitted). (2) "If you got conflicting or different reports of the same news story from radio, television, the magazines, and the newspapers, which of the four versions would you be most inclined to believe — the one on the radio or television or magazines or newspapers?" (only one answer permitted).
Source: Television Information Office, "America's Watching 30th Anniversary 1959–1989" (New York: Television Information Office, 1989), pp. 27, 28.

compression that makes it possible for you to lift it from the doorstep and read it in about an hour.[16]

Whatever flaws may be inherent in the ways the media function, the mass media are still a key link in making the democratic process work. They communicate back and forth between the government and the people. Without proper expression of public opinion to the government and a proper response by the government to public opinion, a democracy in the sense of "government by the people" becomes highly questionable. The relationships among government, the mass media, and public opinion pose important questions and prompt diverse interpretations about their strengths and weaknesses in American constitutional democracy.

? ISSUES TO ANALYZE

ISSUE 1   *ARE THE MASS MEDIA TOO POWERFUL?*

REASONS WHY THE MASS MEDIA ARE TOO POWERFUL

Aleksandr Solzhenitsyn declared that the American press is "more powerful than the legislature, the executive and judiciary" and that it is guilty of making heroes out of terrorists, giving away national secrets, unnecessarily invading the privacy of public figures, and violating the public's right *not* to know. Concerning the last charge, Solzhenitsyn contended that the press prints information the public cares nothing about reading or hearing. His indictment also stated that the press misinforms, distorts the news, and does not correct its errors. Finally, he said that the press limits the thoughts and ideas it prints to a very narrow range that fits with its preconceptions about what is right and best.[17] Solzhenitsyn may have been too severe in his description of the media's power. But these certainly are legitimate grounds for concern about the power of the media, as can be seen when we examine the concentration of the media and the effect of commercialism.

Concentration. The journalist A. J. Liebling once noted that "a large number of competing newspapers, permitting representation of various shades of thought, are a country's best defense against being stampeded into barbarism." The United States no longer has this defense, for virtual monopolies exist on all phases of mass communications. As Liebling observed, "The American newspaper industry has become a series of local elimination tournaments, like Golden Gloves boxing."[18]

As shown in Table 6.3, daily newspapers, once the major source of news in the United States, are gradually disappearing. In 1920 there were just over 2000 dailies; by 1992 there were under 1600. Of the 50 largest cities in the country, about one-half are served by a single newspaper. Most American cities, regardless of size, have only one newspaper.

Pressure to concentrate ownership has been intensified by recent Supreme Court decisions limiting the protections granted to newspapers under the First Amendment's guarantee of freedom of the press (discussed in Chapter 14). Independent newspapers now find it more difficult to defend themselves against lawsuits charging them with libel or infringement on the right to a fair trial. Legal costs as well as loss of lawsuits present major financial burdens.

TABLE 6.3 DAILY NEWSPAPERS IN AMERICA: 1920–1992	
Date	Number
1920	2042
1930	1942
1940	1878
1950	1772
1960	1763
1970	1748
1980	1745
1990	1611
1992	1586

Source: *Historical Statistics of the United States*, p. 809; *Editor and Publisher Yearbook*, 1992, p. 1.

Just six media companies—CBS, RCA, Time-Warner, Times Mirror, *The New York Times*, and *The Washington Post*—generate more than $10 billion annually in revenues, and they own radio and television stations as well as book and magazine publishing houses. All but RCA publish magazines, and all but CBS and RCA publish newspapers.

Television, with its enormous potential for educating and informing the public, reaches into about 100 million American homes. Yet only the Public Broadcasting System (PBS) and the Cable News Network (CNN) provide any significant nationwide competition for the news services of the three major networks—ABC, CBS, and NBC—and, at the local level, only scattered religious and independent channels with limited viewing audiences offer alternatives to the public. By the early 1990s the FOX network was competing successfully for a national audience with its entertainment programs, but was offering very little in the way of news or public service.

Although there is not as much concentration in radio ownership, local stations customarily depend on national networks for national and international news. In addition to the three major networks, the Mutual Broadcasting System and the wire services (such as the Associated Press) provide news for local affiliates.

The same corporation sometimes owns both radio and television stations as well as a daily newspaper in the same city. For example, in Chicago, *The Chicago Tribune* newspaper owns both WGN radio and WGN-TV as well as media outlets in other cities, providing that conglomerate with a larger circulation than any other newspaper in the United States.

Commercialism. The Federal Communications Act of 1934 granted owners of commercial broadcasting stations the rights to public airways without charging a penny, which is somewhat like giving away oil drilling rights on public property. Besides this, however, the commercial incentive has several broad effects.

First, broadcasting stations and newspapers may oppose changes in laws or regulations that would adversely affect their profits, including changes in the free grant they receive to the public airways. Media owners are not likely to encourage expression of opposing points of view on legal and regulatory changes that might harm their profitability. Second, mass media companies that provide goods or services for defense and space programs, such as RCA, are unlikely to support cuts in defense or space expenditures. Third, many mass media, such as *The New York Times* and *The Los Angeles Times*, own pollution-producing paper mills. They are not likely to support legal and regulatory changes that would impair the profits of these businesses.

Obviously, radio stations do not consider news programming very profitable, since only 5 minutes of every 60 are customarily devoted to news, and the news is a mere summary rather than an in-depth analysis. Exceptions are the few all-news stations in the big cities and National Public Radio (NPR).

Newspapers, except for a few like the *The New York Times* and the *The Christian Science Monitor*, tend to cater to their readers with local and sensational stories rather than national and analytical stories. Since advertisers want to have the widest possible circulation, newspapers tend to concentrate on those stories that will increase their circulation.

Conservatism. Not only does concentration of ownership reduce alternative points of view and commercialism make independent journalism difficult, but there is also a bias toward conservatism that further underscores monopoly control of the media. To illustrate, most newspapers editorially endorse Republican candidates for President, and the most widely syndicated political columnists in daily newspapers are conservatives like James J. Kilpatrick and George Will.

The combination of commercialism, concentration, and conservatism may have led to reduced expenditures devoted to investigative reporting. An **investigative reporter** is a journalist who searches through the activities of public organizations seeking to expose conduct contrary to the public interest. The pioneers in popular journalism—William Randolph Hearst, Joseph Pulitzer, and E. W. Scripps—protected ordinary citizens from giant corporations and utilities, unfeeling governments, and even from the status quo. Where there is little competition among the mass media the public lacks one of the most important safeguards of democracy—the ability to be fully informed. Various reforms have been suggested to remedy the monopoly situation: (1) The government might subsidize newspapers to compete in one-newspaper communities, (2) a board or commission with enforcement powers could be established to serve as a watchdog of media fairness, or (3) corporations that own more than one media outlet in a city might be required to relinquish all but one outlet.

REASONS WHY THE MASS MEDIA ARE NOT TOO POWERFUL

Is concentration necessarily bad? If two newspapers are competing for the same market and therefore for the same advertising, would they not be both tempted to report news in ways (including slanting the news) that would enhance sales and increase advertising? On the other hand, if only one newspaper controls a given market, would it not have more freedom from this temptation? The public and the advertisers in the latter instance would have one newspaper outlet while in the former they could use economic leverage to force the newspapers into a particular editorial position or stance on news. In any case, the government has instituted regulations to help break up concentration of ownership. In 1975 the FCC ruled that a radio station, newspaper, or television station cannot acquire ownership of another media outlet in the same market area.

Commercialism, as reflected in sales of advertising space and copies of publications, is an indicator of public preferences. If neither space nor copies are sold in sufficient quantity, there is reason to believe that the public does not particularly favor the medium—or, at least, its message. This situation itself reflects the mass media's inability to control public opinion. No one is forcing the public to buy what the media produce.

While the owners of the mass media tend to be conservative, their reporters tend to be liberal, particularly on the flagship papers like the *The New York Times* and *The Washington Post*. A recent survey of 1400 American journalists found that around 44 percent identify themselves as Democrats compared to only 16 percent who call themselves Republicans. A little more than 34 percent claim to be independents (Figure 6.1). Their rate of Democratic affiliation runs about 5 to 10 percentage points higher than that of the general public.[19] According to one conservative media analyst, "The media [are] becoming a safe haven for the left in this country."[20]

Yet the liberal bias of reporters does not necessarily get conveyed in the media. Studies of the 1980 and 1984 presidential campaigns suggest that network television news did not give a significantly larger amount of coverage to either the Republican or Democratic candidates, showed essentially no ideological bias in favor of either conservatives or liberals, and generally avoided loaded adverbs and adjectives, such as "far right" and

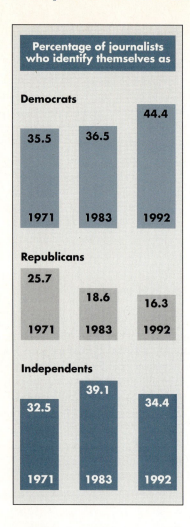

Figure 6.1 THE PRESS AND ITS POLITICS. Source: Freedom Forum survey reported in *The New York Times*, November 18, 1992, p. A20.

"far left," in describing the campaigns' events and personalities.[21] Generally journalists seem more interested in covering candidates who attract attention than in advancing a particular agenda.

Liberals who argue that conservative ownership unfairly skews public opinion may take solace from the outcome of some important political races. In all four of Franklin D. Roosevelt's presidential campaigns, newspaper owners were overwhelmingly opposed to him, but he won every time. In 1960 John F. Kennedy won against this same widespread opposition as did Jimmy Carter in 1976 (see Table 6.4, p. 190).

Another factor reining in media power is that the public does not totally depend on any one source for its news. The public's choices of news sources, allowing for multiple choices, show that 65 percent choose television and 44 percent, newspapers, with a growing number choosing magazines, which have about 20 percent more readers today than in the mid-1970s.[22] And among these sources are a number of alternatives, including independent cable networks, religious channels, and others. Thus, traditional voices in the media have become less influential as alternative voices have increased.

Critics suggest that the news media should devote more of their resources to investigative reporting. There are at least two reasons why this could not or should not be done. First, most media outlets do not have the financial resources to undertake extensive investigative reporting. Second, the media would be duplicating information already provided by the government through such activities as criminal investigations and congressional hearings. The role for the media in investigative reporting should be a supplementary and complementary role rather than a duplicating one. Of course, there are occasional instances when the media *should* act as an adversary to governmental interest. The Watergate scandal in the 1970s and Irangate in the 1980s are two examples of needed media investigation.

Actually, increased concentration of media ownership can benefit the public in this area. Since the large chains have more financial resources at their disposal, they can afford to finance more investigative reporting. Gannett newspapers have won several Pulitzer prizes in noncompetitive markets by upgrading and expanding news coverage following acquisition of newspapers.

Critics also imply that the media should educate the public, even if the public is relentlessly stubborn about becoming educated. To what extent are the media obligated to impose education on the public? Would it be democratic, for instance, to make the three national television networks abandon most of their entertainment programs in favor of news programs? If we assume that the people govern in a democracy, should not the public's tastes and interests dictate more to the media than the reverse?

Finally, there is a growing movement among newspapers to employ an ombudsman who serves as a watchdog over the newspaper to criticize its stories in the interest of improving quality and fairness. Such ombudsmen sometimes write columns in the paper to show readers that something is being done to air their grievances about unfair reporting. Independent watchdog groups, such as Accuracy in the Media, also help to police the media.

ISSUE 1: Summary ★ *Are the Mass Media Too Powerful?*

Although there is substantial concentration of ownership among the media, in recent years public reading and viewing habits have shown greater diversification. And while the media are powerful, they are not overwhelmingly controlled by either conservative or liberal forces; moreover, media watchdogs now help police the media. ■

ISSUE 2 IS COLLUSION BETWEEN THE MASS MEDIA AND THE GOVERNMENT A SERIOUS PROBLEM?

REASONS WHY COLLUSION IS A SERIOUS PROBLEM

Public opinion on many issues reflects the limited or biased information released by the press. But one of the most important factors in limiting and slanting that information is the government itself. During and after the Persian Gulf War, two charges about press coverage stand out: (1) that the government kept the media from reporting fully and fairly on the war, and (2) that some members of the media received

TABLE 6.4 NEWSPAPER ENDORSEMENTS OF PRESIDENTIAL CANDIDATES, SELECTED YEARS 1944–1992

	PAPERS	
	Number	Percentage
1944		
Dewey (R)	796	60%
Roosevelt (D)*	291	22%
Uncommitted	237	18%
1948		
Dewey (R)	771	65%
Truman (D)*	182	15%
Thurmond	45	4%
Wallace	3	0%
Uncommitted	182	15%
1952		
Eisenhower (R)*	933	67%
Stevenson (D)	202	15%
Uncommitted	250	18%
1960		
Nixon (R)	731	58%
Kennedy (D)*	208	16%
Uncommitted	328	26%
1964		
Goldwater (R)	359	35%
Johnson (D)*	440	42%
Uncommitted	237	23%
1968		
Nixon (R)*	634	61%
Humphrey (D)	146	14%
Wallace	12	1%
Uncommitted	250	24%
1976		
Ford (R)	411	60%
Carter (D)*	80	12%
Uncommitted	168	26%
1980		
Reagan (R)*	443	42%
Carter (D)	126	12%
Anderson	40	4%
Uncommitted	439	42%
1988		
Bush (R)*	241	31%
Dukakis (D)	103	13%
Uncommitted	428	55%

(continued)

TABLE 6.4 *(CONTINUED)*

	PAPERS	
	Number	Percentage
1992		
Bush (R)	138	15%
Clinton (D)*	183	20%
Perot	4	0%
Uncommitted	559	63%

* Indicates winner.
Source: *Editor & Publisher* November 4, 1944, p. 9; October 30, 1948, p. 11; November 1, 1952, p. 9; November 5, 1960, p. 10; October 31, 1964, p. 10; November 2, 1968, p. 9; October 30, 1976, p. 5; November 1, 1980, p. 10; November 5, 1988, p. 9; November 7, 1992, p. 15.

favored treatment from the government, allowing them to report stories unavailable to other reporters. Regardless of how the dust settles on these and other charges, the fact remains that during the war, the media, particularly the owners, made no serious effort to resist limitations imposed by the government, such as prohibitions on journalists' interviewing people in private, making interview appointments on their own, or going to their interview appointments without a military escort.

At times the media have acceded to government pressures not to air certain programs or report certain stories. President John F. Kennedy's handling of the press before the ill-fated invasion of Cuba in 1962 is a classic example of manipulation. Several press people, including representatives of *The New York Times, The New Republic,* and *The Miami Herald,* knew that the CIA was training Cuban exiles for an invasion. At the request of the government, they did not report this until it was too late to stop American involvement. After the debacle, Kennedy told the managing editor of *The New York Times:* "If you had printed more about the operation, you would have saved us from a colossal mistake."[23]

In this case, reporters had kept silent out of consideration for national security, at least as it was presented to them. In other instances, motives may be less patriotic. Corporate interests may play a part. The Chandler family, which owns *The Los Angeles Times,* also has substantial investments in television stations, lumber and steel companies, railroads, airlines, food stores, banking, farming, publishing, and oil. Since federal regulation can be vital in such enterprises, the *Times* might be expected to tread carefully where the government is concerned.

The president of the United States, perhaps the most newsworthy public figure in the world, can generally command television time at will. This situation creates enormous potential for collusion between television and the government. The president can dominate television news, with its penchant for brief sound-bites and photo opportunities.* President Reagan used television to go directly to the American public over the heads of the print press, which was frequently hostile to his positions on issues. President Bush refined the technique even more with his quick response to questions as he moved from place to place, such as leaving the White House to board the presidential helicopter for a weekend at Camp David with his advisors. Presidents can also create news that the television networks feel obligated to cover.

The government also has numerous ways of controlling the mass media. Among them are blatant lying, the manipulation of media personnel, and abuse of government information policies.

Lying. Does the government lie to the press and public? The Vietnam War, which ultimately claimed over 58,000 American lives, began without acceptable factual evidence of a provocation against the United States. According to President Lyndon Johnson, three North Vietnamese PT boats attacked two American destroyers, the *Maddox* and the *Turner Joy*, in the Gulf of Tonkin on August 2, 1964. Actually, the first shots were fired by the *Maddox*, there were no American casualties, and only one machine gun bullet fired by a PT boat struck the *Maddox*.[24] The Watergate episode provides a rich trove of examples of government lying. For ten months after the initial break-in at the Democratic party headquarters, aides of President Richard Nixon denied that they were aware of the planning and execution of the incident or that they had participated in a cover-up of the resulting scandal. When the White House later acknowledged some involvement, it termed previous misstatements on the subject "inoperative."

Manipulation of Media Personnel. Reporters depend on government sources for many news stories. Recognizing this fact, departments and agencies of government reward media personnel with information if they write favorable reports and punish them by withholding information if stories are unfavorable. This situation may substantially impair a reporter's professional standards. Washington reporter Robert Walters described the granting and withholding of favors:

> You get invited to the agency's parties. Not that the bureaucrats are consciously trying to co-opt you. They just want to get to know you better and make you feel more kindly toward them. But then if you get into a shoving match with them over some story, you get the stick instead of the carrot. You not only don't get invited to the parties, what's more important you don't get invited to the background briefings. . . . It becomes a totally symbiotic relationship.[25]

The nature of this symbiotic relationship—one in which both sides need and help each other—is further illustrated by a senior reporter: "Send a young reporter to the White House and let him indulge in a presidential trip or two and he isn't worth [anything] for six months. He gets on a first-name basis with these clowns, he gets to indulge in fancy drinks and big hotel rooms that he couldn't otherwise afford, and he's wiped out."[26]

Reporters may be used by government officials to satisfy grudges or conduct quarrels in public. Some reporters have received praise for their investigative reporting

---

* This is not always a good thing, especially when mishaps occur. In January 1992, for example, President Bush visited Japan where, at a state dinner, he became ill and collapsed.

when the real credit belonged to disgruntled bureaucrats who blew the whistle on their bosses by leaking information to the press. Although *The New York Times* credited Neil Sheehan's investigative reporting for the Pentagon Papers story—the revelation of classified documents detailing the government's involvement in the Vietnam conflict—it was an unhappy government analyst, Daniel Ellsberg, who actually gave the story to the newspaper. Newspapers get most of their best stories because somebody wants the story out. Investigative reporters are not necessarily getting material nobody wants them to have.[27]

Officially released government information may be handled in such a way that the press connives in its own manipulation. A major technique in this exercise is the **backgrounder.** Here government officials provide information to reporters on condition that it be relayed without attribution; that is, when the news is released, the identity of the government official must not be revealed. (Hence, stories are attributed to "a high government official" or "White House informants.")

Another factor that strengthens the government's hand in dealing with reporters is reporters' lack of specialized training. A liberal arts graduate in journalism, English, or political science, for example, is usually not trained to assess complex technical issues in economics, space and nuclear science, or military strategy.

Abuse of Government Policies. According to the 1966 Freedom of Information Act, the public is to have relatively easy access to government information, except for that protected by security regulations. To protect itself—and also to prevent the public from acquiring data—the government has classified a good deal of material as secret. Departments and agencies spend millions each year just to stamp documents "secret" and keep them out of general circulation. The government can also refuse to release certain information on the grounds that its release would violate an individual's or company's right to its "trade secret" in government records. Ralph Nader, a consumer advocate since the 1960s, observed a generation ago, "The more I look into the trade secret area, the more I realize that it isn't a trade secret between competitors—they know all about it— it's a trade secret against consumers or against the public."[28]

The government can use delays to avoid releasing information that is supposed to be available to the press and public. It can deny that information exists or maintain that it is being compiled, thus preventing it from being published. In the case of the Pentagon Papers—which had already been leaked—the government succeeded in delaying their publication for 15 days through court action.

REASONS WHY COLLUSION IS NOT A SERIOUS PROBLEM

How much collusion is there, in fact, between the media and government? Certainly a hand-in-glove relationship did not characterize the Vietnam War, the Watergate affair, and the Irangate scandal. Even if one does concede a certain amount of complicity, whether overt or not, the actual effect on public opinion may be exaggerated. Five factors point to the weakness in the collusion argument.

First, what might be called popular skepticism toward both the government and the media is fairly widespread, making it difficult for these forces to control public opinion. In fact, the more the public knows about an event, the more skeptical it is of media accuracy.[29] And the Watergate and Irangate episodes simply added to the distrust already felt for public officials.

Second, primary groups—family, neighborhood, peers, and other person-to-person contacts—are effective filters in the public opinion process. As noted earlier, these groups generally have more influence on the formation of one's opinion than televised speeches. Even if the media promote a certain governmental view, it is often conveyed through, and altered by, family and friends. Parents, for example, often interpret the meaning of an election for their children.

Third, lack of public awareness may inhibit the potential of the media and government to influence public opinion. The public may simply have a "nonopinion." Of course, lack of public awareness may allow the government more latitude to do as it pleases without reference to public opinion. The government must, however, face the danger that its decisions and policies will arouse latent public opinion. Opinion is divided on whether public awareness is a danger or an asset to democracy. Walter Lippmann noted the dangers of the public's being *too* aware and *too* active.

> *Where mass opinion dominates the government, there is a morbid derangement of the true functions of power. The derangement brings about the enfeeblement, verging on paralysis, of the capacity to govern. This breakdown in the Constitutional order is the cause of the precipitate and catastrophic decline of Western society. It may, if it cannot be arrested and reversed, bring about the fall of the West.*[30]

On the other hand, Robert E. Lane has argued that nonparticipation may be a greater liability than participation.[31] While the significance of lack of public awareness is debatable, it does appear that the public is not waiting with bated breath for the next pronouncement from the mass media, whether government-inspired or not.

Fourth, have Washington and the media *prevented* issues from being raised about government performance? Hardly. The media may occasionally neglect to raise important questions, but crusading individuals and public interest organizations, such as Ralph Nader and Common Cause, have stepped in to take up the slack. Nader, for example, raised the issue of automobile safety, and Common Cause pioneered in the issue of congressional ethics.

Fifth, the media and the government often engage in an adversarial relationship, which indicates that the argument about collusion is weak. **Adversary journalism** automatically and relentlessly views the government as an enemy to be distrusted. Retired White House correspondent Vermont Royster has noted that "one consequence is that presidents today try to say no more at a press conference than what might be put as well in a carefully drafted statement. The president has thus lost an opportunity to share his thought processes, which without being the stuff of tomorrow's headlines could help them [reporters] do a better job informing their readers and listeners."[32] President Bush implicitly acknowledged this adversarial relationship by promoting what he called his favorite bumper sticker in the 1992 election campaign: "Annoy the media, Re-elect Bush."

Critics of media-government cooperation appear to assume that the government (the different branches and agencies) should compete with its own position by putting out information adverse to its interests. But what degree of confidence could the public have in its government if the government constantly released information conflicting with existing policy? Its ability to govern would be undermined in such a situation. In

ANNOY THE MEDIA
RE-ELECT BUSH

Occasionally the media and the government find themselves adversaries. George Bush took a swipe at the media for what he thought was biased coverage of the 1992 election.

addition, the public actually benefits from "backgrounders" since more information is provided than if the government and the press did not cooperate. There are times when government officials want the public to have information but do not want to be identified with it. By anonymously releasing such data, the government official makes available information that will help to provide a more complete debate on the issue at stake.

ISSUE 2: Summary ★ *Is Collusion Between the Mass Media and Government a Serious Problem?*

In specific instances close relationships between government and the media have been unhealthy, but there have also been cases of unhealthy adversarial relationships. These examples of collusion on the one hand and adversary journalism on the other are the extreme and not the norm. Just as a relationship dominated by collusion would be detrimental to democracy, so too would one dominated by adversary journalism. Collusion may be in order at times (protecting, for example, identification of military maneuvers), just as at other times (during Watergate, for example) adversarial journalism is preferable. On the whole, however, the press is more of a watchdog than either a friend or an enemy fighting the government. ■

ISSUE 3   *SHOULD ELECTRONIC DEMOCRACY BE USED TO DETERMINE PUBLIC POLICY?*

REASONS WHY ELECTRONIC DEMOCRACY SHOULD BE USED TO DETERMINE PUBLIC POLICY

Inasmuch as the word *democracy* means people govern or rule, public opinion should be allowed to determine public policy. This historic definition, given to us by the Greeks some 400 years B.C., needs to be implemented even more in American public life to improve democracy now that the electronic capability exists to do so. **Electronic democracy** would utilize television, computers, and other electronic means to conduct such events as nationwide town meetings for debate and voting on public policy issues. Third-party candidate Ross Perot recognized this capability during his campaign when he said that if elected he would convene such electronic nationwide town meetings on a regular basis.

Giving the public a greater role in the determination of public policy could serve to increase support for public policies and trust in the government and public officials. Electronic democracy would also be a way to make public officials more responsive to the public will, which would be clearly and definitively expressed through debates and voting by electronic means. For example, the drama of a nationwide town meeting on, say, congressional ethics could cause members of Congress to stop using legislative procedures to delay or to conceal what they are doing.

Allowing the public a greater voice in public policy could foster more interest in government as well as support for what government does, since the public would recognize its role in what is being decided. Our nation has sometimes pursued policies that the public opposed or was not adequately informed about, such as the Vietnam War. If America's involvement in Vietnam had been thoroughly debated through the use of electronic means, America's involvement there would have been less likely.

Finally, the idea of granting the public greater influence in determining public policy might lead to the creation of the initiative and referendum nationwide, devices used in many states that allow the public to initiate legislation and constitutional amendments or to vote directly on legislative proposals. The **initiative** permits the public to bypass the legislature by petitioning to put a proposition on the ballot and then to vote on that proposition, while the **referendum** allows the public to check the action of the legislature by petitioning to vote on a proposal of the legislature.

REASONS WHY ELECTRONIC DEMOCRACY SHOULD NOT BE USED TO DETERMINE PUBLIC POLICY

The reasons just stated in favor of electronic democracy not only are simplistic, but also overlook the liabilities of increasing the public's role in determining public policy. First, today's issues are complex, defying easy solutions that can be encapsulated in a nutshell on television and in speedy voting by computers. Environmental proposals can be simplistically presented to gain overwhelming public support, but the same public might significantly modify its position if it knew all of the consequences of a particular proposal, such as loss of jobs. Public policymaking should not become the

Hello, this is the Clinton White House. If you think we should attack the deficit first, punch 1 on your touch-tone phone. If you think growth is more important, punch 2. If you think a gas tax is OK, punch 3. If you think entitlements are the problem, punch 4. If you think health care....

captive of the simplistic sloganeering opportunities that television and computers make possible.

Second, popular decisions usually reflect immediate desires and personal interests rather than the long-term interests of society as a whole. Elected representatives are in a better position to set aside immediate personal and partisan considerations to vote for what is in the national interest. In California, the public has voted for initiatives that in the long run have been costly to their interests, particularly limitations on taxes that later undermined the ability of state and local governments to maintain roads and highways and to support public schools.

Third, decisions must often be made in a crisis, especially in foreign policy, and should not be subjected to the delay of debates. Here again, sophisticated understanding of the nuances and subtleties of foreign policy is essential in making wise decisions.

Fourth, American democracy is representative, or republican: The people elect representatives to make decisions for them. Electronic democracy would undermine this fundamental idea of the Founders, which is clearly embodied in the Constitution. The Founders emphasized thought and reflection by representatives in the making of public policy, not speed and action by the populace. Extended debate and hearings over a long period of time are more likely to produce the best public policy than brief electronically conducted, nationwide town meetings and their computerized voting results.

ISSUE 3: Summary ★ *Should Electronic Democracy Be Used to Determine Public Policy?*

Electronic democracy would truly allow the people to increase their ability to rule. A greater role in determining policy would serve to increase support for government, interest in what it does, and trust in its actions. It could also lead to institution of the initiative and the referendum on a nationwide basis. Arguments against electronic democracy emphasize the complexity of issues today, the need to take into acount long-term national interests rather than short-term personal concerns, and the necessity of making some decisions quickly, especially in the area of foreign policy. Moreover, our Founders established a republican form of government in which representatives were intended to make decisions on behalf of the public. ■

COMPARISONS WITH OTHER NATIONS

PUBLIC OPINION AND THE MASS MEDIA IN DEMOCRACIES

The Media

Like Americans, other Western democratic societies also enjoy a vast amount of freedom of expression. And they do express themselves. The arrival of cable television, VCRs, personal computers, fax machines, and even vision phones has accelerated a relentless process of personal and political communication that has been well under way for generations. The revolution of technology has been contagious across the globe. The democracies, in particular, tend to watch one another's television programs and see one another's movies. But before the Soviet Union dissolved, Russians were fond of smuggling in videotapes from the United States and Western Europe whose subject matter ranged from comedies such as the 1960s film hit, *The Russians Are Coming, The Russians Are Coming,* to pornography. Most people in the industrial world depend on television for most of their political information and, as a direct result, for most of their political opinions. But newspapers do reach a large market as well, more so in Western Europe and Japan than in the United States, as Figure 6.2 shows.

Both technology and insatiable public interest have also produced a new dimension of politics for democracies: the exposure of the most intimate details of personal lives of government leaders. It can be argued that the public has the right and perhaps the obligation to stay informed about presidential health problems. But in the United States national careers can be easily ruined on the basis of a single sexual indiscretion, as former Colorado Democratic senator Gary Hart can testify. Not even the families of public figures are safe. The biography of Nancy Reagan by Kitty Kelley suggested that the former first lady had engaged in premarital sex, smoked marijuana, and committed adultery, activities that Mrs. Reagan had spent a good deal of time publicly condemning.[33]

It isn't much different elsewhere. Members of the British royal family often read about themselves in the morning newspapers. During Prince Andrew's career as a bachelor, for example, wide coverage was given to his alleged escapades with a soft porn movie star. The breakup of his marriage to Sarah Ferguson ("Fergy," as she is sometimes known in irreverent tabloids) in 1992 was front-page news for a week or so. His older brother and heir to the throne, Charles, found that his marital troubles with Princess Diana were even more newsworthy. The way politicians and ceremonial heads of state and their families behave in their private lives has become public domain in most democracies.

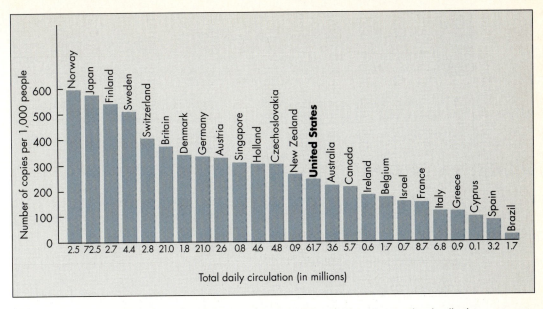

Figure 6.2 NEWSPAPER READERSHIP AND CIRCULATION, 1991. Norway leads all other nations in newspaper readership, with sales of close to 600 copies a day per 1000 people. The United States falls fairly low on the list: Its daily sales total only 244 copies per 1000 people. At the bottom of the graph are figures on total daily circulation of papers. Notice that Japan tops the list with 72.5 million papers, shared among just 124 titles. Source: *The Economist*, November 28, 1992, p. 119. Data from "World Press Trends, 1992."

Americans are unfamiliar with a muzzled or censured press, but much of the world isn't. According to Freedom House, barely two out of five countries enjoy the type of free press that would be familiar to a citizen living in a full-fledged democracy. As Figure 6.3 suggests, government control of the media varies substantially. And it is important to point out that even within the democratic societies there is not complete consistency. Notice, for example, the slight difference in media control between the United Kingdom and the United States. It can be fairly stated that the United States has maximized freedom of the press with barely any restraints. But Britain does not have a totally unrestrained press. During the years of Prime Minister Thatcher's government (1979–1990), Britain

> banned several books and news reports about [Irish terrorists], and limited television coverage. . . . The courts, belatedly, have not sustained the bans. Bills before Parliament would empower government appointees to oversee the content of broadcast programming, and refuse to license an independent television company if it is judged "not in the public interest." The U.K. still has a lively, free press. But it exists without the protection of a written constitution, and not without threats.[34]

The contrast between American and British approaches to media control was highlighted in 1986 when the British Broadcasting Corporation (BBC) refused to air an

A VIEW FROM THE STATES
Trashing the Royal Family

That great lady Queen Elizabeth II said in a speech at the Guildhall marking the 40th year of her reign that 1992 has been an "annus horribilis."

The banquet hall at Windsor Castle, her favorite residence, burned. Some of her subjects in Parliament want her to pay taxes (which she had told the prime minister privately she would be glad to do), even though her voluntary contributions and those of the Prince of Wales to the Treasury probably dwarf the allowance she draws to maintain her position, the so-called civil list. Worse, her younger in-laws have been making spectacles of themselves, literally so in the case of the Duchess of York.

Some of the trouble is self-inflicted, but more of the recent deterioration is a product of the great media revolution of our day. London tabloids, feasting on royal scandal, make America's National Enquirer look as staid, by comparison, as the Christian Science Monitor. Royal scandal is an old story, and so is the odd outburst of republican sentiment in England. The novelty is that the rags of Fleet Street observe less restraint than ever.

Even admirers of the great institution of press freedom have to wonder at times what we think we're getting in exchange for all these dreary and prurient invasions of privacy. It is now the creed on both sides of the Atlantic that public personages have no entitlement to privacy. Yet as recently as the abdication crisis of 1936, brought on by the present queen's uncle's love affair with an American divorcee, the press kept the lid on for a remarkably long time. Some sense then still survived of the fragility of institutions whose foundations are primarily mythic and symbolic.

Britain has tough libel laws, more protective of privacy than America's. But the tabloid press is well aware that the queen and her family are at their mercy. She could sue, but only at the cost of amplifying the gossip and fiction. She asked, the other day, for a bit of "gentleness and humor" in the journalistic treatment of the "firm," as I gather she likes to call the monarchy. Good luck!

Source: Edwin M. Yoder, Jr. (Washington Post Writers Group), "Why Trash This Symbol of Civility?" *International Herald Tribune*, December 2, 1992.

interview with Martin McGuiness, a leader of the Irish Republican Army, because of the pressure exerted by the government, which is instrumental in renewing its broadcasting charter. Around the same time the National Broadcasting Company (NBC) aired an interview with Abul Abbas, the leader of the Palestine Liberation Front, an organization that has promised to bring political violence to the United States.[35] The American government was officially upset by the fact that the Abbas interview was conducted and even more so since NBC apparently knew where Abbas was then residing and the government didn't, but it did nothing to try to prevent the broadcast.

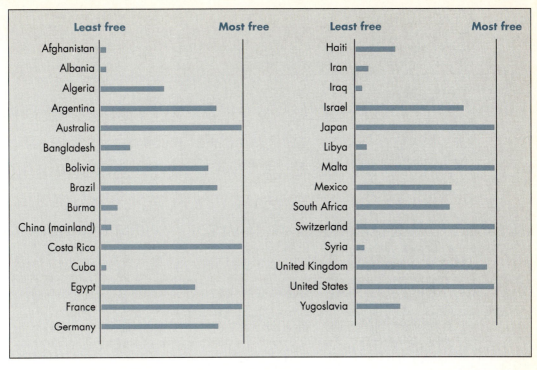

Figure 6.3 NEWS MEDIA CONTROL, BY SELECTED COUNTRIES. Source: "News Media Control by Countries," *Freedom Review*, Vol. 22, No. 1 (1991), pp. 32–33, Freedom House, New York, NY 10005.

Responding to Public Opinion

In a political democracy the elected government carefully monitors public opinions expressed about various issues. Parliamentary systems have another reason for watching public opinion polls very closely. In contrast to the United States, where the timing of elections is constitutionally prescribed, a prime minister in a parliamentary government can, within limitations, decide to have an election just when the polls show that he or she is most popular. In 1983 British Prime Minister Thatcher decided to call for an election immediately after Britain had won back the Falkland Islands from Argentina. President Bush might have done something similar in 1991 after humbling Saddam Hussein in the Persian Gulf War had Article I, section 2, of the Constitution not stipulated that national legislative elections would be held "every second year."

Advocates of political democracy agree that an informed public is essential for the functioning of a polity. Most members of democracies have access to political information but don't take regular advantage of it. It is unfair to blame this lack of interest solely on people's apathy: They are swamped with information (much of it contradictory). In fact, they have too much information to consume properly. The number of issues and opinions about them are historically unprecedented: "In nineteenth-century England, it was probably easier for the electorate to understand issues than it is today. Fewer big political problems faced government, and often these required a straight decision in principle, such as whether or not to expand the franchise. Today, many more problems are defined as political."[36] All of this becomes especially cumbersome in democracies, if only because it is relatively easy to politicize many issues. Increasingly, democracy's citizens look to government to resolve problems.

Governments, like people, are very sensitive to criticism. But in democracies, governments must also learn to be tolerant—even to the point of allowing wholesale indictments to be published. A case in point is P. J. O'Rourke's *Parliament of Whores: A Lone Humorist's Attempt to Explain the Entire Federal Government*.[37] To be sure, this is an extreme example. The author refers to the American federal system as the "great slime engine of government."[38] Perhaps this is a slight and rather harsh exaggeration, but it has a great deal of public sympathy. And it is safe to say that its counterpart can be found in other political systems.

PUBLIC OPINION AND THE MASS MEDIA IN TOTALITARIAN SYSTEMS

Hundreds of millions of people in the Soviet Union and all over the world got to see pictures of Russian President Boris Yeltsin standing on top of a Soviet tank in August 1991 in a gesture of defiance toward the hardliners' coup. His personal and political courage went a long way toward ensuring his own popularity as well as the collapse of the coup. The coup revealed, among other things, that even a totalitarian system can no longer avoid becoming a media event. A global network of sophisticated electronic communications has probably doomed totalitarianism, if we allow for some isolated exceptions such as North Korea, Cuba, and the remaining major totalitarian state of China.

For about 95 percent of its history, however, opinions in the Soviet Union were submerged. Public curiosity about political leaders in nondemocratic societies is rarely aroused let alone satisfied. While still a thoroughgoing totalitarian system, the Soviet Union began to both manufacture and manipulate the opinions of children. The theory was that the younger the mind the easier it is to create lasting impressions that are consistent with the desires of the regime.

This process of socialization worked for about three-quarters of a century. In fact, it worked all too well since Soviet education discouraged children from asking questions or coming up with innovative solutions to problems. A quick look at the Soviet curriculum helps to explain why: Courses in the social sciences, humanities, and history were ideological in their content, and a tenth of class time was consumed by political concerns.[39] In the early 1980s expressing an unauthorized opinion was still a physically dangerous thing to do. By the early 1990s, however, as democratization swept over the communist bloc, the Soviets began to expect more from their government. It became almost fashionable to express an opinion. A close observer of this trend, Hedrick Smith, made a pertinent observation:

> The most widely watched program [in the Soviet Union] is the nightly 600 Seconds (Shestot Sekunduv), a graphic, ten-minute news kaleidoscope, featuring crime, corruption, and sensation. Its anchor, Alexandr Nevzorov, was once a movie stuntman and singer in a church choir. Now, at thirty-one years old [in 1990], he is a full-tilt ambulance chaser. He can cover thirteen news bits in ten minutes. His topics range from how rotting meat is ground into sausages at a Leningrad factory, to how radioactivity emanates from old Soviet

Totalitarian systems cannot control the images that get beamed around the globe via modern media technology. The sight of a lone man challenging Chinese tanks in Beijing during the student unrest of June 1989 made a huge impression throughout the world.

helicopters in a children's park, to a trip to the morgue to report on the tragic suicide leap of a woman and her two small children.[40]

Communist systems control the media but the task is not as easy as it might appear since the government may face both a literate population and radio broadcasts originating from abroad. They must also deal with international media within their borders. In June 1989, Chinese university students protesting against the oppression of their own government became victims themselves in Beijing's Tiananmen Square. The tragedy angered and sickened a great many people who believed that Chinese communism was finally beginning to mellow. The government denied that anything very important had occurred and disavowed the stains of dried blood in the square, but since foreign correspondents were in the capital city at the time, a more accurate and horrifying story emerged. Even in as tightly controlled a totalitarian system as China's the necessity of compromise with modern media technology and the desire to belong to the rest of the world, at least commercially, precluded complete control over information. The picture of a lone student defying an advancing tank electrified the world and completed the political bankruptcy of this last major totalitarian system.

In totalitarian societies the media behave as agents of government policy, as responsible as any governmental ministry for successfully carrying out policy. In fact, in some cases, public opinion has the status of a cabinet ministry. In Nazi Germany, for example, the Ministry of Propaganda and Culture provided the print and electronic media with "information" demonstrating that all of Germany's problems were the result of a conspiracy among American capitalists, Soviet communists, and international Jewry.

Subsequent totalitarian systems have not been slow to pick up on the convenient device of scapegoating. By attributing all sorts of troubles to a single person or a collective of people regarded as enemies of the state, the regime escapes responsibility for economic and social ills, at least for a while. The scapegoat, of course, is usually completely defenseless as well as innocent, and probably suffers from the same problems as everyone else. No matter. The government can pursue the policy of scapegoatism even to the point of genocide. More frighteningly, the policy may have a modicum of public support. Table 6.5 summarizes two extreme and violent examples in this century.

While totalitarian systems have an aversion to bad news, a constant habit of producing nothing but good news is boring. Aware that the Soviet public could handle only so many record grain harvest reports, the evening news (the most popular program on Soviet television) until its last years spiced up its diet of happiness with features on terrible conditions in the United States. This news emphasis was especially noticeable during the turbulent years of the 1960s. Soviet television enthusiastically featured race riots in the cities and antiwar demonstrations all over the country. The United States was portrayed as a decadent and violent capitalist society whose inequities would soon bring about its inevitable demise while the Soviet system was attaining economic and social justice.

All governments like to rave about their accomplishments and dread having to admit failures, especially totalitarian systems. The former Soviet Union offers some striking and tragic examples. The Soviet government took several years to admit that a small number of its citizens had contracted the HIV virus. Since AIDS had long been described by the Soviet media as a feature of moral decadence in the West it could not be acknowledged as a problem in morally upright societies such as the Soviet Union. A perfect society does not have the problems of the less fortunate imperfect societies. The worst nuclear accident in history occurred at a nuclear power plant in Chernobyl (in the northern Ukraine) in April 1986. The Soviet government kept the accident from public view for as long as possible. Tens, perhaps hundreds, of thousands of people in mortal danger of dying from radiation sickness were not warned for at least 36 hours. The Soviet government waited almost two weeks before informing the outside world that something had gone wrong (and only after radiation-monitoring machines in Sweden had detected a sudden increase in radioactivity).

Chernobyl may eventually cost 300,000 lives.[41] This tragedy was so overwhelm-

TABLE 6.5 USEFUL SCAPEGOATS IN TOTALITARIAN SYSTEMS		
System	Scapegoats	Official Characteristics
Nazi Germany (1933–1945)	Jews, Gypsies, homosexuals	Subhuman, socially unsuitable, racially inferior
Stalinist (1924–1953)	Capitalists, American spies, cosmopolitans	Unprogressive, counterrevolutionary, bourgeoisie

ing that no cover-up was feasible. The Soviet regime was revealed as one that had lied to its own citizens by long maintaining that the flawed nuclear technology was quite safe. As one close observer pointed out, "An abscess, long hidden within our society, had just burst; the abscess of complacency and self-flattery, of corruption and protectionism, of narrow-mindedness and self-serving privilege."[42]

An institutionalized inability to admit there is something wrong can eventually destroy both governments and their citizenry. The Soviet handling of Chernobyl contrasts with a similar though less dramatic nuclear accident at Three Mile Island in Pennsylvania several years earlier. In this case, the government acted quickly to evacuate nearby residents and inform the nation of what happened. But the government could (and did) place most of the blame for the accident on the private sector.

Perhaps the most comprehensive attempt in history to formulate and control public opinion occurred during China's Great Cultural Revolution during the late 1960s and early 1970s. Even songs had to receive official approval before being sung. Popular songs of this period were noted for their political message and adulation of the Chinese communist leader Mao Tse-tung. A song that was at the top of the hit list during this period was "East is Red":

> The East is Red,
> The sun rises,
> China has brought forth a Mao Tse-tung
> He works for the people's happiness,
> He is the people's savior.
> Chairman Mao loves the people,
> He is our guide
> He leads us onward
> To build the new China
> The Communist Party is like the sun,
> Wherever it shines, there is light
> Where there's the Communist Party,
> There people will win liberation.[43]

Totalitarian systems are reluctant to learn how to monitor public opinion, but at the end of its career the Soviet Union at least tried. It wasn't an easy lesson. The Soviet government discovered to its dismay in the spring of 1991 that only 10 percent of its citizenry had confidence in the government's ability to deal effectively with a worsening economic crisis.[44] No democratically chosen government could survive such low esteem, nor ultimately did the communist system in the Soviet Union.

PUBLIC OPINION AND THE MASS MEDIA IN AUTHORITARIAN SYSTEMS

In authoritarian systems, public opinion is also manipulated by the government, but such systems have a distinct advantage over communist regimes such as the Soviet Union: Their citizenries are often less well informed and less literate. Dictators can get away with a lot in such societies, especially if the country's only really modern institutions include a technologically sophisticated secret police and army. Bad news is rarely reported unless it is about the regime's enemies. Dictatorships are loath to admit having problems.

Authoritarian dictators are often megalomaniacs who build monuments to themselves in a frenzied fashion. They are also paranoid (not without some justification) and believe that lying is a justifiable act of self-defense. The more clever ones mobilize popular support by trying to be anything they believe people want them to be. During the last months of 1990 and the early months of 1991, Iraq's Saddam Hussein appeared at various intervals as a warrior for Arab freedom, a hero to the Palestinian cause, a pious Muslim fighting Western infidels, and even a socialist attempting to enlist Soviet support. Hussein was trying (with some obvious success, since his regime survived) to secure favorable opinions with a variety of publics in Iraq and throughout the Middle East.[45] Politicians in democratic societies religiously listen to public opinion, mainly because they want to be elected or reelected to office. Dictators have no such concern as free elections, but they still yearn to be liked.

Dictators usually achieve widespread fear and loathing because they often come to power in a coup by shooting or exiling their predecessors. But they understandably crave legitimacy and respect. Public opinion can furnish both, if the population is constantly reminded of the dynamic qualities of the leader. A dictator will have huge picture posters displayed all over the country and, like Saddam Hussein, construct statues of himself that may be as large as any building in the country. Both pictures and postcards frequently show the leader smiling and waving, assuring the populace that everything is fine. Unlike American presidents, dictators are never shown in an unguarded moment. And on public occasions their secret police ensure they need not be worried about being embarrassed by hecklers.

One of the more humane ways for a nondemocratic system to manipulate public opinion and to discourage dissent is through the use of the **plebiscite**. The electorate is simply asked to vote yea or nay on a particular issue. Usually the government can count on at least a 95 percent endorsement and often receives over 99 percent. (Few dictatorships have had the gall to claim a 100 percent approval rating, although why they seem convinced that 99 percent is more believable remains a mystery.) Technically, the ballots are secret. In reality, relentless intimidation on the part of the government works very well to encourage voters to cast their ballots "correctly." Besides, it's the government that counts the ballots.

Even the most brutal of dictatorships prefer a political consensus. And they know they can usually create one. Whether it is fictitious or not isn't a major concern. There is no guarantee that truth will eventually surface, anyway. With sophisticated communications technology, governments have the ability to get a large number of their citizens to believe complete fabrications. This point was appreciated even before the technology was available. As philosopher John Stuart Mill notes: "Indeed, the dictum that truth always triumphs over persecution is one of those pleasant falsehoods which men repeat after one another till they pass into commonplaces, but which all experience refutes. History teems with instances of truth put down by persecution."[46]

Authoritarian and totalitarian states have a great deal in common when it comes to dealing with the media. It is important in a dictatorship for the leader to impress the public as the personification of the state. In order to accomplish this, dictators carefully control and manipulate media and public opinion in the following ways:

1. Secret police agencies: They are usually several in number. They not only spy on the population but on one another to ensure that no dissension goes undetected.

2. Control of the media: Only those messages the government approves of are broadcast or published. This usually means there is no bad news.

3. Family operations. Relatives of the dictator are all placed in key government and military positions to maintain control over and manipulate the public mood.

4. Deification. Through the government-controlled media most dictators attempt to convince their subjects that they are totally devoted to the welfare of the state. Frequently enough they do so with some success. Any dissent against the leader therefore becomes an act of state treason.

Restraints and brutality are favorite ways governments and their agents deal with an uncooperative or critical press. As the following list suggests, journalism is not a particularly safe profession. The statistics refer only to physical and psychological harassment of the media for 1990. They don't include other forms of editorial censorship or ways of putting economic or political pressure on the mass media. They should give a clue, however, to the extent journalists in authoritarian systems practice self-censorship.

Journalists killed: 43 in 19 countries

Kidnapped or disappeared: 16 in 8 countries

Arrested or detained: 155 in 45 countries

Expelled: 31 in 14 countries

Wounded: 41 in 9 countries

Beaten: 16 in 9 countries

Otherwise assaulted: 82 in 25 countries

Death threats and other threats: 50 in 22 countries

Homes raided or destroyed: 3 in 1 country

Films or manuscripts confiscated: 43 in 23 countries

Press credentials withdrawn or refused, or expulsion threatened: 43 in 17 countries

Harassed: 170 in 60 countries

Closed publications or radio stations: 50 in 16 countries

Banned publications or radio programs: 37 in 12 countries

Bombed or burned publications or radios: 12 in 11 countries

Occupied publications or radios: 30 in 20 countries

Total cases of all forms of attack, harassments: 855 in 92 countries[47]

In nondemocratic societies the natural (and probably politically healthy) adversarial role between the government and the media has been resolved in the government's favor, and society overall is the loser. The government not only controls the media, but in effect makes them worthless since only government-approved information is published. Many societies are so underdeveloped that the central government is actually the only source of information any average citizen has of the outside world or even of her or his country. In these cases inaccurate or misleading information may be better than no news at all.

Governments that embrace a particular and exclusive ideology or theology are often excessively intolerant of anyone else who tries to provide facts to better inform the public. Too many unpleasant regimes still thrive on censorship. Interestingly, though, some governments, such as Iran's, permit differences of opinion to be published as long as they do not contradict legitimate theological pronouncements. During the regime of the Ayatollah Khomeini (1979–1990), for instance, government-owned newspapers were encouraged to compete with one another, but only to expose scandals and corruption. No criticism of Khomeini and no suggestion of allowing religious freedom were permitted.[48]

Summary

1. Public opinion in the political sphere refers to those beliefs held by the public that influence government. Different issues generate interest among differing and often opposing publics, called special publics.

2. Five characteristics important to an understanding of public opinion are salience, stability or fluidity, intensity, latency, and distribution.

3. There are different types of public opinion. These include permissive, directive, supportive, and divisive public opinion.

4. In a process known as political socialization public opinion is shaped from early childhood by family, school, peers, the media, and an individual's own ethnic, religious, and social class background.

5. Public opinion is measured through surveys known as polls. Polls must be constructed carefully to obtain reliable and valid results.

6. The media in the United States have evolved through four phases: the partisan political press, popular press, reform press, and (currently) the electronic media. Television is the medium through which most Americans get their news and form their opinions about political candidates.

7. The media may be considered too powerful because of their ability to immediately reach audiences in the tens of millions, because of the declining competition among newspapers and the growing monopoly of media markets, because of the emphasis on making profits rather than on public affairs, and because of the conservative ideological posture of media owners. And yet the media may not seem so powerful if one considers the variety of media sources and the rise in alternative voices, and not exceptionally conservative since several "flagship papers" have comparatively liberal editorial policies and reporters tend to be increasingly Democratic.

8. While government and the media are often natural adversaries they can at times also seem to be in collusion. They may agree, for example, that national security requires a tacit silence on some issues.

9. Electronic democracy would allow average citizens to have decision-making power. This would increase support for and trust in government. But some issues are too complex to be decided in a nationwide town meeting, and long-term national interests may be overwhelmed by the public's short-term political and economic concerns.

10. Democratic polities usually thrive on an informed citizenry, and democratic governments carefully monitor public opinion.

11. Public opinion polls in most parliamentary systems are watched very carefully by the government in order to determine the optimal time to call a national election. The American Congress and the president lack this luxury since the timing of elections is constitutionally prescribed, without reference to polls.

12. Totalitarian governments tend to use the media to manipulate public opinion. The Chernobyl tragedy in the Soviet Union was an example of institutionalized reluctance of a communist government to admit even obvious and widespread mistakes. The Chinese communists attempted to cover up a massacre of protesting students in 1989. But literate populations and global media technology make such cover-ups difficult.

13. Control of the media is essential to government control in a modern dictatorship, and freedom of the press has no real meaning. Many countries of the world are authoritarian and have a muzzled or censured press. Journalists who oppose the government are subject to restraint and brutality. Such nondemocratic systems frequently use the plebiscite to legitimate their governments. Usually the plebiscite is a vote arranged to ensure that a dictatorship receives an almost unanimous approval rating.

Terms to Define

Adversary journalism	Plebiscite
Backgrounder	Political socialization
Directive public opinion	Polls
Divisive public opinion	Public opinion
Electronic democracy	Random sample
Initiative	Referendum
Investigative reporter	Selective perception
Mass media	Special publics
Muckraking	Supportive public opinion
Permissive public opinion	Universe

Suggested Readings

Asher, Herbert. *Polling and the Public: What Every Citizen Should Know*. Washington, D.C.: Congressional Quarterly Press, 1988. Relates polling methods to campaign polls.

Crespi, Irving. *Public Opinion, Polls, and Democracy*. Boulder, Colo.: Westview Press, 1989. Assesses how the media use public opinion polls to their advantage.

Bozell, L. Brent, III, and Brent H. Baker, eds. *And That's the Way It Isn't*. Alexandria, Va.: Media Research Center, 1990. Documents the liberal media bias from a conservative perspective.

Entman, Robert. *Democracy Without Citizens: Media and the Decay of American Politics*. New York: Oxford University Press, 1989. Contends that the media do not do a better job of reporting news because the public does not demand it.

Graber, Doris A. *Media Power and Politics*, 2nd ed. Washington, D.C.: Congressional Quarterly Press, 1990. Leading essays on political journalism and the media.

Ichilov, Orit. *Political Socialization, Citizenship Education, and Democracy*. New York: Teachers College Press, 1990. Cross-national comparisons about how people acquire political attitudes.

Iyengar, Shanto, and Donald R. Kinder. *News That Matters: Television and American Opinion*. Chicago: University of Chicago Press, 1987. Assesses the substantial impact of television news on public opinion.

Kellner, Douglas. *Television and the Crisis of Democracy*. Boulder, Colo.: Westview Press, 1990. Analyzes from a liberal perspective the relationship between the mass media and political culture.

Niemi, Richard G., John Mueller, and Tom W. Smith. *Trends in Public Opinion*. New York: Greenwood Press, 1989. Essays and data on 50 years of public opinion polling.

Sanders, Arthur. *Making Sense of Politics*. Ames: Iowa State University Press, 1990. Defends the proposition that people focus more on the style of decision making than the substance of decisions to make sense of politics.

Notes

1. V. O. Key, Jr., *Public Opinion and American Democracy* (New York: Alfred A. Knopf, 1961), p. 7.
2. Ibid., p. 10.
3. For studies of the structure of public opinion, see Key, *Public Opinion and American Democracy*; Robert E. Lane and David O. Sears, *Public Opinion* (Englewood Cliffs, NJ.: Prentice-Hall, 1964); and Norman R. Luttbeg, "The Structure of Beliefs Among Leaders and the Public," *Public Opinion Quarterly* 32 (Fall 1968): 308–400.
4. Lane and Sears, *Public Opinion*, p. 15.
5. For a summary of studies on child-parent agreement on party preference, see Gardner Lindzey and Elliot Aronson, "Political Behavior," in *The Handbook of Social Psychology*, 2nd ed. (Reading, Mass.: Addison-Wesley, 1969), vol. 5, p. 376.
6. M. Kent Jennings and Kenneth P. Langton, "Mothers and Fathers: The Formation of Political Orientation Among Young Americans," *Journal of Politics* 31 (May 1969): 357.
7. Ibid.
8. Robert D. Hess and Judith V. Torney, *The Development of Basic Attitudes and Values Toward Government and Citizenship During the Elementary School Years*, Part I (Washington, D.C.: U.S. Office of Education, 1965), p. 193.
9. M. Kent Jennings and Richard G. Niemi, "The Transmission of Political Values from Parent to Child," *American Political Science Review* 68 (March, 1968), 179.
10. Confused about what capital gains are or how you should feel about them? See Michael Kinsley, "A Capital Gains Primer," *The New Republic*, February 10, 1992, pp. 17–18 and 20.
11. *Washington Post*, November 4, 1992, p. A24.
12. Kurt Lang and Gladys Engel Lang, *Politics and Television* (New York: Quadrangle Books, 1968), p. 303.
13. Quoted in Hobart Rowen, "Investing in Our Children," *The Washington Post National Weekly Edition*, February 3–9, 1992, p. 5.

14. See, for instance, the revealing insight offered in Randy Shilts, *And the Band Played On* (New York: St. Martin's Press, 1988). In this work the press is taken to task for poor journalism that included some reporters' making bad jokes.

15. See Larry Sabato's excellent treatment of misdirected journalism in *Feeding Frenzy* (New York: Free Press, 1991). Ironically, Governor Clinton's wife, Hillary, actually benefited among some people from press coverage, insisting that she was supportive of her husband without being "long suffering." See David Sussman, "Hear Her Roar," *The Wall Street Journal*, January 31, 1992, p. A1.

16. *The Washington Post,* June 3, 1979, p. D1.

17. *The Washington Post,* June 16, 1978, p. A3.

18. *The Washington Post,* September 17, 1975, p. B8.

19. Freedom Forum survey reported in *The New York Times*, November 18, 1992, p. A20.

20. Quoted ibid.

21. *Public Opinion*, February/March 1985, pp. 43–48.

22. *Public Opinion*, April/May 1984, p. 2.

23. Victor Bernstein and Jesse Gordon, "The Press and the Bay of Pigs," *The Columbia University Forum* (Fall 1967): 4–15.

24. David Wise, *The Politics of Lying* (New York: Vintage Books, 1973), pp. 62–66.

25. Quoted in Sherrill, *Why They Call It Politics* (New York: Harcourt Brace Jovanovich, 1974), p. 309.

26. Ibid., p. 308.

27. Ibid., pp. 299–300.

28. *The New York Times*, January 24, 1971, sec. 3, p. 1.

29. *Newsweek*, November 9, 1970, pp. 22–25.

30. *The Essential Lippman*, edited by Clinton Rossiter and James Lare (New York: Random House, 1963), p. 241.

31. Robert E. Lane, *Political Life* (New York: Free Press, 1959), p. 344.

32. *The Washington Post*, December 25, 1978, p. A19.

33. Kitty Kelley, *Nancy Reagan: An Unauthorized Biography* (New York: Simon & Schuster, 1991).

34. Leonard R. Sussman, "The Press 1990: Contrary Trends," p. 59, *Freedom Review*, Vol. 22, No. 1, Freedom House, 1991.

35. An excellent summary of this episode is provided by Rushworth M. Kidder, "Unmasking Terrorism: Manipulation of the Media," *The Christian Science Monitor*, May 16, 1986, pp. 18–20.

36. Richard Rose, *Politics in England: An Interpretation for the 1980s*, 3rd ed. (Boston: Little, Brown, 1980), p. 203.

37. Boston: Atlantic Monthly Press, 1991.

38. Quoted in *The Washington Post National Weekly Edition*, June 10–16, 1991, p. 37.

39. See Mervyn Matthews, *Education in the Soviet Union* (London: George Allen & Unwin, 1982).

40. Hedrick Smith, *The New Russians* (New York: Random House, 1990), pp. 153–154.

41. Ibid., p. 19.

42. Gregori Medvedev, *The Truth About Chernobyl* (New York: Basic Books, 1991). Quoted in *The Economist*, April 27, 1991, p. 93.

43. *Peking Review*, October 6, 1967.

44. *The Economist*, April 27, 1991, p. 93.

45. For the secrets of Saddam Hussein's success, see Efraim Karsh and Inari Rautsi, *Saddam Hussein: A Political Biography* (Glencoe, Ill.: Free Press, 1991) and Samir al-Khahil, *The Monument* (Berkeley: University of California Press, 1991).

46. John Stuart Mill, *On Liberty*, edited by David Spitz (New York: Norton, 1975), p. 28.

47. *Freedom in the World, 1990–1991: Political Rights and Civil Liberties* (New York: Freedom House, 1991), p. 476.

48. *The Economist*, October 15, 1988, p. 56.

CHAPTER ★ SEVEN

INTEREST GROUPS

The French political observer Alexis de Tocqueville noted that America is a nation of joiners par excellence. On almost any conceivable subject, groups represent varying interests or opinions. Lawyers and physicians join professional organizations, blue-collar workers join unions, people in business look to the Chamber of Commerce, environmentalists join the Sierra Club, political reformers join Common Cause, and so on.

Each of these organizations is an **interest group,** defined as an organized group representing a special segment of society that seeks to influence governmental policies directly affecting its members. Interest groups, also called "lobbies" or "pressure groups," are considered legitimate representatives of various segments of public opinion. That is, they are special publics that take definite positions on specific issues. Labor groups represent the interests of working people, the highway lobby is concerned chiefly with transportation policy, and so forth. **Lobbyists** are the professionals who represent such interest groups. The term *lobbyist* originated in seventeenth-century England, when persons interested in influencing votes in the House of Commons met with members in a nearby lobby. Any citizen can, of course, "lobby" a government official, but professional lobbyists are supposed to register as such and submit written financial reports.

Other nations seem not to be as inundated with interest groups as America is. Those countries with more homogeneous populations may not require them, and in those nations with a tradition of multiple parties, various interests may channel their energies into a political party (such as the environmentalist Green party in Germany). Americans not only join groups more than people in other countries; they also join different types of organizations. For example, Americans are more likely to join political and religious groups, while people in other Western democracies are more likely to join labor unions.[1]

Later in the chapter we will make other comparisons with other nations. But now we will examine why interest groups emerge, what forms they take, what their tactics are, and whether interest groups do (or should) determine the public interest in America.

 ## INTEREST GROUPS IN AMERICA

CAUSES OF INTEREST GROUPS

How may we account for the ever-increasing number and variety of interest groups in America? Among the fundamental causes are (1) the nature of American society, (2) the federal system of government, and (3) the condition of the two major political parties. Unlike many European democratic countries that have a largely homogeneous population, the American population is heterogeneous. The diversity of our population, with its many ethnic, social, economic, and other classifications of people, creates a diversity of interests that need to be represented. Polish-Americans, Italian-Americans, German-Americans, Swedish-Americans, African-Americans, Mexican-Americans: These and many other groups vie for representation of their interests. Our highly complex and diverse economic system produces other sets of interests to be represented, and the intensity and variety of religious beliefs in America provide for still others.

The American federal system of government, with over 82,000 units of government, allows for many access points for interest groups. Thus, there is a potential for interest group influence at each level of government (national, state, and local), as well as within each branch of government (legislative body, executive branch, and courts).

The condition of the parties also contributes to interest group influence. The American two-party system has had periods both of great strength and of great weakness. A cause-effect relationship appears to exist between these periods and the number and strength of American interest groups. When the two-party system is relatively weak, interest groups are both numerous and strong; that was the situation in the late 1980s and early 1990s. But when our two major parties were stronger, as during the 1950s and early 1960s, interest groups were fewer and weaker.

The Democratic and Republican parties, of course, represent tens of thousands of people and many diverse groups, while the very largest interest groups represent only a small portion of the population and only one or a few interests. Since the focus of parties is more general and that of interest groups more specific, times of tension in society are likely to produce new interests that lead to the organization of groups to represent

Hotly disputed issues pave the way for the formation of interest groups. The two sides of the abortion debate are represented by interest groups that formed in opposition to each other.

them. However, during periods of relative calm and stability in society, parties are generally stronger since there is not as much need for people to organize into specialized groups. For example, from the late 1960s through the early 1990s, heatedly disputed issues—such as school busing, prayer in the public schools, abortion, minority rights, and the role of women in society—paved the way for new interest groups. The broadly based major political parties could not address these issues in a way that was completely satisfying to those concerned. Parties require a great deal of compromise to reach consensus among diverse groups, while interest groups form just to focus on one or a few issues. Pro-life and pro-choice advocates may be found in both the Democratic and Republican parties, but a microscope would be required to find a pro-life advocate in the National Organization of Women or a pro-choice advocate in Concerned Women of America.

There are four additional reasons for the rise of interest groups at particular times in history. Economic developments spawn interest groups to represent emerging interests, as has occurred recently in the electronics and computer-based industries. The rise of the railroads in the 1800s and the growth of labor unions earlier in this century stimulated the formation of corresponding interest groups.

Government policy may spawn interest groups. A war produces veterans who demand representation; new social policies such as Medicare and Medicaid produce groups wanting representation; a policy like revenue sharing causes local governments and the benefited citizens to organize to protect that policy from abolition. Sometimes the government needs interest groups to assist it in regulations. The American Medical Association, for example, licenses members of the medical profession.

One interest group may cause others to organize in opposition. Women disagreeing with the policies of the National Organization for Women (NOW) organized rival interest groups, such as Phyllis Schlafly's Eagle Forum and Beverly LaHaye's Concerned Women of America (CWA).

Finally, an interest group may form around a strong leader. The several interest groups associated with consumer activist Ralph Nader required the creative stimulus of his name (associates and supporters sometimes refer to themselves as "Nader's Raiders"), mind, and personality; the Christian Coalition required the same from television evangelist Pat Robertson.

TYPES OF INTEREST GROUPS

America offers a dizzying array of interest groups that can vary in size, cause, influence, purpose, and composition. Perhaps the best way to distinguish among the various interest groups is to characterize them by the principal reason for their existence—their common interests. They tend to fall into seven main categories: professional, economic, political, public interest (or consumer), religious, governmental, and single-issue.

Professional. The American Bar Association, organized by lawyers, is an example of a professional interest group. This organization, representing the overwhelming majority of practicing lawyers in the United States (about two-thirds of all the lawyers in the world), is concerned with protecting the interests of the profession from governmental intrusion or regulation. Some other professional interest groups are the American Medical Association and the National Association of Realtors. In some instances, professionals have spawned more than one interest group: educators have developed the National Education Association, the American Federation of Teachers, and the American Association of University Professors, among others.

Economic. Interest groups organized around economic lines are many and varied. Among the leading business organizations are the Chamber of Commerce of the United States, the National Small Business Association, and the National Association of Manufacturers. Some business groups have much more specialized interests, such as the American Bankers' Association. Representing farmers are the American Farm Bureau Federation, the Farmers' Union, and the National Farmers Organization. Specialized farm groups include the National Cattlemen's Association, the National Wool Growers Association, and the American Meat Institute. Labor's major interest group is the AFL-CIO, which was formed in a 1955 merger of the American Federation of Labor and the Congress of Industrial Organizations. The AFL grouped craft unions, such as those of bricklayers or carpenters; the industrial unions of the CIO organized all the workers in a given industry, such as steel. These many separate groups still exist within the AFL-CIO. Two other powerful labor organizations are the International Brotherhood of Teamsters (transportation workers) and the United Auto Workers.

Ideological. Americans for Democratic Action (ADA), a liberal organization, and the Americans for Constitutional Action (ACA), a conservative association, illustrate ideological interest groups. Both the ADA and the ACA rate members of Congress according to how they vote on critical issues. These ratings may play a key role in election campaigns. In a conservative district, for example, a member of Congress can use a high ACA rating to advantage. Senator Strom Thurmond (R-S.C.) publicizes his very high rating by the ACA, while Senator Edward Kennedy (D-Mass.) does the same with his ADA rating.

Public Interest. **Public interest groups** represent the general public on a wide range of issues and typically have no economic self-interest at stake. Common Cause, the various consumer groups founded by Ralph Nader, environmental organizations, and the American Civil Liberties Union are prime examples.

Religious. The liberal National Council of Churches, the conservative Christian Coalition, the U.S. Conference of Catholic Bishops, and the Anti-Defamation League of the B'Nai B'rith are examples of religious interest groups. Some represent people from a variety of religious backgrounds while others represent only those of a particular denomination.

Governmental. Included in this category are the National Governors' Conference, the National Association of Counties, and the U.S. Conference of Mayors. They organize, of course, to protect their common interests in public policy. Both the National Association of Counties and the U.S. Conference of Mayors have been vitally interested in the preservation of federal grant programs. The various departments and agencies of government may also constitute interest groups. For example, the Department of Education seeks to influence Congress on educational issues, while the Department of Defense constitutes a kind of lobby concerned with military affairs.

Single-Issue. **Single-issue groups,** largely the product of the last 20 years, focus narrowly on one issue (abortion being the best-known example). They typically have little tolerance of the opposing side and probably even less desire to compromise. The intensity with which they hold their positions make them more likely to engage in protest demonstrations, such as at abortion clinics, than more traditional interest groups like the American Farm Bureau Federation or the American Bar Association.

We have just seen that one way to classify interest groups is by their area of common interest. Another way to distinguish interest groups is by their position on the ideological spectrum, from far left to far right. Most groups would be located somewhere near the middle, in the moderate category, or would include people from a wide range of ideologies. Most business groups can be classified as conservative and most labor groups as liberal. Typically, the moderate, conservative, and liberal groups in the United States believe in working within the established political system, while radicals on both extremes of the spectrum are more apt to advocate violence as a tactic. The sprinkling of radical organizations ranges from the Weathermen (an extremist student organization that advocated violent overthrow of the government during the 1960s and 1970s) on the left, to the Posse Comitatus of the 1980s (a racist and ethnocentric movement with followers mainly in the midwestern and northwestern states) on the right.

INTEREST GROUP TACTICS

How does an interest group try to exert influence on government? Lobbyists testify before congressional committees or meet personally with regulators. Groups provide campaign contributions to office-seekers. Mass media advertising and public relations campaigns build grass-roots pressure and support. Demonstrations and petitions call attention to various causes. Finally, lawsuits bring interest group views to the courtroom.

An interest group may use all these methods in a well-devised strategy to influence the government. The methods described above may be loosely divided into several categories: direct lobbying, grassroots lobbying, information campaigns, and coalition building. Direct lobbying occurs, for example, when a lobbyist goes to Congress to present arguments in support of the interest group's positions. Of course, direct lobbying may also occur in the courts when interest groups file suit to accomplish a lobbying objective. On the issue of abortion, both proponents and opponents have presented their arguments directly to Congress and also sought judicial remedies in the courts.

Another important method of direct lobbying takes the form of campaign donations. **Political action committees** (PACs) are the financial lobbying arms of interest groups. They solicit voluntary contributions from members and donate these funds to political candidates. A PAC's direct contributions may not exceed $5000 per candidate, but services and indirect contributions greatly increase the value of PAC donations. Congressional candidates (especially incumbents) rely more on PACs than on any other single source for their fundraising (see Table 7.1). This reliance creates undue (and sometimes addictive) dependence on them as well as independence from the candidates' own political parties.

Grass-roots lobbying involves such things as letter-writing and telephone-call campaigns from rank-and-file constituents to representatives of the government. Since members of Congress are especially responsive to constituents' calls and letters, a good

TABLE 7.1	CONTRIBUTIONS TO CONGRESSIONAL CAMPAIGNS BY POLITICAL ACTION COMMITTEES, 1980–1990 (in Millions of Dollars)					
Election Year	Total	Democrats	Republicans	Incumbents	Challengers	Open Seats
U.S. House						
1980	$37.9	$20.5	$17.2	$24.9	$7.9	$5.1
1982	$61.1	$34.2	$26.8	$40.8	$10.9	$9.4
1984	$87.4	$54.7	$32.6	$65.9	$9.1	$12.4
1988	$102.2	$67.4	$34.7	$82.2	$10.0	$10.0
1990	$108.5	$72.2	$36.2	$87.5	$7.3	$13.6
U.S. Senate						
1980	$17.3	$8.4	$9.0	$8.6	$6.6	$2.1
1982	$22.6	$11.2	$11.4	$14.3	$5.2	$3.0
1984	$29.7	$14.0	$15.6	$17.9	$6.3	$5.4
1986	$45.3	$20.2	$25.1	$23.7	$10.2	$11.4
1988	$45.7	$24.2	$21.5	$28.7	$8.0	$9.0
1990	$41.2	$20.2	$21.0	$29.5	$8.2	$3.5

Source: *U.S. Statistical Abstract, 1992, p. 275.*

lobbying strategy will look for ways to encourage constituents to contact their members of Congress. When President Bill Clinton first proposed lifting the ban on homosexuals in the military, both the White House and Congress were flooded with protest calls from constituents who had been activated by conservative organizations. The National Rifle Association (NRA) is particularly adept at getting its members to contact Congress when gun control laws are being debated. Grass-roots lobbying may also include gathering petitions and protest demonstrations, as occurred in the 1960s before the passage of the 1964 Civil Rights Act and the 1965 Voting Rights Act.

Well-financed lobbying campaigns, such as those run by the oil industry, may use television and other media to inform the public of their positions in an attempt to obtain popular support. Public relations efforts of this nature are indirect rather than direct in their approach to the government. Lobbyists may provide research to back up their information campaign. Both proponents and opponents of abortion have retained survey research firms to conduct public opinion surveys to show popular sentiment on this issue.

Sometimes it is mutually beneficial for interest groups to work together on an issue. Abortion, business, civil rights, education, labor, and other issues may lead to coalition building among interest groups that are similarly affected. Higher-education interest groups in Washington join together to lobby for common concerns like increased funding for scholarly exchanges with other countries. A coalition of civil rights interest groups was very effective during the 1980s in limiting or reversing the impact of court decisions on their interests.

THE PUBLIC INTEREST

What is the public interest? Realistically, the public interest is determined by the result of interest group competition. On an issue, the law that emerges from the compromises made among the concerned groups becomes the public interest. This practical definition of the public interest, of course, does not address the question of what the public interest *should* be. As we will see, some scholars contend that the public interest should be distinguished from the result of interest group competition.

The impact of interest groups on American democracy is heatedly debated. Some observers believe that they undermine our democracy; others contend that interest groups are democracy's very essence and lifeblood. Gabriel Almond and Sidney Verba have stated that interest groups permit the individual "to relate himself effectively and mean-ingfully to the political system."[2] On the other hand, Theodore Lowi has argued that interest groups do not lead to "strong, positive government . . . but impotent govern-ment."[3] According to Lowi, to the extent that the public interest is determined by the resolution of conflict among private interest groups, government is amoral. Yet, as C. Wright Mills suggests, government depends on this resolution for its ideals and values in forming public policy. He finds that interest groups are a crucial ingredient of successful political democracy:

Mass democracy means the struggle of powerful and large-scale interest groups and associa-tions, which stand between the big decisions that are made by state, corporation, army, and the will of the individual citizen as a member of the public. Since these middle-level associations are the citizens' major link with decision making, his relation to them is of decisive importance. For it is only through them that he exercises such power as he may have.[4]

Which position is right? That question provides the focus of the analysis that follows.

? ISSUES TO ANALYZE

ISSUE 1   *ARE BUSINESS AND INDUSTRIAL LOBBIES TOO POWERFUL?*

REASONS WHY BUSINESS AND INDUSTRIAL LOBBIES ARE TOO POWERFUL

Industrial and business lobbies predominate both in number and expenditure over other types of interest groups.[5] As might be expected, business organizations spend more money on lobbying than do any other groups. And that just represents the expenditures lobbyists are *required* to report because they are used to influence public policy directly. Unreported expenditures for indirect lobbying would raise the total considerably. Thus, an oil company's expenses in producing a television commercial focusing on the search for new energy sources need not be reported. The huge funds at their disposal give business and industrial groups an enormous advantage in the interest group struggle. They can recruit and finance the best lobbyists, employ the best minds, and conduct the most effective campaigns to influence public opinion.

Business and industrial lobbies increase their clout through their well-financed and well-organized PACs. In the last 20 years the number of business PACs has soared (Table 7.2). While it cannot be said that campaign contributions from business interest PACs actually *buy* the legislators' votes (rarely is there obvious evidence and it is impolite to even make such a suggestion), they certainly do provide access to the lawmakers and promote friendly attitudes. Less affluent interest groups thus start out at a disadvantage in the legislative marketplace. (See Figure 7.1.)

Another source of power for the business and industrial lobbies is access to information. Gathering information requires both time and money. Here again, business and industry have an advantage. Should one be surprised by General Electric's lobbying success? Not when one looks at the array of lobbying talent GE has bought, including the former chairman of the Nuclear Regulatory Commission and general counsel to the Atomic Energy Commission, the former chairman of the Democratic Congressional Campaign Committee, a former chief staff member of the House Armed Services and Science and Technology committees, three former Air Force generals—and the list could continue. Big companies buy knowledge and contacts.

In 1978 Congress passed legislation to restrict private-sector groups in hiring former government workers to lobby on their behalf, a practice known as the **revolving door.** The act required that a substantial time elapse before the former government employee could represent a private interest. But, because this restriction led many employees either to leave or threaten to leave their government positions, Congress later

TABLE 7.2 NUMBER OF POLITICAL ACTION COMMITTEES (PACs), 1974–1992*

| | | | CONNECTED† | | | | |
Date	Corporate	Labor	Trade/ Membership/ Health	Cooperative	Corporation Without Stock	Nonconnected‡	Total
1974	89	201	318§	NA	NA	NA	608
1976	433	224	489§	NA	NA	NA	1146
1978	785	217	453	12	24	162	1653
1980	1206	297	576	42	56	374	2551
1982	1469	380	649	47	103	723	3371
1984	1682	394	698	52	130	1053	4009
1986	1744	384	745	56	151	1077	4157
1988	1816	354	786	59	138	1115	4268
1990	1795	346	774	59	136	1062	4172
1992	1893	365	818	59	147	1303	4585

* **Note:** The counts reflect federally registered PACs. Registration does not necessarily imply financial activity.
† Connected PACs are associated with a sponsoring organization that may pay operating and fund-raising expenses. They are typically subdivided by the type of sponsor: corporate (with stockholders), labor (unions), membership/ trade/health (professional groups and associations of corporations), cooperatives (primarily agricultural), and corporations without stock.
‡ Nonconnected PACs do not have a sponsoring organization. A family or a group of friends or associates may organize in this way.
§ For the years 1974–1976, trade/membership/health category includes all PACs except corporate and labor; no further breakdown available.
Source: Federal Election Commission, "FEC Releases 1990 Year-end PAC Count," press release, January 11, 1991.

modified the act to impose the restriction for only one year. President Clinton has imposed a five-year limit on his appointees.

Another aspect to the revolving door is that business and industry also have the aid of representatives of their interests *within* the government itself, among both elected and appointed officials. Many leading state and national officials have come from corporate management, prominent law firms, and large banking and other financial institutions. According to one view, "Elected and appointed . . . policy makers are overwhelmingly from the more favored classes; in the federal government 60 percent of them come from business and professional families."[6] They understandably are more closely associated with and respectful of corporate clout. In late 1991, for example, it was revealed that breast implants, which had been a common surgical procedure since 1963, had not been tested for retroactive safety before 1976, and even after 1976 the law was not especially binding on this issue.[7] It was not until a public outcry on behalf of 2 million women with implants that the Federal Drug Administration (FDA) finally declared a moratorium on the operation until the safety of implants could be determined. Public interest had finally prevailed over corporate reassurances to the FDA that all was well. But the outcry was, of course, assisted by another interest group, the National Trial Lawyers' Association,

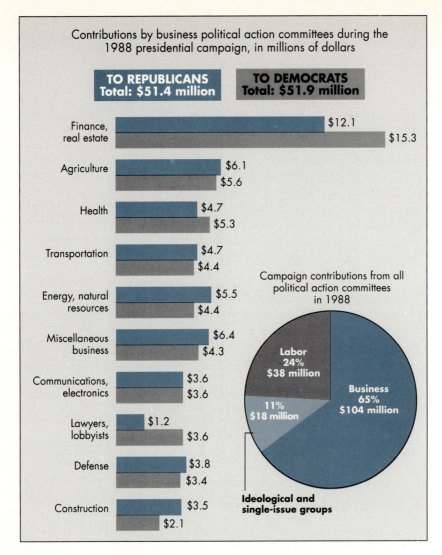

Contributions by business political action committees during the 1988 presidential campaign, in millions of dollars

TO REPUBLICANS Total: $51.4 million	TO DEMOCRATS Total: $51.9 million

Finance, real estate — $12.1 / $15.3

Agriculture — $6.1 / $5.6

Health — $4.7 / $5.3

Transportation — $4.7 / $4.4

Energy, natural resources — $5.5 / $4.4

Miscellaneous business — $6.4 / $4.3

Communications, electronics — $3.6 / $3.6

Lawyers, lobbyists — $1.2 / $3.6

Defense — $3.8 / $3.4

Construction — $3.5 / $2.1

Campaign contributions from all political action committees in 1988

Labor 24% $38 million

11% $18 million

Business 65% $104 million

Ideological and single-issue groups

Figure 7.1 WHERE THE PAC MONEY COMES FROM. As the pie chart shows, the large majority of PAC campaign contributions come from business political action committees. In the 1988 presidential campaign these funds were distributed about equally to the Republican and Democratic candidates. There were variations among the different professions and industries, however. Source: *The New York Times*, September 16, 1990, p. 18A. Data from Center for Responsive Politics.

which immediately recognized how well its members' bank accounts would be served by the formation of a "breast implant litigation group."[8]

What is called an **iron triangle** often develops among key members of Congress, bureaucrats, and interest groups (Figure 7.2). For example, Federal Highway Administration officials, in concert with business lobbyists and relevant committee members of

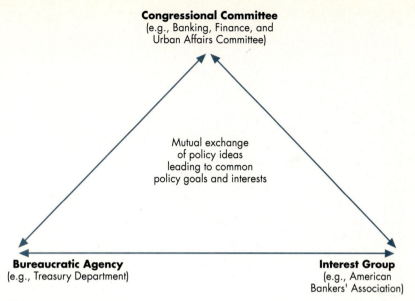

Congressional Committee
(e.g., Banking, Finance, and
Urban Affairs Committee)

Mutual exchange
of policy ideas
leading to common
policy goals and interests

Bureaucratic Agency
(e.g., Treasury Department)

Interest Group
(e.g., American
Bankers' Association)

Figure 7.2 THE IRON TRIANGLE.

Congress, carefully gutted a plan to remove billboards from federal roads. Working together, this triangle changed a rule and gave the taxpayers two ugly choices: either leave the 9000 billboards where they were or spend $18 million to take them down. In effect, the rule change turned the Highway Beautification Act into a billboard protection law.

Another factor favoring business and industry is the **built-in constituency** that these interest groups can call on to support their positions on a public issue. How was the financially beleaguered Chrysler Corporation able to obtain $1.5 billion in federal loan guarantees in the early 1980s? One of the most sophisticated lobbying efforts in history put it together for Chrysler. Local Chrysler dealers around the nation wrote to and personally lobbied members of Congress on behalf of the measure. Suppliers of parts and services to Chrysler throughout the nation did likewise. Chrysler itself retained some of the best-known and most effective lobbyists in Washington. Combining money, knowledge, and built-in constituencies, Chrysler averted bankruptcy.

No other interest group has sufficient authority to balance the overwhelming power of business and industrial interests. Two groups, labor and agriculture, have been most often regarded as **countervailing forces**, acting as checks on business and industry. Labor leaders, however, are not consulted by government officials as much as business leaders are. In January 1992, for example, President Bush made a state visit to Japan and brought with him several dozen of America's highest-paid corporate executives, but no labor leaders. Labor's countervailing influence is also weakened by the fact that labor's interests sometimes coincide with those of business, as in the case of the Chrysler bailout. As for agriculture, the number of small family farms has declined steadily throughout the twentieth century. There were 6.5 million farms in 1925, but only 2 million in 1990. At the same time farming is increasingly becoming big business; agribusiness has more in common with industry than with the individual farmer.

When President George Bush made a state visit to Japan in 1992, he took along several heads of American auto companies to get their input on trade issues. But no labor leaders or consumer group representatives were invited. On the left is Robert Stempel, Chairman of General Motors; Prime Minister Kiichi Miyazawa is on the right.

The federal government has tried to regulate lobbying, but its controls are ineffectual. The Federal Regulation of Lobbying Act (1948) required lobbyists to register and to report their lobbying expenses. The Supreme Court's interpretation of the law a few years later limited its scope. For instance, organizations must register only if lobbying is their "principal purpose." This exempts many groups that do lobby, but not as their main goal. As indicated earlier, lobbyists are required to report only those expenses incurred in *direct contact with members of Congress*. Thus, they need not report money spent contacting members of the executive department. This provision also effectively exempts overhead expenses and the major portion of lobbyists' salaries.

Political parties are no more effective than the government at counteracting the power of business and industrial interest groups. American political parties today lack the clout to force legislators and other elected officials to adhere to established party positions and thus lessen their susceptibility to interest group pressure.

The massive pressure that the affluent interest groups are able to place on government may contribute to the frustration of those who have *no* resources to influence government and feel alienated from the American system. In the 1960s and 1970s some of these Americans, many of them college students, turned to radical and sometimes violent leftist ideologies and movements; in the 1980s others turned to radical and violent rightist ones. Without money and other more acceptable forms of influence, they chose violence as a technique of persuasion.

REASONS WHY BUSINESS AND INDUSTRIAL LOBBIES ARE NOT TOO POWERFUL

It is true that more interest groups represent business and industry than any other segment of our society, but some qualifying points should be made. First, in a largely capitalist economy, such representation is only natural. Second, despite their numerical superiority, business and industrial interest groups do not necessarily dominate public policy. For example, the major social and economic innovations of the twentieth century did not originate with the Chamber of Commerce or the National Association of Manufacturers. The New Deal, for instance, forged a coalition of labor unions, big cities, and the mostly rural and agriculturally dominated South largely through a brain trust of liberal intellectuals.

Sometimes, despite their best efforts, business lobbies *lose* key battles. Public opinion and government bureaucrats teamed up to get Medicare and Medicaid programs passed in 1965 in the face of strong opposition from the powerful American Medical Association. (The AMA had considered these programs to be forms of "socialized medicine," an impolite term for national health insurance, which might threaten the independence of medical practitioners.)

In response to the assertion that PACs enable business and industry to improperly influence election results and legislative decisions, one should note that business and industrial PACs constitute only a plurality of all PACs, not a majority, and that their winning percentage for candidates they support is not higher than that for many other PACs, like labor. Moreover, a PAC contribution may harm more than it helps a member of Congress if that PAC represents a position contrary to the public's general consensus on the issue. Would a candidate want a contribution from an oil PAC if clean air is an issue in the campaign? Or would a candidate be eager to accept a contribution from the National Rifle Association if some lunatic has shot to death dozens of people taking lunch in a restaurant in her or his congressional district? Five thousand dollars is not really worth losing the public support that is crucial in elections.

In any case, PACs are not the exclusive province of business and industry. The PACs also give millions of otherwise unrepresented people a voice in the interest group struggle. By combining their limited financial resources, the PACs of small organizations can substantially increase their political impact.

A number of **emerging interest groups** have placed checks on the more powerful and affluent traditional interest groups. As lobbyists representing oil companies, shippers, and medical associations leave a legislator's office they may encounter younger lobbyists representing the Energy Action Committee, the Sierra Club, the Tax Reform Research Group, or the Health Research Group, which have been responsible for helping pass new laws regulating campaign finance, automobile safety, air pollution, and government secrecy. Once considered omnipotent in setting national sugar policy, the cane sugar lobby now must battle consumer and labor lobbyists as well as the corn sweetener industry. From a relatively unorganized beginning with Earth Day celebrations in the late 1960s, the environmental lobby grew to a position where it could challenge business and industrial interests on Alaskan land use.

New interest group involvement occurred in the Roman Catholic Church, with the National Conference of Catholic Bishops taking well-publicized positions on nuclear arms, abortion, human rights, and economic justice. Because their pastoral letters are read

Earth First is one of many emerging interest groups that are now challenging traditional interest groups.

in every Roman Catholic parish, they are in a position to influence millions of grass-roots Americans.

Critics of interest group influence call for more regulation, but regulation of lobbyists can create its own dangers. What if interest groups were to be abolished or their activities substantially restricted? The result would be catastrophic for the First Amendment freedoms of religion, speech, press, and assembly, which are fundamental to any democracy. If we do not accept interest groups, we must necessarily allow a single "truth" to prevail. Competing interest groups at least give both the public and those in government competing points of view. This would not be necessary if we were governed by omniscient philosopher-kings. But, as James Madison warned, "It is vain to say the enlightened statesmen will be able to adjust these clashing interests, and render them all subservient to the public good. Enlightened statesmen will not always be at the helm."[9]

Another question to consider is how concerned we should be about government employees who once worked for the businesses they are now charged with regulating. It is simplistic to think that the business automatically benefits from such an arrangement. Just as neither President Lyndon Johnson nor President Jimmy Carter represented the view of the South on civil rights (although they both came from that region), so a government employee does not necessarily represent the interests of a previous employer. In fact, the business or industry may be adversely affected by the employee's desire to avoid even the *appearance* of benefiting the previous employer. Peer-group pressure also helps to maintain high professional standards.

Finally, we should note that many issues settled by competition among interest groups are not generally of concern to business and industry. For example, one of the most visible and dramatic interest group battles in recent years has taken place between pro-life and pro-choice forces over the issue of abortion. The pro-life forces, with a large grass-roots constituency, have spawned several interest groups, including the Life Amendment Political Action Committee (which wants a constitutional amendment banning abortion once and for all) and Americans for Life. The National Abortion Rights Action League (NARAL) is the principal pro-choice group and, of course, fights vigorously against such a possible amendment.

ISSUE 1:   Summary   ★   *Are Business and Industrial Lobbies Too Powerful?*

With an emphatic capitalist base to the American economy, the large number of business and industrial interest groups is no surprise. The danger is that their affluence and access to information will unduly influence legislators and elected officials in their favor. On balance, however, it does not seem that their influence is overpowering. There are many other types of interest groups, and even interest groups within each category differ in their desires to influence public policy. Not only do interest groups check other interest groups, but new interest groups usually emerge to fill voids in group representation. Additionally, the government and public opinion may perform useful checks on business activities that do more harm than good to consumer interests. Just as democracy is itself imperfect, however, interest groups do not fully and accurately reflect *all* American interests, and sometimes checks do not work properly.

ISSUE 2   ARE INTEREST GROUPS A LIABILITY OR AN ASSET IN DETERMINING THE PUBLIC INTEREST?

REASONS WHY INTEREST GROUPS ARE A LIABILITY IN DETERMINING THE PUBLIC INTEREST

There are three main reasons why interest groups are a liability in determining the public interest. One, just discussed at length, is that the balance of interests may be tipped in certain groups' favor. Another is that the emergence of single-issue groups is distorting the interest group struggle. Finally, the interests of group leaders and rank-and-file members may not coincide.

Imbalance of Power. Here is an example of how one group may have too much power: Weapons manufacturers pressured Congress to pass the Extraordinary Contractual Relief Act, a "cradle-to-the-grave" protection plan that (1) ensures that few defense contractors fail, (2) adds a hidden surcharge to every military budget for this protection, (3) picks up the tab for even unsolicited and unsuccessful proposals, and (4) dispenses termination fees to companies whose weapons are no longer purchased. Another example is tax code legislation during the 1980s. It was supposedly drafted to tighten the loopholes used by big business, but it actually helped such companies as American Motors, Bethlehem Steel, Texas Industries, Allis Chalmers, John Deere, Mercedes-Benz, and the tobacco industry by providing for major tax loopholes. Tax-exempt bonds were to be restricted, but 12 members of the Senate Finance Committee put into the bill 27 exceptions for projects in their states in deference to those financial interests that wanted tax-free income and were, by interesting coincidence, campaign contributors.[10] (See the accompanying box for an example of clout wielded by the pharmaceutical industry.)

Single-Issue Groups. Single-issue groups, those that care about only one issue, were first seen in the 1970s and are still a dominant force today. Their allegiance is solely to their particular position on that one issue. As a result, a public official who votes on the wrong side on that issue, regardless of how well he or she performed in other areas, would be vehemently opposed by the single-issue group. Its position cannot be compromised. This rather emphatic inflexibility caused *Washington Post* columnist David Broder to comment:

> Some call them special-interest groups. Some call them single-interest groups. Whatever the name, it's agreed they're a shame. "Strident and self-righteous," as one senator terms them, the single-issue groups are accused of fragmenting the political consensus, whipsawing conscientious public officials with non-negotiable demands, and generally playing havoc with responsible government and politics.[11]

Women's rights, gun control, and abortion are some of the issues that have spawned single-issue groups. Antiabortion interest groups, for example, have been given primary credit for defeating about ten incumbent U.S. Senators in 1978, 1980, and 1982. This record of success was not sustained, however, since it provoked just as strident pro-choice groups to be formed and apply equal pressures on the other side, causing pro-life candidates to be more careful about how they approach the issue and leading some to change their positions. In the aftermath of the 1992 election, Republicans began a major internal debate on the party's pro-life position, which it had held under Presidents Reagan and Bush.

Misrepresentation. Both conservative and liberal interest groups have been accused of misrepresenting their members. The American Farm Bureau Federation and its state affiliates, for example, have large insurance companies. The tie that binds members to the organization may not be representation of interests, but service of financial needs. Rank-and-file members may allow enormous discretion to their leaders in return for services provided. In the process the members' interests may actually get misrepresented.

Edward Norman and Ernest Lefever contend that the World Council of Churches (WCC) misrepresents the interests of many members, particularly those of American churches like the United Methodist, Episcopal, and Presbyterian.[12] Examples of this misrepresentation include WCC's financing of revolution in Africa. Although Ralph Nader tries to represent the public interest, S. Robert Lichter and Stanley Rothman found that his associates are decidedly different from the general public in both composition and belief, including differences in race, sex, geographical location, partisan identification, education, ideology, and religion.[13] Linda S. Lichter, in a study of African-American leaders and rank-and-file African-Americans, found a gulf of difference between them, suggesting that the leaders may not be accurately representing their followers (Table 7.3).

A VIEW FROM THE STATES
The Other Drug Lords

The scene was right out of middle America's worst nightmare about what goes on under the Capitol dome. Special-interest lobbyists prowled the halls buttonholing lawmakers. Debating in the chamber, senators parroted industry-supplied talking points and attacked the legislation at hand as a threat to the American way of life. Senators trotted out charts and graphs, the snazziest of them provided by industry.

At the end of the wearying eight-hour debate last March, Senator David Pryor's (D-Ark.) amendment to restrict a tax break enjoyed by U.S. pharmaceutical makers with factories in Puerto Rico went down by a margin of almost two-to-one.

Chalk up another one for the drug industry, a lobby that ranks among the most muscular in town, adept at deploying plenty of both PAC money and lobbyists—many of them former congressional aides—to make arguments and usually carry the day. . . .

A look at how this industry operates in Washington gives a glimpse of how tough it will be to enact any meaningful national health-care reform. At even the hint that Congress might curb the skyrocketing price of prescription drugs, the drug lobby enters with guns blazing:

- When Congress tried to control drug prices for the Medicaid program, the industry persuaded minority leaders to warn of "second-class medicine" for the poor. . . .

- When lawmakers were debating a landmark Medicare bill to cover catastrophic illness, the drug industry helped whip up senior citizens, ultimately bringing the law crashing down—because it included a prescription drug benefit that might have led to cost controls. . . .

. . . Unlike physicians and hospitals, drug makers have so far fended off virtually all government attempts to control prices.

It's the public that pays, through inflated health-care costs and medications that are often priced beyond the reach of many who need them. . . .

It doesn't have to be like this. In Europe, where most countries regulate drug costs, consumers pay 54 percent less for pharmaceuticals than Americans. . . .

But underestimating the drug lobby is a proven mistake. . . .

"If the debate and vote on [the Puerto Rico tax breaks] is any indication of how long it is going to take to reform the health-care system in this country," says Pryor, "it is clear to me that we have a very long way to go. If Congress cannot stand up to the pharmaceutical industry—for which we spend less than 10 percent of our health-care dollars—how in the world are we going to stand up to the other entrenched health-care interests?"

Source: Viveca Novak, "The Other Drug Lords," *Common Cause Magazine*, reprinted in *The National Times*, mini-edition, December 1992, pp. 1, 10–14.

TABLE 7.3 PROPORTION OF LEADING AND RANK-AND-FILE AFRICAN-AMERICANS FAVORING SELECTED ISSUES		
	Leaders	Rank and File
Prayer in public schools	40%	83%
Death penalty	33%	55%
Ban on all abortions	14%	44%
School busing	68%	47%
Affirmative action	77%	23%
Allowing homosexuals to teach in public schools	59%	40%
Termination of corporate investment in South Africa	59%	40%

Source: Linda S. Lichter, "Who Speaks for Black America?" *Public Opinion* 8 (August/September 1985): 41–44. Reprinted with the permission of The American Enterprise Institute for Public Policy Research, Washington, D.C.

REASONS WHY INTEREST GROUPS ARE AN ASSET IN DETERMINING THE PUBLIC INTEREST

Sometimes public policy or the public interest is considered to be the balance achieved in the competition among interest groups. This definition provides a clue to five significant contributions interest groups make to American democracy.

1. They supplement the constitutional system of checks and balances.
2. They provide another form of representation.
3. They help maintain an open society by offering alternatives to government policies.
4. They educate the public in the complexities of government.
5. They stabilize American society.

A Supplement to Checks and Balances.   Although James Madison did not consider factions an ideal arrangement, he did provide a rationale for allowing group interaction and conflict to operate freely:

> By a faction, I understand a number of citizens, whether amounting to a majority or minority of the whole, who are united and actuated by some common impulse of passion, or of interest, adverse to the rights of other citizens, or to the permanent and aggregate interests of the community. . . .
>
> The latent causes of faction are . . . sown in the nature of man, and we see them everywhere brought into different degrees of activity, according to the different circumstances of civil society. A zeal for different opinions concerning religion, concerning government, and many other points, as well of speculation as of practice; and attachment to different leaders ambitiously contending for preeminence and power . . . have, in turn, divided mankind into parties, inflamed them with mutual animosity, and rendered them much more disposed to vex and oppress each other than to cooperate for their common good. . . .

The inference to which we are brought is, that the cause of faction cannot be removed, and that relief is only to be sought in the means of controlling its effects.[14]

Group competition and conflict are natural ways to control the effects of faction. As groups challenge each other, they serve as an informal supplement to the constitutional system of checks and balances. Competing interests vie with one another for the support of public opinion and the various branches of government. The Sierra Club and other environmental groups are often opposed by real estate development interests. Right-to-life groups are opposed by pro-choice groups. State aid to parochial schools, supported by many Roman Catholic and Lutheran groups, has frequently been challenged by some Jewish and Protestant groups.

Indeed, where one interest may have the upper hand with the legislature, another interest may have the upper hand with the executive or with the courts. In that respect, no one group can dominate the development of public policy on a permanent basis. A vivid example occurred during the early New Deal period, when President Franklin D. Roosevelt obtained passage of major legislation only to have the Supreme Court declare much of it unconstitutional.

Grass-roots lobbying, as we saw earlier, provides a way to give ordinary citizens, when they act in large enough numbers, influence on the policymakers. It is very easy to write, phone, or fax a legislator and often very effective in concert with action by others.

Additional Representation. In a democratic society based on republican principles, representation enables the citizen's point of view to be heard in the councils of government. Obviously, political parties and the electoral system provide representation, but it is usefully supplemented by interest groups. Unlike political parties, interest groups generally represent persons with similar concerns about a narrow range of interests. In many respects, interest group representation is superior to party and electoral representation, because the bond holding the interest group members together tends to be stronger. For example, African-Americans stood to gain more by working through the National Association for the Advancement of Colored People (NAACP) and seeking to win their rights in the courts than they did by working through the Democratic party. Indeed, party affiliation had no meaning until they could vote.

Aiding an Open Society. As Madison said, groups will exist in any form of government that allows people some measure of freedom to express their views. A free and open society is endangered if all information comes from one or a few sources, or if there are no alternatives to government policies and decisions. All kinds of groups need the liberty to express their opinions and to try to influence government about their needs and interests. Only in this way can we prevent the dominance of one or a few groups and the stagnation of ideas.

A relevant example concerns the funding of public schools. Traditionally local property taxes have supported them, with the result that the wealthier the community, the better the schools. Groups in many states have successfully organized to contend in the courts that such financing denied equal protection of the laws under the Fourteenth Amendment.

Without interest group agitation, there would have been no alternative to the Vietnam War policies of Presidents Johnson and Nixon. In this instance, interest groups such as the Vietnam Veterans Against the War organized for the specific purpose of opposing the war. They marched and picketed in the streets, petitioned the government,

Interest groups aid in maintaining an open society by giving a voice to those who oppose government policy. The activities of Vietnam Veterans Against the War served as a powerful reminder to the Nixon administration that its policy in Vietnam was not working.

gave testimony in congressional hearings, and challenged the presidents' actions in the courts.

When interest groups provide a challenge, the government must constantly evaluate and defend its policies. The public benefits from this interchange. Consider the NAACP's challenge to race discrimination, Ralph Nader's challenge to auto manufacturers, and the Sierra Club's challenge to lumbering interests. Without the work of these groups, it is safe to say that white supremacy, unsafe automobiles, and unchecked deforestation would be far bigger problems than they are today.

Educating the Public. The public, looking at a mass of 535 persons serving in the Congress, finds it hard to distinguish the corrupt and inept from the honest and competent. Interest groups help people cope with this problem through their ratings of members of Congress. A variety of organizations— liberal and conservative, business and labor—rate legislators. Their ratings can have a substantial impact on public thinking.

Stabilization of Society. The abundance of interest groups means that change in American society occurs gradually. Interest groups face competition from other groups. Each must convince the government of the validity of its positions. All this takes time, so the evils of too-rapid change are avoided.

Preceding most major public policy innovations is an "incubation period" of several years during which the new idea is discussed. With certain issues like federal aid to education and federal medical programs, this period may last several decades. The incubation period allows groups to present their views before Congress. During this time the public benefits by receiving news accounts and analyses of the ongoing national debate on major new proposals.

Without interest groups it would be difficult, if not impossible, to define the public interest. If there were no interest groups, they would most likely be invented because they are essential to the effective working of democracy. The public depends on them for representation of group interests, and elected officials depend on them for information on which to make decisions.

ISSUE 2: Summary ★ *Are Interest Groups an Asset or a Liability in Determining the Public Interest?*

Whether interest groups are an asset or a liability in determining the public interest depends on the compromise achieved in the interest group struggle. Are sufficient points of view represented effectively as interest groups compete to influence public policy? It is true that not all Americans are fairly represented by interest groups, but the groups still contribute to the American political system by supplementing the checks and balances of our government, providing another form of representation, offering alternatives to existing government policy, educating the public about government, and stabilizing American society. Interest groups cause problems, but without them there could be no public interest other than what one person or group specified. The system allows a variety of interest groups rather than just one or a few to determine the public interest.

COMPARISONS WITH OTHER NATIONS

INTEREST GROUPS IN DEMOCRACIES

Many democracies have interest groups that very much resemble our own. In the United Kingdom, for example, there are single-issue groups that Americans would not find unfamiliar: the Abortion Law Reform Society and the Campaign for Homosexual Equality, for instance, have their counterparts in the United States.

But it is unusual for an interest group in another democracy to possess either the financial resources or the political influence of several of the more powerful interest groups in the United States. There are several reasons for this distinction:

1. Many American interest groups (such as the National Rifle Association) have tremendous influence because of their large memberships, a great advantage at election time.
2. Many American interest groups (such as the American Medical Association) have substantial amounts of money to contribute to a political campaign to help elect (or defeat) a candidate.
3. Interest groups abroad (farmers or ethnic minorities, for example) often form themselves into political parties.

Naturally, interest groups in other countries lobby on behalf of their cause. However, the target of the lobbying is often quite different than what is found in the United States. The American textile industry, for instance, expends a great deal of time (and, presumably, money) in an effort to develop a close relationship with members of the House of Representatives whose constituencies include a large number of textile plants. The members of Congress are already sympathetic with the concerns of the industry or they might not have gotten elected in the first place. The textile lobbyists count on their votes in legislation affecting the industry.

In contrast, lobbying in Britain is carried on in a very different context. In a parliamentary system, the executive controls the majority of seats in the House of Commons, so the focus of lobbying is on the ministry, not the Commons.

Party discipline (or the lack of it) also has something to do with the success of interest group lobbying. It is not at all uncommon for House and Senate Democrats and Republicans to defy their party leadership and vote either their conscience or, more likely, the sentiment of their constituents. But in most parliamentary systems, legislators who want to pursue a long-term political career must vote in almost every case the way their party leadership has told them to vote. This practice makes it nearly a waste of time to focus lobbying efforts on individual legislators. As one distinguished scholar has pointed out: "Attempts to lobby Parliament or to maintain regular contact on a scale analogous to that maintained on Capitol Hill are notable for their rarity. Many groups maintain friendly contact with members of Parliament, but few sectional groups mount or would even know how to mount an effective lobby."[15]

In many countries with multiparty systems a number of interest groups evolve into full-fledged political parties. They tend to be unsuccessful in the long term, but they can make an impact for an election or two. In France one of the most successful (if short-lived) single-issue groups, an organization vehemently opposed to paying taxes, became a political party: The Union for the Defense of Shopkeepers and Artisans, founded by Pierre Poujade. While hatred of taxes was its greatest appeal, this party also was anti-big business and anti-Semitic, but these were less advertised characteristics. In the parliamentary elections of 1956 the "Poujadists" won 12 percent of the popular vote and 53 parliamentary seats. They then merged with larger conservative political parties and disappeared. Such parties are less common (and less successful) in the United States and the United Kingdom, but they do spring up from time to time. Single-issue groups still in existence as parties in our country include the Vegetarian party and the Prohibition party. The former wants people to stop eating meat; the latter wants them to stop consuming alcoholic beverages. One predominating issue motivates each party.

More and more countries are developing an equivalent of the Green party, one of the strongest environmentalist and antinuclear movements. The Greens have appeared in most Western European party systems. By the early 1990s they were beginning to organize in Eastern Europe, Japan, and even parts of the former Soviet Union. In the German national parliamentary elections of 1983 and 1987 the Green party won several dozen seats. A relatively new Green party in Britain managed to receive about 5 percent of the votes cast in local elections held throughout the country in May 1991.[16] While the environmentalist movement in the United States is strong, none of the movement's organizations have seriously attempted to form a political party (with the exception of California's Green party) that would have any electoral significance. They prefer instead to persuade Democrats and Republicans that a clean environment benefits everyone.

In multiparty countries, particular interests may organize into political parties. Many nations have some variation of what is known as the Green party, an environmental and antinuclear movement. Shown here is Antoine Waechter, the leader of the Green party in France. His sign reads, "Ecology. That's the Greens. Beware of imitations."

In some democracies, notably the newer ones such as India, Spain, and Israel, interest groups that take the form of political parties are frequently based on ethnic and/or religious communities. Table 7.4 summarizes the more prevalent ones. These parties function in great part because their supporters have not been (or are not willing to be) integrated into the overall political system. They either have a memory of political independence in the past or a desire for it in the future. Even the older democracies are not immune to this phenomenon. Scotch and Welsh separatists in the United Kingdom, for instance, have formed their own parties as part of an effort to secure political independence from England.

Disrupting Influences

It would be difficult to imagine politics in the United States or in any other democracy being conducted without the activities of interest groups. Even so their presence is not

TABLE 7.4	ETHNIC/RELIGIOUS POLITICAL PARTIES IN SELECTED DEMOCRACIES	
Country	Ethnic or Religious Party	Political Agenda
India	Akali Dal	Autonomy for India's Sikh community
Israel	Sephardic Torah Guardians	Religious orthodoxy in the country
Spain	Basque Nationalist Party	Political independence from Spain

always a welcome one. In France, for example, interest group activity has been equated with factionalism, a dangerous phenomenon in a country that has endured a great many political fissures throughout its modern history. When Charles de Gaulle founded the Fifth Republic in 1958 he intentionally, if unsuccessfully, discouraged interest groups from participating in the political process.[17]

He preferred the concept of concertation (or harmonization[18]) in an effort to unify the French people. Like Madison two centuries earlier, de Gaulle was concerned that interest groups might detract from a nation's much-needed political unity.

Sometimes a country's interest groups will have a disruptive effect on relations with other nations. Take the example of Israel and the United States. In the late 1980s and early 1990s private political and religious organizations as well as government-sponsored ones in Israel accelerated the establishment of Jewish settlements in the West Bank in open defiance of official American government preferences. Because organizers of the settlements have a great deal of popular support, the Israeli government felt compelled to support the settlements. This further annoyed the United States government because such efforts could seriously damage the American-sponsored peace talks between Israelis and Palestinians. Thus, the same interest group has been successful in promoting not only its own agenda, but also in influencing how two governments view one another. Nor is this phenomenon unusual. The United States is composed of millions of citizens who have relatives in or sympathies with their countries of origin, so there is no shortage of attempts to influence American foreign policy.

The Influence of Unions

Industrialized democracies usually have very powerful labor unions that try, with frequent success, to influence the outcome of national elections. (One of the two major parties in Britain, in fact, is the *Labour* party.) In this respect, the United States differs from its democratic counterparts in Western Europe and Japan. As Table 7.5 points out, American workers are less likely to join unions than elsewhere. They are also apparently more likely to leave one. Between 1975 and 1985, for example, union membership in the United States declined by 4 million, even as the labor force grew in absolute numbers.[19] But other industrialized societies have experienced declines in trade union membership too,

TABLE 7.5 UNION MEMBERSHIP IN SELECTED INDUSTRIALIZED DEMOCRACIES, 1987

Country	Percent of Labor Force in Unions
United Kingdom	50%
Italy	43%
Germany (excluding eastern Germany)	40%
Japan	28%
France	22%
United States	**18%**

Approximate percentages adapted from *The Economist*, February 14, 1987.

and they probably will continue to do so as long as economic progress convinces workers that security can be guaranteed by means other than joining a union.

The union movement in any of the democracies shows how an interest group takes its chances. As union strength has declined in the United States and, to a lesser extent, elsewhere, so has its influence. The Labour party in Britain, for example, has no hope of winning a national election without a large union block vote. Much the same could be said for the Social Democrats in Germany. In both countries, as union membership has declined so have the political fortunes of the left-of-center political parties. Labour has been out of power since 1979 and the Social Democrats since 1982. And, in the United States, the Democratic party, traditionally supported by labor, lost three consecutive presidential elections between 1980 and 1992. Of course, none of these parties can win a national election solely on solid support from labor, but none can win *without* such support.

Emerging "International" Interest Groups

The labor movement has at times attempted to develop an international posture under the assumption that working men and women have similar problems in every industrial society. By and large, though, different sorts of interest groups have risen in response to different problems. Since Western societies developed industrial economies at their own pace, even similar interest groups tended to form at different intervals.

This tradition may now be changing. The increasing globalization of domestic economies and the common challenges facing the world are having an effect. Global concerns require global interest groups. The Green movement has already been mentioned. The environment is quite properly being regarded more and more as a concern for everyone on the planet, since pollution doesn't stop at a country's national borders. In addition, over the last decade there have been international conferences and permanent organizations established on the AIDS epidemic, political terrorism, the rights of women, and abortion. The Union of Concerned Scientists, an international organization based in the United States, monitors nuclear energy installations around the globe. The breakdown in the nuclear power plant at Chernobyl in the Ukraine demonstrated that a nuclear meltdown in one country can affect the health and lives of millions of people in numerous neighboring societies.

The ecology movement is another focus of international interest. Organizations such as the Worldwide Fund for Nature and the World Rainforest Movement are attempting to save the remaining rainforest regions of the world. The destruction of the rainforests will ultimately affect the entire planet since the disappearance of the forests will also eliminate plant and animal species that could feed millions of people and cure or prevent innumerable diseases.[20] There is a realization that like-minded groups in several countries must work together if they are to have any hope of success. Increasingly, these global interest groups will influence the internal politics of a number of countries.

Some issues are old but are receiving new emphases. The British, for example, have a long tradition of being kind to animals, well before the issue of animal rights became politicized. Britain's venerable Royal Society for the Prevention of Cruelty to Animals (RSPCA) has inspired more recently organized animal lovers in the United States to make life miserable for American cosmetic manufacturers. Animal welfare and rights groups in America are boycotting companies that produce lipsticks whose chemical

Some interest groups are international in scope. They operate in the global arena. The World Wildlife Fund joined with America's National Wildlife Federation to create this advertisement on behalf of chimpanzees whose natural habitats in Africa are shrinking.

ingredients have been force-fed to rabbits, for instance.[21] Sometimes a global organization will be formed to voice concern for only one animal, even one not usually found outside its natural habitat. The Koala Preservation Society of New South Wales in Australia, for example, has an executive director for North America (equipped with an 800 phone number), even though koalas are not found on the North American continent except, rarely, in zoos.[22]

Simple but profound demographic change is also promoting the emergence of new interest groups whose need was neither obvious nor foreseen only several years ago. During the 1980s, strong interest groups formed in south Florida, for example, to promote the establishment of Spanish as an official language in America along with English. Other groups have formed for the precise purpose of opposing placing Spanish on a par with English. The pro-Spanish interest groups maintain that with a million transplanted Cubans and south Florida's proximity to the Caribbean Basin (much of which is Spanish-speaking) it makes perfectly good sense to adopt Spanish as at least the coequal language with English. The pro-English groups maintain that, regardless of its geographical location, south Florida is part of the United States and Americans speak English. This debate may be repeated in other states that border on Spanish-speaking countries and contain large communities of Spanish-speaking residents.

Most Americans may not even be aware of the rise of language as a political issue. But it already is one in other democracies. For example, Canadians have long debated the primacy of English versus French, and Wales has been modestly successful in reviving Gaelic. The United States has perhaps always been a *multi*lingual nation. If you travel on a New York subway through the borough of Queens, you can sometimes hear nearly every language *except* English.[23]

The Persistence of Tribal Interest Groups

Ironically, at the same time that many interests are becoming more progressive and increasingly global, other interest groups that are tribal in nature retain a strong hold on the political process, even in countries with democratic systems. These are the greatest actual and potential source of international violence. They are also perhaps the greatest challenge to the establishment and durability of political democracy. Even countries that are relatively linguistically and religiously homogeneous—that is, countries that should be conducive to democracy—can be destroyed by primordial tribal or clan loyalties. The African nation of Somalia clearly demonstrated this danger in 1992 and 1993 as competing clan families, despite speaking the same language and adhering to the same religious beliefs, completely wrecked the economy and political stability of an entire society.[24]

India is a case in point of a developing democracy. It is a society in which one-sixth of the human race resides. Yet India is a segregated society whose interest groups (and, to some extent, political parties) are frequently based on social rank or caste. Certainly, not all interest groups in India are based on the caste system. The familiar business, military, bureaucratic, and professional associations also have political concerns. But caste is the overwhelming character of social divisions because caste permeates so much of daily life. For hundreds of millions of Indians, "caste shapes almost every aspect of life: the food they eat, and who can cook it; how they bathe; the colour of their clothes; the length of a sari; how the dhoti is tied; which way a man's moustaches are trained and whether he can carry an umbrella. Nothing is left to chance."[25]

Indian society retains a great deal of social rigidity that in large part prevents or at least delays the integration of castes (see Table 7.6). To become a thoroughly modern society India requires modern interest groups that transcend caste differences, such as professional associations that admit members without regard to caste origin and that publicly encourage qualified applicants regardless of social background. So far, these have not fully arrived on the scene.

There are perhaps a hundred countries in the Third World. Most of these are far from fully integrated politically. In these countries tribal, ethnic, and religious associations take precedence over professional ones. The sense of a national community with competing but politically loyal interest groups is still a predominantly Western concept. The lack of a national identity may not be the fault of those without it. Many African and several Asian countries, for instance, had their boundary lines drawn by Europeans in the nineteenth century; these boundaries were at best oblivious of and at worst insensitive to the preferences of the local inhabitants. Many of these inhabitants became reluctant neighbors in a single political society whose various regions had little if anything in common. Tribal associations, which preceded national ones by many centuries, are the focal points of political loyalties.

TABLE 7.6 INDIA'S SOCIAL SYSTEM: A MANY-LAYERED THING	
India's Population	Proportion of Total
Upper castes	17.58%
Backward castes	43.70%
Untouchables	15.05%
Tribesmen	7.51%
Muslims (other than tribes)	11.19%
Christians (other than tribes)	2.16%
Sikhs	1.67%
Buddhists (other than tribes)	0.67%
Jains	0.47%
Source: *The Economist,* June 8, 1991, p. 22.	

As a result, some of these nations' interest groups have not yet developed beyond narrow sectional or sectarian concerns to the point where they can be tolerant of other interests. Such a divisive environment can threaten to destroy a political system altogether. This has already happened in places such as Cyprus and Lebanon, two countries that at one point showed some promise of becoming democratic, and in Somalia and Yugoslavia. It could still happen in India and Malaysia. It is difficult to convince the various interests of a nation to accept the "win some-lose some" perspective of interest groups in Western Europe and North America. There have been too many massacres to entertain that possibility as a viable one.

INTEREST GROUPS IN TOTALITARIAN SYSTEMS

Not even totalitarian systems are without interest groups or without competition between them. The regular military, for example, is often at odds with the secret police, which usually has its own fairly sophisticated military apparatus. The totalitarian party bureaucracy competes with and frequently duplicates the state bureaucracy. And within the party itself various factions compete with one another for political power and economic influence.

In former communist societies the emergence of new and demanding groups, a few of which have a potential for violence, is changing the political character of their countries. At the same time, the sorts of interest groups with which Americans are familiar—environmental, labor, consumer, for example—are also beginning to emerge, bumping into the more established and often un- or antidemocratic interests.

The former Soviet Union remains a useful example. The old interests in August 1991 attempted in a miserably failed coup to turn back the clock, remove Gorbachev from power, and reestablish the Communist party's supremacy. It didn't work, but the coup did reveal the desperate measures some interest groups will take to stay in power. The list below summarizes the recalcitrant interest groups:

A VIEW FROM ABROAD
Time to Lobby in Russia

One of the most important institutions that we urgently need to develop is that of lobbying. The very term was considered virtually a swear word in Russia until just recently. But lobbying is one of the leading instruments of market-style democracy.

Several different interests can lobby at the same time, including mutually exclusive ones. In other words, there is competition here. And this competition, as a rule, is open—official registration is mandatory.

To idealize the institution of lobbying would be as unjustified as minimizing its importance. There is no panacea for all evils in politics. And yet, the overall democratic potential of lobbying is obvious.

A debate about whether we need lobbying is pointless. We already have it. In fact, we have it in its worst form—"wildcat," wide-scale lobbying, uncontrolled by anything or anybody. So the real choice today is not whether lobbying will exist or not but what kind it will be: dominated by the elite, pro-communist, or civilized.

. . . Inevitably, the question arises of the right of foreigners to exert influence on our bodies of government. In today's world, community lobbying by foreign interests is a commonly accepted practice. Besides, our need for foreign investments dictates the necessity of official lobbying by foreign interests. This issue has a flip side—lobbying by Russian interests in other countries. It is time to begin to make effective use of a commonly accepted international practice.

Source: Viktor Danilenko, "Izvestia" (Moscow). Reprinted in *World Press Review,* December 1992.

1. Communist nomenclatura—the top 250,000 party bureaucrats
2. Military-industrial complex—elitist alliance of high-ranking officers and major officials of defense related industries
3. Managers of state and collective farms
4. Managers of factories

Notice that the Communists have ceased to be a political party and have really been transformed into an interest group. The higher party officials, the nomenclatura, worked hard to protect their special privileges. Their appendages, high-ranking military officers and the managers of collective farms and state-run factories, acted out of fear as well. And, of course, even though the old Soviet Union concluded its career in December 1991, the old interests are still around. Taking no chances, Russian President Boris Yeltsin made sure he was in Moscow on the first anniversary of the August coup to forestall another one (Gorbachev a year earlier had gone for a vacation to the Crimea on the Black Sea).

The Soviet Union's most enduring political legacy is based on ethnicity. Many of the hundred or so different nationalities in the former Soviet Union are beginning to reemerge from the wreckage of communism. They come equipped with their old religious and territorial motivations and ambitions. It remains uncertain whether these ethnic and religiously based interest groups can or even want to contribute to the democratization of the countries that belong to the new Commonwealth of Independent States.

The Communist party is still in control in China but an interesting experiment is under way. Since the late 1970s China "has quietly encouraged the non-state, market-oriented sector to flourish. Most of the industrial growth in China's economy derives from the non-state sector, which includes private enterprises, foreign-invested and joint venture firms, and entrepreneurial village and township companies."[26] Unlike Russia, which "went for shock therapy, the big bang, sudden price decontrol, and almost overnight privatization of state-run enterprises," China more or less backed into capitalism with its gradual, trial-and-error approach.[27] The Chinese now have money to spend: In 1978 only 1 in 300 Chinese owned a television set and 1 in 10,000 a washing machine; in 1992, 13 in 100 owned a TV set and 7 in 100 a washing machine.[28]

China's experiment consists in seeing whether communism can retain political power while permitting capitalism to thrive in the economic system. The experiment also raises a curious question: Is a totalitarian system actually helping to create the kinds of interest groups—business, labor, professional—that tend to thrive in democracies? If the answer is yes, the government in China could face a future opposition from interest groups that understand how to work in the give-and-take politics of democratic societies but find their aspirations ignored by an insensitive totalitarianism.

INTEREST GROUPS IN AUTHORITARIAN SYSTEMS

There are important differences between democratic and nondemocratic interest groups in their agendas and their activities. Some of the more obvious ones are suggested in Table 7.7. But we should avoid sneering at those nations whose interest groups often behave in a criminal fashion. Our own history, for example, includes ugly episodes of violence directed against racial or religious minorities by intolerant groups. In the American and other democracies, however, groups generally tend to retain their strong identities in more or less quiet ways.*

Authoritarian systems are often patriarchal as well, which can leave the interests of women unrepresented. In some Islamic countries, for example, feminists are not legally allowed to exist, let alone form an interest group. In Iran women cannot show more than their faces and hands (and cannot apply nail polish). The only perfume allowed is rose water. Women cannot organize themselves. Husbands can divorce wives without giving a reason (wives need 16 of them) and can keep any children. Wives cannot travel abroad if their husbands object.[29] Women in Iran and other Islamic societies such as Pakistan

---

* Notorious exceptions remain, of course. They include religious groups in Northern Ireland and occasional separatist ethnic movements in Corsica (an island in the Mediterranean Sea considered by the French government to be part of metropolitan France), and in the Basque provinces of Spain. Increasingly, though, these exceptions are characterized by terrorism and have lost credibility in world opinion.

	Typical Interest Group	Agenda	Activities
TABLE 7.7 DIFFERENCES BETWEEN DEMOCRATIC AND AUTHORITARIAN INTEREST GROUPS			
Democratic	Professional	Safeguard interests of membership	Lobbying; public awareness; petitioning
Nondemocratic	Ethnic/religious	Cultural and/or political autonomy	Boycotting of central government policies; resistance and political violence

and Saudi Arabia (where they are still forbidden to drive) are worth only one-half of their male counterparts when it comes to inheritance.

As the 1990s began, interest groups in nondemocratic, mostly authoritarian systems were still based in substantial part on ethnic and/or religious affiliations. Two of the more notorious examples include Iraq and Yugoslavia. In the case of the former, the incumbent political coalition of Saddam Hussein is based on extensive family and tribal associations, support from most of the Iraqi Sunni majority, and the military (again dominated by family, tribal connections, and coreligionists). Professional and worker associations exist, but are controlled by the government. In this sort of atmosphere, those groups that do not fit into the scheme experience varying degrees of difficulty. The sizable Iraqi Christian community encounters discrimination, while Shia Muslims and Iraqi Kurds are the victims of near-genocidal activities by the military. In Iraq the dominating interest groups are clearly divisive.

Much the same could be said for the former Yugoslav republic of Bosnia. Fragmented into three distinct ethnic or religious communities—Serbian, Croatian, and Muslim—Bosnians include no groups that have an interest in keeping the country together. In fact, each group has felt as though the republic had to be destroyed and partitioned in order to guarantee its own physical survival. In most modern democracies, interest groups engage in economic competition or political rivalry within certain humane guidelines. But Bosnia and Iraq possess populations divided into communities that have been in conflict for centuries; their collective memories are permeated with occasional persecutions and massacres of one another. When Serbian Christians interned Bosnian Muslims in concentration camps in early 1992, it seemed strongly reminiscent of German atrocities during World War II. Outsiders were reminded that interest group activities in much of the world are still based on almost primordial associations with one's tribal or ethnic community. As we have seen in Somalia, family clans can also supersede all other loyalties. Ethnic and/or religious affiliations or clans override all other considerations, an obviously unhealthy development for any polity.[30]

Nation-building is a tenuous affair at best. It may very well be that political evolution requires the moderation of ethnic and subnationalist rivalries. If that is the case, many countries have a long and hard road to travel.

Summary

1. Interest groups are particularly prevalent in the United States; Americans tend to "join" much more enthusiastically than citizens of other nations.

2. Interest groups arise out of the heterogeneous nature of the American population, the division of power among several levels of government (permitting multiple access points), and the declining strength of political parties.

3. There are various types of interest groups—including professional, economic, political, public interest, religious, governmental, and single. The question remains as to whether they serve the public interest or more narrow concerns.

4. Interest group tactics include direct lobbying, grass-roots lobbying, information campaigns, and coalition building. Political action committees (PACs) are the financial lobbying arms of interest groups.

5. Some interest groups, such as business and industrial interests, may be too powerful for the proper conduct of democratic politics since they often command huge sums of money and can influence electoral outcomes at all levels. Business and industry also enjoy built-in constituencies because entire communities may have their economies and tax base tied to a single corporation.

6. Business and industrial PACs, however, represent only a plurality of all PACs, and they must face competition from numerous other PACs, with their own agendas and resources. In addition, several emerging interest groups are increasingly placing checks on the more traditional and well-established groups.

7. Interest groups may be considered a liability in determining the public interest because of the imbalance of power among various groups, the distortion caused by single-issue groups, and the divergence between the interests of group leaders and rank-and-file members.

8. On the other hand, interest groups may stabilize and support political democracy because they supplement existing checks and balances, provide additional forms of representation, give voice to diverse interests, educate the public and expose it to the public policy choices available, and slow down the pace of change.

9. Interest groups in other democratic societies rarely have the resources that their American counterparts do, but they are present and are a political force.

10. Party discipline in parliamentary societies means that legislators there are not as susceptible to lobbying efforts as they are in the United States. Interest groups are also not as effective in multiparty systems, where a political party may take on the interests of a group.

11. Some interest groups are basing their programs on international concerns, such as the environment or eradication of disease, that do not respect national frontiers.

12. Tribal associations still dominate politics in many societies. Tribes have become interest groups and can detract from building a national consensus.

13.   In totalitarian societies, interest groups certainly exist, but they are generally part of and protected by the overall power structure. The former Soviet Union and the current communist regime in China are examples of political systems in which the party dominates and controls all other interests.

14.   In authoritarian societies the emergence of aggrieved ethnic and religious groups is especially likely. Such groups may use violent tactics and encounter resistance from governing powers.

Terms to Define

Built-in constituency	Lobbyist
Countervailing force	Political action committees
Emerging interest group	Public interest group
Interest group	Revolving door
Iron triangle	Single-issue group

Suggested Readings

Berry, Jeffrey M. *The Interest Group Society*, 2nd ed. Glenview, Ill.: Scott, Foresman/Little, Brown, 1989. Addresses the growing pervasiveness of interest-group politics in the United States.

Cigler, Allan J., and Burdette A. Loomis, eds. *Interest Group Politics*, 3rd ed. Washington, D.C.: Congressional Quarterly Press, 1991. Eighteen essays explore facets of interest group behavior.

Lowi, Theodore J. *The End of Liberalism*, 2nd ed. New York: Norton, 1979. Leading critical analysis of the impact of interest groups on American society.

Mansbridge, Jane J. *Why We Lost the ERA*. Chicago: University of Chicago Press, 1986. Analyzes the ERA campaign based on organization, incentives, and tactics.

Olson, Mancur. *The Logic of Collective Action*. Cambridge: Harvard University Press, 1965. Study of individuals' reasons for joining interest groups.

Sabato, Larry. *PAC Power*. New York: Norton, 1985. Complete assessment of the formation and functions of political action committees.

Schlozman, Kay Lehman, and John T. Tierney. *Organized Interests and American Democracy*. New York: Harper & Row, 1985. Comprehensive analysis of interest groups based on a survey of Washington lobbyists.

Truman, David B. *The Governmental Process*, 2nd ed. New York: Knopf, 1971. Classic defense of interest group politics.

Vogel, David. *Fluctuating Fortunes*. New York: Basic Books, 1989. Studies the cyclical nature of American business and industrial power.

Wilson, James Q. *Political Organizations*. New York: Basic Books, 1973. Develops a theory about how interest group incentives are used to attract members.

Notes

1. Gabriel Almond and Sidney Verba, *The Civic Culture: Political Attitudes and Democracy in Five Nations* (Boston: Little, Brown, 1965), p. 302.

2. Ibid., p. 245.

3. Theodore Lowi, *The End of Liberalism* (New York: Norton, 1969), p. x.

4. C. Wright Mills, *The Power Elite* (New York: Oxford University Press, 1956), p. 307.

5. See generally Thomas R. Dye, *Who's Running America* (Englewood Cliffs, N.J.: Prentice-Hall, 1986) and John R. Munkirs, *The Transformation of American Capitalism* (New York: M. E. Sharpe, 1984).

6. Charles Lindbloom, *The Policy-Making Process* (Englewood Cliffs, N.J.: Prentice-Hall, 1968), p. 68.

7. See "On Implants, Safety First," *The Washington Post Weekly Edition*, January 13–19, 1992, p. 26.

8. "Tat for Tit," *The Economist*, February 15, 1992, p. 33.

9. *The Federalist*, edited by Henry Cabot Lodge (New York: G. P. Putnam's Sons, 1902), p. 55.

10. *The Washington Post National Weekly Edition*, April 9, 1984, p. 8.

11. *The Washington Post*, January 7, 1979, p. D1.

12. *The Washington Post*, August 27, 1979, p. D7.

13. *Public Opinion*, April/May 1983, pp. 44–48.

14. *The Federalist*, pp. 54–55.

15. Philip Norton, *The British Polity* (New York and London: Longmans, 1984), p. 151.

16. For details see *The Economist*, May 11, 1991, pp. 53–55.

17. William Safran, *The French Polity* (New York and London: Longmans, 1985), p. 110.

18. Ibid.

19. *The Economist*, February 14, 1987.

20. "The Vanishing Jungle," *The Economist*, October 15, 1988, pp. 25–28.

21. *The Economist*, February 9, 1991, p. 74.

22. *The New York Times*, June 5, 1991, p. A14.

23. *The Economist*, May 11, 1991, p. 20.

24. See Jane Perlez, "Somali Clans Planning Last Grab for Advantage," *The New York Times*, December 9, 1992.

25. *The Economist*, June 8, 1991, p. 21.

26. Andrew Tanzer, "The Chinese Way," *Forbes*, reprinted in *The National Times*, mini-edition, December 1992, p. 8.

27. Ibid.

28. "Soaking the Rich," *The Economist*, June 6, 1992, p. 32.

29. "Cover Up, Quick," *The Economist*, August 22, 1992, pp. 30–31.

30. "The Arts of War and the Guiles of Peace," *The Economist*, August 15, 1992, pp. 37–40.

POLITICAL PARTIES

The Constitution makes no provision for political parties, yet they have become a vital force in our government. Indeed, some would argue that parties have been the glue holding together the American system and that democratic government would not be possible without them.

A **political party** is an organization that selects and sponsors candidates for office under the party name. That is its primary function. But parties also help organize government, especially the legislative branch; educate voters; provide teams of officials who can work together when elected; maintain communication between the voters and government officials; and give citizens a commitment to the government even when their party is out of power.

In totalitarian countries, where there is only a single party, these functions are carried out without giving voters any choice at all. In the multiparty systems of many

European countries, loyalty to specialized parties, such as a religious or ideological party, may be so strong that adherents never learn to compromise for the sake of winning an election. But in a two-party system, such as that in the United States, diverse groups must learn to work together under the umbrella of one party or the other.

American society is less partisan than most societies. In communist nations the political party is inseparable from the governing process and actively determines educational, social, and economic policies. Even in other Western democratic nations, political parties normally influence more areas of life than in the United States. On those infrequent occasions when Americans become involved in a political party, it is generally because they like the excitement of partisan politics, just as a baseball fan follows a favorite team, or because they hope to get something out of the party that will personally advance them, or because they have deep ideological convictions they want to promote through the party. For example, strongly conservative persons since the mid-1960s have increasingly identified with and worked in the Republican party to make it more conservative and to influence government policy through it. In most respects, however, Americans should be considered as no more than passive participants in the American party system.

In the first part of this chapter we will be looking at the development of American political parties and of the two-party system in particular. We will also take a look at how parties are structured. Then we'll examine some areas of controversy: whether there are any real differences between the two parties, whether the two-party system inhibits constructive change, and whether parties are in fact becoming obsolete. We then conclude with a comparison with other party systems.

THE PARTY SYSTEM IN AMERICA

PARTY DEVELOPMENT

Many leaders of the early Republic disliked the idea of political parties. George Washington warned against "the baneful effects of the spirit of party" in his farewell address, while John Adams said, "There is nothing I dread so much as the division of the Republic into two great parties, each under its leader."[1] James Madison had already foreseen the emergence of parties, however, when he wrote in *The Federalist* that the job of resolving conflicting interests would necessarily involve "the spirit of party and faction in the necessary and ordinary operation of the government."

The First Parties

The first American parties emerged out of the continuing debate over a strong versus a weak central government. Those who favored a strong central government formed the *Federalist party*, under the leadership of Alexander Hamilton. In the other camp were the *Democratic-Republicans*, under Thomas Jefferson's leadership. The Federalists appealed primarily to banking, commercial, and financial interests. The Democratic-Republicans drew support from small farmers, debtors, southern planters, and frontier settlers.

Federalist ideas were in the ascendant during the administrations of Washington and John Adams. The party went into decline, however, when Jefferson's election in 1800 began a 28-year period of Democratic-Republican dominance. After 1816, the Federalists no longer even offered a candidate for the presidency.

Democrats and Whigs

Democratic-Republican strength began to wane when irreconcilable factions developed within the party. Those under the influence of the populist president Andrew Jackson stood for popular rule and the hopes of the common people. Anti-Jackson forces united initially as National Republicans. Under the leadership of Henry Clay, William Henry Harrison and Daniel Webster, they subsequently formed the *Whig party* from a coalition of bankers, merchants, and southern planters. Thus the two dominant parties from 1824 until just before the Civil War were the Democratic-Republicans (generally called *Democrats* after 1828) and the National Republicans followed by the Whigs. (See Figure 8.1.)

Both major parties successfully competed for the presidency during this period. Out of their competition grew the modern party system, with its concerted emphasis on winning the presidency, the intermittent rise of third parties, patronage, national nominating conventions, and party bosses. **Patronage** is the awarding of government positions to the party faithful. **Party bosses** have usually been strong party leaders in big cities, such as Chicago under Mayor Richard Daley from the late 1950s to the late 1970s. His son was to become mayor in 1989.

Democrats Versus Republicans

With the coming of the Civil War, both the Democrats and the Whigs experienced the same divisions that were tearing asunder American society in general. After passage of the Kansas-Nebraska Act in 1854 (which permitted slavery in the territories), Whigs, antislavery Democrats, and others formed a new party to fight the further expansion of slavery. This organization, the *Republican party*, became the only successful third-party movement in American history; it eventually supplanted the disintegrating Whig party and quickly became the chief rival of the Democrats. Following a North-South split among the Democrats over the slavery issue, the Republicans elected their first president, Abraham Lincoln in 1860.

Although the Republicans represented mainly the North and the West, they remained the party with the largest following until the Great Depression of the 1930s. Then Franklin D. Roosevelt, elected in 1932, formed the New Deal Democratic coalition, a large party composed of southern interests, big city voters, and labor. From the 1930s until 1980, Republicans had congressional majorities only from 1947 to 1948 and from 1953 to 1954, and occupied the White House for only 16 years.

Ronald Reagan's 1980 and 1984 victories and the Republican majority in the Senate from 1981 through 1986 gave Republicans a ray of hope that they might reclaim their former status. George Bush's election in 1988 continued a modern pattern of Republican control of the White House, but Democratic control of Congress. The Democrats, however, broke that pattern by winning both the presidency and Congress in 1992. Still, both parties remain dominated by more or less moderate forces. And in both parties,

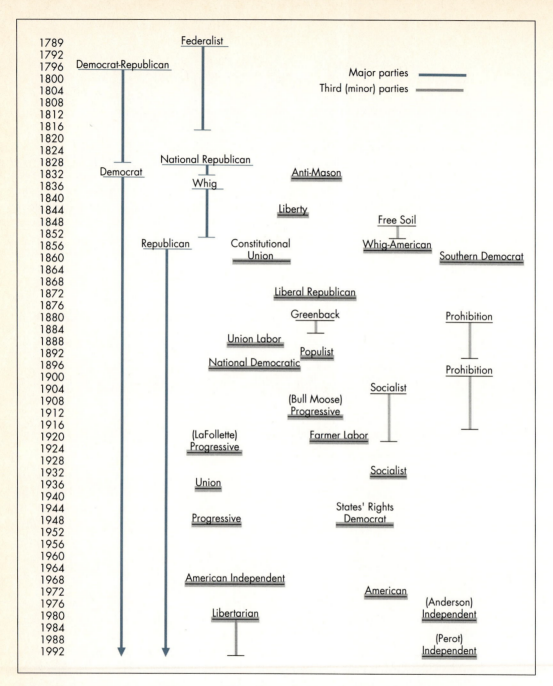

Figure 8.1 AMERICAN POLITICAL PARTIES SINCE 1789. The chart indicates the years in which the presidential candidate of a political party received 1 percent or more of the popular vote. Third parties are not included if the candidate is also the candidate of one of the two major parties. Party candidates sometimes run under different designations in different states. In such cases, the total vote for the candidate is given under a single party designation. Sources: 1789–1984: Congressional Quarterly, *Congressional Quarterly's Guide to U.S. Elections*, 2nd ed (Washington, D.C.: Congressional Quarterly, 1985), pp. 329–377; 1988: *Congressional Quarterly Weekly Report* (1989), p. 139.

public identification and loyalty have declined, as more and more people declare themselves **independents**, voters who are determined to remain unaffiliated with any party.

THE TWO-PARTY SYSTEM

In a **two-party system**, two major parties can count on regularly winning elections. The party that has the largest following is known as the **majority party**, while the **minority party** is the other major party with the next-largest following. Minor parties are known collectively as **third parties**. They rarely have a chance of winning a national election, but they occasionally will win state or local contests.

Why Two Parties?

What actually accounts for the rise of the two-party system in America? Although America's Founders in Philadelphia in 1787 opposed political parties, issues that persisted while our government was being implemented contributed to the forging of a two-party system. The Constitution itself balanced the interests of those favoring a strong national government versus those preferring strong state governments. But since this issue was not resolved to everyone's satisfaction by the Constitutional Convention, parties formed to reflect those two positions: Federalists to represent the nationalists, and Democratic-Republicans to represent the states' rightists. The parties coalesced around strong personalities who advocated these positions—especially Hamilton and Jefferson (as we saw earlier). Ever since then, a strong two-party system has dominated American politics.

Other factors have also contributed to the formation and continuation of the two-party system. One of these is the **single-member district**, which allows the election of only one candidate to represent a designated set of constituents (such as an election district). Since most American elections are conducted in winner-take-all, single-member election districts, practical politics dictates that unity and cohesion rather than disunity and division are necessary for challengers to unseat the incumbent candidate or party. There is no reward in governing for losers; only the winner can directly exert influence and power on government policy. Competing interests must, then, form coalitions to mount a successful challenge to the incumbent candidate or party. Since the Civil War, those coalitions have been the Democratic and Republican parties.

In the process of appealing to the center of the American electorate, the two major parties have reached a general political consensus on many issues. For example, both parties accept the social security system, originally a Democratic initiative, and federal aid to state and local governments. There is also a bipartisan acceptance of basic liberties and rights. The broad consensus between the two parties lessens the ideological debate and focuses attention on the pragmatic objective of organizing to win elections. The general consensus also helps to keep our parties and society from fragmenting, a phenomenon that occurs in countries where multiple parties disagree on fundamental issues.

While our two major parties tend to be more pragmatic than ideological, making the winning of elections more important than advocating a principle, still there are discernible ideological differences that contribute to the formation of two parties. Conservatives are more likely to identify with the Republican party and liberals with the

Democratic party. Both parties include conservatives and liberals, but the concentration differs between the two. In addition, on the issue of nationalists versus states' rightists, the Democratic party has had more nationalists and the Republican more states' rightists, particularly since the New Deal, when the Democratic-controlled Congress and the Democratic president substantially enlarged the role of the national government.

Of course, ideological differences can also be *intra*party, a consideration revealed in the 1992 race for the Republican nomination. It is unusual, for example, for a sitting president to face determined opposition for renomination. George Bush did, though, from conservative journalist Pat Buchanan. The Bush-Buchanan competition was really a continuation of a struggle between a conservative and isolationist wing of the Republican party and a more moderate internationalist wing. Buchanan, for instance, had opposed the American intervention in the Persian Gulf to remove Iraqi soldiers from Kuwait in early 1991. The internationalist wing was considered to have betrayed the *true* conservative cause.[2] The following list* suggests some of the ideological splits the Republicans have experienced in this century between the internationalist and isolationist wings.[3] (The Democrats have experienced intra-party ideological differences too. Bill Clinton's triumph in 1992 represented the rise of a more centrist wing of the party at the expense of its more liberal elements.)

1912:   The conservative President William Howard Taft challenged by the more progressive former President Theodore Roosevelt

1944–1952:   The more internationalist forces led first by Governor Thomas E. Dewey of New York and then by General Dwight D. Eisenhower versus the conservative forces led by Ohio's Senator Robert A. Taft

1964:   Intense competition for the presidential nomination between Senator Barry Goldwater of Arizona, representing conservatives, and Governor Nelson Rockefeller of New York, representing the liberal wing

1972:   President Richard Nixon annoyed some Republican conservatives by his opening to China and faced modest opposition in the early primaries

1992:   Conservative Pat Buchanan challenged President George Bush because of the latter's call for higher taxes and refusal to adopt strong protectionist policies

Third-Party Contributions

Although the two-party system is eminently suitable for the American people and their government, third parties have made meaningful contributions. They bring voters' attention to issues that major parties avoid. Their names alone provide a clue to this function: the Free Soil party advocated the abolition of slavery; the Greenback party urged the government to print more paper money. Indeed, third parties first advocated abolition of

---

* Adapted from Thomas B. Edsall, "How to Conquer an Elephant," The Washington Post Weekly Edition, March 2–8, 1992, p. 116. © 1992 The Washington Post.

slavery, women's suffrage, direct election of senators, a progressive income tax, the Fourteenth Amendment (equal protection of the laws), regulation of monopolies, and social security. Since the emergence of the modern two-party system between 1840 and 1860, there have been more than 100 third parties. The four main types are summarized below.

Single-Issue. These parties advocate one policy idea, which is usually reflected in their name. Their life span may be short, if either or both major parties adopt the single-issue idea, or long, if the idea cannot be absorbed into the two-party mainstream. Examples:

- Free Soil (1848–1856) opposed the spread of slavery.
- American (or "Know Nothing") appeared in 1856 elections to oppose immigration of Catholics.
- Prohibition (1869–1990s) opposed the sale and consumption of liquor.
- Women's (1913–1920) supported women's suffrage.
- Vegetarian (1950s–1960s) opposed sale and consumption of meat products.
- Green (beginning in early 1990s) advocates restriction of industrial growth in favor of the environment.

Economic-Protest. Often regional and tied to economically depressed conditions, especially agriculture, these parties usually disappear as conditions improve. Examples:

- Farmer-Labor (1930s–1940s) was a working-class alliance restricted mostly to Minnesota, with organizations in neighboring states.
- Greenback (1876–1884) advocated monetary changes to help farmers.
- Populist (1892–1908) supported governmental reforms to assist farmers.
- Independent candidacy of Ross Perot in 1992 made an issue of the federal deficit as well as the overall state of the national economy.

Factional. A split in a major party over an important issue and the support of a popular political personality may lead to the creation of a factional party. The split usually is restricted to one national election. Examples:

- The Whigs experienced a fatal split in 1854 when many members defected to the newly formed Republican party on the issue of slavery and other Whigs created the short-lived American party, which participated in the 1856 presidential election.
- The Republicans have experienced two serious splits: the "Bull Moose" party (1912) led by former President Theodore Roosevelt and the Progressive party (1924) led by Wisconsin Senator Robert La Follette. There has been one modestly serious split: the independent candidacy of former Representative John Anderson (in 1980).

- The Democrats have had three major splits in the twentieth century, including two in a single election year: States' Rights (1948) led by Senator (then Governor) Strom Thurmond; Progressive (1948) led by former Vice President Henry A. Wallace; and American Independent (1968) led by Alabama's Governor George Wallace.

Ideological. Advocating radically different policies with a pronounced ideological orientation, ideological parties cannot (and often will not) be absorbed by the major pragmatic parties. Most ideological parties in this century have had a leftist perspective, except for the Libertarian party (whose members brag about being the third-largest party in the United States), which advocates minimum or "bare bones" government in all areas of American life. Unlike the first three types, ideological parties are not discouraged by consistent and massive electoral defeats and exhibit remarkable staying power. Examples:

- Socialist (1901–1960s)
- Socialist Labor (1886–1990s)
- Socialist Workers (1938–1990s)
- Communist (1920s–1990s)
- Libertarian (1972–1990s)

Third parties or independent candidacies have also provided an important political fulcrum for leaders who were frozen out of the two-party system: Eugene Debs, Robert La Follette, Norman Thomas, Henry Wallace, George Wallace, and Ross Perot. Each of these men articulated positions that challenged those taken by the major parties. Their success in calling attention to issues has been phenomenal. Norman Thomas, the Socialist Party standard-bearer for many years, remarked in his later years that he was proud of his political achievements. Most of the proposals he had advocated through his party were ultimately adopted into law through the efforts of the two major parties. For example, Thomas claimed credit for being the first to call for social welfare measures, such as social security, that were later adopted as policy by the major parties.

Third parties also provide a way for interest groups to organize on a key issue. Both the 1948 States' Rights Party and the 1968 American Independent Party attracted support from those who opposed the federal government's role in enforcing civil rights legislation.

The presidential race of 1980 sparked substantial interest in third parties and independent candidacies, including the Libertarian party, John Anderson's independent candidacy, Barry Commoner's Citizens' party, the Communist party, the Right to Life party, and the Socialist party. In 1992 independent candidate Ross Perot won close to one-fifth of the national vote. Perot's candidacy may eventually be considered the basis of a new third-party movement.

In order to get on the ballot as a third-party candidate in the presidential election of 1992, Ross Perot had to obtain thousands of validated signatures on voter petitions in every state. He is shown here addressing a crowd in Texas above stacks of boxes containing petitions.

Transferring Party Power

What may seem like a confusing seesaw between the two major parties makes more sense when we categorize elections as either realigning, deviating, reinstating, or maintaining. In a **realigning election**, the minority party comes to the fore to assume a long-lasting majority position. This happened in 1860, when the Civil War paved the way for the dominance of the new Republican party. It happened again in 1932, when the Great Depression helped sweep the Republicans out and made the Democratic party dominant. The minority party remained competitive during both periods, however, with occasional **deviating elections**, in which the minority party won the presidency on a short-run basis. Such were the victories of Democrat Woodrow Wilson in 1912 and 1916 and of Republican Dwight D. Eisenhower in 1952 and 1956.

When the majority party returns to its dominant position, it is known as a **reinstating election**. The Republicans won back the presidency in 1920 with Warren G.

Harding, the Democrats with John F. Kennedy in 1960. Finally, **maintaining elections** simply continue the status quo between the parties. The party in power stays in power.

How are we to view the 1980 and 1984 victories of Ronald Reagan and the 1988 election of George Bush? Some observers categorize them as deviating. They point out that the Republican party's voter identification was not consistently above that of the Democrats during the 1980s and early 1990s. Moreover, the Republicans' increase in voter support in those elections came about largely through economic issues, a fragile foundation given the vagaries of the economy. In any case, the Democrats continued to control Congress and more governorships and state legislatures than the Republicans, as well as winning back the presidency in 1992.

Those favoring realignment put forth several arguments. First, the Democratic party has lost control of its most important areas, the solid south and the industrial states. Not since 1944 has the South voted solidly for a Democratic candidate for president, not even in 1976 when Georgian Jimmy Carter ran, or 1992 when the ticket itself was solidly southern (Clinton from Arkansas and Gore from Tennessee). The Democratic party has not won with large margins in the industrial states since 1964. Second, in 1984 the Republicans won 20 of the 25 largest metropolitan areas, all of which President Carter had won in 1976. And President Bush followed in 1988 with equally convincing inroads into traditionally Democratic party strongholds. In 1992 the Republicans' strongest constituency consisted of white southerners.[4] Third, Republicans sometimes bested Democrats in recent years as the party of prosperity and peace, a first since the 1940s.

A third view of the two parties' current seesaw battle, however, emphasizes the deterioration of both parties. The fact that one-fourth to one-third of the electorate now identifies itself as independent suggests that a **dealignment** is taking place—that is, voters are avoiding identifying with *either* major party. By 1991 about one-third of the American electorate referred to themselves as Democrats and a third Republican. Another third insisted on telling pollsters that they were independent.[5] Ross Perot's popularity with both Democrats and Republicans in 1992 underscored the dealignment theory.

The American two-party system is constantly under attack. Some contend that it is on the decline because of the rising number of independents. Others believe the two major parties are weakening because they don't take clear enough ideological positions. Some argue that the Republican party should become the Conservative party and the Democratic party, the Liberal party, in order to strengthen the identification and loyalty of the people to a party and also to increase a party's responsibility to stand for a consistent ideology and set of positions on issues.

POLITICAL PARTY STRUCTURE

The organization of America's two major parties follows closely the outline of our federal system of government: there are three levels of party structure—national, state, and local—and power is diffused, in keeping with the federal system itself. Actually, the party organizations are much more like a confederation, loosely joined together, than either a stronger federation or unitary system. Each party has three principal parts at the national level.

TABLE 8.1 THE HOOPLA INDEX AT PARTY CONVENTIONS

	1992 Republican National Convention (Houston)	1992 Democratic National Convention (New York)
Balloons	250,000	60,000
Protests	50–52 (planned)	52
Senators	26 of 43 (60%)	50 of 57 (87%)
Representatives	92 of 166 (55%)	240 of 265 (94%)
Video walls	2	1
Police	2,000	3,000
Security budget	$2.4 million	$6.6 million

Source: Interviews, news reports, Democratic National Committee, Republican National Committee.

- *National Convention.* Several thousand delegates and alternates in each party gather every four years at a national convention to nominate presidential and vice-presidential candidates, to adopt a platform, to establish party rules, and to choose a national committee to conduct party business until the next national convention. These are occasions for party hoopla more than anything else (see Table 8.1). Candidates have generally already been selected through primaries.

- *National Committee.* Each state has representation on the national committee, and other representation may be added from such groups as youth and ethnic constituencies. Approximately 150 and 350, respectively, serve on the Republican and Democratic National Committees. The chair of the National Committee is usually chosen by a party's presidential nominee, subject to approval by the committee itself. The party losing the presidential election may decide to replace the committee chairman.

- *Congressional Campaign Committees.* These committees, which exist for each party in both houses of Congress, raise funds to help candidates in their reelection campaigns. They function independently of the national party organization.

State and local party organizations usually follow the governmental organization of a state in the counties and cities. From the bottom to the top, a typical pattern consists of precinct captains or committee persons elected in the local voting precincts, a county convention composed of all precinct committee persons, a state convention composed of delegates from county conventions, and a state central committee composed of members selected by the state convention.

The loosely structured American two-party system allows for different types of organization in different regions; it adapts to state and local political cultures. In the large northern states of Illinois, Ohio, New York, and Michigan, a very competitive two-party system exists. In other states, although the two parties compete, one is dominant. In Maryland, for example, the Democratic party is dominant, but the Republican party wins enough offices to be competitive on a statewide basis. In much of the South until recent years, the Republican party hardly existed, and the Democratic party elected all officials. In some localities there is a powerful central party organization, resembling the Chicago Democratic machine under Mayor Richard Daley; in other areas there is a loosely knit structure, such as the California Democratic party.

Party structure in America with its diffused power has led to a weaker party system here than in many other nations. Traditionally, America's parties have had their principal power base at the local and state levels of government. In recent years, however, some power has shifted to the national level. The Democrats have given the national party greater authority in determining rules and procedures for the state and local parties, and the Republicans have developed sophisticated fund-raising and campaign management techniques at the national level.

In this century political parties have gradually opened to greater popular participation as caucuses and conventions gave way to the primary as a method of nominating candidates. **Caucuses** and **conventions** are relatively small groups of party members who meet to determine party nominees and policy. Party members elect delegates to represent them at conventions, while caucuses are usually simply composed of interested party members. Caucuses are typically held at the precinct level; conventions are normally held at the county, state, and national levels. **Primaries** are elections in which all party members are allowed to vote for a nominee. With more people now participating in political parties through primaries, party leaders have less control over the nominating process. This is especially true in some states with an **open primary**, in which Democrats may cross over to vote in a Republican primary and vice versa.

Since the 1960s both major party organizations have gradually lost power to interest groups, which have been able to raise and contribute money to candidates. Because the candidates feel less beholden to the party organization than they used to, the tenuous hold of party discipline is further weakened. There is even some talk that American political parties are becoming obsolete. This is one of the issues we will consider in the next section.

? ISSUES TO ANALYZE

ISSUE 1   ARE THERE MEANINGFUL DIFFERENCES BETWEEN THE DEMOCRATIC AND REPUBLICAN PARTIES?

REASONS WHY THERE ARE NO MEANINGFUL DIFFERENCES

Except for their names, what is the difference between the parties? On basic and fundamental issues, there is little difference, if any. Both parties uphold the sanctity of private property, advocate a free enterprise economy, support individual freedom, view government's role as limited, and adhere to majority rule and due process of the law. Both parties support the major domestic policies developed since 1930—social security, a graduated income tax, and welfare and unemployment compensation. Both parties have generally supported the same foreign and military policies in this period. Party agreement on fundamental issues restricts the alternatives presented to the electorate. Rather than having a wide range of choices, Americans are presented with a very limited selection.

The mass of the American public is in the center of the ideological spectrum, neither to the left nor to the right. Whenever a major party has nominated a presidential candidate with pronounced ideological bias, the party has been defeated. After all, the majority of American voters are, as one study put it, "unyoung, unpoor, and unblack." Naturally, candidates who take moderate positions on issues—close to the "political center"—are more likely to be elected than those advocating more extreme positions."[6]

The basic purpose of American political parties is to win office, not to raise issues. Thus, the parties advocate positions only on issues that fit an already established view of what is acceptable. They would lose rather than gain votes by advocating positions outside the areas of consensus. Democrats and Republicans disagree mainly over which party is better qualified to achieve the goals both accept. The chief competition is therefore not between policies but between different types of packaging.

Late in the 1980s, under the auspices of the Democratic Leadership Council, the Democrats moved toward the political center and away from what many voters considered too far to the left. In 1992 they convinced the electorate that they had learned the lessons of previous elections. In the immediate aftermath of their 1992 presidential defeat, moderate Republicans formed the Republican Majority Coalition to help move their party away from the religious right and more toward the center. One of its founders maintained that "our purpose is to exclude issues of morality and conscience as litmus tests of being a Republican."[7]

The similarity between the parties has led to a decrease in party identification, as more people identify themselves as independents (Table 8.2). In addition, the party identification that does exist is at a rather crude level of understanding. It is frequently based on influences like family and socioeconomic class rather than a rational assessment of issue differences. Nor can party identification be relied on to predict the behavior of either the electorate or those elected. In 1972, one-third of all registered Democrats voted for Richard Nixon; an extremely large number voted for Dwight D. Eisenhower in 1952 and 1956. The Republican party's 1980, 1984, and 1988 victories depended on substantial numbers of votes from Democrats (sometimes known as "Reagan Democrats"). Many Jewish and Roman Catholic voters, previously dominantly Democratic, changed their votes to the Republican party. In 1992, however, Ross Perot demonstrated that voters still respond to a clear choice. He attracted many voters by his strong positions on issues that the major party candidates tried to sidestep.

REASONS WHY THERE ARE MEANINGFUL DIFFERENCES

McDonald's, Burger King, Hardee's, and Wendy's are alike in that they all sell hamburgers, but they are still different. So it is with the two major parties.

Critics enjoy arguing that Democrats and Republicans are like fraternal twins, or like Tweedledum and Tweedledee, but the evidence supports meaningful differences between the two parties. According to one journalist: "When times get tough, it turns out that there really is more than a minute difference between Republicans and Demo-

TABLE 8.2 PARTY IDENTIFICATION, 1937–1992			
	Republican	Democrat	Independent
1992	29%	39%	33%
1988	30%	42%	28%
1984	31%	40%	29%
1980	24%	46%	30%
1976	23%	47%	30%
1972	28%	43%	29%
1968	27%	46%	27%
1964	25%	53%	22%
1960	30%	47%	23%
1954	34%	46%	20%
1950	33%	45%	22%
1946	40%	39%	21%
1937	34%	50%	16%

Source: These data were kindly furnished by Ed Jimerson of the Gallup Poll Organization, Inc. on January 26, 1993.

crats. There is a whole lot of difference—and there is going to be more."[8] Some areas in which clear differences can be seen are in the composition of parties and their ideology.

Composition. In 1917 the economic historian Charles Beard said that the "center of gravity of wealth is on the Republican side while the center of gravity of poverty is on the Democratic side."[9] That characterization is still valid. Membership of the two parties differs not only in wealth, but also in education, occupation, religion, and race, as shown in Table 8.3. Moreover, studies of delegates to the national conventions of the two parties since 1956 have shown differences in income, ideology, race, sex, political experience, and religion. Both parties attract support from all groups, but the *base* of power in the two parties differs.

Ideology. The two parties have clear policy and ideological differences, which are evident among party members and their legislative representatives, among the judiciary, among party leaders, and in party platforms. In analyzing these differences, David Broder concluded:

> There is not just a dime's worth of difference between the parties. There are dollars and livelihoods at stake, to say nothing of the balance between private enterprise and government in our economy and the reliance on public officials or private citizens to decide the basic issues that affect all our lives. If voters won't turn out and make such a choice, then we might as well admit that politics is what pollster Pat Caddell called it—one of the less popular spectator sports.[10]

Lest anyone think that the differences summarized are the product of very recent history, consider the following data from presidential elections: In 1948, most of those persons opposed to the Taft-Hartley Act, which weakened the role of big labor unions,

TABLE 8.3 REPUBLICANS, DEMOCRATS, AND INDEPENDENTS: 1992 GROUP COMPOSITION

	Republicans	Democrats	Independents
Race			
White	32%	34%	34%
Nonwhite	11%	65%	24%
Black	9%	70%	21%
Hispanic	21%	52%	27%
Region			
East	24%	41%	35%
Midwest	29%	33%	38%
South	31%	40%	29%
West	32%	38%	30%
Income			
$40,000 and above	34%	33%	33%
$25,000–$40,000	32%	34%	34%
$15,000–$25,000	26%	41%	33%
Under $15,000	22%	50%	38%
$25,000 and over	33%	33%	33%
Under $25,000	24%	46%	30%
Sex			
Men	30%	36%	34%
Women	28%	40%	32%
Age			
18–29	28%	35%	37%
18–24	27%	36%	37%
25–29	30%	33%	37%
30–49	28%	37%	38%
50 and older	30%	41%	38%
65 and older	32%	42%	25%
Education			
College graduate	36%	32%	32%
Some college	32%	34%	33%
High school graduate	27%	39%	34%
Less than high school graduate	21%	49%	30%
Grade school	20%	55%	25%

Source: These data were kindly furnished on January 26, 1993, by Ed Jimerson of the Gallup Organization, Inc., which publishes the Gallup Poll.

voted Democratic. In 1952, most of the Americans who thought the government had gone too far in dealing with problems of unemployment and housing voted Republican. In 1960, most persons who favored greater government involvement to stimulate the economy voted Democratic. In 1964, those who thought the government should do more to advance the cause of civil rights voted overwhelmingly Democratic. In 1968 and 1972, those who believed that more concern should be shown for victims of crime than for the rights of the accused voted heavily Republican.[11]

A glance at the types of delegates who attended the Democratic party convention *(left)* and the Republican party convention *(right)* in 1992 gives an idea of the differences in composition and ideology between the two parties.

The *Washington Post* and the Harvard Center for International Affairs found substantial differences between Democratic and Republican party workers (state, city, and county officials) in their ranking in importance of ten national goals. This national survey of 155 Republicans and 128 Democrats showed that they agree on the priority of only one of the ten goals. For example, Republican party workers considered reducing the role of government as the second-highest goal, but Democratic party workers viewed the same goal as last in order of importance.[12] The same survey showed that both party workers and the rank-and-file party members differed ideologically: Democrats were more liberal and Republicans were more conservative.

Historically, Democrats and Republicans have differed most in the legislative arena on the issues of the tariff, agriculture, labor, and social legislation. Republicans have tended to favor higher tariffs, less government support for agriculture, less assistance to labor, and fewer new social programs. The two parties have differed least on public works, states' rights, civil service, and women's rights. In foreign policy, the two parties had very different views between 1933 and 1948 and very similar views from 1948 to the 1960s. In the 1970s and 1980s, a divergence seemed to be emerging. Most Republicans, for example, were more interested in maintaining a strong national defense, while Democrats were more committed to the peace initiatives of international organizations.

Among judges, clear differences may be seen between Republicans and Democrats. Studies show that "Democratic judges are more likely than Republican judges to vote for the defense in criminal cases, for the claimant in unemployment cases, . . . for the government in tax cases, for the tenant in landlord-tenant cases, for the consumer in sale-of-goods cases . . . and for the employee in employee injury cases."[13]

A landmark study of party leadership, completed in 1956, documented sharp differences between the leaders of the two parties. Herbert McClosky studied delegates to the two national conventions. He concluded that the active members of the two parties "are obviously separated by large and important differences. The differences, moreover, conform to the popular image in which the Democratic party is seen as the more 'progressive' or 'radical,' the Republican as the more 'moderate' or 'conservative' of the two."[14]

Are there differences in the subjects addressed by the **party platforms**, the policy positions on which a party or candidate runs for office? Are these platforms specific? Are they implemented? The answer in each case is yes. The 1980, 1984, 1988, and 1992 Republican platforms differed dramatically from the Democratic platform on many issues. (See Table 8.4.) Republican platforms, for example, have been opposed to abortion, the equal rights amendment, and school busing, while Democratic platforms have generally supported them. Gerald Pomper's study of platforms between 1944 and 1964 showed that Republicans made more pledges about defense and government; Democrats emphasized labor and welfare. As for the language of platforms, the pledges tended to be very specific: 60 percent had to do with continuing or repealing an existing and very specific program or policy. Pomper ascertained that of the 2245 pledges made in the platforms, 72 percent had been implemented by 1966. He concluded that "Democrats and Republicans are not 'Tweedledee' and 'Tweedledum.' "[15]

ISSUE 1:   Summary   ★   *Are There Meaningful Differences Between the Democratic and Republican Parties?*

No, not if one is looking for dramatic ideological differences such as between Communist and Libertarian parties; yes, if one is looking for more subtle differences concerning composition, shades of ideological differences, and varied approaches to reaching essentially the same ends. Franklin D. Roosevelt and the New Deal brought about a different public policy than what Herbert Hoover and the Republican party would have pursued in the 1930s. In 1964 Lyndon Johnson's Great Society could be readily distinguished from Barry Goldwater's Republican plans, and the Reagan-Bush conservatism was distinctly different from Michael Dukakis's liberalism in 1988 and even Bill Clinton's more centrist position in 1992. Thus, the two parties have meaningful differences. The question is whether they are meaningful enough for those who want parties strongly based on ideology.

ISSUE 2   DOES THE TWO-PARTY SYSTEM INHIBIT CONSTRUCTIVE POLITICAL CHANGE?

REASONS WHY THE TWO-PARTY SYSTEM INHIBITS CONSTRUCTIVE POLITICAL CHANGE

The two-party system is an outdated relic that actually impairs the democratic process. The lack of alternatives presented to American voters means that elections are determined primarily by factors other than party differences on issues. This result ill serves the voter. Disadvantaged groups are underrepresented, national party conventions merely rubber-stamp status quo platforms and nominate middle-of-the road candidates, and elections are decided by useless publicity contests.

There are many ways by which the two-party system inhibits change, but we will focus on only three: (1) being unresponsive to the electorate, (2) favoring middle-of-the-road candidates with unoriginal ideas, and (3) discouraging minor parties and their differing views.

TABLE 8.4 COMPARE AND CONTRAST: QUOTES FROM THE 1992 PLATFORMS

	Republicans	Democrats
The 1980's	We launched an era of growth and prosperity, such as the world had never seen. . . . During the 1980's and into the present decade, the U.S. economy once again became the engine of global growth.	We need to rebuild America by abandoning the something-for-nothing ethic of the last decade. . . . It is wrong to borrow on ourselves, leaving our children to pay our debts.
The Ecomomy	Inflation has fallen to the lowest level in 30 years. Interest rates dropped 15 percentage points. Productivity has sharply risen. Exports are booming. Despite a global downturn in late 1990, real economic growth resumed last year and has continued for five consecutive quarters. With low interest rates and low inflation, the American economy is poised for stronger growth through the rest of the 1990's.	America is on the wrong track. The American people are hurting. The American dream of expanding opportunity has faded. Middle-class families are working hard, playing by the rules, but still falling behind. Poverty has exploded.
Role of Government	We believe government has a legitimate role to play in our national life, but government must never dominate that life. . . . The Democrats argue that government must constantly override the market. Republicans regard the worst market failure as the failure to have a market.	We believe in an activist government, but it must work in a different, more responsive way. . . . We believe in . . . the power of market forces. But economic growth will not come without a national economic strategy.
Abortion	We believe the unborn child has a fundamental individual right to life which cannot be infringed . . . reaffirm our support for a human life amendment to the Constitution . . . endorse legislation to make clear that the Fourteenth Amendment's protections apply to unborn children. We oppose using public revenues for abortion and will not fund organizations which advocate it.	Democrats stand behind the right of every woman to choose, consistent with Roe v. Wade, regardless of ability to pay, and support a national law to protect that right. It is a fundamental constitutional liberty that individual Americans—not government—can best take responsibility for making the most difficult and intensely personal decisions regarding reproduction. The goal of our nation must be to make abortion less necessary, not more difficult or dangerous.

(continued)

TABLE 8.4 *(CONTINUED)*

	Republicans	Democrats
Homosexual Rights	We oppose efforts by the Democratic Party to include sexual preference as a protected minority receiving preferential status under civil rights statutes at the Federal, state and local level.	Democrats will continue to lead the fight to ensure that no Americans suffer discrimination or deprivation of rights on the basis of . . . sexual orientation or other characteristics irrelevant to ability.
Arts	We . . . condemn the use of public funds to subsidize obscenity and blasphemy masquerading as art. . . . No artist has an inherent right to claim taxpayer support for his or her private vision of art if that vision mocks the moral and spiritual basis on which our society is founded.	We believe in public support for the arts . . . that is free from political manipulation and firmly rooted in the First Amendment's freedom of expression guarantee.
The Environment	We have taught the world three vital lessons. First environmental progress is integrally related to economic advancement. Second, economic growth generates the capital to pay for environmental gains. Third, private ownership and economic freedom are the best security against environmental degradation.	We will protect our old-growth forests, preserve critical habitats, provide a genuine "no net loss" policy on wetlands, conserve the critical resources of soil, water and air, oppose new offshore oil drilling and mineral exploration and production in our nation's many environmentally critical areas and address ocean pollution by reducing oil and toxic waste spills at sea.
Gun Control	Republicans defend the constitutional right to keep and bear arms. We call for mandatory sentences for those who use firearms in a crime. We note that those who seek to disarm citizens in their homes are the same liberals who tried to disarm our nation during the cold war.	We support a reasonable waiting period to permit background checks for the purchases of handguns, as well as assault weapons controls to ban the possession, sale, importation and manufacture of the most deadly assault weapons. . . . We will work for . . . stronger sentences for criminals who use guns.
Health	Republicans believe government control of health care is irresponsible and ineffective. We believe health care choices should remain in the hands of the people, not government bureaucrats.	All Americans should have universal access to quality, affordable health care—not as a privilege but as a right.

Source: *The New York Times,* August 16, 1992, Section 1, p. 26. Copyright © 1992 by The New York Times Company. Reprinted by permission.

Lack of Responsiveness. The most frequent criticism of the two major parties is their lack of responsiveness to the electorate. A committee of the American Political Science Association reported that the parties lack the discipline and organization to ensure that their programs are passed by Congress and signed by the president.[16] As we have seen, the Republican and Democratic parties are loose coalitions or confederations of 50 state parties. Power in the parties tends to flow up to, rather than down from, the national leadership. State and local party organizations function relatively free from national party direction. The late Mayor Richard Daley of Chicago, for example, ruled the Cook County Democratic party; he did not take orders from either the state or the national party. At the national level, neither the president nor the national party chairman dictate to their respective party members in Congress. As a result, American parties have far less party discipline than their West European counterparts, which are much more coherent and centralized.

Voters have no rational way of ensuring that the national party leadership is responsive to policy positions. Indeed, neither party *has* a policy position except for a platform and other vague statements emanating from the national convention and national committee meetings, which are not binding on either the president or the congressional leaders.

During the 1970s and early 1980s, the Democratic party tried to develop precise policy proposals. They even held national conventions in nonpresidential election years to develop party policy. Elected Democratic officials in Congress and elsewhere, however, were not bound by them, and the exercise itself divided the Democratic party to the point that such efforts were abolished after the 1984 election.

In this situation, compromise becomes the dominant theme. Both Congress and the president must sometimes reconcile their stances in order to implement a policy requiring action from both. This may dilute the effect of what was originally intended. Compromise tends to force differences to the center and to undermine major change or reform. During the recessionary years of 1991 to 1992, for example, President Bush agreed with many in Congress to raise taxes to restrain the growth of the deficit, even though he had pledged "no new taxes" in his 1988 campaign.

"Safe" Candidates Preferred. A candidate who wants to achieve a party nomination and then win an election must offend as few people as possible, especially party leaders. To the extent that candidates deviate from this policy, they encounter resistance and opposition and lose financial support. John Anderson alienated most Republicans in the 1980 presidential campaign with his liberal positions on the ERA, abortion, and homosexuality. In the fall he ran as an independent. In 1972, George McGovern's support for party reform offended many Democratic party leaders, including Mayor Daley of Chicago.

Historically, the candidate with unusual views is the one who can't win— whether he is William Jennings Bryan with his "free silver" platform, Barry Goldwater with his plan to abolish social security, or George McGovern with his proposals to increase the taxes of the middle and upper classes. Even if elected to Congress, persons with original ideas may face ostracism, assignment to obscure committees, or redistricting out of their jobs. These possibilities often push public officials to trim their sails and conform to conventional views.

Third Parties Discouraged. In the American federal system, the states make most election laws. But a common thread runs through the 50 sets of election laws: the obstacles confronting minor parties in organizing and in challenging the major parties. Some states require exorbitant filing fees for minor-party candidates. Others demand an extraordinarily large number of signatures of registered voters on third-party petitions before allowing candidates to run for office.

Another major protection for the two-party system in the United States is the winner-take-all single-member district. Any group that endeavors to compete as a third party in this system faces the futility of rarely or never winning. The voter who casts a ballot for a third-party candidate is in effect throwing away his or her vote, unless the minor party has enough strength to affect major-party positions on issues. This was the case with Alabama Governor George Wallace's American Independent party in 1968, which raised conservative social issues later adopted by Richard Nixon and the Republicans. Perot certainly lost some votes in the 1992 presidential election because those who otherwise supported him did not want to "throw away" their vote on a candidate who did not have a chance of winning the necessary electoral college votes. Still, his strong showing at the polls will no doubt have some effect on President Clinton's agenda and policies.

REASONS WHY THE TWO-PARTY SYSTEM DOES NOT INHIBIT CONSTRUCTIVE POLITICAL CHANGE

The two-party system in America has numerous values. It provides for electoral competition by nominating candidates, simplifies choice, promotes stability, and bridges divisions.

Provision of Candidates. The national party conventions are not mere rubber stamps for nominating presidents; for the most part they make meaningful and responsible decisions. The Brookings Institution analyzed 65 national conventions held between 1832 and 1960 and identified five types of nominations:

1. *Confirmation.* An existing president or party titular leader is confirmed as the party's choice.

2. *Inheritance.* A political understudy or previous leader inherits the party mantle.

3. *Inner group selection.* Dominant party leaders get together and agree on the nominee.

4. *Compromise in stalemate.* A deadlocked convention turns to a dark horse or unexpected candidate.

5. *Factional victory.* One of several competing factions within the party succeeds in nominating its candidate.[17]

Only 23 conventions were of the "confirmation" type. Twenty fell in the category of "factional victory." This is evidence that genuine competition has characterized national nominating conventions a good part of the time. Since 1960, there have been eight factional victories (Republicans in 1964, 1968, and 1980; Democrats in 1972, 1976, 1984, 1988, and 1992), six confirmations (Republicans in 1972, 1976, 1984, and 1992;

Democrats in 1964 and 1980), and two inheritances (Democrats in 1968, Republicans in 1988).

Simplification of Voter Choice. In a multiparty system, voters confront a bewildering array of choices that may confuse the democratic process. With only two major parties, voter choices are limited to two principal candidates and options on issues. This is especially important in a nation with diverse racial, geographic, and social interests. To compete effectively and successfully within the system of single-member districts, American parties must unite a variety of groups behind one candidate and position. Thus the parties ease group differences. Each one, in trying to achieve a broad base of support, becomes generally representative of many groups in American society.

The two-party system helps to ensure that issues are not only joined in campaign debate, but also clearly crystallized in the public's mind. A multiparty system would tend to diffuse issues rather than to focus popular thought on two competing alternatives and candidacies. For example, in 1991, Democrats, searching for an issue against incumbent George Bush, raised a question that came back to haunt Bush days before the 1992 election: As vice president, did George Bush know of or participate in an arms-for-hostages deal with Iran before it became public? The two-party system allows an issue like this to be clearly focused and explored in the news media as the two sides trumpet their respective pieces of evidence. Bush consistently denied being "in the loop" on this issue, but contradictory testimony by a former defense secretary that was leaked five days before the election hurt Bush at the polls.

On occasion, bipartisanship prevails within our two-party system. During the Persian Gulf War in 1991, for example, President George Bush consulted with Democratic congressional leaders: Speaker of the House Thomas Foley *(left)* and Senate Majority Leader George Mitchell *(right)*.

Promotion of Stability. Compromising differences at the party level reduces the amount of time the government might otherwise have to spend on resolving conflicts (already an enormous task). Suppose the United States had a multiparty system with a strong ideological orientation: The government would undoubtedly have to devote more time to resolving disputes among parties than it currently does. Also, in such a system, there is a greater potential for too-rapid, even chaotic, change when one party replaces another in office. The pragmatic, mildly ideological American two-party system ensures that changes occur gradually and incrementally.

A Bridge for Communication. As it is organized, the two-party system serves as a bridge between and among the branches of the national government and between the national government and state and local governments. Democratic and Republican leaders in Congress can communicate with state and local party leaders, such as governors and mayors of sizable cities. The system also helps to foster **bipartisanship**—cooperation between the two major parties. During the 1940s and 1950s, Democratic President Harry Truman turned to certain Republican congressional leaders to obtain passage of crucial foreign policy legislation. Similarly, Republican President Dwight D. Eisenhower called upon Democratic leaders for support in Congress. President Ronald Reagan cultivated the congressional leadership structure of both parties to obtain support for his economic program in 1981, as did President Bill Clinton in 1993. What would result from the constitutional separation of powers structure if there were no two-party system to provide this kind of interaction?

ISSUE 2: Summary ★ *Does the Two-Party System Inhibit Constructive Political Change?*

The two-party system can be faulted for creating a political world in which unoriginality is rewarded and compromise smothers sudden or drastic change. But these characteristics can also be regarded as virtues if they protect the nation from radical candidates whose programs might result in social instability and unbridgeable party differences.

ISSUE 3 ARE POLITICAL PARTIES IN AMERICA BECOMING OBSOLETE?

REASONS WHY POLITICAL PARTIES IN AMERICA ARE BECOMING OBSOLETE

Many political observers and scholars have commented on the weaknesses of the party system during the past two or more decades. David Broder stated: "What is missing from our politics is the mechanism which once helped organize . . . voter choices in a sensible fashion, which channeled the individual ambitions of eager aspirants and the conflicting claims of various interest groups into a coherent ticket and platform. That agency was the political party, and it is in a shambles today."[18] Broder points for evidence to the steady decline in voter turnout, the steady increase in **ticket-splitting** (splitting one's vote among candidates of different parties for different offices), the increase of voters calling themselves independent, the increased tendency of candidates to downplay rather than to emphasize their party affiliation, and the substitution of television for party organization in campaigns.

One problem is campaign finance. As we saw in Chapter 7, candidates have become more dependent on the PACs of interest groups for their campaign contributions and less dependent on political party organizations.

Another major cause of the breakdown of the parties began in the late 1940s when party primary elections allowed aspiring candidates to challenge and beat incumbents with or without the endorsement of party leaders. Primaries came to replace the "smoke-filled rooms" where party bosses had held sway and designated the party's candidates. Gerald Ford, John F. Kennedy, and Richard Nixon were part of that new breed when they first entered politics in 1946. Rather than working their way up the political party ladder, each of these men first campaigned for a seat in the U. S. House of Representatives, defeating the preferred candidates of the party leaders in primaries.

Perhaps the most dramatic single setback to party leaders occurred within the Democratic party in 1968 when the McGovern-Fraser Commission was established to encourage more open participation in presidential nominating politics. The McGovern-Fraser reforms required state delegations to the convention to reflect such factors as the racial and sexual makeup of the voters. As a result, long-time Democratic kingmakers, such as Chicago's Mayor Richard Daley and AFL-CIO Chairman George Meany, who had exercised extraordinary power in determining Democratic presidential nominees, were not even seated as delegates at the 1972 Democratic Convention in Miami. The party's overwhelming defeat in 1972 and the hostile reaction of traditional Democratic leaders to the reforms led to their modification, but not abolition. While party leaders secured more representation, rank-and-file delegates continued to reflect proportionately the various voting constituencies. For example, delegates are generally evenly divided between male and female. The Republican party, meanwhile, has voluntarily moved to more diverse representation at their national conventions. As might be expected, however, the Democratic party mandates produce a more precise representation of the makeup of the American electorate.

The fact that presidential primaries are now held in most states has caused a proliferation of candidates who previously would not have been contenders. A person like Jimmy Carter, for example, would not have been a serious candidate for president prior to the 1970s because he was not a major figure in the Democratic party. The primary system allowed him to bypass the party leadership.

Individuals from this new breed of candidates who win office can behave much more independently toward the party organization. The candidates have obligations only to themselves and the narrow range of interests that supported them. They become, in effect, political parties of one. The interests that supported the winning candidates become more powerful in the policymaking process, because the elected officials do not have a strong party organization to help them stand up to the opposition the interests can generate.

The growth of single-issue groups has caused many people to transfer their loyalty from a political party to one group that emotionally motivates them, such as gun control and abortion interest groups. Single-issue groups have had their effect on Congress. It now has not only the two major party organizations with their elected leaders, but also 60 other caucuses and groups with elected leaders on such subjects as mushrooms, gasohol, textiles, solar energy, steel, and tourism. Each of these groups makes establishing and carrying out policy more difficult for the party.

A VIEW FROM THE STATES
The Death of Party Discipline

Back in the Pleistocene era of American politics, which ended about the same time the Vietnam War heated up, there was something called party discipline. It gave a phrase to the language: either "toe the party line," they said, or get in trouble with its elders.

With the popular rebellion against the fighting in Vietnam and the attendant changes in social values, insurgency became a more or less permanent political condition, especially in the Democratic Party. Big-city bosses and ward heelers passed from the scene. Congressional and legislative leaders lost their clout. Smoke-filled rooms were replaced by primary elections.

Now there is no party line, no party discipline and no party elders (or, to be more accurate, none that anyone pays much attention to).

. . . It is every man or woman for himself or herself in American politics these days, and there are no real sanctions anyone can take against the naysayers.

Source: R. W. Apple, Jr., "Lack of Party Discipline Makes Contest Untidy," *The New York Times*, April 28, 1992, p. A19.

The technology of modern campaigns has also contributed to party obsolescence. Pollsters can provide voter opinion directly to the candidates, bypassing the advice and counsel of political leaders. Computerized direct-mail techniques enable well-financed candidates to go over the heads of political party leaders directly to the people to generate support and to raise more campaign money. Television, too, enables candidates to bypass the party organization in campaigns by personalizing their appeal to the electorate. As political historian Arthur Schlesinger, Jr., pointed out about the electronic revolution: "Television presents the politician directly to the voter, who makes his judgment more on what [television] show[s] him than on what the party leaders tell him. Moreover, television, as political scientist Austin Ranney suggests, has become the main source not just of information but of 'reality' for the voter."[19] Ross Perot's ample use of economic tables and charts on hour-long television commercials demonstrated that it is possible to conduct an effective campaign without any formal party organization.

Laying bare the problem of the obsolescence of the two-party system, David Broder concluded: "The result is that independent, autonomous officeholders are confronting independent, autonomous interest groups in a kind of unmediated power struggle that leaves the national interest in shreds and helps persuade voters to express their dissatisfaction in the most dramatic way possible—by not voting."[20]

Without much awareness of politics and public issues, or encouragement to assume leadership, the electorate retreats to the sidelines. Interest groups assume more and more power. In effect, interest groups dominate the making of public policy because parties are too weak, inept, and divided to stand up against them.

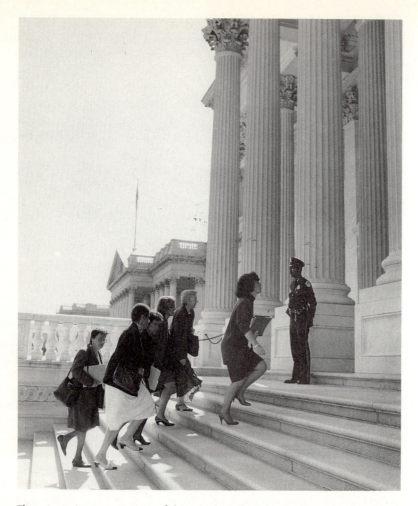

The women's caucus is one of the many single-issue groups in Congress that make party discipline difficult to achieve today. This bipartisan group of congressional women marched to the Senate side of the Capitol to seek a delay in the vote on the nomination of Clarence Thomas to the Supreme Court in October 1991.

REASONS WHY POLITICAL PARTIES IN AMERICA ARE NOT BECOMING OBSOLETE

Arthur Schlesinger, Jr., once noted that "the crumbling away of the historic parties would leave political power concentrated in the adventurers, in the interest groups that finance them and in the executive bureaucracy. Without parties, our politics would grow angrier, wilder and more irresponsible."[21] How would an independent like Ross Perot, for example, have governed the United States without a political party base to support him? An independent would lack an organized broad base of public support and the means to obtain support from party leaders in Congress.

Today there is too much excitement about the decline of parties and too little historical understanding of political parties. This is not the first time in American history that the two-party system has deteriorated and interest groups have become extraordinarily powerful. The abolitionists, prohibitionists, and many other single-interest groups proliferated during other eras, and in the post-Civil War era, major business and industrial interest groups were exceedingly influential. Each time, however, the party system survived the onslaught of the interest groups.

Those who argue for party centralization and discipline overlook the fact that centralization and discipline run against the grain of greatness in the two-party system. For example, during the late 1800s, the parties were very disciplined, but interest groups were also at a zenith. Compared with other eras, the times produced neither great party leaders nor great ideas. Party centralization and discipline often thwart imagination and initiative by stifling new ideas. Many of the most respected American political leaders, such as the two Roosevelts and Woodrow Wilson, have had to fight their parties either to participate in or to gain approval for their new ideas.

When a party's leader, such as Abraham Lincoln in the Civil War era or Franklin D. Roosevelt during the Great Depression, begins to touch the heartstrings of the public's needs and interests, rejuvenation of the party tends to follow. We might say that our parties are now awaiting leadership that will spark public interest and loyalty by addressing public needs and issues in more appealing ways. Some people sense that President Clinton is capable of doing that. The issues that spawn interest groups are real and cannot be swept under the rug. Topics like abortion, the insolvency of banks and savings and loan companies, health care, gun control, and nuclear power merit the attention of the parties. People shift from party loyalty to interest-group loyalty when their issue interests are not addressed. The faults in the parties stem from the failure of party leaders, not from the system itself.

Parties remain of value to American society for a variety of reasons. First, it would be difficult to imagine American society *without* its two-party system. Since the Federalists faced off against the Anti-Federalists, the system has become deeply ingrained in our way of thinking. It is a part of our political culture.

Advocates of strengthening America's parties believe that "at their fullest potential, political parties are mediating institutions that provide some measure of continuity, stability and orderliness in politics."[22] Accordingly, they recommend that the party system be strengthened by

- Increasing the use of partisan elections at the municipal level to enhance party responsibility and strength at the grassroots,

- Removing the expenditure restrictions parties have on how much money they can spend in support of their candidates,

- Diminishing the strength of PACs in relationship to the parties, and

- Allowing more use of the electronic media for partisan political debates sponsored by the parties.

A VIEW FROM ABROAD
Why We Need Parties

There are all sorts of things wrong with political parties as they exist in practically every democratic country. But that does not mean that representative government can function without parties—except on the smallest scale, where everybody knows who everybody is.

The idea that it is possible "to represent all the people" denies the very basis of democratic pluralism, the acceptance and expression of difference. Disagreements and perception of conflicting interests are inevitable, and the role of politics is to provide the means for decision, compromise and conciliation without violence or force. . . . [A]nti-politics advocates do not deny the im-portance of the rule of law essential to government by consent of the governed. But they neglect to consider that laws must be made. For that, people must find poles of coalition and opposition to define their views.

. . . [T]he organizing skills of politics and political debate are essential. They can be distorted, degraded, used to manipulate, to mystify and cheat, but they cannot be simply discarded without bringing paralysis or chaos.

For politics to do its job, there have to be politicians. . . .

Further, rival parties have proved to be the most intelligent, efficient way for politicians to develop and practice their skills.

Source: Flora Lewis, "One Cheer for Our Politicians," *International Herald Tribune,* December 3, 1992, p. 4.

ISSUE 3: Summary ★ *Are Political Parties in America Becoming Obsolete?*

Is the party over? This is a question that is asked frequently. Parties seem to be overtaken by independent candidates, powerful interest groups, and modern technology. For the "party" to continue it must adjust to late-twentieth-century technology, not an easy task for an institution established nearly two centuries ago. And so must its candidates for office. Parties will be obsolete if they nominate obsolete candidates. Leaders need to be recruited from those who are educated about and are sensitive to legitimate issues and who come equipped with both education and integrity.

 ## COMPARISONS WITH OTHER NATIONS

POLITICAL PARTIES IN DEMOCRACIES

Our Constitution says nothing about political parties. In contrast, some democracies' constitutions take great pains to stipulate in detail the role of parties in the political process. The German and French constitutions even warn parties that they must behave themselves according to democratic norms.

Even though there are no real guidelines for the conduct of political parties in the United States, our system (along with those of most other democracies) does not make it especially easy for new or third-party movements to compete successfully. Several American states require, for example, tens of thousands of registered voter signatures on petitions in order for a political party to place its candidates on the ballot. In Germany, it is easier to get on the ballot, but no party can win parliamentary seats unless it secures at least 5 percent of the total national vote.

Two-Party Systems

While some observers regard the similarity between the Republican and Democratic parties as a liability, it may in fact simply reflect our political stability. Compared with other major democracies, American parties apparently have the *least* difference between them when it comes to the voter's economic bracket and party preference, as shown in Table 8.5.

American parties very often find themselves in a situation of divided government, with one party controlling Congress and the other in control of the presidency. It's useful for the parties: Each gets to blame the other for how little gets done. No other major democracy deliberately functions this way, however. Sometimes, by accident, the French stumble into the same situation. Because presidential and parliamentary elections are usually held at different times, it is possible for the branches to be in the hands of different parties. This has occurred only twice in the history of the Fifth Republic (which began in 1958). In 1981 the French elected a Socialist president, François Mitterand, to a seven-

TABLE 8.5 SOCIAL CLASS AND PARTY VOTING

	PERCENTAGE VOTING FOR PARTY	
Party	Upper Class	Lower Class
United States		
Left: Democrats	53%	60%
Right: Republicans	47%	40%
United Kingdom		
Left: Labour	15%	54%
Right: Conservative	66%	28%
Germany (before unification)		
Left: Social Democrats	27%	53%
Right: Christian Democrats	54%	39%
France		
Left: Socialist	35%	62%
Right: Conservative/Gaullist	44%	17%

Note: Since only major parties are cited, totals may not add up to 100 percent.
Source: Adapted from R. J. Dalton, *Citizen Politics in Western Democracies* (Chatham, N.J.: Chatham Books, 1988), p. 155.

year term and then five years later returned a conservative majority to parliament.[23] Two years later they reelected Mitterand, who proceeded to dissolve the parliament. The subsequent election provided him with a socialist majority. But legislative elections in 1993 again brought in a conservative majority, an expression of the French lack of confidence in President Mitterand's socialist policies.

The American political party system tends to be similar to those of other English-speaking democracies—Australia, Canada, New Zealand, and the United Kingdom—all of which have two major parties that receive the overwhelming portion of the vote at election time. In great part this is because of the single-member district system. Yet there are some differences. The more important ones are listed below:

1. The other English-speaking democracies are all parliamentary systems; the winning party therefore controls the executive branch through its majority in the legislative branch. This ensures that there will be no divided government, as so often occurs in the United States.

2. Parties in the other English-speaking democracies concentrate on winning a majority of the lower house of the legislature (no problem for the New Zealanders, since they have only one house).The upper house is a good deal less powerful because it is not popularly elected. Its members either are appointed or inherit their seats. In fact, the United States is practically alone among the democracies in having an upper chamber that is both popularly elected and powerful.

3. While two major parties usually dominate the political scene, an occasional third-party movement can score enough electoral successes to enable it to secure parliamentary seats. Canada and the United Kingdom are cases in point. Third parties in the United States, on the other hand, tend to make very little effort to furnish candidates for national legislative office.

What does seem to be common to the American and other two-party systems is the myth that the two parties are of relatively equal strength, especially when it comes to controlling the executive branch. Reality is different. The Republicans, for example, dominated the presidency for 20 of the 24 years between 1968 and 1992. In the four decades between 1951 and 1992 the Conservatives controlled Parliament (and therefore the prime ministership) for a total of 30 years, compared with only 11 for the Labour opposition. In Germany between 1949 and 1992 the Christian Democratic party controlled the Bundestag and the chancellorship for 30 years; the main opposition, the Social Democrats, had to make do with only 13. Thus, regular turnover of parties is not a given in two-party systems. A traumatic event, such as the Great Depression, is sometimes needed to dislodge an incumbent party from government. As we have seen, the Republican party ascendancy that began with Lincoln in 1860 did not really end until the election of the Democratic candidate, Franklin D. Roosevelt, in 1932.

Multiparty Systems

Democracies with two-party systems differ in major ways from democracies with multiparty systems. Most multiparty systems include two or three larger parties and perhaps half a dozen or more small ones. The electoral system often encourages the modest hopes of smaller parties through **proportional representation:** A political party receives the number of seats that accurately reflects the proportion of the vote it received in a national election. For example, if a party wins 20 percent of the vote it will win 20 percent of the seats in the legislature. It is a more democratic electoral device than is the system of winner-take-all single-member districts. But it is also less efficient. Instead of an election yielding a clear-cut winner (a party with a majority of legislative seats), proportional representation provides (with occasional exceptions) only confusion. If no party has a majority, who is to form a government? Usually, the party with a plurality of seats attempts to form a **coalition government**, sharing power with one or more smaller parties that are ideologically compatible.

Some multiparty systems have become less "multi" over the years. When Germany's sovereignty was restored in 1949, as many as a dozen separate parties contested national elections, but for a variety of reasons the smaller parties declined until the only minor party remaining was the Free Democrats. The Free Democrats typically manage only 8 to 10 percent of the vote, but this is often enough to deny either of the major parties a parliamentary majority. The German system is referred to as a two-and-one-half party system because of the ability of the Free Democrats to be a coalition partner in nearly every German government since 1949.

France experienced a similar process. During the period of the Fourth Republic (1946–1958) its multiparty system was so chaotic that governments formed and collapsed on the average of every seven months. But by the 1960s two major party blocks, the Socialist and two conservative parties, plus a small but still significant Communist party, dominated French politics.

Even the United States can be thought of in terms of coalition politics. Both major parties in the United States are, in a very real sense, coalitions themselves. Can, for example, the Democratic party be imagined without steadfast supporting factions such as African-Americans and organized labor, or the Republican party without the business community and religious conservatives? Over and over it has been suggested that our two parties are really no more than a loose coalition of several interests that meet once every four years to agree on candidates for national office. In recent years Republican presidents have felt compelled to form coalitions with conservative Democrats in the Democratic-dominated Congress in order to secure passage of their legislation.

Any political party would prefer to govern without partners, if only because finding compatible coalition partners is often a difficult task for the leading party in a multiparty system. Consider, for example, the Italian government between 1982 and 1991: Five political parties were included in the cabinet in proportions that roughly represented their parliamentary strength (as of 1987):

Christian Democrats	234
Socialists	74
Social Democratic	17
Republicans	21
Liberals	11

Together these parties controlled 357 seats out of 630, a safe majority. But the two largest, the Christian Democrats and Socialists (rightist and leftist parties, respectively), are unnatural allies. If the Socialists departed from the cabinet because of a policy dispute, the government would fall because it would lose its majority.

Coalition governments, then, can be precarious affairs. In Italy they fall apart at regular intervals: Between 1945 and 1988 the Italians watched a total of 50 governments come and go. Usually, a cabinet minister is in the government because he or she is a party leader and rarely because the prime minister likes the person. In fact, the prime minister may have good reason to fear other ministers from other parties as potential and actual rivals. The fall of a government may present an opportunity to replace a prime minister. It is no wonder that the Italians have so many governments in rapid succession.

A multiparty system doesn't necessitate a coalition government. India and Japan, for example, have multiparty systems, but the Congress party in India, with infrequent interruptions since 1947, and the Liberal Democratic party in Japan, uninterrupted since 1955, have governed without the need of partners. This arrangement is unusual. In India's case a viable opposition to the Congress party has yet to form, while in Japan the Liberal Democratic party is associated with the country's leap into economic prosperity that began in the middle 1950s.[24]

Ideology

Ideology tends to play a stronger role in multiparty systems than in two-party systems. In two-party systems there are ideological differences between the parties, but since both parties tend to be centrist, these differences are often played down—unless, that is, the party gives in to one or another of its extreme wings. The Republicans did this in 1964 when the ultraconservative wing of the party secured the presidential nomination for Barry Goldwater, who lost the election in a landslide. As if to demonstrate their refusal to learn from history, the Democratic party allowed its ultraliberal wing to nominate George McGovern in 1972. McGovern's electoral defeat was even more decisive than Goldwater's.* The lesson for the major parties is not to stray too far from the center.

Multiparty systems, in contrast, can offer an ideological home for nearly every political persuasion. Even political movements that are traditionally un- or antidemocratic in their ideological outlook are often found in such systems. The Italian Social Movement, for example, is a neofascist party. Such parties can win parliamentary seats through the system of proportional representation. Similar undemocratic movements have failed (so far) in the United States because they are not acceptable to the political center.

In the United States the Democrats and the Republicans are more pragmatic than ideological. Their main objective: to win elections, whether for a single seat in the House of Representatives or the presidency. When they think too long about ideological righteousness they tend to lose, usually in a big way (as in 1964 and 1972). In multiparty systems, few parties entertain the idea of winning a national election because their ideological appeal is often very narrow. Keep in mind, though, that, since it is often impossible for any single party to win a majority of parliamentary seats, even a party that wins a small percentage of seats can dictate terms to a bigger party trying to form a government. They become especially persuasive if they are needed to join a coalition

---

* Goldwater won five states in 1964; in 1972 McGovern won only one, Massachusetts, and the District of Columbia.

TABLE 8.6	TYPES OF IDEOLOGICAL SMALLER PARTIES IN MULTIPARTY SYSTEMS	
Country	Party	Political Agenda
Israel	Degel Torah	Enforcement of religious laws regarding compliance with the Sabbath; diet; marriage and divorce, educational programs
France	National Front	Expulsion of foreigners; anti-Semitism
Italy	Italian Social Movement	Xenophobic; restoration of Roman greatness; neofascist
Spain	Basque National Party	Secession from Spain and formation of independent state
Netherlands	Party for Better Housing	Better housing

government. A small party can thus exercise power far beyond its ability to draw votes. Table 8.6 gives examples of small parties that may not require a national electoral victory to achieve their limited goals.

Figure 8.2 helps to summarize the ideological directions of standard political parties in North America and Western Europe. At the extremes of *left* and *right* are parties with ideologies that are often considered hostile to democracy; these parties are rarely, if ever, invited to participate in those governments that necessitate coalitions. Most Western European democracies have parties that are mainstream (conservative and socialist), issue-oriented (ecological and religious), and radical (communist and neofascist). The list is certainly not all-inclusive, but simply includes the most likely parties.

The most permanent radical party in Western European multiparty systems seems to be the communists. Most of these communist parties were formed soon after the 1917 Bolshevik Revolution in Russia. Around the same time a communist party was also formed in the United States. It contested elections as early as 1924, including nominating candidates for the presidency and vice presidency, but it never won more than 100,000

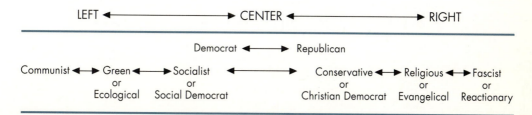

Figure 8.2 IDEOLOGICAL SPECTRUM OF POLITICAL PARTIES.

TABLE 8.7 THE DECLINE OF COMMUNISM IN FRANCE, 1978–1988	
Parliamentary Election Year	Proportion of First Ballot Votes Won by Communist Party
1978	20.5%
1981	16.1%
1986	9.8%
1988	11.3%

Source: Adapted from *The Economist*, June 11, 1988, p. 49.

votes (even in the midst of the Great Depression). In Western Europe, however, communist parties became both a permanent fixture and an electoral consideration. They were even part of coalition governments in France in the late 1940s. However, beginning in the 1980s Western European communist parties experienced a decline, which was accelerated by the collapse of communist regimes in Eastern Europe in the late 1980s. Table 8.7 suggests the decline may have bottomed out. Even with its decline, the Communist party in Europe has achieved a degree of political respectability. In contrast, American communists have always been regarded as simply a foreign element in the body politic, and a menacing one at that.

Across the globe democracy appears to be accumulating converts, but it is important to remember that the democratic process can include the participation of those who are in fact relentlessly hostile to this process. With the waning of communism, the hostility has been increasingly monopolized by parties with a fanatical political agenda controlled by religious orthodoxy. This is particularly apparent in the Third World, but is by no means restricted to it. Table 8.8 suggests just a few of the more electorally successful religious fundamentalist movements that are experiencing substantial popular support.

Religious ideals as political issues are certainly evident in the established democracies as well. In the United States Pat Robertson's Christian Coalition is a case in point. But fundamentalist movements in the United States tend to work within the Republican party as one of that party's most intense and influential interest groups. They have not seriously entertained the prospect of running their own candidates under a new party label. That is just as well. There is no evidence to suggest that working outside the two-party system would further their political agenda.

TABLE 8.8 RELIGIOUS PARTIES IN THIRD WORLD COUNTRIES		
Country	Religious Party	Level of Electoral Support*
Algeria	Islamic Resistance Front	Perhaps 50%
India	Bharatiya Janata Party	40%
Jordan	Islamic Salvation Front	40%

* These are estimates only, as of 1991.

A rally of the Islamic Resistance Front in Algeria in 1992. Radical fundamentalist parties in the Third World are meeting with substantial electoral success.

POLITICAL PARTIES IN TOTALITARIAN SYSTEMS

Totalitarian systems, whether characterized by the extreme left or right, tend to be defined as well as organized by a single legal party. The Germans between 1933 and 1945 were governed by a regime completely dominated by one political party, the National Socialists (Nazis). Like their communist counterparts in the former Soviet Union or in today's China, the Nazis made every other political party illegal. The totalitarian political party typically represents an uncompromising ideology that by definition excludes any movement or political ideals opposed to the goals of what is, practically speaking, a party-state.

In a totalitarian system the government itself becomes an appendage of the party. In China, for example, the Communist party leadership in effect determines economic and social policy in the country. The party leadership is so dominant that a Communist dictator need not even hold state office in order to exercise power. Communist party General Secretary Josef Stalin, for example, ruled the Soviet Union for nearly two decades before assuming a state office. Party leader Deng Xao-ping has dominated Chinese politics since the late 1970s, but through most of that time only held the state office of vice premier (there are usually about 15 vice premiers in China). Government is not allowed to interfere with the supremacy of the party.

The totalitarian party incorporates what, in democracies, are normally considered state institutions: It has its own para-military force, spies, youth organizations, bureaucracy, and, sometimes, even its own universities. Nor do totalitarian parties function the way democratic ones do. They can easily be distinguished from democratic parties in the following ways:

1. Their elections are not free since there is no competition for the single party.

2. An all-inclusive ideology determines how the party will conduct economic and social activities (without the usual democratic consideration of what will work).

3. They desire to completely control the daily activities of each citizen throughout his or her life; democratic parties simply want to get people to vote for them.

4. They do not expect ever to relinquish power: Having come to power either violently or through political subterfuge, a totalitarian party sees no reason to give up power.

For the totalitarian leader, the party is the most important and most visible vehicle of social control.

In the former Soviet Union and in the countries of Eastern Europe we are witnessing the extraordinary sight of totalitarian parties being transformed into multiparty systems. The Soviet Communist party itself broke into five factions that ranged from orthodox adherents to extreme reformers (dubbed Entrepreneurial Communists[25]) before the party was technically banned altogether in early 1992. Some of the new parties in Russia are democratically inclined and some are not. One, for example, is unabashedly fascist: Its leader, who received 6 percent of the popular vote when he ran for president of the Russian republic in 1990, wants Russia to reclaim Lithuania by threatening to dump radioactive waste there if the Lithuanians aren't cooperative.[26] Some former one-party states have gone on a party spree. In Poland, for example, literally dozens of parties have seats in Parliament.

This sudden appearance of political movements is almost unprecedented. In the West, political parties developed over a period of decades or even generations. In Russia and other former Soviet republics, unless the process is violently snuffed out, new parties are being formed virtually as we watch. Unlike some countries in Eastern Europe, such as Poland and Hungary, many of the newly independent republics of the former Soviet Union have no past experience of political development that enables parties to take form in a leisurely fashion. After all, the country didn't even have a parliament before 1906. This fact alone made the Soviet Union the least politically evolved country in Europe. Christian Democrats and Social Democrats, two of Europe's most popular (and politically centrist) parties, lacked any significant equivalents in the former Soviet Union.

POLITICAL PARTIES IN AUTHORITARIAN SYSTEMS

Authoritarian systems often tend to be without parties altogether. Many times the government bans them as a divisive and an unaffordable luxury for a society that feels rushed to develop economically. Parties may also be viewed as a potential source of competition for the leader. Many traditionalist regimes, such as Saudi Arabia and other Persian Gulf monarchies, discourage the growth of parties and rely on a royal network of dozens or even hundreds of blood relatives to effectively control the bureaucracy, army, and overall workings of the government. Where parties do exist, as in the case of Nigeria, they are frequently based on tribal or regional constituencies. It is unusual to find political parties that are truly national in the newer countries.

In the more sophisticated authoritarian systems and the ones without monarchies, such as Iraq and Syria, a one-party system may flourish, but it is almost expected to be the personalized political vehicle of the dictator. Hafez al-Assad of Syria and Saddam Hussein of Iraq, for example, use the single legal party in each country as a personal political machine. In such a situation, the party provides positions for close relatives and devoted followers. The party has its own print and electronic media that monopolize the distribution of information throughout the society.

While all of this is similar to what has already been described in communist systems it is important to remember that even if a party does exist in an authoritarian state, the dictator can probably survive nicely without it. In a communist system an ambitious politician must work *through* the party to get anywhere; in an authoritarian state the dictator more often than not has come to power through the military and requires military support to remain in power.

If parties exist in authoritarian states it is because they are useful to the dictatorial regimes. They are rarely independent of government control, and their primary purpose is to assist the regime's quest to remain in power. Authoritarian parties, like communist ones, are instrumental in the systematic prevention of democratic development.

Summary

1. A political party's most important function is to select and sponsor candidates for political office.

2. The Constitution says nothing about political parties. They developed primarily out of the debate over a strong versus weak central government. Federalists favored a strong central government and Democratic-Republicans favored more power for the states. These parties eventually developed into the Democratic and Republican parties that we know today.

3. The United States' two-party system is attributable to the nationalist versus states' rightists debate, the single-member election districts, conservative/liberal cleavages, and a general political consensus on many issues that discourages the formation of multiple parties.

4. Third (or minor) parties have been successful at calling attention to issues ignored by the major parties, but they have not succeeded in winning national elections.

5. The two parties trade power through realigning, deviating, and reinstating elections, and keep hold of power through maintaining elections. Recently there has been a dealignment in the electorate as more and more voters identify themselves as independent.

6. American political parties are loosely organized along federal lines, with national, state, and local structures.

7. The American party system has been weakened through diffusion of power within the structural levels, the rise of primaries and consequent loss of influence of party leaders, and the rise of interest groups.

8. Some critics maintain that the two major parties have no meaningful differences. Both parties pitch their appeal to the ideological center of the electorate, leaving the voters little choice. But proponents of the party system argue that the two parties still differ in clear-cut ways in both composition and ideology.

9. Critics also accuse the two-party system of inhibiting constructive political change. They claim that the two major parties are largely unresponsive to the electorate, encourage only "safe" candidates, and discourage third parties. Defenders of the system point out that it provides candidates, simplifies choices, promotes stability, and bridges divisions among the branches and levels of government.

10. Are political parties becoming obsolete? Yes, if one considers the low voter turnout, weakening of party leaders, increase of political independents, growing reliance of candidates on interest groups, breakdown of party discipline, and substitution of television for party organization in campaigns.

11. However, political parties have undergone cycles of strength and weakness for their entire history. Defenders of the parties point out that the system is too ingrained in our political culture to fade away. What is needed is an adjustment to technology and the emergence of strong party leaders.

12. America's two-party system differs significantly from that in parliamentary democracies in that the parliamentary system ensures that the party with a legislative majority controls the government. In all the two-party systems, however, one party tends to dominate the executive branch at the expense of the other party.

13. In multiparty systems elections may not yield clear-cut winners. The party with a plurality of seats in parliament often forms a coalition government with smaller parties that are ideologically compatible.

14. Ideological differences get full play in multiparty systems, whereas two-party systems tend to downplay differences in ideology.

15. In totalitarian systems, such as the communist nations, a single legal party dominates the state. It exerts complete control over the activities of its citizen.

16. Authoritarian systems most often make do without any parties. Parties can be divisive and provide an unwanted source of political competition. In some authoritarian regimes a one-party system that caters to the dictator's needs is allowed to flourish. But most dictators, whose strength lies in the military, can exist without any party organization.

Terms to Define

Bipartisanship	Coalition government
Caucus	Dealignment
Convention	Deviating election

Independents

Maintaining election

Majority party

Minority party

Open primary

Patronage

Party boss

Party platform

Primary

Political party

Proportional representation

Realigning election

Reinstating election

Single-member district

Third party

Ticket-splitting

Two-party system

Suggested Readings

Burnham, Walter Dean. *Critical Elections and the Mainsprings of American Politics*. New York: Norton, 1970. While somewhat dated, this work is an excellent primer on the continuing phenomenon of party realignment.

Goldman, Ralph M. *The National Party Chairmen and Committees: Factionalism at the Top*. Armonk, N.Y.: M. E. Sharpe, 1990. The best (and, so far, the only) history of party leadership in the United States from the 1790s to 1960.

Key, V. O. *Politics, Parties, and Pressure Groups*, 5th ed. New York: Thomas Crowell, 1964. A classic work that analyzes why we have political parties and why we will continue to have them in the American democracy.

Ladd, Everett Carll. "The 1988 Elections: Continuation of the Post-New Deal System." *Political Science Quarterly* 104 (Spring 1989): 1–18. An interesting and incisive discussion of *dealignment* as voter identification with the traditional political parties weakens.

Morgan, Roger. "'La Cohabitation' or 'La Cohabitension'? The Fifth Republic Enters a New Phase." *Government and Opposition* 21 (Summer 1986): 3–21. For two years (1986–1988) the French experienced what Americans have grown accustomed to: one party controlling the legislative branch and another the executive. The French didn't like it.

Notes

1. As quoted in Wilfred E. Binkley, *American Political Parties* (New York: Alfred A. Knopf, 1965), p. 19.
2. See Thomas B. Edsall, "How to Conquer an Elephant," *The Washington Post Weekly Edition*, March 2–8, 1992, p. 16.
3. Adopted ibid.
4. *The Christian Science Monitor*, December 11, 1992, p. 19.
5. Mark Shields, "Democrats: The Party's Almost Over," *The Washington Post National Weekly Edition*, June 17–23, 1991.
6. This is the thesis of Richard M. Scammon and Ben J. Wattenberg in *The Real Majority* (New York: Coward, McCann & Geoghegan, 1970).
7. R. W. Apple Jr., "Republicans Form Group to Regain Centrist Votes," *The New York Times*, December 16, 1992, p. A24.
8. David Broder, "Widening Party Differences," *The Washington Post*, February 9, 1975, p. B6.
9. *National Municipal Review* 6 (1917): 204.
10. Broder, "Widening Party Differences," p. B6.
11. Arthur L. Peterson and William C. Louthan, *The Republicans and the Democrats—Similarities and Differences* (New York: The Robert A. Taft Institute of Government, 1976), p. 10.
12. *The Washington Post*, September 27, 1976, p. A2.
13. Herbert Jacob, *Justice in America* (Boston: Little, Brown, 1972), pp. 117–118; see also Stuart

Nagel, "Political Party Affiliation and Judges' Decisions," *American Political Science Review* 55 (1961): 843–850.

14. Herbert McClosky, ed., "Issue Conflict and Consensus Among Party Leaders and Followers," *American Political Science Review* 54 (June 1960): 409.

15. Gerald Pomper, *Elections in America* (New York: Dodd, Mead, 1968), p. 200.

16. American Political Science Association, *Toward a More Responsible Two-Party System* (New York: Holt, Rinehart and Winston, 1950).

17. Paul T. David et. al., *The Politics of National Party Conventions* (New York: Vintage Books, 1964), chap. 7.

18. *The Washington Post*, February 4, 1979, p. C5.

19. *The Wall Street Journal*, May 14, 1979, p. 20.

20. Ibid.

21. *The Wall Street Journal*, May 10, 1979, p. 30.

22. "The Future of American Political Parties," The American Assembly, Columbia University, Arden House, Harriman, N.Y.: 1982, April 15–18.

23. Roger Morgan, " 'La Cohabitation' or 'La Cohabitension'? The French Republic Enters a New Phase," *Government and Opposition* 21 (Summer 1986):3–21.

24. For a useful discussion of multiparty systems that "work" and those that tend to produce crises in governing, see the old but still applicable treatment by Arend Lijphart, "Typologies of Democratic Systems," in Arend Lijphart, ed., *Politics in Europe: Comparisons and Interpretations* (Englewood Cliffs, N.J.: Prentice-Hall, 1969), pp. 46–80.

25. *The Economist*, May 25, 1991, p. 52.

26. *The Economist*, February 29, 1992, p. 55.

VOTING, CAMPAIGNS, AND ELECTIONS

We tend to think of our right to vote as one of our most precious democratic privileges. Indeed, various groups initially excluded from the franchise fought long and hard to exercise that right. And yet America has a surprisingly low rate of voter turnout. Even in our most important elections—the presidential contests every four years—the proportion of eligible voters turning out has rarely exceeded 55 percent in recent decades. By contrast most other democracies can boast percentages of 75, 80, and even over 90 percent.

But it is well to keep in mind also that Americans vote in more elections and more frequently than most other citizenries. Millions of Americans vote every year or every other year in local, state, and national elections. They cast their ballots for judges, school board members, city council members, mayors, state legislators, governors, members of Congress, and president, as well as for propositions, amendments, and referendums

Moir/Sydney Morning Herald

(approval or disapproval of existing state and local legislation). And if that isn't enough to exhaust the American voter, there are primaries and run-off elections as well. Probably no other nation has as many different types of elections and elective offices as the United States.

Not only are Americans treated to more elections, they are also exposed to the longest political campaigns of any nation on earth. It's not unusual for presidential campaigns to begin two years before the election, and they are carried out in earnest for an intense three months after the national conventions select their candidates. (The traditional start-up point is Labor Day in early September; the campaign then reaches a white heat by election day in early November.) Even candidates for local offices may have to spend months on the campaign trail seeking the party nomination and then the victory in the general election. When parliamentary democracies hold an election, candidates generally have a mercifully brief six weeks in which to do all their campaigning.

The American electoral process is complex and often confusing. It is understandable that Americans sometimes fail to exercise their right to vote. Still, it is a matter of concern when a bare majority in a democracy determines its elective leaders. In this chapter we will examine more closely the factors contributing to low turnout, as well as who votes and how they make their voting decisions. We'll also take a look at the types of elections we participate in and the scope of political campaigns. Our electoral process raises some serious issues: How rational are voters in their decision making? Do political campaigns focus enough on matters of substance? Is the electoral college an outmoded institution? Should political campaigns be publicly financed? Finally, we'll see how our electoral system stacks up against those in other nations.

THE ELECTORAL PROCESS IN AMERICA

VOTING

Who votes? And why do they vote as they do? These are probably two of the most studied issues in American politics, and we will be considering the results of these studies. First, however, it is important to understand a little of the history of voting in America, especially the expansion of **suffrage** (the right to vote).

An Expanded Electorate

The Constitution specifies that state laws will determine voter qualifications. For generations, these laws effectively eliminated from the electorate people without property, women, African-Americans, and everyone under the age of 21. Over the course of two centuries, since the Constitution went into effect, constitutional amendments and changes in state laws gradually eliminated these restrictions and greatly expanded the electorate (Table 9.1). In some cases, however, these changes were not accomplished without years of struggle.

Property Qualifications. Originally, someone who owned property was thought to have a more legitimate stake in governmental affairs than someone who didn't (the idea being that if you owned the country you ought to be allowed to run it). After all, property-owners needed to protect their property rights from government intrusion. The poor, it was argued, might just sell their votes to the rich. These attitudes, modified as Jacksonian democracy (ushered in by the presidency of Andrew Jackson, 1829–1837), brought an increasingly egalitarian mood to politics—and as politicians found it increasingly desirable to win additional votes. By the mid-1800s, property restrictions on voting had been abolished.

Women's Suffrage. Women were denied the right to vote for many and various reasons; one premise held that a man voted the interests of his whole family. Agitation for women's suffrage began in the latter half of the nineteenth century. It eventually involved parades, petitions, the organization of a Washington lobby, picketing of the White House, arrests, and hunger strikes in jail. In 1874 the Supreme Court explicitly held that the Constitution did not grant women the right to vote.[1] But by the 1890s women had won the right to vote in some state elections, and then finally gained national suffrage with passage of the Nineteenth Amendment in 1920. The Western European democracies were more or less in concert. The British, for example, extended the franchise to women in 1927. The laggards were the Swiss, who were the last Western European nation to do so, in the 1970s.

African-American Suffrage. In recent history, the most significant broadening of the vote broke down barriers to African-American suffrage. Although African-Amer-

TABLE 9.1 EXTENSION OF THE FRANCHISE IN THE UNITED STATES		
Amendment	Year Ratified	Effective Electoral Extension
Fifteenth	1870	To African-Americans
Nineteenth	1920	To women
Twenty-Third	1961	To residents of the District of Columbia in presidential elections
Twenty-Fourth	1964	To voters unable to pay the poll tax
Twenty-Sixth	1971	To 18- through 20-year-olds

ican males theoretically gained the right to vote with the Fifteenth Amendment, adopted in 1870, numerous state restrictions effectively kept most of them from the polls. Some states adopted a **grandfather clause**, which prevented anyone from voting whose grandfather had not voted before the Civil War. Since most African-Americans were slaves before the war and slaves could not vote, this restriction effectively prohibited African-Americans from voting. **Literacy tests** required citizens to have a minimum knowledge of American government before they could register. These tests were often administered unfairly to African-Americans. **White primaries** were a device used by the Democratic party in the South: The party declared that it was a private club and only members of the club could vote in primaries to nominate its candidates for office. Since the Democratic party nearly always won general elections in southern states, the white primary effectively prevented African-Americans from having any say in who took office. Citizens in some states had to pay a **poll tax** before voting; those who could not afford the tax could not vote.

It took close to a century to get rid of these restrictions. The Supreme Court outlawed the grandfather clause in 1915 and white primaries in 1944.[2] Extensive litigation, sit-ins, and marches led to passage of the Voting Rights Act of 1965, which prohibited voting tests and spurred registration of African-Americans in the South. The Twenty-Fourth Amendment (1964) outlawed the poll tax in national elections, and a 1966 Supreme Court decision did away with taxes on state and local elections.[3]

Lowered Voting Age. The fourth extension of suffrage centered on the movement to lower the voting age from 21 to 18. Proponents argued that 18-year-olds had enough education to vote intelligently and that requiring them to enter military service, perhaps to die, without allowing them the right to vote was undemocratic. This movement took place when there was a draft to meet manpower needs of the Vietnam War. The Twenty-Sixth Amendment, lowering the voting age to 18, was ratified in 1971.

Actually, the United States was emulating the direction being taken by many of its democratic counterparts. The British lowered their voting age to 18 around the same time, as did most of the Western European democracies. Other countries remain less trusting of teenagers: Austria's voting age is 19; Japan's, 20; Denmark's, 21; and Monaco's, 25.

It is perhaps ironic that despite the expansion of the electorate, the level of voter turnout has generally declined since its height of close to 80 percent in the 1880s (Figure 9.1). The three-way presidential race in 1992 sparked a slight increase in voter turnout, from 50.1 in 1988 to 55.2 in 1992. In the following discussion we'll try to make some sense of this situation.

Who Votes?

And who doesn't? And why? Because of the changing electorate, the picture has not always been clear. Nevertheless, it seems safe to say that older people, those of higher socioeconomic status, and those with greater education are the most likely to vote. African-Americans are slightly less likely to vote than whites, while Hispanics are much less likely to vote than either whites or African-Americans. To a great extent these differences in race can be attributed to differences in socioeconomic status. Males and females vote in about equal numbers. Young people are the *least* likely to vote of any age

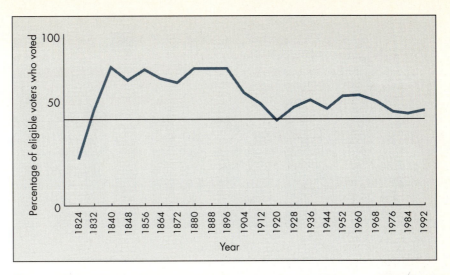

Figure 9.1 VOTER TURNOUT IN PRESIDENTIAL ELECTIONS, 1824–1992. Sources: *Historical Statistics of the United States*, Part 2, 1975, pp. 1071–1072; *Statistical Abstract of the U.S.*, 1991, p. 270; 1992: *The New York Times*, December 7, 1992, p. A1.

group (Figure 9.2). This fact may explain why overall voting turnout declined even further after extension of the suffrage to 18-year-olds in 1971.[4]

The reasons for not voting can be categorized as motivational or mechanical. That is, people either don't *want* to vote for some reason or another, or find it too difficult to do so. To both confuse matters and make them worse, many nonvoters want others to believe that they vote when they have no intention of doing so and tend to take particular delight in lying to pollsters.[5]

Within the first category of nonvoters are those who don't think their vote makes any difference—that it doesn't matter whether a Democrat or a Republican is elected. Voters who live in an area dominated by one party may be disinclined to vote because of the lack of competition. Arthur Hadley, author of *The Empty Polling Booth*, attributes the dramatic decline in voter participation to a single factor: "whether you believe you can plan ahead in life or whether you believe life too much a matter of luck to plan ahead."[6] Curtis Gans, Director of the Committee for the Study of the American Electorate, calls apathy too mild a word to describe the nonvoting phenomenon. "There are substantial numbers of Americans," he said, "who are disenchanted with the political process, disgusted with their leaders, and disillusioned by the failure of government and of both political parties to meet their needs."[7]

This disillusionment appears to characterize those of lower socioeconomic status more than those who are affluent. Indifference to voting may also be more characteristic of younger voters; older voters tend to make efforts to get informed and feel duty-bound to vote. They also have a greater stake in electoral outcomes, since they generally pay more taxes and may have children in public schools.

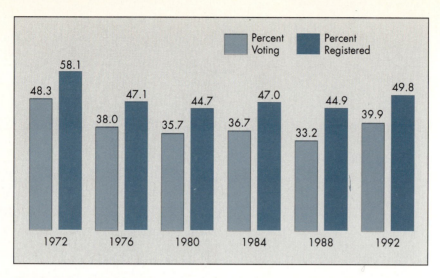

Figure 9.2 PARTICIPATION OF 18- TO 21-YEAR-OLDS IN PRESIDENTIAL ELEC-
TIONS, 1972–1992. Source: *The Christian Science Monitor*, October
28, 1991. All data from U.S. Census Bureau.

There are exceptions to this general indifference. A particular candidate may
generate electoral excitement in otherwise uninterested communities. The Reverend Jesse
Jackson, for example, did this during his 1988 campaign for the Democratic party presidential nomination. African-Americans turned out in record numbers to vote for Jackson.
In the 1988 Alabama Democratic primary, African-Americans furnished 45 percent of
the voters, even though they constituted only 25 percent of the population. In Virginia
they accounted for 38 percent of the primary's total even though they make up less than
20 percent of the state's population.[8] Another exception is Ross Perot, the independent
candidate for president who won intense support from a cross-section of voters in 1992.

The mechanics of voting can be bothersome and even intimidating to many
would-be voters, particularly for those who are less educated, less literate, and less patient.
Long ballots, used in localities with numerous elected officials, and unfamiliar voting
machines will probably require instruction, which may cause embarrassment. The different
kinds and numbers of primaries (discussed below) also confuse voters. Bad weather may
keep voters away from the polls, especially among voters of lower socioeconomic status
(who often lack convenient transportation). Finally, some people don't want to take time
off from work to vote, are unable to get to the polls on their own, or are discouraged by
lines at the polling place. The disconcerting habit of holding elections on Tuesday also
discourages voting because it is normally a work day (most Western parliamentary democracies hold their elections on Sunday).

Forty percent of the eligible voting age population can't vote because they are
not *registered* to vote—that is, they haven't fulfilled the state requirements to prove their
eligibility. Registering to vote often requires that a citizen go to the courthouse or some
other unfamiliar public building. Moreover, the period for registration may begin—and
end—well before an election, when political interest is at a low level. States differ in
their registration requirements. Some make it easy—with postcard registration, for in-

stance—but others throw up obstacles. Stiff registration requirements are especially hard on younger voters, who are mobile and not yet rooted in a community.

In 1993 Congress passed what is known as the "motor voter bill," which requires states to let qualified citizens register when they apply for or renew a driver's license and also to permit registration by mail. These procedures are expected to register as much as 90 percent of eligible voters (compared with the current 60 percent) when they take effect in 1995.[9] Before the motor voter bill became law, eight states (Maine, Michigan, Minnesota, Montana, Nevada, North Carolina, Oregon, and Washington) and the District of Columbia had motor voter programs. Turnout increased more in these states between 1988 and 1992 than it did for non–"motor-voter" states. (See Table 9.2)

Does it matter that we have a low voter turnout in America? Those who take a bleak view think that nonvoting is indicative of alienation from the political system, a sense of powerlessness to bring about change. But others view the situation more charitably. In fact, many leading political theorists throughout history, such as Aristotle, Plato, John Stuart Mill, and John Locke, believed that democratic government was better served by *fewer* voters—or none at all: Plato's *Republic* envisioned rulership so wise there was no point to holding elections. Thomas Jefferson thought only high school graduates should be able to vote. As we have seen, the franchise at the founding of our nation empowered only propertied white males. Our early political leaders were worried about intemperate votes by an uneducated and uninformed electorate. There is some evidence that nonvoters include a number of individuals low in political sophistication, who are susceptible to authoritarian appeals.[10] A case could be made that democracy is better off without the input of such voters. On the whole, however, Americans have been motivated by the view that voting is important for a democracy and that the more who vote, the better.

Voting Decisions

How does the voter decide which candidate to vote for? Three factors help explain voting decisions: party affiliation, personal characteristics of the candidate, and the candidate's record and stand on issues. Hardcore Democrats and Republicans will rarely switch allegiances, even if they find that the candidate of their party is personally repulsive. Millions of American families have voted Democrat or Republican for generations. This phenomenon is changing as the number of independents continues to grow, especially among younger voters, but it remains a strong consideration in national and state races.

TABLE 9.2 MOTOR VOTER TURNOUT		
	1988	1992
"Motor voter" states	53.5%	59.8%
Non–"motor voter" states	49.3%	52.0%
Total National Vote	50.1%	55.2%

In 1988 and 1992 the personal characteristics of candidates, by tradition much neglected by the media, became increasingly well known to the electorate. Was a candidate a draft dodger, unfaithful to a spouse, or guilty of sexual harassment?* Does the candidate have a happy family life? Is the candidate's spouse good-looking? What is the candidate's state of health? How much these questions (or their answers) determine voting behavior remains uncertain, but there is little doubt that they do matter.

In several recent presidential campaigns the front-runner lost substantial ground, losing the election in one (Dukakis in 1988) and very nearly losing in others (Carter in 1976 and Nixon in 1968). This indicates that voters watch closely to see how candidates hold up to the rigors of campaigning. Candidates who are not equipped to withstand intensive campaigning could hardly be expected to thrive on the extraordinary demands of the presidential office. In such situations voters are exercising **prospective voting**, casting their vote on the basis of how well they think their choice will perform in the future.

But perhaps an even more powerful influence on voters is their retrospective judgment—their opinion of the candidates' records, particularly in the case of incumbents and incumbent parties. **Retrospective voting** eliminated Carter in 1980, reelected Reagan in 1984, and rejected George Bush in 1992. So conclusive is past performance that two political scientists who have studied presidential campaigns all the way back to the Civil War claim that "debates, television appearances, fund-raising, advertising, news coverage, and campaign strategies—the usual grist for the punditry mills—count for virtually nothing on Election Day. The only issues that matter are the ones for which the results are already in."[11] Among the 13 keys to winning the presidency that they list are the administration's performance in such areas as the economy, social unrest, scandal, and foreign and military policy successes.

Part of a candidate's record is his or her stand on issues. Candidates for major state or national office are fond of authoring position papers on issues of the day. During the 1992 primary campaigns, for example, the economic recession was on the minds of most Americans. That issue prompted a plethora of candidate pronouncements on how to cure economic ills, ranging from tax cuts (Bush) to cutting government spending (Perot) to protectionism (Buchanan) to "invest and grow" (Clinton). Bread-and-butter issues predominate in most national campaigns. Both parties woo voters with the promise that they will make things better economically. And when the economy is badly off, as in the 1992 campaign season, the candidates are at least spared excessive concern with their views on issues they dread such as abortion, gun control, and what they intend to do about rising crime rates. Exit polls after the 1992 election showed that Clinton benefited from voters concerned about jobs, government services, and the need for change; Bush drew support for his foreign policy, his stand on taxes, his emphasis on family values, and his experience, while Perot rated high on his position on the federal deficit and concern with family values (Table 9.3).

---

* Such an accusation can destroy a political career. Senator Brock Adams (D-Wash.) decided against running for reelection in 1992 in great part because of anonymous accusations (from eight women) of sexual harassment (*The New York Times*, March 2, 1992, p. A7).

TABLE 9.3	EXIT POLLS: A COMPARISON OF CLINTON, BUSH, AND PEROT VOTERS ON SELECTED ISSUES			
Issues		Clinton	Bush	Perot
More government services and higher taxes		55%	20%	26%
Fewer government services and lower taxes		36%	72%	66%
Traditional family values		53%	87%	75%
Tolerance of nontraditional families		42%	9%	19%
Economy/jobs		53%	24%	23%
Federal budget deficit		37%	26%	37%
Taxes		27%	56%	17%
Foreign policy		8%	87%	5%
Has the right experience		23%	63%	14%
Will bring needed change		59%	19%	22%
Cares about people like me		57%	24%	20%
Has the best plan for the country		52%	26%	21%

Source: Rapaport in *The Christian Science Monitor,* December 11, 1992, p. 19; *Washington Post,* November 4, 1992, p. A24. © 1992 TCSPS.

CAMPAIGNS AND ELECTIONS

Types of Elections

We've already mentioned how Americans are inundated with elections. Electoral contests come in a bewildering array of types and sizes, from the local election for dogcatcher to the national election for president. They include elections to nominate candidates, known as **primaries**, as well as elections to actually fill the public office, called **general elections**.

Primary elections differ from state to state and from congressional to presidential contests. In a **closed primary**, only registered members of a party may vote in the party's primary; in an **open primary**, independent voters may vote in either party's primary. (They can cause havoc occasionally by voting in heavier numbers than the party faithful.) In a **blanket primary**, all candidates of all parties appear on the same ballot, which makes it possible to choose a Democratic party candidate for one office and a Republican for another. To ensure even greater confusion, in some states party nominees are chosen by a **caucus** (a meeting of party workers that is the closest modern equivalent of "smoked-filled room" selections by party leaders) or in a **convention** (a larger meeting of party delegates). Most nominees for seats in the United States Congress are chosen directly in statewide (for the Senate) or district-wide (for the House) primaries. It is unusual for an incumbent who is seeking another term to be opposed in a primary, but it does happen. It is even more unusual for an incumbent to then lose a primary.

Presidential nominees are formally selected by delegates to a national convention. But within each state those delegates may be chosen by a caucus, a convention, a primary, or a combination of all three. By 1992, 37 states held presidential primaries (a record number), in which voters chose delegates committed to a particular candidate. Voters in some states cast ballots in a **presidential preference primary**. This vote merely records a *preference* for a presidential candidate that is not binding on the delegates, who are chosen separately by caucuses and local conventions.

The general election is the contest between the major parties that decides which candidate will take office. This is the contest that is most likely to attract a voter's attention, and it is the one we will focus on in our discussion of campaigns. But don't forget that those running for office, unless they are secure incumbents, often must first mount competitive campaigns against other members of their own party in the primaries.

Campaign Strategies

Like other areas of American life, political campaigning has changed from a personal, often folksy form to a sophisticated electronic form. It has been a century since a successful presidential candidate, William McKinley, was able to conduct his campaign from the front porch of his home. The days of stump meetings and courthouse debates have all but passed from the scene as candidates have turned to television and radio to reach and attract the voters.

One of the major goals of the Clinton campaign in 1992 was to dominate local television news coverage. National field director Craig Smith described the effort this way:

> In this campaign we have a G.O.T.V. program, but it doesn't mean Get Out the Vote. It means Get On TV. Each state has two or three staffers whose whole job is Get on TV. We don't evaluate our people on the ground by how many voter-I.D. phone calls they make each day. We evaluate them by how they do in media placement each day: Did you get on TV? Did you make it on the front page? What was the tone of the coverage? How good was the play?[12]

Public opinion polling is also very much a part of contemporary campaigning: poll-taking helps to determine public response on certain issues and, of course, gives information as to who is ahead in the race and, just as importantly, why.

The structure of presidential and many congressional and gubernatorial campaigns reveals the sophistication of today's campaign. The four main categories of campaign staff workers are

1. *Professionals*. These individuals are paid to perform such functions as press relations, advertising, fund-raising, public opinion polling, and scheduling.

2. *Senior advisers*. Usually a candidate for a major office has close friends, often wealthy, who advise and help raise funds. If the candidate is elected, they become a "kitchen cabinet" of personal advisers who may or may not hold office. Jim Baker, long-time friend of President Bush, was rewarded for his substantial efforts during the 1988 campaign with appointment as Secretary of State. Thomas McLarty, a trusted friend of Bill Clinton since kindergarten, was named Clinton's chief of staff.

3. *Citizen volunteers*. Many Americans like the excitement of politics and have the time to volunteer for stuffing envelopes, making telephone calls, and knocking on doors.

4. *Issue advisers*. Other Americans work their ways into campaigns through their knowledge of issues. Professors, lawyers, and others with specialized training help map out candidates' positions on issues and write important speeches.

The staff organization attempts to manage and mold campaign variables to a candidate's advantage. Elements in their campaign strategy include

- Whether and when to conduct a positive campaign (running on one's own record or positions) or a negative campaign (attacking the opposition);

- What theme(s) to use for the campaign;

- When a candidate should hold press conferences and make speeches on major issues (better known as timing);

- Who should be reached in the electorate and what method of communication should be used (television, radio, newspaper, direct mail, etc.); and

- How to raise funds and how the funds should be allocated.

American presidential campaigns provide many examples of these crucial elements of strategy. In 1948 President Harry S. Truman attacked what he called the "do-nothing" Republican Congress as he traveled by train on a whistle-stop tour that crisscrossed the continental United States. He went from expected loser to decisive winner. In 1960 John F. Kennedy spoke of the need to "get the country moving again" and through the use of televised debates moved from underdog status to narrow victor over Richard M. Nixon. In 1976 Jimmy Carter ran against Washington and the bureaucrats on the theme "you can trust me." In 1980 and 1984 President Reagan won decisively with campaigns that portrayed his warm personality, confidence, and conservative positions on issues. President Bush, using similar themes and strategies, enjoyed similar success in 1988. Bill Clinton won the presidency in 1992 by focusing unrelentingly on the state of the economy and blitzing the media. A sign hanging in Clinton headquarters in Little Rock put it succinctly: "It's the economy, stupid." Ross Perot made effective use of the media in his campaign, including hour-long "infomercials."

Much of a candidate's time must be spent raising funds.* In fact, it is almost as though a politician needs to raise money in order to remain in office in order to raise more money to keep winning office. Campaign strategists also need to be concerned with where the funds will be most effectively spent (print ads, TV commercials, radio spots?) and when (how much in the early part of the campaign and how much at the end?). In 1992, both major-party candidates favored grass-roots strategies that catered to the heart-

---

* Public financing has eased this burden somewhat on presidential candidates.

The 1992 election saw a return to old-fashioned, grass-roots campaign strategies: down-home bus tours and whistle-stop train tours. George Bush is greeting supporters in Columbus, Ohio, from the platform of his campaign train.

land while attracting free media attention—Clinton's down-home bus tours through small midwestern and southern towns, Bush's whistle-stop train trip across the Midwest.

Campaign Finance

Money seriously matters in political campaigns, and financing itself has become an issue. Those candidates able to raise more funds (usually incumbents) obviously have a big advantage over their less well-financed challengers. Then there is the question of whether large contributors have an undue influence on those they help put into office. We like to think that in a democracy all citizens have equal access to and influence on those that represent them. But reality is quite different.

Marlin Fitzwater, the White House spokesman during the Bush years, was asked whether wealthy contributors were giving money to have access to high-ranking government officials. In a moment of remarkable candor, he responded: "It's buying access to the system, yes. That's what the political parties and the political operation is all about." Fitzwater said all donors to political parties are "buying into the political process of the

A View from Abroad
Six Reasons Not to Run for Office

"Why," one so often hears, "do we have such lousy politicians?" As a person who has seriously considered a career in politics, I find this question not at all perplexing; far more difficult for me is understanding why any sane and talented person *would* run for office. . . .

Here are some very good reasons for keeping your hat out of the ring:

- *Life in the fishbowl:* Every move you make is scrutinized. Peccadillos, personal and professional, are fair game. You and your family become public property; your relatives and friends had better get used to reading about their most private problems at breakfast.

- *Fun with figures:* As far as the media and your constituents are concerned, you are grossly overpaid. Never mind that you make a fraction of what your equivalents do in the private sector.

- *It does not matter:* If you keep your campaign promises, you are an ideologue, fanatic, or fiscal fritterer; if you do not, you are a hypocrite. If you do not consult widely, you have "got blinders on." If you do, you are "governing by referendum" or "afraid to lead."

- *If it's Tuesday, this must be Kenora:* Give your family and friends a rain check. You will not be seeing much of them. You do not have a life; you have a schedule. On a weekday, you are in cabinet, caucus, and legislative meetings all day (and sometimes all night). This is followed in the evening by a public meeting or rubber-chicken dinner with a community group in your district (and the obligatory handshaking until midnight). Then a few hours of fitful sleep spent worrying about what the media will have decided you screwed up today.

  On weekends, you meet with disgruntled constituents all day before feasting once again on rubber chicken.

- *Twenty-five thousand of my closest friends:* You will be forgiven if you wonder how you got so "popular." Everyone and his dog wants to see you, and as far as they are concerned, they have a right to. Loquacious lobbyists, slick solicitors, and craven consultants slap you on the back as if you went to summer camp together. Bus rides, visits to the corner store, and having one too many with dinner present a new challenge: You never know who is going to waltz right up and appropriate "a few moments of your time."

- *Is that a rug I see under your feet?* "Job security" is a phrase from a foreign lexicon. Should you lose your job, do not expect a homecoming parade from your grateful constituents or the thanks of all your erstwhile friends and colleagues. You will fade like an old letter.

Source: Michael Melling, *Toronto Star,* quoted in *World Press Review,* June 1992, p. 25.

participant in the sense of saying, 'I want to give money. I want the system to continue to work the way it has.'" Asked how other, less wealthy citizens could buy into the system, Fitzwater said, "They have to demand access in other ways."[13]

What immediate benefits did large donations to the Republican party in 1992 get for the donors? Here is a breakdown from the Bush campaign:

$1500—an intimate dinner with the president and 4300 other $1500 donors

$15,000—an invitation to attend a White House reception hosted by President and Mrs. Bush

$92,000—a photo opportunity with President Bush[14]

Democracies are not always perfect examples of political equality.

Congress has made a number of efforts to reform campaign finance (Table 9.4), including proposals to limit the influence of PACs (political action committees) in 1993. These efforts have used four basic approaches:

1. Limitations on how much a candidate could spend on a campaign;
2. Limitations on contributions to candidates and parties, such as $1000 per person, which must be reported to the Federal Election Commission;
3. Requirements that campaign committees file detailed reports with the government on receipts and expenditures of $100 and above; and
4. Subsidies of presidential campaigns (public financing), beginning with the 1976 campaigns.

Both candidates and contributors have found loopholes in the laws that enable them to spend and contribute more than is prescribed. For example, contributions made to parties rather than candidates are not restricted. Such donations, known as "soft money," can be used for party activities that directly aid those running for office. In addition, each of these approaches to reform raises serious questions. Should the national government regulate campaign finance? Should tax dollars be used for political campaigns? Is the government restricting freedom of speech and press by limiting the amount of money a person can contribute to a political candidate? Will public subsidies to candidates, rather than parties, further weaken the latter, making campaigns even more fragmented and personalized? We will be looking at some of these questions in the next section.

? ISSUES TO ANALYZE

ISSUE 1   ARE AMERICAN VOTERS RATIONAL?

REASONS WHY AMERICAN VOTERS ARE RATIONAL

Some political observers believe that many voters cast their ballots for superficial or even nonsensical reasons, without any depth of understanding of either the issues or the candidates' positions on them. But voting is not an irrational and irrespon-

TABLE 9.4 CHRONOLOGY OF CAMPAIGN FINANCE REFORM

Date	Act/Decision/Proposal	Nature of Reform
1907	Tillman Act	Prohibited business groups from contributing directly to federal candidates
	President Theodore Roosevelt	Advocated public financing of presidential and congressional elections
1925	Federal Corrupt Practices Act	Limited contributions and required disclosure of receipts and expenditures by federal candidates
1943	Smith-Connally Act	Prohibited unions from contributing directly to federal elections from union treasury funds until after World War II
1947	Taft-Hartley Act	Made Smith-Connally ban permanent and extended it to primaries and conventions
1971	Federal Election Campaign (FEC) Act	Required (1) reports of all contributions and expenses over $100, (2) political action committees (PACs) with annual receipts over $1000 to file statement of organization, (3) TV stations to sell candidates time at lowest rate. Limited (1) spending on media ads and (2) personal and/or family contributions to a person's campaign
1971	Revenue Act	(1) Established public funding of presidential campaigns, (2) granted tax benefits in exchange for political contributions, (3) allowed annual $1 checkoff on income tax statements for presidential campaigns, and (4) created guidelines for Presidential Election Campaign Fund
1974	Amendments to FEC Act (1971)	(1) Limited size of contributions, (2) placed caps on candidate spending, (3) created Federal Election Commission (FEC), (4) abolished limits on media ads, (5) limited contributions to congressional campaigns from individuals and political action committees, and (6) established spending limits on congressional campaigns
1976	*Buckley* v. *Valeo* (Supreme Court)	Declared spending limits in 1974 FEC Amendments unconstitutional as a violation of free speech
1989	U. S. House Resolution	Banned speech honoraria for House members beginning in 1991
1991	U. S. Senate Resolution	Banned speech honoraria for Senators beginning in 1991

sible act. Take the example of African-American voters. In presidential elections, between 85 and 95 percent of these voters cast their ballots for the Democratic candidate. They have been doing so since the 1930s. They have perceived the Democratic party and its candidates as more representative of African-American interests because major civil rights legislation bears the principal imprint of the Democratic party. Moreover, beginning in 1969, Republican administrations frequently sought to abolish or to limit programs in which African-Americans were especially interested, such as the Office of Economic Opportunity (OEO) programs.

As this example indicates, segments of the electorate (1) know how a specific government policy affects them; (2) are aware of how the parties stand on government policies that affect them; (3) know whether the major group or groups to which they belong will benefit more from one party or another; and (4) are aware of whether the condition of the nation merits the retention of the incumbent party, administration, or candidate.

The shift of a majority of Roman Catholic voters to the Republican party in 1984, which had been gradually taking place for about two decades, reveals the perception they have of how the Republican party stands on such issues as abortion. Most Jewish voters identify with Democratic concerns. In the ten presidential elections prior to 1992 an average of 28 percent of American Jews voted Republican. A high point was hit in 1980 when Ronald Reagan got 39 percent, but returned to average in 1988 when only 27 percent voted for George Bush,[15] and only 11 percent in 1992.[16] While some Jewish voters had temporarily shifted toward the Republican party because of its strong pro-Israel position, the perceived hostility of Secretary of State James Baker toward Israeli settlement policies probably drove many of these Jewish voters back to the Democratic party column.[17] (See Table 9.5 for a breakdown of how various groups voted in 1992.)

V. O. Key, Jr., has described three types of voters, all of whom, in his opinion, conduct themselves rationally: the "standpatters," who stick with one party election after election because they understand the party's ideology and policies and perceive them favorably; the "switchers," who tend to have more than average education, information,

TABLE 9.5 COMPARISON OF CLINTON, BUSH, AND PEROT VOTERS BY GROUP, 1992			
	Voted for . . .		
	Clinton	Bush	Perot
Asians	31%	55%	15%
Blacks	83%	10%	7%
Hispanics	61%	25%	14%
Jews	80%	11%	9%
White Catholics	42%	37%	22%
White Northern Protestants	36%	44%	20%
White Southern Protestants	30%	53%	17%
Born-Again/Fundamentalists	31%	56%	14%
Attend religious services weekly	36%	48%	15%

Source: *The Christian Science Monitor*, December 11, 1992, p. 19.

and interests, and who base their voting decisions on what they know about candidates and thus vary their choices; and the "new voters"—that is, those who have never before voted or have not voted for some years—who make their decisions on the basis of their personal interests. Of course, rational conduct is not limited to the act of voting. People may know how to get the political process to work for them in other ways—for instance, through appeals to their legislators.[18]

Research by Norman H. Nie and associates in *The Changing American Voter* suggests that the increasing number of independents results from an increased awareness of issues and ideologies among the electorate.[19] Traditionally, American voters have been pragmatic "centrists" or "moderates." However, between 1956 and 1973, middle-of-the-road voters declined from 41 to 23 percent of the electorate, while those on the left of the political spectrum increased from 12 to 21 percent, and those on the right from 13 to 23 percent. This larger bloc of independents has continued into the 1990s.[20] Their increasing awareness of issues and ideology may lead to major changes in the two parties.

Nie and associates also show that the American electorate is taking more consistent positions on issues and making more use of issues to evaluate candidates. President Clinton's success may be largely attributable to his efforts to move the Democratic party from the left to the center of the electorate and also to appeal to independent voters on issues. Of course, his appeal was very successful on economic issues, as shown in Table 9.2. If the Republican party has moved too far to the right, as moderate and liberal Republicans contend, then it will need to adjust its positions to appeal to a changing electorate. However, since the 1992 election was more of a referendum on the economy than on moral and social issues, that debate cannot be answered based solely on 1992 results.

People tend to vote in ways that reflect their group memberships, party affiliation, socioeconomic class, religion, and/or race. These are obviously rational considerations. The increasing number of independents may also be seen as a sign of rational decision making. Quite properly, many voters are not influenced by predetermined party ties or established positions on issues. Since independents often determine the outcome of an election, parties and candidates must appeal to them.

Campaign ads on television and in other media do not necessarily manipulate voters. As pointed out in Chapter 6, slick appeals don't always fool the public. Political consultants have come to recognize that the electorate can see through campaign advertising that does not reflect the genuine character of the candidate. Political scientists Thomas Patterson and Robert McClure concluded that "what the voters are reacting to is substance. The most effective campaign ad is based on substance, not flimsy image appeal."[21]

Increasingly, there seems to be another consideration at work that influences rational voting behavior. It can easily be referred to as the "fed-up" factor. Voters by the early 1990s were making decisions very much on the basis of whether the incumbents in Congress and state legislatures were actually doing a good job. Some apparently weren't. Democratic primary voters in Illinois in March 1992 achieved notoriety by dismissing several incumbents from office: One sitting senator, 2 sitting members of the House, and 11 state legislators lost in primaries. The elections were exciting (one candidate was shot at but lived to defeat an incumbent House member) and in the end Democratic party candidates for Congress included an African-American female, a former leader of the Black Panthers (a radical group of the 1960s), and a former Rhodes Scholar.[22] Voters in

One of the beneficiaries of the "fed-up" vote in the 1992 elections was Carol Moseley-Braun, shown here being sworn into the Senate by Vice-President Dan Quayle and Senate Majority Leader George Mitchell. Moseley-Braun upset the incumbent Illinois senator in the Democratic party primary and then went on to win the general election.

the presidential election sent Bush packing because he had presided over the slowest-growing economy since the Hoover administration 60 years earlier.[23]

REASONS WHY AMERICAN VOTERS ARE NOT RATIONAL

For a variety of reasons, the American electorate is unable to make rational choices. Voters do not know enough to vote intelligently. They make irrational decisions and are easily manipulated.

Ignorance. The Survey Research Center at the University of Michigan concluded that one of the greatest limits on political participation in presidential elections is "sheer ignorance" of major social and economic problems.[24] Indeed, political scientist Philip Converse has said, "large portions of the electorate do not have meaningful beliefs, even on those issues that have formed the basis for intense political controversy among elites for substantial periods of time."[25] Moreover, a recent study has found that independents are not necessarily better informed or more sophisticated voters than the more consistent Democrats and Republicans, and their rationales for their electoral choices may actually be more superficial.[26]

Lack of knowledge about issues is not the only impediment to rational voting. For elections to be meaningful, the electorate must have some basic knowledge about the structure of government within which issues are decided and policies established. But the American people are amazingly ignorant about how their government works. A study of American teenagers showed that

- Fewer than half could name even one of their U.S. senators or their representative in the U.S. House of Representatives;

- Approximately one-third did not know that a U.S. senator is elected;

- Over one-third believed that a newspaper should not be permitted to criticize elected officials;

- One-fourth did not know that the U.S. Senate is a part of the U.S. Congress; and

- One-third did not know that the U.S. Constitution specifies our individual rights.[27]

Earlier studies of the public's knowledge of government revealed essentially the same conclusions for the populace as a whole. As might be expected, those with higher education were better acquainted with the issues.[28] This is small consolation, however. More recent studies suggest that most Americans, and particularly younger people, are blithely ignorant of political issues.[29]

Irrational Decisions. Studies on the degree of change in public opinion over a period of time show that, except for party identification, public opinion is very unstable. Philip Converse has shown statistically that only about 13 of 20 persons (65 percent) are likely to take the same position on the same issue consistently. Of these 13, 10 (50 percent) may be expected to take the same position merely because of chance rather than because of an understanding of and commitment to a principle.[30]

Voters do not necessarily make rational decisions based on analysis of information. For one thing, people are highly selective in accepting political messages; as one political scientist put it, they reject "too strenuous an overload of incoming information."[31] For another, they are impressed by appearances. How was Dwight D. Eisenhower able to defeat Adlai Stevenson in 1952 and 1956, when Democrats outnumbered Republicans by about 45 to 33 percent? Eisenhower's personal appeal—his smile, his image as an outstanding military hero of World War II—did much to offset normal party loyalties. Ronald Reagan was widely perceived as warm and genial, a perception that certainly contributed to his substantial victories over Jimmy Carter and Walter Mondale in 1980 and 1984.

What are the overriding issues in congressional campaigns? Reflecting on a study which found that the candidate's personality and constituent service, not well-conceived and well-reasoned positions on issues, are most important, the columnist James J. Kilpatrick put it this way: "What many Americans appear to want in Congress is a friendly neighborhood druggist, well supplied with Band-Aids, cough syrup and something to soothe the aching back."[32] Important questions are these: Is the candidate friendly, energetic, and accessible? If an incumbent, does he or she take care of such problems as social security difficulties faced by constituents?

Some might argue that voters made rational decisions based on the issues when they were presented with ideologically clear choices in the presidential elections of 1964 and 1972. In the first instance, Barry Goldwater's brand of Republican conservatism ("A choice, not an echo" was his campaign theme) was clearly at odds with Lyndon Johnson's Democratic liberalism. In 1972, Democrat George McGovern's liberal positions and policies had little in common with those of Republican Richard Nixon. But did the election results actually indicate thoughtful decision making? Seymour Martin Lipset saw the 1972 vote not as a choice on issues and policies but rather as a rejection of extreme change: "The basic threat perceived by the electorate in the McGovern candidacy was not so much to existing social arrangements as to the social order itself."[33]

Why, then, do we persist in the view that democracy depends on people making rational choices about public issues? The idea, said Murray Edelman, "may persist in our folklore because it so effectively sanctifies prevailing policies and permits us to avoid worrying about them."[34]

Are We Like Sheep?. If voters reject an overload of information and are influenced by factors other than issues, several questions are in order. Is the great mass of American voters manipulated by Madison Avenue image makers? Does a candidate's image so captivate our minds that we vote against our own interests? Do elites control the decision-making process because of electoral apathy? At least one student of the subject, Murray Edelman, thought so:

> The mass public does not study and analyze detailed data about secondary boycotts, provisions for stock ownership and control in a proposed space communications corporation, or missile installation in Cuba. . . . It ignores these things until political actions and speeches make them symbolically threatening or reassuring and it then responds to the cues furnished by the actions and speeches, not to direct knowledge of the facts.[35]

Substantial portions of a candidate's campaign dollar go into television because it reaches so many people. In this medium issues can easily be blurred, as pointed out by Marshall McLuhan: "The TV image is of low intensity or definition, and therefore, unlike film, it does not afford detailed information about objects. The TV producer will point out that speech on television must not have the careful precision necessary in the theater. In the TV image we have the supremacy of the blurred outline."[36]

After John F. Kennedy won in 1960, Richard Nixon felt that he had devoted too much time to issues and too little time to his physical appearance. With the increasing influence of advertising and public relations executives, the electorate is asked to choose not between candidates, but rather between prepackaged images. Campaign slogans suggest the low level of the appeals made to voters. No better and no worse than most were the meaningless phrases shouted by Nixon supporters in 1972: "Nixon's the One" and "Four More Years."

ISSUE 1:　Summary　★　*Are American Voters Rational?*

A balanced answer requires that we say American voters exhibit both rationality and irrationality. Voters generally do not have a great deal of in-depth knowledge of candidates and issues. In that way, we can see the basis for the irrationality. On the other hand, they generally have a *rough* idea about whether a candidate and his or her positions are helpful or harmful to their interests, and vote rationally on that basis.

ISSUE 2   DO POLITICAL CAMPAIGNS FOCUS TOO MUCH ON IMAGE AND NOT ENOUGH ON SUBSTANCE?

REASONS WHY CAMPAIGNS FOCUS TOO MUCH ON IMAGE

Where's the Beef? In the 1984 contest for the Democratic presidential nomination, Walter Mondale chided his fellow candidates for a lack of substance in their campaign pronouncements. Echoing a popular commercial for a fast-food chain that poked fun at the small burgers of its main competitors, he asked "Where's the beef?" That slogan caught the fancy of the electorate, many of whom must have been wondering the same thing.

Political campaigns are too chaotic, complex, and chancy to allow much time for attention to matters of substance. It almost seems that the longer campaigns have stretched, the less substance has been included. Modern campaigns involve long hours, fatigue (on the part of both the candidates and their staffs), and momentous decisions made at a moment's notice. Those who conduct campaigns are often overwhelmed by the tasks of raising money, doing research, organizing volunteers, conducting polls, writing speeches, and handling public relations. Few of these chores have anything to do with the real issues of the campaign. The many claims on the candidate's attention and the demands of the media for actions and statements that make good "sound bites" leave little time for thoughtful analysis of important, if not stirring, issues.

Some issues today are too complex for the electorate to understand, or too controversial for a candidate to take a clear-cut stand on. It is close to impossible to craft a comprehensive and winning strategy on domestic issues because 252 million Americans are so diverse in their needs and aspirations. Every thoughtful position taken by a candidate on a controversial issue produces many negative reactions from a variety of interest groups. Candidates find it far more convenient to concentrate on safe issues that have an instant appeal to a large number of voters, regardless of their backgrounds: "no new taxes" (or cutting old ones), a constitutional amendment to protect the American flag, or bashing Japanese trade practices. Such pronouncements may have little chance of becoming policy, but they sound good.

Finally, political campaigns can owe much to the element of chance. Small states like Iowa and New Hampshire have a large impact on determining the fate of presidential candidates because they are among the first states to hold a caucus or primary. They give "momentum" to the winning candidates (or the "Big Mo," a term coined in 1980 by George Bush when he thought his quest for the Republican nomination would be successful after winning the Iowa caucus. He subsequently lost out to Ronald Reagan). The electorates of these small states may be unrepresentative of either party, let alone the entire nation. Yet the candidate who spends a great deal of time and resources wooing the voters in these states has a head start on the also-rans in the race, no matter how much attention they may give to the issues. In 1976 Jimmy Carter came "out of nowhere" to take the lead in the race for the Democratic nomination after winning in Iowa. In 1992 Bill Clinton was the first candidate ever to lose the New Hampshire primary (he came in second), yet win the party's nomination.

Candidates for Sale. Close to 20 percent of the total cost of a campaign goes to the professionals responsible for packaging the candidate—the specialists in direct mail,

A VIEW FROM THE STATES
Political Star Search

This article first appeared in a newsletter addressed to the needs of women in politics in the 1990s. It gives some practical advice on how to reach for the stars.

Drawing attention to your political campaign can often be accomplished by inviting a sympathetic celebrity to a special event or fund-raiser. By adding a celebrity to your campaign plan, you are earning heightened voter attention and enhancing your ability to promote your message.

Republicans angling for Arnold Schwarzenegger may find him busy with President George Bush; Barbra Streisand may have her hands full with top-line Democratic contenders. But there are plenty of celebrities who want to be involved politically and who will help your campaign. You just have to know how to find them.

It takes research to find the right celebrity. Start with your state party headquarters and ask for a list of celebrities who support your party. As a "downballot" [local] candidate, you should be particularly interested in those who come from your own area. The "hometown" approach is one of the best ways to convince a celebrity to help with your campaign. If celebrities find the right candidate in their own backyard, they have a chance to demonstrate their community involvement.

As a downballot candidate, you should try to attend senatorial and gubernatorial events in your state that you know will feature a celebrity. This coattail approach will reduce your costs; if you make the right contacts, it may result in a secondary endorsement of your campaign. All you really need is a picture of you and the celebrity at a happy moment and the right to publish it in your next mailing. Get a comment from the celebrity about your campaign, and you're golden.

Using a celebrity in your campaign takes an investment of time and some money, but the payoff will be considerable in additional publicity and fundraising dollars. Plus, the inclusion of a celebrity grabs the attention of the electorate and makes you stand out from the crowd.

POSSIBLE CELEBRITY ENDORSEMENTS

Republicans	Democrats
Ann-Margret	Rhea Perlman
Cheryl Ladd	Goldie Hawn
Mary Hart	Whoopi Goldberg
Brooke Shields	Roseanne Arnold
Tom Selleck	Morgan Fairchild
Pat Boone	Rob Lowe
Scott Baio	Judd Nelson

Source: Harper's Magazine (October 1992), pp. 18–19. Reprinted from Chris Carroll and Marc Goldman, "The Art of Using Celebrity Endorsements," *Majority Rules!*, July 1992.

polling, film-making, advertising, public relations, and so on. Unfortunately, the image of the candidate that is projected in the media is often a distorted one. Joe McGinnis described Richard Nixon's 1968 campaign this way: "It was as if they were building not a President but an Astrodome, where the wind would never blow, the temperature never rise or fall, and the ball never bounce erratically on the artificial grass."[37]

Campaign advertising frequently does little to enlighten the electorate on the issues of a campaign. Consider these television commercials for Senator Bill Bradley (D-N.J.), a former professional basketball star with the New York Knicks:

1. Bradley seated at a desk and talking on the telephone. A narrator describes Bradley's political record. Near the end of the spot, Bradley wads up a piece of paper and shoots it through a small basketball hoop above a wastepaper basket.

2. A man's hands pouring plaster into a mold. When the mold is opened the bust of a man is revealed. The hands use a brush to paint the plaster man and place him on a shelf with other similar busts. A narrator intones that Bradley is not tied to any special interests, but is "cast in a different mold."

Bradley barely won reelection to the Senate. New Jersey voters may have preferred that Bradley speak out more forthrightly on delicate issues such as tax reform.

A campaign may be decided simply on the basis of contributions if one candidate has a good deal more money than the other. Usually it is the incumbent who has the deepest campaign war chest. Even in presidential races, where public financing is available, wealthier candidates have a chance to prosper more. Ross Perot's vast wealth (estimated at $3.5 billion, give or take a hundred million) allowed him to forgo public financing and spend enough to get on the ballot in every state as an independent candidate. It's unlikely he would have been a candidate without personal wealth.

REASONS WHY CAMPAIGNS ARE SUBSTANTIVE

No one could conduct a campaign without *some* regard to issues. Candidates are expected to produce issue papers—statements on where they stand. These have to be crafted with some care since their author must defend them when questioned by the media and in debates with competing candidates. Many observers felt that Ross Perot's reluctance to come up with detailed positions on issues and defend them publicly may have led him to pull out of the presidential race in July 1992. When he reentered the race in October he joined the debates and bought hours of prime TV time to present his views in detail.

Presidential elections usually allow for two to three face-to-face wide-ranging debates between the major party candidates. Most debates center on questions to candidates from members of the news media, but in 1992 the debate format was varied so that at least one evening was given over to questions from a pool of voters. The participants in this "town meeting" insisted on focusing attention on substantive issues instead of personal characteristics of the candidates.

George Bush, Ross Perot, and Bill Clinton engaging in a campaign debate in 1992. Debates help focus attention on substantive issues and give voters an idea of the communication skills of the candidates.

A political campaign also offers voters the opportunity to make several judgments about the candidates:

- How well do the candidates define their themes and issues?
- How well do they handle adversity?
- How good are their organizational skills?
- How do they respond to the rigorous demands of political campaigning?
- How sound are their judgments and decisions under pressure?
- How good is their sense of timing about when to act or speak on an issue?
- How thorough is their knowledge of issues?
- How effective are they in communicating to diverse groups of voters?

Several examples from recent presidential campaigns illustrate one or more of these tests that voters can make of the candidates.

In 1984, Walter Mondale tried to increase his credibility with the American people by proposing a tax increase to balance the budget, but the American people frowned on the idea.

In 1976, candidate Jimmy Carter asked, "Why not the best?" and in 1980, President Carter suggested, "It could be worse." The positive strategy worked, but the negative failed. Carter's efforts to portray Ronald Reagan as simplistic and poorly equipped to be president failed when the public compared the two on television. By contrast, Ronald Reagan's principal strategy was to show people how bad life had become during the Carter administration. He repeatedly asked: "Are you better off than you were four years ago?" The strategies of the two candidates were not missed by the voters in 1980. They accepted one and rejected the other.

When George Bush overcame an initial 17 percentage point deficit to beat Michael Dukakis in 1988 it was not because the election was "Dukakis's to lose." According to Allan Lichtman and Ken DeCell:

> As compelling as this account may be, it is dead wrong. George Bush did not "come from behind" to snatch victory from the Democrats in 1988. Michael Dukakis did not "blow" an election that was within his party's grasp. The American public did not succumb to the manipulation of cynical, media-savvy political strategists or the influence of sound bites and television images. . . .
>
> In choosing George Bush to be the 41st president of the United States, the electorate responded to identifiable social, political, and economic circumstances in a pragmatic, and clearly predictable manner—a manner clearly consistent with the historical pattern of presidential-election results since Republicans and Democrats emerged as the two major parties.[38]

In the 1992 campaign voters were obviously impressed by Clinton's ability to handle the revelation of scandals that would have sunk a less steady candidate. His grasp of a wide range of issues and focus on a positive campaign also won the voters' approval.

ISSUE 2:   Summary   ★   *Do Political Campaigns Focus Too Much on Image and Not Enough on Substance?*

American political campaigns are criticized for their reliance on large sums of money and Madison Avenue showmanship techniques, and their reluctance to grapple with issues. Despite these faults, the electorate can use political campaigns to judge campaign themes and formal positions on issues, how candidates handle adversity, their organizational skills, and a variety of other tests.

ISSUE 3   *SHOULD THE ELECTORAL COLLEGE BE ABOLISHED?*

REASONS WHY THE ELECTORAL COLLEGE SHOULD BE ABOLISHED

Delegates to the Constitutional Convention in 1787 designed the electoral college to prevent the people from voting directly for president. They didn't trust the mass of voters to make wise choices. A group of electors from each state who made up the **electoral college** are the ones who formally elect the president a month after the general election. Originally designated by the state legislatures, they are now chosen

(a)

(b)

(c)

BENJAMIN HARRISON

What do these three presidents have in common? None won the popular vote in the general election. (a) John Quincy Adams, (b) Rutherford B. Hayes, and (c) Benjamin Harrison were elected by a majority of *electoral college* votes.

by popular election and reflect the number of members each state has in Congress. In a presidential election, then, one's vote is actually cast for a *slate of electors* committed to a candidate and not directly for the presidential candidate. (In states where the slate of electors does not appear on the ballot, votes go to a presidential candidate, whose slate of electors has previously been chosen by the candidate's party.) The electoral college has been criticized as having serious defects as a method of electing our nation's highest official.

First, if a presidential candidate wins a state by even one popular vote, he or she receives *all* the state's electoral votes. (Maine is the one exception to this rule: under the district method Maine allocates electoral votes according to who wins the congressional districts; two electoral votes go to the candidate who wins statewide.) One result of the prevailing winner-take-all method is that a candidate who has lost the total popular vote may still be elected president. This has indeed happened three times: in 1824, with John Quincy Adams; in 1876, with Rutherford B. Hayes; and in 1888, with Benjamin Harrison. The losing candidates in these races actually won a majority or a plurality of the *popular* vote, but they did not win a sufficient number of states to receive a majority of the nation's *electoral college* votes.

Second, the electoral college system does not fairly represent all states. In the North, for instance, substantial minority groups may exert undue influence. This occurs because large northern states are often fairly evenly divided between parties, at least in close presidential elections, giving minority groups the pivotal strength to determine to whom *all* of the state's electoral votes will be given. The NAACP opposed an amendment to allow for direct popular election because it would have reduced the political power of African-American voters in key northern states. The electoral college system also over-represents the nation's smallest states; each has at least three electoral votes regardless of its population (two for its senators and one for each representative).

Third, electors in some states do not have to vote for the candidate to whom they are pledged. Throughout our nation's history, a total of ten electors have defected from this pledge. For example, in 1972, a Virginia elector who was pledged to Nixon voted for the Libertarian party candidate, and in 1976, a Washington state elector pledged to Ford voted for Reagan. In 1988 an elector in West Virginia pledged to vote for Dukakis instead gave her vote to Dukakis's running mate, Senator Lloyd Bentsen.

Fourth, the system can result in a deadlock in the electoral college if minor party candidates win enough electoral votes. If no candidate receives a majority of electoral votes, the election must be decided by the House of Representatives (as happened in 1824). In 1992 many people had feared that Ross Perot, running as an independent, would receive enough electoral votes to deprive either George Bush or Bill Clinton of their necessary majority of electoral votes. Perot, in fact, cited this concern as a major reason for pulling out of the race during the summer. A deadlock would have led to bargaining for votes and determination of the winner in the House. Each state has one vote in this situation, which gives the least populated states equal weight with the most populous.

Fifth, the electoral college system exacerbates regionalism. The battle between the so-called Frostbelt and Sunbelt states has heightened as governors, members of Congress, and other elected officials debate federal policies that favor the Sunbelt. Between 1950 and the 1980s, the Frostbelt suffered a net loss of about 70 electoral college votes to the Sunbelt. This shift has strengthened the conservative movement, which is stronger in the Sunbelt than in the Frostbelt.

A substantial majority of the population as well as groups as diverse as the American Bar Association and the AFL-CIO support direct popular election of the president. In 1970 the House of Representatives approved a Constitutional amendment but the Senate did not. In 1977 President Jimmy Carter proposed abolition of the electoral college.

REASONS WHY THE ELECTORAL COLLEGE SHOULD BE RETAINED

The electoral college system has several advantages. First, it forces a candidate to seek broad support throughout the country instead of relying on piling up huge majorities in just one region. Moreover, since the winner of a state receives all its electoral votes, the system allows candidates to cut down campaigning time in states they are likely to either win or lose easily. They can then concentrate on states in which the partisan balance between the two major parties appears to be about even. Typically these are populous states—Illinois, New York, California, Pennsylvania, and the like—with a cross-section of voters: rich and poor; African-American and white; industrial and agricultural; urban, suburban, and rural. Candidates thus project their views to voters who represent divergent interests rather than appeal to a narrow ideological or geographic spectrum.

Second, the electoral college has worked for nearly two hundred years. Why change an existing system for something that might be less stable? As one professor of law has noted, "It would take a Constitutional Amendment to change it. And people start to worry that when you tinker with the system, who knows what we'll be left with?"[39]

Third, direct popular election, the principal alternative to the electoral college, has many disadvantages. Minority parties would be more likely to emerge, thereby fragmenting American politics and endangering the two-party system. The proposal for direct election under consideration in Congress in 1970 required that a candidate receive at least 40 percent of the vote in order to win. With the knowledge that denying a major candidate 40 percent of the vote could force a run-off election, fringe candidates might enter simply to enhance their bargaining power. The electoral college helps the two-party system resolve social conflict and manage the transfer of power by forcing serious presidential candidates to develop a national base of support.

Fourth, the electoral college system tends to create stability, which gives voters more confidence in the government and its ability to govern. It avoids the kind of trouble that would probably have resulted in 1960 when Kennedy narrowly edged Nixon by less than one vote per precinct. With direct popular election, a vote recount might have put a cloud over the American government until the recount was completed and perhaps long afterward. As Figure 9.3 shows, the electoral college vote normally provides the winner of the popular vote with an even greater margin of victory. In close elections, such as 1960, the winner's proportion of the electoral college vote is significantly greater than the proportion of the popular vote. Thus, the electoral college has the effect of strengthening the popular-vote winner.

Fifth, by emphasizing the importance of the states through the distribution and counting of electoral votes, federalism itself is the beneficiary. The electoral college system highlights symbolically and substantively the importance of the states within our federal system.

As Wallace Sayre points out in his study of the electoral college:

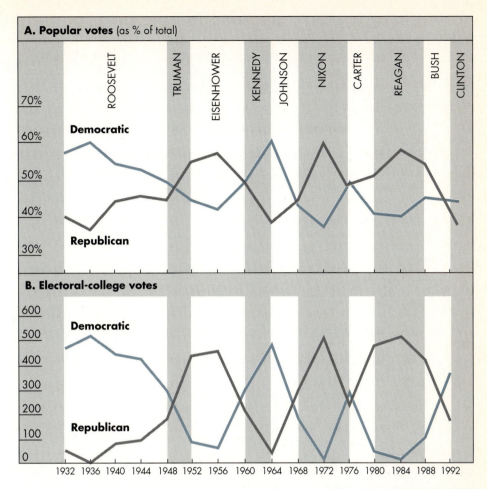

Figure 9.3   A COMPARISON OF POPULAR VOTE AND ELECTORAL COLLEGE VOTE, 1932–1992. Figure 9.3A charts the percentage of popular votes for the two major parties in presidential elections over the last 60 years; Figure 9.3B shows the number of electoral votes for the same elections. The electoral college gives a greater winning margin for a candidate than does the popular vote, thus helping to provide greater legitimacy for winners of elections with close popular votes. Source: *The Economist,* November 7, 1992, p. 29. Data from U.S. Census Bureau.

> *It has evolved along with the nation and has in every era produced presidents accepted as legitimate and capable of governing effectively. . . . It has encouraged political leaders to wage their struggles within two great parties. It has provided a point of access for metropolitan interests that are often ignored elsewhere. It has promoted national stability in the battle for the presidency. We see no reason to abandon, and many reasons to support, an institution whose assets have been very tangible and whose liabilities have been largely conjectural.*[40]

The principal criticism of the electoral college system is that it allows the possibility of electing a president who has not won the plurality or majority of the popular vote. But this problem can be addressed without abandoning the electoral college. The National Bonus Plan would award a bonus of 102 electoral votes (two for each state and the District of Columbia) to the candidate who received the most popular votes nationwide. Had this plan been in effect, no candidate in U.S. history would have been elected who had not won the plurality or majority of the popular vote.

ISSUE 3:   Summary   ★   *Should the Electoral College Be Abolished?*

To some extent, what critics see as weaknesses, advocates see as strengths of the electoral college. Critics say that the system causes candidates to concentrate too much on the large industrial states with major blocks of electoral votes. Advocates say that these states are a microcosm or representation in miniature of the whole of the United States. Critics say the system has almost failed to work on occasion, but advocates say that it *has* worked for more than two hundred years and that the principal alternative, direct popular election, might create more problems than it would solve.

ISSUE 4   *SHOULD POLITICAL CAMPAIGNS BE PUBLICLY FINANCED?*

REASONS WHY POLITICAL CAMPAIGNS SHOULD BE PUBLICLY FINANCED

Presidential elections, including the primary campaigns, have been publicly financed since the 1976 election. A candidate may opt out of receiving federal funds (as Ross Perot did), but those who do accept the funds must agree not to spend more than the total allowed. This system helps to hold campaign spending down and provides a level playing field for all those who agree to use the public funds. Thus, incumbency provides less of an advantage because it won't necessarily draw greater campaign contributions.

Many people would like to see public financing extended to the other federal elections—for the Senate and the House of Representatives. In these races, as we have seen, candidates must typically spend a great deal of time fund raising and catering to the "fat cats" whose contributions they depend on. Moreover, as mentioned earlier, it is these contributors who tend to have greatest access to the legislators who get elected.

Particularly troublesome is the influence of the PACs, the political action committees established as the fund-raising arms of corporations and interest groups. In 1990, winning candidates for the House of Representatives spent an average of $407,000, 50 percent of which was contributed by PACs.[41] From 1988 to 1990, as Figure 9.4 shows, various types of political action committees had significantly increased their contributions to political campaigns. As PAC giving has increased, candidates have had to depend less on political parties and individual citizens for their campaign finances. Naturally, the candidates will spend more time cultivating their relationships with PACs, where more money can be raised in less time. And once elected, candidates may be expected to respond more to the wishes of PACs than to individuals or their party leadership.

In fact, the very idea of a responsible two-party system, which clarifies and simplifies issues for American citizens, has been threatened by PACs. Party leaders, including the president and congressional leaders, find it more difficult to enlist support for a party position on an issue when a representative's party loyalty has been diluted by

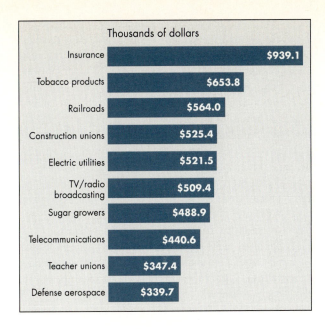

Figure 9.4 DOLLAR INCREASES IN PAC GIVING FROM 1988 TO 1990. Source: *The Christian Science Monitor,* March 5, 1992, p. 11. Data from the Center for Responsive Politics.

PAC influence. Members of Congress have effectively become pawns on the PAC chessboard.

Another problem with PAC influence is that the campaign contributions pour into incumbents' war chests at a far greater rate than into those of challengers. In 1990 PACs gave $89 million to incumbent candidates for the House of Representatives and only $7.6 million to challengers.[42] As Figure 9.5 shows, both PAC and non-PAC finance sources significantly favor incumbents. Not surprisingly, campaign spending by incum-

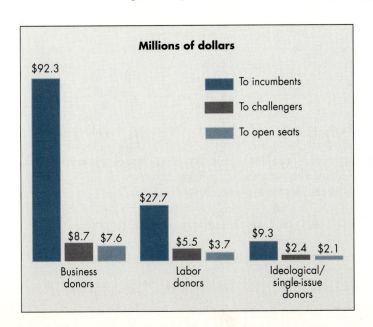

Figure 9.5 TOTAL CAMPAIGN CONTRIBUTIONS TO INCUMBENTS, CHALLENGERS, AND CANDIDATES FOR OPEN SEATS, 1989–1990. Source: *The Christian Science Monitor,* March 5, 1992, p. 11.

bents has greatly increased relative to campaign spending by challengers (Figure 9.6). Democrats, who currently account for more incumbents than Republicans, thus receive greater benefits from campaign contributions. In the 1990 races for the House, the ten incumbent winners who had raised over $500,000 each were Democrats.

Those who defend the status quo point out that federal election laws set limits on contributions and require careful accounting of expenditures. After all, how much influence can one have if an individual is limited to a contribution of $1,000 and a PAC to a contribution of $5,000 for any one candidate and $20,000 for a party? But both candidates and parties have found ways around these restrictions. Someone who aspires to be a "fat cat" can make the usual legal donations and then use his or her influence to "convince" business colleagues, friends, and family members to do the same. Political parties can receive extra unrestricted contributions for what are termed "party-building activities," such as voter registration drives and get-out-the-vote campaigns. But these "soft money" funds often end up directly benefiting the party's political candidates.

The fund-raising system today has fertilized the seedbed of citizen cynicism. First, by giving great influence to PACs, it has distanced ordinary citizens from politics. Second, by decreasing electoral competitiveness through large PAC donations to incumbents, it has given citizens less of a reason to participate in campaigns and elections.

REASONS WHY POLITICAL CAMPAIGNS SHOULD NOT BE PUBLICLY FINANCED

Publicly financed political campaigns, if private funding were disallowed, would violate a citizen's right to self-expression under the First Amendment and would also impair democracy. For example, had Ross Perot not been allowed to spend his own money during his 1992 presidential campaign, the American public would not have had the opportunity to consider this alternative to the two major party candidates.

While much criticism focuses on the large amounts of money spent on campaigns, critics fail to put expenditures in perspective. An expenditure of half a million dollars for a House seat comes to almost $1 dollar per resident. Total costs in 1987–1988 for all national, state, and local campaigns in a nation of 250 million were $2.7 billion, the same as the combined 1987–1988 advertising budgets of Philip Morris and Procter & Gamble.[42] In any case, large campaign budgets are required to fund media advertising, campaign staff, travel, opinion polls, and organizational efforts. When put in that light, fund raising becomes more defensible.

Fund raising is a legitimate test of a candidate's communication and organization abilities. If a presidential candidate cannot conduct an effective fund-raising campaign, can that person serve effectively as president? The vast administrative apparatus of the presidency requires superb communication and organization skills, which can be at least partially tested through presidential campaign fund raising.

Critics worry about PAC funding but they overlook contributions by individual citizens and political parties, which still account for the majority of campaign contributions given to the U.S. House and Senate candidates.[43] Thus, while PAC funding of campaigns has increased, it is not the dominant player in the fund-raising game.

Sometimes candidates are charged with spending too much money to win an election. It is generally well known that U.S. Senator Jesse Helms (R-N.C.) spent about $17 million to win his last race in 1990, but it is not well known that he spent $6.5

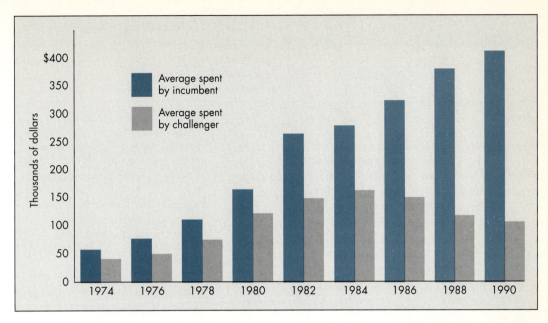

Figure 9.6 AVERAGE CAMPAIGN SPENDING BY INCUMBENTS AND CHALLENGERS, 1974–1990. Source: *The Christian Science Monitor,* March 5, 1992, p. 9. Data from Center for Responsive Politics.

million to raise that amount in small sums in 50 states.[44] In this case, at least, private fund raising served to increase citizen participation in the electoral process.

Public financing, as practiced in the presidential elections, actually works far from perfectly. Candidates still can be influenced by large donors who operate through a variety of loopholes. For example, committees that are nominally independent of a candidate's campaign organization are able to spend money freely on a candidate's behalf. And the "soft money" that is given to political parties can wind up in a presidential candidate's coffers. Both major parties admit that their actual expenses greatly exceed the limit imposed by the Federal Election Commission.

ISSUE 4: **Summary ★** *Should Political Campaigns Be Publicly Financed?*

When both sides are considered, this is not an easy question to answer. Perhaps that is why Congress has had such difficulty in solving the dilemmas of campaign funding since its first reform efforts in 1907. Republicans generally oppose governmental solutions to problems like this, but they might benefit more than Democrats from publicly financed campaigns. Democrats, who might be expected to support this reform initiative, have incumbency advantages in attracting private funds. Both Republicans and Democrats must wrestle with the First Amendment issues of freedom of expression. The combination of constitutional issues and partisan questions are likely to ensure that this will continue to be an intractable problem. As Table 9.6 shows, other countries have found various solutions to the question of campaign financing.

TABLE 9.6   FINANCING POLITICAL CAMPAIGNS ELSEWHERE

	Public Financing	Limits on Fund Raising or Spending	Television
Britain	No	Yes	Free time, allocated according to party's strength in previous election
Denmark	Allowance to parties, based on strength in previous election	No	Parties given equal and free time on public stations
France	Reimbursement to candidates, according to votes received	Yes	Free and equal time to candidates
Italy	Reimbursement to candidates according to votes received	No	Free and equal time to candidates on state-run stations, but parties control major private stations
Israel	No	No	Parties given equal and free time on public stations
Japan	No	Yes	Candidates given some free time for speeches; no negative advertising
Germany	Reimbursement to parties, according to votes received	No	Free time to candidates on public stations

Source: *The New York Times,* March 21, 1990, p. A12.

 ## COMPARISONS WITH OTHER NATIONS

THE ELECTORAL PROCESS IN DEMOCRACIES

Voter Participation

Generally, when a society has the opportunity to vote in a free, secret, and competitive fashion, its members take full advantage. This point is especially noticeable in a fledgling democracy, as the recent elections in several Eastern European countries have increasingly made clear. But even in the more established democracies of Western Europe voter participation is consistently in greater evidence than in the United States (see Table 9.7, p. 328). Many reasons have been offered to explain the discrepancy. Here are some of the more important ones:

1. European elections are generally held on Sunday. Most people have the day off and find it convenient to get to their polling places. Americans make do with Tuesday, a difficult day at best. American voters have to struggle to get to their polling place during a day when they must also deliver children to school, go to work, and attend to all those daily necessities that leave little desire to stand in line to cast a ballot.

2. European elections, particularly in parliamentary systems, occur less frequently than in the United States. Voters in Europe and in other democratic societies normally only go to the polls every four years or so, when the national election determines the

Campaign rallies in European countries (such as this one in Italy) tend to be festive and well-attended affairs. One reason for the enthusiasm may be that election campaigns in Europe are far less frequent and are far briefer than campaigns in the United States.

composition of the government. Americans are confronted with elections, it seems, almost every time they turn around.

3. Election campaigns in Europe (and almost everywhere else where elections are held) are mercifully brief, rarely consuming six weeks before their culmination. The British general election campaign in 1992 barely lasted a month, for instance. Very few countries have anything equivalent to the institution of the political primary. Americans, in contrast, experience seemingly endless political campaigns that take several months and often a couple of years. Prior to the 1992 congressional and presidential elections it was commonplace for some candidates to announce their candidacy early in the year preceding the election. By the time the election is finally held, many voters are weary of and perhaps even bored by the candidates.

4. Europeans are more partisan than Americans. A large core of voters see a big difference between voting socialist or conservative. This may be slowly changing as political parties worry more about being elected than preserving ideological purity. Moreover, ideologies matter less when economies grow wealthier. Prosperity leaves socialist parties with fewer issues. Ironically, those Americans who do vote are reacting more the way Europeans used to, feeling that one party or the other is ideologically too far to the left or right of the political spectrum.

5. In most European systems, the candidates are far more dependent on their official party positions than are their American counterparts. In the United Kingdom, for example, parliamentary candidates generally tend to stick very close to their party's position. A Conservative party candidate will hold to the party line even if standing for

Remember how tiresome the 1992 political campaigning became? That's probably because it all started in 1991. Americans suffer through the longest campaigns in the world. One British member of Parliament contrasts the American campaign season to his own.

The British general election is under way. Ahead lies a grueling campaign, lasting a full three weeks ... at the end of which the public will be thoroughly fed up with all things political. ...

During the campaign I, like any politician, shall keep an eye on the finances. After all, I have to raise $15,000 to fight the election in my constituency; if I spend more, I get disqualified. So the close watch is not on raising the money but on seeing that there is no overspending. There are no political action committees, no Friends of Dudley Fishburn and no slush funds. But $15,000 is enough, since I know that it is all my opponents will have as well.

Then there is, as in America, the all-important television coverage to be thought out. What I will say, not how much time I can buy, is the question. Each candidate gets exactly the same amount of free air time. Each candidate, too, is allowed, courtesy of the Royal Mail, free postage on a single election leaflet that goes out to every voter. ...

My American political friends, aghast at the presumption that I dare call myself a politician with such puny resources at my command, ask, "How do you get anyone to vote for you?" ... But note, if you will, that on April 9 about 75 percent of the electors in my constituency will turn out to vote. Note, too, that 95 percent of my constituents will be registered to vote. In Britain it is easy to register; indeed hard not to do so: the lists are updated annually and the onus to get the right names on the list rests as much with the public authorities as with the private individual. ...

In the polling station, voters are handed a pencil (no, it's not on a piece of string) and a slip of paper with the names of three or four candidates and their parties printed on it. A simple X in the appropriate box is all that is required, and off they go. That's it. There is not the long list of political offices, Electoral College candidates, propositions, symbols, fine print and columns that greet the bewildered American voter.

One other difference—it sends a shudder through my American friends in elective office—is that the incumbent enjoys few advantages over the challenger. ...

There is a particular advantage to this. In Britain, people float in and out of office. You don't have to be a politician to get into politics: Margaret Thatcher was a chemist, John Major was a banker and I was executive editor of *The Economist* before becoming incarcerated in the House of Commons. The ease of getting into, and of being booted out of, British politics attracts better people, not worse. A healthy legislature draws its representatives from the public at large, warts and all, and returns them to a useful life after a spell in office.

Source: Dudley Fishburn, "British Campaigning—How Civilized!" *The New York Times*, March 14, 1992, p. A25.

election in a strongly working-class district that has voted Labour for three or four generations. This party line makes it easier for the electorate to make voting decisions. A party vote is meaningful. (Of course, party loyalty is neither engraved in concrete nor irreversible. One study, for example, has revealed that in the United Kingdom, people also vote very much on the basis of their pocketbooks, punishing their government for economic downturns.[45] This is why many observers thought the Conservative party would be thrown out of power in the 1992 elections, which were held in the midst of a severe recession. The Conservatives squeaked through with a much reduced parliamentary majority. Apparently, many voters believed that as bad as the economy was under the Conservatives, it could only get worse under Labour.)

6. Some democracies make voting compulsory. Australian law, for example, requires eligible voters to cast ballots. Austria also makes voting legally compulsory, but only for elections to the presidency, an essentially ceremonial office. In all likelihood, any attempt to require voting in American elections would be found unconstitutional and, at the very least, would certainly go against a long-standing political tradition: the American custom of ignoring elections. There is a certain amount of democracy associated with the decision (or, perhaps, the nondecision) to vote. Americans take full advantage of the observation that the right to vote also implies the right not to vote.

7. The discrepancy in voter turnouts between the United States and other democracies may actually not be as great as is widely perceived because of the way voter turnout data are calculated. First, while other countries generally compute voter turnout as a percentage of *registered voters*, the United States computes it as a percentage of *voting age population.* (see Table 9.7). But as of 1992 only three-fifths of that population was even registered to vote. Second, while other countries count both invalid and blank ballots in their voter turnout figures, the United States counts only valid ballots. As a result, voter turnout in the United States as compared with other nations is skewed to the low side.

Winner-Take-All Versus Proportional Representation

Americans and the other English-speaking democracies are accustomed to a "winner-take-all" system of voting. The British refer to this electoral rule as "first past the post." Such a system provides an efficient method of selecting a government. But as we saw in Chapter 8, it also is less democratic than a system of **proportional representation**, which provides precisely the political power a political party deserves as the outcome of a free election, by allocating seats on the basis of the proportion of votes received.

Consider, for example, the Israeli electoral method. The entire country is treated as a single constituency. The 120-member unicameral legislature, the Knesset, is composed of parties that have received seats on the basis of their percentage of the total national vote. Simply put, a party that received 30 percent of the total national vote (an electoral success by Israeli standards) would receive 36 Knesset seats. Each party puts up a list of up to 120 candidates. The voter casts a ballot for a party list of names. He or she is probably unfamiliar with most of the names, but does recognize the names at the top of the list. The first name, of course, is that party's choice for prime minister.

If a party does well and, say, gets those 36 seats, what then happens to number 37 on the list? Nothing, unless he or she moves up to 36 because of the death or resignation of one of the candidates who won a seat. The numerical ordering of names is, of course,

TABLE 9.7 COMPARATIVE CALCULATIONS OF VOTER TURNOUT

Calculation A: Voter Turnout As a Percentage of Voting Age Population		Calculation B: Voter Turnout As a Percentage of Registered Voters	
Austria	89.3%	Belgium	94.6%
Belgium	88.7%	Australia	94.5%
Sweden	85.8%	Austria	91.6%
Netherlands	84.7%	Sweden	90.7%
Australia	83.1%	New Zealand	89.0%
Denmark	82.1%	West Germany	88.6%
Norway	81.8%	Netherlands	87.0%
West Germany	81.1%	**United States**	**86.8%**
New Zealand	78.5%	France	85.9%
France	78.0%	Denmark	83.2%
United Kingdom	76.0%	Norway	82.0%
Japan	74.4%	United Kingdom	76.3%
Canada	67.4%	Japan	74.5%
Finland	63.0%	Canada	69.3%
United States	**52.6%**	Finland	64.3%
Switzerland	39.4%	Switzerland	48.3%

Source: Table adapted from tables in David Glass et al., "Voter Turnout: An International Comparison," *Public Opinion* (Dec.–Jan., 1984): 50, 54.

the undemocratic element in this scenario. It is the party leadership that determines the list, and the leaders consistently ensure that their names are placed in *safe* positions on the list. The ones in *marginal* places are usually the candidates with ulcers: Their fate is questionable. Those toward the bottom of the list understand they have no chance of winning a seat and therefore don't worry about it. Generally, this is how the positions work out for the larger Israeli parties:

Safe: 1 through 35

Marginal: 36 through 45

Unsafe: 46 through 120

The German electoral system uses both the winner-take-all system *and* proportional representation. For all practical purposes the German voter actually casts two ballots: one in her or his single-member district for a particular candidate and one for a party list. Each method produces half of the membership of the Bundestag, the lower house of the German parliament. This two-ballot system enables the German electoral system to satisfy both the advocates of winner-take-all single-member districts (SM) and proportional representation (PR).

There is an on-going debate as to whether the "winner-take-all" SM or PR is more effective. The question really revolves around whether one prefers more efficiency or a maximized democracy. In SM, for instance, the losing party's supporters get no representation. Since SM contributes strongly to the dominance of two major parties, a government is almost certainly to be dominated by one party. The stability this arrangement provides is preferable, according to SM advocates, to the coalition governments so frequently produced in multiparty PR systems (as in case of the Italian government, discussed in Chapter 8).

People in SM systems sometimes begin thinking more about PR after some blatant unfairness is revealed. The United Kingdom has become a celebrated example of a political democracy in which one party can secure a majority of parliamentary seats with a bare plurality of popular votes, as Table 9.8 suggests. With less than 42 percent of the vote the conservatives secured nearly 52 percent of the House of Commons seats, a clear majority. Labour did even better: With around 34 percent of the national vote, Labour still secured almost 42 percent of the seats. The most unfortunate party in British politics is the Liberal Democrats (Liberals). Despite winning more than one-sixth of the popular vote the Liberals won just 3 percent of the seats in the Commons.

It is obvious that the two major parties would have the most to lose and Liberals the most to gain should seats be distributed proportionally. What is just as obvious is that no one party would then control a majority of seats, necessitating a coalition government between two of the parties. This is a situation that the British have refused to tolerate since the early 1920s, a time when there actually was a viable three-party system. The only comparable experience Americans may have had goes all the way back to the 1850s when the Whig party and its spinoff, the Republicans, opposed the Democrats and each other. This three-way competition lasted for only a few elections; by 1860 the Whig party had disappeared. The Americans and the British both seem to be very impatient with third parties, preferring the neatness and the electoral certainties that two major parties offer.

One other electoral formulation should be mentioned. Some democracies use the **multi-member district**. The most important country that has this sort of system is Japan, where each of its 171 electoral districts has three to five seats available. This kind of electoral system is complicated even for the Japanese voter who simply casts a ballot

TABLE 9.8   POPULAR VOTE AND SEAT DISTRIBUTION IN THE HOUSE OF COMMONS, 1992

Political Party	Percentage of Popular Vote	Percentage of Seats	Number of Actual Seats*	Number of Seats if PR System Used
Conservative	41.9%	51.7%	336	272
Labour	34.2%	41.6%	271	222
Liberal Democrat	17.9%	3.1%	20	116
Others	6.0%	3.6%	23	39

* A minimum of 326 seats is required for a parliamentary majority.
Source: Adapted from *The New York Times*, April 11, 1992, p. A5.

along party lines. This is because there may be too many party candidates running for too few seats. Supporters of the largest party, the Liberal Democrats, still may find that they have to choose among several members of their own party. This makes intraparty competition very intense.

The only election that comes even close to this sort of internecine political warfare is the American primary system. Party members compete for the nomination in the primaries, with the Republican and Democratic winners facing each other in the general election. But at least in the United States the lack of party harmony is confined to the primary, and is not evident in the official election that determines who wins a political office. In Japan, there is no primary. Since 1955 the majority party has had to face its greatest electoral challenge from within, with occasional rebellions against an aging leadership by younger party members.[46]

Every country that has elections restricts its electorate in some ways. The democracies have removed all of the more unreasonable restrictions. Early qualifications based on religion, race, or gender have disappeared, with rare exceptions. When Switzerland extended the franchise to women in 1970, it was at least half a century behind every other established democracy.

Some restrictions remain. Members of the royal family in Britain and other constitutional monarchies cannot vote. This is not an unreasonable rule since royal families in democracies need to observe strict political impartiality. And no democracy permits prisoners to vote; after being convicted of a felonious crime, they legally lose several constitutional rights. As we shall see below, the modest restrictions on voting in democracies pale into insignificance compared with the ones in nondemocratic systems.

THE ELECTORAL PROCESS IN TOTALITARIAN SYSTEMS

Having an election in a strict communist system may seem to be a waste of time. The candidates are approved only by the party leadership, opposition is nonexistent, and the outcome is easily anticipated. Yet elections in communist systems are not as absurd as one might at first believe. The regularly held elections confer a degree of legitimacy, however weak, on the regime. They can also indicate to the regime the level of dissatisfaction among its constituency. Throughout most of the history of the Soviet Union, for example, it was possible for a candidate, chosen and approved by the Communist party, to run unopposed and still not get elected. Communist-sponsored candidates were occasionally so unpopular that they received many "no" votes, the only option remaining to the Soviet voter. If a candidate failed to obtain a majority of votes cast, a second candidate had to be nominated.

But even if voting in communist systems was sometimes worthwhile, the results wouldn't be. In every communist society it is the party and not the government that is the effective policymaker. The party hierarchy (which, in effect, selects itself and recruits its own successors) formulates and dictates policy to the government bureaucracy, which then implements it. Legislative bodies that are "elected" in China resemble those in the former Soviet system. These bodies meet irregularly and rarely. When they do meet they tend to simply rubber-stamp whatever the party has already decided.

In totalitarian societies a political opposition not only is legally forbidden, but is an alien concept. Moreover, the government insists on high voting turnouts, and the right not to vote is not a highly valued privilege. Rather, not voting is considered an antisocial act. And the authorities know who doesn't vote since the secret ballot is also a bizarre notion in a totalitarian society.

Ironically, the last legislative election conducted in the Soviet Union before its demise was also the most free. The communist government in March 1989 agreed to hold contested elections for the Congress of People's Deputies if the party was guaranteed 750 of the 2250 seats. It was, and so there was competition in a total of 1101 electoral districts, where communists proceeded to lose disastrously. From that point on communist power in the Soviet Union unraveled rapidly.[47]

The end of communist totalitarianism and the Soviet Union does not, however, ensure normal democratic elections. For example, one of the former Soviet republics, Latvia, is a small country on the Baltic Sea. The Soviet government over several decades encouraged Russians to move to Latvia. Many did, in great part because living standards were better than in the Russian Republic. When the Latvians regained their sovereignty they found themselves sharing full citizenship with the 48 percent of the population that is non-Latvian, mostly Russian. This large minority has retained its own language and culture and even lives in its own neighborhoods. Latvia is a voluntarily segregated society. Can Latvia become a full democracy knowing that nearly half the population is ethnically and politically tied to another country? If nearly half the voters in Latvia are not indigenous, is it fair to expect them to vote for Latvians?

Before answering, try to keep in mind that the United States, like many established democracies, is hardly in a position to point fingers. Soon after the 1990 census was completed the decennial task of redrawing congressional districts was begun. Usually district lines are redrawn to favor one political party over another, a process known as **gerrymandering**. But one of the questions being entertained was whether congressional lines should be drawn to ensure that African-Americans or Hispanics would be elected to Congress. The American South offered the most serious problem: 20 percent of the region's population is black, but African-Americans make up less than 12 percent of its congressional representatives.[48] One proposed solution was to create congressional districts so full of African-American majorities that more African-Americans would surely be elected to Congress (see Figure 9.7). In other words, ethnic voting patterns, even in democracies, are not a thing of the past. Some might question whether voting district lines are drawn to accommodate racial concerns or whether Americans are imitating South Africa's Black Homelands and resegregating. The charge that several new districts are emulating South Africa is not a compliment. The idea that blacks should only vote for blacks and whites for whites discredits democracy and has been condemned by both African-American and white politicians.[49]

THE ELECTORAL PROCESS IN AUTHORITARIAN SYSTEMS

The voter in an authoritarian system is often surprisingly active. Even if a regime is autocratic, it may still crave legitimacy. There are, of course, ample holdouts. Some regimes simply feel no need for elections. This is because they base their legitimacy on other considerations, much the way medieval European monarchs justified their autocracies on the basis of divine right: They did not feel their actions were answerable to any earthly power.

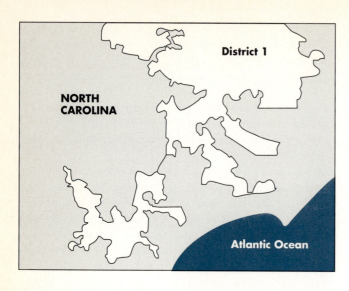

Figure 9.7 CONGRESSIONAL DISTRICT 1 IN NORTH CAROLINA. This district was gerrymandered (redrawn) after the 1990 census to provide a majority of African-American voters. At one point the new district is no wider than Interstate 85's lanes. Source: *The Wall Street Journal,* "America's Segremanders," April 2, 1992, p. A14.

Several countries don't permit free elections and would face great inconvenience if they did. This reluctance is based in great part on the nature of the electorate or, more properly, the nonelectorate. A number of countries in the Middle East, for example, have rather incongruous demographics. Table 9.9 lists countries whose populations include majorities or very large minorities of alien residents. It is simply not as easy as it sounds to provide for the universal franchise. For some governments to do so would be tantamount to surrendering their sovereignty.

Some current regimes that refrain from elections consider democracy a social abomination as well as a source of political instability. Often found in countries dominated by a single, usually royal, family and a single industry (in many cases this means oil and natural gas), such regimes generally govern small and traditionalist societies. The Sultanate of Brunei and the Kingdom of Saudi Arabia are examples. The Saudi government's discomfort with democracy was clear during the Persian Gulf crisis in 1990–1991. The Saudi government insisted that American military personnel, 11,000 of whom were women, remain segregated from the indigenous population. Why? They set a "bad" example. Not only were these Americans eligible to vote, but men and women freely mingled with one another. Worse, women wore pants and even issued orders to men they outranked. The last straw may have been the sight of women driving jeeps. So much for democracy. Even a hint of it was disconcerting to the Saudi political establishment.

TABLE 9.9 DECLINING NATIVE CITIZENRIES		
Country	Percentage of Native Citizens	Elected Legislature?
Bahrain	63%	Not since 1975
Kuwait	28%	Not since 1986
Qatar	40%	No
United Arab Emirates	19%	No

Until the early 1990s, when the system of apartheid (racial segregation) began to wind down, the Republic of South Africa did have universal suffrage: at least in theory. Everyone over the age of 18 could vote, but voting rights were racially based. One could vote only for or against candidates of one's own race for seats in a racially segregated legislature.

In most of the world voting is still a political luxury. And it is important to point out that voting does not always lead to or guarantee a working democracy. It can do the opposite. In Algeria and Jordan, for example, radical Islamic fundamentalists have formed political parties and won substantial numbers of seats in the first free elections these countries have had in decades. But radical fundamentalists compete in the elections only to destroy democracy, not build it. If they are voted into power, they have promised to establish a society based on the religious authority of holy scripture (which doesn't permit political opposition).[50] The relatively mild authoritarian regimes in these countries may be convinced more than ever that voting in free elections is a dubious activity.

Summary

1. The history of voting is the history of the gradual extension of the franchise. None of the older democracies began their electoral institutions with a universal electorate. Within the United States suffrage was gradually extended to those without property, African-Americans, women, and youths between the ages of 18 and 21.

2. Overall, Americans have a relatively low voter turnout. But whites vote in greater proportions than African-Americans, and African-Americans vote in higher proportions than Hispanics. This equation may reflect the greater proportions of non-white Americans in the lower socioeconomic ranks. People in those ranks tend to be less motivated to vote than those in the more prosperous strata. Nonvoting may itself be a way to express a political opinion. But, more likely, nonvoting may be the result of obstacles to voting that include too many elections, overly long campaigns, and strict registration requirements.

3. Voters make their decisions based on their party affiliation, personality traits of the candidate, and the candidates' records and issue positions.

4. American elections are both frequent and numerous. They are also seemingly never-ending because the general election is preceded by primaries, caucuses, and, every four years, a national convention.

5. Campaign strategies have fostered an important political industry that includes professional campaign coordinators, citizen volunteers, issue advisers, and, of course, crucial fund-raising efforts.

6. The soaring costs of campaigns have led to congressional efforts to limit contributions and monitor expenses. Presidential campaigns have been publicly financed since 1976.

7. Are American voters rational? There is some evidence that groups vote for those who best represent their interests. Overall, however, thoughtful candidates may not be as attractive as those who are simply perceived as friendly and can project well on television.

8. "Sound bites" that may not have any substantive message seem preferable to the electorate than making an informed voting decision on the basis of detailed information, although voters tend to respond more favorably to messages that are themselves favorable rather than negative.

9. Abolishing the electoral college in favor of popular elections would create a more thorough democracy, but would also dilute the current voting advantages of ethnic and religious minorities. The electoral college has also encouraged a stable two-party system that provides a real contrast between the major candidates.

10. The argument on behalf of public financing of political campaigns is based on the notion that office-holders would not then be obligated to special interests and that well-financed incumbents would not have a monetary advantage over challengers. However, an opposing argument holds that fund raising is an indication of the candidate's ability to communicate and organize, and attempts to restrict private giving might impinge on First Amendment rights.

11. Voter turnout in America is far below that of the other democracies because of registration obstacles, timing of elections, and statistical ways of calculating turnout.

12. While the American and other English-speaking electoral systems use the winner-take-all single-member district system (SM), most democracies prefer proportional representation (PR). The former is more efficient in that it almost guarantees a strong two-party system and a one-party government, whereas the latter produces greater democracy but a less efficient multiparty system and coalition government.

13. Totalitarian systems insist on high voter turnout and regular elections, but political opposition to the one party is not permitted and the ballot is rarely secret.

14. Some countries, including a few democracies, may be reluctant to extend the franchise to growing ethnic and/or religious minorities who may not have citizen status, but are long-term residents.

15. Several countries see no point to holding elections. These authoritarian systems tend to be absolutist and traditionalist monarchies.

Terms to Define

Blanket primary	Open primary
Caucus	Poll tax
Closed primary	Presidential preference primary
Convention	Primary
Electoral college	Proportional representation
General election	Prospective voting
Gerrymandering	Retrospective voting
Grandfather clause	Suffrage
Literacy test	White primary
Multimember district	

Selected Readings

Burnham, Walter Dean. *Critical Elections and the Mainsprings of American Politics*. New York: Norton, 1970. A focus on the historical lessons of critical elections as well as an analysis of the phenomenon of increasing voter disinterest in election participation.

Ginsberg, Benjamin and Alan Stone, eds. *Do Elections Matter?* 2nd ed. Armonk, N.Y.: M. E. Sharpe, Inc., 1991. This question is often asked. In this collection of 13 essays an attempt is made to provide some answers.

Jamieson, Kathleen Hall. *Packaging the Presidency: A History and Criticism of Presidential Campaign Advertising*. New York: Oxford University Press, 1984. An interesting analysis of how presidential candidates are manufactured like any other consumer product and then sold to their clientele, the American electorate.

McGinniss, Joe. *The Selling of the President, 1968*. New York: Trident Press, 1968. An easily readable classic that emphasizes the first modern "packaging" of a presidential candidate.

Sorauf, Frank J. *Money in American Elections*. New York: HarperCollins, 1988. How campaign financing defines electoral politics and annoys many voters is analyzed in a study that also explains how financing itself has become a political issue.

Notes

1. Minor v. *Happerset*, 88 U.S. 162 (1874).
2. *Guinn and Beall* v. *U.S.*, 238 U.S. 347 (1915); *Smith* v. *Allwright*, 321 U.S. 649 (1944).
3. *Harper* v. *Virginia State Board of Elections*, 383 U.S. 663 (1966).
4. See Lester W. Milbraith and M. L. Goel, *Political Participation*, 2nd ed. (Chicago: Rand McNally, 1977), pp. 98–116 and Raymond E. Eolfinger and Steven J. Rosenstone, *Who Votes?* (New Haven: Yale University Press, 1980).
5. Seymour Martin Lipset, "Polls Don't Lie, People Do," *The New York Times*, September 10, 1992, p. A19.
6. *The Washington Post*, August 12, 1978, p. B1.
7. *The New York Times*, March 2, 1992, p. A9.
8. *The New York Times*, October 31, 1991.
9. *The New York Times*, October 31, 1991, p. A5.
10. Seymour Martin Lipset, "Working-Class Authoritarianism," in Seymour Martin Lipset, ed., *Political Man* (New York: Doubleday, 1960), pp. 97–130.
11. Allan J. Lichtman and Ken DeCell, *The Keys to the Presidency* (Lanham, Md.: Madison Books, 1990), pp. 4–6.
12. Quoted in *The New York Times*, September 30, 1992, p. A21.
13. "President's Dinner Party Draws Big Contributions, and Criticism," *The New York Times*, April 28, 1992, p. A19.
14. Ibid.
15. "An Awkward Balance," *The Economist*, August 29, 1992, p. 22.
16. AIPAC Newsletter, December 1992.
17. Ibid.
18. V. O. Key, *The Responsible Electorate* (Cambridge: Harvard University Press, 1966, pp. 9–28.
19. Norman H. Nie et al., *The Changing American Voter* (Cambridge: Harvard University Press, 1976), chaps. 4–6, 8–10, and 12–14.
20. See surveys by the Gallup Organization, 1937–1990 and the 1988 CPS National Election Study.
21. *The Washington Post*, July 30, 1976, p. A9.
22. "St Patrick's Curse," *The Economist*, March 21, 1992, p. 26.
23. *The Economist*, December 26, 1992–January 8, 1993, p. 6.
24. Angus Campbell et al., *The American Voter* (New York: John Wiley, 1960), p. 175.

25. Philip Converse, "The Nature of Belief Systems in Mass Publics," in David Apter, ed., *Ideology and Discontent* (New York: Free Press, 1964), p. 210.
26. See William Flanigan and Nancy Zingale, *Political Behavior of the American Electorate*, 6th ed. (Dubuque, Iowa: Brown, 1988), pp. 37–42.
27. *The Washington Post*, February 2, 1978, p. A1.
28. Campbell et al., *The American Voter*, p. 175.
29. *The Economist*, July 6, 1991, p. 25.
30. Converse, "The Nature of Belief Systems," p. 240.
31. Murray Edelman, *The Symbolic Uses of Politics* (Urbana: University of Illinois Press, 1964), pp. 171–172.
32. *Greenville News*, August 15, 1978, p. 4A.
33. Seymour Martin Lipset and Earl Raab, "The Election and the National Mood," *Commentary* 55 (January 1973): 44.
34. Edelman, *The Symbolic Uses of Politics*, p. 172 .
35. Ibid.
36. Marshall McLuhan, *Understanding Media: The Extensions of Man* (New York: McGraw-Hill, 1964), pp. 276, 280.
37. Joe McGinniss, *The Selling of a President* (New York: Trident Press, 1968), pp. 39–40.
38. Allan J. Lichtman and Ken DeCell, *The Keys to the Presidency* (Lanham, Md.: Madison Books, 1990), pp. 4–6.
39. *The New York Times*, December 15, 1992, p. B12.
40. Wallace S. Sayre and Judith L. Parris, *Voting for President* (Washington, D.C.: The Brookings Institution, 1970), pp. 150–151.
41. *The Christian Science Monitor*, March 5, 1992, p. 11.
42. Ibid., p. 9.
43. Ibid., p. 11.
44. Ibid., p. 9.
45. Ian Budge and David McKay, *The Changing British Political System in the 1990s*, 2nd ed. (London and New York: Longman, 1988), p. 88.
46. "Young Turks," *The Economist*, December 19, 1992, p. 37.
47. Hedrick Smith, *The New Russians* (New York: Random House, 1990), p. 443.
48. "The Battle of the Pastry Cooks," *The Economist*, May 18, 1991, p. 27.
49. "America's Segremanders," *The Wall Street Journal*, April 2, 1992, p. A14.
50. *The Economist*, September 5, 1992, pp. 46–47.

THE PRESIDENCY

The Constitutional qualifications for the presidency are simple: A president must be at least 35 years old, a native-born American, and a resident of the United States for at least 14 years. Beyond that the qualifications become less clear-cut and far more subjective. Experience in politics is generally considered desirable. Many presidents had previously served in Congress, some had been state governors, yet a few had held no previous political office. Presidents George Washington, Andrew Jackson, Ulysses S. Grant, and Dwight D. Eisenhower gained office by being war heroes. Up until the middle of this century every president was a Protestant. John F. Kennedy, a Roman Catholic, broke that mold with his election in 1960. There is no requirement that a president be a white male, but this represents a mold yet to be broken.

    There does not seem to be one standard presidential "personality" that gets elected. Presidents differ greatly in their outlook and in their philosophy of office. Theodore Roosevelt, along with some other activist presidents, viewed the office as a "bully pulpit," a place from which a leader exhorts and motivates a nation. He believed in using presidential power. As Roosevelt noted, "My belief was that it was not [the president's] right but his duty to do anything that the needs of the nation demanded, unless such action was forbidden by the Constitution or the laws."[1] Others regard their job as president more as a caretaking position. They contend that the chief executive can exercise only those powers explicitly spelled out in the Constitution or in laws passed pursuant to it. William Howard Taft, for example, stated that "there is no undefined residuum of power which can be exercised which seems to him to be in the public interest."[2]

Political scientist James David Barber has attempted to categorize twentieth-century presidents according to whether they were active or passive in office and how much they enjoyed their position. Table 10.1 shows the results of his analysis. Generally, Americans tend to rank active, powerful presidents higher than passive, less powerful ones. This does not mean that active presidents are always popular while in office. They may receive a great deal of criticism for the strong measures they take, some of which may even be undemocratic, as we will see later in the chapter.

In what follows we will be taking a look at a president's specified duties, how the executive branch is organized, and how undefined presidential powers have necessarily expanded over time. We will then consider to what extent a president may or may not have too much power. Are there enough controls on presidential power? How much executive power can a democracy afford? Some ask these questions, while others wonder if the presidency has *enough* power to cope with its growing burdens. Finally, we'll compare our presidential system with other executive systems in other countries.

TABLE 10.1   PRESIDENTIAL CHARACTER

Type	Characteristics	Examples
Active-positive	Confident, flexible, enjoys exercise of power, goal-oriented	Franklin D. Roosevelt, Harry S. Truman, John F. Kennedy, George Bush
Active-negative	Compulsive, anxious, rigid, uses power without enjoying it, aggressive	Woodrow Wilson, Herbert Hoover, Lyndon Johnson, Richard Nixon
Passive-positive	Compliant, receptive, superficially optimistic but inwardly self-doubting, unwilling to take risks	Warren G. Harding, William Howard Taft, Ronald Reagan
Passive-negative	Doesn't enjoy power, motivated by sense of duty, emphasizes principles and procedures, avoids conflict	Calvin Coolidge, Dwight D. Eisenhower

Source: Adapted from James Barber, *Presidential Character: Predicting Performance in the White House,* 4th ed. Englewood Cliffs, N.J.: Prentice-Hall, 1992.

THE AMERICAN PRESIDENT

THE FUNCTIONS OF THE PRESIDENT

In a single day, a president may, as head of state, host a state dinner; as chief executive, meet with economic advisers; as commander in chief, order the movement of American troops; as diplomatic leader, sign a treaty; as legislative leader, submit a bill to Congress; and as party chieftain, deliver a campaign speech. This list of presidential roles gives some idea of the awesome burden of the office. Harry Truman said: "The Presidency is a killing job—a six man job. . . . It requires young men—young in physical and mental ability, if not necessarily young in age."[3]

Article II of the Constitution stipulates five of the major functions of the president—head of state, chief executive, diplomatic leader, commander in chief, and legislative leader. In each of these constitutional functions, the president's power has increased enormously since the days of George Washington. A sixth function, that of party chieftain, was not even envisioned by the framers of the Constitution.

Head of State

In many democracies, such as the United Kingdom, there are two national leaders: a ceremonial leader (the monarch) and a governmental leader (the prime minister). In the United States, the ceremonial and governmental functions are combined in the president as head of state. The role combines the mystique of monarchy with the power of political leadership.

As head of state, the president lays wreaths on the tomb of the Unknown Soldier, entertains visiting dignitaries, issues proclamations on holidays, presents awards, lights the White House Christmas tree, and throws out the first ball of the baseball season. These functions may appear trivial, but they have ceremonial value. Failure to perform them would offend many people; performing them well enhances a president's stature.

The symbolic, almost mystical, power of the presidency is revealed when a president dies in office or is the victim of an attempted assassination. President Reagan's popularity and political power rose dramatically after an attempted assassination outside the Washington Hilton Hotel in March 1981. The deaths of Abraham Lincoln, Franklin Roosevelt, and John Kennedy brought outpourings of grief. Just a medical checkup for a president can affect the stock market.

Chief Executive

According to Article II of the Constitution, "The executive Power shall be vested in a President. . . . [who] shall take Care that the Laws be faithfully executed." This means that the president is a chief administrator: The president not only signs bills into law, but also implements them. For example, a law providing for additional federal judges would oblige the president to nominate persons to the judgeships. A law mandating clean air requires the chief executive to see that it is carried out. The vagueness of the phrase "take care" in Article II has encouraged some presidents to broaden their powers as chief executive.

Perhaps the president's most important task is to manage the nation's economy. Since the 1930s, that role has greatly increased. For example, by act of Congress a president must now name a Council of Economic Advisors and also submit an annual economic message and budget to the Congress. A president's popularity frequently rises or falls with the upward and downward swings in economic activity. In late 1991 and early 1992, President Bush's popularity plummeted in large part due to an economic recession. But in the weeks following the devastation in Florida caused by Hurricane Andrew and in Hawaii by Hurricane Iniki, President Bush demonstrated both the economic and political power available to his office by rushing billions of dollars and thousands of soldiers to assist the hundreds of thousands of people who had lost homes and jobs. That and other acts of largess in the months before the election were not enough to keep him in office, however.

The chief executive is helped in administrative tasks by a huge bureaucracy, including 14 Cabinet departments, the Executive Office of the President, and more than 50 regulatory agencies, boards, and commissions. The president nominates or appoints people to fill upper-echelon positions: the top personnel in the cabinet departments, members of the Executive Office, and upper-level executives in regulatory agencies. The appointees for the regulatory agencies, however, must be representative of both major parties. (Once hired, they do not report to the president but function as independent members of the bureaucracy.) Senate confirmation of these presidential nominations and appointments is generally required, except for most positions in the Executive Office of the President.

The presidential power of appointment also implicitly includes by custom and practice the authority to *remove* officials. The president can remove without cause all presidential appointees except those named to regulatory agencies.

Diplomatic Leader

Article II also provides that the president "shall have Power, by and with the Advice and Consent of the Senate, to make Treaties, provided two thirds of the Senators present concur; and he shall nominate, and by and with the Advice and Consent of the Senate, shall appoint Ambassadors, other Public Ministers and Consuls." These powers are part of the president's role as diplomatic leader.

The president also has sole power to recognize foreign governments, a power that provides substantial leverage in executing American foreign policy. One far-reaching instance of diplomatic recognition occurred in 1933, when Franklin Roosevelt recognized the Soviet Union, 16 years after the Russian Revolution. Another occurred in 1972, when Nixon's historic trip to Peking (now Beijing) precipitated a new era of diplomatic contacts between the United States and China.

How a president chooses to work with foreign governments may greatly affect the issues of war and peace. Presidents Reagan and Bush chose to work constructively with former Soviet leader Mikhail Gorbachev, significantly diminishing friction between the two countries and leading to many exchanges of students, business leaders, and performing artists. President Bush worked cooperatively with many countries throughout the world in building opposition to Iraq's aggression against Kuwait during 1990–1991. The United States also gained the support of the United Nations in what President Bush called the building of a "New World Order."

As president, Bill Clinton must wear many hats. Some of his roles shown here are chief executive (meeting with his economic advisors), diplomatic leader (summit talk with Russian President Boris Yeltsin), legislative leader (signing the Family and Medical Leave Act into law), and head of state (throwing out the first ball of the baseball season).

Commander in Chief

An important principle of American government is civilian supremacy over the military. This principle finds its constitutional basis in Article II, section 2, which says that "the President shall be Commander in Chief of the Army and Navy of the United States." Thus, presidential command can move troops and promote and retire generals. This power could be seen in Truman's order to drop the atomic bomb on Hiroshima and Nagasaki in 1945 and his firing of General Douglas MacArthur during the Korean War; Reagan's military invasion of Grenada in 1983, his forced landing of an Egyptian plane carrying PLO terrorists who had killed an American citizen in 1985, and his 1986 military response to Libyan terrorism; and Bush's decisions to invade Panama in 1989, to forcefully prosecute the Persian Gulf War, and to send troops to Somalia to safeguard the distribution of food to its starving citizens.

The most ominous reminder of the president's role as commander in chief is a locked briefcase, sometimes called the "black box" or "football." This briefcase, always kept near the president, contains the coded orders that authorize nuclear retaliation in the event of a nuclear attack on the United States or its bases abroad.

Legislative Leader

Article II, section 3, reads in part that the president "shall from time to time give to the Congress information of the State of the Union, and recommend to their Consideration such Measures as he shall judge necessary and expedient." The president annually gives a State of the Union speech to Congress that outlines major legislative goals. After World War II Congress required the president to submit an annual budget message as well as an annual economic message.

The president's function as legislative leader evolved into a principal source of presidential power only in this century. In the early years of this century Woodrow Wilson became the first president in modern times to deliver his State of the Union messages to Congress personally. He and a predecessor, Theodore Roosevelt, also were the first to develop legislative programs for congressional action. Today it is the president's detailed legislative program that drives the Congress.

By commanding prime network television time to deliver their addresses to Congress, presidents communicate their legislative ideas to the American public as well. Special follow-up legislative messages can mobilize voters on behalf of the president's program as its specific components are submitted to Congress. Many of President Reagan's early successes with Congress were attributed to his ability to communicate to the public, which in turn pressured Congress on behalf of his programs.

The president's legislative power is not limited to the delivery of legislative messages. Skilled legislative technicians assist the president by monitoring the flow of legislation through Congress on a day-by-day basis. The congressional liaison office, another post–World War II phenomenon, helps make the president not only the chief legislator, but also the chief lobbyist on Capitol Hill. One of President Bill Clinton's first acts was to visit legislative leaders on the Hill to help solidify his working relationships with them.

The Constitution gives the president the power to **veto** (refuse to sign) bills passed by Congress if the president acts within ten days. Congress can override an ordinary veto by a two-thirds vote in each house. Another presidential weapon is the **pocket veto**: A bill is automatically vetoed if the president chooses to take no action on it within a ten-day period while Congress is adjourned. Congress has no opportunity to override a pocket veto because the president does not return the bill to it. Usually a veto threat alone forces Congress to modify legislation to accommodate the president's wishes. Table 10.2 shows the presidential record in vetoes and veto overrides.

Other constitutional powers allow the president to adjourn Congress if the House and Senate disagree about when to do so (a power no president has ever exercised) and to call Congress into special session. Although seldom used, the power to call a special session can be a great advantage to a president. When President Truman called Congress into special session in 1948 to act on his legislative proposals, the Republican majority failed to give him what he wanted. In his presidential campaign that year, he attacked the "do nothing" Congress, a political strategy that many credit for his unexpected election victory.

Theoretically, Congress cannot delegate legislative authority to the president. Practically, however, the chief executive does exercise legislative authority through **administrative law**. This refers to the guidelines and rules established by executive-branch agencies to implement and enforce acts of Congress. Critics contend that administrative rulings give the president too much legislative authority. In addition, for about 40 years Congress granted the president the power to restructure the executive departments and agencies; if one house of the Congress did not disapprove such a reorganization plan within 60 days, it became effective. In 1981, however, Congress discontinued that authority. Now reorganization plans must proceed through Congress as a regular bill.

Party Chieftain

The function of party chieftain is the only one not mentioned in the Constitution, yet in some respects it is the most crucial. No president has been elected without first obtaining the support of a political party. After nomination, the presidential candidate customarily names a national chairman of the party, and, if elected, continues to control most of the party's affairs.

Beyond being nominated and elected through the party process, a president also relies on the party to obtain support in Congress and among state governors. A president who commands overwhelming support among the majority party in Congress, as did Lyndon Johnson, can accomplish major changes in national policy. A president who lacks such support, like John F. Kennedy, may have difficulty pushing through major or innovative legislation. The size of a President's electoral victory helps determine the level of congressional support. Kennedy won by a narrow margin; Johnson, by a large one. A large margin of victory also helps those presidents, such as Nixon, Reagan, and Bush, whose party is in the minority in Congress. By winning easily they could claim that they had "mandates" to get legislation passed. Reagan achieved significant success early in his administration by getting southern and conservative Democrats to join ranks with Republicans. Soon after his election Bill Clinton made a point of visiting Washington in order to shore up party support in Congress.

Perhaps more than any other president—certainly more than any other modern president—Franklin D. Roosevelt utilized each of the presidential functions to maximum

TABLE 10.2 PRESIDENTIAL VETOES, 1789–1992

Years	President	Regular Vetoes	Vetoes Overridden	Pocket Vetoes	Total Vetoes
1789–1797	Washington	2	0	0	2
1797–1801	J. Adams	0	0	0	0
1801–1809	Jefferson	0	0	0	0
1809–1817	Madison	5	0	2	7
1817–1825	Monroe	1	0	0	1
1825–1829	J. Q. Adams	0	0	0	0
1829–1837	Jackson	5	0	7	12
1837–1841	Van Buren	0	0	1	1
1841–1841	Harrison	0	0	0	0
1841–1845	Tyler	6	1	4	10
1845–1849	Polk	2	0	1	3
1849–1850	Taylor	0	0	0	0
1850–1853	Fillmore	0	0	0	0
1853–1857	Pierce	9	5	0	9
1857–1861	Buchanan	4	0	3	7
1861–1865	Lincoln	2	0	5	7
1865–1869	A. Johnson	21	15	8	29
1869–1877	Grant	45	4	48	93
1877–1881	Hayes	12	1	1	13
1881–1881	Garfield	0	0	0	0
1881–1885	Arthur	4	1	8	12
1885–1889	Cleveland	304	2	110	414
1889–1893	Harrison	19	1	25	44
1893–1897	Cleveland	42	5	128	170
1897–1901	McKinley	6	0	36	42
1901–1909	T. Roosevelt	42	1	40	82
1909–1913	Taft	30	1	9	39
1913–1921	Wilson	33	6	11	44
1921–1923	Harding	5	0	1	6
1923–1929	Coolidge	20	4	30	50
1929–1933	Hoover	21	3	16	37
1933–1945	F. Roosevelt	372	9	263	635
1945–1953	Truman	180	12	70	250
1953–1961	Eisenhower	73	2	108	181
1961–1963	Kennedy	12	0	9	21
1963–1969	L. Johnson	16	0	14	30
1969–1974	Nixon	26*	7	17	43
1974–1977	Ford	48	12	18	66
1977–1981	Carter	13	2	18	31
1981–1989	Reagan	39	9	39	78
1989–1993	Bush	31	1	15	46
Total		1,451	104	1,065	2,508

* Two pocket vetoes, overruled in the courts, are counted here as regular vetoes.

Sources: *Congressional Quarterly Weekly Report* (1989), 7; Louis Fisher, *The Politics of Shared Power: Congress and the Executive,* 2nd ed. (Washington, D.C.: Congressional Quarterly Press, 1987), 30; *Congressional Quarterly Weekly Report,* July 27, 1991, p. 2044 and May 16, 1992, p. 1384.

Franklin Delano Roosevelt was a consummate user of presidential power. He is shown here with his wife, Eleanor, returning from his third inauguration (1941).

advantage. For this reason political scientist Richard Neustadt regarded him as a prime example of how a president should use his power: "No president in this century has had a sharper sense of personal power, a sense of what it is and where it comes from; none has had more hunger for it, few have had more use for it, and only one or two could match his faith in his own competence to use it."[4]

ORGANIZATIONAL STRUCTURE OF THE EXECUTIVE BRANCH

Presidents carry out their functions through a complex structure of subordinate offices that include the independent regulatory agencies, the 14 executive departments of the Cabinet, and the Executive Office of the President. The total executive structure employs nearly six million persons (including military personnel, which account for about one-fifth of the total). Chapter 11 will describe the organization of the federal bureaucracy in detail. Here we are concerned with those parts of the bureaucracy most directly controlled by the president.

Vice President

Before examining the organizational structure of the presidency, we should make note of an office that typically does not even appear on the organization charts of the executive branch, that of vice president. A vice president, whose only constitutional duty is to preside over the Senate (a duty rarely performed), is generally chosen for political reasons to balance a ticket. John F. Kennedy, for example, chose Lyndon Johnson, a Protestant southerner, to balance his own Roman Catholic, northern background. Dan Quayle, a recognized young conservative leader from the heartland of midwestern Republicanism, balanced the older, more moderate George Bush. As a result, vice presidents do not necessarily bring with them administrative skill or experience. Typically, a vice president's political ambitions and policy positions must be subordinated to those of the president. For example, while competing against Ronald Reagan for the Republican presidential nomination in 1980, George Bush supported the right to an abortion and the Equal Rights Amendment, both of which Reagan vehemently opposed. Part of the price Bush paid for subsequently getting the vice presidential nomination was renouncing his positions on these issues. Clinton's choice of Senator Al Gore as vice president surprised many observers because Gore, as a fellow southerner, did not "balance" the ticket nor, with his experience and prestige, did he seem likely to remain a shadow figure in the Clinton administration.

Vice presidential duties, other than occasionally presiding over the Senate and voting in the case of a tie (most vice presidents never get a chance to), usually depend on what a president gives the vice president to do. President Reagan was fond of sending Vice President Bush to the funerals of foreign leaders. President Bush gave Vice President Quayle the responsibility of overseeing and making changes in the regulatory process of the executive branch. Vice President Gore has substantial duties coordinating environmental and economic policy strategies. Typically, however, most vice presidential duties are ceremonial and political: doing what a president does not have time to do and helping a president get reelected by giving speeches and meeting with important groups.

In at least one respect the position of vice president is not inconsequential. In this century, five vice presidents became president through the death or resignation of the president: Theodore Roosevelt, Calvin Coolidge, Harry S. Truman, Lyndon Johnson, and Gerald Ford. Two other vice presidents were subsequently elected president: Richard Nixon and George Bush.

In case a vice president was not available to assume the presidency, Congress provided for presidential succession by law, either following a line of succession through the Cabinet departments, beginning with the Secretary of State, or through Congressional leaders, beginning with the Speaker of the House of Representatives. At times the line of succession has included both Cabinet secretaries and Congressional leaders. Following President Kennedy's assassination, Congress proposed and the states ratified the Twenty-Fifth Amendment, which is designed to provide for a vacancy in the vice presidency. The president nominates a vice president, who must then be confirmed by a majority vote in both houses of Congress. In the 1970s Gerald Ford and Nelson Rockefeller gained the vice presidency in this way. This amendment also provides for the removal of a president from office if in the view of the vice president and a majority of Cabinet officers it is determined that a president is unable to discharge the duties of office. Conditions for reassuming the duties of office are also stated in this amendment.

The Cabinet

The **Cabinet** includes the vice president and the head of each executive department (see Table 10.3.) At a president's discretion, other officials may have Cabinet status, such as the Director of the Office of Management and Budget and the Ambassador to the United Nations. Beginning with the Departments of State and Treasury in 1789, the Cabinet has generally grown in response to societal pressures and problems, mirroring to some degree the growth of the United States itself. Westward expansion led to creation of the Department of the Interior in 1849; housing problems in the twentieth century resulted in a Department of Housing and Urban Development (1965). In 1977 Congress created a Department of Energy to coordinate the various parts of the executive branch with responsibility for energy decisions. The Cabinet, as a body of advisers, exists for the president to utilize as desired. There is no legal requirement for the president to hold Cabinet meetings. In fact, presidents tend to rely more on their personal staffs for advice and policymaking than they do on their Cabinets.

Not all Cabinet departments are equal in prestige and power. Historically, the

TABLE 10.3	CREATION OF CURRENT EXECUTIVE DEPARTMENTS OF THE CABINET
Year Created	**Executive Department**
1789	State
1789	Treasury
1849	Interior
1870	Justice*
1889	Agriculture
1913	Commerce
1913	Labor
1947	Defense[†]
1965	Housing and Urban Development
1966	Transportation
1977	Energy
1979	Education[‡]
1979	Health and Human Services[‡]
1988	Veterans' Affairs

* Established in 1789 but reorganized in 1870.
[†] Previously the Department of War, established in 1789.
[‡] Created from the division of the Department of Health, Education, and Welfare, which had been established in 1953.

departments of State, Defense, and Justice have been among the most powerful and prestigious while the departments of Education and Veterans' Affairs have been among the least powerful and prestigious. Recognizing a pecking order among Cabinet departments, President Richard Nixon proposed a reorganization plan that would have created several supersecretaries with authority over several departments. Although his proposal was not adopted, it confronted the reality of a Cabinet pecking order. The power of a Cabinet secretary, of course, also depends on such factors as the relationship of a secretary to the president and the problems that may be confronting a department. Under President Reagan, for example, Treasury Secretary James Baker had more power and influence than usual because of his presidential access and the severe economic problems that the Reagan administration faced, particularly the budget deficit. Not all Treasury secretaries have been equally influential.

The Executive Office of the President

As government became bigger during the New Deal era of the 1930s, questions arose about the president's ability to manage and administer an ever-growing bureaucracy. A study commissioned at that time determined that "the president needs help." The solution was to create the **Executive Office of the President,** the staff arm of the presidency. Like the Cabinet, the Executive Office has grown in response to national problems. Its principal components are the White House Office, the National Security Council, the Office of Management and Budget, the Council of Economic Advisers, and the newly added National Economic Council.

 The White House Office. Those who staff the White House Office are generally those closest to the president. They have the president's ear and their advice carries great weight. The White House chief of staff normally has immediate unconditional access to the president. The authority of these assistants flows from that of the president; they hold their positions at the president's pleasure, and their purpose is to help the president coordinate and administer the executive branch. Other key aides in the White House Office are the press secretary, the congressional liaison staff, and speech writers. Many personal assistants have had an enormous impact on American history through the years—Wilson's Colonel House; Franklin Roosevelt's Harry Hopkins; Eisenhower's Sherman Adams; Kennedy's Theodore Sorensen; Johnson's Bill Moyers; Nixon's H. R. Haldeman and John Ehrlichman; Carter's Hamilton Jordan and Jody Powell; Reagan's Ed Meese, James Baker, and Donald Regan; and Bush's John Sununu and James Baker.

 Presidents use the White House Office in different ways, depending on their personal administrative styles. Presidents who give more power to the secretaries of the Cabinet departments do not delegate as much power to the White House staff, while presidents who concentrate decision making and policymaking in the White House strengthen the role of their staff at the expense of the Cabinet. Presidents Reagan and Bush illustrate the former, and Presidents Johnson and Nixon, the latter.

 The National Security Council (NSC). This council, created by the National Security Act of 1947, includes the president, vice president, the secretaries of State and Defense, the director of the Central Intelligence Agency, the chairman of the Joint Chiefs of Staff, and the assistant to the president for national security affairs. The National Security Council provides advice on foreign and military policy, coordinates day-to-day security policy, and plays a key role in helping the president handle crises, such as Iraq's invasion of Kuwait in August 1990.

The Office of Management and Budget (OMB). Formerly the Bureau of the Budget in the Treasury Department, the OMB has two principal tasks—preparing the federal budget (its original function) and assisting the president with management chores (a function added by President Nixon). For example, the OMB must fit the budget requests from various agencies within the overall federal budget limits.

The Council of Economic Advisers (CEA). This council was created to help combat economic problems after World War II. The three members of this body advise the president on such matters as wage and price controls, taxes, spending, and unemployment. They also prepare an annual report. To enhance the prestige and importance of economic policymaking, President Clinton also called for the establishment of a National Economic Council.

THE EXPANSION OF PRESIDENTIAL POWER

As we will see later, many people argue about whether presidents today enjoy too much power. Few, however, would deny that presidential power *has* expanded a great deal over the years. So before we get into the debate over presidential power, let us examine the factors that have led to that expansion and the attempts to contain it.

Causes of the Expansion

With about six million civilian and military personnel and a budget of $1 trillion (bigger than the gross domestic product of all but five countries in the world), the executive establishment is gigantic. How did it get so big? Domestic and foreign crises, the weakening of Congress, a changing society, and the chief executives themselves have all served to enlarge presidential power.

Domestic Crises. As Wilfred E. Binkley points out, the Civil War offers a prime example of how presidential power grew to resolve a domestic crisis:

> Unquestionably, the high-water mark of the exercise of the executive power in the United States is found in the administration of Abraham Lincoln. No President before or since has pushed about the degrees of executive power so far into the legislative sphere. . . . Under the war power he proclaimed the slaves of those in rebellion emancipated. He devised and put into execution his peculiar plan of reconstruction. With disregard of law he increased the army and navy beyond the limits set by statute. The privilege of the writ of habeas corpus was suspended wholesale and martial law declared. Public money in the sum of millions was deliberately spent without congressional appropriation. Nor was any of this done innocently. Lincoln understood his Constitution. He knew, in many cases, just how he was transgressing, and his infractions were consequently deliberate. It is all the more astonishing that his audacity was the work of a minority president performed in the presence of a bitter congressional opposition even in his own party.[5]

Another watershed in domestic policymaking was the crisis of the Great Depression and the measures taken to overcome its effects. Many would agree with the scholar Edwin S. Corwin, who noted that the New Deal created "social acceptance of the idea that government should be active and reformist, rather than simply protective of the established order of things."[6] As a result the executive establishment today, under presidential leadership, has broad powers to solve problems in race relations, health care, education, and a host of other fields.

Foreign Crises. A number of crises abroad in the last four decades have helped to develop presidential power: breaking the Soviet blockade of West Berlin in 1948–1949, the Korean War, the landing of American troops in Lebanon in 1958, the 1962 Cuban missile crisis, the invasion of Grenada in 1983, the air attack on Libya in 1986, and the Persian Gulf War in 1991. Presidents have ranged widely in foreign affairs, broadly interpreting treaty commitments and their power as commander in chief, and confident that they are better informed than anyone else. (Lyndon Johnson's memoirs are entitled *The Vantage Point.*) Johnson immersed the country in the Vietnam conflict without a congressional declaration of war. When President Carter undertook an abortive 1980 rescue mission of American hostages in Iran, he did not consult with the leaders of Congress. President Reagan showed little concern for congressional opinion during the 1983 Grenadian invasion, the 1985 capture of Palestinian terrorists, or the 1986 response to Libyan terrorism. Although President Bush consulted with Congress on the Persian Gulf War, he ultimately acted independently.

With the escalation of presidential power in international affairs, foreign policymaking has tended to overshadow domestic policymaking. One reason for the dominance of international affairs on the presidential calendar is the interrelationship of events in different parts of the world. A change in America's policy toward Japan could have ripple effects on our policy toward China, for example. Another reason is the speed with which foreign events can move. A president must devote extraordinary time and energy and use large staffs just to keep abreast of them.

Congressional Weakening. The framers intended for Congress to be the most powerful of the three branches of government. During the twentieth century, however, Congress has yielded more and more power to the president. As the government took on expanded functions in the New Deal era, Congress decided to respond to problems by simply extending broad grants of authority to the president. (One of the standard jokes about Franklin Roosevelt's first hundred days in office was that a representative on the floor of the House waved a blank piece of paper, which he claimed was a bill the president wanted in his New Deal program; the House passed it.)

Congress enabled the president to take the initiative in policymaking by providing greater budgetary authority under the Budget and Accounting Act of 1921 and increased administrative authority under the Administrative Reorganization Act of 1939. The former authorized the president to submit a presidential budget to Congress, which became the centerpiece of Congressional debate about the budget, while the latter allowed the president to have an Executive Office of the President, in addition to granting broad authority to reorganize the executive branch.

Social and Technological Changes. Many people found the presidency a logical place to look for help in coping with the social tensions of modern America. Dealing with a single individual is easier than with a Congress of 535 members. African-Americans, for instance, have primarily used the presidency and the courts for relief of their grievances. They found that moving the president and the courts as levers of governmental power was easier and quicker than prodding a rural- and southern-dominated Congress

President Clinton finds nationally televised town meetings a very effective form for communicating his political agenda to the public. He used this 1993 town meeting in Detroit to "sell" his economic plan.

to action. In addition, presidents—especially liberal Democrats—turned to such minority groups in building coalitions to win presidential elections.

The mass media have been powerful forces in making the president larger than life. Television, newspapers, and magazines try to cover the president's every move, even revealing personal habits and idiosyncrasies. This magnification of the president's image affects the national mood, shapes the times, and even causes fluctuations in the stock market. With access to prime television time on request, a president has the means to influence vast numbers of people in a way that no other public official can. President Clinton's nationally televised "town meetings" are another method of communicating the chief executive's agenda to the public.

Presidential Initiative. No assessment of the expansion of presidential power would be complete without mentioning the role of presidents themselves. Most of those in the modern era have had a rather aggressive attitude toward their role. Woodrow Wilson said that the president's office is "anything he has the sagacity and force to make it. . . . The President is at liberty, both in law and conscience, to be as big a man as he can."[7] John F. Kennedy stated boldly that the president "must be prepared to exercise the fullest powers of his office—all that are specified and some that are not."[8]

Even a president like Jimmy Carter, who came to Washington pledging to reduce centralized power in the White House, changed his view within two years and followed the pathway cut out for him by his predecessors. President Reagan used his charismatic qualities to build popular support that undercut congressional opposition to his policy proposals. President Bush's high popularity level at the beginning of his term gave him unusual latitude and independence in the exercise of presidential power. Bill Clinton showed his aggressive approach to making policy even before he took office. His two-day economic conference of 300 business and labor leaders and economists during the transition showcased his ability to grasp issues and articulate the problems. Clinton also was interested in being visible, in the belief that Presidents Carter and Bush stayed away from public exposure more than was good for them or their policies.[9]

Another way in which presidents have expanded their authority is in their use of executive privilege. First invoked against Congress by President Washington in 1796, **executive privilege** is an assertion of the right of the president to withhold information, documents, or testimony from either Congress or the courts in the interest of national security or the proper functioning of the executive branch. The president's right of executive privilege has also been extended to presidential advisers and Cabinet members to ensure that they can be completely candid in their conversations with the president.

The Constitution has no specific provisions dealing with executive privilege; it is a right predicated on the independence of the branches. Although invoked by presidents many times, the doctrine did not come under severe attack until the Watergate scandal, when Nixon declined to give tape-recorded conversations that took place in the Oval Office to either the courts or Congress. In the case of *United States* v. *Nixon* (1974), the Supreme Court unanimously ruled that executive privilege is constitutional, although it does not extend to criminal cases in which the public interest in a fair trial outweighs the necessity for presidential confidentiality. Even in these situations, we do not know what a strong president, unencumbered by a scandal like Watergate, might do if challenged. It is difficult to imagine the Court employing sanctions against a powerful and popular president, such as Franklin Roosevelt, who used executive privilege just as he pleased.

Attempts to Limit Presidential Power. In 1960 the political scientist Richard Neustadt published *Presidential Power,* in which he admonished presidents to conduct themselves in ways that would maximize their power.[10] Americans were taught to believe that the chief executive, the only official elected by all the people, would use the presidential authority to "do good." Then, in quick succession, two presidents challenged almost everything the liberal intellectual community had been assuming about the virtue of a strong presidency. First came Lyndon Johnson and the Vietnam War; next came Richard Nixon and Watergate. As a result, serious questions arose about the strong presidency, and Congress took steps to limit the presidency in the areas of foreign affairs and the budget.

War Powers Act. The principal challenge to presidential power in the field of foreign affairs was the War Powers Act of 1973, a direct response to the Vietnam War. Congress intended to prevent presidents from committing troops for extended periods of time without the approval of Congress and thus to reassert congressional authority to declare war. The act has four main provisions:

1. If Congress has not declared war, military force may be committed only to repel an armed attack on the United States or to forestall the "direct and imminent threat of such an attack," to repel an armed attack on American armed forces outside the United States or forestall the threat of one, to protect American citizens in another country if their lives are threatened, or to carry out specific statutory authorization by Congress.

2. The president is to report promptly to Congress the commitment of forces for such purposes.

3. Forces may be committed for a period of up to 60 days, unless Congress authorizes their continued use, or for an additional 30 days if the president certifies that the time is needed for their safe withdrawal.

4. Congress is authorized to terminate a presidential commitment by a concurrent resolution (which does not require presidential approval).

It is debatable whether this act decreased the power of the president in foreign affairs. There are also questions about its constitutionality. The War Powers Act, if it accomplished anything at all, merely strengthened the president's power to commit troops in the short term. But political scientist William Lasser argues that the War Powers Act is a political check on presidential power. He sees the Act's significance as "a constant warning to Congress not to follow blindly the president's lead in a foreign-policy crisis but to assert itself as a co-equal branch of government. Congress can fulfill the spirit of the War Powers Act with or without its formal procedures, regardless of whether the act is, in some academic sense, unconstitutional."[11]

The Budget. Although the Constitution gives Congress the "power of the purse," the president has had the upper hand in making budgets ever since the Budget and Accounting Act of 1921 gave that power to the president. Budgetary recommendations originate with executive departments and agencies, are channeled through the Office of Management and Budget, and are submitted to Congress in the president's budget message. Because of this one package backed by enormous research, the chief executive in effect takes the offensive, and Congress takes the position of reacting to proposals.

In the 1970s and 1980s Congress acted to win back some of its budgeting powers. In 1974 it passed legislation to create a streamlined budgetary process, complete with a well-staffed Congressional Budget Office and budget committees in each house. Congressional leaders hoped that these moves would provide them with expertise in dealing with the presidential budget and tax proposals. Congress also made the director and deputy director of the Office of Management and Budget subject to Senate confirmation, and now the Senate interrogates these important budget officers before the nominees take office. Then, in the late 1980s, Congress passed the Gramm-Rudman-Hollings Act, which required that if the president and Congress fail to meet budget targets for reducing the deficit, automatic budget cuts would take effect.

The president, however, is armed with another budgetary weapon. This is **impoundment**—the refusal to spend certain funds appropriated by Congress in a given fiscal year. Before the twentieth century, only Jefferson and Grant made significant use of impoundment, but it has become more common since Franklin Roosevelt's time. Nixon practiced impoundment more freely than any of his predecessors, withholding millions of dollars from social welfare programs of which he disapproved. Congress retaliated with the Budget Impoundment and Control Act of 1973, which established procedures for the president to obtain congressional approval before impounding funds.

The growth of presidential power has led to a debate about whether presidents have too much power these days—and, if so, what can be done about it. That is the main focus of the issues we analyze in the following section.

? ISSUES TO ANALYZE

ISSUE 1   DOES PRESIDENTIAL POWER POSE A DANGER TO AMERICAN DEMOCRACY?

REASONS WHY PRESIDENTIAL POWER POSES A DANGER

The previous discussion has suggested some of the disadvantages of a presidency bloated with power: a chief executive distracted from domestic problems by foreign concerns; an imbalance in the governmental system, with a weakened Congress trying to recover lost authority; and an unhealthy reliance on the president to solve all the nation's ills. Other dangers include unrealistic hero worship, undue influence by special interests, and hasty—possibly unconstitutional—interference in the affairs of foreign nations.

Man or Superman? Alexander Hamilton wanted a strong executive, yet he asserted that the president could not become a monarch "decorated with attributes superior in dignity and splendor to those of the king of Great Britain . . . with the diadem sparkling in his brow and the imperial purple flowing in his train . . . seated on a throne surrounded with minions and mistresses, giving audience to the envoys of foreign potentates, in all the supercilious pomp of majesty."[12] In many respects, Hamilton was wrong.

Thomas Cronin, a leading student of the presidency, has chronicled many developments of presidential power, including the presidency's veneration by scholars and journalists. According to one, the president is the "great engine of democracy." Another calls the president the "American people's one authentic trumpet." A third extols presidential government as "a superb planning institution," while a fourth reverently declares that the White House "is the pulpit of the nation and the president is its chaplain."[13]

Americans have placed the president on a pedestal of power far above what the Founders ever intended. They have invested the president with almost supernatural qualities. In the words of Woodrow Wilson: "Let him once win the admiration and confidence of the country, and no other single force can withstand him, no combination of forces will easily overpower him."[14]

This reverential attitude can have negative consequences. First, with so much power committed to one person, the risk of failure is too great. If the president fails, we all fail. If Watergate had been looked on as a failure of one man and not as a failure of the presidential office, the whole affair could probably have been resolved in a shorter period of time. The extreme reluctance to act against President Nixon stemmed from the public's attachment to and worship of the office, and the close linkage of the person and the office in the public's mind.

Second, there is the "parent" syndrome, with the president looking on the people as children. Nixon said that "the average American is just like the child in the family."[15] A third negative result of too much reverence is the "monarch and court" syndrome, with the president growing increasingly out of touch with American life. Two writers say presidential isolation occurs because "the President, needing 'access to reality' in order to govern effectively, too often has access, instead, only to a self-serving court of flunkies, knights, earls, and dukes in business suits, whose best chances of advancing their separate fortunes usually lie in diverting reality before it can reach the President."[16]

Despite some harsh criticisms of the presidency over the past 20 years, the problems remain. Because Americans continue to be attached to the presidency as the catalyst for good causes, presidents are often held responsible for problems they did not create and likely cannot resolve. Neither Jimmy Carter nor George Bush were responsible for the economic problems confronting them, but the electorate insisted on holding them responsible. Presidents, lacking ways to measure up to the responsibility placed in them, turn to leading through image, providing the people with the *impression* of leadership, when in reality they are constrained from leading.

Harvey Mansfield's *Taming of the Prince* puts the problem in yet another way as he addresses how presidential power can be properly controlled:

> *Some years ago it was still a question whether executives would do better by being trained in a science or by learning in the "school of hard knocks." Now it is clear that the business schools and their methods have won a victory: the executive has been professionalized. Professionalized means collectivized. Today's executive is so packaged by consultants and confined by bureaucracy that he yearns atavistically to do something on his own, by himself.[17]*

It is these presidential yearnings to "prove themselves" that often end up being their undoing.

The Role of Special Interests. Those who become presidents have made compromises to gain votes for nomination and election. They are captives of their compromises. As a result, a president's power tends to be used in only one way—to protect the interests that helped win the election. Even President Kennedy, considered a champion of the have-nots in American society, capitulated to the special interests. According to Bernard Nossiter: "In every significant area—wage policy, tax policy, international trade and finance, federal spending—[Kennedy] showed a keen understanding and ready response to the essential corporate program."[18]

President Carter's decision to renounce a treaty with Nationalist China (Taiwan) served to open the door to potentially huge markets in the People's Republic of (Communist) China for products of American industry, including Coca-Cola, which is headquartered in Carter's native Georgia. Presidents Reagan and Bush predictably generated decisions favorable to their native states, California and Texas, in federal grants and appointments to important posts. The award of the multibillion dollar Super Collider project to Texas was a major bonanza in the Bush administration.

Foreign Intervention. The Constitution suggests that its framers intended the United States to establish relationships with other nations only by treaty, an action that requires Senate ratification. If this is so, their intention has been subverted; executive agreements between a U.S. president and another nation are now five times more common than treaties. An **executive agreement** has the legal status of a treaty but does not require Senate approval. Some of the foremost examples of executive agreements are the Atlantic Charter of 1941, the Yalta Agreement of 1944, and the Potsdam Agreement in 1945, all of which established major portions of American foreign policy during and after World War II.

Presidents can even undo treaties without Senate approval. When President Carter unilaterally abrogated the Taiwan Treaty, Senator Barry Goldwater (R-Ariz.) contended in the federal courts that a president could not do so without approval since the Senate had had to ratify the treaty in the first instance. A lower court decision upheld Goldwater's contention, but the U.S. Supreme Court reversed it, thereby strengthening the president's hand in foreign policymaking.[19]

The entire American military establishment is at the disposal of the president as commander in chief. About ten times in the past 25 years, presidents have militarily intervened in foreign countries without previously consulting with Congress. When public outcry against the Vietnam War became intense, congressional leaders tried to recoup their lost leadership and power in international crises by passing the War Powers Act. But, as we saw earlier, this act only serves to allow presidents to wage "60-day wars" unchallenged by Congress.

Because the Constitution gives Congress the power to declare war it would seem to follow that presidential deployment of troops without a declaration of war is unconstitutional. Such may not be the case, as Saul K. Padover has said:

> There is nothing in the Constitution that says that the President may not wage war abroad at his discretion. The Constitution merely states that Congress can "declare" war. But it does not say that a war has to be "declared" before it can be waged [emphasis added].[20]

Whether or not such presidential discretion is constitutional, the fact remains that it gives the chief executive enormous resources and the potential for a disastrous decision.

REASONS WHY PRESIDENTIAL POWER DOES NOT POSE A DANGER

Fundamentally, there are two reasons why presidential power does not pose a danger to American democracy: (1) the need for adequate presidential power in important instances, and (2) the restraints that inhibit abuses of presidential power.

Presidents have the U.S. military establishment at their disposal. Without consulting Congress, President Bush intervened in Panama in December 1989 to remove General Manuel Antonio Noriega from power. These soldiers are surrounding the Vatican embassy in Panama City, where Noriega took refuge.

The Need for a Powerful President. In a time of complex change and rapid communications, the United States *needs* an executive with the authority to act decisively. A few questions will serve to illustrate why. Could another nation negotiate in confidence with an American president who lacked the power to follow through on the results of the negotiations? Can we rely on 535 members of Congress to make fast decisions in the midst of a critical energy crisis? Should all of Congress have unlimited access to data gathered by our intelligence agencies?

Each of these questions can be answered only with a resounding "no." In response to the first question: A president without the power to implement international agreements would soon lose the respect of other nations and their leaders. As for the second question: During the energy crises of the early 1970s, Congress spent years debating and haggling with the president without solving the problem. Finally, much of the intelligence data gathered by the CIA and other agencies must remain confidential. The likelihood of information leaks increases when Congress is apprised of these data, and leaks endanger intelligence officers and undermine their future effectiveness.

Although Congress began checking presidential power in the mid-1970s, even critics admit the need to maintain a strong presidential position in foreign affairs (including a major role for the Central Intelligence Agency). Presidents must act quickly in protecting the national interest. Some people believe that, far from having too much power, the president does not have enough, particularly in domestic affairs, an area in which Congress likes to assert itself. For example, while we hold presidents accountable for the administration of a budget, we limit their power to control the budget. In addition, well-organized interest groups can wield power through the "iron triangle," whereby key committee chairmen, bureaucrats, and interest groups combine to thwart presidential leadership, even when the president enjoys strong public support.

In *The Federalist*, No. 70, Alexander Hamilton argued convincingly on behalf of an "energized executive":

> There is an idea, which is not without its advocates, that a vigorous executive is inconsistent with the genius of republican government. . . . Energy in the executive is a leading character in the definition of good government. It is essential to the protection of the community against foreign attacks; it is not less essential to the steady administration of the laws; to the protection of property against those irregular and high-handed combinations which sometimes interrupt the ordinary course of justice; to the security of liberty against the enterprises and assaults of ambition, of faction, and of anarchy.
>
> . . . A feeble executive implies a feeble execution of the government. A feeble execution is but another phrase for a bad execution; and a government ill executed, whatever it may be in theory, must be, in practice, a bad government.
>
> Taking it for granted, therefore, that all men of sense will agree in the necessity of an energetic executive, it will only remain to inquire what are the ingredients which constitute this energy? . . .
>
> The ingredients which constitute energy in the executive are unity; duration; and adequate provision for its support; and competent powers.[21]

Arguments about presidential power are inextricably linked to the larger debate about the future of the nation. Clinton Rossiter put it this way: "Few men get heated up over the presidency alone. Their arguments over its powers are really arguments over the American way of life and the direction in which it is moving."[22] The presidency, linked to the future of the United States more closely than any other governmental institution, must necessarily be involved in debates about the direction of the country. Will presidential powers be used for war or peace? Will a president's economic program benefit one class more than another? Such questions underline the importance of not allowing our distaste for a given president's policies to color our view of presidential power itself; the same authority used by a different president may bring about great accomplishments in what we regard as the public interest.

Built-in Restraints on Presidential Power. The American system of government, with its checks and balances, makes it impossible for presidents to act without some restraints. Governmental power in the United States is shared, not concentrated in the hands of one person or one office. The Constitution provides several very important checks on presidential power, including those exercised by Congress and the courts. State and local governments and the two-party system provide additional curbs. Other restraints, subtler but no less effective, include such factors as the need to persuade others to act, economic and social change, and international pressures.

Congressional Checks. Congress has at its disposal several means to check presidential actions. Probably the most important is the "power of the purse," the budgetary power. The president can spend only money that has been appropriated, and Congress alone can do this. Taxes cannot be raised or lowered without congressional action. A president who needs funds to finance programs must go to Congress hat in hand. Congress has recently strengthened its budget staffs to better challenge presidential control over budgeting information.

Another congressional weapon is the veto override. A president's veto is not the last word on whether a bill will become a law. Congress can and does (however infrequently) override presidential vetoes with a two-thirds majority in each house.

A third check Congress can use is the Senate's constitutional privilege to vote on presidential nominations. The Senate has many times either rejected nominations made by a president or forced their withdrawal. For example, President Bush's nomination of former U.S. Senator John Tower to be Secretary of Defense and President Reagan's nomination of Robert Bork to the Supreme Court were both voted down by the Senate. In 1993 Zöe Baird, President Clinton's nominee for Attorney General, withdrew her nomination when it became clear the Senate Judiciary Committee would not recommend her confirmation.

A fourth congressional check on the president is the constitutional amendment. If the presidency is too powerful an institution, what prevents Congress from limiting that power by amendment, a process that bypasses the White House? This right to propose amendments to the Constitution, including amendments that restrict presidential power, provides an ample safeguard against an authoritarian president.

A fifth important congressional power, the right to investigate presidential performance, has been used many times. Such investigations serve as reminders that presidential power is limited and that the president can be held accountable for the abuse of that power. The congressional investigation of Watergate forced President Nixon's resignation in 1974. In 1991 Democrats initiated an investigation of charges that Bush had participated in an alleged secret deal with Iran to hold American hostages until after the November election in 1980. (After the 1992 presidential election, Congress issued a report that cleared Bush of these charges.) Also during 1992, Congress investigated America's foreign policy in Iraq prior to the Gulf War.

Summing up congressional control of presidential power, the historian Arthur Schlesinger, Jr., compared the president with European parliamentary leaders: "Where a parliamentary prime minister can be reasonably sure that anything he suggests will become law in short order, the president of the United States cannot even be sure that his proposals will get to the floor of Congress for debate and vote."[23] Because congressional power is diffused among many committees and leaders, the president has to deal with a number of individuals and small groups. Clashes with recalcitrant representatives and senators are not infrequent. Even congressional members of the president's party are not as responsive to party leadership as they used to be.

The Courts. Throughout history, presidents have had to face the possibility that their actions would be tested in the courts. Franklin Roosevelt saw several of his New Deal programs declared unconstitutional by the Supreme Court. The Court also ruled against Truman's seizure of the nation's steel mills in 1952. In the 1970s, several federal courts held that Nixon could not impound congressionally appropriated funds, leading to the establishment of congressional guidelines for impoundment.

Roosevelt, understanding too well the special role of the judiciary, proposed in the 1930s that the number of Supreme Court justices be increased from 9 to 15; in this way he hoped to appoint a majority of justices who would be loyal to his New Deal programs. Public and congressional opposition put an end to this "court-packing" scheme.

State and Local Interests. Although the national government and its executive branch are powerful, they must reckon with state and local governments throughout the country. The diffusion of governmental power in the federal system forces a chief executive to take into account the wishes and needs of state and local political officials. This is especially true when nominations and elections are at stake. During the 1992 presidential campaign, both Bill Clinton and George Bush courted state and local officials with promises of help. President Bush was able to actually deliver grants and contracts during the campaign in key electoral vote states such as Texas. He was merely using a long-standing political weapon of incumbent presidents.

The Two-Party System. The diffused nature of the two-party system, with more power at the bottom than at the top, hinders presidential control of political parties. Presidents have no way to discipline their parties or force party members to support their policies. They must use compromise and often sacrifice some power to achieve their ends. For example, when President Kennedy made judicial appointments, good politics dictated that he reward the southern Democrats who had supported him in 1960. As a result, he appointed some segregationists, even though he publicly opposed segregation. Reagan named several moderate-to-liberal Republicans to high positions to retain the allegiance of that wing of his party. President Bush appointed some conservatives with more extreme views than his in order to retain the support of conservative Republicans.

The Need to Persuade. The president is at the top of the executive branch and is therefore assumed to be in command of those below. This is hardly the case. Harry Truman put it well: "The principal power the president has is to bring people in and try

President Lyndon Johnson was famed for his persuasive powers. In this photo he is putting them to work on Senator Richard Russell. According to Harry Truman, the powers of the presidency amount to the power to persuade.

to persuade them to do what they ought to do without persuasion. That's what I spent most of my time doing. That's what the powers of the presidency amount to."[24]

Why? The answer lies in the nature of relationships between presidents and their subordinates, and between presidents and other political leaders. No other person or group has the same perspective as the president. Even Cabinet members have their own departments with their own constituencies and loyalties. A president's appointees are responsible not just to the chief executive but also to Congress, to the groups and individuals that helped them get their appointments, and to the people working in their departments or agencies, as well as to themselves. The president is only one of five masters. As a result, Cabinet secretaries are sometimes referred to as a president's natural enemies. The chief executive's job is not so much one of commanding subordinates as of persuading them that what the president wants done is what they should do, despite their own interests or loyalties.

A president's personal and professional reputation assists in cultivating the art of persuasion. President Dwight D. Eisenhower had tremendous prestige among the people but lacked a Washington reputation as a professional who could manipulate effectively. In contrast, President Lyndon Johnson was esteemed in the capital as a professional politician but lost favor in the country at large with his Vietnam policy. When he referred to "the awesome power and the immense fragility of executive authority," he spoke as one who had witnessed the collapse, like a row of dominoes, of all that had gone into constructing his power base. Among the dominoes were relations with the public, Congress, the bureaucracy, and the press. Presidential power is built on the shaky foundations of relationships that necessitate persuasion, not command.

Other Restraints. What about control of the economic and societal forces in the United States? Presidents may influence such forces, but they cannot command them. Johnson could not control the demonstrations that ignited urban ghettos and campuses in the 1960s. Carter could not control inflation. Bush could not control the deficit.

Nor are presidents free agents in effecting basic social change. They must share power with other elected officials, bureaucrats, interest groups, elites, and politicians. Public opinion also prescribes boundaries for the exercise of presidential power. For example, public discontent with incumbents in 1992 forced George Bush to reinvent himself as a reformer ready to do battle with the system, particularly (the Democratic-controlled) Congress.

Second-term presidents are handicapped by the Twenty-Second Amendment, which prevents them from being elected to serve more than two terms (or ten years if as a vice president, a person replaces a president in office). After one term the president is in effect a four-year **lame duck,** one who no longer can use the threat to go to the polls to rally widespread public support.

The ebb-and-flow (or tide) theory of presidential power holds that the flow of history itself places limits on the chief executive; activity or passivity seems to run in cycles. According to this argument, Eisenhower's times in part shaped him as a passive president. The American people, having lived through the Great Depression, World War II, and the Korean War, wanted tranquility. If Eisenhower had tried to be an active and powerful president like his predecessors, he would have cut against the grain of public feelings.

American allies can also restrict presidential power. In preparing for action against Iraq during the Persian Gulf War, President Bush had to resist or overcome the opposition of such longtime allies as Jordan, to cultivate the diplomatic and military support of such allies as Germany and Japan, and to put pressure on Israel to remain out of the conflict. In making economic decisions the president must weigh and delicately balance the interests of other countries before he acts. For example, the president must give something to the European Community countries in exchange for their opening doors to an influx of American agricultural products.

ISSUE 1:   Summary   ★   *Does Presidential Power Pose a Danger to American Democracy?*

According to the critics, the presidency has assumed power far beyond that intended by the Founders. Presidents have become objects of unrealistic hero worship, putting them out of touch with American life and reality. Their power is used in a distorted fashion—to protect the special interests that elected them. And they have been given too much latitude to interfere in foreign affairs.

Defenders of presidential power point to the many pluses of a strong presidency and the many checks and restraints imposed by Congress, the courts, the parties, state and local governments, subordinates with other loyalties, and international obligations, among other factors. Those who believe presidential power is too great generally do not like the policies that a given president is pursuing, while those who support the expansion of presidential power tend to approve of those policy directions. ■

ISSUE 2   ARE PROVISIONS FOR THE REMOVAL OF A PRESIDENT ADEQUATE?

REASONS WHY PROVISIONS ARE NOT ADEQUATE

Removing a president from office is difficult. The simplest way, of course, is through defeat in an election, but elections take place only at prescribed times. And, in any case, presidents have a way of being reelected. In this century, only five incumbents who ran for reelection have been defeated—Taft (1912), Hoover (1932), Ford (1976), Carter (1980), and Bush (1992)—while nine incumbents have been returned to office—Theodore Roosevelt (1904), Wilson (1916), Coolidge (1924), Franklin Roosevelt (1936, 1940, and 1944), Truman (1948), Eisenhower (1956), Johnson (1964), Nixon (1972), and Reagan (1984). Normally presidents *increase* their margins of victory when they run for a second term, as did Nixon in 1972, Eisenhower in 1956, and Reagan in 1984.

The Constitution provides that a president (and certain other federal officials) may be removed by **impeachment.** In this case the House of Representatives adopts an impeachment resolution (brings charges) by a majority vote; the Senate tries the official and convicts with a two-thirds vote. The grounds for impeachment are "Treason, Bribery, or other high crimes and Misdemeanors." Only one president—Andrew Johnson, in 1868—has ever been impeached by the House and tried by the Senate. The Senate fell one vote short of conviction, and he remained in office. President Nixon, when faced with the certainty of impeachment proceedings in 1974, became the only American president to resign from office.

Congress has been reluctant to use impeachment, the only means it has for removing the highest official in the nation. Some fear that the process might too easily become a political weapon used by the opposition party to remove a president on slight provocation. Time is another factor. A Congress must be willing to commit a substantial amount of time and energy to the issue of impeachment, and to sacrifice other important business.

Not only is impeachment a laborious process, but, as spelled out in the Constitution, it is also far from precise in its meaning and implications. Can a president be indicted by a court before impeachment? Does the phrase "high crimes and misdemeanors" mean that a president can be impeached and convicted only for actual crimes, or may serious abuses of the office that fall short of indictable crimes be sufficient cause for removal? Opinion is divided on both questions. The most commonly held view is that judges and other officials, including the vice president, may be indicted and convicted in judicial proceedings before Congress impeaches. This view holds, however, that a president must be impeached and removed before prosecution, lest the nation find its president behind bars while still in office. As for what acts constitute impeachable offenses, several authorities feel that they should be limited to actual crimes; if a president can be impeached and convicted for something less, the president is more likely to be removed for purely political reasons.

The result is that the president is almost completely safe from the prospect of removal by Congress for any political actions. Presidential power is enhanced because the means for removal, uncertain as it is, remains essentially unused. By contrast, parliamentary systems can dispose of their executive by a simple **vote of no confidence** in the legislature. This vote calls for an immediate election or the selection of a new government by the majority party.

What if a president becomes physically or mentally unable to function while in office? The Twenty-Fifth Amendment, ratified in 1967, provides that the vice president will become acting president if (1) the president informs Congress in writing that "he is unable to discharge the powers and duties of his office," or (2) the vice president and a majority of the Cabinet make that judgment. If there is a disagreement between the president and the vice president and Cabinet about whether an inability exists, Congress has to vote (by a two-thirds majority of both houses) within three weeks on whether to support the vice president as chief executive. In essence, the balance of power rests with the president.

As we saw earlier, if the office of vice president becomes vacant, the president nominates someone to fill the position, subject to confirmation by a majority vote of both houses of Congress. President Nixon nominated Gerald Ford to replace Spiro Agnew, who resigned from office. After Nixon resigned Ford nominated Nelson Rockefeller to replace himself. In this unusual situation *both* the president and vice president had been forced to resign. That left the two top executive positions in the nation in the hands of men who had *not* been elected by the people. The extraordinary power of the president is obvious. Richard Nixon could name the person who would ultimately succeed (and later pardon) him. Gerald Ford in turn named the man with the potential to succeed him. Thus far, these are the only times the Twenty-Fifth Amendment has been implemented.

For two years (1974–1976) the United States was governed by two *unelected* leaders: President Gerald Ford *(right)* and Vice President Nelson Rockefeller *(left)*.

REASONS WHY PROVISIONS FOR REMOVAL OF A PRESIDENT ARE ADEQUATE

Five recent presidencies—those of Lyndon Johnson, Richard Nixon, Gerald Ford, Jimmy Carter, and George Bush—demonstrated that presidents *can* be removed from office. President Johnson decided not to run for reelection in 1968 after recognizing that he had lost substantial public support even within his own party. President Nixon resigned from office in the middle of his second term, when it became apparent that the Senate had enough votes to convict him if the House of Representatives impeached him. President Ford lost to Carter in 1976 after just two years in office. President Carter simply lost his reelection bid in 1980 and President Bush lost his in 1992.

Impeachment may be an arduous and time-consuming task, but should the nation's highest elected official be removed without a thorough investigation? Removal of the only official (other than the vice president) who is elected by all the people *should* be an awesome undertaking. In the post–Civil War era, the lengthy deliberations in Andrew Johnson's impeachment trial helped to exonerate him and protect him from extremists who wanted him removed from office for refusing to deal harshly with the South.

Impeachment, if taken lightly and acted upon quickly, might lead to the removal of presidents solely for political reasons rather than for violations of the law. In the case of President Nixon, a majority in favor of impeachment in the House of Representatives developed only after Judiciary Committee hearings had demonstrated Nixon's constitutional and legal violations. Because the impeachment process requires substantial time, the president is more likely to get a fair and impartial investigation with minimal partisan prejudice.

ISSUE 2: Summary ★ *Are Provisions for Removal of a President Adequate?*

The response to this question hinges in part on whether one thinks removing a president should be easy or difficult. Impeachment is a difficult and time-consuming process. A vote of no confidence in a parliamentary system is easy by contrast, but there, politics plays a larger role. The two-thirds majority requirement in the Senate for impeachment conviction makes strictly partisan politics unlikely to lead to a president's removal. Of course, the ballot box can always remove presidents, as has occurred five times in this century. And the Twenty-Fifth Amendment, however cumbersome, does make provisions for removing presidents with crippling disabilities. ■

ISSUE 3   *SHOULD THERE BE MAJOR REFORMS OF THE PRESIDENCY?*

REASONS WHY THERE SHOULD BE MAJOR REFORMS

The executive office can be restored to its proper role only by major reforms of the presidency. Several alternatives are possible.

A constitutional amendment allowing the president to serve only one 6-year term would free the president from spending so much time, energy, and money (at least during the first term) running for reelection. Power could be concentrated on constructive ends rather than on the pettiness of party politics.

Another possible reform is a constitutional amendment allowing Congress a vote of no confidence. As in a parliamentary system, a new election would be called. The incumbent president would have the right to run for reelection. In this way, the putrid air of an event like Watergate could be cleared without the extensive and counterproductive consequences of impeachment proceedings. In the election following a majority vote of no confidence, people could either remove or restate their faith in a president.

A third option is a multiple executive established by constitutional amendment. Too much power is now concentrated in one person. A president cannot properly fulfill all duties, and often sacrifices domestic interests to concentrate on foreign policy. One president could handle foreign affairs, for example, and another oversee domestic affairs. The concept of a multiple executive is not new. Many local governments have several elected executive officials performing different functions. The multiheaded executive would reduce the concentration of power in the hands of one president.

A fourth plan calls for a new amendment to provide for an election when the vice presidency falls vacant. This would prevent the awesome power of the presidency from ever being placed in the hands of a person who had never been popularly elected, as happened when Gerald Ford became president in 1974.

A more likely reform at some point in the future is the line-item veto or some variation of it. The **line-item veto** is a device that would allow the president to eliminate individual items in a bill without having to veto the entire bill. Most governors have this power, which enables them to cut what they consider unnecessary or excessive spending.

A VIEW FROM THE STATES
A Battle for the Power of the Purse

The renewed arguments over whether President Bill Clinton should have what President Bush wanted—devices he could use to cut spending, like the "line item veto" and its feebler cousin "enhanced rescission authority"—are not really about cutting the deficit. [Enhanced rescission authority would allow a president to propose budget cuts but would require a majority vote by both houses of Congress to implement them.]

Nobody, not even Mr. Clinton, argues that either device would affect the deficit very much, even though they would allow a President to strike individual items from spending bills without having to veto the entire measure.

Instead, the engine behind this discussion is perceived political necessity, an urgent need to convey to constituents that lawmakers are willing to take a bold step to curb Federal spending.

For opponents of both notions, the issue is as old as the Republic, the contest for power between the executive and legislative branches. And the foremost opponent is the chairman of the Senate Appropriations Committee, Senator Robert C. Byrd of West Virginia, who has said Congress would have to be crazy to surrender any of the power of the purse to any President of either party. . . .

"The power over the purse is the taproot of the tree of Anglo-Saxon liberty," Mr. Byrd said. "The item-veto debate, when shorn of all of its fancy trappings, is a debate about power, and control of the purse is the bone and sinew of power." . . .

An enhanced-rescission bill will almost surely pass the House fairly early next year. The test will come in the Senate, though perhaps not quickly, and it will be a measure of how much political capital Mr. Clinton is prepared to spend on a war with the Senate's senior Democrat. He will not want to lose such a war, but neither is he likely to want to retreat from a fight.

With this reform, Congress could reinstate the item only by making it a new bill that the president would be free to veto; a two-thirds majority in both houses would be required to override.

REASONS WHY THERE SHOULD NOT BE MAJOR REFORMS

Carrying out structural reforms to limit the power of the presidency would be extremely difficult. Reforms tend to come only when a crisis focuses continuing attention on the need for major changes. As far as the presidency is concerned, this time passed when the Watergate furor abated. In any case, let's consider the constructive value of the reform proposals described above.

The adoption of one 6-year term could certainly remove a president from partisan politics—that is, from the necessity to prepare for reelection—but such a policy also has a negative impact. A president who must keep reelection in mind is more likely to respond to public and congressional pressures as well as to political party interests. For example, in preparing for the 1972 election, President Nixon began troop withdrawal from Vietnam to counter antiwar criticism during the campaign.

Another problem generated by the one 6-year term plan is that members of Congress would feel less restraint in opposing the president's legislative program, making it more difficult for the president to govern. The Twentieth Amendment (ending the presidential term in January rather than March) was ratified to keep the president from being a lame duck for four months, and many people now doubt the wisdom of the lame-duck feature of the Twenty-Second Amendment (limiting the president to two full terms or ten years). Would we want a lame-duck president for *six years*?

The idea of a vote of no confidence mixes parliamentary and presidential systems, thereby creating a hybrid with unknown prospects for success. Frequent partisan no-confidence votes could hamper the proper functioning of our government.

A multiple executive would add more confusion to our complex and diffuse governmental structure. Where would the power of one president end and the power of another president begin? Would there be struggles *between* the presidents?

The line-item veto takes the power of the purse away from the Congress, where it constitutionally belongs. Moreover, just because state governors have it is not a reason for the national executive to have it. The line-item veto is not the solution to the budget deficit, since Congress and the president already have the authority to eliminate it. If the argument for the line-item veto is that it will help eliminate deficit spending, many economists would rebut by saying that there are times when deficit spending may be necessary, such as during a war or a recession.

In sum, retaining the existing form of the presidency is better than imposing reforms that might do more harm than good. What is needed, however, is a more realistic attitude toward the presidency. We need to understand the difference between the characteristics of an appealing candidate and those of a good president. Then, we will be in a position to evaluate performance better and more fairly.

ISSUE 3: Summary ★ *Should There Be Major Reforms of the Presidency?*

A number of major reforms have been proposed such as one 6-year term, a vote of no confidence in Congress, a multiple executive, and the line-item veto, but such reforms might substantially alter the separation of powers between the executive and legislative branches. Achieving constitutional reforms requires use of the constitutional amending process. With the extraordinary majorities necessary in the Congress and among the states, these reforms are probably unlikely. Their unrealistic nature and unknown impact lead to the conclusion that major reforms require a more compelling case. ■

⊕ COMPARISONS WITH OTHER NATIONS

The American presidency was a historically unprecedented office when it was created. Few countries anywhere had either an elective head of government or anything more sophisticated than an autocratic monarch. Europe and much of the rest of world ignored the American precedent. As most of Western Europe and, later, its former colonies in Africa and Asia developed parliamentary systems, political power devolved into the hands of their prime ministers. In systems that eventually established a presidential office, the president was frequently chosen by the parliaments, not by popular election, and was no more than a ceremonial head of state. Those countries that retained monarchies—the United Kingdom, the Scandinavian countries, and Japan, for example—allowed their monarchs little or no actual power and simply used them as national symbols.

There was some emulation of the American presidency, mostly in Latin America. But for most of their history, Latin American countries produced presidents through revolutions and militarily inspired coups d'etat rather than through elections. Happily, this is changing, and only a minority of countries in Latin America currently have dictatorial regimes. Most of the region's elected presidents are strictly limited in how long they can hold office. In this sense, the United States emulated Latin America when, in 1951, it ratified the Twenty-Second Amendment, restricting presidents to two terms.

THE EXECUTIVE IN DEMOCRACIES

Prime Ministerial Systems

Often an American president seems to come from nowhere. Jimmy Carter was a one-term governor of Georgia, little known outside his own state, who surprised many of the experts by winning the Democratic nomination in 1976. Bill Clinton had spent his entire political career in the Arkansas state house. Ronald Reagan was a movie actor who hadn't entered elective politics until he was well into his fifties. Other presidents, such as Dwight D. Eisenhower, had never been in politics at all until they ran for the presidency itself. Even Abraham Lincoln became president after a lackluster political career: He had briefly served in the House of Representatives before being defeated in a bid for reelection and had lost a Senate race.

Quite the opposite is true in prime ministerial systems. Generally, no one becomes prime minister without being a long-time parliamentary apprentice. This apprenticeship often lasts as long as 20 or 25 years. Common requirements for being a prime minister include the following:

1. Must have long-time service in lower house of parliament,
2. Must have previous Cabinet service,
3. Must hold position of party leader,
4. Must belong to party winning parliamentary majority in the most recent election, and
5. Must not be a member of the royal family, if there is one.

Many American presidents first established their political careers in Congress. But John F. Kennedy's election in 1960 was the last one of a president who was a sitting member of either house of Congress. A prime minister, in contrast, is *always* a sitting member of parliament. Earlier in this chapter we noted that the president of the United States is the chief legislator (regardless of legislative experience; Bill Clinton, for example, has none, nor did Ronald Reagan). But the president is not, and by law cannot be, a member of Congress. This fact greatly distinguishes the presidential from the prime ministerial system. There, an aspiring politician *must* be a member of parliament before he or she can become prime minister. And the prime minister must remain in parliament to be an effective legislator.

In certain countries, other (often unwritten) requirements may apply: In Canada the prime minister must be bilingual (fluent in French and English); in Britain the prime minister in all likelihood will not be Catholic; in Israel the prime minister will not be from the 15 percent of the population that is not Jewish; in India the prime minister will be Hindu. It would be unheard of in any of these countries for a military hero such as Eisenhower to become head of government. Popular generals are not considered political figures. As noted earlier, there have been unwritten requirements in the United States as well. However, it is important to point out that old biases are probably on the downturn. For example, John Kennedy, a Catholic, was elected president in 1960, and in 1984 Geraldine Ferraro was the first female vice presidential candidate on a major party ticket. Several European countries, including the United Kingdom and Norway, have had female prime ministers, and so have India, Pakistan, Sri Lanka, Canada, and Israel. Presidential systems seem much more resistant than parliamentary ones to heads of government being recruited from the female gender. Two recent exceptions include Corazan Aquino (1986–1992) of the Philippines and Violeta Barrios de Chamorro of Nicaragua.

The American president's Cabinet can include secretaries who are actually opposed to presidential policy. If so, at least the president has the option of dismissing such people (usually by asking for their resignations). And, even when presidents keep Cabinet secretaries who may oppose a particular policy, they generally don't have to worry about being in competition with the secretaries. That is because these individuals carry a low profile, unless they become controversial or hold a key position (such as secretary of State).

Prime ministers are not as fortunate. They are influenced (sometimes almost coerced) in their choices of ministers by serious political considerations. The Cabinet ministers represent powerful factions within the party. They are usually well known. They have probably been in national politics for a long time, and it is a safe bet that they have sat in previous Cabinets. The result is that the prime minister's Cabinet always includes a few would-be successors who are keen for the top job. It was an open secret, for example, that Britain's Prime Minister Margaret Thatcher and several of her Cabinet secretaries were frequently in conflict over both policy and the extraordinary length of Mrs. Thatcher's tenure as prime minister (1979–1990).

Unlike presidents and their Cabinets, prime ministers and their Cabinets attend parliamentary sessions with the regularity of any other member of parliament—even more so, since they are expected to respond to inquiries from the opposition. This exposure ensures that a Cabinet minister must constantly be aware of what is going on in her or his ministry. In the United States, knowledge of one's own department is valuable, but can also be fudged. Cabinet secretaries normally appear in Congress only at the request of a concerned committee. Some on occasion have refused to appear and gotten away with it. The president appears in Congress only at carefully selected intervals, usually no

British Prime Ministers and their cabinet ministers are members of Parliament and attend parliamentary sessions regularly. They also must respond to questions by other members on a regular basis. Prime Minister John Major is shown here making a point during question time in the House of Commons.

more than once a year to deliver the State of the Union Address (at which no questions are taken).

There have been frequent comparisons of the British prime minister and the American president in terms of how democratic or how politically powerful each office is. It is difficult to decide either matter. Instead of trying to do so we urge the reader to consider the points summarized in Table 10.4.

There are advantages to being a prime minister that the president lacks. As both head of state and head of government, the president of the United States is obligated to perform many ceremonial duties. In Britain, the monarch takes on those functions. A renowned observer of the British political scene has succinctly summarized the difference between the American president and the British monarch:

> In the United States, the head of state is the president. In the United Kingdom, the head of state is the monarch. Both fulfill certain formal duties associated with the position. Beyond that there is little similarity between the two. In terms of history, determination of incumbency, powers, and current responsibilities, the United States presidency and the British monarchy have virtually nothing in common. The president is both head of state and political head of the administration. He operates directly and personally at the heart of the political decision-making process. The monarch, as head of state, stands above political decision-making. In political terms, he or she serves not to decide but, primarily, to perform a symbolic role. The president serves by virtue of election; the monarch by virtue of birth.[25]

	President	Prime Minister
TABLE 10.4 DISTINCTIONS BETWEEN THE AMERICAN PRESIDENT AND THE BRITISH PRIME MINISTER		
Term of office	Two 4-year terms (or 10 years)	No limit on terms of up to 5 years
Elections	Constitutionally prescribed	Prime Minister can give 6 weeks' notice
Selection method	Electoral college majority	Leadership of majority party in Parliament
Removal	Impeachment	Loss of majority (vote of no confidence)
Relationship to legislature	Often faces majority opposition	Guaranteed majority support

Some American presidents have utilized their vice presidents for time-consuming but politically irrelevant chores, such as attending weddings and funerals of important but not crucial (or no longer crucial) personages. As George Bush learned, however, this is an excellent way to cultivate future contacts if a vice president subsequently becomes president.

Ceremonial presidents tend to appear in parliamentary systems that lack monarchies and therefore require someone to handle the basically symbolic tasks that the prime minister can easily do without. Such individuals also tend to have been politically inoffensive throughout their careers (which is why former prime ministers almost never become presidents—they've made too many enemies). In fact, these presidents are frequently from outside politics altogether. The Israeli presidency, for example, has twice been occupied by professional scientists of international repute.

Other ceremonial presidencies, such as those in Germany and Austria, often choose a president among candidates who have held high and distinguished diplomatic posts over a long career. President Kurt Waldheim of Austria is a well-known, if controversial, example.* The Austrian situation is interesting for another reason. Usually, a ceremonial president is elected by the country's parliament or by a special electoral college to ensure that he or she will not be able to claim the mandate a popular election would normally provide. Austria, however, does elect its president, but still denies him or her substantial power anyway.

Without substantial powers, then, what do ceremonial presidents do? Probably their most important obligation occurs whenever there is a national election. The president must ask someone to form a government. Usually this is a cut-and-dried affair. The leader of the party with a parliamentary majority normally gets the nod, since there is no

---

* Ceremonial presidents aren't supposed to be controversial. Waldheim served as United Nations Secretary General, but his military activities as an officer in the German army during World War II were subsequently linked to war crimes. See Robert Edwin Herzstein, *Waldheim: The Missing Years* (New York: Paragon House, 1989).

choice in the matter. The head of state, however, may have some discretion in those rare situations when the electoral outcome is close or cloudy, and no party or combination of parties emerges with a majority. Between elections, the ceremonial president keeps busy dedicating new bridges or schools, paying calls on other heads of state, and being cheered by crowds at sporting events.

Other Presidential Systems

There is much to be said for dividing up the heads of government and state, as is regularly found in parliamentary systems. Most democracies (and even most nondemocratic systems) do this. It is also an easy way to avoid the excesses of the **imperial presidency**, a syndrome that grew out of difficulties of the Nixon administration when members of the president's staff placed themselves above the law. There is no lack of corruption in any political system. However, prime ministers are considered unseemly if they appear to the public to be overly concerned with their own importance. That is what ceremonial heads of state are for.

But some countries *like* monarchical presidents and appreciate executive arrogance as long as it is dignified. France is the only major European country to disavow parliamentary government in favor of a presidential system and the only other major democracy to adopt it. Since the creation of the Fifth Republic in 1958, French presidents have been nearly as monarchical as democratically permissible. Having long given up their monarchy, the French still retain a nostalgic appreciation of a strong executive. For example, French presidents can

- Serve as many 7-year terms as they can win
- Declare themselves a constitutional dictator for a period of up to six months in a national emergency[26]
- Dissolve the lower house of parliament and call for new elections
- Call for a national referendum (a national vote on an issue), the results of which become law (without the need of legislative approval)
- Be guaranteed of a popular mandate by having to win an absolute majority of votes in a presidential election

American presidents cannot do any of the first four things (unless they want to guarantee impeachment proceedings) and can only hope for a popular vote majority. It is no wonder that French presidents are often accused of arrogance. Their powers almost require it.* The French combined their long and often contradictory traditions of monarchy and republicanism into a democratically chosen but very powerful executive.

In a sense the French presidency deserves to be more powerful than the American

---

* American presidents may eschew arrogance, but they do occasionally recruit arrogant aides. President George Bush's first chief of staff, John Sununu, exhibited rampant and even uncontrollable arrogance. See Richard Cohen, "Sununu's Arrogance," *The Washington Post Weekly Edition*, July 1–7, 1991, p. 29. One story, perhaps apocryphal, alleges that when Sununu was asked why people take an instant dislike to him he replied, "To save time."

one. The insistence on a popular majority sometimes requires a runoff election between the two highest vote-getters. The United States lacks any constitutional provisions for a runoff. A candidate who can secure a majority of the electoral college (at least 270 votes out of 538) wins. As we saw earlier in this chapter, several American presidential candidates have won their elections in the electoral college while losing in the popular vote column to the "runner-up." The French abolished their electoral college in 1962, determined to provide their president with an undeniable popular majority.

The electoral college also explains why we occasionally elect minority presidents. The most recent occasion was the three-way race in 1992 when Bill Clinton won with 43.2 percent of the vote. An election result like this would have required a runoff in France between the two top candidates.

The Head of Government and Political Democracy

The American presidency is far from being a thoroughly democratic institution. It is a good deal less democratically selected than the one in France or the majority of other presidential systems. This fact doesn't seem to bother most Americans. Nor does it seem really to disadvantage democracy. As Figure 10.1 suggests, there are other democracies without purely democratically chosen heads of government. In no parliamentary system, for example, is the prime minister directly elected by the voters at large. The voter does understand, of course, that by voting to elect, say, a conservative from his or her district, an indirect ballot is cast for the leader of the conservative party to form a government. What both presidential and parliamentary systems tend to completely agree on is that the legislature ought to be popularly elected, either in winner-take-all single-member districts or through proportional representation, and that should be enough democracy for most people.

Perhaps the most democratic feature of the typical prime ministership is that it is renewable indefinitely. With the exception of that in France, presidential systems lack a similar trust. Most presidential systems, even ceremonial ones, limit terms and years in office. (See Table 10.5 for a sample.)

Political Succession in Democracies

In most instances political succession in the United States proceeds smoothly. After election in early November the president-elect forms a new government and takes office

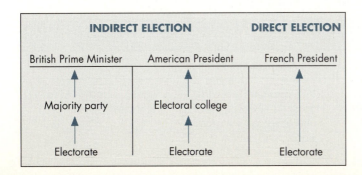

Figure 10.1 INDIRECT AND DIRECT WAYS OF SELECTING THE CHIEF EXECUTIVE.

TABLE 10.5	PRESIDENTIAL TERM LIMITATIONS IN SELECTED COUNTRIES	
Country	Length of Term	Renewable?
Costa Rica	4 years	No
France	7 years	Indefinite
Mexico	6 years	No
Switzerland	1 year	No
United States	**4 years**	**Once**

January 20. But the American presidential system allows for "accidental presidents." In other words, people can become president instantly without securing a single popular vote for that office. Of our 42 presidents, 8 have been accidental: vice presidents assuming the office after the death or resignation of the elected president. While hardly a democratic procedure this succession apparatus in the United States is not unusual for presidential systems.

France again is the major exception. A presidential vacancy constitutionally necessitates a presidential election. There is no vice president hanging around to succeed to the office. A national election is held within several weeks of a presidential departure. The winner receives a 7-year term regardless of how long the previous term still had to run. The French believe that a president, any president, requires at a minimum a popular endorsement to have a chance of doing well. It is difficult to be sure whether this rule gives the French president any substantial advantage over other executives. Greater democracy may or may not produce greater stability, although many would like to believe that it does. For purposes of clarification, the three main examples of political succession in democracies following a sudden vacancy in the executive are summarized in Table 10.6.

Some countries, such as Costa Rica (one of the oldest and most successful democracies in Latin America), disqualify immediate relations from succeeding to presidential office. They are understandably frightened of a family dynasty that doesn't allow democratic institutions to grow or destroys already existing ones. This is exactly what has occurred in countries such as Argentina, Paraguay, and Nicaragua.

TABLE 10.6 THREE WAYS TO FILL A VACANCY IN THE EXECUTIVE		
British Prime Minister	American President	French President
Majority party members of House of Commons select new party leader, who then is asked to form a government	Vice president succeeds; appoints new vice president subject to congressional confirmation	National election for a new president

A VIEW FROM ABROAD
The Ten-Year Itch

In marriage they call it the seven-year itch: the time when things start to go wrong. Remember the Marilyn Monroe film? In politics it is the ten-year itch—the movie, one day, in which Madonna makes the role of Margaret Thatcher her own.

Ten years, it seems, is about as long as any leader ought sensibly to stay in power in a modern democracy. Mrs. Thatcher is merely the most striking recent example. She should have gone gracefully after a decade—instead of getting kicked out ignominiously after 11 years. After 11 years, too, France said *non* to General de Gaulle. Now François Mitterand, France's president since 1981, is developing a bad case of the ten-year itch. Of late he seems to have been losing his touch abroad and his popularity rating at home.

A whole batch of European leaders are experiencing a Mitterand-like *malaise*. The booming 1980s helped keep them in power; the troubled 1990s will make it harder for them to stay there. . . .

What goes wrong after a decade? Po-litical palsy sets in. Symptoms commonly include delusions of grandeur (Mrs. Thatcher behaving like a queen, Mr. Mitterand like Louis XIV), aversion to criticism, boredom with party politics, preference for foreign affairs and, often, an obsession with what future history books will say. But it is what voters say—or party colleagues waiting for their turn in power—that forces a change.

The one known cure is worse than the disease: be a dictator, not a democrat. Colonel Qaddafi has led Libya for 22 years, Kim Il Sung has been North Korea's "great leader" for 46 years. If only a ten-year rule had applied to dictators too—Stalin would barely have had time to begin his purges, [Romania's] Ceausescu might have been remembered as a reformer, and Saddam Hussein would have gone before invading Kuwait. . . .

"Old politicians chew on wisdoms past, and totter on in business to the last," wrote Pope. The great thing about democracy is that it gives totterers the push.

Source: The Economist, "The Ten-Year Itch," August 17, 1991, p. 16.

Life After Power

In the United States we tend to dump former presidents onto golf courses and keep them busy building presidential libraries. Only three presidents ever held public office after leaving the White House, and none have since 1930.* But former prime ministers pop

---

* The sixth president, John Quincy Adams, enjoyed an illustrious 18-year career in the House of Representatives (1831–1848); the 17th, Andrew Johnson, went back to the Senate and died there in 1875; the 28th, William Howard Taft, became a Supreme Court Chief Justice (1921–1930). All three had experienced unhappy presidencies that lasted a single term.

Political succession proceeds smoothly in the United States. President and Mrs. Bush and Millie (the dog) welcome the Clintons to their new home on Inauguration Day in 1993.

up quite often in Cabinet ministries, or they may eventually be appointed to the House of Lords, where they enjoy a title and prestige, even though by accepting the position they give up any hope of exercising real political power.

Even more importantly, a former prime minister may and often does aspire to a political comeback. If, for example, a majority party is transformed into the minority after parliamentary elections and becomes the opposition, its party leader is often the former prime minister. If that party then regains the majority, the party leader is once more the prime minister. In contrast, our one-term presidents, such as Herbert Hoover or Jimmy Carter, are expected simply to retire from national politics and never run for anything again. Only one president, Grover Cleveland, ever made a comeback: he won the election of 1884, lost in 1888, and won again in 1892.

In 1993 there were five living former American presidents—Richard Nixon, Gerald Ford, Jimmy Carter, Ronald Reagan, and George Bush—a record number. It seems a waste to put former presidents out to pasture. With four or eight years of experience at the highest political level, their talents could be put to good use in other offices, such as Secretary of State. But the public and traditional bias against such a practice seems very strong. Once presidents retire they are supposed to stay retired. In any case, former presidents seem reluctant to become involved in politics again. To be sure, they may feel that they have earned their rest.

THE EXECUTIVE IN TOTALITARIAN SYSTEMS

The executive office in totalitarian political systems is little more than an appendage of the party state. During his first 20 years as General Secretary of the Communist party of the Soviet Union, Joseph Stalin didn't even bother to hold a government post. And in China between 1968 and 1983 the state presidency was unoccupied altogether. No one seemed to have noticed.*

Both China and the former Soviet Union did create political structures that appeared familiar to the West, including the presidential and prime ministerial offices. However, it should be kept in mind that the most powerful office in the typical communist state is not technically a government office at all. The party leader, usually the general secretary, determines who becomes president and prime minister. Sometimes, he chooses himself for at least one of those offices. After politely waiting in vain for Soviet President Nikolai Podgorny to die, for example, General Secretary Leonid Brezhnev finally shunted him off to retirement and then appointed himself president in the 1970s. Assuming a government office serves more for convenience than to increase power: When meeting heads of government in the West it was useful protocol to meet as technical equals rather than simply as the leader of a political party.

When totalitarian dictators do hold high public office they seem to enjoy it. The leader of Nazi Germany, Adolf Hitler, was first appointed Chancellor (roughly the equivalent of prime minister) in 1933 and then assumed the post of German president the next year when the incumbent died. Again, though, totalitarian leaders normally acquire power through the party they either found (as in the case of Hitler) or in which they have worked their way up through the ranks (as in the case of Soviet leaders after Stalin). Assuming the highest government office in a totalitarian state simply provides a sense of political legitimacy that the party leader understandably craves.

In the former communist societies, popularly elected presidents are apparently now gaining a foothold. In the spring of 1991, for the first time in its history, the Russian Republic in what was still the Soviet Union popularly elected Boris Yeltsin over three other candidates for president. The Czechoslovaks and the Poles had earlier elected presidents. Eastern Europe seems to be evolving a combination of presidential and parliamentary systems, with a popularly elected president who appoints a prime minister and Cabinet that represents the majority party or a coalition of parties in the legislature.

It is premature to guess how political evolution will proceed in Eastern Europe. Yugoslavia deteriorated into civil war in the early 1990s and the Soviet Union finally dissolved in December 1991. Bulgaria and Romania have yet to commit completely to

---

* Greater attention has been given to the office since the early 1980s, at least to the extent of regularly filling it. See "On the Revision of the Constitution," *Beijing Review*, 25:18 (May 3, 1982), 15–18.

democracy. Several of these countries have a past that includes some democratic institutions. Each country's democratic development (assuming it will proceed) will be related to its own peculiar political culture and history. It seems safe to say that an abundance of popular heroes— Lech Walesa in Poland, Vaslev Havel in what was Czechoslovakia, Boris Yeltsin in Russia—makes a popularly elected presidency relevant and easy to accomplish in these countries. However, the parliamentary system that pervades most of neighboring Western Europe will remain an influence in the evolution of Eastern European political institutions. The happy fact is that democracies historically live in peace with one another, regardless of how any democracy develops.

THE EXECUTIVE IN AUTHORITARIAN SYSTEMS

The many political leaders in nondemocratic regimes who refer to themselves as presidents simply enjoy the title. They are, in fact, dictators. They tend to come from military backgrounds and, in a coup, promptly appoint themselves to the office. Many of these are political thugs, like Saddam Hussein of Iraq or Hafez el-Assad of Syria. They appoint their own prime ministers, who are simply obedient sycophants. However, some authoritarian dictators prefer to remain in the background and simply install presidents whenever it suits them. This was certainly the case of General Manuel Noriega of Panama. Before becoming an inmate in a Miami jail in 1989, Noriega manufactured presidential elections in Panama to ensure that his personally chosen candidate would win. The Panamanian president was at all times aware that his term of office depended on how pleased Noriega was with him.

Many successor regimes to collapsed communist governments are decidedly authoritarian. They are attempting to confirm their legitimacy by being especially brutal in consolidating their power. Hence, the Serbian regime of President Slobodan Milosevic has committed criminal acts in neighboring Bosnia. Such regimes retain the loyalty of their military and a good part of the population by pursuing inhumane policies against ethnic or religious communities long perceived as enemies.

Most authoritarian leaders are unexcited about the prospect of term limitations. Haiti's "Papa" Doc Duvalier, for example, declared himself "president for life" in the 1960s and served as the Haitian leader for nearly two decades until his death. But the modern world record may be held by North Korea's Kim Il Sung. Kim has ruled since 1945, is determined to guarantee the succession to his son, Kim Jong Il, and happily presides over the increasing impoverishment of his country.*

Summary

1. Different presidents have differing views on what the actual powers and prerogatives of the presidency are and how they should be exercised. Both active and passive presidents have left their imprint on the office, but the former are generally ranked higher.

---

* One estimate suggested that North Korea's economy declined by 30 percent in 1992. "Morning edition," April 2, 1993, National Public Radio.

2. The functions of the American president as head of state, chief executive, diplomat, military leader, legislative leader, and party leader are very demanding. A prime minister is at least free of the duties of head of state.

3. American presidents have the support of an executive bureaucracy, especially the vice president, the 14 executive departments, and the Executive Office of the President with its staff of personal advisors.

4. Presidential power has expanded as government has steadily centralized. Domestic and foreign crises, a weakening of Congress, a changing society, and presidential initiative have all contributed to the expansion of power. Congress has attempted to limit that power in recent years by passing a War Powers Act and increasing its own expertise in budgetary matters.

5. Too much presidential power may pose a danger for democracy by creating a "superman" in the presidency, by having presidential powers used on behalf of special interests, and by allowing presidents to interfere unilaterally in other countries. In a democracy, however, there are still important restraints to presidential power, including the other branches and levels of government, the parties, the president's need to persuade, and social and economic forces.

6. Presidents are generally removed through elections. The threat of impeachment remains as the last resort of getting rid of an unruly president. It was invoked only once, in 1868, and seriously considered in 1974 before Richard Nixon resigned from office. Prime ministers, on the other hand, don't have to worry about impeachment, but they can be removed by a vote of no confidence among their own parliamentary supporters.

7. Some suggested reforms for the presidency include providing for one 6-year term, transforming the American political system into a quasi-parliamentary one requiring a congressional vote of confidence, creating a multiple executive, requiring an election for our president whenever there is a vacancy in the office, and giving the president a line-item veto. But the impact of these reforms is uncertain, and the prospect of their being passed in the amending process is unlikely.

8. Presidents and prime ministers differ in significant ways. Presidents can take office with very little political experience, whereas prime ministers must put in a long parliamentary apprenticeship before becoming party leader. Presidents don't generally have political rivals within the Cabinet, whereas prime ministers often do. The prime minister enjoys the advantage of having a head of state available, either a monarch or a ceremonial president, to handle nonessential duties, leaving the prime minister free for important policy matters. The American president is both head of government and head of state but may employ the vice president as a sometime ceremonial official.

9. French presidents are more authoritarian and constitutionally powerful than American presidents, but they have an electoral mandate by being elected directly by a majority of the people.

10. Presidents and prime ministers are both chosen in relatively democratic fashion. The popularly elected president (as in France) is the most democratically chosen.

Prime ministers are always the leaders of the parliamentary majority but are never chosen directly by the popular electorate. American presidents are indirectly elected through the electoral college. There is no such thing as a lame duck prime minister, since their terms can be renewed indefinitely. Most presidential systems (France being an important exception) have constitutional limitations on how long one individual can remain in office.

11. While the United States has occasionally been governed by an unelected "accidental" president, this is an exception rather than a rule. Other systems ensure that the president is always an elected one.

12. While former American presidents are put out to pasture, if only because they are disqualified from serving again after two terms, former prime ministers often continue to serve in lesser offices or may again hold the top job.

13. In totalitarian systems the title of executive is more a convenience than a sign of power. Real power lies in the hands of the party leader.

14. In authoritarian systems dictators appoint themselves to office or appoint presidents and prime ministers who do their bidding. Their intention is to hold power for life.

Terms to Define

Administrative law	Imperial presidency
Cabinet	Impoundment
Ceremonial president	Lame duck
Executive agreement	Line-item veto
Executive Office of the President	Pocket veto
Executive privilege	Veto
Impeachment	Vote of no confidence

Suggested Readings

Barber, James David. *The Presidential Character*, 4th ed. Englewood Cliffs, N.J.: Prentice-Hall, 1992. Assesses the relationship between a president's character and presidential leadership.

Ferrell, Robert H. *Ill-Advised: Presidential Health and Public Trust*. Columbia and London: University of Missouri Press, 1992. Presidents are sometimes sicker than they want the public to know. As the author indicates, there is a "deplorable situation" regarding the cover-up of presidential illnesses that has been going on at least since the administration of Grover Cleveland and through the administration of George Bush.

Greenstein, Fred I., ed. *Leadership in the Modern Presidency*. Cambridge: Harvard University Press, 1988. Analysis of leadership styles of presidents from Franklin Roosevelt through Ronald Reagan.

Lichtman, Allan J., and Ken DeCell. *The Keys to the Presidency*. Lanham, Md.: Madison Books, 1990. Presents and tests a useful model for predicting presidential elections from the Civil War through 1988.

Mansfield, Harvey, Jr. *Taming the Prince: The Ambivalence of Modern Executive Power*. New York: Free Press, 1989. Exhaustive analysis of the historical and philosophical underpinnings of the presidency.

Neustadt, Richard E. *Presidential Power and the Modern Presidents*. New York: John Wiley, 1990. A new edition of a classic study of the relationship between power and leadership.

Wildavsky, Aaron. *The Beleaguered Presidency*. New Brunswick, N.J.: Transaction, 1991. Assesses relationships between American culture and presidential leadership and how presidents have tried to cope with their beleaguered status.

Notes

1. Arthur B. Tourtellot, *Presidents on the Presidency* (Garden City, N.Y.: Doubleday, 1964), pp. 55–56.
2. William Howard Taft, *Our Chief Magistrate and His Powers* (New York: Columbia University Press, 1938), p. 138.
3. Mark Goodman, ed., *Give 'em Hell, Harry!* (New York: Award Books, 1974), p. 108.
4. Richard E. Neustadt, *Presidential Power* (New York: John Wiley, 1960), p. 161.
5. Wilfred E. Binkley, *President and Congress* (New York: Alfred A. Knopf, 1947), p. 127.
6. Edward S. Corwin, *The Presidents, Office and Powers 1787–1957* (New York: New York University Press, 1957), p. 311.
7. Emmet John Hughes, *The Living Presidency* (New York: Coward, McCann and Geoghegan, 1973), p. 52.
8. Ibid., p. 57.
9. *The Economist*, December 19, 1992, p. 23.
10. Neustadt, *Presidential Power*, p. vii.
11. *The Atlanta Constitution*, November 4, 1983, p. 19A.
12. *The Federalist*, edited by Henry Cabot Lodge (New York: G.P. Putnam's Sons, 1902), p. 419.
13. For a full assessment of these and similar quotations about the American presidency, see Thomas E. Cronin, "The Textbook Presidency and Political Science," *Congressional Record*, October 5, 1970, pp. S17102–17115.
14. Quoted in James MacGregor Burns, *Presidential Government* (Boston: Houghton Mifflin, 1965), p. 96.
15. Marquis Childs syndicated column, *The Washington Post*, November 17, 1972, p. 17.
16. Russell Baker and Charles Peters, "The Prince and His Courtiers: At the White House, the Kremlin, and the Reichchancellery," *The Washington Monthly*, March 1971, p. 34.
17. Harvey Mansfield, *Taming the Prince* (New York: Basic Books, 1991), p. 297.
18. Bernard Nossiter, *The Mythmakers* (Boston: Beacon Press, 1964), p. 40.
19. For a discussion of the circumstances of this case, see *Congressional Quarterly*, December 22, 1979, p. 2919.
20. Saul K. Padover, "The Power of the President," *Commonwealth*, August 9, 1968, p. 524.
21. Robert Maynard Hutchins, ed., *Great Books of the Western World:* Volume 43, *American Papers.* "The Federalist" (Chicago: Encyclopaedia Britannica, 1952), pp. 210–214.
22. Clinton Rossiter, *The American Presidency* (New York: Harcourt Brace Jovanovich, 1960), p. 257.
23. Arthur M. Schlesinger, Jr., "The Limits and Excesses of Presidential Power," *Saturday Review*, May 3, 1969, pp. 18–19.
24. Goodman, *Give 'em Hell, Harry!* p. 111.
25. Philip Norton, *The British Polity*, (New York and London: Longman, 1984), p. 294.
26. See Article 16 of the French Constitution of 1958.

BUREAUCRACY

I n the United States the government is responsible for the administration of social welfare, the armed forces, foreign policy, postal service, and space exploration and for the regulation of agriculture, commerce, transportation, communications—just to name some of the more important and highly visible functions. In many other Western democracies government goes beyond regulation in owning and operating extensive public housing projects, radio and television communications, railroads, airlines, utilities, and full health and medical insurance programs. The organizational system through which government carries out its various administrative responsibilities is known as the bureaucracy. More formally, a **bureaucracy** is any administrative system that implements policy pursuant to law, that follows standardized procedures, and that assigns specialized duties to its employees.

Most of us encounter very few bureaucrats as we go about our daily lives, yet hardly any aspect of our lives escapes a bureaucratic touch: the interstate highways we travel on, the prescription drugs we take, the grade of meat we buy, and the federal loan that puts us through college. Perhaps because bureaucrats are so "faceless" we tend to vent our aggravations about government in general on the bureaucracy more than any other institution of government. Liberals and conservatives; Democrats, Republicans, and independents all eagerly join the ranks of bureaucratic critics. After we examine various aspects of America's federal bureaucracy we will consider what some of these complaints are: Is the bureaucracy too large and powerful? Is it partial in whom it serves? Are bureaucrats typically incompetent and unfeeling? As we will see, such problems exist also in other countries.

★ THE FEDERAL BUREAUCRACY IN AMERICA

BUREAUCRATIC ORGANIZATION

When our nation started out, President Washington found he could make do with 9 bureaucratic units and about 1,000 employees. Today the federal bureaucracy employs more than 3 million nonmilitary personnel (around the total number of Americans during Washington's presidency): 15,000 in the judicial branch, 40,000 in the legislative branch, and all the rest in the executive branch.[1] They are organized into more than 1,000 major units and subunits.

As Figure 11.1 shows, the president is at the apex of the federal bureaucracy. Under the president is the Executive Office of the President (EOP). As we saw in Chapter 10, the EOP includes such organizations as the White House Office, the Office of Management and Budget, the National Security Council, and the Council of Economic Advisers. These agencies are primarily concerned with gathering information and advising the president. The makeup of these agencies as well as their tasks can vary from president to president. When President Bill Clinton took office, he reshaped the EOP to suit his needs and purposes. The other parts of the bureaucracy, which generally remain the same from one president to another, are charged with carrying out executive policy and congressional statutes and providing service.

Fourteen executive departments make up a second major element of the bureaucracy. Each is headed by a Cabinet secretary who is nominated by the president and subject to senatorial confirmation. Typically, each secretary has an undersecretary and several assistant secretaries, all of whom serve at the president's pleasure. Beneath them are the directors of bureaus and other offices within the department. Figure 11.2 shows how a typical Cabinet department is organized.

The third and fourth major elements of the bureaucracy appear in Figure 11.1 under the heading of "Administrative Agencies, Independent Establishments, and Government Corporations." Those elements are the administrative or service agencies—such as the Small Business Administration, the National Aeronautics and Space Administration (NASA), and the General Services Administration—and the independent regulatory agencies and government corporations. The directors of administrative or service agencies are nominated by the president, subject to senatorial confirmation. They report to the president, who can also remove them at any time.

By contrast, the commissioners or board members of the independent regulatory agencies and government corporations, although nominated by the president and con-

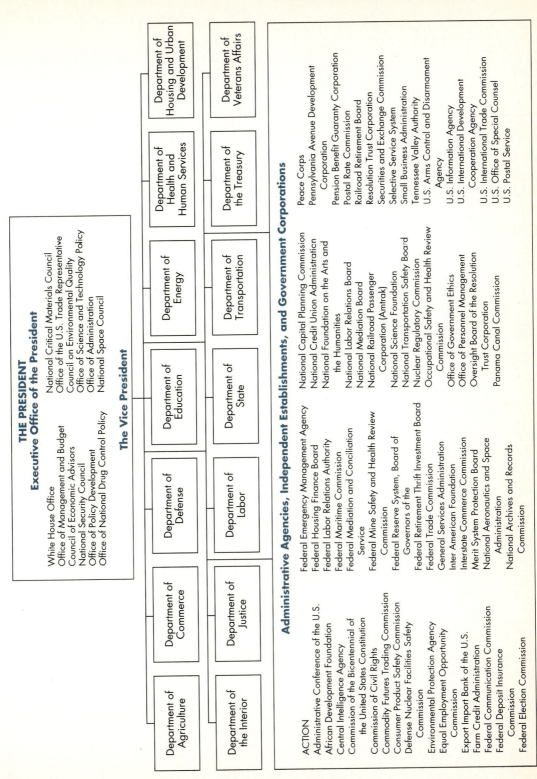

THE PRESIDENT
Executive Office of the President

White House Office
Office of Management and Budget
Council of Economic Advisors
National Security Council
Office of Policy Development
Office of National Drug Control Policy

National Critical Materials Council
Office of the U.S. Trade Representative
Council on Environmental Quality
Office of Science and Technology Policy
Office of Administration
National Space Council

The Vice President

Department of Agriculture

Department of Commerce

Department of Defense

Department of Education

Department of Energy

Department of Health and Human Services

Department of Housing and Urban Development

Department of the Interior

Department of Justice

Department of Labor

Department of State

Department of Transportation

Department of the Treasury

Department of Veterans Affairs

Administrative Agencies, Independent Establishments, and Government Corporations

ACTION
Administrative Conference of the U.S.
African Development Foundation
Central Intelligence Agency
Commission of the Bicentennial of the United States Constitution
Commission of Civil Rights
Commodity Futures Trading Commission
Consumer Product Safety Commission
Defense Nuclear Facilities Safety Commission
Environmental Protection Agency
Equal Employment Opportunity Commission
Export Import Bank of the U.S.
Farm Credit Administration
Federal Communication Commission
Federal Deposit Insurance Commission
Federal Election Commission

Federal Emergency Management Agency
Federal Housing Finance Board
Federal Labor Relations Authority
Federal Maritime Commission
Federal Mediation and Conciliation Service
Federal Mine Safety and Health Review Commission
Federal Reserve System, Board of Governors of the
Federal Retirement Thrift Investment Board
Federal Trade Commission
General Services Administration
Inter American Foundation
Interstate Commerce Commission
Merit System Protection Board
National Aeronautics and Space Administration
National Archives and Records Commission

National Capital Planning Commission
National Credit Union Administration
National Foundation on the Arts and the Humanities
National Labor Relations Board
National Mediation Board
National Railroad Passenger Corporation (Amtrak)
National Science Foundation
National Transportation Safety Board
Nuclear Regulatory Commission
Occupational Safety and Health Review Commission
Office of Government Ethics
Office of Personnel Management
Oversight Board of the Resolution Trust Corporation
Panama Canal Commission

Peace Corps
Pennsylvania Avenue Development Corporation
Pension Benefit Guaranty Corporation
Postal Rate Commission
Railroad Retirement Board
Resolution Trust Corporation
Securities and Exchange Commission
Selective Service System
Small Business Administration
Tennessee Valley Authority
U.S. Arms Control and Disarmament Agency
U.S. Information Agency
U.S. International Development Cooperation Agency
U.S. International Trade Commission
U.S. Office of Special Counsel
U.S. Postal Service

Figure 11.1   ORGANIZATION OF THE FEDERAL BUREAUCRACY. Source: *U.S. Government Manual,* 1991, p. 21.

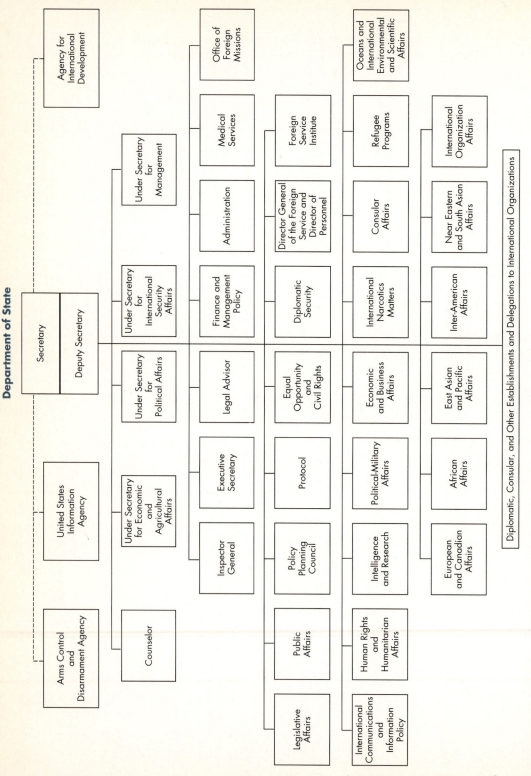

Figure 11.2 ORGANIZATION OF A CABINET DEPARTMENT. *Source: U.S. Government Manual, 1991, p. 426.*

firmed by the Senate, are not responsible to the chief executive for their decisions, and the president cannot remove them from office, except for cause as specified by Congress. The regulatory agencies have broad powers to regulate certain areas of the economy, such as trade (Federal Trade Commission), securities (Securities and Exchange Commission), and labor relations (National Labor Relations Board). Although their agendas are supposed to be independent of both the chief executive and the social and economic interests they regulate, sometimes these agencies are "captured" by one or the other or both. The government corporations run various functions much as a private business would; the U.S. Postal Service and the Federal Deposit Insurance Corporation are examples of government corporations.

Increasingly in recent years, many government agencies have contracted out work to private institutions like the RAND Corporation, a "think tank." Although not formally and officially a part of the bureaucracy, such institutions are certainly adjuncts, providing it with assistance and depending on it for their survival.

Although the president and his subordinates are able to make political appoint-

---

A VIEW FROM THE STATES
The Consequences of Contracting Out Federal Work

As developed over the past decade, the practice of contracting out federal government responsibilities to private firms was seen as a way to trim bureaucratic waste and inefficiency. As it turns outs, the practice has bred its own kinds of waste and fraud.

A White House report, prepared for the Office of Management and Budget, details widespread misuse of public monies by companies hired to carry out such government business as environmental cleanup. Lavish entertainment expenses and unreasonably high salaries are among the abuses listed. The loss to the government is in the billions of dollars. Investigators put much of the blame on the shortage of government auditors to monitor contracts and spot illegal use of funds.

That's part of the problem, but the implication that a larger corps of inspec-

tors general would solve everything is flimsy.

It would take a huge army of auditors to keep an adequate eye on all the contracts signed under current procedures.

Some experts who have studied the problem underscore the extreme complexity of government contracts and the preponderance of experience and know-how on the private-sector side of the dealings. The mountains of paperwork invite deception and fraud, they argue.

The overall solution? Design a system of letting federal contracts that makes it clearer what is expected of a contractor. Spell out how the firm's performance will be assessed, so that unmistakable signals of government watchfulness are given at the beginning of the process. And do a better job of training government employees who negotiate the contracts.

Source: "Private/Public Waste," *Christian Science Monitor* (editorial), December 8, 1992, p. 20. Reprinted by permission from *The Christian Science Monitor.* © 1992 The Christian Science Publishing Society. All rights reserved.

ments for more than 5,000 high-level positions in the bureaucracy, most federal employees are hired under the **civil service** system. This system requires that candidates for jobs be chosen on the basis of ability, not political allegiance. Within the civil service, positions are classified according to the type of work performed. Under the General Schedule (GS) rating, for example, a job might be classified as GS-5 or GS-14. Persons with the same rating do essentially the same type of work and get the same pay. The benefits of the civil service system are that it simplifies the recruitment and selection of personnel, provides equal pay for equal work, institutes agreed-on lines of authority and responsibility among employees, allows clear avenues of promotion and transfer, and treats all cases alike that have similar circumstances. There are some disadvantages, too: For example, the system makes it difficult to fire incompetent civil servants.

BUREAUCRATIC FUNCTIONS

Federal government departments and agencies perform a variety of functions that might be categorized under the headings of administration, legislation, adjudication, and enforcement. Each of these functions derives from Article II of the Constitution, which states that the president "shall take care that the laws be faithfully executed."

In its *administrative* function, the bureaucracy carries out laws. Thus, when the Civil Rights Act of 1964 and the Voting Rights Act of 1965 became law, the Department of Justice had the primary responsibility for implementing them. Almost every law passed by Congress requires some part of the bureaucracy to implement it.

In the area of *legislation*, the bureaucracy performs two tasks. It recommends legislative proposals to the president, which are customarily filtered through the Office of Management and Budget. The second legislative function is to implement statutory law through administrative law. Bills passed by Congress are called **statutory law**; they are usually general in nature. Spelling out more specific rules, guidelines, and regulations is the job of **administrative law**.

How is administrative law created? A common method occurs when an agency is asked to provide more detail about the provisions of a given law. For example, the Federal Election Commission (FEC) was established to develop rules and regulations for a new federal election law. It has been asked to interpret election law on such questions as (1) Will funds donated for purchase of a van for constituent services be considered political campaign contributions? (2) Can expenses incurred in taking constituents to dinner or lunch in Washington be considered part of a senator's position or must they be considered political expenses? The FEC's application of statutory law to each of these questions becomes administrative law. The decisions made by the Federal Election Commission on these (and other) matters form just one part of a huge body of administrative law. These laws are, of course, a principal source of bureaucratic power. Each year thousands of administrative laws are compiled in the Federal Register, a publication several inches thick. During his term President George Bush designated Vice President Dan Quayle to streamline the complicated administrative lawmaking process so that it would be more responsive to the public interest, as perceived by the president. Bush had performed a similar function as vice president under President Ronald Reagan.

Adjudication comes about when a department or agency resolves conflict between parties. For example, the National Labor Relations Board issues decisions on disputes between labor and management. In a dispute between a consumer group and a manufacturer, the Federal Trade Commission may rule whether a television commercial advertises a product honestly.

Enforcement is an important task, especially for the Justice Department. In enforcing federal criminal law, the department maintains a large staff to investigate and prosecute violators. Other departments also have enforcement powers. For example, the Bureau of Customs of the Treasury Department enforces laws against importing drugs and other illegal goods.

With its complex organization and numerous functions, the bureaucracy obviously has substantial power. Some people feel it acts as a "fourth branch" of government. Discussions often center around whether its exercise of power is an asset or a liability to American democracy. Several recent presidents have tried to control and/or to reduce the bureaucracy's size, and Congress has been particularly concerned about *administrative discretion*, the latitude or leeway Congress gives the bureaucracy to make policy decisions consistent with the spirit of its mission. Congress has neither the time nor the specialized knowledge to spell out precise policies in all areas. But the more vaguely Congress defines an agency's mission, the more administrative discretion the agency has, thereby creating greater potential for conflict with the legislative branch. For example, Congress frequently criticizes the Food and Drug Administration for moving either too slowly or too quickly to suit congressional wishes in approving new medications.

BUREAUCRATIC CONTROLS

The bureaucracy has two main sources of power: administrative law and control of information. The vast body of administrative law, establishing the rules and regulations for carrying out statutes, allows bureaucrats (who really prefer to be called civil servants) to shape policy according to their own goals and expectations (and sometimes according to the wishes of the special interests that bureaucracy caters to). Control of information is another important weapon. Max Weber, perhaps the foremost student of bureaucracy, held that the first line of defense for any bureaucracy is the ability to withhold information.[2] Private citizens may request release of information through the Freedom of Information Act, but the release may be delayed or, if it is classified as secret, denied. Information can also take the form of propaganda. Large public information budgets are common throughout the bureaucracy. Some of the larger departments like Defense spend millions of dollars each year on public information.

Sometimes it seems that the bureaucracy is impossible to tame. One critic in state government described the fight to reduce and control the bureaucracy as follows: "Can you imagine trying to fight a revolution against a huge, righteous marshmallow? Even if you had enough troops not to be suffocated by it, the best you can hope for is to eat it. And, as you all know, you become what you eat."[3] Fortunately, there are some institutional controls to rein in bureaucracy.

Congressional Controls

The chief job of the bureaucracy is to interpret, implement, and enforce acts of Congress. Whenever it fails to do so properly, Congress has numerous remedies. It may amend the law to make its intent clearer. It may call on the courts to require the bureaucracy to implement a law properly or to enjoin it from interpreting a law contrary to congressional intent. Congress may conduct a public investigation of the bureaucracy; this method is especially useful to focus public attention on a specific issue.

Congress has also used the **legislative veto** of federal regulations to change policy made by the bureaucracy. Members of Congress frequently contend that in making administrative law the bureaucracy violates congressional intent and Congress has the right to "veto" the regulation. Federal courts have ruled that a legislative veto of executive-branch decisions is unconstitutional because it violates the doctrine of separation of powers,[4] but since Congress persists in using it, the stage has been set for another Supreme Court case on whether the legislative veto is a violation of that doctrine.

Federal employees, well aware of their dependence on Congress for funds, are not likely to abuse their power if Congress asserts itself. Congress may ask the General Accounting Office (GAO) to conduct a special investigation to determine whether an agency is functioning properly. The GAO's principal technique is the audit of expenditures, but it may also investigate the effectiveness of other ways of achieving the same bureaucratic goals.

In the Administrative Procedures Act of 1946, Congress has specified several procedures that the bureaucracy must follow. Government agencies must make public their administrative organizations. They must provide interested persons with advance information on proposed rules, allow them to present information and arguments on pending cases, and allow their counsel to cross-examine witnesses.

Presidential Controls

Through the Office of Management and Budget (OMB), the president can review the budget and administrative operation of each agency and make appropriate recommendations to Congress. The OMB, together with the president's annual budgetary recommendations, can restrain the bureaucracy. Budgetary authority was one of President Bush's principal tools to gain control over the bureaucracy.

The president's influence on public opinion and ability to create new agencies provide further opportunities to control the bureaucracy. To avoid having his programs lost in the bowels of the bureaucracy, Franklin Roosevelt created many new agencies outside the structure of existing departments and agencies. In fact, most of the New Deal's so-called alphabet agencies were established in this way. They included the Works Progress Administration (WPA), the Public Works Administration (PWA), and the Civilian Conservation Corps (CCC).

Court Checks

Citizens who believe they have been wronged by bureaucratic action have judicial recourse. A private citizen may seek an injunction against a bureaucratic agency to stop a particular action or to seek enforcement of a law not being enforced. The United States Court of Claims and the United States Tax Court are examples of special courts designed to adjudicate citizen complaints against bureaucratic decisions. A citizen with an income tax complaint, for instance, can take the case to the Tax Court.

The bureaucracy is hardly an island unto itself. It is a part of a whole political process with numerous and diverse relationships with competing private groups and other government agencies and departments.

BUREAUCRATIC REFORMS

Another way to control the bureaucracy is to reform its worst defects. Perhaps the most drastic change was made in 1883 when the civil service was introduced. Up until then government employees were hired and fired at will by elected public officials under the **patronage system**. The assassination of President James A. Garfield by a distraught and disappointed, perhaps mentally ill, seeker of a patronage job prompted a reform of the system. After 1883 the bulk of government employees (the civil service) were to be hired on the basis of a **merit system**—that is, based on ability—and protected from arbitrary firing. Republicans, then in control of both the presidency and the Congress, also saw civil service as a way of preventing the wholesale turnover of federal government employees that would follow a partisan shift in control of the White House.

One of the highly praised achievements of President Jimmy Carter's administration in the late 1970s was civil service reform. An Office of Personnel Management now manages the vast civil service bureaucracy, and the Merit Systems Protection Board

An artist's conception of the assassination of President James A. Garfield by a disappointed seeker of a patronage job in the Garfield administration. This event in 1883 led to civil service reform: Government employees were to be hired strictly according to a merit system.

protects employees from unfair dismissal or transfer. This reform measure also specifies procedures for investigating and punishing prohibited personnel practices and makes it easier to fire incompetent employees. Finally, the new civil service reform created a Senior Executive Service of 8,000 individuals who previously would have stayed in the same department or agency throughout their careers. Now they can be transferred from one department or agency to another, according to where the government needs their management skills. Bonuses and other incentives are calculated to improve the performance of this group. Under this system the best bureaucrats can use their creativity to solve new problems instead of stagnating in one position.

Any organization as large as the federal bureaucracy can be improved. To its credit, the bureaucracy itself has experimented with a variety of new organizational techniques. One is **program budgeting**, commonly called PPBS (Planning, Programming, Budgeting System). Under this plan, agencies must put a price tag on what they are trying to accomplish before they request new programs and appropriations. Continued experimentation with interdepartmental committees and coordinating bodies may also improve bureaucratic efficiency.

Both specific and general reforms have been proposed for federal and state bureaucracies:

1. *Sunset laws.* First conceived in Colorado, **sunset laws** provide for the automatic abolition of every governmental agency after a prescribed time period unless good reasons justify continuing it. This dramatic reform, supported by both conservatives and liberals, fights bureaucratic obesity through automatic termination. It shifts the proof of an agency's value to the agency itself and encourages the legislature to perform its oversight function better by requiring legislative hearings on the continuation of agencies (with the public having a voice in determining whether an agency should live or die).

2. *Zero-based budgeting.* Traditionally, every governmental agency has assumed that the funds received the previous year will be provided for the next year. The agency's task, then, has been not to justify the past year's budget but to justify an increase. **Zero-based budgeting** would force an agency to justify the previous year's budget before seeking an *increase*. That is, its budget for the coming year is assumed to be zero until the agency's rationale for its expenditures convinces Congress to appropriate more funds.

3. *Party leadership.* V. O. Key, Jr., once said that "it is through . . . persons who owe their posts to the victorious party that popular control over government is maintained." Key places the burden of controlling the bureaucracy on the party that elects the president who is supposed to administer the government. If parties placed more emphasis on recruiting outstanding administrative talent rather than outstanding political talent, the party process could improve relationships between bureaucracy and democracy.[5]

4. *Ombudsman.* To make the bureaucracy more responsive to average citizens'

needs, organizations have begun establishing the office of **ombudsman** (from the Swedish word for commissioner). This office investigates citizen complaints against government, giving people an alternative to accepting (as most often happens) the decision of a faceless bureaucrat. Members of Congress already perform the role of ombudsman for their constituents in a major way.

5. *Public confrontation.* Several federal regulatory agencies now provide funds to financially disadvantaged groups that would not otherwise be able to participate in the making of federal regulations. Congress has been considering the extension of this program to allow greater citizen participation in influencing bureaucratic rules and regulations.

6. *Improving presidential control.* The regulatory agencies exist in a kind of "no-man's-land" as quasi-judicial and quasi-executive bodies. If they were under the president's direct control, the public would have an opportunity to disapprove of their actions at the polls by holding the president accountable. As it is, the president cannot remove the commissioners on these bodies. They are in a highly independent position, aloof from control by the political process.

7. *Burden of proof.* Another proposal would shift the burden of proof in citizen suits against bureaucratic regulations from the citizen to the bureaucracy. At present, courts presume bureaucratic regulations to be valid, and citizens must take on the challenge of proving them invalid.

8. *Cost-benefit analysis.* Which alternative regulations under consideration would make the most economic sense? This question is now being raised as another reform that would require cost-benefit analyses of alternative regulations before one is implemented. For example, a proposed regulation that had fewer benefits but much less cost might be chosen over one with more benefits and greater cost. The costs considered include both bureaucratic costs to implement and enforce the regulation and the costs to business and others to abide by the regulation.

9. *Presidential involvement.* Some reformers believe that the White House should review all regulations before implementation to determine whether they conform with the president's wishes. Public participation in the regulatory process would increase because the public could lobby the White House.

While there is not universal agreement on what reforms to implement or how far to carry them, there is widespread agreement that bureaucracy does not work properly at this time. Like several previous presidents, President Bill Clinton named a commission to devise reforms of the bureaucracy. Vice President Al Gore heads more than 100 managers and experts from throughout the federal government in this task. Called a National Performance Review, their plan proposes ways to eliminate unnecessary layers of management and to improve services. We will now turn to consider some of the more current issues surrounding this "imperfect" bureaucracy.

? ISSUES TO ANALYZE

ISSUE 1   *IS THE BUREAUCRACY TOO LARGE AND TOO POWERFUL?*

REASONS WHY BUREAUCRACY IS TOO LARGE AND TOO POWERFUL

The growth of the federal bureaucracy has been phenomenal. The number of civilians employed by the federal government has increased more than sevenfold since the early twentieth century. This staggering growth requires an increasingly large share of the tax dollar to support salaries, equipment, buildings, retirement funds, and other expenses.

The presidential Grace Commission, which was asked to study cost control in the bureaucracy, found that costs in government greatly exceeded comparable costs in the public sector. For example:

- Civil service and military retirees collect 3 and 6 times, respectively, the total lifetime pension benefits of their counterparts in the private sector.

- The General Services Administration employs 17 times more people and spends almost 14 times more money to manage its facilities than does a private firm with comparable responsibilities.

- After 6 years at a job, a federal blue-collar worker earns 12 percent more than the average private sector employee for similar work.

- The cost of health-care benefits for federal employees is $450 million greater than for a comparable group of private sector employees.

- Postal workers receive an average of 28 percent higher wages than their private-sector counterparts.[6]

Understanding *why* bureaucracy grows and spends in a seemingly unstoppable fashion is important. One theory of employment growth comes from C. Northcote Parkinson, most noted for his development of "Parkinson's Law," which holds that work expands to fill the amount of time available. In another vein, Parkinson argues that because agencies do not have rigid boundary lines, bureaucracy is able to expand continually. Bureaucracies tend to be self-perpetuating and self-protecting; they expand in order to perpetuate and protect. Employees will make work to justify their existence; as they make work, more employees are needed to handle the work they have created.[7]

A modification of Parkinson's Law, devised by Norman John Powell, holds that bureaucratic growth necessitates more personnel to help manage the employees.[8] For example, the Executive Office of the President was created in the late 1930s to help the president manage the bureaucracy. Since then, it too has expanded, creating management problems that, ironically, it was supposed to solve. In effect, the bureaucracy expands in a never-ending spiral. Each executive needs subordinates. Subordinates need work to justify their existence. With more work, more employees are hired.

Budgetary growth, obviously affected by employment growth, involves two important principles. The first is that bureaucrats must compete with rival agencies for funds. The second is that each unit wants an increase over the previous year's budget (the strategy of **incrementalism**). To compete effectively, departments and agencies may propose new programs that require new personnel and a larger budget. Even if no new programs are proposed, however, bureaucratic units still want more money every year. One popular strategy is to ask for more than what is needed in order to be sure of obtaining the amount actually desired. After all, if a budget proposal must pass through three channels—for example, an executive department, the White House, and Congress—it makes sense to inflate the request to allow for the possibility of three cuts. Bureaucrats expend an inordinate amount of time justifying their expansion rather than their accomplishments. They subtly shift the focus of debate from the past to the future. This ploy makes denial of their requests difficult, because opponents have to argue against prospective plans as well as past performance.

Another important part of an agency's strategy is to spend all available funds in each fiscal year. For example, the General Services Administration has been known to increase its spending in the last several weeks of a fiscal year by as much as 40 percent in order to use up any surplus funds.

As was pointed out earlier, a major contention of Presidents Ronald Reagan and George Bush was that the most dangerous growth of the federal bureaucracy has been in the issuance of administrative laws. They argued that far too many people are employed by the federal government to just write, review, and enforce some type of regulation and that too much time is required for administrative law judges to make decisions; these judges hear and decide disputes between the government and private citizens on such issues as business licenses and social security claims.

REASONS WHY BUREAUCRACY IS NOT TOO LARGE AND TOO POWERFUL

The common impression is that the federal bureaucracy is like an octopus extending its tentacles everywhere. As shown in Figure 11.3, the principal bureaucratic growth today is in state and local governments, which employ over 82 percent of all government employees. Also, during the decade of the 1980s, the percentage of American workers employed by the federal government as civilians declined from 3.7 to 2.7 percent.[9] In any case, as Table 11.1 reveals, Americans do not disapprove of a larger role for the federal government.

Most government growth has occurred in response to problems. The bureaucracy grows because the American people *ask* government for services, not because bureaucrats demand programs. Think about any government program, even one you dislike, and you will probably find substantial public support for it. That is why we have a Federal Communications Commission, a Food and Drug Administration, a Federal Election Commission, and a Social Security Administration, among many others.

Myths about the Washington bureaucracy are legion. Politicians can count on

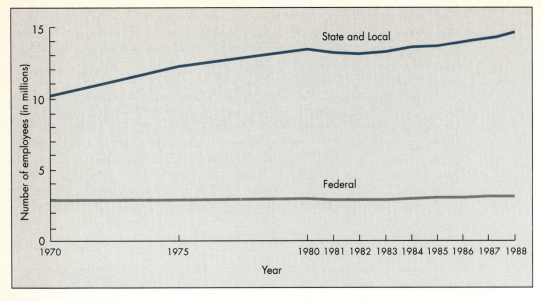

Figure 11.3 GROWTH OF STATE AND LOCAL AND FEDERAL GOVERNMENT EMPLOYMENT, 1970–1988. Source: *U.S. Statistical Abstract,* 1991, p. 305.

applause when they promise that, if elected, they will go to the capital and throw the briefcases of bureaucrats into the Potomac River. In fact, however, the Washington metropolitan area contains only a small proportion of the federal government's civilian employees—about 12 percent. To get rid of bureaucrats' briefcases, politicians would have to travel throughout the United States; in California alone they would find over 250,000 federal bureaucrats. They would also discover that a mere 10 percent of all bureaucrats work for welfare agencies like the Social Security Administration, which are frequently attacked for being bloated. (Federal regulatory agencies, also frequently criticized, employ an even smaller proportion of the federal work force than do the social service agencies.)

This same enlarged bureaucracy that is so often condemned is also responsible for many things that few Americans would want to sacrifice. For example, environmental and energy laws have helped to clean up the environment and conserve energy. Product safety standards have helped to save lives. Federal highway safety standards have made highway travel more safe.

Moreover, bureaucracy does not perform in a vacuum without curbs. Professional ethics; the advice and criticism of experts; and the views of political figures, interest groups, and private citizens restrain bureaucracy. In addition, Congress, the president, and the courts have power to limit the bureaucracy. Whether these institutions actually exercise their rights of control is not the responsibility of the bureaucracy.

ISSUE 1: Summary ★ *Is the Bureaucracy Too Large and Too Powerful?*

Those who answer "yes" point to (1) bureaucracy's penchant for creating more work in order to justify its existence, (2) its inflated budget requests, and (3) the overwhelming

TABLE 11.1 PUBLIC OPINION ON THE ROLE OF THE FEDERAL GOVERNMENT		
	The federal government should be . . .	The federal government should not be . . .
Regulating airline prices and schedules.	38%	55%
Upholding traditional moral values.	53%	41%
Seeing to it that everyone who wants a job has one.	71%	26%
Guaranteeing medical care for all people.	78%	19%
Seeing to it that day care and after-school care for children are available.	62%	35%

Question: I'd like to know what you think the responsibilities of government are. For each of these items, please tell me if you think this is something the government in Washington, D.C., should or should not be doing.
Source: Reported in Gary C. Jacobson, "Meager Patrimony," in Larry Berman, ed., *Looking Back on the Reagan Presidency* (Baltimore: Johns Hopkins University Press, 1990), p. 307. Adapted from *The New York Times*/CBS News poll in November 1987.

number of administrative laws. Supporters of bureaucracy, on the other hand, contend that its growth merely mirrors what is happening to the country as a whole. Bureaucracy acquires more power to resolve the disputes created by the increased complexity of American society. In any case, there are controls in place to restrain overbearing bureaucracy. ■

ISSUE 2   *DOES THE BUREAUCRACY SERVE SOME GROUPS MORE THAN OTHERS?*

REASONS WHY THE BUREAUCRACY SERVES SOME GROUPS MORE THAN OTHERS

A study of senior federal bureaucrats by Stanley Rothman and S. Robert Lichter shows that they are decidedly different from the general public in income, race, sex, education, ideology, religion, and moral values.

- 100 percent have annual family income in excess of $50,000.
- 94 percent are white.
- 93 percent are male.
- 77 percent have postgraduate degrees.

- 56 percent are political liberals compared with only 21 percent of the public.

- 33 percent report no religious affiliation compared with only 10 percent of the public.

- 33 percent believe adultery is wrong compared with 85 percent of the public.[10]

　　If the senior bureaucrats charged with implementing and enforcing our laws are not representative of the public as a whole, tension potentially exists between the public and its bureaucratic servants. Most commonly, this tension arises in the field of social welfare legislation. Here the interests of poor and otherwise deprived Americans, the beneficiaries of such laws, differ from the interests of the middle-class Americans who implement and enforce the laws (and pay a large proportion of the taxes to support their programs). One study concluded that "bureaucratic systems are the key medium through which the middle class maintains its advantaged position vis-à-vis the lower class."[11] In appointing his Cabinet, President Clinton strove for diversity—African-Americans, Hispanics, and women were included—but they all came from the upper middle class, most were lawyers, and several had been highly paid lobbyists.

　　Networking. According to Hugh Heclo, bureaucrats generally recruit fellow employees who think the way they think.[12] He calls the pool from which they draw recruits **issue networks.** These networks are composed of persons inside and outside government who are interested in the same issues. For instance, a bureaucrat in the Federal Communications Commission is likely to employ someone he or she knows in the private sector who is knowledgable about the broadcasting industry. The employing

· THE DIVERSITY CABINET ·

HISPANIC LAWYER　BLACK LAWYER　PRESIDENT LAWYER　WHITE LAWYER　FEMALE LAWYER　BL LA

bureaucrat must send a job vacancy form to the Office of Personnel Management, but sometimes the job is so precisely described that only the person whom the bureaucrat wants to hire meets the qualifications.

The "Iron Triangle." Bureaucratic efficiency and effectiveness are often related to what groups bureaucracy serves. Bureaucrats are not politically neutral. They tend to respond more quickly and favorably to business interests than to those of the poor. For example, the Department of Housing and Urban Development is better attuned to the needs of realtors and contractors than to the situation of the ghetto residents for whom many housing laws were designed. These close relationships with special interests cede portions of public authority to private groups seeking to benefit only themselves. In addition, bureaucratic units fall under the influence of the congressional subcommittees that oversee them. Since these subcommittees also form close ties with special interests within their jurisdiction, the bureaucrats, key members of Congress, and special interest groups coexist in what is known as an **iron triangle** (see also Chapter 7).

The iron triangle enables bureaucracy to defy the public interest. For example, one would like to think that the Department of Agriculture (and every other executive department) serves the public interest. Every American has a legitimate stake in farm production and prices. However, the Department of Agriculture has allowed farming to become neither a public nor a private enterprise, according to Theodore Lowi:

> It is a system of self-government in which each leading farm interest controls a segment of agriculture through a delegation of national sovereignty. Agriculture has emerged as a largely self-governing federal estate within the federal structure of the United States . . . through a line [of power] unbroken by personality or party in the White House.[13]

Agriculture Department decisions have not always been in the public interest. Take the content of meat products like hot dogs or hash: As pointed out by one critic, "Standards are ordinarily based on prevailing industry practices," not on what is best for consumers.[14]

Clientelism. The special relationship between industries and the federal commissions that regulate them—**clientelism**—is prevalent and potentially harmful. Because of it, cases can drag on for years without resolution. A glaring example involved the patent medicine Geritol. A case accusing the maker of misleading advertising was pending for nearly a decade. Through a combination of Federal Trade Commission timidity and the legal and financial resources available to the manufacturer, the company stalled a final decision until it had subtly changed its advertising program (from a claim that Geritol provides strength to one implying that it would keep users young). However, clientelism can best be illustrated through a series of pointed questions: Why have large numbers of high-ranking employees in the Food and Drug Administration come from regulated industries, and why do so many of them return to regulated industries? Why have substantial numbers of the top energy officials in the government previously worked for private companies holding government contracts, licenses, or permits?

Whistle-blowers, those who try to reveal an impropriety between a government agency and its client groups, often receive adverse treatment from their superiors and peers. When a Pentagon auditor accused a major defense contractor of padding labor costs by $150 million and questioned a $1 million bill for entertainment expenses, the De-

Ernest Fitzgerald, a civilian cost expert at the Pentagon, blew the whistle on soaring defense contractor costs in 1969. His position as deputy for management systems was subsequently eliminated.

partment of Defense had him criminally investigated, tried not to respond to his professional audit, lowered his job performance ratings, attempted to transfer him, and sought to persuade him to retire. Only intervention by the FBI and the press protected the auditor.[15] In still another case, a veterinarian in the U.S. Department of Agriculture who persisted in revealing inadequate USDA meat inspections was reprimanded twice, transferred to another part of the country, and given a job unrelated to his training.[16] These examples and questions lead to the conclusion that public government has become private government and that the public interest has become secondary to private interests.

REASONS WHY BUREAUCRACY DOES NOT SERVE SOME GROUPS MORE THAN OTHERS

Critics espouse the theory that an iron triangle exists among the bureaucracy, interest groups, and Congress. However, not all interest groups have the same concerns in the same department. For example, the Farmers' Union and the American Farm Bureau Federation have distinctly different interests in the affairs of the Department of Agriculture. The former is concerned with the small farmer and the latter with larger farm enterprises. Moreover, not all members of a congressional committee share the same interests in the department or agency overseen by the committee. To illustrate, liberal Democrats and conservative Republicans on the House and Senate Armed Services Committees differ in their views on the defense budget, even though the Cold War is apparently over. Liberal Democrats are more likely to support cuts and conservative Republicans, increases.

Critics also argue that interest groups shuffle top personnel into and out of the bureaucracy to serve their interests. Certainly this occurs, but why not? Should the bureaucracy be denied the right to employ the best-trained personnel available? Should bureaucrats be denied the freedom to earn a livelihood in the private sector that they previously helped to regulate? To answer "yes" to these questions is to acknowledge that one does not want (1) bureaucracy to benefit from the enormous expertise of such groups, (2) bureaucrats to have the right to obtain the best possible positions for themselves, or (3) the private sector to have the right to hire the best applicants.

Bureaucrats are not unrepresentative of the public, nor are they unrestrained advocates of special interests. As V. O. Key, Jr., points out, bureaucrats are sometimes the *only* participants in the policymaking process who are devoted to the public interest.[17] Contrary to what many Americans believe, bureaucrats are not of any one political or ideological persuasion. Indeed, according to Hugh Heclo, "Taken as a whole the U.S. federal bureaucracy appears open and broadly representative of the American population in education, income, and social status (as indicated by father's occupation)."[18]

Even if bureaucracy favors some groups, this is not necessarily harmful to American democracy. As groups struggle to have their interests represented, not all of them can dominate bureaucratic policymaking all of the time. In some instances, about the only place where some groups disadvantaged elsewhere can gain a hearing is before the bureaucracy. In such cases the bureaucracy becomes a definite asset to democracy.

ISSUE 2:   Summary   ★   *Does the Bureaucracy Serve Some Groups More than Others?*

Those who argue that bureaucracy serves some groups more than others point to the middle-class bias of bureaucrats, to the tendency of bureaucracy to hire like-minded people, and to the special relationships bureaucrats form with interest groups and key members of Congress that help support business interests. But others point out that the competition among interest groups helps to even out the balance of power. Moreover, while bureaucracy responds in part to the interest group struggle (as it should), it may also articulate a public interest that is distinct from the interest group struggle. ■

ISSUE 3   ARE BUREAUCRATS TYPICALLY INCOMPETENT AND SLOW TO ACT?

REASONS WHY BUREAUCRATS ARE TYPICALLY INCOMPETENT AND SLOW TO ACT

Even if the bureaucracy were not so involved with special interests, it would have difficulty accomplishing a great deal. Inherent defects render it weak and sometimes harmful. Among the most significant faults are inertia and downright incompetence.

Bureaucratic Inertia. The bureaucracy's lack of response is seen most clearly in the relationship between it and the presidency. Of the 3 million civilian federal employees, the president directly appoints only about 850, who in turn make a few thousand appointments. The executive branch employs 3,072,000 nonmilitary personnel.* The president *directly* appoints

- About 200 members of the White House staff
- 14 Cabinet heads
- 400 to 500 members of the sub-Cabinet
- About 150 ambassadors (subject to Senate confirmation)

Agency and Department heads appoint

- 600 to 800 members of the Senior Executive Service
- About 1,800 special aides exempted from civil service regulations

In all, the president and subordinates directly appoint about 5,200 people. But the vast majority of executive branch officials are career civil servants. The relatively few policy-making appointments the president makes do not provide the necessary leverage to ensure that the bureaucracy responds to the national interest. A presidential directive may take two or three years to be translated into agency guidelines and reach the action level.

One reason for this delay is that a new presidential policy threatens the way the bureaucracy has been doing things. President Lyndon Johnson wanted his poverty programs administered primarily by a new agency (the Office of Economic Opportunity) in the Executive Office of the President partly because he feared what existing bureaucratic organizations in the executive departments might do to them. The Department of Labor, for example, had its own programs and policies, and the new poverty programs would have threatened the status quo.

The bureaucracy has a built-in asset in resisting or subverting presidential (and congressional) initiatives: its continuing identity. The bureaucracy was there before and will be there after the president; it has only to wait. Moreover, the president, encumbered with many interests and problems, cannot focus completely on persuading foot-dragging bureaucrats to cooperate. Should the president's interest wane, no one prods the bureaucracy. The department secretaries and other political appointees usually do not have a lifetime career commitment. Their attempts to make major changes or to control the bureaucracy more effectively might well result in a battle that bureaucrats would win by virtue of their longevity in office. Considering that presidents are limited to eight years to accomplish their objectives and that a bureaucracy has until eternity to resist them, it is remarkable that presidential authority has any meaning at all.

The political scientist Richard Nathan in *The Plot That Failed* shows the difficulty a conservative Republican president has in trying to get a liberal Democratic bureaucracy to follow his policy leadership.[20] The plot that burned up in the ashes of Watergate had

---

* This information and the lists below are from *The Christian Science Monitor*, February 1, 1993, p. 3. Data from *Statistical Abstracts of the United States, 1991*; Congressional Quarterly's Guide to the Presidency; Office of Personnel Management. Reprinted by permission from The Christian Science Monitor. © 1993 The Christian Science Publishing Society. All rights reserved.

President Nixon placing key loyalists, including former White House staffers, lower in the bureaucracy to exert greater pressure. Nixon discovered that the bureaucracy can subvert presidential policy if administrative direction comes only from the top. He needed his loyalists closer to where policy was executed. Policy direction and policy execution must be closely connected if the direction is not to be subverted in the execution. Presidents Reagan and Bush also followed the plot that Nathan outlined in an attempt to gain control over the bureaucracy.

Bureaucratic Bungling. Why is the level of competence so low in the bureaucracy? Laurence J. Peter and Raymond Hull would see it as an application of what they call the Peter Principle—the theory that "in a hierarchy, every employee tends to rise to his level of incompetence." Peter and Hull hold that there are two main reasons for promoting and one for retaining employees in a bureaucracy. Promotion gets rid of people by "kicking them upstairs" or advances them because of merit; in the latter case, a person ultimately reaches a position that he or she cannot handle. Rigid (and, to appearances, unreasonable) civil service regulations that protect employees tend to retain incompetents, since getting rid of anyone is not worth the effort. Clearly, if these conditions apply, every position will sooner or later be occupied by an incompetent.[21]

Incompetence also results from the personality type that bureaucracy tends to foster. Since bureaucratic organizations have long life spans, the institution takes on more importance than the individual. In this context, the successful bureaucrat is the person who fits into the agency's expected mold of behavior, neither too far to the left nor too far to the right, with no desire for personal publicity—in short, a person in tune with the aim of perpetuating the agency. One critic outlined five rules of behavior that successful bureaucrats follow: (1) maintain your tenure, (2) keep the boss from getting embarrassed, (3) make sure that all appropriated funds are spent by the end of the fiscal year, (4) keep the program alive, and (5) maintain a stable and well-circumscribed constituency.[22]

For the bureaucrat who adheres to these rules, the priorities are not individualism and the opportunity for personal creativity (which may be threatening), but protection of one's job and prospects for advancement. The result of this process throughout the bureaucracy can be massive depersonalization ("facelessness") and mediocrity. Peter Drucker has noted that bureaucrats have no incentives to achieve excellence:

> The best we get from government in the welfare state is competent mediocrity. More often we do not get even that: we get incompetence such as we would not tolerate in an insurance company. . . . And the more we expand the welfare state, the less capable even of routine mediocrity does it seem to become.[23]

REASONS WHY BUREAUCRATS ARE NOT TYPICALLY INCOMPETENT AND SLOW TO ACT

Bureaucrats, much maligned today by both public and private citizens, are human beings like the rest of us. Understanding why they resist change and knowing something about the special pressures under which they operate will put their accomplishments in perspective.

Understanding Resistance to Change. Bureaucrats may seem to resist change and reform because of the natural human tendency to concentrate energy on activities that may garner praise and promotion. Bureaucrats understand that to change a program, even to improve it, is to change the status quo, introducing risk. Risks threaten not only oneself, but also one's superiors, subordinates, and peers.

Like most people, bureaucrats do not want others to control them. They may oppose reform proposals (and other types of proposals as well) because of the possibility of an agency's becoming controlled by another organization. One reform proposal would, for example, move the Federal Trade Commission (FTC), now an independent regulatory agency, to the Department of Justice. The change has been proposed because the FTC has allegedly become the captive of regulated interests and thus insensitive to the public interest. Under the Attorney General in the Department of Justice, the FTC would be in a clear line of accountability to the president, who could more effectively respond to public concerns about this agency.

Special Pressures. The federal bureaucracy, unlike private business, functions under public scrutiny. Its actions are subject to analysis and criticism by journalists, scholars, and politicians. This scrutiny is political as well as public, and the bureaucracy is subject to the vicissitudes of political fortune. The same bureaucratic decision may be praised at one time and later condemned. This uncertain bureaucratic environment is illustrated by the Federal Bureau of Investigation. For most of the FBI's history, the public viewed the bureau as the epitome of efficiency. Who dared criticize it? But as public attitudes toward the role of intelligence agencies became more critical after Watergate, the FBI's position diminished accordingly. Evidence suggests that the FBI was the same agency making the same kind of decisions, with but one difference—the political environment had changed.

Not only do bureaucrats function in a very open and intensely political environment, they also must make decisions on the most controversial of issues and problems.

As a result of public pressure and the conflicting demands of interest groups, Congress tends to place prickly problems in the hands of the bureaucracy. But doing so does not make the problems and pressures disappear. For example, Congress's replacement of the United States Post Office Department with the United States Postal Corporation did not reduce the problems of the postal service; authority for solving them was simply transferred from an executive department to a public corporation.

Whatever decision a bureaucrat makes is bound to meet with adverse criticism from those whom it does not favor. Attacks on bureaucracy are one way the public has of "letting off steam," according to Peter Blau:

> Frustrated clients can relieve their pent-up aggression in discussions of bureaucratic stupidity and red tape. Whereas the organization's ruthlessness, not its inefficiency, is the source of their antagonism, by expressing it in the form of an apparently disinterested criticism of performance, clients derive a feeling of superiority over the "blundering bureaucrats" that serves as psychological compensation for being under their power.[24]

Politicians can run for reelection to seek vindication for their decisions. What can bureaucrats do? They have no place to appeal for protection from the public's natural inclination to criticize.

Bureaucracy's Accomplishments. People often complain that only bad news makes news. To a considerable extent, this is true of bureaucracy. We hear about its failures and shortcomings, but pay less attention to the many government programs that are run efficiently and in the public interest. Take the case of the Social Security Administration. In 1935, less than 15 percent of the jobs in the United States were covered by any retirement system. Today about 95 percent of all Americans are eligible for social security benefits at age 65, and for disability insurance at any age. Without social security, the incomes of 60 percent of all couples over age 65 would be below the poverty line as defined by the federal government. This same agency also enrolled 19 million people in Medicare and set up the organizational procedures to pay their medical bills in all 50 states in less than a year's time. For another example, year after year, the Bureau of the Census provides detailed and reliable data on almost every facet of American society. And the National Bureau of Standards and the National Institutes of Health are highly regarded for their contributions to the quality of American life.

Admittedly, some bureaucratic programs fail or are abused, but the proportion is not large. Putting the issue another way, we might ask ourselves just which governmental programs we would like to abolish. The answer is probably very few. Americans actually think rather highly of the work of bureaucrats. Four psychologists who carried out a study of a range of government services found that the percentage of people who are satisfied with bureaucracy far exceeds those who are dissatisfied. Their report concludes:

> Bureaucrats have had a bad press. The vision is of a petty tyrant who wraps the cloak of office around inadequate shoulders, dominates those below him, and crouches sheepishly before those above him. That image has been with us a long time. . . . It turns out, however, that for all the snickering at the stereotype, Americans like the bureaucrats they deal with pretty well.[25]

The prevailing myth is that somehow private business is much more efficient than government. If this is so, why do major corporations have huge cost overruns in executing military contracts? Business produces its share of failures. Chrysler had to seek federal loan guarantees to survive. Ford produced the Edsel, and the big moviemakers regularly produce box-office flops.

ISSUE 3:   Summary   ★   *Are Bureaucrats Typically Incompetent and Slow to Act?*

According to critics, bureaucrats can get away with being unresponsive and resistant to change because their continuing identity is independent of whatever president is in office. Their mediocrity is a function of the need to protect their programs and maintain the status quo. Bureaucracy's supporters, however, maintain that such an attitude is only human. Moreover, bureaucrats fall under intense public and political scrutiny and must decide on highly controversial issues. Despite its shortcomings, bureaucracy can claim some genuine accomplishments over the long run and can count on long-term public support. ■

⊕ COMPARISONS WITH OTHER NATIONS

Modern political society would be both impossible and unimaginable without the services and occasional grief reliably provided by governmental bureaucracy. All of our lives and all through our lives bureaucracy is a given, always present to assist or to interfere. Often we can't tell the difference. What we can be confident of is that bureaucracy is a permanent feature in daily life in every nation and one that all of us would most likely be lost without.

Bureaucracy, then, allows for the presence of government in our daily existence. Even terminating that existence may, in the future, require bureaucratic assistance or approval. For example, the European Parliament, the meeting place for legislators elected from a dozen Western European nations, began to debate in the early 1990s the question of whether physicians should accede to the request of terminally ill patients to help end their lives.[26] The decision about how and whether life should end may ultimately be a political one administered and monitored by a bureaucratic agency. In every society that is modern or hopes to become so, both bureaucrats and the services they provide will remain vital.

BUREAUCRACY IN DEMOCRACIES

Most bureaucracies have grown as the explosion of technology and economic prosperity, particularly in the West, enables government to do more and more for its citizenry (which, at the same time, demands more and more). The services of public education, unemployment compensation, and social security are relatively recent undertakings by government. Most were simply either unfeasible and/or unaffordable until only a few generations ago. Many democratic countries have proceeded even further along the path to welfare states. The United States, by comparison, lags behind. For example, in the early 1990s the

United States was the only industrialized society to be without a national health insurance program. Of course, the lack of national health insurance has not meant the absence of government bureaucracy in the medical profession. In fact, this practice goes as far back as at least 4,000 years ago, when the Babylonian government regulated fees of physicians and applied punishments if they injured their patients.[27]

There was actually a great deal of idealism attached to the creation of modern bureaucracies. The idea was that bureaucrats would administer the delivery of vital public services to a desirous population and that this would be done in an efficient and professional fashion. The French, for example, created the Ecole Nationale d'Administration. This institution is the elite of about 300 grandes écoles whose job it is to prepare students to become professional and dedicated civil servants. The training must be excellent since businesses in the private sector eagerly recruit many of the graduates.

Most countries, including the United States, have no equivalent of the grandes écoles. Perhaps they should. It makes sense for civil servants to receive training for their profession. Otherwise, bureaucracies can become, as some undoubtedly have, both bloated and incompetent. Apparently, the grandes écoles are also useful in producing civil servants who are not at all squeamish about planning where, how, and when the state will intervene in critical areas. In contrast, civil servants in both the United Kingdom and the United States are squeamish. Bureaucracies in these democracies tend to wait for a need to arise rather than attempt to anticipate future needs.

Governments that have tried to diminish the role of bureaucracy have not been especially successful in doing so. Republican presidents in the United States, for example, consistently promise with hand on heart to reduce public expenditures, but, as a rule, are unable to do so. One of the most conservative Western governments (and one of the most hostile toward big government) was Prime Minister Margaret Thatcher's administration in the United Kingdom (1979–1990). Yet, even Mrs. Thatcher (dubbed the "Iron Lady" by civil servants worried about their jobs) was incapable of substantially reducing, let alone dismantling, Britain's welfare state:

> Britain still remains more of a welfare state than an enterprise society. Education vouchers and "workfare"—no benefits for the jobless, unless they take the training or do the work that the state offers—are still Thatcherite pipe-dreams. One of her most paradoxical achievements may have been to strengthen the welfare state by stopping it from indulging itself to death.[28]

During the 1980s Mrs. Thatcher did manage to reduce public expenditure from 44 percent of the national gross domestic product to about 40 percent.[29] No modern presidency in America has been able to do more than dream of that kind of achievement.

In modern industrialized societies, however, it is probably futile to try to reduce the role of government in any appreciable fashion. The demands of a population that is aging, increasingly dependent on medical and dental care (and constantly worried about fast-rising costs), and concerned about the relationship between monthly social security payments and the rate of inflation are not going to diminish. This gets back to an undeniable truth: Nations have "big government" because their citizens want it. We like having things done for us; we simply resent having to pay for them through taxation. The best that government can hope for is to maximize return on investment and keep expenses from going out of sight.

When Margaret Thatcher was prime minister in Britain, she became known as the "Iron Lady" for her fierce attempts to control the ballooning bureaucracy of a welfare state.

Many governments, especially elected ones desirous of staying in power, spend much of their time finding ways to make the delivery of public services both cost-efficient and palatable for the citizens who are paying for them. During the decade of the 1980s, for example, the British government worked long hours on such a project. The result was a document entitled Citizen Charter. The charter called for reforms that may provide a model for other industrialized democracies whose national bureaucracies include a significant proportion of the total labor force.

The charter insists that public employees be held accountable for how they respond to and treat citizens. Anyone dealing with the public, for instance, is required to give her or his name to help ensure courteous treatment. The Charter also "relies on popular but surprisingly inexpensive ideas like guaranteed maximums for hospital waiting times, and fines for over-long road works."[30]

In a democracy, the bureaucracy must strive to be responsive to the citizens. But doing so may create a problem. The public's right to know must be balanced against the government's obligation to protect the national interest. The bureaucracy, particularly that part involved in security matters, is the most secretive part of the government. The United States is at the more permissive end of revealing the workings and decisions of inner government, mostly because of its Freedom of Information Act. That act allows citizens access to government information that is unclassified. The United Kingdom is at the opposite extreme: The Official Secrets Act of 1911 makes any "unauthorized disclosure of official information a criminal offense."[31] Other democracies, such as France and Israel, are more secretive than the United States but much less so than Britain.[32]

Sometimes bureaucracies must deliver services to populations that have done little or nothing to earn or pay for them. For example, a long-term source of irritation to

New York City officials was the great number of people who lived out of the state but worked in the city: they drove on the city's roads to get to work, used its public transportation system, and enjoyed police and fire protection during the eight to ten hours of each business day they were in New York. A commuter tax now helps to pay for some of these services. Because of the compactness of its population, Germany has a similar problem. One of its largest urban areas, Hamburg, is a city state in the north-central part of the country. Hamburg would like compensation from the federal government "because of commuters who use the city's services but live beyond city limits in other states and pay their taxes there."[33] In the future, similar situations could grow even more complicated. As metropolitan areas spill into one another across national boundary lines (a phenomenon already well underway in a few border locations between the United States and Canada and the United States and Mexico), bureaucracies will almost certainly have to merge jurisdictions and perhaps pool their resources, often to provide services for culturally disparate, but geographically linked communities.

Bureaucracies grow for a reason. They appear, at least ostensibly, in order to accomplish some good deeds. Unfortunately, life is rarely so simple. Many bureaucrats are in their jobs not only to implement laws, but to formulate the guidelines by which the rules will be enforced and monitored. For example, through the 1980s and into the 1990s the United States and a few other Western democracies stepped up the insistence that more and greater pollution controls become part of the design of new cars. This is "good" bureaucracy at work: civil servants working to make sure we all breathe better. One resultant problem, however, is that the controls add substantially to the price of a new car. Thus, pollution controls that increase price may also increase pollution as people decide against the purchase of a new car because of the higher price and keep their old air-polluting cars.[34]

BUREAUCRACY IN TOTALITARIAN SYSTEMS

Bureaucracy is basically the instrument by which the policy decisions of government are implemented. But what happens if a government is controlled by the worst possible elements in a society? It is a question worth asking because a nightmarish government is not uncommon in our century. We have seen such governments in communist and other totalitarian systems. The two most lethal ones in modern history were the Soviet Union under Stalin (1924–1953) and Germany under Hitler (1933–1945). As a result of their policies, perhaps 50 million died. At least two-thirds of this number were civilians who were worked to death, died of disease or hunger, froze, or were gassed. Around 12 million adults and children perished in German concentration camps. Some estimates range up to 17 million in Siberian counterparts.[35]

Death on such a massive scale would have been impossible were it not for two crucial considerations: modern technology (the construction of gas chambers made it possible to efficiently murder thousands of people daily) and a compliant and hard-working bureaucracy. How did the bureaucracy become a death machine? Mainly because bureaucrats were convinced they were doing their jobs and performing a necessary public service.

During the Nazi dictatorship in Germany, for example, the top bureaucrat was probably Albert Speer, the minister of armaments. He was hardly an ideological fanatic or even a convinced Nazi. He simply had a job to do. Speer has been described as "a calm executive in a menagerie of zealots."[36] And possibly he did more harm than the zealots:

> *The next time one hears it said that not everyone need study politics, particularly to become only a technician, or an executive, or a mere voter . . . think on Albert Speer. . . . Speer's memoirs, like his other products, were detailed, efficient, and craftsmanlike. They remain highly useful to students of the period. And yet they are more analytical than profound. They peel off layer after layer of description and explanation, revealing an emotional emptiness at the core. At the news of his death, one wondered: Was he ever alive?*[37]

The system that produced Speer also produced Adolf Eichmann. Eichmann was given the responsibility of ensuring that millions of Jews marked for extermination in German concentration camps arrived at their last destinations by train on schedule. He took great pride in the fact that he completed his job in a most efficient manner and complained only that he was not promoted to a higher rank.[38]

Totalitarian systems can easily be referred to as bureaucratic states. The Soviet Union was called a party-state because the Communist party, at least until the end of the 1980s, dominated the entire political and bureaucratic structure of Soviet society. This kept the communists in power for the better part of a century. The bureaucracy in a totalitarian state is charged with keeping not only the regime in power, but also the party that created the regime. And, of course, it is the bureaucracy that has the resources to maintain its position. Thus, it is not easy to reform a *successful* totalitarian regime.

Both economic and political reforms in the Soviet Union kept running into the wall of bureaucratic intransigence. Bureaucrats saw their function as not providing services to their society or even to their regime, but as preserving their own favored positions, which would be destroyed with the reforms that only they were capable of implementing. One journalist who spent many years covering the Soviet Union observed, shortly before communism's final collapse in December 1991, that "an entrenched bureaucracy of party and Government officials—18 million strong by Gorbachev's count—has been blocking and sabotaging many reforms, clinging to power and privilege."[39]

If anything, the current Chinese bureaucracy is at least as entrenched as the Soviet counterpart was before the collapse of the Soviet system. Indeed, in Beijing in 1989 the tragedy that befell Chinese university students who were clamoring for political reform revealed the strength of the communist bureaucracy in China as much as the desire for democracy. The Chinese Communist party's political apparatus is probably the largest in the world. Literally, tens of millions of Chinese communists are employed to keep the regime (and, therefore, themselves) in power. Before some apparently meager reforms were enacted in the early 1980s, the party bureaucracy (which is separate from the state's) peaked at about 20 million. The major reform of this most totalitarian bureaucracy was to encourage a mandatory retirement age of 65. Ironically, this proposal was suggested by the party's leader, Deng Xiaoping, who was in his 80s at the time and who remained in power in his 90s.[40]

The totalitarian bureaucracy, then, is built to withstand reform. This is mainly because there is no other institution available to reform it. All other political agencies, including the government itself, are either appendages of the party bureaucracy or creations of it.

BUREAUCRACY IN AUTHORITARIAN SYSTEMS

Bureaucracies in nondemocratic societies range from inept and corrupt to horrifying and murderous. They tend often to be the former in the Third World. Frequently the creations of personalized dictatorships, they have no mandate to respond in any significant way to public needs. What is worse, they usually couldn't even if they wanted to, since resources are often minimal and occasionally nonexistent. When bureaucracies are horrifying and murderous they serve (in quite enthusiastic and efficient fashion) the rather nefarious purposes of a totalitarian regime determined to remake society in its own image, as we have seen.

In an authoritarian society the bureaucracy may well be the most developed aspect of the state. While much of the society's economic and political development may be languishing and even regressing, as is the case in several African and Middle Eastern states, the bureaucracy can include the most talented and the most educated segment of the population. In fact, the bureaucrats may have been recruited into government for two interrelated reasons: (1) By contrast with the United States and Western Europe, here the private sector is not developed enough to offer attractive alternatives to qualified people; and (2) the regime itself may see its best hope for preservation in placing educated people (and, therefore, the most likely political opponents) *within* the system, thereby co-opting them.

Bureaucracies in the Middle East are often family affairs. This is certainly true in the case of the monarchical regimes such as Kuwait and Saudi Arabia, where large royal families may include literally dozens if not hundreds of half-brothers and -sisters. The closer the ties of blood and kinship to the king or emir, the better and more prestigious the job. Even when the regime is not monarchical, the effective head of government often will appoint a close relative as defense minister since it is unlikely he could count on as much loyalty from anyone else. Syria's long-time president, Hafez al-Assad, put his brother in charge of the Syrian military, but was forced to remove him because of an increasingly public link to drugs.

Nepotism is the practice of appointing one's relatives to political office. In the early days of his administration President Bill Clinton appointed his wife, Hillary Rodham Clinton, to chair (nonsalaried) a commission on the problem of national health care. But this is not nepotism in the sense of sharing political power with one's family members. Dictators appoint family members to important and powerful posts because they really can't trust other people. It is a traditionally accepted way of running a country in much of the developing world. Moreover, it is an effective way for a dictator to stay in power. For example, Iraqi President Saddam Hussein remained in power even after losing a costly war to the allied nations because he had placed the right people in the right jobs. The most important bureaucratic and political posts belong to Saddam's relatives:

Internal Security Police:	Sibawi al Tikriti (half-brother)
Special Security Police:	Qusay Hussein (son)
Minister of Defense:	Hussein Kamel (son-in-law)
Minister of Interior:	Ali Hassan Majid (cousin)

These offices are vital for the survival of the regime, for they are charged with protecting the ruler and rooting out dissent and opposition to his government. Other jobs, such as Minister of Foreign Affairs, can be safely left to nonrelatives and professional civil servants, because they are in no position to threaten the regime. Bureaucracies such as Iraq's are ineffective in the Western and democratic sense as servants of the people, but they are effective in the dictatorial sense: If the bureaucracy is doing its job, the government survives.

The United States was once a developing country. But the American bureaucracy, for all its faults, grew gradually as a reaction to the growth of the country demographically, economically, and even geographically. Newly independent countries in the Third World don't have the luxury or, in a sad number of cases, the realistic expectation of gradual or even eventual growth (except in terms of population). Many of these countries have the following characteristics:

1. Lack of sustained economic growth to provide the tax revenue required to deliver and improve public services;

2. Relentless population growth that outpaces economic development and the ability of the bureaucracy to respond adequately to crucial public needs—education, health care, sanitation, and so on; and

3. Low morale on the part of rank-and-file bureaucrats whose wages and prestige are also low.[41]

All these characteristics are found throughout the developing world. And there is little that can be done to prevent a bad situation from becoming worse. For example, Cairo, the capital city of Egypt, is home to perhaps 16 million people, or one out of every four Egyptians. Yet the bureaucratic and technological structure is geared to deliver public services to a city of perhaps four million. Cairo is an example of a major Third World city that is breaking down. Americans have had a taste of how problems can outstrip the ability to deal with them, but their problems pale in comparison to Egypt's. For example, while New York City residents become upset if a number of school teachers are laid off, in Cairo attending school at all, even in overcrowded classrooms, is becoming a luxury.

It is unlikely the situation will improve soon. Many developing countries depend on foreign assistance from the richer nations to bolster their ability to provide services. Egypt, for instance, receives more foreign assistance from the United States than any other country except Israel. All of this $3 billion of aid goes to the bureaucracy.[42] It is hardly enough, of course, and Egyptians and other Third World populations, which are doubling every 25 years,* will probably have to make do with less rather than more help. This is because new priorities are emerging for the West:

---

* To have some sense of what that kind of population growth means, imagine the United States by 2015 with a population of over 500 million (compared to 250 million in 1990). Even in a country as rich as this one, the bureaucracy would be extremely hard put to keep up an acceptable level of services.

Central Europe's and the Soviet Union's reconstruction will divert resources from third-world aid programs. Meanwhile, the overdue domestic agenda in Western Europe and North America demands new investments to counter Northeast Asia's competitiveness and technological prowess.[43]

When fewer resources are available for development, third world bureaucracies will surely be the culprits in the eyes of the populations they are charged with serving. Authoritarianism can at least seem to be an efficient manager of public services if the alternative is social breakdown and chaos.

All of this is, of course, in great contrast to Western democratic bureaucracies. However imperfect, these civil services are not solely concerned with their own preservation because they don't have to be. Their job security is not usually dependent on a particular political party and their loyalty to its program, but on legal guidelines.

Summary

1. Bureaucracies have a very profound effect on all of our lives nearly every day. They are necessary to our well-being and provide many services we tend to take for granted and would find it exceedingly difficult to do without. The federal bureaucracy began with a very modest size and grew as the ability to provide services and the demand to receive them grew.

2. The huge federal bureaucracy is covered by the civil service system for the most part. The main exception is 5,000 top positions secured normally by presidential and subordinate appointment.

3. A body of administrative law provides much of the federal bureaucracy's authority to adjudicate disputes and enforce federal statute. Checks on the bureaucracy itself are effected through the Congress, the presidency, and the courts. There have also been reforms suggested to discourage bureaucratic abuse in the form of sunset laws, zero-based budgeting, and cost-benefit analysis, among others.

4. The bureaucracy is generally considered to be too large and unwieldy, an outcome of Parkinson's law and increasing regulatory activities. Yet bureaucracy grows in response to citizens' demands for services. Moreover, most federal bureaucrats are not located in Washington, D.C., and most bureaucrats aren't federal. More than four-fifths of all government employees are to be found at the state and local levels.

5. Bureaucracies may perform services more efficiently and more effectively for some groups than others because bureaucrats tend to be drawn from and be representative of the white, male, middle-class components of the population. When "whistle-blowers" attempt to correct bureaucratic corruption they are usually made to feel uncomfortable in their jobs.

6. Bureaucrats, however, are not the only ones involved in the policymaking process. Interest groups are also at work and their competition for the ear of bureaucrats results in a range of views heard. Moreover, bureaucrats may be more representative of the public than legislators and politically appointed executives.

7. Bureaucrats are difficult to remove from their jobs. Because they tend to endure endlessly, they outlast presidents and often frustrate presidential policy. Bureaucrats are not necessarily well regarded for competence but they are noted for their ability to spend their budgets and remain loyal to their administrative superiors.

8. For better or worse, however, bureaucrats are necessary for the proper maintenance of government. They actually deliver the proper amount of services most of the time to most of the intended recipients. It is the occasional bad news about bureaucracy that makes the news, not its consistent and quiet accomplishments.

9. Every industrial society requires a substantial bureaucracy to carry out the government's obligations to public service. Those governments that attempt to reduce the size of government programs are rarely successful.

10. Some governments, such as the French, provide special training schools for bureaucrats. While they do have a good record for producing competent civil servants, the negative side is that the better ones are lured away to the private sector with the promise of better salaries.

11. In many societies, including our own, bureaucracies are now having to provide services with much reduced resources. In some instances services are provided to populations that don't pay for them, as happens in metropolitan areas that spill over state or national borders.

12. Bureaucracies in modern totalitarian systems, such as the Soviet Union and Nazi Germany, were disconcertingly competent. They were notorious for assisting the dictatorship in illegal and immoral policies, including wholesale violations of human rights and genocide.

13. Most Third World bureaucracies are corrupt and/or inept, even though they include most of the educated and trained citizens of the country. Some Third World countries are run as family estates. The bureaucracy is co-opted into helping to control the society on behalf of the dictator, who gives a new and reinforced meaning to the term *nepotism* by employing family members in high-level administrative positions.

Terms to Define

Administrative law
Bureaucracy
Civil service
Clientelism
Incrementalism
Iron triangle
Issue networks
Legislative veto
Merit system

Nepotism
Ombudsman
Patronage system
Program budgeting
Statutory law
Sunset law
Whistle-blowers
Zero-based budgeting

Suggested Readings

Arendt, Hannah. *Eichmann in Jerusalem: The Banality of Evil.* New York: Viking Press, 1963. A classic analysis of the darker and amoral side of bureaucracy and bureaucrats.

Burke, John P. *Bureaucratic Responsibility.* Baltimore: Johns Hopkins University Press, 1986. Assesses the role of "whistle-blowers" in the bureaucracy.

Heclo, Hugh. *A Government of Strangers.* Washington, D.C.: Brookings Institute, 1977. Analyzes how political appointees try to control the bureaucracy and how the bureaucracy resists, with frequent success, control.

Parkinson, C. Northcote. *Parkinson's Law.* New York: Ballentine Books, 1957. Tongue-in-cheek, but incisive explanation of how the bureaucracy always seems to grow.

Rourke, Francis E. *Bureaucracy, Politics, and Public Policy,* 3rd ed. Boston: Little, Brown, 1984. Good introduction to bureaucracy and relationships between bureaucratic agencies and their clients.

Wilson, James Q., ed. *Bureaucracy.* New York: Basic Books, 1989. Thorough analysis of American bureaucratic behavior.

Notes

1. *The Christian Science Monitor,* February 1, 1993, p. 3. See also Bruce D. Porter, "Parkinson's Law: War and the Growth of American Government," *Public Interest,* Summer 1980.
2. Max Weber, *The Protestant Ethic and the Spirit of Capitalism,* translated by Talcott Parsons (New York: Scribner's, 1930). First published, 1904.
3. *The Washington Post,* October 21, 1979, p. A1.
4. *Immigration and Naturalization Service* v. *Chadha,* 103 S. Ct. 2764 (1983); *Maine* v. *Thiboutot,* 100 S. Ct. 2502 (1980).
5. V. O. Key, Jr., *Politics, Parties and Pressure Groups,* 5th ed. (New York: Crowell, 1964), pp. 711–712.
6. *War on Waste* (Washington, D.C.: U.S. Government Printing Office, 1984).
7. C. Northcote Parkinson, *Parkinson's Law* (New York: Ballantine Books, 1957), p. 17.
8. Norman John Powell, *Responsible Public Bureaucracy in the United States* (Boston: Allyn & Bacon, 1967), pp. 175–176.
9. *U.S. Statistical Abstract,* 1991, p. 330.
10. S. Robert Lichter and Stanley Rothman, "What Interests the Public and What Interests the Public Interest?" *Public Opinion* 6(1983): 44–48. Reprinted with the permission of The American Enterprise Institute for Public Policy Research, Washington, D. C.
11. Gideon Sjoberg et al., "Bureaucracy and the Lower Class," in Francis Rourke, ed., *Bureaucratic Power and National Politics* (Boston: Little, Brown, 1972), pp. 395–396.
12. Hugh Heclo, "Issue Networks and the Executive Establishment," in Anthony King, ed., *The New American Political System* (Washington, D.C.: American Enterprise Institute, 1978), pp. 87–124.
13. Theodore Lowi, *The End of Liberalism* (New York: Norton, 1969), pp. 103–104.
14. Michael Jacobson, *Eater's Digest* (Garden City, N.Y.: Doubleday, 1972), p. 200.
15. *Washington Post National Weekly Edition,* January 2, 1984, p. 32.
16. *Washington Post National Weekly Edition,* January 28, 1985, p. 34.
17. V. O. Key, Jr., *Politics, Parties and Pressure Groups,* 5th ed. (New York: Crowell, 1964), p. 710.
18. Hugh Heclo, *A Government of Strangers: Executive Politics in Washington* (Washington, D.C.: Brookings Institute, 1977), p. 114.
19. *The Christian Science Monitor,* February 1, 1993, p. 3. Data from *Statistical Abstract of the United States, 1991;* Congressional Quarterly's Guide to the Presidency; Office of Personnel Management.
20. Richard Nathan, *The Plot That Failed* (New York: John Wiley, 1975).
21. See generally Laurence J. Peter and Raymond Hull, *The Peter Principle* (New York: Bantam Books, 1969).

22. Matthew P. Dumont, "Down the Bureaucracy!" *Transaction*, October 1970, pp. 10–12.
23. Peter Drucker, *The Age of Discontinuity* (New York: Harper & Row, 1969), pp. 212–220.
24. Peter Blau, *Bureaucracy in Modern Society* (New York: Random House, 1956), p. 103.
25. Robert L. Kahn et al., "Americans Love Their Bureaucrats," *Psychology Today*, June 1975, p. 66.
26. "Euthanasia," *The Economist*, July 20, 1991, p. 24.
27. "Health Care," *The Economist*, July 6, 1991, p. 1. Even more restrictive rules were in place in China, where physicians got paid only if their patients remained in good health (Ibid).
28. "The Thatcher Record," *The Economist*, November 24, 1990, p. 19.
29. Ibid.
30. "Taking on the Public Sector," *The Economist*, July 27, 1991, p. 54.
31. Ian Budge and David McKay, *The Changing British Political System: Into the 1990s*, 2nd ed. (London and New York: Longman, 1988), p. 41.
32. Ibid., p. 42.
33. "Federal Jigsaw," *The Economist*, June 2, 1990, p. 51.
34. "Do the Right Thing," *The Economist*, June 2, 1990, p. 74.
35. The best and most comprehensive history of the Siberian camps is found in Robert Conquest, *The Great Terror* (New York: Oxford University Press, 1990).
36. Paul Greenberg, "But Albert Speer Was a Great Manager," *Shreveport Journal*, September 12, 1981.
37. Ibid.
38. For a chilling analysis of a totally insensitive bureaucrat see Hannah Arendt, *Eichmann in Jersualem* (New York: Viking Press, 1963).
39. Hedrick Smith, "The Russian Character," *The New York Times Magazine*, October 28, 1990.
40. See *The New York Times*, January 20, 1982, and Trong R. Chai, "Communist Party Control over the Bureaucracy: The Case of China," *Comparative Politics*, 11:3 (Spring 1979), 359–370.
41. These and other observations of Third World bureaucracies are discussed in Monte Palmer, Ali Leila, and El Sayed Yassin, *The Egyptian Bureaucracy* (Syracuse: Syracuse University Press, 1988).
42. Ibid.
43. James Clad, "'Democratic' Unraveling in Third World," *The Christian Science Monitor*, July 24, 1991, p. 19.

CHAPTER ★ TWELVE

CONGRESS

Among the legislative bodies in the world, America's Congress is unique for many reasons. Certainly no legislative body, it is fair to say, has been the butt of more jokes than the U.S. Congress. Humorist Artemus Ward wrote in the last century: "It's easy enough to see why a man goes to the poorhouse or the penitentiary. It's because he can't help it. But why he should voluntarily go and live in Washington is entirely beyond my comprehension."[1] A twentieth-century politician in county government said: "I can make a decision, order it implemented and in six months see if it has worked or not. But in Congress, it is like elephants making love. It takes two years before you can see whether what you've done has had any results."[2] Mark Twain once referred to members of Congress as probably the only "distinctly native American criminal class." Twain was only indulging in a favorite American pastime, mocking the national legislature.

A more substantive characteristic that distinguishes our Congress from legislative bodies in other countries is separation of powers. The United States is one of the few democracies that allows for the possibility of **divided government**, with Congress controlled by one party and the presidency by another. Until the 1992 election, most Americans had grown accustomed to a Congress in the hands of the Democrats and a presidency in the hands of the Republicans. For the better part of two generations this division became the natural political order of things. The result was that when the president of the United States proposed legislation, there was a respectable chance that it would go nowhere.

This system seems both strange and chaotic to most other nations. In parliamentary democracies, for example, the legislative majority normally forms a government. These democracies could not even function if one party or coalition of parties did not control both the executive and legislative branches. When a Western European government proposes legislation, there is little doubt the legislation will be approved at the parliamentary level.

The fact that the U.S. Congress has two houses that both exercise significant power is also bewildering to the average European. Only Germany has an upper house approaching the power and status of the U.S. Senate and some countries have no upper house at all. The American system is one of a very few to have an upper house that is popularly elected as well as politically powerful. The only other major democracy with a popularly elected house is Japan, but its legislative body is far less influential than the U.S. Senate.

The schizophrenic quality of our Congress was a very deliberate creation on the part of the framers of the government. It was born out of a conflict between proponents of a strong executive and others favoring a strong legislature. The former wanted to avoid the pitfalls of the overly powerful legislature under the Articles of Confederation; the latter recalled the troubles caused by an overbearing executive in the form of the British monarch. There is still disagreement on the role of the legislature, which contributes to the ambivalent attitude many Americans bear toward the institution of government that is closest to them. In what follows we will examine the functions of Congress, how it is organized, and how it conducts its business. We'll then consider some controversial issues surrounding Congress: Is it truly representative? Does politics take precedence over deliberation? Is the institution in need of reform? Should terms be limited? Finally, we'll compare our system with those in parliamentary, totalitarian, and authoritarian countries.

★ THE AMERICAN CONGRESS

FUNCTIONS OF CONGRESS

Congress is entrusted with, or has evolved, many functions. Some of these stem from constitutional duties and some from the fact that each member is a representative of a certain number of constituents, whose interests need tending. Sometimes one function conflicts with another and, always, a member must decide how to divide his or her time. Should it be spent legislating? Overseeing? Serving constituents? There is never enough time to do everything.

Constitutional Functions

As enumerated below, the Constitution prescribes some functions for both House and Senate combined and others for just one of the two houses. The most important duty for both houses is lawmaking, the process of deliberating on and passing legislation. This process can be contentious and time-consuming, as we will see later in this section.

CONSTITUTIONAL POWERS (ARTICLE I, SECTION 8)

1. Taxation: To lay and collect taxes, duties, imposts, and excises.
2. Borrowing: To borrow money on the credit of the United States.
3. Commerce: To regulate commerce with foreign nations and among the states.
4. Citizenship/bankruptcy: To establish laws governing naturalization (citizenship) and bankruptcy.
5. Money/measures: To coin money, determine its value, and punish counterfeiting; to fix the standard of weights and measures.
6. Post office: To establish post offices and post roads.
7. Copyrights/patents: To grant authors and inventors, respectively, copyrights and patents.
8. Courts: To create courts below the Supreme Court.
9. High Seas: To define and punish piracies, felonies on the high seas, and crimes against the law of nations.
10. War: To declare war.
11. Military: To raise, support, and establish rules for governing an army and a navy.
12. Militia: To provide for a militia, but allowing the states to name the officers and train the militia consistent with the laws of Congress.
13. Federal property: To govern the District of Columbia and other federal property.
14. "Necessary and proper" laws: To "make all laws which shall be necessary and proper for carrying into execution the foregoing powers, and all other powers vested by this Constitution in the government of the United States."

CONSTITUTIONAL RESTRICTIONS (ARTICLE I, SECTION 9)

1. Slave trade: Shall not be prohibited prior to 1808 although a tax and duty may be imposed not to exceed $10 per person.
2. Habeas corpus: Shall not be suspended except during emergencies.
3. Bill of attainder/ex post facto laws: Shall not pass either a bill of attainder or an ex post facto law.
4. Interstate tariffs: Shall not tax goods transported between states.

5. Treatment of states: Shall not give preferential treatment of one state over another in commerce and revenue matters.

6. Appropriations: Shall not appropriate money except as provided by law.

7. Titles: Shall not grant titles of nobility.

The House and Senate acting together also can propose constitutional amendments, declare war, and determine presidential disability. In impeachment proceedings, the House of Representatives impeaches (in effect, indicts) the official and the Senate acts as a trial court. When the electoral college fails to provide a majority, the House elects the president and the Senate, the vice president. Each house has the constitutional authority to regulate the conduct of its members and to determine whether a prospective member has been properly elected or should be seated.

Certain functions are specified for one house only. The Senate has sole authority to ratify treaties proposed by the president and to confirm presidential nominations (Article II, section 2). In using this confirmation power, the Senate developed the custom of **senatorial courtesy**, whereby senators of the president's party can exercise veto power over presidential appointments in their states (as for a federal judgeship). The House has the power to originate all money bills (Article I, section 7); this authority is based on the theory that the branch of government closest to the people should exercise the closest control over tax dollars.

Legitimating Function

Individuals and groups have conflicting ideas on public policy. Should there be a national health insurance program? Should railroads be nationalized? Should there be a national land-use policy? A principal function of Congress is to resolve such questions through compromise—that is, by devising a solution that competing groups will accept. In this way it *legitimates* public policy.

Another phase of the legitimating function occurs during military emergencies, when the president commits military forces. Since World War II this has happened in Korea, Lebanon, Cuba, Vietnam, Grenada, Panama, the Persian Gulf, and Somalia. Typically, Congressional leaders announce their bipartisan support for the president's action. Only on rare occasions have rank-and-file party members differed with their leaders' endorsements of presidential actions, but such disagreement has increased since Vietnam. In the 1991 war against Iraq, for example, a substantial number of Senate Democrats voted against President George Bush's proposal to send troops into combat.

Investigatory Function

One of the most visible congressional functions is that of investigating the executive branch. Congress conducts such inquiries to determine whether the executive is administrating properly and spending money wisely. The most dramatic contemporary example of this role was represented by the Senate Watergate hearings of 1973, which investigated the alleged involvement of President Richard Nixon in illegal and unethical activities: this investigation contributed to the fall of the Nixon presidency. In 1987 another well-

Congress can oversee and investigate the executive branch. In 1987 Congress held investigatory hearings on the illegal sale of arms to Iran and the funneling of profits to the Contras in Nicaragua. White House aide Lieutenant-Colonel Oliver North is shown here being sworn in as a witness.

publicized hearing investigated the Reagan administration's sale of arms to Iran and the funneling of profits to the Contras, a rebel group in Nicaragua. Both acts were prohibited under laws and policy in effect then.

Checking Executive Power

Congress has a role in checking executive power. The Founders, who wanted to guard against a monopoly of governmental authority in the hands of any one branch, considered this role extremely important. Congress has the power to bring even a strong executive to heel, as its severest critics would admit in the light of the Vietnam War and the Watergate scandal. Without congressional criticism of his Vietnam policy, would President Nixon have carried out troop withdrawal? Without the threat of congressional impeachment and conviction, would he have resigned from office? Without congressional criticism, would President Jimmy Carter have changed his style from a closed, aloof position to a more open one that solicited congressional advice? Presidents Reagan and

Bush, realizing the power of Congress, quickly established good personal relationships with both Democrats and Republicans and organized an effective White House–congressional liaison team. Their early legislative victories were generally attributable to their efforts to build goodwill in Congress.

Washington Post columnist David Broder appropriately described the value of Congress in delaying presidential actions: "Nothing that bugs presidents as much as Congress does can be all bad. Presidents come to office thinking the world was born anew on the day they were sworn in. Congress knows better."[3] President Clinton quickly learned, over the issue of removing the ban on homosexuals in the military, that his power could be checked by Congress: In the first week of his administration he had to make a compromise with the chairman of the Senate Armed Services Committee, Sam Nunn (D-Ga.).

Ombudsman Function

In the ombudsman role, a legislator acts as an agent representing a constituent's interest, usually against some aspect of the bureaucracy. The large number and variety of cases has led to the creation of staff specialists in congressional offices who do nothing but casework. Members of Congress value this function highly, because it enables the member to act personally and directly on behalf of constituents and prospective voters. Voters' problems with government agencies may range from lost social security checks to reduced veterans' benefits to immigration visas. Of course, members of Congress also represent cities, counties, states, groups, and institutions in such matters as obtaining federal grants or contracts.

ORGANIZATION OF CONGRESS

Congress carries out its several functions in a complex organizational setting. For our purposes, the four most important aspects of this structure are party organization, informal organization, committee organization, and staff organization.

Party Organization

From the party leadership emerges the leadership of Congress as a whole. The majority party in the House of Representatives provides the *Speaker*, who is the presiding officer and most powerful member. The Speaker is theoretically chosen by all members of the House but in reality is elected by the majority party. As parliamentary leader, the Speaker can recognize persons on the floor and thus influence the flow of legislation. The Speaker also controls appointments to the Rules Committee, which governs what legislation is debated and how. In addition, the Speaker serves as a member of the Steering and Policy Committee, which allocates committee assignments.

Each party in the House also has a *majority* or *minority floor leader* and *whip*. They are responsible for party leadership in debate and for lining up members' votes on issues that divide along party lines. All party members belong to either the Democratic Caucus or the Republican Conference. Each of these groups has a chairman. The Caucus and the Conference select the party leaders within Congress and may also establish party policies on issues.

The vice president has the constitutional duty of presiding over the Senate, but in actuality does so only if a tie vote needs to be broken. For example, in 1991, Vice President Dan Quayle presided over the confirmation vote of Judge Clarence Thomas to the Supreme Court because a close vote was expected. In the vice president's absence the presiding officer is the *president pro tempore* of the Senate. Although this individual is the senior member of the majority party, the president pro tempore has little real power. The principal party voice and power in the Senate is the Senate *majority leader*, but even this leader's power is not as great as that of the Speaker of the House. Power is much more centralized in the House, with its 435 members, than in the Senate, which has just 100 members. The Senate party leadership also includes a *minority leader* and *whips* from both parties, who serve the same function as House whips. (See Table 12.1.)

Party committees in the two houses include (1) the campaign committees, which raise and disburse funds for congressional candidates; (2) the policy committees, which establish party policy on key issues; and (3) the committee on committees (Republicans) and steering and policy committees (Democrats), which make committee assignments (a process discussed in more detail later). Democrats with majorities in both houses also have patronage or personnel committees, which make appointments to positions that serve the entire House and Senate. Traditionally, Congress's large patronage system, including Capitol elevator operators and police, has been controlled by the majority party.

Informal Organization

In addition to the formal party organization, informal groups also have a great deal of influence on member behavior. Republicans have the Wednesday Club, the Chowder

TABLE 12.1 PARTY ORGANIZATION IN CONGRESS

	House (with a Democratic majority)	Senate (with a Democratic majority)
Democrats	Speaker Chairman of Caucus* Majority Leader Majority Whip Steering and Policy Committee Democratic National Congressional Committee Patronage Committee	Majority Leader Majority Whip Chairman of Caucus* Policy Committee Steering Committee Senatorial Campaign Committee
Republicans	Minority Leader Chairman of Conference* Minority Whip Committee on Committees Policy Committee National Republican Congressional Campaign Committee	Minority Leader Minority Whip Chairman of Conference* Policy Committee Committee on Committees Senatorial Campaign Committee

* Caucus and conference include all members of party.

and Marching Society, and an organization of conservative members. The Wednesday Club consists of moderate-to-liberal Republicans in the House (a similar organization exists for Senate Republicans); they develop and sponsor legislation as a group. Three of the best-known Democratic organizations are the Democratic Study Group, which has been in the forefront of efforts to modernize the House of Representatives; the African-American Caucus; and the Boll Weevils, who represent conservative Democratic interests.

During the last 30 years, numerous caucuses of individual members have been organized. At the last estimate more than 60 caucuses had formed on single-issue subjects. Bipartisan caucuses, such as Women's, Textile, Tourism, and others, represent special interests that cross party lines. The caucuses help diffuse the power structure of Congress, because each caucus or group has its own leadership and policy on a narrow issue.

Committee Organization

The most crucial unit in legislative organization is the committee, because that is where the fate of the thousands of bills and resolutions introduced each year is determined. **Standing committees** are permanent and continue their work from one session to the next. There are 22 standing committees in the House and 16 in the Senate (Table 12.2). In addition to standing committees, there are several **joint committees**, such as the Economic and Taxation Committees, which include members from both House and Senate. Each house also creates special **select committees** from time to time to explore subjects of extraordinary interest; there have been, for example, Senate select committees on aging, hunger, and intelligence.

Each standing committee has numerous subcommittees, which enable legislators to divide the workload and develop expertise in different areas. Committee members and their staffs are often the most knowledgeable people in the United States about the subjects under their jurisdiction, and Congress has been increasing its staff to provide even more assistance. As of 1993, there were 300 full committees and subcommittees.

Standing committees dealing with appropriations and finance (the Ways and Means Committee handles finance in the House) are among the most powerful in both the House and Senate. The prestige of other committees varies between the two houses. In the House of Representatives, with its large and complex organization, the Rules Committee is powerful. In the Senate, the Foreign Relations Committee occupies a preeminent position because of the Senate's constitutional obligations to confirm ambassadors and ratify treaties. Committees can change in status over time. For instance, the House Committee on Science and Technology was relatively unimportant when first created and thus consisted of new and uninfluential members. Later, as its subject matter became more important to American society, it gained prestige and desirability. The Budget committees in the two houses have also gained in stature.

Service on the more prestigious and powerful committees is almost universally the prerogative of more senior members. The senior members dominate the committee selection process and look for trustworthy members (that is, those loyal to the party) to place on committees. Obviously, a member generally needs an apprenticeship in Congress to be judged trustworthy by senior members.

For House Republicans, a Committee on Committees, dominated by the senior members from states with large numbers of Republican representatives, controls the committee assignment process. For example, the senior Republican from a state with 12

TABLE 12.2   STANDING COMMITTEES OF THE SENATE AND HOUSE, 1993

Senate	House

Major (13)
(Limit of two per senator)
  Agriculture, Nutrition, and Forestry
  Appropriations
  Armed Services
  Banking, Housing, and Urban Affairs
  Budget
  Commerce, Science, and Transportation
  Energy and Natural Resources
  Environment and Public Works
  Finance
  Foreign Relations
  Governmental Affairs
  Judiciary
  Labor and Human Resources
Minor (3)
(Limit of one per senator)
  Rules and Administration
  Small Business
  Veterans' Affairs
	Exclusive (3)
	(No other assignment allowed except
	  Budget)
	  Appropriations
	  Rules
	  Ways and Means
	Major (8)
	(Limit of one per member)
	  Agriculture
	  Armed Services
	  Banking, Finance, and Urban Affairs
	  Education and Labor
	  Energy and Commerce
	  Foreign Affairs
	  Judiciary
	  Public Works and Transportation
	Nonmajor (11)
	(Limit of one major and one nonmajor or
	  two nonmajor committees per member)
	  Budget
	  District of Columbia
	  Government Operations
	  House Administration
	  Interior and Insular Affairs
	  Merchant Marine and Fisheries
	  Post Office and Civil Service
	  Science, Space, and Technology
	  Small Business
	  Standards of Official Conduct
	  Veterans' Affairs

Note: In the Senate, membership limitations are not always observed. In the House, Republicans are not bound by the classification scheme, which is the product of the Democratic Caucus, but normally they make assignments consistent with it.

Republican representatives has 12 votes in the Committee on Committees. House Democrats have a Steering and Policy Committee chaired and generally controlled by the party leader. In the Senate, veteran-dominated steering committees make committee assignments for both parties. According to the **seniority system,** committee chairmanships generally go to persons of the majority party with the longest continuous service on the committee.

Both the House and the Senate modified their seniority system in the 1970s to allow challenges by secret ballot to committee leadership. But seniority challenges are rare. The seniority system enables committees to avoid the conflicts that could occur every two years if chairmen were elected in hard-fought popularity contests. In short, seniority provides continuity.

Staff Organization

While each member of the House represented about 212,000 people in 1910, today each House district is home to nearly 600,000 people. Every decade, following the census, this number increases. In 1940, 331,000 people received social security benefits and each congressman represented, on the average, 761 social security recipients. Today, more than 20 million Americans, an average of 48,000 in each congressional district, receive social security benefits. As for senators, they generally find themselves representing increasing numbers of constituents *each year* as state populations grow. How can a member of Congress handle the casework generated by population growth, new programs such as social security, and the large number of demands citizens make? The only answer is more staff. Between 1947 and 1993 staff for individual members and congressional committees increased from 1,440 to 12,446 in the House and from 590 to 7,620 in the Senate.[4]

Several types of staff members work for the Congress, totaling approximately 38,500 in all (see Table 12.3). First and most numerous are the staffers of individual representatives and senators. Generally each member has an administrative assistant, a

TABLE 12.3 STAFFING ON CAPITOL HILL	
Agency/Branch	Total Employees
Senate	7,620
House of Representatives	12,446
Commission on Security and Cooperation in Europe	18
Architect of the Capitol	2,346
Botanic Garden	53
Commission on Agricultural Workers	13
Commission on Interstate Child Support	2
Congressional Budget Office	224
Copyright Royalty Tribunal	8
General Accounting Office	5,274
Government Printing Office	4,910
John C. Stennis Center for Public Development	6
Library of Congress	5,033
National Commission on AIDS	22
National Commission to Prevent Infant Mortality	11
Office of Technology Assessment	190
Physician Payment Review Commission	1
Prospective Payment Assessment Commission	13
U.S. Tax Court	319
Total Staff Members	38,509

Source: *The Christian Science Monitor*, February 16, 1993, p. 3. Data from Office of Personnel Management.

press secretary, several legislative aides, caseworkers to handle concerns of constituents, and secretarial personnel. Every House member is entitled to 18 full-time and 4 part-time staffers. Second are committee staffers, including the majority and minority counsels, other professional staff, and secretaries. Committee counsels are among the most prestigious staffers for their role in setting up committee hearings, scheduling witnesses, asking questions of witnesses, and drafting legislation. Third are the members of the service staff who support Congress as an institution, such as the Sergeant at Arms, Architect of the Capitol, Clerk of the House, and many others. Fourth are the members of the leadership staff. The Speaker of the House and the majority and minority leaders in both houses, for example, have extra staff who serve them in their leadership capacities.

Congressional staff working for individual members have no established salary or working guidelines. They can be fired immediately without advance notice or reason given. Many are underpaid, and their hours are usually longer than the normal eight-hour day. Through their bosses, the members of Congress, they must answer to the electorate. If their bosses are not returned, they lose their jobs. Committee staffs also face job tenure difficulties when the chairmanship of the committee changes and when the minority party becomes the majority party. Those employees of the legislative branch whose jobs are permanent include the service staffs of the Library of Congress, the General Accounting Office, and parts of the Government Printing Office.

Legislative staff members perform a variety of useful functions including speech writing, bill drafting and research, press relations, and casework. Committee staff workers prepare for committee hearings, write committee reports, and draft legislation. The technical support staffs in such agencies as the Congressional Budget Office and the Office of Technology Assessment enable Congress to obtain the best available information and analysis on crucial subjects. In prestige, generally the party leadership staff and committee counsels rank highest, then a senator's senior staff, followed by the House staff. By law, congressional staff cannot work on the political campaign of a member unless they take unpaid leave for that purpose. Of course, this is a difficult law to enforce if for no other reason than that the line between staff and campaign work is very fine.

THE LEGISLATIVE PROCESS

Congress is, first and foremost, a legislative body. And it is a deliberative body. That means that laws generally have a long gestation period. A bill does not just appear on the floor and get passed overnight. It almost always works its way through committees and subcommittees and may undergo numerous drafts and revisions before it comes up for debate in the full chamber (*if* it comes up for debate at all). In addition, many bills take separate paths through the Senate and the House and must be reconciled before final passage.

Types of Legislative Proposals

Proposals may take the form of resolutions or bills. Resolutions are of three types. A **simple resolution** requires the action of only one house, does not have the force of law, and merely expresses the opinion of that house. Simple resolutions are also used to conduct business pertaining to only one house, such as internal administrative issues. Also without the force of law is the **concurrent resolution,** which requires action by both houses and expresses the opinion of both houses. A **joint resolution,** passed by both houses, has the force of law but does not require the president's signature. A constitutional amendment proposed by Congress does not require action by the president; hence, it would be introduced as a joint resolution. Joint resolutions also deal with internal administrative issues pertaining to both houses.

There are two kinds of bills. A **private bill** concerns the private interests of an individual or corporation, such as a financial claim against the government. A **public bill,** as the name suggests, deals with matters of concern to the whole population. Both must go through committees.

Legislative Stages

A bill goes through a number of basic stages en route to becoming a law (Figure 12.1). Not all stages are equally important for the bill's survival, but each has some part to play in the legislative process. First, a bill is developed and prepared for introduction. This stage may take from several hours to several years. The idea for the bill may come from constituents, a lobby, the president or an executive branch agency, one or more representatives or senators, or congressional staff members. Both House and Senate have staffs that can provide background data for bills and put bills into proper form.

Second, a member introduces the bill, which is then referred to a committee, in the House by the speaker and in the Senate by the presiding officer. Since committee jurisdictions are fairly well defined, there is usually no controversy about where a bill is assigned. On some occasions, the referral of a bill may be contested, and also on some occasions, a bill may be referred to more than one committee. Sometimes, this can get out of hand: some 40 committees and subcommittees routinely demand a say in energy legislation. Resolution of a contested referral is normally worked out through informal negotiation among the interested members or committees. The full House or Senate hardly ever votes on these disputes.

Third, the appropriate committees (or specialized subcommittees) hold hearings and make recommendations. If the committee recommends passage, a bill is "marked up"—that is, put in final form for presentation to the full House or Senate. If the committee has radically altered the bill, it may be redrafted; it is then known as a **clean bill,** which the committee reports to the House or Senate with a new number, making it a committee bill rather than that of an individual member. When a committee makes no recommendation on a bill it is dead. A **discharge petition** signed by a majority of House members can bring a dead bill out of a committee before the full House, but this is rarely used. The discharge rule has removed only 26 bills from the House since its adoption in 1926. Sometimes, however, the mere threat of a discharge petition can force a committee chairman to act on a bill. Even so, the reality is that *most* bills never get out of committee (see Figure 12.2). Of the 10,352 bills and joint resolutions introduced in the 101st Congress (1989–1990), only 411 were passed by Congress.[5] Committees are the cemeteries for most bills and joints resolutions.

The fourth stage applies only in the House. Although some bills, such as those dealing with appropriations, may be brought directly to the floor from committee, most must be brought to the Rules Committee to be assigned a rule to be followed in debate. Even committees with direct access to the House floor, however, usually prefer to obtain

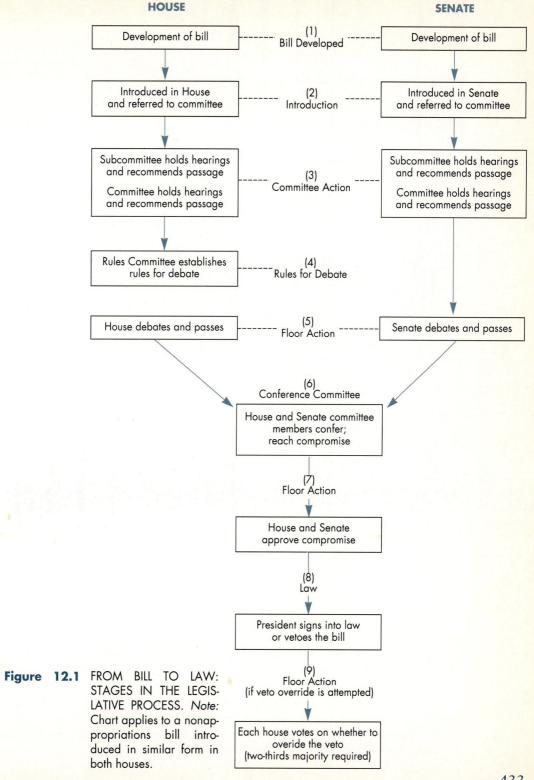

HOUSE   **SENATE**

| Development of bill | (1)
Bill Developed | Development of bill |

| Introduced in House
and referred to committee | (2)
Introduction | Introduced in Senate
and referred to committee |

| Subcommittee holds hearings
and recommends passage

Committee holds hearings
and recommends passage | (3)
Committee Action | Subcommittee holds hearings
and recommends passage

Committee holds hearings
and recommends passage |

| Rules Committee establishes
rules for debate | (4)
Rules for Debate |

| House debates and passes | (5)
Floor Action | Senate debates and passes |

(6)
Conference Committee

| House and Senate committee
members confer;
reach compromise |

(7)
Floor Action

| House and Senate
approve compromise |

(8)
Law

| President signs into law
or vetoes the bill |

(9)
Floor Action
(if veto override is attempted)

| Each house votes on whether to
override the veto
(two-thirds majority required) |

Figure 12.1 FROM BILL TO LAW: STAGES IN THE LEGISLATIVE PROCESS. *Note:* Chart applies to a nonappropriations bill introduced in similar form in both houses.

433

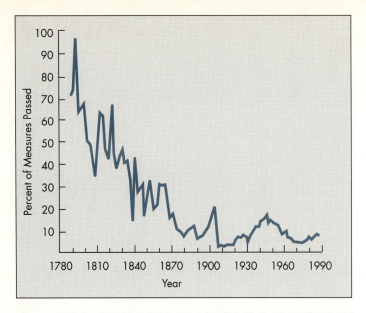

Figure 12.2 PROPORTION OF MEASURES INTRODUCED IN CONGRESS THAT WERE PASSED, 1789–1988. Congress passed nearly all the bills it considered in its very early days; now less than 10 percent make it through the legislative process. *Note:* Measures include acts, bills, and joint resolutions. Prior to 1824 only bills and acts are included. Source: Harold W. Stanley and Richard G. Niemi, *Vital Statistics on American Politics* (Washington, D.C.: Congressional Quarterly Press, 1992), p. 212.

a rule from the Rules Committee, because of the protections it may offer. A **closed rule** prevents any amendment from being offered on the House floor; an **open rule** allows amendments; a **modified closed rule** allows amendments on only some portions of a bill. Each rule also specifies how much time may be devoted to debate. The Rules Committee can effectively save members from having to vote on issues they want to avoid by disallowing amendments to be introduced on the subjects. The Rules Committee actually provides an invaluable service, much as a traffic cop does. If every bill had an equal right to the House floor, and if all bills were subject to amendments from all 435 members of the House, chaos would always be just around the corner.

The Senate, with only 100 members, does not have the same need for a traffic cop. Although different from a House rule, the Senate's **unanimous consent agreement** is also used at times to expedite action. To do this, Senate leaders agree to procedures for debating and voting on a bill, and then they ask the entire Senate to accept that agreement.

In the fifth stage, a bill is placed on the legislative calendar and then sent to the floor for debate and a vote. Although the Senate has only one legislative calendar, the

House has five: (1) *Private*, for private bills affecting specific persons; (2) *Union*, for bills that pertain to the appropriation of money or the raising of revenue; (3) *House*, for bills that do not appropriate money or raise revenue; (4) *Consent*, for noncontroversial bills; and (5) *Discharge*, for bills that have been removed from a committee by a discharge petition, signed by at least 218 members (a majority). During debate, the chairman (or the person the chairman assigns) and the ranking minority member (or the person that member assigns) of the committee that marked up the bill are in charge of the majority and minority positions on debate. The time alloted for debate on both sides is strictly monitored.

The Senate has no limits on debate (unless the senators unanimously consent to a limit). That means a minority of members are able to carry on a **filibuster**—that is, try to talk a bill to death. Some senators have talked over twenty hours nonstop in efforts to kill a bill. In 1992, when Senator Alphonse D'Amato (R-N.Y.) filibustered a bill that would have put some New Yorkers out of work, he had the aid of his New York colleague Democratic Senator Daniel Moynihan. Moynihan fed D'Amato long questions so that he could rest his voice during the 15-hour talkathon. At one point D'Amato broke into song to relieve the tedium. A filibuster may be ended only by a form of termination called **cloture:** 16 senators introduce cloture by petition, and 60 members must approve it. Without cloture, the Senate simply cannot act on a bill that is the subject of a filibuster, even though the bill may have already passed every other stage in the legislative process.

At each stage, a majority must be developed in the bill's favor or it will die. Every program that involves appropriations must pass through the stages twice—first, to have funds authorized (for example, Judiciary Committee action authorizing appropriations for the Department of Justice) and second, to have funds appropriated (for example, Appropriations Committee action on the authorization legislation). In funding a program, therefore, the number of obstacles approximately doubles.

The sixth stage takes place if the two houses have passed similar bills in different forms. A **conference committee**—usually consisting of ranking members from the House and Senate committees that handled the bill earlier—is appointed to reconcile differences.

Seventh, the conference committee reports the bill back to both houses, where a final vote is taken. The bill must be accepted or rejected without amendment. Debate on the bill at that point is generally and mercifully minimal.

Eighth, the bill goes to the president, who may take one of several courses of action, as we saw in Chapter 10: (1) sign the bill into law; (2) veto and return the bill to Congress within ten days; (3) allow the bill to become law without his signature, which occurs if he has neither signed nor vetoed a bill while Congress is in session; and (4) "pocket veto" a bill by neglecting to act on it after Congress has adjourned.

Ninth, if the president vetoes a bill, Congress may choose to override the veto by a vote of two-thirds of the members of each house, in which case the bill becomes law.

Roadblocks to Legislation

It should be clear that the complex structure and slow movement of Congress raise formidable roadblocks to the passage of legislation. Each of the stages discussed above can also be an opportunity to delay or kill the bill:

1. The chairman of the House or Senate committee may try to prevent the committee from considering the bill.

2. The subcommittee chairman may hold up progress on the bill.

3. The House or Senate committee may decide not to move the bill along to the chamber.

4. The Rules Committee chairman may neglect to act on the bill.

5. The House Rules Committee may decline to act.

6. A Senate filibuster may prevent action on the bill.

7. The House or Senate (or both) may vote against the bill.

8. The conference committee of the two houses may not be able to resolve the differences between the two versions of the bill.

9. Either the House or the Senate (or both) may decline to approve the conference committee's action on the bill.

Of course, in a democracy, issues are supposed to be thoroughly debated so that voters can make intelligent decisions based on the best data available. Research to get the facts, debate to determine the alternatives, and compromise to achieve agreement require a good deal of time. Assembly-line speed is not necessarily a virtue in the resolution of serious social and economic problems. By deliberating at length on legislation, Congress performs the useful function of gradually educating society and preparing people for change. One has only to imagine what could have happened throughout the country without extensive debate on civil rights laws. Debate and deliberation help cushion the impact of change and stabilize our society with its diverse volatile interests.

Even so, Congress can move with surprising speed when the members' personal interests are at stake. **Pork barrel** refers to the practice of loading down legislation with something for most, if not all, members. The biggest parks bill in history, with 150 park projects in 44 states at a total cost of $1.4 billion, cleared the House Rules Committee in just five minutes in 1979. (The action caused the historic term "pork barrel" to be renamed in this instance "park barrel.") Congress has also acted quickly on pay raises for members, sometimes using parliamentary procedures to avoid a roll-call vote.

How Legislators Vote

What should influence how a legislator votes? The views of constituents? Advice from colleagues? Party loyalty? The president and the executive branch? The legislator's conscience? A member of Congress must maintain a balance among these five important influences on congressional voting. To vote according to party loyalty every time, for instance, suggests a crippling inflexibility. But if constituents were the most important influence on each vote, then a legislator might too often be voting against the national interest.

A legislator's perception of his or her role largely determines the manner in which these forces are weighed. Three types of roles have been ascribed to members of Congress: delegate, trustee and politico.[6] The **delegate** tries to determine what constituents want and votes accordingly. The **trustee** attempts to work out a position using both factual analysis and conscience, even though that position may conflict with constituent interests. The **politico** votes as a trustee on some issues and as a delegate on others.

The three congressional roles are most easily seen in operation when lawmakers vote on a bill. Take the example of a representative from the South, where support for both high tariffs on textile imports and a large defense budget are strong. The southern representative would act as a delegate by consistently representing constituents' views on these issues. This same southern representative would be acting as a politico by supporting high tariffs but favoring defense cuts. A trustee would consistently take an independent position, regardless of constituent desires. A trustee's support for constituent wishes would come only from his or her own reasoned judgment, not from constituents' views. Most members of Congress are either delegates or politicos; the trustee role is fraught with reelection dangers.

? ISSUES TO ANALYZE

ISSUE 1   IS CONGRESS A TRULY REPRESENTATIVE BODY?

REASONS WHY CONGRESS IS NOT A TRULY REPRESENTATIVE BODY

It is natural to assume that in a representative democracy, those who do the representing—the legislature—would be a cross section of the whole population. The legislative body should reflect race, sex, age, religion, and other groupings in a roughly proportionate way. If the legislature does not mirror the people, questions arise about how much of a representative democracy exists. The Founders were deeply concerned about this problem, which they deemed important to address in *Federalist, No. 57* by James Madison, who said: "The charge against the House of Representatives is that it will be taken from that class of citizens which will have least sympathy with the mass of the people, and be most likely to aim at an ambitious sacrifice of the many to the aggrandizement of the few." His answer to the charge was simple: "Who are to be the electors of the federal representatives? Not the rich, more than the poor; not the learned, more than the ignorant; not the haughty heirs of distinguished names, more than the humble sons of obscure and unpropitious fortune."[7]

Madison's efforts to lay the issue to rest failed. To this day problems with congressional representation arise. Representation in the U.S. Congress is distorted along three dimensions. Some groups are seriously underrepresented, others are overrepresented, and influential individual constituents receive the best representation.

Underrepresentation. African-Americans, women, and Hispanics get short shrift in Congress. Although 13 percent of the American population is African-American, in the 103rd Congress (1993–1994) the Senate had 1 African-American member (1 percent) and the House just under 9 percent, or 33 members. Slightly more than half the population is female, but only 47 women serve in the House, something over 10 percent, and just 6 in the Senate (precisely 6 percent). (See Figure 12.3 A and B.)

If African-Americans and women were represented in proportion to the population, approximately 56 African-Americans would be in the House and 13 in the Senate, and women would constitute half of both houses. Hispanic membership would also increase from 17 to over 20 in the House. What difference would such proportional representation make? Take the case of women. It could legitimately be argued that women

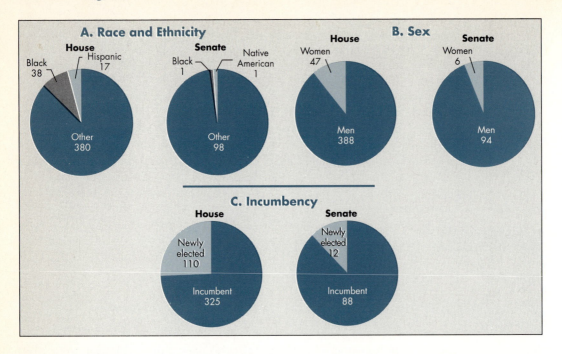

A. Race and Ethnicity

House
- Black 38
- Hispanic 17
- Other 380

Senate
- Black 1
- Native American 1
- Other 98

B. Sex

House
- Women 47
- Men 388

Senate
- Women 6
- Men 94

C. Incumbency

House
- Newly elected 110
- Incumbent 325

Senate
- Newly elected 12
- Incumbent 88

D. OCCUPATIONS

	HOUSE			SENATE			Congress Total*
	D	R	Total*	D	R	Total*	
Actor/entertainer	0	1	1	0	0	0	1
Aeronautics	0	2	2	1	0	1	3
Agriculture	7	12	19	3	5	8	27
Business or banking	56	75	131	12	12	24	155
Clergy	1	1	2	0	1	1	3
Education	45	20	66	6	5	11	77
Engineering	2	3	5	0	0	0	5
Homemaking	0	1	1	0	0	0	1
Journalism	11	12	24	7	2	9	33
Labor officials	2	0	2	0	0	0	2
Law	122	59	181	33	25	58	239
Law enforcement	8	2	10	0	0	0	10
Medicine	4	2	6	0	0	0	6
Military	0	0	0	0	1	1	1
Professional sports	0	1	1	1	0	1	2
Public service	51	36	87	8	2	10	97
Real estate	9	17	26	2	3	5	31

Note: Because some members have more than one occupation, totals are higher than total membership.

E. RELIGIOUS AFFILIATIONS

	HOUSE			SENATE			Congress
	D	R	Total	D	R	Total	Total
African Methodist	4	0	4	0	0	0	4
Apostolic Christian	0	1	1	0	0	0	1
Baptist	38	13	51	4	7	11	62
Christian Church	1	0	1	0	0	0	1
Christian Reformed	0	2	2	0	0	0	2
Christian Scientist	0	4	4	0	0	0	4
Church of Christ	4	1	5	0	0	0	5
Disciples of Christ	1	0	1	0	0	0	1
Episcopalian	18	17	35	4	11	15	50
French Huguenot	0	1	1	0	0	0	1
Greek Orthodox	0	4	4	1	0	1	5
Jewish	26	5	32	9	1	10	42
Lutheran	9	8	17	3	1	4	21
Methodist	31	23	54	7	4	11	65
Mormon	2	7	9	1	2	3	12
Presbyterian	20	26	46	5	3	8	54
Roman Catholic	77	41	118	15	8	23	141
Seventh Day Adventist	0	2	2	0	0	0	2
Unitarian	4	1	5	0	2	2	7
United Church of Christ/Congregationalist	5	2	7	4	3	7	14
Unspecified	9	0	9	1	0	1	10
Unspecified Protestant	10	17	27	2	0	2	29

F. A COMPARISON OF FRESHMEN AND INCUMBENTS IN THE HOUSE

	Freshmen	Incumbents
Under age 45	50.0%	19.1%
Prior military service	18.2%	47.7%
Prior elected office	71.8%	68.3%
Advanced degrees	65.5%	63.1%
Racial or ethnic minorities	23.6%	10.5%
Women	20.9%	8.0%

Figure 12.3 A PROFILE OF THE 103RD CONGRESS (1993–1994): WHO ARE THEY? Source: A, B, and C: *The New York Times*, January 5, 1993, p. A9; D, E, and F: *Congressional Quarterly Weekly Report*, November 7, 1992, pp. 7, 9.

would be more concerned than men about such issues as infant mortality, child care, consumer fraud, health centers, and world peace (and that both men and women would therefore be better off?).

Overrepresentation. An examination of congressional backgrounds reveals overrepresentation in several categories. Members of Congress come largely from middle-class and upper-class families, with fathers who were primarily professionals or business executives. Almost half of those in the 103rd Congress are lawyers, and banking and business are heavily represented as well (Figure 12.3D).

For most of the last hundred years, rural and southern members of Congress dominated committee leadership. A combination of retirements, defeats, increased political competition in the South, increased seniority for liberal northern members from urban areas, and the effects of reapportionment decisions in the 1960s, however, significantly increased the number of chairmen from outside the South during the 1970s. The shift in committee chairmen, therefore, has generally been from the one-party rural South that is more conservative to the one-party urban North that is more liberal.

The proportion of incumbents winning reelection reached over 98 percent in 1990; only 2 percent did not return to Congress. This low rate of turnover means less new blood and fewer new ideas in Congress. During the 1800s, an average of over 40 percent of House members were serving their first terms, but by the 1900s that percentage had dropped to under 20 percent, the backdrop to the extraordinarily low turnover rate in recent years. Low turnover rates can be thought of as the overrepresentation of experience. Experience, of course, is not bad unless it becomes stale. While the turnover rate in the 1992 congressional election was higher than in recent years (7 percent of incumbents were not returned), its causes related to such factors as redistricting, the House banking scandal, and running for other offices and not to any fundamental reforms that would make it easier for challengers to compete on an equal footing with incumbents. (Another significant factor was that members who retired in 1992 could keep leftover campaign funds which they would have lost had they stayed in Congress.) The year 1992 is likely, therefore, to be an anomaly rather than a harbinger of things to come.

Tunnel Vision. Who is important to members of Congress? Special interest groups! They are the people and groups who know the most about politics and how to influence politicians. Two scholars have written that "the communication most congressmen have with their districts inevitably puts them in touch with organized groups and individuals who are relatively well informed about policies. . . . As a result, [a representative's] sample of contacts with a constituency . . . is heavily biased."[8] A national survey has shown that only 59 percent of those questioned could identify even one senator from their state; only 46 percent could identify their own representative in the House. Indeed, 20 percent believed that Congress also included the United States Supreme Court.[9] A small percentage of people do know about Congress and how to influence it, and members of Congress pay more attention to them than to the masses. Tunnel vision makes political sense for these members.

REASONS WHY CONGRESS IS A TRULY REPRESENTATIVE BODY

It has been charged that Congress is not a representative body because some groups are underrepresented. There is not a perfect relationship between groups in the population and their numbers in Congress, but is such a perfect congruence really

Women are still overwhelmingly underrepresented in Congress in proportion to the population. But the addition of 4 female senators in 1992 (and 1 by a special election in 1993) more than tripled the complement of women in that body. The new look is exemplified here by the Banking, Housing and Urban Affairs Committee, which includes three new female members: Barbara Boxer (D-Ca.), Carol Moseley-Braun (D-Il.), and Patty Murray (D-Wa.)

necessary? Can only African-Americans represent African-Americans? Must only women represent women? Important laws favoring both groups have been enacted by members of Congress who were neither African-American nor female. Arguments involving representation can be carried to ludicrous extremes. After all, who represents the handicapped? The handicapped housewife? The handicapped Italian-American housewife? The handicapped Italian-American housewife on social security? In any case, women and minorities are gradually increasing their representation in Congress.

What about the charge that some groups, such as lawyers, southerners, and rural interests, are overrepresented? A body that drafts legislation probably ought to contain many lawyers. Southern and rural strength in Congress has been caused by **safe seats**, districts in which a member has little or no competition for the office. But these are now declining in number. For example, southerners no longer chair the influential Ways and Means or Rules Committees of the House.

What matters most is that members of Congress are responsive to the public that elects them. While the president and vice president are elected by a national constituency, members of Congress represent smaller constituencies and are thus closer to group and individual interests. The American public is not a large shapeless mass. Its differing values and concerns all merit representation in a democracy. A bureaucracy tends to establish uniform rules for everyone and overlook the myriad of individual, regional, and group differences. In a society with more than 250 million citizens, the standards relevant for some may not be the best for all. Unity and uniformity have their virtues, but so does diversity, especially in the United States. Congress is uniquely equipped to represent

A VIEW FROM THE STATES
The New Face of Congress

The young black woman with the gold sneakers, slacks, braided hair and Mickey Mouse watch stepped into the elevator in the Capitol.

"This elevator is for members only," the elevator operator said frostily.

"Yes, thank you," Cynthia McKinney replied, her glittering shoes planted firmly in place.

"This elevator is for members only," the woman running the elevator repeated, even more coldly.

"Yes, thank you," Ms. McKinney said, even more insistently.

"This elevator is for members only," the operator tried once more, before finally spotting the blue pin with the Congressional seal, worn by members, hanging on a gold chain around Ms. McKinney's neck.

"The elevator lady was very apologetic, and I told her that it's wonderful now that members of Congress come in all shapes and hues," the freshman Representative from Georgia said, recalling the recent standoff.

Cynthia McKinney is the startling new face of Congress: A 37-year-old former college professor and single mother from Atlanta with uncommon poise and a decidedly unpinstriped wardrobe.

... In 1992, a year of domestic concerns and disgust with business as usual, historic numbers of women were propelled into the cloistered world long dominated by white middle-aged men. The number of women jumped by 200 percent, or four seats, in the Senate, and by 68 percent, or 19 seats, in the House.

Source: Maureen Dowd, "Growing Sorority in Congress Edges Into the Ol' Boys' Club," *The New York Times,* March 5, 1993, p. A.

diversity. Because of their local concerns, members of Congress can balance the interests of a diverse population against the forces of uniformity.

The legislature is much more accessible to the public than either the judiciary or the executive. Its members must campaign for office every two (or six) years in a district or state where they are held accountable for their action and inaction. Federal judges do not have to face the public in this way and, in the executive branch, only the president and vice president are similarly accountable. The courts are solemn, the executive bureaucracy is impersonal, but Congress is open. A citizen may incur tremendous costs in bringing a lawsuit and enormous frustration in getting a response from the bureaucracy, while a simple letter or phone call to his or her representative or senator frequently produces the help needed. In fact, casework, or the ombudsman role, is a major part of all congressional offices. A little-known but very important aspect of their work is the passage of private bills for individuals who have not obtained relief from the bureaucracy and the courts. For example, when the General Services Administration (GSA) refused to honor a commitment to buy the old building of the First Baptist Church of Paducah, Kentucky, Senator Wendell Ford (D-Ky.) introduced a private bill that led to compensation of the church for GSA's refusal.[10]

Members of Congress generally pay attention to constituent demands. Senator Paul Simon (D-Il.), wearing his trademark bowtie, is shown here meeting in a constituent's home.

Congress represents the public interest when congressional opinion shifts along with public opinion. For instance, in the aftermath of World War II and the Korean War, veterans' organizations developed tremendous political muscle, prompting some critics to observe that this "iron triangle" of the bureaucracy, Congress, and the interest groups could produce pretty much what it wanted for veterans. Public opinion, of course, generally supported such actions at the time. However, public opinion changed after the Vietnam War during the 1970s; as a result the veterans' organizations could no longer count on easy victories in Congress. Then after the successful Persian Gulf War against Iraq in 1991, public opinion about the military shifted once again, making it easier for the military and veterans' organizations to get a favorable hearing in Congress. Thus we can say that congressional opinion shifts as public opinion redefines the public interest.

Within Congress itself, power ebbs and flows. For example, during the late 1950s a group of liberal Democrats in the House formed the Democratic Study Group and had substantial influence in legislative affairs. But with the conservative resurgence in the general public in the 1980s, conservative Republicans in both House and Senate organized to have greater impact on legislation.

Lest we give the impression that Congress is merely a yo-yo on a string responding to public opinion, we should note that while a representative body must obviously respond to, it does not have to necessarily *follow* public opinion. When the public, as measured by the polls, strongly supported a balanced budget amendment in the late 1970s, Congress did not. Recognizing that the citizens were saying, "We want a tighter budgetary policy," Congress instead began to tighten the budgetary and appropriations process as bills went through the Congress. This action, according to some observers, benefited the public interest more in the long run because it did not straitjacket the country with a balanced-budget requirement regardless of our economic or international situation. That is, a balanced budget is not necessarily desirable or advisable during a depression or a major war.

ISSUE 1:　Summary　★　*Is Congress a Truly Representative Body?*

Although considered the world's premier representative body, Congress underrepresents some groups while overrepresenting others. Critics contend that areas of under- and overrepresentation may cause Congress to distort the public interest in their legislative decisions. Congressional advocates, on the other hand, point out that a member of Congress does not have to be, for example, African-American to represent African-American interests effectively. Moreover, congressional representation provides Americans with another point of access to government that is much easier for the average citizen to use than either the executive or judicial branches. Also, Congress is a dynamic and not a static institution and therefore responds to changes in society; in recent years as society became more conservative, so did Congress. ■

ISSUE 2　DO MEMBERS OF CONGRESS PLAY TOO MUCH POLITICS?

REASONS WHY THEY PLAY TOO MUCH POLITICS

Alan Ehrenhalt in his book *The Politics of Ambition: Politicians, Power and the Pursuit of Office* argues that politics has become a profession, attracting people who love to play politics: "As politics turns into full-time work . . . it attracts people for whom political life itself is the reward."[11] According to one representative: "Although legislative matters theoretically consume most of a congressman's time, this is rarely true in practice. The energies of a great many of us are spent primarily in feathering the elective nests. Many members of Congress use their official facilities and staff help for various forms of constant campaigning."[12] The situation is especially bad in the House, because members must run for election every two years.

This state of affairs resembles a "misdirection play" in football, when the ball is apparently going one way but is really being carried in another direction. Members of Congress appear to be legislating when they are playing politics, and playing politics can be a demanding chore:

> *Infant-care booklets, provided free, may be mailed to all new mothers along with rhapsodical notes on the subject of motherhood. Home-district newspapers may be so carefully clipped that no new Tenderfoot Boy Scout, bathing beauty, or bake-off contest winner goes unremarked by the Congressman. . . . Sometimes there is no rest even for the dead: their survivors may be sent weepy letters of condolence.*[13]

Staff Growth. When former Senator William Proxmire (D-Wis.) bestowed his Golden Fleece Award, a "booby prize" for wasting government money, on Congress, he said: "While bread is the staff of life, it can now be said that too much of the taxpayer's bread has been used to give too much life to the congressional staff."[14] Since World War II, personal staff for House members have increased from 2 to over 20 and for senators, from an average of 4 aides each to over 40. Personal staff for members in both houses, totaling less than 1,500 before World War II, have increased to over 12,000. Of these personal staff, 34 and 44 percent, respectively, in the Senate and House, work outside of Washington in state and district offices. (These personal staff members paid for by taxpayers do not include congressional committee staff, leadership staff, and other support staff, all of which have had comparable growth.) No other legislator in any democracy has a staff anywhere near this size. Much of the staff time is devoted to enhancing a member's image.

Computer Technology. An incumbent's chances of winning reelection are enhanced by computerized direct mail to the voters. Although the **frank**—the free mailing privilege members enjoy—does not include the right to send campaign literature to key groups of voters, members may target groups in their districts and states with newsletters of interest to them, thus circumventing the rule against using the franking privilege to campaign. On a controversial issue, such as American policy in the Middle East, a member may send a pro-Israeli newsletter to Jewish constituents and another type of letter to those hostile or indifferent to Israel. In domestic politics, issues such as gun control lend themselves to this approach.

Congressional Myopia. Senators and representatives are elected by states and districts. Logically, therefore, members of Congress should be more concerned with the interests of their own constituencies than with larger, national concerns—and they are. Since congressional campaign money and other help come almost entirely from localities and special interest groups, members are practically forced to concentrate on narrow issues.

Examples of congressional myopia are legion, but one of the best is military base closings. Time after time recommendations to close obsolete military installations have been fought, usually successfully, by members of Congress. The representatives from the state where the bases are located lead the fight, but they get support from their colleagues because Congress is a sort of mutual benefit society in which back-scratching dominates. The theme is "I'll vote for your bill if you'll vote for mine."

REASONS WHY THEY DO NOT PLAY TOO MUCH POLITICS

To say that members of Congress are too busy playing politics to fulfill their real duties is unfair. For one thing, blanket characterizations are misleading. Numerous differences between the House and Senate affect how the members of each body approach their jobs. For another, the major business of Congress—handling legislation—does get accomplished, and both houses contribute to achieving this goal.

Different Approaches. The two houses differ in many ways that balance and complement each other (Table 12.4). First, senators have a larger constituency (except in those states with only one representative) and thus naturally deal with a wider range

TABLE 12.4 MAJOR DIFFERENCES BETWEEN HOUSE AND SENATE

	House	Senate
Size	435	100
Formality	More	Less
Terms	Two years	Six years
Hierarchical organization	More	Less
Action	Faster	Slower
Power distribution	Very uneven	More even
Apprenticeship	Longer	Shorter
Relationships	More impersonal	More personal
Committee assignments	One major	Two or more major
Policy interests	Specialist	Generalist
Prestige	Less	More
Ideology	More conservative	More liberal
Bill referral	Difficult to challenge	Easy to challenge
Committee consideration	Difficult to bypass	Easily bypassed
Debate	Limited	Unlimited
Nongermane amendments	Disallowed	Allowed
Rules committee	Powerful	Weak
Scheduling of legislation	Majority party control	Majority/minority—leaders usually agree
Rules	Rigid	Flexible
Media coverage	Less	More
Staff reliance	Less	More
Foreign Policy role	Less	More

of interests. Senators from states with large metropolitan areas confront diverse racial and social pressures. Second, senators don't have to worry about campaigning as often as representatives, but they are more likely to face significant competition for reelection. In the House, the number of safe seats—those for which there is little or no competition—has historically been much higher.

Another way in which the two houses balance each other has to do with the role of **mavericks**—legislators with unorthodox views or positions—who challenge congressional leadership on important issues. The House, a large body with a need for rules to restrain the freedom of its members, has produced few effective mavericks. The smaller, less formal Senate, on the other hand, has boasted many such people; they have made important contributions, especially in championing minority views. Senators Howard Metzenbaum (liberal, D-Ohio) and Jesse Helms (conservative, R-N.C.) performed this role in the 1980s and early 1990s, contesting the dominant views and offering alternatives. Mavericks do not play or enjoy politics as usual. Although an inner circle—a so-called Senate Club—has been accused of running the upper house, mavericks have actually been free to challenge the establishment with unusual and sometimes annoying ideas.

The size of the Senate is not the only factor here. Senators have large staffs, a great deal of social prestige in Washington, and a high degree of visibility. There are always several who are regularly mentioned as future presidential or vice presidential possibilities by the media or by their staffs (or even by themselves). There are usually several around, such as Robert Dole (R-Kans.), who have already run in presidential primaries. These factors enable them to get publicity for their views and to develop a following outside the Senate hierarchy. Senators are, of course, better situated to address international issues than members of the House of Representatives, because of their constitutional duty to confirm ambassadors and ratify treaties.

Legislative Accomplishments. Critics are quick to point out all the legislation on which Congress does not act. In any given year, members of Congress may introduce some 10,000 bills and resolutions and pass fewer than 1,000 or even 500. But critics are slow to praise the legislature for the number and type of laws it does pass. Moreover, Congress can represent the public interest just as much by killing a bill as by passing one. Many bills have no future and should have none.

Often the president receives credit for legislative accomplishments. Yet in many instances, a president's program, especially for major, innovative legislation, has had its incubation period in Congress. For example, Great Society legislation proposed and enacted during the Johnson administration had been culled in part from bills developed and introduced earlier by members of Congress, just as were Richard Nixon's revenue-sharing legislation and President Ronald Reagan's economic reform package.

Political leadership in Congress is often necessary to take a program through countless political land mines. President Lyndon Johnson could not have obtained passage of the landmark Civil Rights Act of 1964 and the Voting Rights Act of 1965 without the senatorial leadership of Republican floor leader Everett M. Dirksen (R-Ill.), nor could President Ronald Reagan have enjoyed his success on economic reform legislation without substantial Democratic party support. Presidents may take credit for great legislative accomplishments, but the genesis of the idea usually comes from Congress, as does the necessary political leadership.

The physical, mental, emotional, and financial costs for serving as a member of Congress are high and generally not well known to the public. Former Representative Leon E. Panetta (D-Calif.), a leader in Congress until chosen to head an executive agency under President Clinton, shared a townhouse with three other members, where he slept in the living room for $400 a month. As a West Coast member, he had to fly back and forth to Washington each week, leaving his wife and three sons behind in California.[15] Considerable dedication and sacrifice are required to meet the seemingly relentless demands of congressional life.

ISSUE 2: Summary ★ *Do Members of Congress Play Too Much Politics?*

Before a person can influence the legislative process, he or she must be able to win a political election and then practice politics astutely enough to remain in office. Members of Congress do engage in political activities that don't relate directly to their purpose of considering important national and international issues and passing legislation. In that sense, they do play too much politics. But if one believes that the primary purpose of politics is to win and that the primary purpose of serving in Congress is to consider the momentous issues of the day, then a built-in conflict is apparent between the two goals. Some legislators, known as mavericks, make a point of not playing politics as usual. And

A VIEW FROM THE STATES
A Day in the Life of a California Congressman

Leon Panetta left the Congress in 1993 to serve as President Clinton's Director of the Office of Management and Budget, the OMB. The following news story describes what his life was like when he represented a California district in the House of Representatives.

[M]r.] Panetta's workweek typically begins at Dulles International Airport outside Washington, where he lands after a long working weekend in California.

Last week, as is often the case, he landed at 6 A.M. Tuesday, having caught a couple of hours' sleep on the red-eye flight from San Francisco. "Welcome to the morning shift," he said in mock ebullience to the Budget Committee aide who picked him up.

Dropped at his townhouse, the Congressman napped for an hour before walking to work.

When he arrived at his cramped office in the Cannon building, his press secretary, Barry Toiv, was waiting. With Mr. Toiv producing, Mr. Panetta took a news release on a Medicaid reform bill into his makeshift office radio studio—a closet full of paint cans and a beat-up refrigerator—to record some sound bites for a radio station back home.

There were few votes that day, but nevertheless Mr. Panetta's schedule ended at midnight. He met with the Budget Committee staff to plot hearings for a balanced-budget amendment, participated in a strategy meeting for a balanced-budget amendment, participated in a strategy meeting with other Democratic leaders and conferred with the president of San Jose State University about the possible conversion of part of a military base into a marine biology school.

He also joined a luncheon attended by Italian-American business leaders and lawmakers. . . . But the meal was disrupted when one businessman rose to coarsely admonish lawmakers for arrogance and ineptitude.

After the luncheon, Mr. Panetta was driven to a downtown hotel to follow President Bush and several newspaper columnists in addressing a business group. Tired of all the Washington-speak, a third of the audience walked out as Mr. Panetta stepped up to speak.

Back at his office, a stream of constituents came by, bearing small gifts and asking favors. Such visitors are a minefield that every lawmaker has to go through without breaking ethical rules or offending influential constituents or fundraisers.

"Anybody who takes this job for the perks," Mr. Panetta said, "is barking up the wrong tree."

Congress as a whole does manage to turn its attention away from personal political concerns long enough to pass up to 1,000 bills each year. ■

ISSUE 3   IS CONGRESS CORRUPT AND IN NEED OF REFORM?

REASONS WHY CONGRESS IS CORRUPT AND IN NEED OF REFORM

Congressional wrongdoing has ranged from the slightly shady to the downright illegal. During the early 1990s, five prominent U.S. senators, including the Majority Whip of the Senate, were charged with illegal and unethical conduct in representing the interests of the Lincoln Savings and Loan Association, which had bilked investors out of millions of dollars. During the 1980s, others were found guilty of filing expense vouchers for non-incurred expenses, filing false campaign donations, padding payrolls, accepting kickbacks from employees, illegally converting campaign funds to personal use, and accepting bribes. And in 1992, the House bank scandal revealed that House members enjoyed and took full advantage of free overdraft protection for bounced checks, a previously undisclosed service that had been available for about a century and a half. News of this scandal induced 43 House members to announce their retirements.[16]* Little wonder that the percentage of Americans having a great deal of confidence in Congress dropped from 28 percent in 1984 to 10 percent in 1992.[17] (See also Table 12.5.)

A common and well-documented type of congressional wrongdoing is **junketing,** ostensibly travel on government business, but in reality for pleasure at government expense. Costs for congressional overseas travel skyrocketed from approximately $1 million in 1975 to some $10 million by 1990. Although some of these costs were for legitimate purposes, a substantial portion paid for junketing. Other instances of abuse include **nepotism,** placing relatives on the payroll (such as one's spouse and then junketing with her or him); and having committee staff aides work on an election campaign while on the government payroll. Some members of Congress have also used their franking privilege to mail campaign literature. As it is, taxpayers fund between $80 and $90 million of free postage for members for presumably legitimate uses.[18]

Congress polices its own ethics violations. But some observers favor creation of an outside group, composed perhaps of retired judges, to do fact-finding when ethics of a member are questioned.

In addition to policing itself, Congress exempts itself from many of the laws it passes to regulate the lives of other citizens. To name just a few, the Civil Rights Act of 1964, the Equal Employment Opportunity Act of 1972, the Equal Pay Act, the Freedom of Information Act, the Age Discrimination Act, the Ethics in Government Act of 1978, the Privacy Act, the Family and Medical Leave Act, and the Americans with Disabilities Act do not apply to either the Senate or House. Representative Christopher Shays (R-Conn.) notes the effect of this: "By exempting ourselves from laws, we are depriving members of the opportunity to experience firsthand the effects of the legislation we adopt."[19]

---

* Another 19 had been defeated in primaries, a suggestion that voters can and do inflict the worst punishment; 13 others had decided to run for other offices.

TABLE 12.5   PUBLIC RATINGS OF PROFESSIONAL ETHICS

Profession	Percentage of People Rating Honesty and Ethical Standards of Profession as High or Very High
Druggists/pharmacists	66%
Clergy	54%
Medical doctors	52%
College teachers	50%
Dentists	50%
Police	42%
Funeral directors	35%
TV reporters/commentators	31%
Bankers	27%
Newspaper reporters	25%
Building contractors	19%
Lawyers	18%
Business executives	18%
Local officeholders	15%
Real estate agents	14%
Labor union leaders	14%
Stockbrokers	13%
U.S. Senators	**13%**
State officeholders	11%
U.S. Representatives	**11%**
Advertising executives	10%
Insurance salespeople	9%
Car salespeople	5%

Source: *The Christian Science Monitor*, February 9, 1993, p. 4. Data from Gallup Poll, June 1992.

Another important area of reform is campaign finance. Members of Congress spend too much of their time seeking funds for reelection, and they are too beholden to the special interests who help put them in office. Public financing of congressional elections, lower caps on political action committee contributions, and greater accountability would help restrain some of the abuses of campaign financing.

Congress is bloated and does not perform efficiently. As Table 12.6 shows, the cost of running Congress has increased by 705 percent since 1970, during which time defense spending increased by only 311 percent and inflation by only 280 percent. Special perks and generous pensions enjoyed by former members elevate the cost of running Congress, as do the salaries for the thousands of staff members. The number of legislative and committee staff has increased tenfold since 1947, while the population of the country increased only 50 percent. Congressional bookkeeping is not easy to determine. For example, congressional salaries and benefits are excluded from the congressional budget by considering them a permanent appropriation not in need of annual authorization and appropriation.

What can be done to correct the abuses? First, reduce the number of staff for

"But how do you know for sure you've got power unless you abuse it?"

both individual members and committees. As Congressman Andrew Jacobs (D-Ind.) stated: "Legislators would be forced actually to know something about the issues that they're voting on and not rely so much on their staff."[20] Second, audit the congressional budget each year and cut back on the subsidized privileges members enjoy.

Congress could also improve the process of legislating. It votes at least twice (often more) on every dollar it appropriates. Combining the authorization and appropriations committees might make this process more efficient. Providing more general guidelines and less detailed provisions in the bills it passes could also streamline Congress's work. Less time would be needed for hearings in committee, and more time could be devoted to debate on the floor—an arena sadly neglected in recent decades.

Finally, the franking privilege could be limited to answering constituents' letters, at a potential savings of $100 to $150 million every two years. Staff presently required to handle the large volume of mail that is not in response to constituents inquiries could be cut sharply.[21]

TABLE 12.6 THE COST OF RUNNING CONGRESS (IN MILLIONS)

	1970	1980	1992
House	$108	$325	$ 722
Senate	58	184	488
Other Congressional agencies and joint committee staffs	177	709	1,550
Totals	$343	$1218	$2760

Source: *Money,* August 1992, p. 131.

REASONS WHY CONGRESS IS NOT CORRUPT AND IN NEED OF REFORM

The illegal and unethical activities of a few members ought not to be condoned, but they should be understood in the context of the society and the times in which they occurred. The Watergate scandal in the 1970s led to new laws and ethical standards, an aroused public, and a press corps that exposed and condemned activities that were previously unknown or quietly tolerated. Congress now functions in much more of a fishbowl environment.

Young and articulate new members entered Congress during the 1970s and 1980s with a zeal for making Congress run more effectively and more openly. Although critics do not agree entirely on the success of the 1970s reforms, Congress has clearly made major changes.

Charges about the large number of congressional employees are often made without understanding what has been accomplished with them. Congress not only created the Congressional Budget Office (CBO), the Congressional Research Service (CRS), and the Office of Technology Assessment (OTA) to make Congress more effective in the policymaking process, but also helped to energize the long-established Government Accounting Office (GAO), the primary investigative arm of Congress. Through its approximately 1,200 annual reports, GAO spotlights waste, fraud, mismanagement, and misdirected government programs.

One of the most severe charges levied at Congress has been that it is unable to challenge the president on budgetary matters. The Congressional Budget Reform Act of 1974 created a standing Budget Committee for each house, in addition to the Congressional Budget Office. These new organizations allow Congress to more effectively determine the government's revenue and appropriations needs each year. The legislature can now gather its own data without relying on the executive branch and can consequently establish priorities for revenue and spending within its own budget timetable. Before 1974, Congress acted on each appropriations bill separately without regard for other appropriations bills or anticipated federal revenues. Now Congress can relate each appropriations bill to the entire revenue and expenditure picture.

For many years it was charged that Congress was a closed system dominated by senior members and that antiquated procedures prevented the majority from working its will. Major changes in these areas during the 1970s have made the Congress a far more open legislative body. First, the seniority system has been modified to allow challenges to the automatic ascension of the senior member of a committee to chairmanship. Second, committee proceedings are now open to the public unless a public vote closes them. Since important legislative work takes place in mark-up sessions, where language in the bill is put into final form, opening these sessions has made Congress more responsive to the public interest. Third, new rules or procedures implemented in the 1970s have improved committee processes. Democrats, the majority in the House, have established several reforms of their party:

1. No House member may chair more than one legislative subcommittee. This change breaks the lock that senior conservative Democrats had on key subcommittees.

2. According to a "bill of rights" for committees, chairmen must share authority with other party members. Committee chairmen can no longer "pocket veto" legislation by ignoring it. They must refer all bills to subcommittees within two weeks.

3. To prevent chairmen from concentrating power in their own hands, the rules also provide for subcommittees.

4. All committees require written rules, which provides another way to check the arbitrary exercise of power by committee chairmen.

5. Each subcommittee must have at least one staff member for the chairman and one for the ranking minority member.

6. Senior Democrats may belong to only two of a committee's subcommittees.

7. The chairmen of all Appropriations subcommittees must be approved by the House Democratic Caucus.

8. Each House Democrat must have one major committee assignment before any member can have another committee assignment. This rule increases the opportunity for junior members to serve on important committees. House Democrats now mandate the same rule for subcommittee assignments.

The Senate restructured its committee system by (1) reducing the number of committees, (2) limiting the number on which a senator could serve, (3) providing the minority party with one-third of each committee staff, and (4) establishing computerized scheduling to reduce the number of overlapping meetings. The new system decreased the number of all types of committees from 31 to 25. Before the restructuring, some members had as many as 30 assignments; the current maximum is 11. The Senate also acted to prevent abuses of the filibuster. Once the Senate has voted to end a filibuster, a final vote on a bill must be taken after no more than 100 hours of debate, regardless of pending amendments. Previously, senators would introduce endless amendments to a bill they didn't want, thereby holding up action on it.

The reformers of the 1970s probably overlooked what may have been the reform of the 1980s, the revitalization of congressional parties. Most members are nominated and elected without any significant degree of dependence on local, state, national, or congressional party leaders. They have been free, therefore, to defy the wishes of party leaders, but now that interest groups are buffeting them members are beginning to look for cover. Strengthened party organizations enable members to use their loyalty to a party and its policies as an excuse to avoid making commitments to interest groups.

The unusually large number of new members elected in 1992 together with the backdrop of congressional scandals will undoubtedly lead to more substantive reforms of the Congress. In fact, a joint congressional committee was named in 1993 to propose specific changes. Even before the 1992 elections, however, exposure of congressional perks by the press caused some of them to be abolished, such as the special check-writing privileges in the House bank.

ISSUE 3: Summary ★ *Is Congress Corrupt and in Need of Reform?*

In some ways Congress is like a herd of elephants, hard to get going and difficult to stop. A lot of momentum must be established before Congress acts on a matter. Sometimes Congress appears to be overlooking the need to censure corruption among its members or to adopt some needed reform. Once Congress begins to act on such matters, however, it often acts so thoroughly that critics think it has gone too far. The 1970s saw a great deal of reform in committee processes. In the 1980s party organizations in Congress were strengthened. In the early 1990s momentum seemed to be gathering for a new generation of legislators to "clean up" the institution of Congress. ■

ISSUE 4   SHOULD MEMBERS OF CONGRESS BE LIMITED TO 12 YEARS IN OFFICE?

REASONS WHY THEY SHOULD BE LIMITED TO 12 YEARS IN OFFICE

Public pressure for limiting terms is dramatically increasing. In 1992, President George Bush called for congressional term limits. By the end of that year, 14 states had adopted congressional term limitations and a number of others had approved state legislative limits. As shown in Table 12.7, public support for congressional term limitations was substantial in all 14 states voting on the proposition in 1992. (These 14, together with Colorado's previous ratification, bring the total to 15.) Adopting term limitations would place the United States nearly alone among the democracies. Why the sudden support for this proposal?

First, between 1948 and 1988 the proportion of incumbents winning reelection to the U.S. Congress increased from 79.3 to 98.3 percent in the House and from 60.0 to 85.2 percent in the Senate. Congress became a safe haven for entrenched incumbents. During the first eight decades of American history, 1791 to 1870, the U.S. House of Representatives averaged 52 percent new members after every election. During the decade just past, that figure was 13.2 percent. Members of Congress averaged about 4 years in office during the last century, but today they *average* about 12 years. Representatives and senators serving 12 or more consecutive years increased between 1959 and 1989 from about 22 to 33 percent in the House and from approximately 21 to 38 percent in the Senate.[22] In the 1990 congressional elections, only one sitting senator lost his seat, and in 1992, only three.

TABLE 12.7   STATE ACTION ON CONGRESSIONAL TERM LIMITATIONS, 1992

State	Senate	House	Percentage For/Against
Arizona	12 years	6 years	74 to 26
Arkansas	12 years	6 years	60 to 40
California	12 years	6 years	63 to 37
Florida	12 years	8 years	77 to 23
Michigan	12 years	6 years	59 to 41
Missouri	12 years	8 years	74 to 26
Montana	12 years	6 years	67 to 33
Nebraska	12 years	8 years	68 to 32
North Dakota	12 years	12 years	55 to 45
Ohio	12 years	8 years	66 to 34
Oregon	12 years	6 years	69 to 31
South Dakota	12 years	12 years	63 to 37
Washington	12 years	6 years	52 to 48
Wyoming	12 years	6 years	77 to 23

Source: *Congressional Quarterly Weekly Report,* November 7, 1992, p. 3594.

Second, ethics scandals in Congress have jarred the public trust. The 1992 House banking scandal implicated over 300 present and former members for bouncing checks. Members who receive campaign contributions from corporations they are helping and who accept large fees for speeches from organizations seeking to influence their votes have caused public opinion to become critical of their lengthy terms in office.

Third, blacks and females, conservatives and Republicans, have good reason to support a limitation on terms. Most members of Congress, protected by the advantages of incumbency, are white, male Democrats. As of 1993, African-Americans, Hispanics, and females together constituted only about 21 percent of the membership in the U.S. House of Representatives.

Conservatives and Republicans cite 1984 to illustrate how they are disenfranchised: 36.57 million Americans voted for Republican congressional candidates while 36.61 million voted for Democrats, but 253 Democrats and 182 Republicans were elected. Since Democrats control most state legislatures, they have been able to redraw districts for the U.S. House of Representatives in such a way as to make it improbable, if not impossible, for Republicans to win their share of seats. Term limits would give conservatives and Republicans more opportunities to run against opponents who do not have the advantages of seniority and incumbency.

Fourth, for many years policy gridlock between Congress and the president, illustrated most recently by the budget stalemate in 1990, made it difficult for a Republican president enjoying an overwhelming popular mandate to get a program through a Congress controlled by Democrats. More frequent turnover of members of Congress might produce a more receptive legislature for a president in a divided government.

Fifth, state and national legislative election contests are no longer conducted on a level playing field. For example, at taxpayer expense Congress has written its own "Incumbent Reelection Insurance Policy" in the form of increased staffs and more district and state offices. Challengers, of course, have no access to these taxpayer-provided resources, including the franking privilege, which allows incumbents to send mail to every household in a district or state at taxpayers' expense.

Sixth, studies of campaign finance show that most political action committees clearly prefer to give to the campaigns of incumbents. Once elected, House members have two years and Senators, six years, to curry favors with PACs by casting votes favorable to them.

Seventh, limiting congressional terms would place Congress and the president on a more equal footing: The president is already limited to two terms or ten years. The lame-duck status of presidents limits their ability to influence Congress and the bureaucracy, while the longevity of members of Congress strengthens their control over the bureaucracy that the president is elected to head.

REASONS WHY THEY SHOULD NOT BE LIMITED TO 12 YEARS IN OFFICE

The countervailing arguments are quite strong and easily stated:

- Should voters in a democracy be arbitrarily denied the right to elect whomever they wish without regard to tenure in office?

- Should an outstanding legislator be arbitrarily removed from office by limitation on tenure?

- Should the power and influence of lobbyists, bureaucrats, and legislative staff, who serve indefinitely, be increased by arbitrarily removing senior members of Congress who have the knowledge and ability to combat their power and influence?

- Should we risk losing the institutional memory of senior members of Congress who know how legislative bodies can and should function?

- Should we diminish the power of the smaller, less populous states by forcing their senior (and probably influential) members to retire?

- Should we risk creating a lame-duck mentality among members of Congress who might lose their incentive to perform well since they could not run for reelection after 12 years?

ISSUE 4: Summary ★ *Should Members of Congress Be Limited To 12 Years in Office?*

The principal advantage of term limitations would be the greater likelihood of fresh blood and new ideas, while the principal disadvantage would be loss of experience. In the short run, conservatives, women, minorities, and Republicans would probably benefit from term limitations. They would be expected to have more success running for an open seat than for one held by an incumbent. But term limitations would deny voters the right to vote for well-qualified persons whose terms are expired. Moreover, the power relationships

A VIEW FROM THE STATES
Term Limits Limit Choice

Leaders of the campaign to limit Congressional terms call it "the largest grass-roots citizens' movement in U.S. history." Maybe so, but it is also the most mischievous proposal of the year. It would give voters less choice while claiming to give them more. . . .

The concept of rotation is older than the Government; there were term limits in the Articles of Confederation. Wisely, the Founding Fathers did not continue them in the Constitution.

The philosophical appeal of term limitation is a Congress of "citizen politicians" rather than "careerists"—the current negative buzzword. The philosophical flaw is that term limits deny voters the right to vote for anyone they want, including deserving incumbents. And while supposedly opening the way for fresh blood, term limits could also discourage potential candidates who see public office as a professional calling.

The practical flaw is that term limitation punishes experience. If no senator can serve more than 12 years, and if representatives are even more severely limited, continuity and real power would pass from elected politicians to unelected staff employees and lobbyists. By the same token, this would also reduce the power of Congress in relation to the President. . . .

In the end, what matters most is that voters have a choice, and that they exercise it. The best way of all to control who holds office is to protect, not limit, people's power to vote.

Source: "Term Limits Limit Choice," editorial in *The New York Times*, October 13, 1992, p. A22. Copyright © 1992 by The New York Times Company. Reprinted by permission.

between members of Congress and others, such as congressional staff, the bureaucracy, and lobbyists, would likely be altered as relatively junior members of Congress confronted these more seasoned individuals. ■

 COMPARISONS WITH OTHER NATIONS

LEGISLATURES IN DEMOCRACIES

As we saw in Chapter 9, Americans are asked to go to the polls to the point of physical exhaustion. The term of office is almost always longer elsewhere. Our Constitution requires an election for the entire House of Representatives every two years. Most other democracies take their time, allowing up to five years between national elections (see Table 12.8). Unless otherwise indicated, of course, we are speaking here only of the lower house. The upper houses are not politically significant (with certain exceptions). It is prestigious to belong to one but not especially important. Table 12.9 shows how upper houses are chosen in certain major democracies.

TABLE 12.8   ELECTIONS OF SELECTED NATIONAL LEGISLATURES

Country	Timing of National Election	Features
Canada	Every 5 years	Election intervals are mandated. But legislature can also be dissolved and new elections called by the government.
France	Every 5 years	
Germany	Every 4 years	
Japan	Every 4 years	
United Kingdom	Up to 5 years	Average time between elections is 3 to 4 years
United States	**Every 2 years**	**Constitutionally mandated**

Many upper houses provide links with a national past. In an even more symbolic fashion, they are links with the heritage of the Western political tradition. For example, several democracies (such as Canada, France, and the United States) have named their upper houses the "Senate" in respect for the ancient upper house of the Roman Republic.

Why are upper houses usually devoid of influence in legislation? It wasn't always so. Many upper houses, such as the British House of Lords, are ancient institutions. The House of Lords, whose pedigree can be traced back nearly a millennium, is the oldest legislative chamber in the world that is still functioning. The typical upper house, however, came to represent a special elitist land-owning class that, by the early nineteenth century, was becoming out of step with increasingly democratic times. As countries in Western Europe and elsewhere democratized, politicians realized that anyone serious about a career in national politics had better get elected to a seat in the lower house. At the end of that career in Britain a successful politician might finally arrive at the House of Lords with a life peerage. Former Prime Minister Margaret Thatcher (1979–1990), for example, was given a life peerage in 1992.

In most systems there is not even a pretense of equality between the two houses. In fact, in many bicameral legislatures it is entirely possible for the lower house to abolish the upper house. Left-wing members of Britain's Labour party call for this all the time since they consider the House of Lords both useless and a political anachronism. Being

TABLE 12.9   SELECTION PROCEDURES FOR UPPER HOUSES IN MAJOR DEMOCRACIES

Country	Upper House	Method of Selection
Canada	Senate	Appointed
France	Senate	Special electoral college
Germany	Bundesrat	Chosen by state governments
Japan	House of Councillors	Popular election
United Kingdom	House of Lords	Inherited or appointed position
United States	**Senate**	**Popular election**

The British House of Lords is unelected, not very popular, and not at all powerful, but it has lasted nearly a millennium and still serves some use as a check on the work of the House of Commons.

unelected and unpopular and, for the most part, unpowerful, does not necessarily mean ineffective. The Lords (and several Ladies, since the house admitted women in the 1960s for the first time in about 700 years) have the luxury of reviewing legislation passed by the Commons, making recommendations, and not worrying about how their actions will influence the electorate.

Many parliamentary systems have given up on bicameral legislatures altogether. These relatively small countries—Denmark, Greece, Iceland, Israel, New Zealand, and Sweden—simply see no purpose in having more than one legislative chamber, elected or otherwise. There is no indication, however, that legislation is any more efficient in unicameral systems.

Another crucial difference between the American and most other democratic systems is the striking clarity of the legislative process in parliamentary systems. Simply put, no parliamentary government can lose a legislative vote and remain the government. Such governments are based, after all, on retaining control of a majority of parliamentary seats. It stands to reason, therefore, that if a government's policy loses a vote it no longer enjoys majority support. Either there must be new elections or a prime minister (either the current one or a successor) must form a new government that will be acceptable to a parliamentary majority.

When a new prime minister must be chosen in the midst of a parliamentary term, part of the parliament, usually the lower house, can serve as an electoral college. For example, when British Prime Minister Margaret Thatcher resigned in 1990 her successor, John Major, was selected not by the electorate voting on a new Parliament and not even by the House of Commons as a whole. Instead, it was the 376 Conservative party members of the Commons who voted on their new party leader (who would then be asked by the Queen to become her prime minister). A majority of the Conservative parliamentary party members selected Major. This method for choosing new prime ministers is not uncommon. There is no equivalent in the United States, but there is a similar procedure. It is the majority party members with seats in the House of Representatives who choose the Speaker of the House, a powerful position that follows the vice president in the presidential succession order.

Members of the British House of Commons and members of the American Congress have some similar problems. They both worry about getting reelected and advancing to leadership positions within their party ranks. In both systems there is also dissatisfaction and impatience with the slowness of advancement. This characteristic is especially prevalent in the Commons. While representatives in the American Congress often aspire to attain a seat in the more prestigious Senate and many senators are hopeful of securing the nomination of their party for president or vice president, members of the Commons almost automatically dream of becoming Cabinet ministers. Most of them will be disappointed:

> Politics has become a profession, with a well-understood career structure. By this standard, most MPs [members of Parliament] are doomed to fail; at any one time, only around 14% of them are members of the government. The consequences are obvious. In the Commons bars and offices lurk many bored, soured souls. A few are dim-witted drones, but most are talented, frustrated, wasted people. The still-ambitious ones (often career politicians who have had no other job) are voting-fodder, humiliatingly dependent on the goodwill of the party bosses and whips.[23]

In parliamentary systems there is no equivalent of a presidential veto because there is no need for one. A piece of legislation that is defeated can mean the end of the government, and almost any legislation that passes had the advocacy of the government to begin with. In fact, the overwhelming portion of legislation (as much as 90 percent) that gets passed in parliaments is sponsored by the government. Only infrequently are private members' bills brought to the house floor.

It might seem that the parliamentary minority opposition is faced with an impossible task. If it opposes the government's legislation it must do so in debate, knowing all the while that its position will be soundly defeated when a vote is taken. That is exactly what will happen. So, why bother? The opposition's legislative role is to explain in public forum (namely, from the floor of parliament) why it opposes the bill in question and how it would provide a better one. It will then go on to campaign on that basis the next time there is a general election.

Figure 12.4 FOR UNIFIED CONTROL OF PRESIDENCY AND CONGRESS. Source: *The New York Times,* November 4, 1992, p. B1. Copyright © 1992 by The New York Times Company. Reprinted by permission. Data from Voter Research and Surveys exit poll of 13,471 voters.

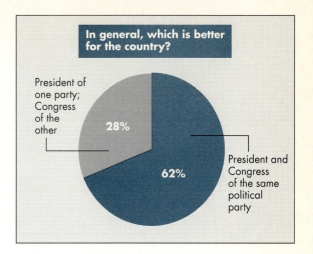

In general, which is better for the country?

President of one party; Congress of the other — 28%

President and Congress of the same political party — 62%

From time to time a proposal surfaces that would transform the current political system in the United States into a parliamentary one. Its advocates claim that more would get done because the president and the Congress would then belong to the same party, legislative impasses would be easily avoided, and government would become more efficient. Maybe. As Figure 12.4 shows, most Americans do favor unified control of the presidency and Congress. It is interesting to note, however, that at the same time political reforms are being proposed in parliamentary systems that might make them resemble us. Britons have discussed the possibility, for example, of transforming the House of Lords into a Senate and making all or part of the membership popularly elected. Indeed, Americans may well wonder why the British keep the House of Lords around if it is an unelected body that "is not particularly popular."[24]

One other crucial difference between American and most European or European-style democracies needs to be mentioned. Most parliamentarians are more dependent on party affiliation and party leadership than are their American counterparts. Party organizations, not primary elections, normally select parliamentary candidates. In Britain, the local party officials interview prospective candidates for a district's parliamentary seat and make a selection. Similar procedures apply in other English-speaking democracies such as Australia and Canada. In Israel, where the entire country is treated as a single constituency, the party leadership determines whose name gets onto its election list and in what place—the higher the ranking, the better the chance to win a seat. Of course, Israel has a unitary political system, quite suitable for its size and population of only 5 million. As a federal system of 250 million people, the United States has diverse constituencies with diverse needs, making party discipline difficult if not impossible to achieve.

Some very viable legislatures are emerging in developing countries. Several in East Asia and Latin America include a competitive political party system. These tend to follow the American model with two houses that are collectively called Congress, although some of the Caribbean islands that are former British colonies have parliamentary systems. In East Asia, economically prosperous societies such as South Korea and Singapore have developed legislatures with extensive powers. In October 1992, the Brazilian Congress was strong enough to impeach and remove from office the Brazilian president on charges of corruption.

Legislatures in the Third World are increasingly becoming the single most important vehicle for political democracy. They are also increasingly courageous. For example, in Thailand in May 1992, the parliament added amendments to the constitution to ensure that future prime ministers would be civilians who hold legislative seats, in order to preclude any repetition of military officers' assuming the office.

Every legislative system that functions in a democracy must evolve with the times. Political evolution is certainly preferable and a lot easier on the nervous system than sudden or violent change. The American Senate evolved rather substantially when the Seventeenth Amendment (1913) made it a popularly elected body, rather than elected by state legislatures. But while legislatures may evolve into something better (more responsive to what people want and need), they also have natural limitations:

> You cannot legislate to create good citizens, sensible politicians or industrious workers. You can, however, improve a system that has failed to evolve. By doing so you can, eventually, produce better laws. They, in time, may make people happier and more industrious (though not, alas, prettier or younger).[25]

LEGISLATURES IN TOTALITARIAN SYSTEMS

Prior to the early 1990s Western political scientists thought little about and spent even less time studying the legislative process in communist systems. There was simply no reason to do so. Legislatures in most communist societies met less frequently than American state legislatures. Typically they would meet for only two sessions a year, each being less than a week long. Most legislators took off time from their regular jobs to dutifully approve policies that had already been decided upon by the Communist party leadership.

One important reason for the diminished role of the legislature in communist societies has to do with the diminished status of the state itself. The party, much more than the government, is responsible for formulating and implementing policy. In the former Soviet Union, for example, the members of the Supreme Soviet, the national legislature, for seven decades monotonously voted unanimously on legislation. That was, after all, their job. For the vast majority of the 750 rank-and-file members of each house, the Soviet of the Union and the Soviet of Nationalities, the sessions were merely pleasant (but usually boring) breaks from the routine of their regular jobs. The house memberships were intentionally large and turnover was substantial. Membership was basically an honor provided to deserving party members. As in most federated systems, one house's membership was based on population throughout the country while the other was composed of representatives from the various regions (in this case republics and autonomous areas) of the country.

As the deterioration of the Soviet economy became increasingly obvious in the late 1980s its political system opened up more and more. A new Congress of People's Deputies was elected in April 1989 and for the first time was filled with deputies representing a variety of political factions, including some distinctly hostile to the communist regime. The plan was for the Congress to elect from its membership a new Supreme Soviet, a sort of inner parliament of the Congress. Its other main responsibility was to

By MOCHALOV in Izvestia (Moscow). C&W Syndicate.

Following the breakup of the Soviet Union, the members of the Russian legislature, representing a variety of factions, frequently came to blows on the question of how best to manage the transfer from a communist to a democratic system.

choose the Soviet President, Mikhail Gorbachev (who later resigned as the Soviet Union dissolved in December 1991).

If all of this sounds somewhat confusing, it was. Political institutions had never developed appreciably in the Soviet Union because of the predominance of the party and its various agencies. The political reforms were not at all helped by the fact that several of the 15 Soviet republics were hostile to the central government in Moscow. All of the republics have their own legislative bodies, which in the waning months of the Soviet Union were not at all eager to yield control to a political center in Moscow. As one reporter noted at the time, the "republican parliaments are mostly inward-looking, concerned more with their backyards than with the fare of the union."[26] This perspective was in even greater evidence after the weak Commonwealth of Independent States (CIS) was established in 1991 by 11 former Soviet republics. It is probably safe to assume that these republics, 2 or 3 of which are in the midst of civil strife because of ethnic conflict, have much less incentive and reason to want to retain their association than the 13 American states had when the Constitutional Convention was held in 1787.

There has been an uneven development of legislative prowess in the former Soviet republics. Several, including the three Baltic states, are relatively responsive to public input, while others, including the majority of the Islamic republics, remain uncertain experiments in a still uncertain democratic process. The latter are developing legal codes that reflect the influence of Turkey, a secularized republic with an Islamic population, and Iran, a fundamentalist Islamic republic.

The typical problem of communist system parliaments is either that no one would miss them if they didn't exist, as is the case in China or North Korea, because they do so little; or that they are composed of (sometimes unwilling) legislators who would prefer simply to attend their own national assemblies. In the former Yugoslavia the legislatures of its member republics, such as Croatia and Slovenia, decided that their areas are sovereign as well. They completely ignored the national legislature, or Federal Assembly, which they regarded as dominated by Serbia, the biggest republic and the one the others lived in dread of. Only Serbia maintains the fiction that there is still a Yugoslav federation and a Yugoslav legislature.

What may eventually come out of all of the difficulty in the former communist systems is a confederation of sorts (perhaps remotely similar to the American experiment between 1777 and 1787) in which national sovereignty will be economic for the most part and perhaps a weak "supralegislature" will cede political authority to the republic parliaments.[27]

LEGISLATURES IN AUTHORITARIAN SYSTEMS

Legislatures are meaningless institutions if they are not (1) composed of at least one chamber that is popularly elected and (2) free from the autocratic control of the executive.

> In situations where the "legislative activity is essentially of a 'rubber stamp' character," or "domestic turmoil may make the implementation of legislation impossible," or the "effective executive may prevent the legislature from meeting, or otherwise substantially impede the exercise of its functions," the legislature is considered to be ineffective.[28]

Weak, rubber-stamp, or nonexistent legislatures are still the rule in the majority of developing societies that remain authoritarian. Ancient traditions and current political cultures tend to dictate against a political institution that is directly or indirectly representative of the population. There are even practical (if not necessarily justifiable) reasons that argue against representative assemblies. For example, in several of the Persian Gulf states the indigenous citizenry is outnumbered by their communities of noncitizen guest workers, many of whom have lived there for years or decades and have reared their families far away from their origins. The governments of these countries would have a difficult time deciding how far the franchise should extend, even if they wanted to have one.

When the United States was created, all the founders assumed there would be a legislature. The fact that Article I of the Constitution is devoted to the Congress highlights the extreme importance of the institution. Many societies that we call developing are really very old, but it did not dawn on these societies until late into the twentieth century that political modernity required a legislature of some sort. Those rather authoritarian regimes that did make the concession still retained their own preferences. Table 12.10 suggests some samples of Third World legislatures that are representative, but only of particularized constituencies.

TABLE 12.10	SOME LEGISLATIVE ASSEMBLIES IN THIRD WORLD COUNTRIES	
Country	Name of Legislature	Characteristics
Brunei	Legislative Council	All members appointed by the Sultan, the head of state
Iran	Islamic Consultative Assembly	Several factions furnish deputies; all members must be religiously correct
Iraq	National Assembly	Four ethnic/religious communities; all members of (or adhering to doctrines of) a single party, the Ba'ath
Kenya	National Assembly	One-party legislature

Even Western societies are not immune from what can be referred to as legislative quota systems. The Germans wonder, for example, what to do with nearly 2 million guest workers and their families from Turkey. Should they become citizens? If not, what about the children born in Germany of Turkish parents? The United States, which has long welcomed immigrants, has from time to time debated ways to guarantee minority groups legislative representation. The redrawing of congressional district lines after a census is usually an occasion for this debate, as happened after the 1990 census. In California, for example, a discussion centered on whether congressional districts should be created with Hispanic majorities in order to get more Hispanics elected to Congress. In South Carolina, a small state with six congressional districts, some advocates wanted to ensure that at least one district would have an African-American majority. That way a state with a population that is almost one-third African-American might have at least one congressional representative for the first time since Reconstruction. The plan worked, and an African-American was elected.

It is unusual (and often illegal) for democracies to purposely base representation on ethnic, racial, or religious characteristics of populations. But this happens a great deal of the time in other societies. The membership of the National Assembly in Iraq, for example, is formulated around both ethnic and religious considerations: Kurds make up 15 percent of the total; Christians, 5 percent; Shiite Muslims, 30 percent; and Sunni Muslims, 50 percent. The Sunnis constitute a majority of the Assembly even though they are no longer a majority of the population. In fact, the distribution of seats does not at all reflect the population makeup. Kurds, for example, make up at least one-fourth of the population but only have about one-seventh of the legislative seats. Not that it matters: The Iraqi National Assembly is no more than a rubber stamp for the only legal party, the Ba'ath.

Legislatures are a cornerstone of any political democracy. For most nondemocratic systems they can at least be a hope for a democracy. In Eastern Europe, for example, several political systems are being transformed from communist to pluralist societies in great part because the most serious opposition to the Communist party has shown up as the result of elections in the national legislature. Even Bulgaria, one of the most recalcitrant communist states in the region, saw opposition to its incompetent and destructive economic policies surface first in its legislature (the executive branch and the bureaucracy were still very much in communist hands).

In authoritarian systems the difficulties are much greater. For one thing, there may not even be a legislature. For another, elections may never be scheduled. A traumatic event may be necessary to nudge authoritarian regimes. The monarchical regime of Kuwait, for instance, found itself forced by reform-minded citizens to schedule national elections for a revived legislature after the country was liberated from Iraqi soldiers. Democracy's greatest impetus remains the legislative branch of government.

Summary

1. The American Congress is distinct in that it has a popularly elected upper house with significant power. The U.S. Congress is also distinguished by the fact that one party can control the executive, while the other controls the legislative branch.

2. In addition to its constitutional function of lawmaking, Congress has the responsibility to authorize and legitimate actions of the executive branch, such as American participation in the Persian Gulf conflict. Congress also exercises investigatory and ombudsman functions.

3. Congress is organized along party lines, by various caucuses, by committees, and by staffs. The party leadership provides the leadership in each house. Informal groups, or caucuses of members, focus attention on particular issues and formulate policy of mutual interest.

4. The committees are especially important to the lawmaking process since they decide in effect how far a bill will proceed and whether the entire House or Senate will have an opportunity to vote a bill into law.

5. Staffs have become increasingly important parts of the legislative process as they have grown in size and influence. Each member has a personal staff, and each committee has a staff. In addition, support staff provide crucial services.

6. Legislative proposals may take the form of bills or resolutions. Each bill must proceed through many stages and be signed by the president before it becomes law. Most bills introduced in Congress never survive to emerge from committee.

7. In their voting decisions legislators may act as delegates, reflecting their constituents' preferences; as trustees, using factual analysis and their own conscience; or as politicos, taking on either role as the occasion demands.

8. Ethnic minorities, women, and young people (under the age of 30) are underrepresented in Congress while middle-aged white males are overrepresented. But this does not mean that Congress cannot pass legislation that is good for the whole country or that Congress cannot respond to societal wishes.

9. Do members of Congress play too much politics? They must be politicians to win elections. And they consistently achieve results by helping one another out (usually with their votes) on legislative matters. While this may seem less than ethical, it

would be difficult to imagine very much getting done without mutual back-scratching.

10. There is substantial opportunity for corruption in Congress. In the 1970s and 1980s Congress instituted several reforms to open up the legislative process and to curtail abuses. But abuses have continued, as the 1992 check-bouncing scandal illustrates.

11. Limits on terms for national legislators would produce new blood and fresh ideas, but would result in a loss of experience in Congress. Such a practice would make the United States a rare democracy. While some countries restrict executive terms of office, no democracy has yet seen fit to restrict the service of its legislators.

12. In parliamentary systems the lower house selects from its own membership the members of the Cabinet. The upper house, with notable exceptions, tends to be politically powerless.

13. Some Third World legislatures are viable and important. In recent years, several East Asian and Latin American legislatures, for example, have become the most important institutions for building democratic practices in their countries.

14. Legislatures in totalitarian systems are large, have little to do, and are basically rubber stamps. China provides a classic case in point.

15. In the former Soviet Union national legislatures are taking on increased importance as they reflect more localized sentiment and aspirations.

16. Legislatures in authoritarian systems, as in totalitarian ones, are often rubber stamps. They meet infrequently (if they exist at all) and their members tend to be handpicked by the dictatorial regime.

Terms to Define

Clean bill
Closed rule
Cloture
Concurrent resolution
Conference committee
Delegate
Discharge petition
Divided government
Filibuster
Frank
Join committee
Joint resolution
Junketing
Mavericks
Modified closed rule

Nepotism
Open rule
Politico
Pork barrel
Private bill
Public bill
Safe seat
Select committee
Senatorial courtesy
Seniority system
Simple resolution
Standing committee
Trustee
Unanimous consent agreement

Suggested Readings

Aberbach, Joel D. *Keeping a Watchful Eye*. Washington, D.C.: Brookings Institute, 1990. Assesses the growth of congressional oversight of the bureaucracy.

Cain, Bruce, John Ferejohn, and Morris Fiorina. *The Personal Vote*. Cambridge: Harvard University Press, 1987. Compares constituent services offered by American and British legislators.

Davidson, Roger H., and Walter J. Oleszek. *Congress and Its Members*, 3rd ed. Washington, D.C.: Congressional Quarterly Press, 1990. Offers one of the most thorough accounts of how Congress functions and, to some extent, how it doesn't.

Dodd, Lawrence C., and Bruce I. Oppenheimer. *Congress Reconsidered*, 4th ed. Washington, D.C.: Congressional Quarterly Press, 1989. Presents much of the latest research on Congress in essay form.

Fenno, Richard F., Jr. *Congressmen in Committees*. Boston: Little, Brown, 1973. Examines the different styles of committees and committee members.

Fenno, Richard F., Jr. *Homestyle*. Boston: Little, Brown, 1978. Describes how House members interact with their constituents.

Fowler, Linda L., and Robert D. McClure. *Political Ambition*. New Haven: Yale University Press, 1989. Analyses the recruitment of congressional candidates.

Loomis, Burdett. *The New American Politician*. New York: Basic Books, 1988. Describes how ambition and other factors are changing Congress.

Malbin, Michael J. *Unelected Representatives*. New York: Basic Books, 1980. Illustrates the influence of congressional staff on the legislative process.

Notes

1. *Congressional Quarterly*, April 15, 1979, p. 891.
2. Ibid.
3. *Washington Post*, September 5, 1979, p. A17.
4. *The Christian Science Monitor*, February 16, 1993, p. 3.
5. *Congressional Record, Daily Digest*, "Résumé of Congressional Activity," 100th Cong. (2nd sess., D1399), 101st (lst sess., D1431; 2nd sess., D1449).
6. See Heinz Eulau et al., "The Role of the Representative: Some Empirical Observations on the Theory of Edmund Burke," *American Political Science Review* 59 (September 1959): 742–756.
7. James Madison, *The Federalist*, No. 57, Robert M. Hutchins, ed., in *Great Books of the Western World*, (Chicago: Encyclopedia Britannica, 1952), p. 177.
8. Warren Miller and Donald Stokes, "Constituency Influence in Congress," *American Political Science Review* 57 (March 1963): 55.
9. U.S. Congress, Committee on Government Operations, Subcommittee on Intergovernmental Relations, *Confidence and Concern: Citizens View American Government* (Washington, D.C.: U.S. Government Printing Office, 1973), pp. 72–77.
10. *The Washington Post*, May 24, 1978, p. A2.
11. Quoted in *The Washington Post National Weekly Edition*, July 29–August 4, 1991, p. 23.
12. Paul N. McCloskey, Jr., *Truth and Untruth*, (New York: Simon & Schuster, 1972), p. 107.
13. Ibid.
14. *The Washington Post*, September 24, 1979, p. A2.
15. *The New York Times*, April 15, 1992, p. A22.
16. "Throw the Bums Out, Part Two," *The Economist*, May 16, 1992, p. 27.
17. *Money*, August 1992, p. 131.
18. *Money*, p. 134.
19. *The Christian Science Monitor*, February 23, 1993, p. 3.
20. *Money*., p. 140.
21. These reforms, though proposed elsewhere as well, have most recently been suggested in *Money*, August 1992, p. 140.
22. Statistics compiled from data in *U. S. Statistical Abstract* and other sources.

23. "Bagehot," *The Economist*, August 3, 1991, p. 58.
24. "The British Constitution: A Modest Proposal," *The Economist*, July 6, 1991, p. 19.
25. Ibid.
26. "When the Juggling Has to Stop," *The Economist*, November 24, 1990, p. 48.
27. "Yugoseparatism," *The Economist*, April 14, 1990, p. 45.
28. Zehra F. Arat, *Democracy and Human Rights in Developing Countries* (Boulder and London: Lynne Rienner Publishers, 1991), p. 24.

CHAPTER ★ THIRTEEN

THE JUDICIARY

Among the judicial systems of the world, the American judiciary is perhaps the most controversial. The Founders never clearly defined its precise nature, and its role has been heatedly debated since their time. The question of whether the judiciary clarifies or makes policy, or both, has never been fully resolved. The judiciary has had to render a decision on almost every major controversy in American history: the scope of the national government's power in economic, political, and social matters; the rights of African-Americans and other minorities; the war powers of the president; and the definition of justice itself. Alexis de Tocqueville wrote that "scarcely any political question arises in the United States that is not resolved, sooner or later, into a judicial question."[1]

American lawyers, often the subject of putdowns and bad jokes, are frequently blamed for clogging up the courts through legal maneuvers and disdained because they seem to be everywhere, whether or not they are needed (see Table 13.1). A British writer suggests that America's lawyers deserve at least some of the uncomplimentary names they have been called:

| TABLE 13.1 LAWYERS AROUND THE WORLD ||
Country	Lawyers Per 100,000 Population
Pakistan	508.4
Singapore	396.0
United States	**312.0**
Belgium	214.0
Finland	191.6
Israel	182.5
Argentina	169.4
Canada	168.5
Venezuela	159.1
Australia	145.7
England and Wales	134.0
Chile	104.9
Japan	101.6
Spain	84.6
Italy	81.2
Costa Rica	80.3
Brazil	69.1
Norway	68.7
Egypt	68.2
Nepal	63.2
Switzerland	51.4
France	49.1
Turkey	42.1
Former Soviet Union	36.3
Holland	35.2
India	34.4

Source: *The Economist,* July 18, 1992, p. 4. Based on data from the Institute for Legal Studies, University of Wisconsin.

As their [lawyers'] fees and incomes have headed for the stratosphere, so have their numbers. In 1960 America had 260,000 lawyers. Ten years later the number had risen by a third, to 355,000. Then the real fun began. By 1980 541,000 lawyers were in practice; this year [1990] the number has swelled to 756,000—more, it is said, than in the rest of the world put together. In the 30 years from 1960, the number of lawyers per 100,000 Americans has gone up from 145 to 312. Much of the "demand" for the output of this swollen industry is created not by clients but by other members of the industry, as if doctors went around injecting diseases for other doctors to cure.[2]

America is the world's leader in product liability, medical malpractice suits, and other types of tort. **Torts** are suits in which an injured person attempts to recover money for damages: economic, such as medical expenses and lost wages, and noneconomic, such as "pain and suffering."

Cases presented to the courts must meet certain requirements, however. A case must involve a real and not a theoretical question. Courts will not issue advisory decisions on speculative issues; a genuine controversy must be involved. In other words, the American system of justice is based on the **adversary process,** with two sides opposing each other on a specific point of law.

The courts, of course, aim to clarify and apply the law. But there are a number of different types of law. **Constitutional law** is based on a constitution and court decisions that interpret and apply it. **Statutory law** results from action by a legislature and the signature of an executive, while **administrative law** is devised by executive agencies to implement statutory law. **Common law** is made by judges as they decide cases. It customarily develops according to the principle of **stare decisis** (Latin for "to stand by things already decided"): Judges render decisions using decisions in earlier, similar cases as precedents. There are two main areas of law: **Civil law** pertains to disputes between individuals or organizations, and **criminal law** concerns crimes against the government or the public welfare.

Recent hearings on the nominations of Supreme Court justices have focused public attention on another aspect of law, its philosophical foundation. Law as practiced and taught in the United States until this century was generally based on the idea of **natural law** (or divine law). This concept held that humanity possesses absolute rights (divinely ordained) on which a king or government could not trample and that to be legal, all human laws must conform with the unalterable natural law. Perhaps the best illustration of natural law is the Declaration of Independence, which reads that "all men are endowed by their Creator with certain inalienable rights." The point is that natural law remains the same, even though the whims of government may change.

This conception of law rooted in absolutes no longer holds in America. The modern conception of law now looks to economic, technological, and cultural changes in society that mold and form the law. In other words, inherited legal codes and traditions need to be adjusted to contemporary social conditions. This new philosophy provided much of the inspiration for Franklin Roosevelt's New Deal programs.

In recent years some critics of this new conception of law have been advocating a return to absolutes. They contend that if much of the litigation in American courts could be decided by fixed principles, law in America would then be more certain, rather than continually fluctuating as it does now. Abortion, for example, would be settled not by contemporary norms of society, which may change from year to year, decade to decade, or generation to generation, but by fixed principles of natural law. Based on Clarence Thomas's writings, the Supreme Court nominee was suspected of favoring the use of natural law in judicial decisions. His views were questioned closely during his nomination hearings in 1991, at which time he said natural law would *not* influence his decisions.

Using the law to dispense justice in America is no simple matter, then. And the judicial system itself is a complex mechanism. In this chapter we will take a look at how the American judicial system is organized and how it works. We'll consider whether the role of the courts is too powerful and whether the judicial system as a whole works fairly for all Americans. Then we will examine how judicial systems in other countries differ from or are similar to the American system.

★ THE AMERICAN JUDICIAL SYSTEM

ORGANIZATION OF THE COURTS

America has a dual court system—a state and local system existing side by side with a federal court system. There are two main differences between the two systems. One has to do with **jurisdiction**, the type of case a court has the right to hear. In general, federal courts have jurisdiction over cases involving: (1) the Constitution and federal laws and treaties, (2) admiralty and maritime law (the law of the sea), (3) land disputes under titles granted by two or more states, (4) the United States as a party, (5) a state as a party, (6) citizens of different states as litigants, and (7) diplomats. State and local courts have jurisdiction over all other types of legal controversies.

The federal judicial system also differs from most state systems in the method of judicial selection and judicial tenure. Federal judges are nominated by the president and confirmed by the Senate. They have lifetime tenure during good behavior. These features of the federal judiciary are meant to free judges from political battles. In the states judges are generally appointed or elected for fixed terms (see Table 13.2). The limited tenure

TABLE 13.2   METHODS OF SELECTING STATE JUDGES

Type of selection	Number of States	Examples
Partisan election	15*	Illinois, New York, North Carolina, Pennsylvania, Texas
Nonpartisan election	16†	Michigan, Minnesota, Ohio, Wisconsin
Legislative election	4	Connecticut, Rhode Island,‡ South Carolina, Virginia
Gubernatorial appointment	10§	Maryland, Massachusetts, New Jersey
Merit system or "Missouri Plan"‖	16	California, Colorado, Florida,# Indiana,** Iowa, Missouri, Nebraska

* Partisan elections are used for some, but not all, judges in 5 of these states, including New York.
† Nonpartisan election is combined with another method in 5 of these states.
‡ Only state Supreme Court judges are elected by the legislature.
§ Three states combine gubernatorial appointment with another method.
‖ The basic "merit system" pattern is as follows: (1) A screening committee of citizens and lawyers presents a list of candidates to the governor. (2) The governor appoints one from the list. (3) After the first term, a judge's name appears on the ballot with this question: "Shall Judge ____ be retained in office?" If the "yes" votes surpass "no" votes, a judge retains office. Variations from this basic pattern occur in several states.
Appellate judges only.
** Appellate judges only.
Source: Herbert Jacob, "Courts," in Virginia Gray et al., eds. *Politics in American States*, 5th ed. (Boston: Scott Foresman, 1990), p. 238.

and the need to face reelection or reappointment at regular intervals are features intended to make judges more responsive to public opinion.[3]

At the apex of the American judicial system is the *United States Supreme Court*, consisting of eight associate justices and one chief justice. The Supreme Court has both original and appellate jurisdiction. **Original jurisdiction** refers to cases that come directly to it. These cases involve foreign diplomats or one of the states, as specified in Article III of the Constitution. Most of its cases, however, come through **appellate jurisdiction**—the right to review decisions of lower courts. Some of these cases may come to the Supreme Court through appeal as a matter of right, as when a lower court has declared a law unconstitutional. But most litigants must *petition* the Court to review their cases. In this situation they ask the justices to issue a **writ of certiorari** (Latin for "to be made more certain") requesting the lower court to send the record up for review. If at least four justices agree to a petition, the Court issues the writ, indicating its willingness to be "made more certain,"—that is, to hear the case. If the Court denies the request (as it does in 85 percent of the cases), it in effect upholds the decision of the lower court.

Beneath the Supreme Court are the 12 United States *courts of appeals*. Each state and territory as well as the District of Columbia falls within the jurisdiction of one of these courts. They have only appellate jurisdiction, reviewing appeals from lower federal courts and decisions of the federal regulatory agencies. The courts of appeals have no choice in what cases they hear: Most losing litigants in the lower courts have the right to appeal to these federal courts.

The United States *district courts* form the third principal layer in the pyramid of the federal judiciary. Each state has at least one of the 94 district courts, as do four territories and the District of Columbia. Unlike the courts of appeals, the district courts are trial courts where cases begin: These courts have only original jurisdiction and do not hear appeals. They hear both civil and criminal cases involving violations of federal law and disputes between citizens of different states. (See Table 13.3.)

Several additional federal courts handle certain specialized cases. The Claims Court rules on financial claims against the federal government. The Court of Customs and Patent Appeals has jurisdiction over trademark, patent, and tariff appeals cases. The Court of International Trade hears cases arising out of tariff laws. The Court of Military Appeals is the final appellate court in court-martial convictions. The Tax Court has the judicial function of reviewing decisions of the Internal Revenue Service. These specialized courts were established by Congress, and its judges have limited terms.

The precise organization of the state court system varies by state. But every state has a system of lower courts with original jurisdiction and higher courts with appellate jurisdiction. A number of specialized courts may deal with such matters as housing, police, traffic, and family disputes. The highest state court has the final say in any particular case, unless the case involves a federal issue. Then, and only then, the decision may be appealed directly to the Supreme Court. In all other ways the state judicial system operates independently of the federal judicial system.

JUDICIAL PROCEDURES

A civil case involves private parties, with one, the plaintiff, seeking damages from the other, the defendant. For example, if a patient sues a doctor for malpractice, the patient

TABLE 13.3 THE FEDERAL COURTS: JURISDICTION AND CASELOAD

Court	Original Jurisdiction	Appellate Jurisdiction	Caseload
Supreme 1 Court 9 Justices	1. Two or more states 2. The United States and a state 3. Foreign Ambassadors and other diplomats 4. A state and a citizen of a different state (if begun by the state)	1. Lower federal courts 2. Highest state court	1. Approximately 130 signed opinions 2. Approximately 4,500 petitions and appeals 3. Fewer than 10 cases of original jurisdiction
Appeals 12 Courts 135 Judges		1. Federal district courts 2. U.S. regulatory commissions 3. Certain other federal courts	1. Approximately 41,000 cases
District 94 Courts 515 Judges	1. Federal crimes 2. Civil suits under federal law 3. Civil suits between citizens of different states where the amount exceeds $50,000 4. Admiralty and maritime cases 5. Bankruptcy cases 6. Review of actions of certain federal administrative agencies 7. Other matters assigned to them by Congress	(No appellate jurisdiction)	1. Approximately 218,000 civil cases 2. Approximately 49,000 criminal cases

Sources: *Annual Report of the Director of the Administrative Office of the United States Courts* (Washington, D.C.: Government Printing Office, 1990); Harold W. Stanley and Richard G. Niemi, *Vital Statistics on American Politics*, 2nd ed. (Washington, D.C.: Congressional Quarterly Press, 1990); Bureau of the Census, *Statistical Abstract of the United States, 1990* (Washington, D.C.: U.S. Government Printing Office, 1990).

is the plaintiff and the doctor is the defendant. In criminal cases the two parties are the government, acting as prosecutor, and someone accused of a crime, the defendant. Thus, if a patient murders her or his physician, the government as prosecutor brings suit against the patient, the defendant. In each type of case, a jury typically finds the defendant guilty or innocent. If the verdict is guilty, a judge then decides on the proper sentence. In cases that are appealed a panel of judges will review the case and decide whether a decision should stand or be overturned.

The Supreme Court is a unique body, and it has its own special procedures. The highest court is usually in session between October and June to hear cases and render decisions. Meeting in august chambers, with a 44-foot-high ceiling and 24 marble columns, each court session opens with the court marshal pounding the gavel and announcing:

> The honorable, the chief and the associate justices of the Supreme Court of the United States: Oyez, Oyez, Oyez. All persons having to do business before the honorable, the Supreme Court of the United States, are admonished to draw near and give their attention, for the Court is now sitting. God save the United States and this honorable Court.

The robed justices then enter, the Chief Justice first and others in order of seniority. These ceremonial aspects and the Court's grand setting are enough to inspire awe in the most accomplished legal counsels, some of whom, like former justices Thurgood Marshall and Abe Fortas, may eventually be named to the high court themselves. Each year's docket of some 170 cases contains only a relatively few cases of widespread public interest. For those, seats in the courtroom are at a premium. Every Friday—and frequently on Wednesdays as well—the justices meet in secret to discuss and vote on pending cases and to determine which cases from lower courts they will hear.

Before the Supreme Court hears a case, lawyers for each side submit written briefs stating their clients' cases in full. When the case comes before the Court, each side generally has a half-hour to state its case. The justices commonly interrupt with questions during this time. Although each case presented to the Court has two adversaries, others who are not parties to the case may seek to influence the Court by filing an **amicus curiae** (literally, "friend of the court") **brief**. For example, in a case involving freedom of speech, a special interest organization such as the American Civil Liberties Union or the National Civil Liberties Legal Foundation may file an amicus curiae brief containing arguments it hopes will be persuasive.

After a decision is reached, the senior justice (in years of service) on the prevailing side assigns the writing of the **majority opinion,** and the senior justice on the losing side assigns the writing of the **minority opinion.** The chief justice is always senior on one side of the issue, regardless of how many years he or she has served. Individual justices may write **concurring opinions,** in which they agree with the majority but perhaps for different reasons than those stated in the majority opinion, and **dissenting opinions,** in which they disagree with the majority position. Sometimes the Court issues **per curium decisions,** decisions without written opinions.

JUDICIAL REVIEW

Perhaps the single most important power that the federal courts have (and what distinguishes them from their counterparts in most other democracies) is the power of **judicial**

Most of the information on which the Supreme Court will base its decision in a given case is presented to the justices in the form of written briefs. However, oral argument in the chamber of the Court—frequently interrupted by questions from the justices—is nevertheless an important part of the process.

review. This refers to the court's ability to declare unconstitutional acts of the executive and legislative branches of government, on both the state and national level. The ultimate wielder of this great power is the Supreme Court, which is what makes that body so influential in the political system.

The right to declare *state* acts unconstitutional stems from a provision in the Constitution known as the "supremacy clause," which holds that federal laws and treaties and the Constitution are the supreme law of the land binding state officials. The Constitution does not explicitly give the federal judiciary the right to review executive and legislative actions on the *national* level, but many delegates to the Constitutional Con-

A VIEW FROM THE STATES
The Supreme Court: Intimate and Sheltered

With its soaring columns and grand public spaces, the Supreme Court building seems designed to inspire awe. That is especially true of the courtroom itself, a high-ceilinged sanctum of hushed formality where the Justices emerge precisely at 10 o'clock from behind a velvet curtain to face rows of lawyers and tourists standing respectfully at attention.

Reporters stand too, and few would deny having felt a touch of awe on the occasion of a major decision. . . .

But after years of trudging up from the press room, pad in hand, to see the Justices in action, what I often sense is not so much the Court's majesty as its intimacy. The Court's power is vast, but its scale is small.

More than almost any other public officials, the people who embody the Supreme Court put themselves on display day after day. A Senator may visit the Senate floor to cast a vote or read a speech, but the chamber is often nearly deserted even when the Senate is in session.

In the Court, by contrast, every public session is a working session, requiring the Justices to perform without a safety net. Power and vulnerability exist side by side. No aides hand the Justices follow-up questions to ask the lawyers; no chairman gavels a recess when things get sticky. The atmosphere is businesslike. The Justices make nothing so clear as that every second counts. Showmanship

is disfavored; when an inexperienced lawyer makes a florid presentation, a chill almost visibly settles on the bench. . . .

The Justices are not only on view, they are accountable. They explain themselves. Congress and the White House can put off decisions indefinitely; entire agendas sink without a trace. But the Court publicly disposes of everything on its docket, every petition, every motion. Every case argued in a term gets some resolution that term.

Issuing decisions is a bureaucratic function in most courts, handled by a faceless clerk's office. But at the Supreme Court, the author of a majority opinion announces it personally. . . .

But visible as the Justices are in their own home, they remain remarkably free of the baggage of public personality that weighs so heavily on other public officials. Part of the reason, no doubt, is the absence of television from the courtroom, a stunning anachronism for a major government institution in an era when government is often a projection of personality. . . .

The Court shelters its inhabitants from the relentless public exposure that is the modern trade-off for the exercise of great public power. Never quite on center stage, always a bit out of focus, the Justices are not about to give up the intimate and anachronistic little world where fate and politics have placed them for life.

Source: Linda Greenhouse, "Supremely Sheltered," *The New York Times Magazine*, March 7, 1993, p. 84. Copyright © 1992 by The New York Times Company. Reprinted by permission.

vention publicly stated their support for the concept and the power is implied in both Articles III and VI of the Constitution. However, it was not until the important case of *Marbury v. Madison* (1803) that this power was made explicit.

Just before leaving office in 1801, President John Adams and his Federalist party majority in Congress created 59 federal judgeships, to which Adams promptly nominated members of the Federalist party. Adams's secretary of State, John Marshall, was responsible for delivering the commissions for the judgeships, but 17 went undelivered in the pressure of inaugural preparations for the new president, Republican Thomas Jefferson. Recognizing that the Federalists had attempted to pack the judiciary with their members, Jefferson and his secretary of State, James Madison, ignored the undelivered commissions. In the meantime, John Marshall had assumed his new position as chief justice of the Supreme Court.

One of the judges who did not get his commission was William Marbury. He asked the Supreme Court to issue a writ of *mandamus* (Latin for "we command") ordering Secretary of State Madison to give him his judicial commission. Marbury based his request on Section 13 of the Judiciary Act of 1789, which empowered the Supreme Court to issue such writs.

Chief Justice Marshall faced an interesting dilemma. If he issued the writ of mandamus, Madison would undoubtedly ignore it, and the Supreme Court would be powerless to do anything. If he did not issue the writ, the Jeffersonian Republicans would triumph by default. Marshall chose a third alternative. He declared Section 13 of the 1789 Judiciary Act unconstitutional, saying that Congress had no right to expand the original jurisdiction of the Supreme Court by a statute; only a constitutional amendment could confer additional powers.

Thus Marshall had his cake and got to eat it too. He declared that Marbury was entitled to the commission but that the Supreme Court could not act because it lacked jurisdiction. His decision was a reprimand to Jefferson and Madison for not performing their duties, but he avoided a confrontation with them that he could not win. In the process he established the precedent for judicial review. Marshall stated:

> It is emphatically the province and duty of the judicial department to say what the law is. Those who apply the rule to particular cases must of necessity expound and interpret that rule. . . . A law repugnant to the Constitution is void; . . . courts, as well as other departments, are bound by that instrument.[4]

Judicial review is a key to understanding most of the controversies about the Supreme Court since the 1950s. Under Chief Justice Earl Warren's leadership, the Supreme Court in the 1950s and 1960s exercised judicial review:

- To begin desegregation of public schools through the equal protection clause of the Fourteenth Amendment (*Brown v. Board of Education*, 1954)[5]
- To improve state legislative and congressional representation for urban and suburban voters, the former through the equal protection of the laws clause

of the Fourteenth Amendment (*Reynolds* v. *Sims*, 1964)[6] and the latter through the due process clause of the Fifth Amendment (*Wesbury* v. *Sanders*, 1964)[7]

- To spell out the rights of those accused of crimes through the due process clause of the Fourteenth Amendment (*Miranda* v. *Arizona*, 1966)[8]

- To require that indigents be provided with legal counsel through the due process clause of the Fourteenth Amendment (*Gideon* v. *Wainwright*, 1963)[9] and

- To ban prayer and Bible reading in the public schools (*Engel* v. *Vitale*, 1962[10] and *Abington School District* v. *Schempp*, 1963,[11] respectively)

In each of these examples, the Supreme Court used judicial review to negate actions of state and local governments. Since there are 50 state governments and more than 82,000 local governments, it is not surprising that judicial review has affected those governments more than the national government. From the 1970s and into the 1990s, the Supreme Court under the leadership of Chief Justices Warren Burger and William Rehnquist began to retreat from the Warren Court's tendency to declare state and local actions unconstitutional, even modifying or voiding decisions of the Warren Court. Burger and Rehnquist believed that the Court should generally respect the decisions of state and local governments.

Abortion, of course, probably provides the best contemporary example of judicial review at work. Since using judicial review to give abortion constitutional protection in 1973 (*Roe* v. *Wade*),[12] the Supreme Court has subsequently used it to limit abortion. In *Roe* v. *Wade*, the Court held that the due process clause of the Fourteenth Amendment implicitly contains a right to privacy that protects a woman's freedom to choose. In *Webster* v. *Reproductive Health Services* (1989),[13] the Court showed signs of backing away from this dictum. Although the Court still upheld the right to an abortion in the case of *Planned Parenthood* v. *Casey* (1992), it said: "The woman's liberty is not so unlimited . . . that from the outset the state cannot show its concern for the life of the unborn, and at a later point in fetal development the state's interest in life has sufficient force so that the right of the woman to terminate the pregnancy can be restricted."[14]

Liberals have been criticized more than conservatives for using judicial review to make public policy, but conservatives have also done so, especially to undo or limit the decisions of liberal courts. That is the storyline behind the Warren and Burger-Rehnquist Courts.

The American judicial system, including federal, state, and local courts; attorneys; police; and other parts of the system, is regularly criticized for a variety of reasons. Some charge that it is too powerful. Others say it is too slow. Still others contend that it protects the interests of the rich over those of the poor. Many complain that the judiciary (especially the Supreme Court) has usurped legislative and executive functions by formulating political, social, and economic policy. Some think that judges are unrepresentative of the general public and therefore unlikely to render decisions fairly and equitably. These and other criticisms raise a crucial question: Is our judicial system really democratic?

? ISSUES TO ANALYZE

ISSUE 1   *ARE AMERICAN COURTS TOO POWERFUL?*

REASONS WHY AMERICAN COURTS ARE TOO POWERFUL

Robert G. McCloskey, a noted student of the judiciary, has said the U.S. Supreme Court is "the most powerful court known to history."[15] Critics claim that our court system has become too powerful through using the tool of judicial review. The chief result is the unhealthy practice of policymaking by the courts.

Using Judicial Review. The power of the courts to determine whether a law or action of government is constitutional causes clashes between judicial supremacy and democratic ideals. "Scratch a fervent believer in judicial supremacy," said one observer, and "as like as not you will find someone with a bitterness about democracy. The two are as close as skin and skeleton."[16] Studying judicial review as practiced by the Supreme Court provides the best understanding of how this principle makes the judiciary so powerful. Why should a body of nine persons who are not elected by the people have the authority to strike down what the people want? Are not Congress and the president, both elected by the people, capable of judging whether a proposed action is constitutional? Is there any reason to believe that the legislature and the chief executive are less devoted to the Constitution than is the Supreme Court?

The power of judicial review has led to **judicial activism,** in which the Supreme Court plays a vigorous role in trying to bring about social change. The Supreme Court under Chief Justice Earl Warren exemplified this role in the 1950s and 1960s. Its philosophy held that when other branches of government are not capable of responding to the rightful demands and grievances of the people, it is the proper role of the Court to exercise leadership and initiate social change. Most notably, the Warren Court acted to desegregate schools in its *Brown* v. *Board of Education* (1954) decision.

When the Court takes an activist stance, it destroys the concept of "settled law," which is based on precedent or the doctrine of stare decisis. The law shifts as the Court shifts in making its decisions. What one court rules is the law, the next may reverse or modify. One result is that the language of constitutional law loses its timeless quality. If the law has no fixed meaning, it becomes as putty to be molded and remolded. That is why under Chief Justice Rehnquist the Court has gradually modified or reversed some of the "activist" decisions of the Warren Court.

Using Judicial Notice. Although it is commonly believed that justices are bound by the constraints of the adversary system to consider only the facts brought before them in a specific case, they do not always limit their concern to the facts presented to the Court in making their decisions. Rather, while ruling on a case, they may take **judicial notice** of other facts and conduct research for information not provided in the case itself in the oral arguments or legal briefs. *The Model Code of Evidence* of the American Law Institute allows for judicial notice and independent research within narrow limits, but does not specify these limits. Should sociological theory be used by justices in making judicial decisions and writing opinions (as was the case in *Brown*)? More generally, to

The integration of schools was a direct outcome of judicial activism in the 1950s. Proponents of judicial activism think it is acceptable for the courts to initiate needed social change if the other branches of government fail to do so. Opponents regard activism as a form of legislating.

what extent should any nonlegal information, especially in the social sciences, be used in rendering court verdicts? Judicial notice and independent research, if used by some justices and not others, may lead to a hit-or-miss approach to interpretation of the Constitution and may thus undermine the adversary system, which at least theoretically binds the Court to the facts presented to it.

  Making Public Policy. Instead of applying a decision only to the case before it, the Warren Court began to apply many of its decisions to a wide range of public issues. In other words, the Court engaged in **judicial policymaking**, setting policy through its decisions and opening itself up to the charge of judicial activism. Thus, a legislative redistricting decision applied to one state set up public policy for other states. Some argue that the Supreme Court should not make public policy but should merely interpret and apply the law in the case before it. This was the philosophy of Presidents Ronald Reagan and George Bush. Others believe that it is quite appropriate for the Court to set public policy, but because of the adversary process this can be done only in an arbitrary fashion; that is, the Court can establish public policy only on the issues that come before it.

Judges are trained in law and not in science and technology, but they increasingly must decide such complex technological issues as the quality of air, food, and water and the safety of drugs, autos, and power plants. Policymaking by the courts becomes a problem, therefore, when judges must decide on issues for which they lack expertise.

The problem of judicial policymaking is certainly not limited to the Supreme Court. An examination of the unpopular school busing decisions rendered by lower federal courts shows vividly how the judicial process can disregard public opinion. Against a background of strong community opposition, these courts have required hundreds of thousands of children to ride buses to schools outside their neighborhoods. Were the courts considering the health and safety of the children? (Many had to board school buses before daybreak and return home after dark.) Did the judges consider the energy crisis? Did they have incontrovertible evidence that either African-American or white students would benefit from this massive shuffling? Did the courts consider that their decisions would escalate "white flight" from city to suburb, thereby further segregating cities and suburbs and also significantly reducing the middle-class tax base of cities?

After considering all the problems attendant on judicial policymaking, one of the most distinguished jurists ever to serve on the Supreme Court, Felix Frankfurter, remarked that "courts are not representative bodies. They are not designed to be a good reflex of a democratic society. Their judgment is best informed, and therefore most dependable, *within narrow limits*"[17] (italics added).

REASONS WHY AMERICAN COURTS ARE NOT TOO POWERFUL

In our judicial system, the courts indeed have power. This power, with deep historic roots, is needed to protect and promote democratic government. Whether it actually results in the formation of public policy is not the most important issue. In any case, limitations on the courts prevent them from exercising their authority in an irresponsible manner.

The Need for Judicial Review. Those who worry about the power of the judiciary might ponder the question: Who is going to determine whether the legislative and executive branches have exceeded their powers under the Constitution? In *The Federalist*, Hamilton argued that it is the courts "whose duty it must be to declare all acts contrary to the manifest tenor of the Constitution void."[18] The people must have protection against unconstitutional acts committed by the legislative and executive branches; the judiciary is the proper agency to provide this protection. Who should interpret the laws? Hamilton argued that "interpretation of the laws is the proper and peculiar province of the courts."[19]

Is judicial review undemocratic as exercised by the Supreme Court, whereby a small group of justices, appointed for life, can overturn actions of an elected Congress and president? No, because the courts do not capriciously reverse actions of other units of government. The Supreme Court is particularly wary of doing so. From 1798 through 1992, only 142 federal statutes were declared unconstitutional.[20] For example, Congress passed and President Ronald Reagan signed into law the Hyde Amendment, which denied the use of public funds for abortions. Although a lower federal court declared the Hyde Amendment unconstitutional, the Supreme Court reversed the lower court decision and decided in favor of the congressional action.[21]

The Limits of Policymaking. Many critics argue that in exercising judicial review, the courts are to judge, not legislate. What this argument does not explain is where judging ends and legislating begins.

Clear distinctions are difficult. Was the Supreme Court judging or legislating when it declared that mandated nondenominational prayers in public schools were unconstitutional?[22] What function was the Court performing when it held that legislative districts that are unequal in population violate the equal protection clause of the Fourteenth Amendment?[23] Did the Court judge or legislate when it ruled that "separate but equal" educational facilities are a denial of equal protection of the laws?[24]

Those who want prayer in public schools argue that public policy should be determined by a plurality or majority of citizens; thus, if enough people want school prayers, they should be permitted. Yet others contend that prayer in public schools violates the separation of church and state, and the courts are playing a proper judicial role in rejecting it.

What about the decisions affecting legislative redistricting and school desegregation? Certainly the Court was setting public policy here, but would it not also have been setting public policy if it had *upheld* existing practices—or not rendered decisions at all? The answer to the question of whether courts judge or legislate often turns on whose ox is being gored.

The Court's power is held in check, in any case, by three main sources of limitations on the judicial system: the president, Congress, and the courts themselves.

Presidential Checks. Presidents may refuse to enforce court decisions, a fact recognized by Chief Justice Marshall in *Marbury* v. *Madison*. Later, in *Worcester* v. *Georgia* (1832),[25] the Marshall Court ruled that the laws of Georgia were of no effect inside the boundaries of the Cherokee nation. President Andrew Jackson, who did not like the decision, reportedly said: "John Marshall has made his decision; now let him enforce it." Presidents may also try to rally public opinion against the judiciary. Because Court decisions had struck down many of his New Deal programs, Franklin Roosevelt wanted to increase the number of justices on the Supreme Court and sought public support for his plan to do so. Although unsuccessful, Roosevelt was soon receiving Court decisions more favorable to his New Deal proposals.

Another check on the judiciary's exercise of power is provided by the system of presidential nomination. Since federal judges are subject only to confirmation by the Senate, the executive can have enormous influence on the composition of the courts (Figure 13.1). Presidents Bush and Reagan named to the Supreme Court over one-half of the court's current membership (Table 13.4): all of their appointees are recognized as conservative jurists. They have thereby potentially altered for a generation or more the types of decisions rendered by the high court. These presidents have also altered the makeup of the lower federal courts.

Congressional Checks. Congress has several important checks on judicial power. First, it can limit the Supreme Court's jurisdiction. Article III, section 2, of the Constitution states that the Supreme Court has appellate jurisdiction "both as to Law and Fact, with such Exceptions, and under such Regulations as the Congress shall make."

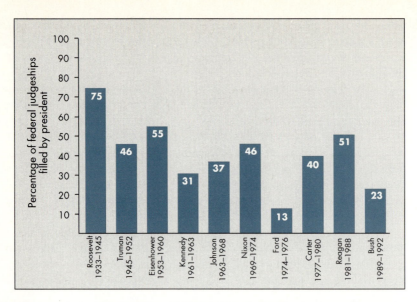

Figure 13.1 PRESIDENTIAL IMPRINTS ON THE BENCH. Depending on the number of years they are in office, presidents are capable of leaving a huge imprint on the nature of the judiciary through their judicial appointments. During his four terms, Franklin D. Roosevelt was able to appoint 75 percent of the federal judges; Gerald Ford, in office for only two years, after filling in for the retired Richard Nixon, appointed only 13 percent of the federal bench. Source: *Congressional Quarterly*, January 19, 1991, p. 173; Administrative Office of the U.S. Courts.

During the past three decades proposals have been introduced in Congress to limit the court's jurisdiction either by statute or by constitutional amendment on such issues as prayer in the public schools and abortion.

Second, the Congress can impeach and try federal judges, and it has impeached and convicted five judges on the lower courts. In 1970 House members led by then-Representative Gerald Ford attempted to impeach Supreme Court Justice William O. Douglas. The criteria for impeachment are ill defined, but conduct unbecoming to the judiciary is either explicit or implicit in impeachment charges. In the instance of Justice Douglas, his eccentric behavior and very liberal political ideology led to the unsuccessful impeachment charges against him. In 1989 Federal Judge Alcee L. Hastings was impeached by the House and convicted by the Senate on charges of perjury and conspiracy to obtain a $150,000 bribe. In 1992 he became the first person elected to the U.S. House of Representatives who had been impeached by that body.

Third, constitutional amendments proposed by Congress can reverse Supreme Court decisions. In 1793, the Court held, in the case of *Chisholm* v. *Georgia*,[26] that a citizen of one state could sue another state; the Eleventh Amendment reversed this decision. The Thirteenth and Fourteenth Amendments in effect reversed the *Dred Scott*

TABLE 13.4 SENIORITY RANKING OF U.S. SUPREME COURT JUSTICES, 1993

	Year Appointed	Appointing President	Law School	Prior Position
Harry A. Blackmun	1970	Nixon (R)	Harvard	Federal Judge
William H. Rehnquist	1972	Nixon (R)	Stanford	Assistant Attorney General
(Became Chief Justice)	1986	Reagan (R)		
John Paul Stevens	1975	Ford (R)	Chicago	Federal Judge
Sandra Day O'Connor	1981	Reagan (R)	Stanford	State Judge
Antonin Scalia	1986	Reagan (R)	Harvard	Federal Judge
Anthony Kennedy	1988	Reagan (R)	Harvard	Federal Judge
David Souter	1990	Bush (R)	Harvard	State Judge
Clarence Thomas	1991	Bush (R)	Yale	Federal Judge
Ruth Ginsburg	1993	Clinton (D)	Harvard	Federal Judge

decision of 1857,[27] which had declared that African-Americans were ineligible for citizenship. The Sixteenth Amendment reversed *Pollack v. Farmer's Loan and Trust Company* (1895),[28] which had declared an income tax unconstitutional. Amendments Nineteen, Twenty-Four, and Twenty-Six also had the effect of reversing Supreme Court decisions.

Fourth, Congress may modify or abort the impact of a court decision. When the Supreme Court ruled that the Endangered Species Act protected the snail darter fish and ordered a halt to construction of a dam that would destroy the fish, Congress reversed the effect of the Court's decision by amending the Endangered Species Act.

Fifth, Congress may exercise limitations on the judiciary through its power to determine the number of judges serving on the courts. While Congress changed the size of the Supreme Court several times in the nineteenth century, it has kept the number at nine in this century. It is much more likely to increase the number of lower federal judgeships.

Sixth, the Senate has the power to confirm the president's judicial nominations. It used this power to reject two of President Nixon's nominations to the Supreme Court, and one of President Reagan's.

Court decisions cannot differ too drastically from opinions of the legislative majority over a long period of time. If this happens, court decisions are likely to be modified or reversed in one way or another.

Self-Imposed Checks. Courts are presented with controversies they must decide according to constitutional principles. A jurist, according to Justice Benjamin Cardozo,

is not to innovate at pleasure. He is not a knight-errant, roaming at will in pursuit of his own ideal of beauty or of goodness. He is to draw his inspiration from consecrated principles. He is not to yield to spasmodic sentiment, to vague and unregulated benevolence. He is to exercise a discretion informed by tradition, methodized by analogy, disciplined by system, and subordinated to "the primordial necessity of order in the social life."[29]

During the era of the activist Warren Court, right-wing organizations campaigned for the impeachment of Chief Justice Earl Warren. Billboards like this one were a familiar sight, particularly in the South.

The Supreme Court cannot rule on a case unless (1) there is a genuine legal controversy between two adversaries, (2) one adversary has suffered or will suffer substantial injury, (3) it involves a clear and substantial constitutional question, and (4) the Court can provide a remedy. In addition, a person cannot first benefit from a statute and then ask the Court to declare the law unconstitutional. These criteria help the courts determine whether a **justiciable issue** exists—that is, an issue that can be decided by law.

Another strong inhibition on court action is the doctrine of stare decisis. It is useful to note that the entire phrase is *stare decisis et quieta non movere*, meaning "stand by things already decided and do not disturb the calm." Pro-choice advocates benefited from *stare decisis* in the 1992 case of *Planned Parenthood* v. *Casey* (1992) when the Court's majority refused to reverse *Roe* v. *Wade* and declare abortion unconstitutional, saying, "It is a rule of law and a component of liberty we cannot renounce."[30] Commonly, courts adhere to precedent except when an error could probably not be corrected by legislative means.

Other limitations on the Court have to do with presumed constitutionality and judicial restraint. **Presumed constitutionality** means that a law is considered to be constitutional as long as there is an interpretation by which it can be declared valid. Chief Justice Charles Evans Hughes wrote that "as between two possible interpretations of a statute, by one of which it would be unconstitutional and the other valid, our plain duty is to adopt that which will save the act."[31] **Judicial restraint** is the avoidance of the urge to set public policy. As Justice Felix Frankfurter stated:

> It is not the business of the Court to pronounce policy. It must observe a fastidious regard for limitations on its own power, and this precludes the Court's giving effect to its own notions of what is wise or politic. That self-restraint is of the essence in the observation of the judicial oath, for the Constitution has not authorized the justices to sit in judgment on the wisdom of what Congress and the executive branch do.[32]

What about cases in which the Supreme Court *does* make policy? For one thing, the Court may subsequently alter its decision. For example, the Burger and Rehnquist Courts have modified crucial Warren Court decisions in the area of criminal law. Second, an earlier decision may be reversed. *Brown v. Board of Education* (1954) reversed the 1896 doctrine of "separate but equal" established in *Plessy v. Ferguson*[33] by calling that doctrine unconstitutional and ordering the integration of public schools with "all deliberate speed."

ISSUE 1:   Summary   ★   *Are American Courts Too Powerful?*

Critics believe that judicial review has allowed the courts to engage in wide-ranging policymaking that was never intended by the Founders. The results, they say, are that the courts make, rather than interpret, law; that increasingly, American law is unsettled and uncertain as the courts change their mind about what the law is; and that the judicial system is clogged with cases that would not have been entertained prior to the courts' engaging in so much judicial activism. Those who defend the courts point to the numerous restraints on the exercise of the courts' powers and the need for judicial review when other branches of government fail to carry out their responsibilities properly. Many advances in the defense of civil rights and liberties have depended on the courts' exercise of power. ■

ISSUE 2   IS THE AMERICAN JUDICIAL SYSTEM FAIR TO ALL AMERICANS?

REASONS WHY THE AMERICAN JUDICIAL SYSTEM IS NOT FAIR TO ALL AMERICANS

Who dispenses justice? How is it dispensed? The first question focuses on the background of the judges who render decisions. The second has to do with the way in which these decisions are made. The answers in both cases indicate that our federal and state judicial system hardly leads to the "justice for all" proclaimed by the Pledge of Allegiance.

Elites in Charge. The range of socioeconomic backgrounds and political attitudes among judges is narrow. Most are white, male, and wealthy; educated in the better law schools; and adherents of solid upper-middle-class values.[34]

Why are persons with uncommon ideas or life-styles unlikely to serve as judges? Why is it that the higher the judgeship, the less likely it is to be occupied by someone with unusual views?

First, most judges are lawyers. This generally means that they have both college and law school educations. Because most minority groups have not had equal access to higher education, this education requirement alone has substantially limited the number of persons with diverse viewpoints. Historically, law schools have been populated largely by white males from the middle and upper-middle classes.

Second, the methods of selecting judges screen out persons with unusual views. In the federal court system, a committee of the American Bar Association (ABA) rates prospective candidates prior to Senate confirmation. Thus, a president who nominates a judge tends to keep in mind the views of the ABA as well as those of the Senate. In addition, the tradition of "senatorial courtesy" allows a senator of the president's party to block a nomination for a federal district judge or U. S. attorney from the senator's home state. As a result, a well-qualified candidate may be blocked solely because of one senator's opposition.

Finally, most judges have some connection with political parties. In state and local courts, where election is common, a judicial candidate typically has participated in party politics. This influence applies even where an appointive system is used. A judicial nominating commission may propose a list of prospective judges from which the governor is to name one. But the governor's appointments to the nominating commission itself may be influenced by party officials.

A profile of the "average" U.S. Supreme Court Justice based on the 107 justices who have served looks like this:

- White male (only two African-Americans and two women ever appointed)
- Anglo-Saxon and Protestant (only nine Roman Catholics and six Jews ever appointed)
- Between 50 and 55 years of age at the time of appointment
- A graduate of a prestigious, Ivy League School
- Upper-middle to high socioeconomic status
- A member of the appointing president's political party
- Having some political and public service experience
- From an urban area
- A lawyer

No nonlawyer has ever been on the Supreme Court, even though being a lawyer is not a prerequisite. Not only might a nonlawyer on the Court have substantial public appeal, but such a person might also bring a fresh dimension of thought to the Court, unencumbered by the nuances and subtleties of the law. A well-trained generalist who is not a lawyer would not be overwhelmed by the Court's work or intellectual challenges.

Even if elitism were eliminated from the judiciary, the American justice system would still not be fair. Among the most serious weaknesses undermining its effectiveness are incompetence, inequitable policing, bail inequities, plea bargaining, inequitable sentencing, case overloads, cost, and jury stackings.

Incompetence. The public sees and hears most about the Supreme Court, where well-qualified persons serve and where justice appears to be dispensed fairly and rationally. But the lower courts, especially those at the municipal and county levels and below, are where the most Americans are directly affected by the judicial process, and it is here that less qualified persons tend to serve as judges, and justice is less equitable. Particularly affected are the poor, whose cases rarely go beyond these local courts.

By contrast, middle- and upper-class people rarely confront the judicial process at these lower levels, except perhaps to pay a traffic fine (often without even appearing in court). They are more likely to have experience with a higher state court or federal district court, where more complex and costly suits are nearer the norm. This contrast leads to important consequences. First, leaders in state and local bar associations and other powerful lawyers seldom represent clients at the lowest levels of the judicial process; therefore, they are not knowledgeable about its inequities. Second, the people least able to challenge and change the judicial process confront it at its weakest point, where the greatest improvement is needed.

Efforts to remove incompetent judges on the federal level are usually unsuccessful. During nearly two hundred years of American constitutional history, the impeachment process has removed only a handful of federal judges from office. Abuse of power, misconduct, corruption, senility, drunkenness, and other behavior problems among judges are frequently overlooked. Every year dozens of complaints against federal judges go unexamined because of insufficient investigatory staff or lack of authority.

It is even more difficult to remove incompetent lawyers from the practice of law. Lawyers can be disbarred for malpractice but the amount of time and effort it takes to do so discourages disciplinary action.

Inequitable Policing. Since the police are part of the judicial system, their behavior is also important to consider. For example, why may country clubs get away with selling alcohol after hours, while lower-class taverns can expect to be raided? Why are affluent-looking drunks generally given a ride home in a taxi, while a "down-and-outer" is usually driven to the police station in a paddy wagon? Why is a well-dressed person less likely to be stopped and frisked than someone who is shabbily dressed? Such examples of police behavior do little to build public confidence in the judicial system, especially among the less fortunate in our society. Rather, these examples breed a callous view that the judicial system exists to help the more fortunate and that there is no such thing as "equal justice under the law."

Bail Inequities. **Bail** is money posted as a guarantee that a person will appear in court at the proper time in exchange for release from jail. The accused can post bail after arrest and before trial, and after conviction and prior to sentencing or appeal. The fact that poorer people are less able to put up funds for bail has a marked effect on the judicial process. Persons on bail have more freedom to help lawyers prepare for a defense in court and obtain lighter sentences if convicted.

Plea Bargaining. The Sixth Amendment of the Bill of Rights reads in part that "in all criminal prosecutions, the accused shall enjoy the right to a speedy and public trial, by an impartial jury." According to the Seventh Amendment, "In suits at common

Police are far more likely to stop and frisk someone who looks "down and out" than someone who has the look of affluence or is conservatively dressed.

law, where the value in controversy shall exceed twenty dollars, the right of trial by jury shall be preserved." What actually happens?

Many cases are never tried because of **plea bargaining**—that is, the plaintiff (or prosecutor) and the defendant, their respective attorneys, and the judge agree that the defendant will plead guilty to a lesser charge in exchange for a reduced sentence. Several unfortunate consequences may result. For one thing, the bargaining skill of defendant and attorney, rather than an examination of the evidence, determines a defendant's sentence. Experienced defendants and attorneys who know the plea-bargaining process generally get lighter sentences than those who are less experienced. Lawyers and their clients make decisions that are properly the province of judges and juries. Moreover, lawyers are often more concerned about caseloads, fees, conviction rates, and time spent on a case than with achieving equitable justice. A defendant who is in fact innocent may be pressured into accepting a guilty plea with a lesser sentence in order to forego the added cost and uncertainty of a trial.

In a criminal case, the prosecutor may offer the defense an attractive bargain to avoid presenting poor or illegal evidence in court (such as evidence obtained through an illegal search or unnecessary force) or to keep secret the identity of an informer. Ironically, the pressure on a defendant to plead guilty is greater if the evidence is weak. A prosecutor with a weak case would rather plea bargain than risk losing a case by going to trial.

Inequitable Sentencing. Do convicted felons who are poor have the same opportunity as upper-class felons to be sentenced to community service work rather than to serve a term behind bars? The answer is obvious. Not only are white-collar criminals more likely to be sentenced to community service work, but if they are imprisoned, their prison stay may be in a far more desirable minimum-security prison. Moreover, in the 33 states that still have capital punishment, poor African-Americans and Hispanics tend to find themselves on death row in disproportionate numbers compared with white middle-class Americans.

Case Overloads. The increasingly litigious nature of American society, the increased number of laws and regulations passed by Congress and state legislatures, and the rising crime rate have contributed to a serious problem of case overload in the judicial system. One consequence is that the accused are often denied their constitutional right to a "speedy trial."

Cost. An affluent person accused of the same crime as a poor person is likely to receive better legal defense because he or she can afford a better lawyer. Cost also creates inequities in civil cases. A person of low to moderate income cannot afford to pay the costs of extensive litigation against adversaries like large companies or the government, which have access to high-priced legal talent.

Jury Selection. What types of persons should be on the jury? Lawyers may invest substantially in determining who should be allowed to serve on a particular jury. They try to develop profiles of the type of jurist most likely to support a client's case. The idea is to "stack" a jury with peers of the person being tried. For example, if an elderly person is being prosecuted, then try to get a jury of elderly persons. Some experts specialize in jury selection and are well paid to advise lawyers on the process. In the well-publicized rape trial of William Kennedy Smith (publicized because Smith is Senator Edward Kennedy's nephew) in 1991 the defense employed such experts to oversee the jury selection.

REASONS WHY THE AMERICAN JUDICIAL SYSTEM IS FAIR TO ALL AMERICANS

Our judicial system exists in a dynamic society. It is not independent of society's problems but rather inherits many of those problems for resolution. In a perfect society, with no conflicts among people, the entire judicial process would be unnecessary. We should ask not whether our courts are perfect, but whether they are improving. The answer is that they are.

Administrative Improvements. At the level of lower courts, improvements have taken a variety of forms. One is the unified court system, which assigns judges where the caseload is greatest so that the constitutional guarantee of a speedy trial can be maintained. In Illinois, for example, rural downstate judges may occasionally be assigned to densely populated areas with heavy caseloads like Chicago. Other elements of a unified court system are the consolidation and simplification of court structure, centralized rules for court operations, centralized budgeting, and statewide financing of all courts. Computerization of records has also helped improve justice at the local level.

Federal courts have also received their share of attention. They, too, have benefited from computerized records, and various proposals to streamline the federal judicial process are under consideration. Congress worked for several years to modernize the federal criminal code.

Another reform, merit selection of judges, provides mixed systems of appointment and election. It is currently used in 16 states. Under the California Plan, the governor nominates a prospective judge. If approved by the three-member Commission of Qualifications, the judge serves for one year, after which he or she runs unopposed for a 12-year term. If a majority of the electorate fails to approve, the governor makes another appointment. Under the Missouri Plan, a nonpartisan nominating board selects three candidates for each vacant judgeship. The governor appoints one of the three for a one-year probationary term, after which the appointee runs in the same type of election as is held in California. Merit selection of judges does not remove the influence of party politics from the scene, but it does allow other interests to have a more effective voice in determining who will serve. Still another reform allows for judicial discipline and removal by a commission before which citizens are able to file charges.

Police training is another area where improvements are taking place. Many universities have instituted criminal justice programs. State and local police personnel now often have college degrees, especially in such states as California and New York. Both federal and state funds have helped finance school programs in criminal justice administration as well as in-service training of police. Several cities have experimented with community policing programs that place police officers in the community to work with residents in preventing crimes.

Other judicial reforms recently implemented or currently being considered include

- Radio and television coverage of courtroom sessions
- Social restitution rather than penal incarceration as a sentence for a convicted defendant who is harmless
- Legal insurance prepaid by interest groups for their members
- More no-fault laws like those in auto and divorce cases to reduce court caseloads
- Storefront legal clinics for people who cannot afford an attorney
- Conflict resolution facilities and personnel to resolve disputes out of court
- Stiffer penalties for malpractice by lawyers

Improving Judicial Representation. More women and minority group members are becoming judges. Because of the increase in female and minority group enrollment in law schools, the pool of legal talent available from these two groups will increase substantially in the near future, helping to eliminate one of the most significant reasons for the underrepresentation of these groups in the judiciary.

Ideological Diversity. Americans benefit from ideological diversity among judges on the federal courts, as shown in Table 13.5. As might be expected, Democratic and Republican judges reflect differing ideological tendencies. Since federal judges do not represent a monolithic ideological viewpoint, neither conservative nor liberal ideology necessarily dominates the courts. Ideological extremes may be checked between genera-

TABLE 13.5 IDEOLOGICAL DIFFERENCES BETWEEN DEMOCRATIC AND REPUBLICAN JUDGES IN U.S. DISTRICT AND APPELLATE COURTS

	Democrats	Republicans
Ideological preference		
Conservative	11%	37%
Liberal	75%	28%
Policies favored		
Less government regulation of business	54%	85%
Preferential hiring of African-Americans	62%	41%
Preferential hiring of women	47%	22%
Oppose government guarantee of jobs	36%	70%
More socialism	19%	4%
Preferred judicial philosophy		
Less protection for criminals	16%	44%
Reduce judicial policy making	51%	69%

Source: Althea K. Nagal, Stanley Rothman, and S. Robert Lichter, "The Verdict on Federal Judges," *Public Opinion* (November/December 1987), pp. 52–56. Reprinted with the permission of The American Enterprise Institute for Public Policy Research, Washington, D.C.

tions, as the more conservative Burger and Rehnquist Courts have balanced the decisions of the more liberal Warren Court, or in a given generation as within the Rehnquist Court, which has balanced pro-life and pro-choice positions on the abortion issue.

Redress Through Crucial Decisions. Certain crucial decisions of federal district courts and the Supreme Court illustrate the importance of the judicial process in assisting the less privileged to seek redress of grievances. Civil liberty guarantees protecting freedom of speech, press, religion, and assembly and other protections in the Bill of Rights are documented in the next chapter. For now, however, we can note that landmark decisions like *Brown* v. *Board of Education* (1954), abolishing segregated education; *Baker* v. *Carr* (1962), establishing the one-person–one-vote doctrine; *Gideon* v. *Wainwright* (1963), mandating legal assistance for indigents; and *Miranda* v. *Arizona* (1966), spelling out the rights of the accused, show how individuals and groups without substantial influence in American society have been able to gain needed protections.

About 1,200 state and 140 federal actions have been ruled unconstitutional by the U.S. Supreme Court during its history.[35] Most of this use of judicial review has occurred in this century, and its concentration has been in the area of civil liberties and civil rights. The importance of judicial review can be summed up in one case: Segregation might still be the law of the land if the Supreme Court had not declared it unconstitutional in 1954 in *Brown* v. *Board of Education*.

ISSUE 2: Summary ★ *Is the American Judicial System Fair to All Americans?*

Charges of elitism and a variety of weaknesses and inequities, such as incompetent judges and lawyers, unequal sentencing and bail imposition, and case overloads, can be fairly lodged against the American judicial system. Taken alone, this evidence appears incontrovertible. However, in the larger context of the dynamics of American constitutional democracy, we can see that the system has on balance substantially strengthened that democracy through administrative improvements, more minority representation among judges, ideological diversity on the courts, and the redress of grievances in crucial judicial decisions. ■

⊕ COMPARISONS WITH OTHER NATIONS

THE JUDICIARY IN DEMOCRACIES

It is unusual for the national judiciary of any democracy to have either the prestige or the authority of the United States Supreme Court. Even the United Kingdom, which possesses a legal heritage similar to that of the United States, displays sharp differences in its court system. Britain, for example, has no equivalent of the Supreme Court. In certain circumstances, the House of Lords can even function as an appellate court. The only time something close to this practice occurs in the United States is during an infrequent impeachment of a high federal official, when the Senate in effect acts as a high court.

The head of the judiciary in the United Kingdom, the Lord Chancellor, is also the highest-ranking official in the House of Lords, over which he or she presides during legislative sessions. British judicial appointments, in which the Lord Chancellor participates, are rarely controversial. The appointees tend to be individuals whose credentials are so impeccable that no reasons can be found to oppose them. There is, in other words, no danger of an appointment being debated either in the news media or the legislature, by contrast with the United States.

In the United States the federal judiciary is not constitutionally inferior to either of the other two branches of government. In Britain, however, the notion of "parliamentary supremacy" is firmly established: A law passed by Parliament cannot be declared unconstitutional by any court decision. This fact provides the courts with an enviable advantage, though, because they easily avoid becoming involved in political controversies. The relative inferiority of British courts compared to American courts can be traced in great part to the fact that the United States has a written constitution and Britain doesn't. Judges are more powerful when they function in systems guided by written constitutions.[36] Their duties are more precisely spelled out and their powers are guaranteed.

The British Parliament is so supreme that it can and does decide what is constitutional and what isn't. One scholar has pointed out that in the United Kingdom:

> The courts do, of course, possess the authority to interpret legislation (which also continually crops up in ordinary litigation), and particularly administrative action based on it—for all government officials are potentially accountable to the courts for their actions. But they may not strike down the law itself.[37]

Therein lies the fundamental difference. The American federal court system can in affect negate a law passed by a state legislature or the national Congress. In Britain no law is wrong unless the legislative branch says it is.

In France, a very limited form of judicial review is in the hands of a body known as the Constitutional Council. Since the creation of the Fifth Republic in 1958 and, more especially, since 1974, when a constitutional amendment enabled the Council to pass on the constitutionality of a legislative bill, the Council has gradually assumed a role that has resulted in the disqualification of certain laws passed by the National Assembly. Usually this process is very politicized, however.

The Council's justices are selected by the presidents of the French Senate, the National Assembly, and the Republic. Each selects three justices who serve nonrenewable nine-year terms. (All former presidents of France are eligible to serve life terms as members of the Constitutional Council. None of the recent ones, though, have chosen to do so.) Because the three presidents may not necessarily be affiliated with the same political party, the justices (three of whom are appointed every three years) can represent a variety of political and social views.

Of all the major democracies, Germany comes closest to practicing judicial review in the American sense. This parallel is more than coincidence. The American influence in German constitutional law is a direct outcome of the occupation of Germany after World War II and American help in writing the German constitution. But there is ample justification as well. Both countries have a history of occasional but very serious disputes between state and federal governments. Some agency was needed to resolve these disputes. In the German case, this agency is the Federal Constitutional Court. The Court was also charged from the beginning with the responsibility of protecting civil liberties. In fact, the German constitution, the Basic Law, clearly states the obligation of the Court to protect the individual against unconstitutional violations of her or his rights.[38] The Court is also required to protect the current democratic political system from forces it perceives as a bona fide threat to the republic.[39] Having no experience with totalitarian regimes, the United States has no equivalent for this precaution.

The executive in Germany is more removed from the process of judicial selection than the American counterpart. The national legislature chooses the Constitutional Court's 16 justices, with each house choosing half. The 16 are divided into two categories: one deals with the disputes between the state and federal governments, while the other has the task of dealing with questions concerning civil liberties.[40] As the following chapter suggests, the latter concern is an even more important focus in Germany than in most other democracies.

There is no way to know whether a defendant's chances for acquittal or a reduced sentence are greater or lesser in the United States than in other democracies. The French have a much higher conviction rate than the United States. But this may be because a higher percentage of cases never get to trial.[41] The French see their judicial authorities and their courts as simply another aspect of their civil service. The noble idea behind the French system of justice is "that justice should be provided quickly, efficiently, inexpensively, and conveniently—very much like any other government service!"[42]

Lawyers in Britain and France are regarded more highly than are lawyers in the United States, where the legal profession as a whole generally is in low repute: "Opinion surveys measuring the public's trust in various professionals generally find lawyers ranked just below plumbers (and journalists) and just above taxi drivers, car salesmen and politicians."[43] Unfortunately, an abundance of lawyers does not ensure an abundance of justice. Japan, for example, with half the population of the United States has only one-sixth the amount of lawyers, but is not known for a lesser system of justice. It *is known* for a much lower crime rate. One observation puts it this way:

> America is undoubtedly over-lawyered and sue-happy. There are . . . three times as many [lawyers] per head as in any other rich country. These besuited sharks are blamed for: a 300-fold increase in medical malpractice suits since 1970; rising insurance premiums; jackpot pay-outs in product-liability cases; and a growing list of "silly suits." A woman in California recently sued her veterinarian for $1m in damages for the emotional distress he caused her by breaking the back of her pet iguana.[44]

The United States has no peer in this respect: No other nations are so wealthy that they can actually afford multimillion-dollar lawsuits as daily occurrences. Figure 13.2 illustrates how in America the costs of lawsuits (expressed as a percentage of gross national product) greatly exceed those of other democracies.

Justice in Developing Democracies

In developing nations that have adopted democracies the judiciary is generally in deservedly low repute. But there are exceptions that offer hope. Costa Rica, for example, is a thorough-going democracy with a strong judiciary. The Costa Rican judicial system is so viable that it even monitors the activities of the legislative and executive branches. Costa Rica has the usual levels of courts that Americans would easily recognize. The highest

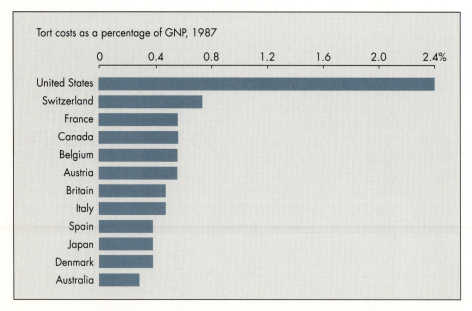

Figure 13.2   THE COSTS OF SUING. Americans spend 2.4 percent of their gross national product (GNP) in legal costs for lawsuits; Australia, by contrast, spends less than 0.4 percent in tort costs. Source: *The Economist,* July 18, 1992, p. 13.

judicial body, the Supreme Court of Justice, is a court of last resort for the protection of individual liberties. To ensure that governments are elected without any hint of fraud the Costa Rican constitution established the Supreme Electoral Tribunal.[45] Because of the Tribunal, Costa Rican elections are both free and honest to an extent unduplicated in all but a very few countries. The Tribunal has no equivalent in the United States. It is designed precisely to guarantee that elections and their preceding campaigns are conducted according to the law, and to resolve disputed elections.

Many governments in developing societies that are struggling to be democratic, however, frequently encounter conditions that remove the possibility of a comprehensive judicial system. Communication and transportation are often primitive or nonexistent, making it difficult to administer justice in disparate regions of the country. The central government may be in control of only a portion of the country, while gangs or guerrillas haphazardly control much of the nonurban regions. Justice is regularly rendered on the basis of who controls the most firepower. More than half of Peru, for example, is dominated by the Shining Path, a Maoist organization that has not hesitated to employ terrorism to

Three female Shining Path guerrillas, ranging in age from 12 to 15. Peru has had to resort to martial law to deal with the terrorism of this widespread Maoist organization, dedicated to overthrowing the government.

dislodge loyalty to and respect for the institutions of the Peruvian government. Peru's legal system is now, in effect, martial law. In any event, it would be unreasonable to expect judges to work in chaotic and sometimes life-threatening circumstances. And no level of justice is immune. For instance, most of the membership of Colombia's Supreme Court was assassinated by terrorists in the middle 1980s.

Even in developed democracies, attempts are made, often successfully, to intimidate the system of justice. Once in a while, a reminder that lawlessness can penetrate the more successful democracies unnerves us. A federal appellate judge was assassinated at his home in Alabama in 1989, for example. Western Europe is no safer:

> "Not everyone has a taste for this sort of thing," says Jean-Claude Vauillemin, a Paris judge.
>   Not everyone indeed. Mr. Vauillemin carries a gun with him and never goes out alone. He and his family are surrounded by bodyguards. He varies his daily itinerary. He keeps his movements, address, and phone number secret. Vauillemin is one of a new breed of "terror judges," investigating magistrates who specialize in understanding the minds and motivations of terrorists.[46]

Now imagine how things would be without a great deal of popular support for the judiciary, with a large guerrilla movement, and with an already high political assassination rate, and you have a common judicial environment in dozens of developing nations.

The Importance of an Independent Judiciary

An independent judiciary is an absolute necessity for any democracy, but it is a luxury many governments think or prefer to think they cannot afford. Even the American government thought so at one time. The Alien and Sedition Acts, passed in 1798, were inspired by a Federalist-controlled Congress and presidency that attempted to snuff out criticism by the opposing Jeffersonian Democrats. The federal courts did not seem very interested. At that time they were still dominated by Federalists, and the Supreme Court itself had not yet asserted itself as a branch of government on a par with the executive and legislative branches (and wouldn't until the appointment of John Marshall in 1801 as Chief Justice).

In an effort to further democratization, Russia established its first independent judiciary, the Constitutional Court, in 1991. Designed to be separate from both the legislative and executive branches, the Constitutional Court is to be Russia's highest court and also to possess judicial review of legislative and executive actions, making it somewhat like the Supreme Court in the United States. The Russian justices may serve until mandatory retirement at age 65 and are not permitted to engage in political activity. Probably the Court's greatest test was to adjudicate the dispute between Boris Yeltsin and the Congress of People's Deputies in 1993 over the issue of executive power and Boris Yeltsin's call for a national referendum on the subject.

Of course, in a democracy, the judiciary does not have to be a coequal branch of the government in order to be effective. But it must be independent, and its decisions must be respected and adhered to by both government and citizenry. If this practice becomes commonplace, even greater respect for international judiciaries is not out of the question. In 1988, for instance, the European Economic Community's Court of Justice banned a Greek law that forbade nationals of other EEC countries from giving private music or dance lessons.[47] This is not an earth-shattering issue, but we are most likely to see an increasing presence of international judiciaries to go along with a wider acceptance of international law.

THE JUDICIARY IN TOTALITARIAN SYSTEMS

It might seem a contradiction in terms to suggest that totalitarian political systems come fully equipped with a judiciary. They do, but the presence of a judicial institution doesn't necessarily imply the application of a system of justice. Totalitarian systems consider a (compliant) judiciary a requirement both for respectability and for the implementation of state policy.

A VIEW FROM ABROAD
A Controversial Supreme Court Decision

Supreme Court decisions are followed regularly abroad. Not all of them are liked. An example of a controversial decision that had repercussions outside the United States is the 1992 6-3 ruling by the high court that justified kidnapping across national borders.

The Supreme Court ruling said that US government agents were not acting illegally when they mounted a covert operation in Mexico to kidnap Doctor Humberto Machian in Guadalajara, and smuggle him back across the border to stand trial for his alleged role in the torture and murder of a US undercover narcotics agent, Enrique Camarena, in 1985.

The Mexican government called the verdict "invalid and unacceptable" in announcing it would no longer co-operate with US drug authorities. The Mexican reaction is expected to be followed by other countries.

In British terms, it is equivalent to granting undercover agents the right to kidnap suspected IRA terrorists from Ireland and bring them back to face British courts without any recognition of the Irish legal system.

The Supreme Court ruling also gives legality to the US seizure of Panamanian ruler Manuel Noriega to stand trial in Miami, and the 1987 capture of Lebanese terrorist Fawaz Yunis on the high seas in the Mediterranean.

"This is a monstrous decision which will shock much of the civilized world. It is unquestionably a flagrant violation of international law," wrote Justice John Paul Stevens, one of the three votes against the decision.

Source: Martin Walker, "US Asserts Right to Kidnap," *The Manchester Guardian*, June 28, 1992, p. 20. Copyright © 1992 The Guardian. (It should be noted that Dr. Machian was later released in the United States for lack of evidence.)

Until the collapse of communism in the Soviet Union, the judicial system was for all practical purposes an important component of the overall security system. Under Stalin during the 1930s, for example, the judiciary was used for perhaps the most cynical of political purposes—allowing a paranoid dictator to get rid of real or imagined enemies. The judiciary ensured that no one in the country could feel safe, including high officials of the government and party. The judiciary was so thoroughly controlled by the government that even lawyers for the defense (always, of course, assigned and employed by the state) would enthusiastically denounce their own clients as enemies of the regime.[48] Sometimes defendants, with the encouragement of physical torture, denounced themselves in the courtroom and asked for (and usually received) the death penalty.

Throughout its history the Soviet Union's court system was charged with emphasizing the rights not of the individual but of the collective. It was actually against the law in the Soviet Union to be antisocial or uncooperative when it came to conforming with the stated goals of the state.

The claim that the courts were technically independent of the government and were encouraged to make their decisions with impartiality[49] was a fiction. True to communist insistence that the Soviet Union was a people's democracy, much of the lower court system was literally in the hands of the people. At the lowest level was what was referred to as the Comrades' Court. Cases that came before this court were minor, and so were the punishments that could be meted out: a comrades' court could "levy reprimands and small fines; order an offender to apologize; administer 'public censure'; propose that an offender be evicted from his dwelling; propose that he be transferred to a job paying less; or require the payment of damages to the victim."[50]

The court system proceeded upward from comrades' courts, through people's courts, through courts of regions and provinces, to the Supreme Court of each of the 15 Union republics. There was also the Supreme Court of the USSR. The Supreme Courts of the republics and the USSR were, like our own state and federal supreme courts, appellate courts. It is not surprising to learn that there was no equivalent of judicial review. The last thing a communist regime would want is a rival power center.

Not all judiciaries in communist systems were established in identical fashion. The Soviet model was imperfectly followed until the late 1980s in much of Eastern Europe. China brought the dispensation of justice to an even more rudimentary level than the Comrades' Courts of the Soviet Union. Mediation committees deal with the sorts of disputes prevalent in a relatively poor society of 1.2 billion people. There are nearly one million such committees throughout the country with a total elected membership of 5.5 million.[51] The committees provide a buffer between the regular courts and the numerous minor problems that would clog them. The Chinese have long evidenced a preference for the informal resolution of disputes.[52]

Ideology superseded law in China by the time of the Great Cultural Revolution (1966–1969) and also intimidated judges. The judiciary, like every other agent of the state, was required to adhere steadfastly to party doctrine. With the beginning of economic reforms in 1979, though, the situation changed drastically. For one thing, as private property became an ingredient of economic life during the 1980s a new set of laws was needed to cope with the phenomenon. Divorce cases had judicial relevance because for the first time there was now property to divide between the spouses. China became a country that actually needed *more* lawyers than it already had.[53]

As China moved away from the strictures of ideology, its legal and judicial

A landlord is on trial here before a Chinese mediation committee. Such committees are composed of ordinary citizens who seek to resolve disputes informally.

systems assumed a perhaps unprecedented position. Laws became suddenly important because they were supposed to be supportive of economic progress. Instead of laws geared to agree with ideology or ignored because of ideology, they now were formulated to encourage and safeguard drastic economic reform (but, as the massacre at Tiananmen Square clearly and tragically demonstrated in June of 1989, not political reform). But the reform also can be invasive of personal privacy. The pressure on Chinese women to restrict themselves to bearing only one child, for example, has legal force behind it: Elderly women known as "grandmothers" are assigned several dozen young married women to inquire about their monthly menstrual cycle; the young women are legally obliged to respond honestly.

In both the ideological and pragmatic stages of the People's Republic of China individual rights were not a strong consideration and were not to be seriously entertained by the judicial process. Whether they will eventually have to be remains to be seen. No national economy has become prosperous without healthy doses of political (that is, democratic) reform.

THE JUDICIARY IN AUTHORITARIAN SYSTEMS

Most authoritarian regimes are understandably insecure and distrust the more familiar judicial procedures. The adjudication of regular criminal cases in Iraq, for instance, is based on the severity of the crime: There are three levels of courts (most of which operate without the inconvenience of juries) that deal with misdemeanors and felonies. However, for crimes against state security there is the Revolutionary Command Council (RCC). The RCC handles cases of treason and "'antistate' activities"[54] and, along with other special security courts, does not hesitate to impose the death penalty.[55] In Saudi Arabia, authorities simply refer to the Quran (the holy book of Islam) for legal remedies. These include the liberal use of the death penalty (often a public beheading, usually on Friday afternoons) for capital crimes (such as prostitution) and the amputation of a hand for thievery. In recent years the amputation has been preceded by a concession to modernity—the administration of a local anesthetic.

Administration of justice in these regimes may be complicated by the fact that within their borders there are often ethnic communities that have little in common with the governing entities. One scholar has pointed out that less than 3 percent of the world's 5,000 national communities enjoy the political luxury of having a state of their own.[56] The remaining 97 percent—communities such as the perhaps 10 million Kurds scattered throughout four countries in the Middle East—do not always accept a legal or judicial system that they regard as alien, exploitive, or hostile to their own political culture and destiny.

The problem of hostile ethnic minorities or, in many cases, the actuality of armed rebellion on the part of some of them provides a beseiged regime all the excuse it needs to declare martial law. The application of martial law enables a government to "legally" ride roughshod over even the pretense of pursuing justice. The army places much or even all of its own country under military occupation in what is most often described as a "state of emergency." The normalcy of constitutional guarantees of individual rights is suspended, usually indefinitely. Even if a rebellion or wave of political terrorism is put down, the government is often hesitant to remove martial law because it works so well in circumventing (sometimes by jailing) the political opposition.

Some authoritarian regimes have laws in place that are contradicted by the generally accepted body of international law. Before it undertook reforms in the early 1990s, South Africa was governed by an authoritarian regime that was a relentless offender of the 1973 *International Convention of Suppression and Punishment of the Crime of Apartheid*. Of course, it is important to keep in mind that most authoritarian regimes don't care about international law as long as they can commit their illegalities with impunity. It is clear that the development of fair, impartial, independent, and unintimidated judiciaries throughout the world still has a long road to travel.

Summary

1. The American judicial system includes both federal and state courts and has assigned activities for each.

2. Courts may have original jurisdiction (trial courts) or appellate jurisdiction (which hear cases on appeal). Judges in the federal courts are unelected and have life tenure, but judges in state courts are either elected or appointed for fixed terms. At the apex of the federal court system is the Supreme Court. Under it are the 12 courts of appeals and 94 district courts where federal cases are tried. The state court system

also includes a tier of lower trial courts and higher appeal courts, but the exact structure varies from state to state.

3. The U.S. Supreme Court's greatest power is judicial review, established in the *Marbury v. Madison* decision in 1803. This power allows the Court to declare the acts of state and federal legislatures and executives unconstitutional. At the same time, the Court can see its decisions reversed by the ratification of constitutional amendments.

4. Some critics think that the Supreme Court has too much power and that it uses its power of judicial review to make policy rather than interpret law.

5. Others defend the Court by noting the limits to its policymaking ability and the checks imposed by Congress, the president, and the Court itself.

6. Many factors suggest that the judicial system does not work fairly for all Americans. Since judges tend to be lawyers, white, middle- or upper-class, and male, they are unrepresentative of large segments of the American population. There are also inequities in bail, sentencing, access to lawyers, policing, and plea bargaining.

7. However, as reforms in the administration of justice are made and more minorities are appointed to the courts, the judicial system will be applied more fairly. Ideological diversity among judges and the ability to redress grievances through legal decisions also help make the system fairer.

8. The United States and the United Kingdom have a similar legal heritage, but the United Kingdom has no parallel tradition of judicial review. France has a limited judicial review. Only Germany among the major democracies has a judicial review similar to ours.

9. The United States is "overlawyered." The other democracies have only a fraction of the number of American lawyers.

10. In some developing democracies the judiciary may be hampered by poor communication and transportation as well as by hostile groups opposing the government.

11. Totalitarian systems make the judiciary powerless to protect individual rights and use it to warp ordinary justice. The Soviet court system was geared to stress the security of the state, the prerogatives of the collective, and ideological purity over the rights of the individual. China is trying to use its judiciary to facilitate economic reform without allowing it to achieve independence or to protect individual rights.

12. Authoritarian regimes often have very weak judiciaries. They also may use unconventional procedures to deal with crimes, and their laws may not conform to international law.

Terms to Define

Administrative law

Adversary process

Amicus curiae brief

Appellate jurisdiction

Bail

Civil law

Common law   Majority opinion
Concurring opinion   Minority opinion
Constitutional law   Natural law
Criminal law   Original jurisdiction
Dissenting opinion   Per curium decision
Judicial activism   Plea bargaining
Judicial notice   Presumed constitutionality
Judicial policymaking   Stare decisis
Judicial restraint   Statutory law
Judicial review   Torts
Jurisdiction   Writ of certiorari
Justiciable issue

Suggested Readings

Abraham, Henry J. *The Judicial Process*, 6th ed. New York: Oxford University Press, 1993. Surveys the organization and functions of the federal court system.

Bork, Robert H. *The Tempting of America*. New York: Free Press, 1990. A dissection of the current state of legal scholarship and its political agenda from a former Supreme Court nominee and federal judge.

Ely, John Hart. *Democracy and Distrust*. Cambridge: Harvard University Press, 1980. Attempts to develop a theory about judicial review that is neither strict constructionist nor activist.

Lasser, William. *The Limits of Judicial Power*. Chapel Hill: University of North Carolina Press, 1988. Demonstrates the Court's capacity to withstand opposition generated by its controversial decisions.

Wasby, Stephen L. *The Supreme Court in the Federal Judicial System*, 3rd ed. Chicago: Nelson-Hall, 1988. Examines the Supreme Court's role in the political system and its internal procedures.

Wice, Paul. *Judges and Lawyers: The Human Side of Justice*. New York: Harper Collins, 1991. Reveals the human dimension of justice through hundreds of interviews in 15 states.

Wolfe, Christopher. *The Rise of Modern Judicial Review*. New York: Basic Books, 1986. Surveys the origins of judicial review from 1787 to the present.

Notes

1. Alexis de Tocqueville, *Democracy in America*, edited by Phillips Bradley (New York: Alfred A. Knopf, 1944), Vol. I, p. 280.
2. "American Living Standards," *The Economist*, November 10, 1990, p. 22.
3. James Eisenstein, *Politics and the Legal Process* (New York: Harper & Row, 1973), pp. 26 and 27.
4. *Marbury v. Madison*, 1 Cranch 137 (1803).
5. *Brown v. Board of Education*, 347 U.S. 483 (1954).
6. *Reynolds v. Sims*, 376 U.S. 1 (1964).
7. *Wesbury v. Sanders*, 376 U.S. 1 (1964).
8. *Miranda v. Arizona*, 384 U.S. 436 (1966).
9. *Gideon v. Wainwright*, 372 U.S. 335 (1963).
10. *Engel v. Vitale*, 370 U.S. 421 (1962).
11. *Abington School District v. Schempp*, 394 U.S. 203 (1963).
12. *Roe v. Wade*, 410 U.S. 113 (1973).
13. *Webster v. Reproductive Health Services*, 109 S.Ct. 3040 (1989).

14. *Planned Parenthood* v. *Casey*, 112 S.Ct. 2791 (1992).
15. Robert G. McCloskey, *The American Supreme Court* (Chicago: University of Chicago Press, 1960), p. 225.
16. Max Lerner, *Ideas Are Weapons* (New York: Viking Press, 1939), p. 474.
17. *Dennis* v. *United States*, 341 U.S. 494 (1951).
18. *The Federalist* (New York: The Modern Library, 1937), p. 505.
19. Ibid. p. 506.
20. Henry J. Abraham, *The Judicial Process*, 6th ed. (New York: Oxford University Press, 1993), p. 300.
21. *Harris* v. *McRae*, 448 U.S. 297 (1980).
22. *Engle* v. *Vitale*, 370 U.S. 107 (1962).
23. *Baker* v. *Carr*, 369 U.S. 186 (1962); *Reynolds* v. *Sims*, 377 U.S. 533 (1964).
24. *Brown* v. *Board of Education*, 347 U.S. 483 (1954).
25. *Worcester* v. *Georgia*, 31 U.S. 515 (1832).
26. *Chisholm* v. *Georgia*, 2 U.S. 419 (1793).
27. *Dred Scott* v. *Sandford*, 19 Howard 393 (1857).
28. *Pollock* v. *Farmers' Loan and Trust Company*, 158 U.S. 429 (1895).
29. Benjamin Cardozo, *The Nature of the Judicial Process* (New Haven: Yale University Press, 1921), p. 168.
30. *Planned Parenthood* v. *Casey*, 112 S.Ct. 2791 (1992).
31. *NLRB* v. *Jones and Laughlin Steel Corporation*, 301 U.S. 1 (1937).
32. *Trop* v. *Dulles*, 356 U.S. 86 (1958).
33. *Plessy* v. *Ferguson*, 163 U.S. 537 (1896).
34. *Congressional Quarterly Weekly Report*, January 19, 1991, pp. 171–174.
35. *Constitution of the United States of America: Annotated and Interpreted* (Washington, D.C.: U.S. Government Printing Office, 1987) and 1988 Supplement.
36. "The British Constitution," *The Economist*, July 6, 1991, p. 22.
37. Henry J. Abraham, *The Judicial Process*, 4th ed. (Oxford and New York: Oxford University Press, 1980), p. 311.
38. Article 93, Section 1.
39. Article 21.
40. See the lucid discussion by David P. Conradt, *The German Polity*, 3rd ed. (New York and London: Longman, 1986), pp. 202–204.
41. Safran, *The French Polity*, p. 235.
42. Abraham, *The Judicial Process*, 4th ed., p. 271.
43. "The Plummeting Price of Justice," *The Economist*, August 10, 1991, p. 53.
44. "A Plague of Lawyers," *The Economist*, August 10, 1991, p. 13.
45. Article 100.
46. Louise Lief, "France's 'Terror' Judges: A New Breed of Risk-Takers," *The Christian Science Monitor*, March 16, 1987, pp. 1, 32.
47. *The Economist*, April 2, 1988, p. 44.
48. For a comprehensive analysis of this nightmare, the best source is Robert Conquest, *The Great Terror: A Reassessment* (New York: Oxford University Press, 1990).
49. Articles 155 and 156.
50. Abraham, *The Judicial Process*, 4th ed., p. 289.
51. James R. Townsend and Brantly Womack, *Politics in China*, 3rd ed. (Glenview, Ill.: Scott, Foresman, 1986), pp. 369–370.
52. Ibid., p. 369.
53. Jonathan D. Spence, *The Search for Modern China* (New York and London: Norton, 1990), pp. 707–708.
54. Mark Lewis et al., *Iraq: A Country Study*, 4th ed. (Washington, D.C.: Library of Congress, 1990), p. 185.
55. Ibid.
56. Bernard Nietschmann, "The Miskito Nation and the Geopolitics of Self-Determination," in Bernard Schechterman and Martin Slann, eds., *The Ethnic Dimension in International Relations* (New York: Praeger, 1993).

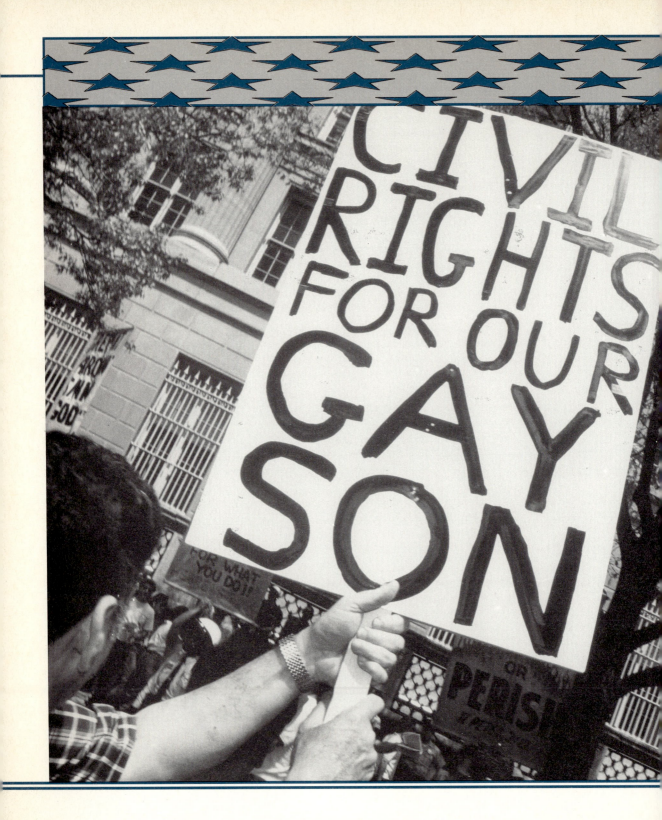

CHAPTER ★ FOURTEEN

CIVIL LIBERTIES AND CIVIL RIGHTS

Civil liberties represent the most fundamental difference between democratic and totalitarian governments. In a totalitarian country the only liberties that exist belong to the government, but in democratic countries, **civil liberties** are those rights that all citizens have that protect them from arbitrary actions by government. They include freedoms of speech, religion, assembly, and petition and guarantees of lawful procedures in the dispensing of justice ("due process of law"). By their very nature, civil liberties mean that government is limited. Government cannot do certain things because citizens have reserved to themselves freedoms and rights with which the government may not interfere.

    In fact, these restrictions on government are so important that the government is not supposed to violate them even if the majority of the people want the government to do so. That is because democracy must embody both majority rule and minority rights. **Civil rights** are protections that government is expected to extend to individuals, regardless of their racial, gender, or ethnic characteristics, to ensure that all citizens are treated equally under the laws. Thus, no category of citizens should claim special privilege nor should any group be discriminated against by other groups or by the government. The majority has its principal protection and strength through governmental procedures, such as voting, that allow the majority to work its will. The minority has its protection and strength through constitutional guarantees of both civil liberties and civil rights.

The principal sources of civil liberties and civil rights in the United States can be traced in part to roots in British constitutional traditions, many of which were transplanted to the North American colonies in the seventeenth and eighteenth centuries. Our own sources include the following:

- The Declaration of Independence, which states that "We hold these truths to be self-evident; that all men are created equal; that they are endowed by their creator with certain inalienable rights; that among these are life, liberty, and the pursuit of happiness."

- The Constitution of 1787, which provided important procedural rights, such as *habeus corpus* (preventing unlawful imprisonment).

- The Bill of Rights, which comprises the first ten amendments to the Constitution and expressly forbids governmental interference, for example, with (1) freedom of religion, speech, press, assembly; (2) "the right of people to be secure in their persons, houses, papers, and effects, against unreasonable searches and seizures"; and (3) the rights of persons accused of crimes.

- The Fourteenth Amendment, which requires that "no State shall make or enforce any law which shall abridge the privileges or immunities of citizens of the United States, nor shall any State deprive any person of life, liberty, or property, without due process of law; nor deny to any person within its jurisdiction the equal protection of the laws." In other words, the same restrictions that the Constitution places on the federal government also apply to state governments.

In this chapter we will examine how our civil liberties and civil rights have evolved and expanded over time. We will consider such issues as how supportive the public is of civil liberties and how we can best assure "equal" protection under the laws. Finally, we will see how our liberties and rights stack up against those of other countries.

★ AMERICAN CIVIL LIBERTIES AND RIGHTS

THE EVOLUTION OF CIVIL LIBERTIES

Civil liberties may seem obvious, until it is necessary to make clear-cut decisions on civil liberty issues. To understand the difficulties involved, put yourself in the place of a Supreme Court justice and decide how you would rule on the following actual cases pertaining to individual rights, freedom of speech, and criminal law:

1. Can abortion counseling be forbidden at publicly funded clinics?
2. Can nude dancing be banned at adults-only clubs?
3. Should a pregnant woman be excluded from a job that might harm a developing fetus?
4. Does freedom of the press in the First Amendment prevent the news media from being sued if they fail to keep promises of confidentiality to their sources?
5. Does a coerced confession, introduced at a trial, automatically taint a conviction?
6. Does life in prison without parole for a first-time drug offense constitute cruel and unusual punishment?
7. Can Congress make burning the American flag unconstitutional?
8. Can police use a low-flying helicopter to search property without a warrant?
9. Can a teenager be sentenced to death?
10. Can a high school principal censor the contents of a student newspaper?

The Supreme Court decided each of these issues by a 5 to 4 vote, except for censorship of a student newspaper, which was decided by a 5 to 3 vote. Following are the Court's decisions:

Issue 1: Can abortion counseling be forbidden at publicly funded clinics? *Rust* v. *Sullivan* (1991)[1]
Decision: The administration may forbid workers at publicly funded clinics from counseling pregnant women on abortion. Title X of the Public Health Service Act can be read to bar not only abortions but also abortion counseling.*

Issue 2: Can nude dancing be banned at adults-only clubs? *Barnes* v. *Glen Theatre* (1991)[2]
Decision: States may ban nude dancing even at adults-only clubs without breaching the First Amendment right of expression.

Issue 3: Should a pregnant woman be excluded from a job that might harm a developing fetus? *United Autoworkers Union* v. *Johnson Controls* (1991)[3]
Decision: Companies may not exclude women from jobs that might harm a developing fetus. Congress intended antidiscrimination laws to forbid all job practices based on workers' ability to have children.

Issue 4: Does freedom of the press in the First Amendment prevent the news media from being sued if they fail to keep promises of confidentiality to their sources? *Cohen* v. *Cowles Media* (1991)[4]
Decision: The First Amendment does not shield news media from lawsuits if they break promises of confidentiality to their sources.

---

* One of President Bill Clinton's first acts was to issue an executive order reversing this ban.

Issue 5: Does a coerced confession, introduced at a trial, automatically taint a conviction? *Arizona* v. *Fulminante* (1991)[5]
Decision: A coerced confession, introduced at trial, does not automatically taint a conviction. It is not in violation of due process of law.

Issue 6: Does life in prison without parole for a first-time drug offense constitute cruel and unusual punishment? *Harmelin* v. *Michigan* (1991)[6]
Decision: A state may require life in prison without parole for a first-time drug offense without violating the constitutional ban on cruel and unusual punishment.

Issue 7: Can Congress make burning the American flag unconstitutional? *U.S.* v. *Eichmann* (1990)[7]
Decision: Burning of the American flag is a form of symbolic speech protected by the freedom of speech clause in the First Amendment; it may not be banned by Congress.

Issue 8: Can police use a low-flying helicopter to search property without a warrant? *Florida* v. *Riley* (1989)[8]
Decision: Use of a low-flying helicopter to conduct a search of private property does not violate the constitutional protection against illegal search and seizure.

Issue 9: Can a teenager be sentenced to death? *Stanford* v. *Kentucky* (1989) and *Wilkins* v. *Missouri* (1989)[9]
Decision: Sentencing a teenager to death does not violate the constitutional prohibition of cruel and unusual punishment.

Issue 10: Can a high school principal censor the contents of a student newspaper? *Hazelwood School District* v. *Kuhlheimer* (1988)[10]
Decision: Censorship of a school newspaper by a school official does not violate freedom of the press under the First Amendment.

The closeness of these decisions indicates how far the Court is from reaching unanimity in applying civil liberties to actual situations. Not only do justices on one Court disagree with one another on these kinds of issues, but justices at different periods of history form different opinions. The result is a confusing array of decisions in which the Supreme Court has seemed to come down on both sides of essentially the same issues. It is important to remember, however, that neither civil liberties nor the judges who interpret and apply them exist in a vacuum. Civil liberties change as society changes, and judges reflect the world in which they live.

Another problem is that civil liberties cannot be absolute. Justice Oliver Wendell Holmes, Jr., once said: "The best test of truth is the power of the thought to get itself accepted in the competition of the market,"[11] a powerful argument for freedom of expression. Some decades later, however, law professor Alexander Bickel noted that a "marketplace of ideas without rules of civil discourse is no marketplace of ideas, but a bull ring."[12] The shade of difference between Holmes and Bickel illustrates the balance that must be obtained between order and freedom—the government's need to maintain order and the individual's right to freedom. Standards and principles embedded in our civil liberties provide a way to establish a proper balance between government and the individual. Thus, the government must have the power to investigate and to maintain order in society; the individual must be free from unreasonable searches and seizures. The government must be able to acquire land by exercising its right of public domain; the individual cannot be arbitrarily deprived of property.

During the 1990s several major issues on college campuses came to pit various groups against one another, particularly on the question of "political correctness," or the use of proper speech. The University of Wisconsin (Madison) and other universities adopted codes of acceptable speech to prevent speech offensive to some students; however, the very existence of the code limited the First Amendment's protection of free speech, and the universities had to either repeal or modify their codes. Other colleges and universities have adopted codes of acceptable classroom speech, such as referring to the presiding officer as "chair" or "chairperson" rather than "chairman." Again, these codes are subject to attack as a violation of the First Amendment and the long-standing respect for academic freedom on campus and especially in the classroom.

As we look more closely at our First Amendment freedoms and procedural rights, we will see the difficulties of finding balances and of adapting to changing times in a dynamic society.

Freedom of Religion

The opening clauses of the First Amendment are known as the **establishment** and **free exercise clauses**. These state: "Congress shall make no law respecting an establishment of religion, or prohibiting the free exercise thereof." What do these clauses mean? They mean what the courts say they mean, and various courts have interpreted them in different ways.

Although Thomas Jefferson said many years after the Constitutional Convention that the First Amendment intended to build a wall of separation between church and state, the wall crumbled in places. Many states have had "blue laws" that require the closing of business establishments on Sundays, the armed forces employ chaplains, Congress begins each day's session with prayer, and our currency affirms "In God We Trust."

The Supreme Court has handed down a number of decisions that tend to blur the establishment clause and break down the wall between church and state:

- Parents may be reimbursed for bus fares to send children to church schools.[13]

- Public schools can release students from part of the compulsory school day to obtain religious instruction outside the school building.[14]

- State bonds may be used to finance the construction of nonreligious buildings on church-related college campuses.[15]

- A state may lend textbooks to church-related schools[16] and furnish textbooks to pupils in private schools (except institutions that exclude students because of race or religion).[17]

- Public school assemblies and programs can include the singing of Christmas carols at official school programs.[18]

- Parents may be able to deduct from their state income tax tuitions paid to nonpublic schools.[19]

Yet, in a number of decisions involving freedom of religion, the Supreme Court has seemingly *strengthened* the establishment clause to reinforce the wall of separation:

- Public schools may not allow any form of prayer, even if the prayer is non-sectarian and voluntary.[20]
- Public schools may not permit religious instructors (even volunteers) to provide religious instruction in public school buildings during the school day.[21]
- Tax funds may not be used to reimburse church-operated elementary and secondary schools or otherwise supplement their financial resources in order to pay for the salaries of teachers, even if they teach secular subjects.[22]
- States may not reimburse parochial and other private schools for the maintenance and repair of school facilities and equipment or for the cost of testing pupils in secular subjects.[23]
- Parents may not be reimbursed by the state for tuition costs for nonpublic schools.[24]

Should prayer be allowed in the public school classroom? Is a nonsectarian prayer acceptable? What about a moment of silence? Such questions are brought before the Supreme Court as constitutional issues. The Court must decide the boundaries between freedom of religion and separation of church and state.

- Public schools may not lend instructional equipment to nonpublic schools.[25]
- The Ten Commandments may not be posted on public school classroom walls.[26]

A basic reason for the seemingly contradictory decisions of the Supreme Court is the principle of *no excessive entanglement* with religion. The Court developed a threefold test to determine whether a law is in agreement with the establishment clause: the law must (1) have a clear secular legislative purpose, (2) have the primary effect of neither advancing nor inhibiting religion, and (3) avoid excessive government entanglement with religion.[27] This test results in some aid to private and parochial schools being permissible and some not.

Sometimes a law requires people to do something that conflicts with the free exercise of their religion. But exempting them from abiding by the law would favor their religion and thus violate the establishment doctrine. Generally, the Court has ruled that religious convictions do not confer any right for a person to violate otherwise valid and nondiscriminatory laws. As long as the law is not violated, however, an individual's freedom of worship should be unrestricted.[28] Some decisions have restricted the free exercise clause:

- Forbidding the religious use of the drug Peyote by American Indians[29]
- Forbidding the practice of polygamy by Mormons[30]
- Requiring the vaccination of schoolchildren who are Christian Scientists[31]
- Upholding a Massachusetts criminal law forbidding boys under 12 and girls under 18 from selling merchandise on the streets (the merchandise at issue was Jehovah's Witness literature).[32]

Other Court decisions have upheld the free exercise doctrine:

- Upholding parents' rights to send their children to parochial schools[33]
- Not requiring Jehovah's Witnesses to participate in a public school flag salute ceremony[34]
- Denying states the right to withhold unemployment compensation from those who refuse on principle to accept positions requiring them to work on their Sabbath[35]
- Allowing Amish parents to withdraw their children from school beyond the eighth grade[36]

The development of private Christian schools since the 1960s has raised other issues. Can they be required to enroll a certain percentage of minority students? Can states impose curriculum standards on them? Reasonable arguments can be made on both sides of these issues. It can be argued that minority students should not be denied access to private Christian education. On the other hand, should those schools be required to enroll students who do not accept the schools' religious doctrines and practices? Certainly a state has an interest in the curriculum taught within its boundaries; however, should a state be allowed to impose a curriculum that undermines the religious doctrines and practices of a school?

More recently, home schooling has become the choice of many parents concerned about crime and violence and other behavioral problems in the public schools. As with the Christian schools, should a state be able to impose curriculum standards, teacher certification standards for the parents, and other requirements imposed on the public schools? Of course, the question of whether the Christian schools and home schools provide adequate opportunity for social development is also debated. A fundamental issue is this: In the matter of educating children, when do parental rights end and the rights of the state begin? Should parents be able to choose for their children the educational environment that they believe is safer and offers greater opportunity for cognitive, character, and personality development or should the state be able to make that decision? That issue will be much debated during the 1990s.

Freedom of Speech

Should all speech receive absolute protection? A quick reading of the First Amendment suggests an affirmative answer. But what about speech that incites a riot or defames another person's character? What about the graphic depiction of sex on television? Protection of all speech might undermine democracy. The flexible interpretation and application of freedom of speech helps to enhance the stability of society.

Several means that the Court has used to test whether speech should be constitutionally protected reveal the Court's flexible interpretation and application. The tests may be summarized as absolutist position, clear and present danger, dangerous tendency, preferred position, and balancing of interests. The test to apply may depend on the condition of society. For example, is the country at war or peace? Is it economically depressed or prosperous? Is there civil unrest or social stability?

Absolutist. According to the **absolutist position**, the First Amendment means just what it says and cannot be qualified. Former Justices Hugo Black and William Douglas took this view. Black argued that "there are 'absolutes' in our Bill of Rights" that cannot be weakened by judicial decisions. Even obscenity and libel cannot be constitutionally limited because they are types of speech. Few justices have agreed with this view.

Clear and Present Danger. Justice Oliver Wendell Holmes used this test in the case of *Schenck v. United States* (1919). During World War I, Congress passed the Espionage Act, which, among other things, prohibited actions leading to insubordination in the armed forces. When Socialist Charles T. Schenck passed out antiwar pamphlets to men eligible for the draft, the government accused him of violating the act. This case pitted the rights of free speech and press against the government's need to protect itself in time of war. The Supreme Court ruled unanimously in favor of the government. Holmes contended that speech loses its constitutional protections if it presents an immediate threat—**a clear and present danger.** The First Amendment would not protect the speech of someone falsely yelling "fire" in a crowded theater because that person would be creating the immediate threat of a stampede. On the other hand, if there were no danger of immediate disturbance harmful to the public, speech would be protected. Wrote Justice Holmes: "When a nation is at war many things that might be said in time of peace are such a hindrance to its effort that their utterance will not be endured so long as men fight, and that no court could regard them as protected by any constitutional right."[37] To use a contemporary example: Neo-Nazis and members of the Ku Klux Klan would likely be allowed to speak on a college campus, because their doing so would not constitute a clear and present danger.

Dangerous Tendency. According to the test of **dangerous tendency**, speech loses its constitutional protection if it tends to lead to a substantive evil. Application of this test would lead to more infringement on freedom of speech than the "clear and present danger" test, since speech must only *tend* to be dangerous, not present an actual threat. Some people might use this test to forbid Neo-Nazis and members of the Ku Klux Klan from speaking, because their speech might incite a hostile reaction, creating a "dangerous tendency."

Preferred Position. Justices using the **preferred position** test contend that First Amendment freedoms have the highest priority in our constitutional hierarchy. Courts bear a special responsibility to scrutinize with extra care any laws that appear to trespass on these freedoms. When freedom of speech is diluted or denied, the channels for correcting errors in the political process become clogged or closed. Any limitation on free speech is presumed unconstitutional *unless there is some overriding justification.* This doctrine would no doubt uphold the free speech rights of Neo-Nazis and members of the Ku Klux Klan.

Balancing of Interests. Does the interest of society in limiting speech outweigh the interest of the person speaking? **Balancing of interests**, instead of placing the First Amendment freedom of speech guarantee on a pedestal, weighs it against the interests of society in maintaining order. In the case of Neo-Nazis and members of the Ku Klux Klan, the Court would ask whether their rights to freedom of speech are outweighed by society's need to maintain order. Since their speaking on a college campus poses no immediate threat to the order of society, their speech might be protected under this test.

Freedom of the Press

One of the principal reasons for civil liberties, especially the First Amendment, is the belief that truth is more likely to be found when freedom of expression is greatest, and freedom of the press provides an outlet for that expression. But free press is subject to some of the same limits as free speech if it harms others or weakens the country. The main issue concerns whether the government can use **prior restraint** to *prevent* publication or broadcast of forbidden material.

A historic Supreme Court decision in 1931, *Near* v. *Minnesota,*[38] contended that although freedom of the press might be abused by "purveyors of scandal," the press should customarily be immune from "previous restraint." The Court did add, however, that exceptions might be necessary in instances concerning national security. The famous Pentagon Papers case of 1971, when Defense Department documents concerning the Vietnam War were leaked to the press, presented the Court with an opportunity to decide whether national security required prior restraint under these circumstances, since many of the documents that *The New York Times* planned to publish were classified. Although ruling against censorship in this instance, the Court did not settle the basic issue of when, if ever, the government can *prevent* publication of a newspaper story by claiming that the national security is endangered.[39]

Can government compel journalists to reveal their sources? In 1976 CBS correspondent Daniel Schorr obtained classified material from the Intelligence Committee of the House of Representatives and arranged for its publication in *The Village Voice*, a New York City newspaper. When Schorr appeared before the Ethics Committee of the House, he refused to disclose his source, citing First Amendment guarantees of freedom of the press. By a vote of six to five, the Ethics Committee refused to recommend to the House of Representatives that Schorr be prosecuted. The committee's vote showed a flexible approach to civil liberties. Still, people inside and outside government differ substantially on how far freedom of the press should be extended. As the Ethics Committee concluded in its majority report: "It is not axiomatic . . . that the news media is always right and the government is always wrong."[40] The fact that Schorr was suspended by his employer, CBS, indicates that even the media may see the need to rein in the press.

During the 1991 Senate hearings and debates about the confirmation of Judge Clarence Thomas to the Supreme Court, there were some embarrassing leaks to the press. Nina Totenberg, a correspondent at National Public Radio, refused to reveal confidential sources and notes, causing some members of the Senate to demand that she be cited for contempt of Congress, but no action was taken.

Another test of freedom of the press arises when pretrial and courtroom publicity might endanger a defendant's right to a fair trial. This situation dramatizes a clear conflict between two elements of the Bill of Rights—freedom of the press and the right of an

Should journalists be required to reveal their sources? Nina Totenberg, a correspondent for National Public Radio, refused to do so at the 1992 Senate hearings investigating leaks in the Clarence Thomas confirmation process.

accused person to a fair trial. This happened in the case of William Kennedy Smith's rape trial in Florida in 1991. Could Smith, a nephew of Senator Edward Kennedy, receive a fair trial in West Palm Beach, site of Kennedy's Florida compound, where the case was thoroughly publicized? Television communication complicates the problem. In 1961 the Supreme Court reversed the convictions of two defendants whose televised confessions presumably influenced the jury.[41] In 1966 the Court overturned the conviction of Samuel H. Sheppard (who had been found guilty of bludgeoning his wife to death) because of excessive news coverage.[42] To ensure a defendant a fair trial, a judge may delay the trial, transfer it to another location, or sequester the jury.

From the mid-1970s through 1991, a long line of cases brought freedom of press issues before the Supreme Court. In *Zurcher* v. *Stanford Daily* (1978),[43] the Court held that law enforcement officials with valid search warrants could not be stopped from examining newsrooms to find evidence of crimes. When *New York Times* reporter Myron Farber refused to turn over documents to a trial court, the New Jersey Supreme Court ruled against Farber and the Supreme Court let the decision stand.[44] In this case, the defendant's Sixth Amendment right to a fair trial prevailed over First Amendment claims of protection of confidential news sources.

Should government officials be allowed to secretly subpoena telephone records of reporters to identify their confidential sources? A lower court ruled that such action was justifiable when those sources have information that may be helpful to a criminal investigation; the U.S. Supreme Court let the lower court ruling stand.[45]

CBS correspondent Mike Wallace and producer Barry Lando were charged with libel by a retired Army colonel, who contended that he was falsely called a liar on CBS's *60 Minutes*. His attorneys sought to question Wallace and Lando about their editorial decisions leading to the charge of lying; that is, they wanted to know what Wallace and Lando were thinking about and what they said to each other before making the charge. In *Herbert* v. *Lando* (1979),[46] the Court held that freedom of the press does not protect a reporter's thoughts, judgments, and newsroom discussions from judicial proceedings. The colonel's right to a fair trial outweighed Lando and Wallace's right to freedom of the press.

In *Gannett Co.* v. *De Pasquale* (1979),[47] the Court said judges could close a criminal trial to the press and public if they believe that pretrial publicity might damage a defendant's right to a fair trial. The Court stated specifically that "members of the public have no constitutional right under the Sixth and Fourteenth Amendments to attend criminal trials."

The conservative political columnist James J. Kilpatrick condemned this decision: "When the press is locked out, the people lose their eyes and their ears and their sense of fishy smell as well. In the case at hand (*Gannett Co.* v. *De Pasquale*), the defendants' rights never were endangered for a moment. The public's rights went down the tube."[48] Responding to these and other charges, Justice William J. Brennan retorted that the press was trying to extend its rights too far under the guise of freedom of speech and freedom of the press. Brennan, a liberal who advocated an almost literal interpretation of freedom of speech and the press, still did not believe these First Amendment rights should be used to deny other rights, such as the right to a fair trial guaranteed in the Sixth Amendment. Brennan said the press either had to accommodate itself to a "variety of important social interests," which "the sad complexity of our society makes . . . inevitable," or it will face "a shrill and impotent isolation."[49]

In 1988, a novel question was raised: Can the administration of a public school censor a school newspaper? The Court said "yes."[50] What about promises of confidentiality made by the news media to their sources? The Court ruled that freedom of press does not protect the media from lawsuits if they break promises of confidentiality to their sources.[51]

These cases and the charges and countercharges about them reveal the delicate balance that must be maintained in the safeguarding of civil liberties. Flexibility in this context becomes an absolute necessity.

Electronic Media. A special application of freedom of the press involves the electronic media: radio and television. Limited air frequencies restrict the number of radio stations and television channels. As a result, the government regulates these media more than it does the print media. The Federal Communications Commission (FCC) assigns stations and channels and reviews licenses at regular intervals (although it seldom revokes them). It may seem ironic that the First Amendment is applied differently to the electronic media than it is to the print media, considering that in recent years radio and TV channels have expanded dramatically while newspapers have been shrinking and becoming more monopolistic.

The FCC has established general standards for the electronic media. One of these, the **fairness doctrine,** enjoins fairness in reporting all sides of community issues. The Supreme Court upheld this doctrine in 1969, declaring that "it is the right of viewers and listeners, not the right of broadcasters, which is paramount." A licensed broadcaster, said the Court, cannot use the First Amendment to "monopolize a radio frequency to the exclusion of his fellow citizens."[52] The combination of the diversity of viewpoints available through cable television and the antiregulatory perspective of the administration of President Ronald Reagan brought about repeal of this doctrine in 1987.

As offensive language, such as four-letter words, becomes more commonplace on the airwaves, questions naturally arise as to what standards may be applied. Is freedom of speech as exercised by broadcasters to be given carte blanche protection? Or will listeners and viewers be able to challenge the use of language deemed offensive to them? This issue creates even more intensity when the issue of children's rights enters the debate.

Access to Information. Should government information be freely available to private citizens? Should the government be allowed to restrict information through a security classification system or executive privilege? Currently, private citizens are entitled to government information unless it falls within one of several categories exempted from the Freedom of Information Act, such as secret records relating to national security information, personnel and medical files, investigatory records such as certain FBI files, and the "internal" communications of an agency. Under the Freedom of Information Act (1966) citizens have the right to go into federal district courts if necessary to force the government to release unclassified information.

Libel. Should you be able to publish what you want to about another person? If you are writing about a public official, yes; if about a private citizen, no. The Supreme Court has ruled that in a free society "debate on public issues should be uninhibited, robust and wide-open, and . . . may well include vehement . . . attacks on government officials."[53] This ruling and subsequent applications of it to include political candidates, some former public officials, and persons involved in events of general or public interest make it almost impossible for a person to be convicted for libeling a public official.[54] Thus, the public has greater freedom to criticize public officials and candidates than to criticize private citizens.

Obscenity. Do freedoms of press and speech extend to obscenity? In 1957 the Court held for the first time that "obscenity is not within the area of constitutionally protected speech or press."[55] But since then the Court's difficulty has been in deciding just what is obscene. The frustrations of this task drove former Justice Potter Stewart to declare that although he could not define hardcore pornography, "I know it when I see it."[56]

In 1966 the Court specified that material could be considered obscene only if (1) its dominant theme as a whole appealed to a "prurient interest in sex," (2) it was "patently offensive" to contemporary community standards, and (3) it was "utterly without redeeming social value."[57] All three elements must be present, the Court declared, before material can be banned as obscene. As a result, almost all restrictions on the content of books and motion pictures were removed, since even the slightest "social value" might redeem them.

In 1973 the Court set up new standards. It declared that a work might be regarded as obscene if (1) the average person, "applying contemporary community standards," found that, taken as a whole, it appealed to "prurient interest," (2) it depicted "in a patently offensive way" sexual conduct prohibited by state law, and (3) if, as a whole, it lacked "serious literary, artistic, political, or scientific value."[58]

Although the 1966 decision aimed to set a nationwide standard, the effect of the 1973 decision—theoretically, at least—was to allow local communities to set their own standards. Justifying the 1973 ruling, former Chief Justice Warren Burger contended that it was unrealistic and constitutionally unsound to impose the standards of Las Vegas or New York City on the people of Maine or Mississippi. In 1974, however, the Court appeared to qualify its own decision when it declared: "It would be a serious misreading of *Miller* to conclude that juries [in local communities] have unbridled discretion in determining what is patently offensive."[59] The Court stated that appellate courts should review carefully the decisions of local juries to make certain that constitutional standards are not violated.[60]

In 1978 the Court approved FCC regulation of obscenity over the airwaves. Writing for the majority, Justice John Paul Stevens gave two reasons:

> First, the broadcast media have established a uniquely pervasive presence in the lives of all Americans. Patently offensive, indecent material presented over the airwaves confronts the citizen . . . in the privacy of the home. . . . To say that one may avoid further offense by turning off the radio when he hears indecent language is like saying that the remedy for an assault is to run away after the first blow. . . .
> Second, broadcasting is uniquely accessible to children, even those too young to read.[61]

Freedom of Assembly

Should Nazis be allowed to march through a predominantly Jewish community, waving the swastika? Skokie, Illinois, officials, facing this issue in 1977, had to observe the Supreme Court's interpretation of the First Amendment right to assemble or to stage a march in a community: Local officials may require a permit, but they cannot deny the permit in order to suppress free speech.[62] If the Court had taken a rigid rather than a flexible position on freedom of assembly, it might have allowed all assemblies, regardless

Should the American Nazi party be allowed to assemble and wave Nazi symbols in a mostly Jewish community? The Supreme Court has held that all Americans have the right to assemble, within appropriate guidelines that safeguard people and property.

of how they affected parks and traffic flow. By upholding the right to assemble freely within appropriate guidelines, the Court promoted both the general public interest and the rights of smaller groups.

Due Process Rights

Due process of law, which has its constitutional basis in the Fifth and Fourteenth Amendments, means that we have protection against arbitrary deprivation of life, liberty, or property. Originally the Bill of Rights applied only to the federal government. In *Barron v. Baltimore* (1833),[63] the Supreme Court held that the Constitution was established by the people of the United States for the national government, not for the governments of the individual states. But in *Gitlow v. New York* (1925),[64] the Court held that the Fourteenth Amendment's due process clause meant that "fundamental personal rights" could not be abridged by the states. With this action, the Supreme Court began the process of **selective incorporation**, or gradual application of specific portions of the Bill of Rights to the states, as shown in Table 14.1. Selective incorporation has taken place over many decades, since specific cases need to be brought before the Court before it can make the application. As state and local governments have grown over the past half-century, extending the application of the Bill of Rights to the states has become even more important.

Generally, due process is interpreted in one of two ways: *substantive due process* means that the laws themselves must be reasonable and fair; *procedural due process* means that laws must be administered in a fair manner. The first meaning focuses on what the law says; the second, on how it is implemented. To understand due process, let us see how it restricts the government in searches and seizures and the rights of the accused, and how it generally contributes to making our civil liberties more secure.

Searches and Seizures. According to the Fourth Amendment, individuals must "be secure in their persons, houses, papers, and effects, against unreasonable searches and seizures." This generally means that a home cannot be thoroughly searched without a search warrant signed by a judicial officer and issued on "probable cause" that the evidence to be seized is in the place to be searched.

The Supreme Court has strengthened the right against unreasonable searches and seizures by stating that police without a warrant cannot ransack a home but must confine their search to the suspect and his or her immediate surroundings.[65] In other cases the Court granted additional protections to the individual by requiring police to obtain warrants before arresting someone in his or her home and before searching patrons of an establishment, even though they already have a warrant to search the establishment itself.[66]

Other decisions have served to protect the interests of society against criminals. For example, the Court has held that police may covertly plant "bugging" devices in a building, even though such devices have not been specifically authorized in the warrant for surveillance.[67] Police can stop and frisk a suspect on the street without a warrant if there is reasonable suspicion that the person is armed or dangerous.[68] Police can also stop and frisk a suspect on suspicion of criminal conduct based on an informant's tip considered to be reliable.[69] However, a police officer who does stop someone on the street must observe the restrictions of the Fourth Amendment relating to searches and seizures.

What are some of these restrictions on police officers that illustrate procedural due process? The Court has ruled that police officers may *not*:

- Stop motorists at random just to check licenses and auto registrations[70]

- Detain a person in custody for questioning if they have less than the probable cause necessary for a traditional arrest[71]

- Seize a large number of items with a search warrant that specifically identifies only two items to be seized[72]

- Stop persons on the street, without any reasonable suspicion to believe they were engaged in criminal conduct, and require them to identify themselves and explain their presence[73]

Wiretapping is a form of search that has been particularly controversial because of its invasion of privacy. It was upheld by the Court in 1928,[74] but in 1967 the Court set limits on the use of wiretapping, declaring that a wiretap or bugging device did not have to involve "physical trespass" to violate the Fourth Amendment and that police could not wiretap without a court warrant.[75] (Exceptions have occasionally been made to these standards.)

TABLE 14.1 SELECTIVE INCORPORATION OF THE BILL OF RIGHTS VIA THE FOURTEENTH AMENDMENT

Right	Applied to States?	Case and Date
First Amendment		
Freedom of speech	Yes	*Gitlow* v. *New York* (1925); *Fiske* v. *Kansas* (1927); *Stromberg* v. *California* (1931)
Freedom of press	Yes	*Near* v. *Minnesota* (1931)
Freedom of assembly	Yes	*DeJonge* v. *Oregon* (1937)
Freedom of religion	Yes	*Cantwell* v. *Connecticut* (1940)
Establishment clause	Yes	*Everson* v. *Board of Education* (1947)
Second Amendment	No	
Third Amendment	No	
Fourth Amendment		
Unreasonable searches	Yes	*Wolf* v. *Colorado* (1949); *Mapp* v. *Ohio* (1961)
Warrants	Yes	*Anguilar* v. *Texas* (1964)
Fifth Amendment		
Grand jury clause	No	
Just compensation clause	Yes	*Chicago, Burlington & Quincy Ry.* v. *Chicago* (1897)
Self-incrimination clause	Yes	*Malloy* v. *Hogan* (1964)
Double jeopardy clause	Yes	*Benton* v. *Maryland* (1969)
Sixth Amendment		
Assistance of counsel	Yes	*Gideon* v. *Wainwright* (1963)
Public trial	Yes	In re *Oliver* (1948)
Confrontation	Yes	*Pointer* v. *Texas* (1965)
Compulsory process	Yes	*Washington* v. *Texas* (1967)
Speedy trial	Yes	*Klopfer* v. *North Carolina* (1967)
Jury trial	Yes	*Duncan* v. *Louisiana* (1968)
Seventh Amendment	No	
Eighth Amendment		
Cruel and unusual punishment clause	Yes	*Robinson* v. *California* (1962)
Excessive fines and bail clause	No	

(continued on next page)

TABLE 14.1 *(CONTINUED)*		
Right	Applied to States?	Case and Date
Ninth Amendment Rights retained by the people	Yes	*Griswold* v. *Connecticut* (1965)
Tenth Amendment	No	

When the Nixon administration claimed that it did not need court approval to use electronic surveillance on domestic groups that it considered a threat to internal security, the Court unanimously ruled against this as a denial of due process of law. Speaking for the Court, Justice Lewis F. Powell said: "The danger to political dissent is acute where the government attempts to act under so vague a concept as the power to protect 'domestic security.' "[76]

Can government make use of evidence that it obtained in an "unreasonable search and seizure"? According to the **exclusionary rule,** such evidence is not admissible in federal criminal trials; in 1961 the exclusionary rule was extended to cover state criminal trials.[77] Since then, this rule has been heatedly attacked. Critics say it permits clearly guilty persons to go free if their rights have been violated by the police while the officers were acquiring evidence. Also, the critics contend, the exclusionary rule does not distinguish between deliberate abuses by government authorities and violations stemming from accidental or minor mistakes.

In a 1975 case the Court modified the exclusionary rule, stating: "If the purpose of the exclusionary rule is to deter unlawful police conduct, then evidence obtained from a search should be suppressed only if it can be said that the law enforcement officer had knowledge, or may properly be charged with knowledge, that the search was unconstitutional."[78] Since then, many holes have appeared in the dike of the exclusionary rule. For example, in 1989, the Court upheld a police search without a warrant by means of a low-flying helicopter over private property.[79]

Rights of the Accused. The Bill of Rights and judicial decisions based on it guarantee several rights to persons accused of a crime:

LIMITS ON CONDUCT OF POLICE AND PROSECUTORS

1. No unreasonable searches and seizure
2. No arrest except on probable cause
3. No coerced confessions or illegal interrogation
4. No entrapment
5. Upon arrest, suspect to be informed of rights

DEFENDENT'S PRETRIAL RIGHTS

1. Writ of habeas corpus
2. Prompt arraignment

4. Reasonable bail

5. Right to remain silent

6. Right to grand jury indictment (in cases of serious crime)

TRIAL RIGHTS

1. Speedy and public trial before a jury

2. Impartial jury selected from a cross section of the community

3. Trial in an atmosphere free of prejudice, fear, and outside interference (right to change venue)

4. Right to confront all witnesses (right of cross-examination)

5. No compulsory self-incrimination (can't be forced to testify against oneself)

6. Right to competent counsel

7. No cruel or unusual punishment

8. No double jeopardy (can't be tried twice for the same crime)

These examples of procedural due process include the right to be indicted by a grand jury if the crime is serious. The accused cannot be tried twice for the same offense **(double jeopardy)** nor be forced to testify against themselves **(self-incrimination).** They have rights to "a speedy and public trial" by jury, to be informed of their legal rights, to summon and cross-examine witnesses, and to be represented by counsel. They cannot be held for "excessive bail," nor be inflicted with "cruel and unusual punishment." These rights, based on the Fifth through the Eighth Amendments, were expanded during the 1950s and 1960s, but in recent years have undergone some modifications after criticism that they sometimes hamstrung police and let criminals go free.

For example, between 1966 and the early 1990s, the Supreme Court changed its mind at least a half-dozen times on the issue of protection of the accused from self-incrimination. The Court ruled in *Miranda* v. *Arizona* (1966)[80] that evidence given by suspects could not be used in either a federal or state trial unless the suspects had first been notified that (1) they were free to remain silent; (2) what they said might be used against them in court; (3) they had a right to have an attorney present during the questioning; (4) if they could not afford to hire a lawyer, an attorney would be provided; and (5) they could terminate the police interrogation at any stage. This notification requirement is now known as the *Miranda* rule. If the prosecution failed to comply with this requirement, a conviction would be reversed, even if other independent evidence was sufficient to establish guilt.

The Court modified this decision in 1974 when it decided that the testimony of a witness could be used even though police had learned the identity of the witness by questioning a defendant without advising him or her of all *Miranda* rights. Here the Court decided that a "fair trial" does not mean a perfect trial; thus, police officers may make some errors in criminal investigations.[81] In 1976 the Court further relaxed the *Miranda* standards by condoning some use of statements made by suspects in custody after the suspect had asked for a lawyer but before the lawyer was present. In this case the accused

Some Americans feel that the Supreme Court has not done enough to protect our basic freedoms and due process rights. These protestors greeted the justices at the opening of the 1991–92 Supreme Court term.

changed his story after the lawyer arrived. Writing for the majority, Justice Harry A. Blackmun said: "The shield provided by *Miranda is* not to be perverted to a license to testify inconsistently, or even perjuriously, free from the risk of confrontation with prior inconsistent utterances."[82]

In 1980 the Court ruled that protection against unconstitutional interrogation as specified in the *Miranda* rule extends only to "words and actions on the part of police officers that they should have known were reasonably likely to elicit an incriminating response."[83] The police in this case merely made a statement in the presence of the suspect that it would be too bad if a child were to find the gun involved in the crime. The suspect, evidently apprehensive about what might happen, incriminated himself by directing the police to the location of the gun, crucial evidence in obtaining his conviction for murder. The Court upheld the conviction on the grounds that the police neither knew their words would lead the suspect to incriminate himself nor did they intentionally attempt to influence him to do so.

Then, in two 1981 cases, the Supreme Court strengthened the *Miranda* ruling. It held that a psychiatrist's testimony could not be used in court if the suspect had not been warned before the psychiatric interview that it might be used as evidence against the accused.[84] And the Court ruled that self-incriminating statements made by a suspect after having asked for counsel and before counsel arrives could not be used in court unless the accused initiated the communication.[85] But in *Arizona* v. *Fulminante* (19 the Supreme Court ruled that a *coerced* confession, introduced at a trial, does not

A VIEW FROM THE STATES
Another Look at the Bill of Rights

This writer takes a tongue-in-cheek look at the Bill of Rights today. He sees our basic rights changed by congressional and judicial actions in the last twenty years.

With quiet efficiency, our understanding of the first 10 amendments to the Constitution has been profoundly revised by the state and Federal judiciary during the last couple decades, sparing us the untidy political melee of a constitutional convention. In light of these changes, a new Bill of Rights, based on current case law, might look something like what follows.

Amendment I.

Congress shall encourage the practice of Judeo-Christian religion by its own public exercise thereof and shall make no laws abridging the freedom of *responsible* speech, unless such speech is in a digitized form or contains material that is copyrighted, classified, proprietary or deeply offensive to non-Europeans, non-males, differently-abled or alternatively preferenced persons; or the right of the people to peaceably assemble, unless such assembly is taking place on corporate or military property or within an electronic environment; or to petition the Government for a redress of grievances, unless those grievances relate to national security. . . .

Amendment IV.

The right of the people to be secure in their persons, houses, papers, and effects, against unreasonable searches and seizures, may be suspended to protect public welfare. Upon the unsupported suspicion of law enforcement officials, any place or conveyance shall be subject to immediate search, and any such places or conveyances or property within them may be permanently confiscated without further judicial proceeding.

Amendment V.

Any person may be held to answer for a capital or otherwise infamous crime involving illicit substances, terrorism or upon any suspicion whatever; and may be subject for the same offense to be twice put in jeopardy of life or limb, once by the state courts and again by the Federal judiciary; and may be compelled by various means, including the forced submission of breath samples, bodily fluids or encryption keys to be a witness against himself, refusal to do so constituting an admission of guilt, and may be deprived of life, liberty, or property without further legal delay; and any private property thereby forfeited shall be dedicated to the discretionary use of law enforcement agents without just compensation.

Amendment VI.

In all criminal prosecutions, the accused shall enjoy the right to a speedy and private plea bargaining session before pleading guilty. He is entitled to the assistance of underpaid and indifferent counsel to negotiate his sentence, except where such sentence falls under Federal mandatory sentencing requirements.

matically taint a conviction and violate a person's due process of law. In this case the state had used a fellow prison inmate to draw Fulminante into a confession of a crime.

Death Penalty. The U.S. Supreme Court has waffled on the issue of whether the death penalty is "cruel and unusual punishment" prohibited by the Eighth Amendment. For a time it allowed the death penalty to be imposed only under very limited circumstances. In 1972 the Court declared virtually all state death penalty laws unconstitutional on the grounds that they left too much discretion to the judge or jury in determining when to impose the death sentence. One justice remarked that the "freakish" manner in which the death penalty was imposed constituted cruel and unusual punishment, "in the same way that being struck by lightning is cruel and unusual."[86]

Responding to this decision, many states drafted new death penalty laws that were more restrictive and less discretionary. But the Court then seemed to reverse itself

A gas chamber used to carry out the death penalty. Does the death penalty violate the prohibition against "cruel and unusual punishment" in the Eighth Amendment? The Supreme Court has waffled on this issue.

in requiring more discretion. In 1976, the Court struck down death penalty laws that made the death penalty mandatory for first-degree murder. The Court said these laws did not allow enough discretion and precluded fair consideration of the individual crime and defendant and other mitigating circumstances.[87] The Court in 1978 ruled an Ohio death penalty law unconstitutional because it defined too narrowly the circumstances that a judge could consider in deciding whether to sentence a person to die.[88] In 1989 the death penalty was upheld for teenagers[89] and for a man of 22 with an IQ of 56 and the mental age of a $6\frac{1}{2}$-year-old.[90]

THE EXPANSION OF CIVIL RIGHTS

As mentioned earlier, civil rights refer to protections that individuals, regardless of racial, gender, or ethnic characteristics, are entitled to in the expectation of being treated equally with other citizens under the law. The history of civil rights in America has been one of gradual (and still incomplete) implementation, restoration, and expansion of rights: for African-Americans and women, over generations and indeed centuries; and for Hispanics, who have arrived in large numbers more recently, over several decades. In recent years homosexuals have been struggling to define their rights. We will focus here primarily on African-Americans and women, because of the long history devoted to seeking their rights through such avenues as the "equal protection of the laws" clause of the Fourteenth Amendment and civil rights legislation. Their successes, of course, have helped pave the way for Hispanics and other groups to secure their rights. We will also take a look at several emerging civil rights issues, including homosexual rights, children's television commercials, smoking, alcohol consumption, and abortion.

The Rights of African-Americans

African-Americans have probably experienced greater expansion of their civil rights than any other group, but they certainly had the farthest to go. They began as slaves in this country (which immediately distinguished them from other immigrant groups more willing to come here), unable to move freely, earn an income, vote, or make any decision that went against their owners. Their struggle has passed through four main stages.

The first was the abolition of slavery, accomplished immediately after the Civil War by the Thirteenth Amendment (ratified in 1865). The Fourteenth Amendment (1868) guaranteed citizenship, due process of law, and equal protection of the laws, and the Fifteenth Amendment (1870) guaranteed the right to vote to male African-Americans. Together, these three amendments are known as the Civil Rights amendments.

The second stage was the era of segregation, when whites in the South passed laws intended to keep the races separate. Thus, African-Americans were not permitted to sit next to whites in public transportation, to stay in the same hotels, to use white toilet facilities, to attend the same schools as whites, and so on. In *Plessy v. Ferguson* (1896)[91] the Supreme Court declared segregation of the races was constitutional as long as the states provided separate public facilities that were equal. This came to be known as the **separate but equal doctrine,** and it prevailed well into this century.

In the third stage various Court decisions between the 1930s and early 1950s gradually whittled away at the separate but equal doctrine. In 1950 in the cases of

McLaurin v. Oklahoma and *Sweatt v. Painter*,[92] the Court held that McLaurin could not be kept in a segregated part of an all-white University of Oklahoma graduate school because such separation inhibited effective learning and rendered his education inferior, and that Sweatt had to be admitted to the all-white University of Texas Law School because its facilities and faculty were superior to those of the separate law school provided for African-Americans.

In the final stage, the Court opened the way for complete integration. The famous *Brown v. Board of Education* decision in 1954 held that separate school facilities are inherently unequal and ordered full integration "with all deliberate speed."[93] The pace with which the states, particularly in the South, have implemented that decision has been more deliberate than speedy, but at least a course was set that has not been substantially altered. Moreover, *Brown* has provided the primary foundation for subsequent efforts to integrate other aspects of American society. During the 1960s the civil rights movement under the leadership of Martin Luther King, Jr., gathered full steam and put pressure on Congress to pass civil rights legislation that integrated public accommodations and transportation and extended voting rights (see Chapter 9).

Women's Rights

In the area of women's rights, the principal efforts have focused on (1) the right to vote; (2) job discrimination and equal pay for equal work; (3) passage of an Equal Rights Amendment (ERA), constitutionally prohibiting discrimination on account of sex; and (4) comparable worth. **Comparable worth** requires that positions with comparable skill

What is wrong with this picture?

levels, responsibilities, working conditions, and so on, receive comparable pay; thus a word processor and a plumber should get approximately the same pay if their job requirements are on a par.

Women were successful in obtaining voting rights (via the Nineteenth Amendment, ratified in 1920), and they have generally been successful in countering job discrimination. In fact, women have made impressive gains in the workplace at the expense of men. In 1980, for example, women held only 30 percent of executive and managerial posts, but by 1990 they filled 42 percent of these positions. Of course, women still account for the great majority of "support jobs"—secretaries, clerks, receptionists, and so on.[94]

Women have not as yet achieved the other two goals. Conflicts between women's interest groups have not helped matters. Two of the largest groups representing women's traditional interests—Concerned Women of America (CWA) and Eagle Forum—oppose the ERA and comparable worth. The primary group supporting these two objectives is NOW (National Organization of Women). There are approximately 700,000 members in CWA, while NOW has about 250,000 members. The ERA fell three states shy of ratification, even after a three-year extension of the seven-year ratification period. The issue of comparable worth awaits a definitive decision by the federal courts.

In distinguishing between women and men, the U.S. Supreme Court has followed the "reasonableness" standard, in some instances denying discrimination between the sexes while in others upholding it, depending on whether a reasonable case could be made for distinguishing between the sexes. Thus, states may not set different ages at which men and women become legal adults,[95] but they may give widows a property tax exemption that is not given to widowers.[96] Women cannot be barred from jobs by arbitrary height and weight requirements,[97] but the U.S. Navy may allow women who are not

A VIEW FROM ABROAD
"Mrs. President"?

This opinion from a German newspaper was published during the American presidential primary season, at a time when Bill Clinton was grabbing attention as the Democratic front-runner.

Hillary Clinton for president? At least a segment of white America would feel transformed and rejuvenated. Another part of the electorate, however, would no longer understand the world. A woman for president? Never.

Hillary Clinton offers several great selling points. She is a Yale graduate, an experienced lawyer and teacher; she received her baptism in politics in the 1968 campaign of anti-war candidate Eugene McCarthy and additional experience working for the congressional committee that planned to impeach Richard Nixon; she is well known for her work on behalf of disadvantaged women and children. She is 44, eloquent, and has a heart. But "Mrs. President" is not running. Her husband is.

Source: Ulrich Schiller, *Die Zeit* (Hamburg), From *World Press Review*, June 1992, p. 39.

promoted to remain officers longer than men in the same situation.[98] In 1991, the Court ruled that women may not be excluded from a job even though it may harm a developing fetus.[99] The Court's rulings have not followed a straight line, but rather a meandering path.

In 1992 women made some striking gains in politics, leading some observers to proclaim it the "year of the woman." More women ran for office and more women contributed to women's campaigns and voted for women candidates than ever before. Four women were elected to the Senate (and one more in 1993) and 47 to the House. Thirty percent of President Clinton's Cabinet are women.

Emerging Civil Rights Issues

Many Americans are now raising questions about other rights pertaining to such issues as discrimination against homosexuals, smoking, alcohol consumption, and abortion. These are issues the founders either never dreamed of or considered uncontroversial at the time.

Homosexual Rights. In one of his first acts as president, Bill Clinton ignited a firestorm of controversy by proposing to eliminate the ban on homosexuals in the military. In the face of opposition from Senate Armed Services Committee Chairman Sam Nunn (D-Ga.) and senior military advisors, the President had to modify his executive order on the subject and postpone final resolution. In the summer of 1993 a compromise (one that may appease no one) was reached: The policy is to be "don't ask, don't tell, don't pursue." In other words, military personnel are not to be asked about nor to reveal their gender orientation, nor are their activities off base to be subject to surveillance. But avowed homosexuality and known homosexual conduct may still be grounds for discharge.

Advocates of homosexuals in the military contend that they should be treated like everyone else and note that other countries allowing them in the military appear to have no problems. Moreover, they point out that homosexuals have always served alongside heterosexuals in the armed forces; they just haven't openly declared their status. America's senior military advisors and some members of Congress have opposed homosexuals in the military on the grounds that their presence would undermine discipline and other traits necessary to a successful fighting force. Some, such as Senator Nunn, believe that we do not have enough knowledge about the impact of homosexuals on the military and that the issue should be carefully studied before making such a major change. The American public is split on this issue (Figure 14.1).

Throughout the United States the issue of homosexual rights is attracting both support and opposition. Some local and state governments have specifically protected the rights of homosexuals and some have limited them. In 1992 Colorado voters in a statewide referendum voted in favor of amending the state constitution to nullify the kinds of protections already afforded homosexuals in several municipalities. But in 1993, the Colorado Supreme Court, upholding a lower court's injunction against the measure, ruled that "fundamental rights may not be submitted to a vote." The Court ruled that the state must demonstrate a "compelling interest" before the measure could take effect, setting a strict standard that many legal experts believed the law could not be shown to meet in a scheduled district court trial. In Florida citizens filed a petition to hold a statewide referendum that would also limit homosexual rights. In other places, particularly in major cities like San Francisco, homosexuals enjoy rights common to other persons.

Few issues in America today spark the degree of intensity on both sides as the

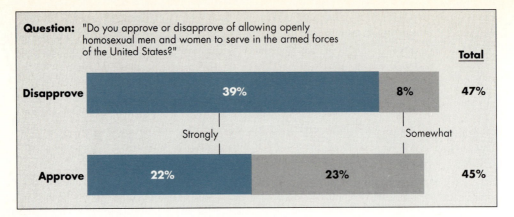

Figure 14.1   PUBLIC VIEWS ON HOMOSEXUALS IN THE MILITARY. Source: *The New York Times,* January 27, 1993, p. A8. Data from *Los Angeles Times* Poll conducted January 14–17, 1993.

issue of homosexuality. On the one hand, advocates of homosexual rights believe they are fighting for democratic progress, while on the other hand, opponents believe they are fighting to stem the tide of moral declension and decay. Both sides agree that a long, hard-fought political battle lies ahead. According to a spokesman for the National Gay and Lesbian Task Force, "We believe civil rights for gay people will be *the* social-change issue of the 1990s." His counterpart and political opponent at the Traditional Values Coalition agrees on this point: "Just as abortion was the issue in the 1980s, in the 1990s there is no doubt it will be homosexuality."[100]

Smoking.   The right of the smokers to puff away and of nonsmokers to be free from the polluted air of smokers has been a subject of debate in recent years. More and more governmental bodies are issuing regulations that impose bans on smoking in public places or require the provision of separate facilities for smokers and nonsmokers, such as on airplanes and in restaurants. Businesses are also providing "smoke-free" workplaces. The Clintons have banned smoking in the White House. U.S. Government health studies on the effects of "passive smoke" on nonsmokers lend support to the need for such restrictions.

Alcohol Abuse.   Mothers Against Drunk Driving (MADD) and other similar groups have fought to strengthen drinking laws to protect human life. Fifty percent of all traffic fatalities, 50 percent of all homicides, and a third of all suicides are directly attributable to alcohol consumption, as are many health problems, including cancer, heart disease, and liver disease. It is also the third-leading cause of birth defects.[101] Groups are now raising questions about how alcohol consumption violates their rights, especially the rights of innocent people killed in traffic fatalities.

Abortion.   Abortion pits the competing claims of those who believe women should have the right to control their bodies against those who believe the unborn have the right to life. Pro-choice groups won a major victory in 1973 when *Roe* v. *Wade* legalized abortion.[102] Since then, pro-life groups have been able to win limitations in the application of that decision. All three branches of the national government plus state and local governments have faced this issue, perhaps the most visible and emotionally intense controversy of the last two decades. The Supreme Court, with a majority of justices named by Republican Presidents Reagan and Bush, has limited application of *Roe v. Wade*. In 1992, without reversing the *Roe* decision, it granted states broad powers to restrict abortions.[103] To counter these efforts, pro-choice groups have organized to influence Congress and state legislatures and also to modify the Republican party's pro-life position and to elect pro-choice candidates. President Clinton's actions to ease the restrictions on abortion and abortion counseling have, in turn, increased the efforts of the pro-life forces. President Clinton pledged during his campaign that he would nominate only pro-choice persons to the U.S. Supreme Court.

The abortion debate is not just about constitutional rights, but also about economic impact. Pro-choice groups contend that abortion strengthens the economy by enabling women to have more continuity in the workplace. Pro-life groups point out that the millions of abortions performed since 1973 are now adversely affecting college enrollments and reducing the number of Americans available to fund social security and replace retiring Americans.

Political and Social Determinants of Civil Rights

The achievement of civil rights depends on eight principal determinants. These are (1) the president, (2) the Justice Department, (3) other executive agencies, (4) Congress, (5) the courts, (6) interest groups, (7) public opinion, and (8) demographic changes.

Since the Supreme Court handed down the *Brown* v. *Board of Education* decision in 1954, each of these eight determinants has helped define the scope of civil rights for African-Americans. President Lyndon Johnson, for example, proposed the Civil Rights Act of 1964 and the Voting Rights Act of 1965, and Congress passed both. Interest groups and public opinion were significant forces in the battle to obtain favorable congressional action. The Civil Rights Commission and the Equal Employment Opportunity Commission have made studies and issued decisions and regulations that have defined civil rights for African-Americans. The Justice Department has brought suits and submitted briefs to bring about action in many areas, such as school busing to achieve integration.

For both African-Americans and women, demographic and social changes set in motion forces to enhance their civil rights. Prior to World War II, African-Americans lived primarily in rural southern areas. During the war African-American men saw the outside world. Many joined the armed forces; others migrated to northern industrial cities. Because of war production needs, women for the first time worked in large numbers at jobs that had always been men's work. Both African-Americans and women might have been much slower to petition for their rights had World War II not led them from their accustomed places into the wider world.

Political and social determinants helped to extend the rights of African-Americans and women until the administration of President Ronald Reagan. Reflecting a growing public backlash to African-American and feminist causes, he altered the course of the executive branch. For example, he changed the composition of the Civil Rights Commission so that it would be less aggressive in its advocacy of civil rights. President George Bush swung the pendulum back to the middle between the civil rights approaches of the pre-Reagan and Reagan eras. President Bill Clinton is moving toward more action on civil rights.

? ISSUES TO ANALYZE

ISSUE 1   *ARE CIVIL LIBERTIES AND RIGHTS ADEQUATELY SUPPORTED BY THE PUBLIC?*

REASONS WHY CIVIL LIBERTIES AND RIGHTS ARE NOT ADEQUATELY SUPPORTED BY THE PUBLIC

Many public opinion surveys have shown that civil liberties do not have consistent support from a majority of Americans.[104] (See Table 14.2.) Such surveys reveal that while Americans *say* they support civil liberties, they frequently do not when they are faced with the realities of specific provisions. Rights like freedom of the

---

TABLE 14.2   THE RIGHT OF ASSEMBLY: WHAT ACTIVITIES SHOULD A COMMUNITY ALLOW?

Should a community allow its civic auditorium to be used by:	Mass Public (Yes/No)	Community Leaders (Yes/No)	Legal Elite (Yes/No)	Police Officials (Yes/No)
Feminists to organize a march for the Equal Rights Amendment (ERA)?	53%/24%	75%/13%	87%/8%	58%/21%
Gay liberation movements to organize for homosexual rights?	26%/59%	46%/40%	65%/26%	21%/63%
Atheists who want to preach against God and religion?	18%/71%	41%/44%	66%/24%	17%/73%
Student protestors who call for a sit-in at city hall to shut down the city's offices?	15%/66%	30%/53%	44%/43%	11%/76%
Patriotic groups to advocate war against some foreign country?	13%/67%	27%/51%	52%/30%	14%/66%
The Jewish Defense League (JDL) to advocate a war against certain Arab countries?	9%/76%	22%/62%	42%/42%	6%/84%
Foreign radicals who want to express their hatred of America?	6%/87%	17%/72%	32%/52%	4%/92%
The Palestine Liberation Organization (PLO) to attack Jews and call for the destruction of Israel?	6%/87%	16%/74%	33%/53%	5%/89%
The American Nazi party to preach race hatred against Jews and other minorities?	6%/89%	18%/74%	37%/51%	3%/92%
Revolutionaries who advocate the violent overthrow of the American government?	5%/89%	11%/81%	21%/68%	2%/96%

Note: Items are rank-ordered, high to low, by responses of the mass public. Totals do not add up to 100% since the undecided category is omitted.
Source: Herbert McCloskey and Alida Brill. *Dimensions of Tolerance: What Americans Believe About Civil Liberties* (New York: Russell Sage Foundation, 1983), pp. 124–125.

press or assembly are fine in the abstract but bad when granted to individuals with whom they disagree. As the table shows, community leaders and lawyers tend to be the most tolerant, while the mass public is far less tolerant and police officials the least tolerant. Similar attitudes apply to civil rights in the abstract and in practice. For example, one poll in early 1993 found that 57 percent of those surveyed did not think homosexuals should be banned from the military, yet only 35 percent thought President Clinton should change military policy to allow homosexuals to serve.[105]

The strength of our civil rights and liberties depends on adequate public support for judicial decisions that apply them. But American history is replete with examples of how rights have been rendered inadequate because the public neither objected to court action or inaction denying them nor supported judicial rulings upholding them.

During the Civil War, President Lincoln denied the writ of habeas corpus to all people arrested for disloyalty to the Union. The writ of **habeas corpus** is a court order directing an official who has a person in custody to bring the prisoner to court and to show cause for that person's detention. It is generally considered to be the most important civil liberty because it prevents arbitrary arrest and imprisonment. Prisoners serving sentences can seek to have their cases reopened based upon alleged illegal detention, such as the denial of rights before or during their trials. The Supreme Court did not declare Lincoln's suspension of habeas corpus in civilian jurisdictions unconstitutional until after the Civil War.[106]

During World War II, the governor of Hawaii suspended the writ of habeas corpus and even declared martial law, again despite the fact that civilian courts remained open. His steps were not ruled unconstitutional until near the end of the war, in 1944.[107] Also during World War II, Americans of Japanese descent were placed in relocation camps in the western United States. Reviewing this action in 1944, the Supreme Court upheld it, saying: "We cannot—by availing ourselves of the calm perspective of hindsight—now say that at that time these actions were unjustified."[108]

These three examples illustrate the inadequate support of significant civil liberties—in this instance, liberties guaranteed in the Fifth and Sixth Amendments. In the first two cases the Supreme Court did not declare the violations unconstitutional until a time when public opinion was more likely to support its decisions. In the third case, the Court actually upheld the government's violation of civil liberties.

In 1954, in *Brown* v. *Board of Education,* the Supreme Court unanimously declared the doctrine of "separate but equal" unconstitutional and a violation of the Fourteenth Amendment's equal protection clause, and ordered school desegregation to begin with "all deliberate speed." Although substantial progress has been made, it has also been marked by numerous incidents of violence and continuing legal disputes. It was not until Congress passed the Civil Rights Act of 1964 and the Voting Rights Act of 1965 that the rights of African-Americans were strengthened in a meaningful way. In other words, civil liberties and rights are truly enforced only when the branches of government closer to the people than the judiciary—that is, the legislature and the executive—step in.

Civil liberties and rights exist independently of the political process only as an abstraction. Despite advances in guaranteeing rights for African-Americans, inadequate public support still precludes their receiving the full benefit of these guarantees in the Constitution. The Colorado referendum limiting homosexual rights and efforts elsewhere to do likewise illustrate the same point. While the political victories women enjoyed in 1992 led some to refer to it as "the year of the woman," women still have a long way to go to fill half the seats in Congress or the federal bureaucracy or the boardrooms of corporate America. As one newspaper editorial put it: "Nobody speaks of the year of the man because it's always the year of the man. When, for the same reason, nobody has to speak of the year of the woman, the year of the woman will have truly arrived."[109] The point is that rights in the abstract are not rights in fact until they are buoyed by public opinion.

REASONS WHY CIVIL LIBERTIES AND RIGHTS ARE ADEQUATELY SUPPORTED BY THE PUBLIC

Critics cite survey research data and wartime examples of failure to enforce civil liberties to suggest inadequate public support for these liberties. What they overlook is the normal daily acceptance of civil liberties by the majority of the American people and their increased public support.

For example, the First Amendment freedoms of speech, press, assembly, and religion are upheld daily in lecture halls, newspapers, streets, and churches. Similar examples could be cited for each of our other civil liberties. Few other societies are as conscientious as the United States in observing and supporting our rights.

Americans have substantially increased their support for various civil liberties over the last few decades. The percentage of people who would allow a speaker against churches and religion has increased from 37 to 62 percent since 1954, while those who would allow a socialist speaker have increased from 59 to 76 percent. Those who would keep an antireligion book in a public library have increased from 35 to 59 percent, and those who would keep a socialist book in a public library have increased from 53 to 69 percent. The percentage that would allow a socialist to hold a university teaching position has increased from 33 to 57 percent.[110]

In a sense, however, it does not matter what percentages of Americans support civil liberties and civil rights. These guarantees are abstract declarations of goals to be attained. By recognizing that they are abstract declarations, we can place them in their proper perspective: They are in a sense the conscience of the nation. They aim society in the right direction and spur it toward broadening its humanitarian goals. Dotting American history are many examples of struggles to attain these goals, and undoubtedly much progress has been made.

For example, quantum leaps were taken toward achieving equal protection of the laws when:

- Indigent defendants were guaranteed the right to legal counsel in *Gideon* v. *Wainwright* (1963)[111]

- Urban and suburban populations were guaranteed their proportion of legislative representation through the doctrine of "one person, one vote" in *Baker* v. *Carr* (1962)[112]

- African-Americans obtained equal access to public accommodations and transportation through the Civil Rights Act of 1964

Granting such liberties in specific situations serves two functions: (1) it redresses wrongs for the person or group adversely affected, and (2) it educates the public at large about the meaning of general phrases and principles.

During this century the Supreme Court responded to the interests of African-Americans long before either the president or Congress addressed the problem of inequality and racial discrimination. By acting against a host of racial abuses, the Court paved the way for the executive and legislature to follow. Without judicial action in interpreting civil liberties, the cause of racial equality might well have made much less progress than it has. The Civil Rights Act of 1964, the Voting Rights Act of 1965, and the Housing Act of 1968 are three instances in which the legislative and executive branches took steps to enforce individual rights as interpreted by the judiciary.

ISSUE 1:   **Summary** ★ *Are Civil Liberties and Rights Adequately Supported by the Public?*

While a clear case can be made that civil liberties do not always receive substantial support in public opinion surveys and that they have been violated on numerous occasions throughout American history, their very existence has enhanced American democracy. Civil liberties and rights are most vulnerable during wartime or when equal protection of the laws is being extended to protect more people, as in the aftermath of the *Brown* v. *Board of Education* decision. In these instances, civil liberties and rights may not be supplied as fully or as quickly as they should be, but still they serve as a type of national conscience to propel further democratic development through the judicial, legislative, and executive branches. In recent decades the public has become more tolerant of the extension of civil liberties and rights. Moreover, each time rights are protected through legislation, executive action, or court decisions the public is educated about the meaning of these general principles. ■

ISSUE 2   SHOULD AFFIRMATIVE ACTION BE USED TO END DISCRIMINATION?

REASONS WHY AFFIRMATIVE ACTION SHOULD BE USED TO END DISCRIMINATION

The purpose of **affirmative action** is to remedy past discrimination against groups by providing them with legal advantages in getting educations and finding jobs, thereby enabling them to compete more effectively with previously advantaged groups. Several arguments in defense of affirmative action are based on the fundamental premise that it is a necessary tool to allow women and African-Americans to compete on an equal footing with white males.

Over the centuries educational and economic discrimination has kept women and African-Americans from entering society's mainstream. Unless this cycle of disadvantage and discrimination is broken, children of subsequent generations will also be disadvantaged. Accordingly, special consideration should be given to hiring women and African-Americans, even to the extent of hiring them ahead of better-qualified white males. In *United Steelworkers of America* v. *Weber* (1979),[113] the Supreme Court upheld the use of employment quotas for African-Americans in a job-training program.

By law we provide special treatment for the physically handicapped; the same needs to be done for those handicapped by long-standing discrimination. Affirmative action allows people to be treated according to their need, just as special facilities for the physically handicapped meet their needs. And it allows a society dominated by white males to help make up for past discrimination of women and African-Americans.

As women and African-Americans improve their economic standing, the entire economy benefits by providing more skilled workers for the work force as well as more prosperous consumers. Stability in society also is enhanced. For instance, in 1992 Los Angeles exploded in riots after the acquittal of four white police officers accused of beating an African-American, Rodney King. One reason for the riots was the lack of jobs for African-Americans. Affirmative action would defuse the explosive tensions between the races and sexes.

REASONS WHY AFFIRMATIVE ACTION SHOULD NOT BE USED TO END DISCRIMINATION

Reverse discrimination occurs when the law favors disadvantaged groups, giving them preference over other groups in such matters as employment. Several arguments have been lodged against affirmative action and its logical consequence, reverse discrimination.

First, reverse discrimination is not better than discrimination itself. Discriminating in order to end discrimination only perpetuates and compounds the problem. Reverse discrimination merely leads to judging people by skin color or gender or both, which is a violation of the equal protection clause of the Fourteenth Amendment and the Supreme Court's decision against racial classification and discrimination in *Brown* v. *Board of Education* (1954).

Second, in critical professions such as medicine, law, engineering, architecture, nursing, and others (like college teaching), should we desire anything other than the most qualified persons? Use of affirmative action to ensure proper proportions of women and African-Americans in professions would dilute quality by basing their entry into a profession on something other than their ability. On balance, this would be a disservice to women and African-Americans themselves, who would know that they had not earned their positions through personal merit.

Third, if affirmative action is carried to its logical conclusion (and affirmative action is the sort of legislation that is usually followed to its logical conclusion), it must be applied to homosexuals and other groups that claim past discrimination. Arbitrating which groups could claim this status would be a legal nightmare and, probably, never-ending. The cost in terms of time, money, and personnel would be prohibitive.

Fourth, women and African Americans, like other ethnic and minority groups, have demonstrated their ability to compete successfully without the benefit of affirmative action. While this process may take longer, it is probably more satisfactory than arbitrary and forced movement into the professions through affirmative action.

In the case of *Regents of the University of California* v. *Bakke*[114] the Supreme Court held that racial quotas may not be used in the school admissions process, but that some consideration of race may be followed in the same way that geography and other criteria

A VIEW FROM ABROAD
U.S. Race Relations

"Racial unrest" is what one calls periodic eruptions of violence [such as the recent rioting in Los Angeles and other cities], but there is more behind them than the old conflict between blacks and whites. The flickering flames of the nights of chaos in [Los Angeles] illuminated the nearness of the end of the American dream: The Society that drew its identity from the melding of immigrants from all the world's countries is disintegrating. . . . [T]olerance and respect for [differing ethnic and racial] groups are diminishing everywhere.

Kurt Kister, *Süddeutsche Zeitung* (Munich)

There is no doubt that the U.S. now is paying the price of "Reaganomics," President Reagan's economic policies that focused on the arms race while ignoring the social and infrastructural problems of the U.S. Twelve years of conservative rule under Reagan and Bush, the blow to the Great Society programs of President Johnson, and the abandonment of care for the black population and other ethnic groups have contributed to a buildup of bitterness, anger, and poverty. . . . All that is necessary is a spark to blow up the barrel of gunpowder.

Al Hamishmar (Tel Aviv)

In a capitalist economy, there are winners and losers. It cannot be otherwise. But any advanced society that allows the development of a huge, under-employed, under-educated, impoverished underclass that lives in violence-racked, drug-ridden slums is storing up for itself the sort of trouble the U.S. is now experiencing.

Hong Kong Standard (Hong Kong)

Source: World Press Review, June 1992, pp. 7–8.

---

are observed to achieve a rough balance in the distribution of students. Bakke, a white male with superior credentials, had twice been denied admission to medical school due to a quota system that reserved specific slots for Hispanics and African-Americans. By declaring this quota system unconstitutional, but still allowing race to be considered as a factor in the admissions decision, the Court took a flexible course of action that removed the harshness of the arbitrary affirmative action approach.

ISSUE 2: Summary ★ *Should Affirmative Action Be Used to End Discrimination?*

By ruling within a year on essentially both sides of the question, the Supreme Court itself has demonstrated that this is not an easy question to answer. How you decide will likely be determined by your response to these questions: Is "reverse discrimination" constitutionally acceptable under the equal protection clause of the Fourteenth Amendment? Can affirmative action be implemented without creating the chaos of too many groups seeking to obtain its benefits? Personal feelings as well as legal and philosophical considerations influence one's position on this issue. ■

🌐 COMPARISONS WITH OTHER NATIONS

Civil liberties and civil rights should be the immediate concern of every government. Too often, however, they aren't. Even the noticeable extension of democratization over the last decade has reached only a relatively small proportion of our planet's population. There are still dozens of despotic governments that haven't given a thought to civil liberties or, if they have, shiver at the idea of guaranteeing any of them to their citizenries.

The United States is a world leader in the development of civil liberties and civil rights. According to one expert on civil rights, "Where rights are concerned, lawyers and judges the world over frequently consult American sources."[115] This is a compliment, of course, but it is also a responsibility. American justice has long symbolized fairness (if not perfection) and has become a model for millions of non-Americans and their governments:

> When life or liberty is at stake, the landmark judgments of the Supreme Court of the United States, giving fresh meaning to the principles of the Bill of Rights, are studied with as much attention in New Delhi or Strasbourg as they are in Washington, D.C., or the State of Washington or Springfield, Illinois.[116]

CIVIL LIBERTIES AND RIGHTS IN DEMOCRACIES

In their protection of civil liberties, democracies tend to be quite similar. The wording used by Lincoln in his Gettysburg Address, "government of the people, by the people and for the people" is found also in Article 2 of the French Constitution of 1958. But the exceptions are interesting. For example, the American Constitution stipulates that there will be no infliction of "cruel and unusual punishments." Some critics view the application of the death penalty as just that. Comparatively speaking, it may be. Yet the United States is the only democracy that still permits capital punishment.

Other nations also deal with details of civil liberties that Americans rarely think about. For instance, the German constitution in its very first article states, "The dignity of man shall be inviolable. To respect and protect it shall be the duty of all state authority." It is as natural for Germans to have this provision as it is for Americans to wonder why it has to be said at all. Human dignity was systematically ravaged during the Nazi regime (1933–1945); hence, the sensitivity of the German constitution-makers.

And there are some issues Americans think about all the time that have been resolved with substantial finality in other democracies. As we saw earlier in the chapter, separation of church and state is an issue that remains controversial in the United States more than two centuries after the ratification of the First Amendment. In the French constitution, however, there is no equivocation or perceived need to debate the issue. Article 2 flatly states that France is a "secular" republic. This means about as absolute separation as possible.

Many civil rights and civil liberty issues have yet to be resolved here or abroad. Some other countries allow homosexuals to serve in their armed forces (sometimes subject to certain restrictions), and others don't (Table 14.3). Even in those countries with no official policy, homosexuals may be expelled from the military if discovered. The United

Country	Policy
TABLE 14.3	**POLICY FOR HOMOSEXUALS IN THE MILITARY IN SELECTED COUNTRIES**
United Kingdom	Expulsion likely if discovered
Italy	Expulsion for overt homosexual behavior
Israel	Drafts all eligible men and women regardless of sexual preference
Russia	Homosexuality is officially illegal; homosexuals are unwelcome in the military
Japan	No official policy
Spain	No official policy
Germany	Homosexuals and heterosexuals have equal rights
Sweden	No restrictions
Norway	No restrictions
Denmark	No restrictions
Holland	No restrictions
Turkey	If discovered to be homosexuals, up to six months' imprisonment

Source: Compiled from *The Greenville News*, November 15, 1992, p. 6E.

States for the most part has done more to protect nonsmokers from the effects of smoking than have European countries, although these democracies have made progress (Figure 14.2).

Japan has built and maintained an exemplary democracy. Yet, the Japanese have emphasized national discipline to the point of sacrificing aspects of individualism most Americans and Western Europeans take for granted, such as who and when to marry. As two journalists discovered:

> *From cram schools for kindergartners to lifetime employment demanding more devotion to company than to family, Japanese accept that to get ahead means to buckle under. Thus when our friend, a government bureaucrat, was told by his boss that he needed a wife by year's end to qualify for his next promotion, he booked a wedding hall for Dec. 29. Then, through a go-between, he found a wife.*[117]

Legal systems in the American and European democracies have long assumed that no individual is above the law. There are exceptions even to this very basic element of democracy. For example, Japan's constitution actually places government ministers above the law, except for the most drastic of crimes (Article 75). The Japanese prime minister has an edge since he or she can give consent for a minister to be subject to legal action. This may be an effective way to get rid of a political rival, but it is an option rarely exercised in Japan.

Although the Japanese have traditionally lacked experience with civil liberties they seemed to make up for lost time with the 1947 constitution. Some 30 articles enumerate and guarantee civil liberties. In contrast to the United States, Japan provides

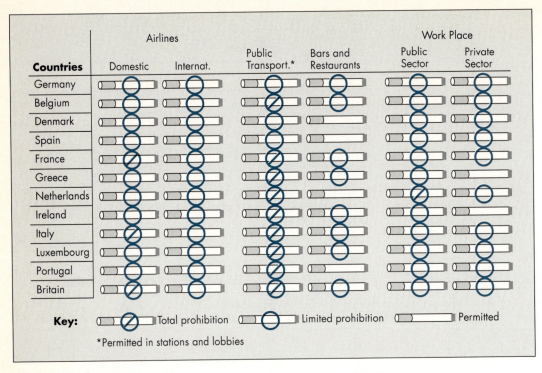

Figure 14.2   SNUFFING OUT CIGARETTES IN EUROPE. Source: *World Press Review,* June 1992, p. 46.

painstaking details that include such items as guaranteeing academic freedom. The Japanese are as meticulous with the protection of constitutional rights as they are with the manufacture of electronic products.

The United States has the shortest constitution of the democracies, in great part because it does not formulate, as do the Japanese and the Germans, a lengthy list of every conceivable civil liberty protection. This is perhaps the greatest distinction between the American and other democratic constitutions. They are all newer than ours and could refer to hundreds of years of political development. The American document did have a reference point: the tradition of English common law and Britain's own development of rights. But the founders understood that it would be self-defeating to try to account for everything. This approach has worked. Constitutional flexibility extends the guarantee of civil liberties whenever necessary.

Or at least up to a point. We need to keep in mind that even maximum and protected guarantees of civil liberties do not completely protect entire national communities. Both petty and serious discriminations are still suffered by Arabs in Israel, Africans in France, Pakistanis in Britain, and Turks in Germany. Overall, though, the democracies are light-years ahead of most of the rest of the world and, perhaps even more important, very much ahead of where they were themselves only a few decades ago.

The advance of technology has raised new questions about issues of privacy. The democracies were the first to enter the information age and experience the impact of

The Japanese often emphasize group discipline over individualism. These employees at a Coca-Cola plant in Japan participate in regular group exercises, as do workers in many Japanese enterprises.

computer technology. With personal computers appearing in the tens of millions, it has become necessary to reevaluate laws having to do with invasion of personal privacy. At the same time, the world, again largely because of computers, has become increasingly small and intimate. Law and the protection of civil liberties have lagged behind the acceleration of technology. Take one example:

> In Britain . . . lawmakers tried to protect information in computers with a recent statute that made unauthorized prying into somebody else's computer a crime punishable up to six months in jail. The first problem is that other countries have not made unauthorized entry into a computer illegal, and it is entirely possible to poke around inside a computer in Britain from a terminal in Japan or Grenada. So to read, say, a business memo from the screen of an executive's computer is a crime, to read a printout lying on his desktop is just bad manners.[118]

The idea that each individual is fully equipped with certain rights that cannot be removed—the right to life, for example, and, usually, property—and that natural law is available to protect and guarantee such rights is a cornerstone of the legal systems of dozens of countries. The concept of private property is important to mention at this juncture. No government in a democracy is able to touch it without the consent of the owner. This is a tradition that goes at least as far back as John Locke in the seventeenth century.[119] And every democracy today accepts the premise that each individual owns his or her own body. But this premise collides with natural rights when it comes to taking one's own life, a collision that helps account for a Western prejudice against suicide. Our bodies are our own, but we can't end their careers unilaterally because we can't abdicate even our own natural rights. The absoluteness of the right to life has begun to be challenged by the issue of what to do about terminally ill individuals who have indicated a preference to die rather than to go on living in pain or in a vegetative state with the assistance of technology but no plausible hope of recovery.[120] The doctrine of natural rights and modern technology seem destined to confront one another.

A final consideration revolves around the economic status of democracies. Most democracies have comparatively thriving economies. But India, the world's largest democracy, is also the poorest. However, as its middle class grows, civil liberty issues already confronted by the longer-established Western democracies are surfacing. Indian homosexuals, for example, began publication of their own magazine in 1991, a generation or more behind similar publications in Western Europe and North America.[121] It does appear that an increasingly middle-class society proceeds, however gingerly, toward an important component in democracy: civil liberties.

CIVIL LIBERTIES AND RIGHTS IN TOTALITARIAN SYSTEMS

This section's title is, in fact, a contradiction in terms. In today's communist societies like China, North Korea, and Cuba the government is unrestrained in its ability to do anything it wants to anybody. However, in China the government seems bent on creating an economic prosperity that will at least take minds off of civil rights.[122] Productivity is being emphasized, which means there is not much toleration for economically unproductive people. For example, some provincial authorities have opted to sterilize retarded citizens to limit the number of future wards of the state:

> The eugenics measures have aroused a ripple of protest abroad, but virtually no opposition in China. In a country where the accent has historically been on the collective interest rather than on individual rights, where a prime slogan is "limit the population quantity, improve the population quality," eugenics seems natural.[123]

Even before the uneven implementation of this policy (the central government is not sponsoring it), the Chinese authorities had long mandated the amount of children each couple should have, preferably one. Neighborhood "grandmothers" regularly inquire of young married women if their menstrual cycle is on schedule, and couples who desire to have a baby often find that they need to have permission of the authorities first. While the American and other Western democracies debate the legality as well as the morality of abortion, and while other countries have either made abortion available on demand or completely outlawed it (see Table 14.4), China is perhaps the only nation in the world where abortion is legally mandatory. It is not uncommon for pregnant women who are well into their second trimester to be pressured into undergoing an abortion.

If even the most intimate private matters are a concern of the state, there is scant hope for civil liberties. And there is little reason to believe that the Chinese

The right to bear children is severely restricted in China. Billboards such as this one in Guangzhou remind the Chinese that they should have "one child only."

government is improving in its recognition of basic rights. One example: "In the 16,000 criminal cases filed last year [1990] in Shanghai, fewer than half of the accused had a lawyer to defend them and only 30 were acquitted."[124]

The Chinese serve as an extreme but telling model of the place of civil liberties in totalitarian societies. In such societies civil liberties can be neither implemented nor tolerated because they detract from the political superiority of the state over the individual and, consequently, from the maximized unity of the society, a hallmark stipulation of every totalitarian system.

In most respects, the remarkable transition of Eastern Europe from totalitarianism to more democratic forms of government and the collapse of the Soviet Union have revealed a new dimension for the study of civil liberties. The decline of totalitarianism has, naturally enough, coincided with the emergence of civil liberties. Last gasps of totalitarian rulership, such as the unsuccessful coup in Moscow in August 1991, are cases in point. The coup-makers understood neither civil liberties nor the fact of their apparently firm establishment within Soviet society in the few years preceding the coup.

Unfortunately, in some former totalitarian societies there is such intense political fragmentation that the extension and guarantee of civil liberties don't go beyond a particular ethnic or religious community. This characteristic is most apparent in several areas of the former Soviet Union and Yugoslavia. There is simply no concept of minority rights. We now understand that communism in these countries was a precariously thin veneer that kept the lid on centuries of old ethnic conflicts. The lid is now off, and the rival ethnic and religious communities have reverted to their old deplorable habit of massacring one another.

TABLE 14.4 WORLD ABORTIONS LAWS

| | When a woman may have an abortion: | | |
	To Save Her Life	Other Health Reasons	Social and Socio-medical Reasons	On Request
Africa	Angola	Algeria	Burundi	Togo
	Benin	Cameroon*	Zambia§	Tunisia
	Botswana	Congo		
	Burkina Faso	Egypt		
	Central African Rep.	Ethiopia		
		Ghana*,§		
	Chad	Guinea		
	Gabon	Kenya		
	Ivory Coast	Lesotho		
	Libya	Liberia*,§		
	Madagascar	Morocco		
	Malawi	Namibia*,§		
	Mali	Rwanda		
	Mauritania	Sierra Leone		
	Mauritius	South Africa*,§		
	Mozambique	Tanzania		
	Niger	Uganda		
	Nigeria	Zimbabwe*,§		
	Senegal			
	Somalia			
	Sudan			
	Zaire			
Asia and Oceania	Afghanistan	Hong Kong*,§	Australia§	China
	Bangladesh	Israel*,§	India*,§	Singapore
	Burma	Jordan*	Japan*,§	Turkey
	Indonesia	Kuwait§	North Korea*,§	Vietnam
	Iran	Malaysia*,§	Taiwan*,§	
	Iraq	Mongolia		
	Laos	Nepal		
	Lebanon	New Zealand*,§		
	Oman	Papua New Guinea		
	Pakistan	Saudi Arabia		
	Philippines	South Korea*,§		
	Sri Lanka			
	Syria	Thailand*		
	United Arab Emirates			
	Yemen			
Europe	Ireland	Albania	Finland*,§,‡	Austria*,§,‡
		Northern Ireland	Former West Germany*,§,‡	Belgium‡
		Portugal*,§		Bulgaria‡
		Spain*,§	Great Britain	Czech‡
		Switzerland	Hungary*,§,‡	Denmark‡

(continued on next page)

TABLE 14.4 *(CONTINUED)*

| | When a woman may have an abortion: | | | |
	To Save Her Life	Other Health Reasons	Social and Socio-medical Reasons	On Request
				Former East Germany‡
				France‡
				Greece‡
				Italy‡
				Netherlands
				Norway‡
				Romania‡
				Ex–Soviet Union‡
				Sweden‡
				Yugoslavia‡
North America	Dominican Republic	Costa Rica		Canada
	Guatemala	El Salvador		Cuba‡
	Haiti	Jamaica		Puerto Rico
	Honduras	Trinidad and Tobago		United States
	Mexico*			
	Nicaragua			
	Panama			
South America	Brazil*	Argentina*	Uruguay*	
	Chile	Bolivia*		
	Colombia	Guyana		
	Ecuador*	Peru		
	Paraguay			
	Venezuela			

* Includes cases of rape and incest.
§ Includes abortion for genetic defects.
‡ Abortion allowed only within limits ranging from 10 to 20 weeks. In other countries with abortion on request, abortion is permitted through 24 weeks or until viability.
Note: Other restrictions may apply. Table does not include countries with fewer than one million inhabitants or where information is not available. Laws in Poland in flux.
Source: Adapted from *The Greenville Piedmont,* Tuesday, March 3, 1992. Data from Stanley K. Henshaw and Evelyn Morrow, "Induced Abortion: A World Review," 1990 supplement.

CIVIL LIBERTIES AND RIGHTS IN AUTHORITARIAN SYSTEMS

Most of the developing nations remain in varying degrees of authoritarianism. So, therefore, does the status of civil liberties. What seems fairly evident is that the richer a nation becomes, the greater and more undeniable the popular demand for greater allowance of civil liberties. If this is true, and the evidence in such places as Taiwan, South Korea, and Singapore strongly suggests that it is, then much of the world is about to experience significant change in this respect.

Authoritarianism, like communist totalitarianism, is increasingly being revealed as both a political and economic anachronism:

> The dramatic increase in the availability and importance of information, made possible by the ability of computers to store huge quantities of information, and retrieve it almost instantaneously, has changed first the nature of economic activities and secondly governmental processes. The revolution initially took place, of course, in open societies; it quickly accelerated the gap in the pace of modernization between open and closed societies. As a consequence, the costs of repression for authoritarian rulers rose sharply, causing most of them to seek at least half-way measures of liberalization. Indeed, the information revolution calls for decentralization and a diffusion of power throughout the society incompatible with centralized authoritarian rule, thereby sharpening the crisis of authority.[125]

Authority in the Third World may be in crisis, but it is still effective in unpleasant ways. Adolescents can still receive the death penalty in Iran, even if their only crime is being a relation of a condemned adult, and prostitutes can still be publicly stoned to death. Civil liberties can also be ignored if the next world is considered more important than this one, as is the case in religious fundamentalist countries. Adolescents were sent by the thousands to clear minefields by blowing themselves up in mindless martyrdom during Iran's eight-year (1980–1988) war with Iraq.[126] The low status of women in several authoritarian societies remains unchanged after centuries. A woman may not drive a car in Saudi Arabia and will be arrested if she tries it. Her total worth in Pakistan is by law half that of a man. And women are still mutilated by the hundreds of thousands in a number of African and Middle Eastern societies when they are circumcised as they reach puberty. Women are also frequently even poorer than men in many authoritarian societies. They are kept poor, illiterate, and frequently pregnant and they have no familiarity with basic rights. Women in wealthier, and usually democratic, societies tend to be well educated and more aware of their rights.[127]

There is hope for both sexes. It may well be that civil liberties will become the rule rather than the exception. It took nearly seven millennia of political experience for rank-and-file citizens to rid themselves of the notion that their civil liberties could be violated arbitrarily and with impunity by dictators. The explosion of communication technology has weakened authoritarianism and enhanced the prospects of the individual. There is at least a modicum of hope that by the dawn of the twenty-first century, would-be dictators will have to look for extremely remote and isolated societies to brutalize.

Summary

1. Civil liberties are those rights that protect citizens from arbitrary actions of government. Civil rights are protections that government extends to citizens to assure that they all are treated equally under the laws.

2. British constitutional tradition, the Declaration of Independence, the Constitution and Bill of Rights, and the Fourteenth Amendment are principal sources of our civil liberties and rights. Civil liberties have also evolved over time through court decisions that have sought to balance freedom and order, a difficult task.

3. The First Amendment freedoms of religion, speech, press, and assembly have been interpreted in various ways in court decisions over several generations. These freedoms are not easily interpreted and will most likely go on being controversial.

4. The Constitution's due process of law clause provides for both *substantive due process* (reasonable and fair laws) and *procedural due process* (the fair administration of laws).

5. Constitutional law protects the accused against double jeopardy and self-incrimination, but recently the Supreme Court has evidenced some equivocation when it comes to what constitutes a "fair trial," indicating that fair trials are not always perfect trials.

6. The expansion of civil rights proceeded in phases for African-Americans through a series of constitutional amendments and Supreme Court decisions, and for women through the Nineteenth Amendment (suffrage) and the removal of discriminatory employment and pay practices.

7. The achievement of civil rights is dependent on eight political and social determinants: the president, the Department of Justice, other executive agencies, the Congress, the courts, interest group activity, public opinion, and demographic changes.

8. Public opinion has occasionally supported or remained silent over such violations of civil liberties as the incarceration of American citizens of Japanese ancestry in 1942. On the other hand, the public has become increasingly tolerant of unpopular speech and the social and economic advance of ethnic and religious minorities in the United States.

9. Affirmative action is considered by many to be the only effective means of redressing generations of unfair treatment of women and African-Americans. But affirmative action leads to "reverse discrimination" and thus remains a controversial constitutional issue.

10. The United States and other democracies have similar attitudes concerning civil liberties and rights. However, there are also stark differences; the United States, for example, is the only democracy that still imposes the death penalty.

11. Totalitarian regimes severely restrict civil liberties and rights in order to maintain control over the daily lives of the citizens. In those totalitarian societies that have collapsed or are on the verge of doing so, old ethnic and/or religious rivalries are resurfacing that have a history of non-acceptance of the rights of other communities.

12. Authoritarian regimes often ignore the protection of civil rights and liberties; some even candidly deny their existence when it comes to such classifications of citizens as women, children, and religious minorities.

Terms to Define

Absolutist position test

Affirmative action

Balancing of interests test

Civil liberties

Civil rights

Clear and present danger test

Comparable worth

Dangerous tendency test

Double jeopardy

Due process of law

Establishment clause

Exclusionary rule

Fairness doctrine

Free exercise clause

Habeas corpus

Preferred position test

Prior restraint

Reverse discrimination

Selective incorporation

Self-incrimination

Separate but equal doctrine

Suggested Readings

Abraham, Henry J. *Freedom and the Court: Civil Rights and Liberties in the United States*, 5th ed. New York: Oxford University Press, 1988. Standard reference on the issues of civil rights and liberties.

Berger, Raoul. *Government by Judiciary. The Transformation of the Fourteenth Amendment*. Cambridge: Harvard University Press, 1977. Well-reasoned analysis of how the courts expanded their judicial policymaking role.

Corwin, Edwin S. *The "Higher Law" Background of American Constitutional Law*. Ithaca: Cornell University Press, 1955. Important work on the legal doctrines that undergird American constitutional law.

McDowell, Gary. *Equity and the Constitution*. Chicago: University of Chicago Press, 1982. Well-reasoned analysis of the issues surrounding equity and the Constitution.

Sowell, Thomas. *Preferential Policies: An International Perspective*. New York: Morrow, 1990. Comparative work on issues related to affirmative action and reverse discrimination.

Tribe, Laurence H. *Abortion: The Clash of Absolutes*. New York: Norton, 1990. Seeks to reach a balance between the conflicting absolute positions on abortion.

Verba, Sidney, and Gary R. Oren. *Equality in America: The View from the Top*. Cambridge: Harvard University Press, 1985. Examines the ideas of equality and equality of results.

Witt, Elder. *The Supreme Court and Individual Rights*, 2nd ed. Washington, D.C.: Congressional Quarterly Press, 1988. Standard reference on Supreme Court decisions related to individual rights.

Notes

1. *Rust* v. *Sullivan*, 111 S.Ct. 1759 (1991).
2. *Barnes* v. *Glen Theatre*, 111 S.Ct. 2456 (1991).
3. *United Autoworkers Union* v. *Johnson Controls*, 111 S.Ct. 1196 (1991).
4. *Cohen* v. *Cowles Media*, 111 S.Ct. 2513 (1991).
5. *Arizona* v. *Fulminante*, 111 S.Ct. 1246 (1991).
6. *Harmelin* v. *Michigan*, 111 S.Ct. 2680 (1991).
7. *U.S.* v. *Eichmann*, 110 S.Ct. 2404 (1990).
8. *Florida* v. *Riley*, 488 U.S. 445 (1989).
9. *Stanford* v. *Kentucky* and *Wilkins* v. *Missouri* , 492 U.S. 361 (1989). These cases were decided together.
10. *Hazelwood School District* v. *Kuhlheimer*, 484 U.S. 260 (1988).

11. *Abrams v. United States*, 250 U.S. 616 (1919).
12. *Commentary*, 54 (November, 1972), 66.
13. *Everson v. Board of Education*, 330 U.S. 1 (1947).
14. *Zorach v. Clausen*, 343 U.S. 306 (1952).
15. *Tilton v. Richardson*, 403 U.S. 672 (1971).
16. *Meek v. Pittinger*, 421 U.S. 349 (1975).
17. *Waltz v. Tax Commission*, 397 U.S. 664 (1970).
18. *Florey v. Sioux Falls*, 449 U.S. 987 (1980).
19. *Muller v. Allen*, 463 U.S. 388 (1983).
20. *Engel v. Vitale*, 370 U.S. 107 (1962); *Lubbock Independent School District v. Lubbock Civil Liberties Union*, 103 S.Ct. 800 (1983).
21. *Illinois ex rel. McCollum v. Board of Education*, 333 U.S. 203 (1948).
22. *Lemon v. Kurtzman*, 403 U.S. 602 (1971).
23. *Committee for Public Education v. Nyquist*, 413 U.S. 756 (1973); *Levitt v. Committee for Public Education*, 413 U.S. 472 (1973).
24. *Sloan v. Lemon*, 413 U.S. 825 (1973).
25. *Meek v. Pittinger*, 421 U.S. 349 (1975).
26. *Stone v. Graham*, 449 U.S. 39 (1980).
27. *Waltz v. Tax Commission*, 397 U.S. 664 (1971); *Lemon v. Kurtzman*, 403 U.S. 602 (1971).
28. *Wisconsin v. Yoder*, 406 U.S. 205 (1972).
29. *Oregon Department of Human Resources v. Smith*, 485 U.S. 660 (1988).
30. *Reynolds v. U.S.*, 98 U.S. 145 (1879).
31. *Jacobson v. Massachusetts*, 197 U.S. 11 (1905).
32. *Prince v. Massachusetts*, 321 U.S. 158 (1944).
33. *Pierce v. Society of Sisters*, 268 U.S. 510 (1925).
34. *West Virginia Board of Education v. Barnette*, 319 U.S. 624 (1943).
35. *Sherbert v. Verner*, 374 U.S. 398 (1963).
36. *Wisconsin v. Yoder* (1972).
37. *Schenck v. U.S.*, 249 U.S. 47 (1919).
38. *Near v. Minnesota*, 283 U.S. 697 (1931).
39. *The New York Times v. U.S.*, 403 U.S. 713 (1971).
40. *Congressional Quarterly Weekly Report*, October 16, 1976, pp. 3019–3021.
41. *Irwin v. Dowd*, 366 U.S. 717 (1961); *Rideau v. Louisiana*, 373 U.S. 723 (1963).
42. *Sheppard v. Maxwell*, 384 U.S. 333 (1966).
43. *Zurcher v. Stanford Daily*, 436 U.S. 547 (1978).
44. *The New York Times v. Jascalevich*, 439 U.S. 130 (1978).
45. *Nebraska Press Assn. v. Stuart*, 427 U.S. 539 (1976).
46. *Herbert v. Lando*, 441 U.S. 153 (1979).
47. *Gannett Co. v. De Pasquale*, 443 U.S. 368 (1979).
48. *The Greenville News*, July 27, 1979, p. A4.
49. *The Washington Post*, October 18, 1979, p. A12.
50. *Hazelwood School District v. Kuhlheimer*, 484 U.S. 260 (1988).
51. *Cohen v. Cowles Media*, 111 S.Ct. 2513 (1991).
52. *Red Lion Broadcasting Co. v. Federal Communications Commission* (1969).
53. *The New York Times v. Sullivan*, 376 U.S. 254 (1964).
54. *Curtis Publishing Co. v. Butts*, 388 U.S. 130 (1967).
55. *Roth v. U.S.*, 354 U.S. 476 (1957).
56. *Jacobellis v. Ohio*, 378 U.S. 184 (1964).
57. *Memoirs v. Massachusetts*, 383 U.S. 413 (1966).
58. *Miller v. California*, 413 U.S. 15 (1973).
59. *Jenkins v. Georgia*, 418 U.S. 153 (1974).
60. *Huffman v. Pursue Ltd.*, 420 U.S. 592 (1976).
61. *FCC v. Pacifica Foundation*, 438 U.S. 726 (1978).
62. *Village of Skokie v. National Socialist Party*, 432 U.S. 43 (1977).
63. *Barron v. Baltimore*, 7 Pet 243 (1833).
64. *Gitlow v. New York*, 268 U.S. 652 (1925).

65. *Chimel v. California*, 395 U.S. 752 (1969).
66. *Payton v. New York*, 445 U.S. 573 (1980) and *Ybarra v. Illinois*, 444 U.S. 85 (1979).
67. *Dalia v. U.S.*, 441 U.S. 238 (1979).
68. *Terry v. Ohio*, 392 U.S. 1 (1968).
69. *Adams v. Williams*, 407 U.S. 143 (1972).
70. *Delaware v. Prouse*, 440 U.S. 648 (1979).
71. *Dunaway v. New York*, 442 U.S. 200 (1979).
72. *Lo-Ji Sales Inc. v. New York*, 442 U.S. 319 (1979).
73. *Brown v. Texas*, 443 U.S. 47 (1979).
74. *Olmstead v. United States*, 277 U.S. 438 (1928).
75. *Katz v. United States*, 389 U.S. 349 (1967).
76. *United States v. U.S. District Court for Eastern District of Michigan*, 407 U.S. 297 (1972).
77. *Mapp v. Ohio*, 367 U.S. 643 (1961).
78. *United States v. Peltier*, 422 U.S. 531 (1975).
79. *Florida v. Riley*, 488 U.S. 445 (1989).
80. *Miranda v. Arizona*, 384 U.S. 436 (1966).
81. *Michigan v. Tucker*, 417 U.S. 433 (1974).
82. *Oregon v. Hass*, 420 U.S. 714 (1976).
83. *Rhode Island v. Innis*, 446 U.S. 291 (1980).
84. *Estelle v. Smith*, 451 U.S. 454 (1981).
85. *Edwards v. Arizona*, 451 U.S. 477 (1981).
86. *Furman v. Georgia*, 408 U.S. 238 (1972).
87. *Gregg v. Georgia*, 428 U.S. 153 (1976); *Woodson v. North Carolina*, 428 U.S. 280 (1976).
88. *Lockett v. Ohio*, 438 U.S. 586 (1978); *Bell v. Ohio*, 438 U.S. 637 (1978).
89. *Stanford v. Kentucky*, 492 U.S. 361 (1989); *Wilkins v. Missouri*, 492 U.S. 361 (1989). As mentioned, these cases were decided together.
90. *Penry v. Lynaugh*, 492 U.S. 302 (1989).
91. *Plessy v. Ferguson*, 163 U.S. 537 (1896).
92. *McLaurin v. Oklahoma*, 339 U.S. 637 (1950) and *Sweatt v. Painter*, 339 U.S. 629 (1950).
93. *Brown v. Board of Education*, 347 U.S. 483 (1954).
94. *The Economist*, January 9, 1993, p. 26.
95. *Stanton v. Stanton*, 421 U.S. 7 (1975).
96. *Craig v. Boren*, 429 U.S. 190 (1976).
97. *Dothard v. Rawlinson*, 433 U.S. 321 (1977).
98. *Schlesinger v. Ballard*, 419 U.S. (1975).
99. *United Auto Workers v. Johnson Controls*, 111 S. Ct. 1196 (1991).
100. Quoted in Brad Knickerbocker, "Gay Rights May Be Social Issue of 1990s," *The Christian Science Monitor*, February 11, 1993, p. 1.
101. *The Washington Post*, October 18, 1978, p. A4.
102. *Roe v. Wade*, 410 U.S. 113 (1973).
103. *Planned Parenthood v. Casey*, 112 S. Ct. 2791 (1992).
104. See generally Herbert McClosky and Alida Brill, *Dimensions of Tolerance: What Americans Believe About Civil Liberties* (New York: Russell Sage Foundation, 1983).
105. *The New York Times*, January 27, 1993, p. A8.
106. *Ex parte Milligan*, 71 U.S. (1866).
107. *Ex parte Endo*, 323 U.S. 283 (1944).
108. *Korematsu v. United States*, 323 U.S. 214 (1944).
109. *The Christian Science Monitor*, November 6, 1992, p. 20.
110. See *Public Opinion*, October 1978, p. 37 and McClosky and Brill, *Dimensions of Tolerance* (1983).
111. *Gideon v. Wainwright*, 372 U.S. 335 (1963).
112. *Baker v. Carr*, 369 U.S. 186 (1962).
113. *United Steelworkers of America v. Weber*, 443 U.S. 197 (1979).
114. *Regents of the University of California v. Bakke*, 438 U.S. 265 (1978).
115. Mary Ann Glendon, *Rights Talk: The Impoverishment of Political Discourse* (New York: Free Press, 1991), p. 159.

116. Quoted in ibid.
117. Fred Hiatt and Margaret Shapiro, "The Two Faces of Japan: Most of What You've Heard Is True, But Then, So Is the Contrary," *The Washington Post National Weekly*, August 27–September 2, 1990, p. 23.
118. "Computers and Privacy: The Eye of the Beholder," *The Economist*, May 4, 1991, p. 21.
119. John Locke, *Two Treatises of Government* (London: Cambridge University Press, 1960).
120. See, for example, "In Matters of Life and Death, The Dying Take Control," *The New York Times*, Section 4, p. 1, August 18, 1991.
121. Edward A. Garga, "Coming Out in India, With a Nod From the Gods," *The New York Times*, August 15, 1991, p. A4.
122. "China's Sort of Freedom," *The Economist*, October 17, 1992, pp. 39–40.
123. Nicholas D. Kristof, "Parts of China Forcibly Sterilizing the Retarded Who Wish to Marry," *The New York Times*, August 16, 1991, p. A1.
124. "First Steps in Human Rights," *The Economist*, August 3, 1991, p. 33.
125. Ibid., pp. 8–9.
126. On why they do this, see G. Hossein Razi, "Legitimacy, Religion, and Nationalism in the Middle East," *American Political Science Review*, 84: 1 (March 1990), 69–91.
127. "Ten Billion Mouths," *The Economist*, January 20, 1990, p. 14.

THE POLITICS OF THE POLICY PROCESS

In our individual lives we all make policy decisions that greatly affect our futures, just as the government does. But while we arrive at *private* policy decisions, the government makes **public policy**, its response to a public issue or problem whereby it establishes a goal and makes decisions to achieve that goal. The following is an example of a typical policy issue, policy goal, and policy decision facing a college student.

POLICY PROBLEM: LAW SCHOOL ADMISSION

1. Policy issue: how to gain admission to law school.
2. Policy goal: attain a high score on the LSAT (Law School Admission Test) and a high GPA (grade point average).
3. Policy decision: take courses that will prepare one for law school while not damaging one's prospects for attaining a high GPA.

Here is an example of a major public policy that was proposed by President Bill Clinton:

POLICY PROBLEM: THE COST OF HIGHER EDUCATION

1. Policy issue: how to enable students who cannot afford college tuition to get a college education
2. Policy goal: Provide higher education for all who want it, regardless of financial need.
3. Policy decision: Establish a national service program that will allow students to repay education loans through community service such as teaching, police work, or health care.

This format looks simple, doesn't it? But in practice policymaking can become enormously complicated. In the case of the policy problem of admission to law school, for example, the student might find conflicts in scheduling easy courses to increase GPA versus harder courses to enhance one's prospects on the LSAT. Moreover, how much diversity can the student bound for law school permit in his or her curriculum choices? And to what extent can he or she afford to get involved in extracurricular activities? The policy goals of getting into law school may conflict with other policy goals of obtaining a broad undergraduate education and having a good time in college.

 Public policy is even more complex since it involves many decision makers who must come to some agreement. Generally, people can agree on what the issues are, but they frequently disagree on goals and on the steps necessary to implement the goals. For example, some labor unions object to the national service plan because they fear low-cost community service workers will steal jobs from union members, and some people are philosophically opposed to government involvement in the private sector. Another problem is that public policies may overlap or conflict. President Clinton's government loan/national service policy requires an infusion of government spending, which undercuts efforts to reduce the federal deficit. Similar problems exist with other policy options. A high tariff policy to protect our textile industry would interfere with a policy of helping developing nations build their own industries. And a policy of subsidizing tobacco farmers would conflict with a health care policy intended to discourage smoking. Debate about policy goals and their decision implementation, then, can be divisive and tortuous, as can be seen in the history of foreign and domestic policymaking in the United States.

 The domestic and foreign policies of our government are each a large *collection* of goals and decisions pertaining to a host of problems or issues. In foreign policy, we have policies on international economic aid, trade, human rights, developing countries, the two Chinas (mainland and Taiwan), the Middle East, and many more. In domestic policy, some of the issue areas are civil rights, welfare, federalism, natural resources, the economy, and agriculture.

 Throughout much of American history, the policies pursued by our government had little direct bearing on the rest of the world. In this century, however, American policy choices have been pivotal in determining, on a worldwide scale, war and peace, food and famine, and resource scarcity and abundance. Policy choices made today by the

United States—the oldest continuously existing democratic nation—ultimately affect all humanity.

In the next section we will take a quick look at the policy choices that have evolved over the past 200 years, as well as a close look at the policymaking process itself. Then we will consider how much influence experts should have in formulating public policy and just how successful the process of policymaking has been in America. Finally, we'll see the ways policy is made (or not made) in other nations.

★ PUBLIC POLICY IN AMERICA

THE HISTORIC CONTEXT OF POLICYMAKING

Public policy is not made in a vacuum. A number of influences help define the issues as well as determine what the policy goals are and delineate how they should be implemented. Among these influences are (1) the mood of the public, (2) statements by national leaders, (3) pressure from special interests, (4) actions of governmental bodies, and (5) crisis situations. Historically, these influences have established the boundary lines for debate about both foreign and domestic policies, as the following review illustrates.

Foreign Policy

When George Washington delivered his "Farewell Address" in 1796, he warned the nation about "entangling alliances" with other nations. With a few exceptions, a mood of isolation dominated American involvement in foreign affairs throughout the nineteenth century. **Isolationism** is a term in foreign policy jargon that means American overseas interests, especially military, are minimal and thus do not require American involvement in foreign affairs. Gradually the climate of opinion began to change, especially as the ideas of "manifest destiny" and "global markets" began to dominate thinking about the role of America in world affairs. Implicit in these ideas was the belief that American culture must be extended first over the whole of the continent and then to other places in the world.

After a period of greater involvement in world affairs early in the twentieth century, culminating in World War I, an isolationist sentiment again dominated foreign policy decisions until the beginning of World War II. Because of the public's isolationist mood, President Franklin Roosevelt found it difficult to implement a military draft and otherwise prepare the United States for the war that was finally declared after the bombing of Hawaii's Pearl Harbor in 1941.

Alarmed by the spread of communism after World War II, the United States devised the policy of **containment**, which called for the government to "contain" Soviet influence in various parts of the world. This effort led to bilateral and multilateral treaties with numerous foreign governments and the deployment of the American military throughout the world. Rather than fighting a "hot war" with weapons and ammunition, we saw ourselves engaged in a "cold war" in which the military was deployed to stand up to communist threats and to fight only if necessary. That occurred, for example, when communist troops from North Korea invaded South Korea in the early 1950s and when communist North Vietnam tangled with U.S.-supported South Vietnam in the mid-1960s.

In the 1970s a policy of seeking detente with communist countries gradually supplanted the containment policy. Under **detente**, American diplomats aimed to reduce tensions by finding areas of common agreement, such as in arms control and disarmament. The United States began to sell grain and other materials to communist nations and established diplomatic relations with mainland China. Presidents Ronald Reagan and George Bush made these objectives the centerpieces of their foreign policy, working closely with the leaders of the former Soviet Union and China.

As the Iron Curtain collapsed and the Berlin Wall crumbled, American policy had to be adjusted to the historic opportunity of helping the devastated economies throughout Eastern Europe and the former republics of the Soviet Union. How the United States could help them establish market economies became a dominant policy issue. With a weakened economy at home, some critics said America could not afford direct financial aid, while others said that without American aid the new birth of freedom in the heartland of communism might be snuffed out. Still other policy issues dealt with the withdrawal of Russian soldiers from Eastern Europe, which reduced the need for American soldiers in Western Europe. Also, what should be the role of NATO (North Atlantic Treaty Organization), which had been established to contain communism? Of course, crucial to the whole world was the dismantling of nuclear weapons, an especially difficult policy issue since the emergence of independent republics raised questions about which government controlled these weapons: for example, the Russian government in Moscow or the government of the Ukraine.

During this momentous time of the collapse of communism, President Bush spoke of a **new world order**, which would utilize collective policymaking by the nations of the world through the United Nations to maintain peace and to enforce standards of human rights. The initial centerfold of the new world order was America's involvement in the Persian Gulf, where President Bush worked in tandem with the United Nations and particularly with the world's major economic and military powers to turn back Iraq's invasion of Kuwait in 1991. As dusk settled on the Bush administration, he followed a similar policy in Somalia. Pursuant to the direction of the United Nations, he sent American troops to establish order and provide food for Somalia's starving population.

The ethnic clash in Bosnia and Herzegovina following the collapse of Yugoslavia tested the new world order in unexpected ways. For example, should America and its allies commit their troops to an area where prospects for success were limited by the difficult terrain and the complicated ethnic rivalries? Yet how could the obvious suffering and the atrocities being committed be ignored? The memory of America's protracted and embarrassing involvement in Vietnam created a reluctance to get our military bogged down in Bosnia. President Clinton indicated during his campaign and early in his administration that his foreign policies would be reasonably consistent with Bush policies. That, of course, has generally been true since World War II, as Democratic and Republican presidents have usually made only marginal changes in their predecessor's foreign policy. Continuity rather than change has been the norm in American foreign policy.

The United States has also used education as an instrument of foreign policy by exchanging scholars and teachers with other countries and by admitting large numbers of foreign nationals to study in the United States. America's Fulbright Program, which has exchanged 200,000 students and faculty with some 130 countries since 1947, is the recognized "flagship" of international educational exchange. **Foreign aid**, a centerpiece of American foreign policy since World War II, features a variety of economic, social, and educational aid programs whose purpose is to help developing nations improve their economies. The Agency for International Development (AID) administers many of these programs, such as the construction of sewers, dams, schools, and other parts of a nation's infrastructure necessary to support a thriving economy.

Domestic Policy

During the late eighteenth and most of the nineteenth centuries, indeed until as late as the 1930s, the common view of the national government was that it should have a very limited role in domestic policymaking. At times the national government did make broad national public policy, such as the Morrill Act, which established land grant colleges during and after the Civil War, but domestic policy was essentially left to state and local governments. **Laissez faire**, allowing the private sector to function without interference from the government, dominated American policy during this period.

The crisis of the Great Depression of the 1930s, however, provided the catalyst for fundamental changes in federalism. The national government assumed a more aggressive and activist role, taking on responsibilities previously left to the states as well as creating new responsibilities. Since the time of the Depression the government has assumed responsibility for social security, unemployment compensation, medical care for

The Great Depression of the 1930s triggered a much more active role of the national government in social policy. As this photo of a breadline in New York City shows, people from all walks of life were affected by the sudden crash of the economy.

the aged and the poor, food stamps, and many other social programs. The private sector also felt the hand of government. New Deal policies instituted during the Depression paved the way for an active daily role for the national government in administering and regulating the economy. Economic policies based on the ideas of the British economist John Maynard Keynes were adopted; they largely determined our economic policy until the 1980s. In **Keynesian economics**, the government spends and taxes in a way that produces deficit budgets in bad economic times and surplus budgets in good times.

World War II also laid the groundwork for changed social policies concerning African-Americans and women, as we saw in Chapter 14. African-American soldiers returned from the war to a largely segregated society that they saw as inequitable. Meanwhile, wartime production needs had led many women to move to workplaces outside the home and to expect equal treatment with (and from) men. During the succeeding decades interest in policies affecting these groups grew. By 1964 and 1965 the Civil Rights and Voting Rights Acts were passed; in the early 1970s the Equal Rights Amendment was proposed (but never ratified). Comparable worth between and among occupations was raised as a policy issue in the 1980s. Health care became a major policy issue during the late 1980s and early 1990s as medical expenses rose, and insurance became more expensive and exceeded the annual rise in the cost of living. Policy alternatives centered on a mixture of government and private sector financing that would provide universal health care.

The advent of the Republican Reagan and Bush administrations in the 1980s brought a fundamental reevaluation of the role of the national government in the American federal system. Their goals focused on greater power for state and local governments and less government regulation of business and industry. This was the first significant challenge to policies that had enlarged the national government's role since the 1930s. Keynesian economics gave way to **supply-side economics**, which emphasized reducing taxes to allow Americans to retain more money to spend and invest. The idea was that the benefits of a stimulated economy would create jobs and increase tax revenues. In theory, supply-side economics leads to both greater savings and investment. As people spend, they generate increased demand for goods and services; thus, new jobs are created and greater tax revenues are available to the government through taxes on increased incomes and sales. As people invest, new companies can be started and older companies can develop new products for sale. President Bush, though sharing some goals with President Reagan, was less insistent upon achieving them. He even (reluctantly) supported a tax increase in 1990 to help reduce the soaring budget deficit.

The 1992 election of a Democratic administration for the first time in 12 years ushered in different approaches to domestic policy problems. President Clinton advocated "growing the economy" through government involvement and investment, indicating that, as far as the deficit would allow, he intended to return the nation's economic policies more in the direction of traditional Democratic ideas. Upon taking office he immediately promised a universal health care program and signed orders reversing restrictions on abortions and fetal tissue research that the two preceding Republican presidents had imposed. In short, the conservative agenda was to be supplanted by programs calling for a more activist role on the part of government.

Many domestic public policies today tend to fall into one of three categories (Table 15.1). A government may use **distributive policies** to encourage private citizens to perform or not perform certain functions. For instance, government subsidies may

TABLE 15.1   TYPES OF PUBLIC POLICIES

Type	Definition	Illustration
Distributive	Encourages citizens to perform tasks they would not do without government financial support	Subsidies to farmers to grow or not to grow certain crops
Regulatory	Specifies how citizens must conduct themselves	Federal Communications Commission (FCC) regulations of radio and television stations
Redistributive	Helps one segment of society at the expense of another	Federal grants and contracts that transfer tax dollars from the industrial North to the rural South

enable a railroad to maintain an otherwise unprofitable passenger service or farmers to keep their farms. **Regulatory policies** specify how private individuals or groups may conduct themselves. The Federal Communications Commission (FCC), for example, sets rules for broadcasters. **Redistributive policies** are used to help one segment of society at the expense of another. For example, many federal grants and contracts have the net effect of transferring tax dollars from industrial northern states to rural southern states. Welfare programs use income tax revenue to help people below the poverty line.

ECONOMIC POLICYMAKING MODELS

Politics and economics are inseparably connected, and assessing that relationship both in the United States and in other countries is important. A different relationship between politics and economics is evident in each of the following models: communist, fascist, socialist, capitalist, and mixed. A look at each of these models will help us chart the course of the United States, with its mixed model combining capitalist and socialist features (see also Table 15.2).

TABLE 15.2 POLITICAL/ECONOMIC MODELS

Model	Characteristics	Sample Nations
Communist	Government ownership of all means of production and control of all economic decision making; loss of political freedom; nominal equal spread of wealth	China, North Korea, former Soviet Union
Fascist	Government supremacy and suppression of dissent but private ownership allowed; no commitment to spreading wealth	Nazi Germany
Socialist	Government ownership of major industries coexisting with private ownership; extensive social welfare; high tax rates; freedom of expression	Sweden, United Kingdom, Israel
Capitalist	All means of production privately owned; free market economy operating according to market forces; politically democratic	South Africa, Switzerland, United States (during nineteenth century)
Mixed	Combines features of socialist and capitalist models: extensive private ownership; some social welfare programs; lightly regulated economy; moderate tax rate; politically democratic	United States, most of Western Europe

Communist Model. In the **communist model**, the government owns all farms and industries and rigidly controls all economic decision making. The objective of this model is to develop the national economy by means of imposed plans, such as the five-year plans of the former Soviet Union. This model is sometimes referred to as an economic democracy, because its stated goal (rarely achieved) is to apportion wealth relatively evenly throughout the society. Political freedom is suppressed in the interest of economic achievement. During the late 1980s and early 1990s, the communist model gave way as people in many communist countries began to demand political freedom and observed the superior economic performance of other (mostly Western) models.

Fascist Model. In the **fascist model**, the government is supreme and does not tolerate dissent, as in the communist model, but private ownership is allowed. A fascist government is not an economic democracy because it has no policy to spread wealth evenly. Historically, the fascist model characterized Nazi Germany, Mussolini's Italy, and Spain under Francisco Franco. Until recently, fascism had its adherents in military dictatorships in several Latin American countries.

Socialist Model. Government ownership of major industries coexists with private ownership in the **socialist model**. The goal is to create maximum economic security for the individual. Most socialist nations allow freedom of expression and other basic human rights characteristic of political democracy and provide extensive social welfare, but the tax rate in such nations is typically very high. Sweden, for example, allows relatively uninhibited human expression, owns major industries, and provides tax-subsidized social welfare programs while still permitting significant private investment, such as the Volvo and Saab corporations.

Capitalist Model. In the **capitalist model**, all the means of production are in private hands. The government does not interfere with economic decision making. The economic system regulates itself through the free market, which operates according to the laws of supply and demand. This model functions within a political democracy, and was characteristic of the United States during the early part of its history. Adam Smith, an eighteenth-century Scottish economist who argued on behalf of free market forces, is generally recognized as the father of the capitalist model through the influence of his book, *The Wealth of Nations*. No nation today has a purely capitalist system, but South Africa and Switzerland probably come the closest.

Mixed Model. The American economic system today is a **mixed model** containing both socialist and capitalist elements. The American system has socialist features, such as government-insured pensions for retired persons, Medicare, and Medicaid, but it retains such capitalist features as privately owned insurance companies. This model, like the socialist model, functions in a political rather than an economic democracy, but it does not seek to create a "cradle-to-grave" sense of security for the individual, as the socialist countries do.

The role of government is an issue of continuing tension between liberals and conservatives in a mixed economy. Liberals believe that government policy should emphasize security over risk for the individual. For example, on the issue of health care, liberals favor universal publicly financed insurance through the federal government, such as that provided in socialist countries like Sweden, while conservatives would emphasize private sector insurance, utilizing the capitalist approach. Personal risk and responsibility are smaller under the liberals' nationalized health care plans and greater under the conservatives' private sector approaches. An individual need not exercise personal responsibility under the typical liberal health care plan: Enrollment is mandatory. Under the typical conservative plan, participation is more voluntary and the public tax burden is less. Liberals feel that the government should make choices *for* the individual in some cases, while conservatives, for the most part, want to maximize the individual's freedom of choice in the expectation that the individual will make fewer bad decisions than the government.

PHASES IN THE POLICYMAKING PROCESS

Perhaps you have heard the statement, "There ought to be a law against that." The person saying this means there should be a policy that prevents whatever actions the speaker opposes. How does one individual with an idea translate the idea to a public policy? The complexity of the policymaking process makes such action nearly impossible. The typical policy, from its inception as an idea to its formulation as a policy proposal to its implementation and possible modification, passes through at least ten phases.

Phase 1: Getting an idea on the agenda. Just to get a policy idea discussed by enough people to get the government listening requires enormous amounts of time and energy, even if the idea is a brilliant one. Press, politicians, and interest groups are among the ingredients generally needed to get the idea on the discussion agenda. Then comes the even more difficult task of pushing the idea through a maze of potential roadblocks in the executive and legislative branches.

Phase 2: Formulation of a policy proposal. An idea for a policy requires that information be collected to support it, that the crucial decision makers in the policy process be apprised, that the policy be measured against alternative policies, and that supporters and opponents support and refute the need for the policy before the decision makers, who will then decide whether to push it.

Phase 3: Legislation. After a policy has been formulated, it is then incorporated into legislation for action by Congress. As we saw in Chapter 12, a proposal must hurdle many legislative roadblocks before it can make its way to the White House for final approval. When the idea for civil rights legislation began to be taken seriously in the 1950s, protracted legislative hearings and congressional debates spanned many years. Finally the Civil Rights Act of 1964 and the Voting Rights Act of 1965 were adopted.

Phase 4: Legitimation. Final action by the Congress in passing a bill and the president in signing it into law legitimates the policy. Even at this stage a veto is not uncommon. In fact, the president may already have threatened to use one if the bill reaches the Oval Office.

Phase 5: Implementation. The bureaucracy is charged with implementing what the president and Congress have approved. Implementation takes the form of administrative law. The bureaucracy, however, can effectively negate congressional intent by creating restrictions, delaying implementation, or simply not enforcing a law. Congress has in turn tried to reverse bureaucratic actions contrary to congressional intent through the use of the legislative veto, a resolution that overrules a decision made in the executive branch (a device that has been ruled unconstitutional).

Phase 6: Cooperation. Often policies require intergovernmental cooperation, such as some social welfare policies that involve national, state, and local governments. Cooperation may be difficult to achieve. After South Carolina and Washington protested that they had become the nuclear dumping ground of the nation, an attempt was made to share the responsibility for disposing of nuclear waste. It took an interstate compact, action by the courts, and years of negotiation to reach an agreement in 1992.

Phase 7: Adjudication. When disputes occur about a policy, the bureaucracy and/or the courts must adjudicate the conflicts. For example, when the bureaucracy began to impose affirmative action standards for admission to schools and for the composition of university faculties, disputes arose over whether the bureaucracy had acted within the scope of its authority. In the case of school admissions, the Supreme Court decided in 1978 that the bureaucracy could not mandate that quotas be met in admissions policies (*Regents of the University of California* v. *Bakke*).[1]

Phase 8: Evaluation. Customarily, the bureaucracy as well as Congress may monitor a policy's effectiveness and determine whether changes should be made. Congress may do this through congressional committee hearings, utilizing their oversight function to determine whether laws are being properly implemented, while the bureaucracy may contract with private firms to review the effectiveness of policies.

Phase 9: Modification debate. Evaluation of a policy may determine that modifications are necessary. This debate may take place in the bureaucracy, in the legislative branch, in the judicial branch, or in any combination of those groups. For example, proposals to modify policies affecting banks and savings and loan institutions in the aftermath of their scandals in the late 1980s and early 1990s were extensively debated within and between the legislative and executive branches.

Phase 10: Implementation of modifications. Once again, the bureaucracy generally has the responsibility for implementing any modifications. When the U.S. Supreme Court ruled that quotas could not be used for school admissions standards, the Department of Education had to implement modifications in its affirmative action guidelines.

CHARACTERISTICS OF THE POLICY PROCESS

Each chapter in this book has provided information on how policy is made in the United States. We can glean from this information several central features of the nature of policymaking. We know that it is incremental, that it involves many decision makers, that influences outside government play a part, that symbols are sometimes as important as substance, and that it is a tentative, ever-changing and, above all, complex process.

Incrementalism. Policy in the United States tends to be made slowly and to evolve over a long period of time. Many discussions in this book have demonstrated this incrementalism; perhaps the most dramatic examples are in the field of civil rights. Although the Supreme Court declared in 1954 that public schools had to be integrated with "all deliberate speed,"[2] well over a decade passed before a concerted effort was made to implement the Court's decision. Only in 1969 did the Court order segregation in the schools to end "at once."[3] In the meantime, the president and Congress began to act in other areas of civil rights with the adoption of the Civil Rights Act of 1964 and the Voting Rights Act of 1965. Some civil rights issues, such as reverse discrimination and comparable worth and special protections for homosexuals, still await resolution through the policy process.

Multiplicity of Policymakers. One factor contributing to incrementalism is the large number of policymakers. All three branches of the federal government were active in determining civil rights policy, and many policymakers were in each branch. In Congress the Judiciary Committees of both houses were involved. In the executive branch, policy first evolved mainly in the Department of Justice, but several other departments and agencies shared the responsibility because civil rights policy had to be enforced in many areas of society. In the judiciary, the lower federal courts played a major role in interpreting and applying Supreme Court decisions. State and local governments were also active in reacting to and implementing policy made by the national government.

Outside Influences. The general public, interest groups, and powerful elite groups may be influential in determining public policy. In most cases the general public participates through their elected representatives, who pay attention to public opinion (since they are normally interested in getting reelected). In some communities, especially in New England, citizens can participate directly in making policy by meeting, discussing, and voting on specific proposals. Sometimes, certain interest groups are powerful enough to bring about policies they favor—witness the long success of the National Rifle Association in protecting their "right to bear arms." When the views of influential groups clash, the result is often compromise, or no action at all. In the fight over ratification of the Equal Rights Amendment, interest groups organized on both sides of the issue. Proponents included the League of Women Voters and the National Organization for Women; opponents formed the STOP-ERA organizations. Some legislators also tested general public reaction by taking their own opinion polls. In the end the proposal died. Finally certain elite groups can forge policy. For example, for many years influential segments of the military-industrial complex were able to allocate resources to defense needs rather than social needs. These various means of public participation in policymaking can be described as the constitutional-republican, participatory, pluralist, and elitist models (see Table 15.3).

Symbol and Substance. The symbolic and substantive aspects of policymaking cannot be separated. To the extent that presidents develop direct support through sym-

TABLE 15.3	MODELS OF POPULAR PARTICIPATION IN DEMOCRATIC POLICYMAKING	
Model	Definition	Illustration
Constitutional-Republican	Public participates through elected representatives	United States Congress
Participatory	Public meets and votes on all policy issues	New England town meeting
Pluralist	Interest groups, representing groups of citizens, compete to influence public policy	Competition between the United Auto Workers (UAW) and the National Association of Manufacturers (NAM) about labor policy
Elitist	Small group of prominent persons determine public policy without popular participation	Invasions of Grenada and Panama

bolic gestures, they generally strengthen their role in policymaking. For example, during the Eisenhower administration, Public Law 480 was adopted to provide food to needy foreign countries. In 1961 the Kennedy administration renamed the program "Food for Peace." The policy was essentially the same, but the Kennedy administration reaped more benefits from it by simply changing its name. The best public policy, if not dressed in the proper attire, will usually accomplish less than policy that is both substantively sound and symbolically stylish.

Through his extraordinary communications skills, President Reagan used the symbolic power of the presidential office to win public support for his policy proposals more effectively than any other president since Franklin D. Roosevelt. Without the use of symbolic power, the conservative Republican Reagan could not have gained the support needed to get his policies accepted by the Democratically controlled House of Representatives. President Bush managed to win American public support as well as the cooperation of other countries, including the Soviet Union, at the time of the Persian Gulf War, by framing the conflict in terms of a "new world order" and aggressively promoting that idea. President Clinton has been skillful at enlisting public opinion for his domestic policies—even those requiring new taxes—by taking the issues directly to the people through televised "town meetings" and weekly radio broadcasts.

Impermanence. However official and permanent policies may *seem*, most bear a stamp of tentativeness. Individuals and groups may work not only to create a new policy but also to change or abolish it. Hardly any American policy seemed more fixed than that of nonrecognition of mainland China after 1949. The same could be said of decisions not to sell wheat to the Soviet Union during the 1960s and 1970s. Both policies changed, however.

Dynamism. Because policymaking is tentative, it is dynamic and not static. Public policy is the result of a struggle at any given time. Observers assessing public policy must determine which forces want to preserve the status quo, which are advocating change, and what levers of power are available to both sides. For example, until civil rights groups gained power in Congress and with the president, their efforts to change policy had little impact.

Complexity. As noted earlier, policies cannot be made in isolation from one another. Links must be considered, such as those between energy and the environment. Because of the interrelationships—and the resulting necessity for numerous policymakers—policymaking is quite complex. A national policy concerning land use would involve at least the Cabinet departments of Agriculture, Commerce, Housing and Urban Development, and Interior, plus the appropriate congressional committees and subcommittees. The courts might become involved, too, as citizens test whether the federal government has the authority to limit use of their own land. Each policymaker would most likely have a different interest in and position on the issue of land use.

Trade-offs are an inevitable part of the complexity of policymaking. For example, Americans have long been attracted by size and speed. These tastes were particularly obvious in the 1950s and 1960s. The public thirsted after bigger, faster, fancier cars; a "love affair with the car" was a term widely used to describe this phenomenon. The automobile industry was only too happy to oblige, with gas-guzzling monsters that sent the automakers' profits upward. New houses were bigger, more elaborate, and set farther apart; business structures were erected higher and higher; real estate developers devoured larger and larger chunks of farmland, escalating real estate taxes and driving farmers off

To celebrate the end of the Persian Gulf War, troops marched in a grand parade down Broadway in New York City.

their land. Food and drink processors turned out quantities of chemically treated products in disposable packages. But these developments seemed to ignore the resulting problems: reduced energy supplies, diminishing resources, and increased trash and pollution. Can our present rate of economic growth continue? Should economic growth be tolerated if it threatens the environment?

In recent years Americans have become increasingly concerned about pollution in many forms. Automobiles, airplanes, buses, and tobacco products cause air pollution. Water pollution results from industrial waste and sewage. Noise pollution is serious in industrial areas and near heavy auto traffic. Toxic waste has alarmed entire neighborhoods

A VIEW FROM THE STATES
Winning Public Opinion and the Gulf War

Just as every movie blockbuster comes with its own set pieces, the movie within the movie, so the Bush Administration devised *its* set piece: a staggeringly successful mini-series called the Gulf War, which demonstrated on an unprecedented scale how events might be given the narrative shape and heady rush of a good action picture.

It is odd, unseemly even, to describe a war as "telegenic," but that is precisely what the Gulf War was. Each network introduced its war coverage with music, a logo and a title—"Crisis in the Gulf" on ABC; "Showdown in the Gulf" on CBS before the hostilities and "War in the Gulf" after the hostilities had begun; "America at War" on NBC. For them it was a new series, and even the correspondents . . . gained a star's celebrity.

Certainly the Gulf War was a lot more telegenic than Vietnam. Vietnam was a long, logy hallucination of a movie—the good guys indistinguishable from the bad, the plot dribbling away to entropy. The Pentagon had learned that if it were to control the media front it couldn't let that happen again. The next war was going to be short, sharp, its narrative lineaments clean, happily unconfused as to heroes and villains. . . .

The casting was impeccable. Articulate, brilliant, rugged, sensitive, heroic H. Norman Schwarzkopf was a figure of Herculean proportions. . . . On the other hand, Saddam Hussein resembled the evil mastermind from a Saturday afternoon serial. As for actual combat, the action we saw, primarily bombs hitting targets, was antiseptic and precise.

Formulated like a World War II movie, the Gulf War even ended like a World War II movie, with the troops marching triumphantly down Broadway or Main Street, bathed in the gratitude of their fellow Americans while the final credits rolled.

Source: "Now Playing Across America: Real Life, the Movie," *The New York Times*, October 20, 1991, p. 32. Copyright © 1991 by The New York Times Company. Reprinted by permission.

in some communities. Americans were even advised to give up sunbathing because the depletion of the ozone layer (by chemicals) was threatening an epidemic of skin cancer.

Cleaning up the environment is a laudable policy objective, especially if it reduces the hazards of such diseases as cancer. But some economists ask whether is is better to live with pollution rather than create a possible recession or depression by slowing down industrial productivity in the interest of a clean environment. The tradeoffs have to be calculated with care. For example, oil is needed to support industrial growth, but oil slicks and spills contaminate ocean waters and threaten marine life, resorts, and the fishing industry. Can offshore drilling be permitted because of its potential benefit to, say, the transportation industry, even though it threatens to harm another industry, like fishing? These are not easy policy choices. In areas short of fuel, many people would accept such a risk.

This cycle of relationships creates another vicious circle, particularly as it relates

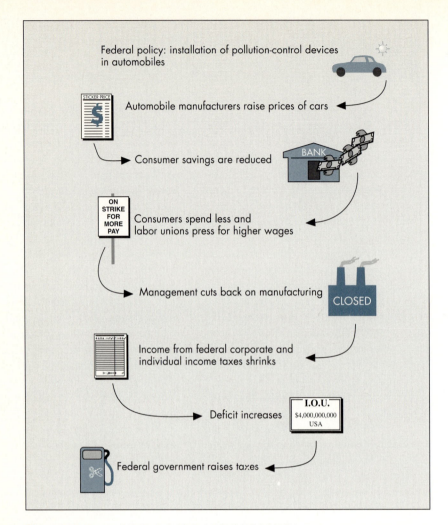

Federal policy: installation of pollution-control devices in automobiles

Automobile manufacturers raise prices of cars

Consumer savings are reduced

Consumers spend less and labor unions press for higher wages

Management cuts back on manufacturing

Income from federal corporate and individual income taxes shrinks

Deficit increases

Federal government raises taxes

Figure 15.1 A VICIOUS CYCLE OF PUBLIC POLICY.

to consumer costs: prices and taxes (Figure 15.1). Automobile manufacturers, forced to comply with federal regulations requiring the installation of pollution-control devices, increase car prices. This increase in turn reduces the purchasing power and savings potential of consumers. Pressures then develop to increase salaries in order to compensate for such reductions. Labor unions may seek higher wages and more fringe benefits to help their members, resulting in labor-management disputes. The government, requiring ever more money (including funds for the support of federal agencies enforcing regulations), contributes to this problem by taking higher taxes out of paychecks. Each of these examples inevitably puts added (usually financial) burdens on consumers.

Economic growth can create economic dislocations. When new businesses become more efficient than older ones, some people lose their jobs. Should the government provide alternative work? Should it retrain people for other jobs? Does the government have an obligation to provide people with jobs commensurate with their education and training? To do so creates another tax burden. Failing to do so fosters discontent and deprives society of the valuable contribution such people may make.

Not even equality has simple solutions. To what extent and under what circumstances should the government act to guarantee equality among all people? Official government policy since passage of the 1964 Civil Rights Act has been to eliminate vestiges of discrimination in a variety of areas, among them education, housing, and employment. But should the government initiate affirmative action on behalf of females and minority groups if such action discriminates against white males? For example, if the government requires a law school to admit a certain proportion of females, this might lead to discrimination against some males who are better qualified. The justification for this action is that females and minority groups have been discriminated against for many years: Affirmative action is necessary to compensate for the past and to train people to serve their own groups. But, as we saw in Chapter 14, the policy goal of eliminating discrimination can itself lead to discrimination.

Trade-offs also occur in the foreign policy area. As developing nations raise the prices of the raw materials that feed the American industrial machine, the cost per unit produced increases, reducing the buying power of American consumers. When the United States sells wheat to the Soviet Union, American farmers may benefit from higher prices, but American consumers may have to pay more for bread. When the United States intervenes overseas, as in Vietnam, American industry may benefit through contracts for military weapons, but thousands may die and American society may be thrown into turmoil. When the United States stations hundreds of thousands of soldiers abroad and when America imports more than it exports, our balance-of-payments problem is aggravated. This problem arises when American dollars spent overseas total more than other currencies that are spent in the United States. Making the dollar less valuable in relationship to other currencies means Americans must pay more for products made abroad. These policy issues show that policymaking, whether domestic or international, is exceedingly complex.

We have defined and illustrated the scope of both public policy and the policy process. In doing so, we have seen that the process raises many questions and produces much conflict, creating diverse interpretations about what is right and wrong with American public policy.

? ISSUES TO ANALYZE

ISSUE 1   *SHOULD EXPERTS HAVE MORE INFLUENCE OVER PUBLIC POLICY THAN THE PUBLIC?*

REASONS WHY EXPERTS SHOULD HAVE MORE INFLUENCE OVER PUBLIC POLICY

From the intricacies of the tax code to the complexities of environmental and energy issues, public policy experts are essential to understanding, analyzing, and making recommendations about important issues. And they are usually expected to be influential because of their specialized training in many fields, such as accounting, law, medicine, biology, and chemistry. The quality of public policymaking would be seriously at risk without their knowledge. Ordinary Americans, confronting an array of complicated policy issues and various types of confusing policies, can hardly be expected to understand the policymaking process that affects them so vitally. The average citizen is like a small boat on a storm-tossed sea with zero visibility. To produce sound policies, the policy process must emphasize factual and logical analysis. The public, however, responds more to the simplicity of slogans and symbols that engender human emotions and passions. Policymakers must endure the vicissitudes of the public-opinion roller coaster and try to prevent good policy from being harmed or killed by public opinion.

The issues discussed in the following examples, no matter which side one is on, reveal serious pitfalls in the policy process: (1) inadequate public knowledge and understanding of policy questions, (2) the potential for politicians to take advantage of popular opposition to proposed policies that are otherwise sound, (3) public moods that may prevent policymakers from developing the best public policy in a timely fashion, (4) the power that interest groups have to thwart policy against their interests, and (5) policy based more on symbol than substance. Each of several examples illustrates one or more of these pitfalls.

Typically, proposals to raise taxes arouse the public's ire even though there may be good reason to do so. There are times when either new taxes or tax increases may be necessary to achieve such goals as the improvement of education. When the public's mood, however, is *irrationally* opposed to new taxes or tax increases, politicians catering to the public's mood can kill a good policy. Most economists agreed during the late 1980s and early 1990s that tax increases would be necessary to reduce the deficit. Yet, few politicians dared challenge the public's opposition, and when George Bush finally agreed to a compromise with Democratic leaders in Congress, increasing taxes in violation of his "read my lips" pledge against a tax increase, he may have signed his political death warrant in 1992.

Policy proposals that had helped President George Bush win the 1988 election met with the opposition of feminist and public school lobbies, which fought his efforts to ban abortion and to provide vouchers for parents to send their children to the private or public school of their choice. Interest groups were thus able to thwart two of Bush's principal platform planks in his landslide victory over Michael Dukakis. However, when Bush twice vetoed the family leave bill, which would have allowed workers in businesses with 50 or more employees to take up to 12 weeks' unpaid leave to take care of a new baby or an old and ill relative, he acted on behalf of interest groups but against public opinion. President Clinton signed this popular legislation into law, his first such act, only 17 days after he took office in 1993.

Many people cannot understand policy unless it is translated into symbols that evoke their support or opposition, but simplistic policies that can be reduced to vivid symbols may not be good policies. Some authorities, for example, argue that Civil War reconstruction policies based on punishment of the South had substantial public support, yet were detrimental to the long-range interest of the nation. Others argue that the fervent anticommunist policies of the post–World War II era also had widespread public support but may have caused us to support doomed colonialist and totalitarian governments and overextend our military commitments in such places as Vietnam.

Symbols can also become more important than substance in wooing popular support. We do not think of interstate highways as national defense highways, but that is how they were packaged to the public in the National Defense Highway Act during the administration of President Dwight D. Eisenhower in the 1950s. Similarly, few people ever studied national defense under the National Defense Education Act of the same era; yet, many obtained their Ph.D. degrees through grants provided by the act. In the aftermath of World War II and the Korean War, national defense was a powerful symbol used to win support for public policies that bore little or no direct relationship to the substance of the policies. Words like *reform, peace, equal rights*, and *national defense* may offer appealing and irresistible titles for policy proposals. It's what's beneath the title, however, that's most important. Emotion-charged titles that misrepresent the substance of a policy proposal may preclude reasoned and reasonable debate.

The public need not totally understand either the policy or the process to appreciate the benefits derived. Countless policies reveal this truth. How many people really understand

- The policy of federal aid to local governments? Despite their lack of understanding, the public can enjoy the benefits of improved sewers and recreation facilities.

- The policy that led to construction of a network of federal highways? Without understanding how and why the various highway construction policies were approved, the public still can appreciate the benefits of easier and safer travel.

- The policy of federal aid to land grant colleges and universities? Yet, the public benefits from the enormous agricultural and technological advances made by these institutions.

Thus, we have ample examples of policies without substantial public involvement and understanding that have benefited our nation, and we have others in which the reverse may be true.

REASONS WHY EXPERTS SHOULD NOT HAVE MORE INFLUENCE OVER PUBLIC POLICY

A public policymaking process wholly controlled by experts and leaders would be undemocratic, and one controlled solely by the general public would be unwise. A balance between the two is necessary.

Experts have knowledge about policy issues that the general public does not possess, but the general public knows what is *acceptable* as public policy. Both elements are needed to make good public policy. While the experts and leaders should prod the public to accept what they consider good public policy, they cannot afford to resist concerted public opposition in a democratic environment.

A dynamic tension exists between the two. For example, school busing to achieve racial integration continued to be imposed as public policy by the courts until violent public protests erupted; in California, a statewide vote against busing demonstrated public opposition to the policy. Finally, some of the leading intellectual architects of the school

When Hillary Rodham Clinton and her task force were developing health care policy, they sought out the opinions of various segments of the public. Here she is listening to comments by steelworkers at Glazer Steel in New Orleans. She is accompanied by Louisiana's two senators and a congressman.

busing policy—the so-called experts—changed their minds. Public policy supporting America's involvement in Vietnam was largely controlled by specialists in foreign and military policy. When the public began to see the disastrous results of this policy, opposition developed that caused America to withdraw from Vietnam. President Bush, recognizing the failure of policy determined by specialists in Vietnam, acted before and during our involvement in the Persian Gulf War to ensure that public opinion was carefully considered and courted.

Of all phases of American government, the policy process is probably least understood. However, the key is not that the public understand the intricacies of the policy process, but that it be able to influence the development of public policy. Through letters, public opinion polls, and interest group representation, the public has opportunities to exercise influence. Even on those issues that do not interest the public, policymakers must develop public policy carefully, lest the public become aroused in opposition to those policies.

American democracy and effective public policymaking are not incompatible; they are essential partners. One without the other leads to disaster. Effective policymaking without democracy is authoritarian, while democracy without effective policymaking is mobocracy or chaos.

ISSUE 1: **Summary** ★ *Should Experts Have More Influence Over Public Policy Than the Public?*

Examples have been cited showing the problems of too much influence from both groups. Neither necessarily has a monopoly on the public interest. The public does not always know and understand its best interests, while experts and specialists do not always know what policy will be acceptable with the general public. A dynamic tension and proper balance need to exist between the two for public policy to serve the public interest. ■

ISSUE 2 SHOULD THE POLICYMAKING PROCESS BE A CAUSE FOR PESSIMISM OR OPTIMISM AMONG AMERICANS?

REASONS WHY THE POLICY PROCESS SHOULD BE A CAUSE FOR PESSIMISM

Americans' views of the world and their role in it deeply affect public policy. The progress of American political history has been marked by bold slogans like "manifest destiny," "fifty-four forty, or fight," and "a war to make the world safe for democracy"—rallying cries fueled by optimism. They ignited in the American spirit a desire either to conquer the North American continent or to spread American democracy throughout the world. Given the drive and determination of Americans, no obstacle seemed too big for American ingenuity. As late as the 1960s, political campaign slogans promising a "New Frontier" and a "Great Society" reinforced this historical belief in the American dream of spreading the good life as widely as possible. Today, however, despair competes with what had seemed to be an endless rhetoric of hope. There are many reasons why we should be pessimistic about the policy process.

Loss of Control. One factor contributing to an ostensibly growing feeling of gloom is the changing role of developing nations in Africa, Latin America, and Asia. Many such countries—longtime suppliers of raw materials for American industry—now wish to use their scarce resources for their own economic development. Their newfound economic muscle may shift the balance of power away from the West. Our economic policy must shift to take account of the scarcity of resources.

Then there are the political hotspots of the world—Bosnia, Somalia, the Middle East, and others—which may erupt without warning at any time. Since American policymakers have little or no control over when, why, and how these eruptions occur, our policy must of necessity be reactive rather than coherent and well planned.

We hear daily of population explosions and fuel shortages, pollution from oil slicks and acid rain, and incalculable and permanent damage to our environment. Are the American people willing to make the sacrifices necessary to solve their social, economic, and political problems? In the early 1990s health care costs were soaring out of control (Figure 15.2). The budget deficit seems to defy solution as Democrats and Republicans exchange charges and countercharges about who is at fault. Meanwhile, the public pays more money in interest, because the federal government absorbs so much money to finance the national debt.

Because people and parties have been unwilling to make the necessary sacrifices to solve problems, the outlook is for change forced on us by external events rather than

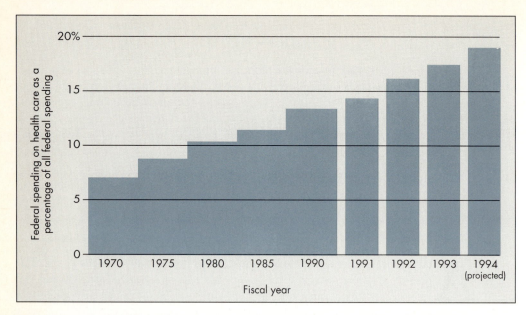

Figure 15.2   HEALTH CARE COSTS, 1970–1994. Source: The *New York Times*, February 3, 1993, p. A16. Copyright © 1993 by The New York Times Company. Reprinted by permission. Data from Congressional Budget Office.

by well-considered decisions, by crisis rather than by wise judgments. Race riots, street crime, drug abuse, airplane hijackings, bombings, and assassinations have created uneasiness and foreboding among Americans: We now question how civilized we really are. There has been a basic change in attitude: a loss of assurance and feeling of control over events, coupled with a growing belief that the quality of life is declining rather than improving. Americans generally used to believe that social change and improvements could be rationally engineered; now we have come to realize that massive expenditures to create a "Great Society" at home or to spread "the American way of life" abroad through foreign aid are not enough. Despite our efforts, poverty and racism abound.

Another symptom of malaise is dissatisfaction with civilization itself. People wonder whether their ancestors, with far fewer material goods, were perhaps happier than they are. Can more money, better food, medical triumphs, and scientific advances bring happiness? The Soviet Union's nuclear disaster at Chernobyl and the United States' disaster with the space shuttle "Challenger" encourage people to question just how beneficial technology is.

Disparities. The irony of the policy process in America is that the people it is supposed to benefit often do not receive the help. Airline and telephone deregulation illustrates how the average person may not benefit from supposed public policy reforms. Rather than bringing lower bills to average Americans, airline and telephone deregulation benefit (1) frequent fliers (usually business people) between large cities, and (2) habitual users (usually businesses) of long distance telephone lines. Many communities that had airline service lost it after airline deregulation, and telephone companies increased the cost of local service. Moreover, while a small business may fail and file for bankruptcy, huge companies like Chrysler merely turn to the government to bail them out.

This man is searching for coins in the burnt-out remains of his apartment in Los Angeles after the riots of April 1992. Such events reinforce the foreboding and pessimism that many Americans feel about the quality of life in their country.

Influence of Special Interests. Increasingly, democratic governments find that they are responding to important substantive decisions that have been made by special-interest groups of one kind or another. For example, when a major corporation decides to raise its prices, the government seems unable to reverse a decision that will feed the inflationary spiral. The same situation exists with respect to labor union demands for higher pay and more fringe benefits. More and more frequently, the policies that vitally affect people are made *outside* the representative institutions of democracy or they are made *through* the influence of special interests on legislators.

American government has been plagued by the **revolving door**, which moves high-level bureaucrats in and out of government and the private sector. An arms-control specialist in the Pentagon may leave to work for a weapons maker and later return to the Pentagon, or a social welfare specialist may leave an interest group to work for the Department of Health and Human Services, only to return later to that or another interest group. (One of President Clinton's first acts limited the revolving door for his senior appointees by requiring that they not lobby the government on matters related to their government work for five years after leaving government office.)

Networks, informal groups of people known to one another who communicate on policy ideas of common interest, are yet another problem. Professionals usually belong to such informal networks, particularly in Washington, which may narrow the scope of advice and counsel the government receives on a policy proposal. Persons or groups outside of these policy networks find it difficult to influence the process. The tendency of network members is to talk only with those with whom they are in general agreement, which limits influences on the making of policy. "Inside the beltway" has become an off-handed phrase to describe the networks inside Washington, which do not consult with or may not even care about popular or professional opinion "outside the beltway," across the 50 states.

The question also arises whether democratic government is even relevant in a highly industrialized society. Can democratically elected representatives rationally and thoroughly debate complex technological issues? Can voters rationally and thoroughly communicate with their elected representatives on these issues? Can such topics be properly discussed in political campaigns characterized by brief television commercials and short newspaper advertisements? These questions undermine the historic premise that the people can govern.

Influence of Organized Crime. Nowhere is the gloom and despair of the policymaking process more justified than in the influence of organized crime, especially at the state and local levels. Historically, the most dramatic example of organized crime's influence on the policy process occurred during prohibition of the sale of alcohol in the 1920s. By corrupting public officials, organized crime effectively negated the national policy.

Contemporary organized crime, now much more sophisticated than in the days of Al Capone, uses a combination of methods to corrupt the policymaking process. First, the standard method of bribery offers public officials sums of money in exchange for favorable policy considerations. Second, accommodation occurs when a politician in need of campaign funds accepts those given by organized crime. In turn, the crime syndicate expects the politician to influence policy decisions on its behalf. Third, by buying into legitimate banks and businesses and controlling labor unions, organized crime can influence public policymaking with hardly anyone suspecting its presence.

REASONS WHY THE POLICYMAKING PROCESS SHOULD BE A CAUSE FOR OPTIMISM

The prophets of doom have overstated their case, and their predictions are unduly influenced by immediate events and short-term considerations. The problems we face can be solved through the application of adequate technology and social engineering. The resources necessary to continue a respectable rate of economic growth do exist, and the technology necessary to acquire those resources is within our grasp.

Recent books such as Joseph Nye's *Bound to Lead*,[4] Michael Barone's *Our Country: The Shaping of America from Roosevelt to Reagan*,[5] Henry R. Nau's *The Myth of America's Decline: Leading the World Economy into the 1990s*,[6] and an earlier book by Ben J. Wattenberg, *The Real America*,[7] make the case that in both domestic and foreign policy, America is doing quite well. Using a wide array of historical and statistical data, they argue that economic indicators, such as income, education, and housing quality, reveal an optimistic picture about America's economy. Workers now have more money, more leisure, and more security than ever before. American economic growth requires the purchase of more raw materials, which helps developing nations. Our indirect contribution to their economies allows them to consume more goods and services. We should allow our technology to develop new resources to support a continually expanding economy.

Because of programs like Medicaid, Medicare, food stamps, housing subsidies, school lunches, and other noncash benefits, as well as general economic growth, the poor in American society have been significantly aided. As shown in Table 15.4, the percentage below the poverty line has dropped from about 22.4 percent in 1959 to about 12.8 percent

TABLE 15.4	PROPORTION OF POPULATION HAVING POVERTY STATUS, 1959–1989			
	White	African-American	Hispanic	Total
1959	18.1%	55.1%	NA	22.4%
1969	9.5%	32.2%	NA	12.1%
1979	9.0%	31.0%	21.8%	11.7%
1989	10.0%	30.7%	26.2%	12.8%

Source: U.S. Bureau of the Census, Current Population Reports, "Money, Income and Poverty Status in the United States: 1989" (Washington, D.C.: U.S. Government Printing Office, 1990), Series P-60, no. 168, 57–58 as reported in Harold W. Stanley and Richard G. Niemi, *Vital Statistics on American Politics*, Third Edition (Washington, D.C.: Congressional Quarterly Press, 1992), p. 375.

in 1989. Also since 1950, the median years of school completed has increased from 9.3 to 12.7 (Table 15.5). Americans have reason to be optimistic when they realize how much less time they have to work than residents of other countries must to acquire basic goods and services. (Figure 15.3).

There are policy crises, such as oil spills, fuel shortages, race riots, and nuclear accidents, but the policy process responds to these crises with methodical and well-considered reactions that permit optimism in the long run. By its very nature the policy process generally must be one of reaction rather than initiation. Often a crisis is necessary to create sufficient public awareness and support for a policy to resolve the problems that precipitated the crisis. For example, until a crisis occurred in America's financial institutions, there was insufficient awareness of the problem to even ignite a debate in Congress on the subject.

Groups disaffected and alienated by policies need not resign themselves to gloom and despair. Rather, they can assert themselves with the goal of changing the offending policy. They may even be joined in the process by previous opponents. Dr. Bernard

TABLE 15.5	MEDIAN YEARS OF SCHOOL COMPLETED, 1950–1989, BY PERSONS AGE 25 AND OVER		
	All Persons	African-Americans	Hispanics
1950	9.3	6.8	NA
1960	10.6	8.0	NA
1970	12.1	9.8	9.1
1980	12.5	12.0	10.8
1989	12.7	12.4	12.0

Sources: 1950–1980: U.S. Bureau of the Census, *Statistical Abstract of the United States, 1990* (Washington, D.C.: U.S. Government Printing Office, 1990), p. 134; 1989: U.S. Bureau of the Census, Current Population Survey, unpublished data as cited in Harold W. Stanley and Richard G. Niemi, *Vital Statistics on American Politics*, Third Edition (Washington, D.C.: Congressional Quarterly Press, 1992), p. 388.

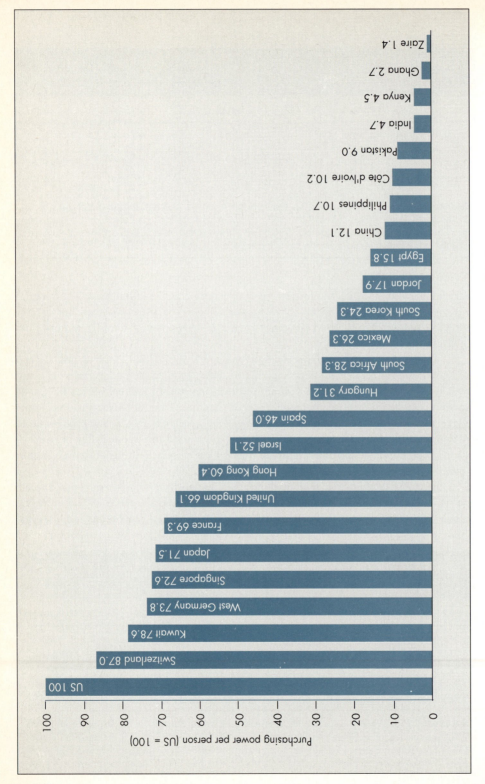

Figure 15.3 PURCHASING POWER PARITY, BY SELECTED COUNTRIES, 1988. Just how well (or how poorly) residents of other countries compare to the United States in purchasing power is shown here by arbitrarily setting U.S. purchasing power equal to 100. The Spanish and the Israelis have approximately half the purchasing power of Americans, while residents of Zaire have only 1.4 percent of the purchasing power of Americans. Source: *The Economist Book of Vital World Statistics: A Portrait of Everything Significant in the World Today* (New York: Time Books, 1990), p. 31.

Nathanson was a leader in the pro-choice movement for ten years and performed several thousand abortions. Then in his book *Aborting America*, he documented his change on this policy issue: "Parents may not abandon their children; why should they be encouraged to abandon their children-to-be? One race ought not exploit another; why should the already-born be allowed to exploit the not-yet-born?"[8]

Conservatives, once on the outside of American politics, organized to elect two presidents in a row, Reagan and Bush, and to alter the course of American public policy domestically and internationally. Their opponents organized and fought to reverse these policies rather than resigning themselves to defeat and despair. They succeeded in electing a more liberal president in 1992 who proceeded to change Republican policies.

Another cause for optimism is that the policy process has been opened up since the mid-1960s in a variety of ways. First, public access to and review of the governmental policy process has increased. Information flows more freely from the policymakers to the public directly, as well as through intermediary groups and elected representatives. Second, equality of representation (implemented with the *Baker* v. *Carr* decision in 1962) has allowed urban and suburban groups proportionate influence in legislative bodies and their policymaking procedures. Third, the greater participation of the public in the selection of presidential nominees through the primaries has made the presidency more responsive to people. This public involvement probably brought about the nomination of different types of presidential candidates and thereby influenced the policy process in the executive branch. If nothing else, the political bosses, where they still exist, no longer have the national influence they had in previous generations.

ISSUE 2: Summary ★ *Should the Policymaking Process Be a Cause for Pessimism or Optimism Among Americans?*

In the short run or with nearsighted vision, the policymaking process provides many examples and good reasons to be pessimistic. The saying, "If you like sausage, don't look how it's made, and if you like the product of congressional action, don't look how the bills are passed," conveys a great deal of truth. The process of making public policy is not neat and tidy, and frequently provides reason for concern. However, if we look at how the policymaking process has adjusted and changed to accommodate differing American needs and public pressures, then there is reason for optimism. In the long run the policymaking process dynamically responds to forces for change. ■

⊕ COMPARISONS WITH OTHER NATIONS

The United States shares many public policy issues and severe problems with most of the other democracies. (Of course, many of the world's nondemocracies, which tend also to be the less economically prosperous countries, would be happy to have our problems.) All of the democracies have mixed economies that offer a blend of private and public sector activities. But not all of them have the same emphasis. There is, as we have already seen, a much greater governmental role in the Scandinavian systems than in the American one. The United States, unlike most democracies, has resisted an expanding role of government in areas such as health care (although the Clinton administration began working early to explore the prospect of national health insurance). The term *welfare state* has frightened more Americans than have been attracted to it.

Part of the discrepancy between the policies of American and Western European democracies is explained by the earlier and unprecedented national wealth achieved by the United States. This was the first country in the world to provide such great conveniences as affordable cars and accessible universities. American industry made it unnecessary for American government to do what national governments were doing in places as diverse as the Soviet Union and Japan as early as the 1930s: developing a cheap and efficient public transportation system for the entire country. Instead, most middle-class Americans were then able to purchase a car of their own (a new one would cost about $500, but with only one choice of color—black). Most Western Europeans had to wait another generation before owning a private car, and most Eastern Europeans and Russians are still waiting.

PUBLIC POLICY IN DEMOCRACIES

As would be expected, the electorate often broadly dictates the direction and impact of public policy in democracies. In 1945, for example, the British elected a Labour government. The Labour party had since the beginning of the century called for the nationalization of selected industries, as in the areas of transportation and steel production. Assuming it had a mandate to act after the election, the government proceeded accordingly. When the Conservatives returned to power in 1951 they denationalized some of what the Labourites had nationalized, again following what they believed to be popular endorsement of policy. By the 1990s both parties had more or less done what they wanted and reached an accord. The goal was to provide adequate services to the people, and the people did not necessarily care whether it was government or private industry that did the job.

Foreign policy among the democracies has a great deal to do with how they view one another. The American-Japanese rivalry is a real one and has engendered a hate-love perspective on both sides. In the United States, even as sales of Japanese products are booming, there are public pressures on the Congress to curb Japanese imports until Japan allows the entrance of more American imports. But the Japanese government has its own and similar problems. Elements within its electorate are every bit as protectionist as their counterparts in the United States. The leading Liberal Democrat party of Japan tries to be "all things to all voters":

> The party is divided into a protectionist wing, devoted to farmers and small shopkeepers, and a modern wing, in favour of city-dwelling consumers and an outward-looking foreign policy. This election might have forced a choice between these tendencies; instead, the party won by forgetting policy and appealing to every special interest it could. A party whose campaign thundered to farmers that "not a single grain of rice will be imported!" is not ideally placed to make Japan a welcome member of the post–cold-war world.[9]

As serious as they are, problems of trade among democracies pale into insignificance compared to the issues of public policy that await them in the closing years of the twentieth century and the opening years of the twenty-first. Large numbers of people are on the move in much of the world, a migration that has no parallel since the fall of the Roman Empire 1,500 years ago.

This creates a public policy issue with a double-edged sword. The good news is that the migrants are mostly young people in search of better lives; they are determined to escape the ruined economies of Eastern Europe or the underdeveloped ones of the Third World. The movement presents a relatively new experience for Western Europeans and a familiar one for the United States. The most-developed industrialized economies are the ones with the aging work forces. New workers may have to be recruited from the outside in substantial numbers. But this could mean that indigenous French, German, and British workers will increasingly be replaced by or will work alongside of African, Middle Eastern, and South Asian ones. Western European governments are already feeling the pressures of nativist organizations that have formed political parties in order to press for stricter immigration laws.

The Japanese too have an aging labor force, but are expected to remain steadfastly opposed to bringing in workers from the outside. Instead, they have adopted the technology of robotics to ease the burden of the Japanese laborer.

Interestingly, this is no problem for the United States. One out of every 12 people in this country is foreign-born (and that figure considers only the legal residents). The Europeans are catching up: In 1990, 1.3 million people moved from Eastern to Western Europe.[10] That is probably only the beginning. A new emigration law in Russia allows up to two million people to leave the country every year, assuming they can find countries willing to accept them. It is safe to assume that most of these will want to migrate either to Western Europe or the United States. Hundreds of thousands of Russian Jews have already left, providing Israel with an oversupply of physicians, engineers, and technicians.

As the United States continues to be a haven for millions of immigrants, primarily from the Third World, Americans will become an even more heterogeneous society. This demographic transition will influence the formulation of both domestic and foreign policy. For example, an increasing number of college and university students will be foreign-born, especially from Asia. These students tend to be serious, and many of them will remain in the United States to pursue productive careers.

In the meantime, the high-priority domestic policy issues of health and education remain. The cost of both worries governments. Americans, for example, spend more on their health than any other country in the world, yet their life span is still lower and infant mortality rate higher than those of many other countries (see Table 15.6). Is this because government-sponsored health care has been lacking in the United States? Not necessarily. The American government has taken the lead in advertising good health habits, such as requiring product warning labels about the dangers of smoking and alcohol. Japan, by contrast, is way behind American policy in this area and has only recently decided to prohibit smoking in certain public places. Two out of three Japanese adult males smoke and drink. Although the Japanese still have lower cancer and heart disease rates than the United States, they are working hard to catch up. They eagerly import American beef and cigarettes. Japanese teenagers are taller than any previous generation, but they are also fatter, and their health may eventually be affected by all the animal fat they are now consuming. Health policies may have to be changed in drastic ways in Japan.

Previous generations of immigrants to America often arrived with little or no

TABLE 15.6   HEALTH INDICATORS IN SELECTED COUNTRIES

Country	LIFE EXPECTANCY		INFANT MORTALITY (PER 1,000 LIVE BIRTHS)	
	Male	Female	Maternal	Infant
Australia	73	80	8	9
Canada	73	80	7	6
France	72	80	8	5
Iceland	75	80	na	na
Italy	72	79	10	10
Japan	75	81	5	5
Netherlands	74	80	5	8
New Zealand	72	80	10	5
Norway	74	80	2	8
Spain	74	80	11	9
Sweden	74	80	5	6
Switzerland	74	80	5	7
United States	**72**	**79**	**9**	**10**

Source: Adopted from *Book of Vital World Statistics: A Portrait of Everything Significant in the World Today* (New York: Time Books, 1990), p. 214.

formal education and worked in sweatshops. The luckier ones were able to open their own small businesses. Today's immigrants, though, are arriving as engineers and physicians or studying for those professions. The newer immigrants are also influencing educational policy in those areas where they are concentrated, particularly huge metropolitan areas such as New York and Los Angeles. The dramatic rise in the number of Asian and Hispanic residents during the 1980s is inducing some curriculum changes in the disciplines of history and popular culture. No longer is it being assumed that American society is the result of strictly European influences. The impact of cultures less familiar to Americans of European descent will surely cause educational policies in several locales to be revised.

The realization that inadequate or nonexistent educations inevitably damage economic progress has not been lost on the industrialized democracies. The United States compares well to the other established democracies in keeping teenagers in school. There is little difference, for example, in the dropout rate between American and Japanese 17-year-olds. But the issue of *quality* of education is another matter. The Japanese school year is substantially longer than ours and Japanese students tend to be in school six days a week. Most other countries have longer school years than we do (Figure 15.4). About 2 percent of American students are now in experimental year-long school systems. This innovative policy change could drastically change the format of public education in the United States.

PUBLIC POLICY IN TOTALITARIAN SYSTEMS

Policymaking in many totalitarian societies has often been guided or enforced by inflexible ideology. In China, for example, the period of the Great Leap Forward (1958–1966)

A VIEW FROM THE STATES
Lessons from Asia

Huge, rich and accustomed to thinking of itself as uniquely successful, the United States has never been good at learning from other countries. This can be a costly blind spot. Answers to many of the woes Americans are struggling to correct in their education system, argues Harold Stevenson, are evident in Asian classrooms.

Mr. Stevenson, professor of psychology at the University of Michigan, and his colleagues have spent more than a decade in meticulous comparison of American, Japanese, Chinese and Taiwan classrooms. Choosing schools in similar-sized cities and students of comparable socioeconomic levels, and using tests in each language of the material in each curriculum, their work confirms that the difference in academic achievement begins by first grade. By fifth grade, what was a narrow gap is a chasm.

In math, only 1 percent of Chinese students scored as low as the American mean. Reading abilities were comparable, although the Chinese students had had to learn thousands of characters and the Japanese the equivalent of several Roman alphabets.

Having confirmed what other studies had shown, Mr. Stevenson asked why. . . . His conclusions . . . make fascinating reading. They shatter a lot of myths.

Television watching is not crucial: Japanese students watch even more than do Americans. Asian elementary schools are not grim drill shops. The school day is longer mostly because of nonacademic activities, although the school year is 60 days longer.

Some findings also highlight the obvious. American children do much less homework—about one-fourth as much as students in Taiwan and half as much as those in Japan. And Americans spend less time reading for pleasure in the kindergarten to high school years. . . .

American teachers spend nearly their whole day in charge of a classroom, and carry a heavy administrative burden to boot. Asian teachers spend only three to five hours that way. . . .

The Asian system does not require money, because fresher, better prepared teachers are able to handle larger classes. Discipline is less of a problem, partly because there is more time for active play—an average of 50 to 60 minutes per day in Japan as compared to 11 minutes per day in the American schools that Mr. Stevenson studied. In Japan there is a play break before every class. . . .

. . . Asian parents see education as vital to their children's future, whether they are college-bound or not. Few Americans feel that way.

Asian children get the message. When asked to make a single wish, 70 percent of the Chinese children wished for something related to education; fewer than 10 percent of the Americans did. At the core of many of these differences is the far greater emphasis Americans place on innate ability in determining achievement. Asians stress effort. . . . The belief in effort as the key to success engages parent, child and teacher in a shared endeavor.

Source: Jessica Mathews, "Schools in Japan, China, Taiwan Have Lessons to Teach America," *The Washington Post*, reprinted in *International Herald Tribune*, December 2, 1992.

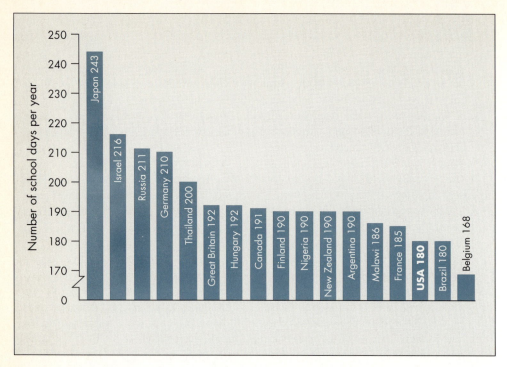

Figure 15.4 SCHOOL DAYS IN SELECTED COUNTRIES. The length of the school year varies in a range of nations around the world. With its six-day school weeks, Japan has the longest school year (243 days). The United States ranks fairly low in number of school days (180). Source: *World Monitor*, September 1992, p. 11. Data from Education Commission of the States' Information Clearinghouse, January 1991; International Institute for Education Planning; Embassy of Brazil.

turned out to be the great leap backward. China's leader Mao Tse-tung had determined that the way for China to catch up with the industrialized West was for hundreds of millions of Chinese to work at backyard steel furnaces which would produce unprecedented amounts of steel. Wrong. For a variety of reasons (not the least of which was the skill level of farmers who were told they had to make steel), it didn't work at all.

China's communist ideologues did not learn their lesson. Mao determined that too many Chinese had too little familiarity with the revolution that had brought the communists to power in 1949. He insisted on self-destructive policy decisions by engaging in the Great Cultural Revolution. From 1966 to 1976, an entire generation was forced to abandon their education and their professions by undertaking simple labor and undergoing ideological indoctrination intended to rekindle revolutionary fervor. All that was achieved was additional economic backwardness and a low standard of living that even in the 1990s is still recovering from long neglect.

But by the early 1980s the Chinese leadership had changed and so had economic (but not political) policy. Government restraints were removed on large segments of the economy. A decade later the Chinese gross national product was growing at the rate of 12 percent a year (the highest growth rate in the world), a remarkable achievement for any economy and one that, if maintained, could produce a larger economy by the middle of the next century than the one currently enjoyed in the United States.[11] And there were smaller signs that by the 1990s China's social policies might be easing. For example, while the Chinese government condemns homosexuality as a "decadent Western import," it has nonetheless allowed a group of homosexuals in Beijing to form China's first "men's club."[12]

As the Soviet Union disintegrated and as the Eastern European communist regimes fell away during the late 1980s and the early 1990s, their intense centralization revealed policy formats that are prescriptions for national disasters. Their controlled economy ensured that production quotas were determined by bureaucrats unknowledgeable about some of the industries for which they had responsibility. It was often said of the former Soviet Union that the state pretended to pay workers and the workers pretended to produce. Even if one had money it wouldn't buy much.

Perhaps the biggest problem for policymaking in a totalitarian system is surviving the aftermath of the system's collapse. After all, once the entrenched leadership was gone, few were around who knew about decision or policymaking. It was a new experience. In the remnants of the Soviet Union, for instance, the gross national product (GNP) declined by unprecedented amounts—amounting to 17 percent of a GNP of perhaps $2.5 trillion in 1991.[13] Without being told how much to produce or even to produce at all, state industries' workers simply stopped producing anything of value. Not enough individual initiative was available to replace the centralized control that had suddenly disappeared. After generations of totalitarianism and centuries of old-fashioned autocracy, many former Soviet citizens were shocked to learn that no one was any longer in a position of absolute power, with the authority to direct the economic and political affairs of the country. Rank-and-file Russians would now have to do that for themselves. They will, if they can figure out how. Factory managers are on the front line of frustration: "Managers who functioned successfully when the Army (indeed, the entire Government) was a reliable supplier and customer now realize that they simply do not know how to operate in a market economy, and that no one is around to tell them."[14] New economic policies must allow for patience and understanding.

PUBLIC POLICY IN AUTHORITARIAN SYSTEMS

The long-standing tradition of central control remains a cornerstone of authoritarian regimes, especially those that view themselves as having a mission. A former president of Iran who went into exile because he disagreed with the religious extremism of the Islamic mullahs, or theological leaders, summed up the Iranian government's policymaking agenda this way: "We don't need to build dams, factories, hospitals, or schools because the goal of the regime is to teach people how to die. For that, all we need to do is to organize violence."[15]

Authoritarian governments tend to neglect domestic needs. Often, they do so deliberately. In fact, impoverishment of the population may actually be a policy goal, since impoverished societies tend to be quiet ones. The overwhelming majority of the population are too sick and malnourished to plan or participate in a revolution. The authoritarian regime feels secure and comfortable this way. It is mindful of the historical

lesson that revolutions occur in societies that are starting to become economically prosperous rather than in those where most people live at a subsistence level.

Some authoritarian regimes, albeit only a minority, do pursue economically
productive policies. Chile actually prospered under the Pinochet dictatorship from 1973
until 1989. But this experiment also proved the point indicated above. As the economy
prospered Chileans became increasingly interested in their own political destiny and
began to demand the end of military dictatorship.

The policy process in authoritarian systems, then, is often deceptively simple.
Since, at any time, an authoritarian regime may be confronted with an armed revolt, its
primary focus is on staying in power. This concern allows the military and police apparatus
to exercise substantial influence in both domestic and foreign policymaking. During the
Cold War era many authoritarian regimes justified their existence on the basis of being a
"bulwark against communism." The military enjoyed enough prestige and influence to
either control the government outright or dominate a nominally civilian government.
For example, the South Korean regime, until it began a democratization process in recent
years, solicited, often successfully, economic and technical assistance from the United
States by pursuing a strong anticommunist policy. Another East Asian society emerging
from authoritarian to democratic political institutions is Taiwan, which, by the late 1980s,
was getting into the habit of free and contested elections.

Perhaps one explanation for the demise of several authoritarian regimes in recent
years is the easily demonstrated bankruptcy of their policies. Remaining in power and
resisting communism tended to be very compatible policies. But the unexpected sudden
collapse of communism in Eastern Europe and the Soviet Union has nearly eliminated
the excuse for such a policy. Even so, there is still a pronounced reluctance in much of
the world to embark on democratization.

And those countries that are attempting to make the transition from authoritarian to democratic regimes are not having an easy time of it, especially in the poorer
countries. Bolivia, for example, has a very low standard of living. Previous authoritarian
regimes neglected the physical well-being and health of the population so thoroughly
that diarrhea become the second leading cause of death.[16] Bolivia's population can be
broken down as follows:

1. Top group of one million who enjoy good health care, high incomes, and
   educational opportunities
2. Middle class of three million who tend to live in cities and have at least
   basic services
3. Urban poor class of two million who live at a subsistence level
4. One million completely removed from the niceties of education, health
   care, adequate housing, and physical security[17]

In a country of only seven million it is difficult to create a productive economy
when nearly half the population is barely making it. The recently installed democratic
Bolivian government has therefore undertaken policies to improve living conditions for
at least the bottom one million, in order to create a work force that is capable of
contributing to the overall economy.[18]

Bolivia's very low standard of living complicates the country's effort to make the transition from an authoritarian to a democratic regime. How can Bolivia hope to generate a productive economy with nearly half the population living at or below a subsistence level?

Democracies that are emerging from the wreckage of authoritarian systems have a long road to travel. Often there is little with which to work. Deposed authoritarians have frequently looted their countries or limited economic growth by discouraging the growth of a middle class. A succeeding democratic government can expect to find an emptied national treasury; scientists, technicians, and intellectuals—the sort of people who help build a middle class—in exile; and little, if any, foreign investment. The policy process for the authoritarian regime was, after all, basically self-serving.

As the Soviet and Yugoslav systems have dissolved, the political direction of their constituent parts seems uncertain. It may be too much to hope that they will all become democratic states. One of the obstacles that may prevent them from doing so is the large number of claims several countries are making on one another's territory. These claims are based on historical or cultural ties and are complicated by the presence of large ethnic minorities in the disputed territory. Ironically, authoritarian systems may in part succeed the communist ones. The foreign policy implications for the United States are impressive and even unprecedented for the following reasons:

1. Millions of Americans have ethnic ancestries that make them sympathetic with claims for sovereignty and territory and to some degree divide them into competing interest groups.

2. Countries that are achieving sovereignty not only may be authoritarian, but also may inherit nuclear weapons and/or technology that could make their neighbors (the ones they are having border disputes with) understandably nervous.

3. New members of the United Nations, especially if they have authoritarian regimes, will surely pursue policies contrary to what the United States would prefer. Discrimination against ethnic minorities and violations of human rights will almost certainly be considerations. American foreign policy may have to undergo reevaluation.

The last years of the twentieth century will be challenging and dangerous ones filled with uncertain and unprecedented policy dilemmas. But they will also be a reminder that government, especially democratic government, must at all times be aware that policy-formulation and implementation require knowledge as well as power.

Summary

1. When a government establishes a goal and makes decisions to achieve that goal, it is making public policy. Public policymaking is a complex process because it involves a number of decision makers who must reach an agreement. Public policies also can overlap and conflict.

2. American foreign policy has gradually changed from an emphasis on isolation to acceptance of a world role, particularly after World War II and during the era of "containment" of communism during the Cold War.

3. Events such as the Great Depression and changing demographics have necessitated new or drastically revised domestic policies, including a large presence of government from the 1930s on, as well as a call for a reduced role in the 1980s.

4. Like most industrialized countries, the United States has a mixed economy of socialist and capitalist ingredients. The latter has been emphasized in this country, while more socialist characteristics have been institutionalized in other democracies, such as the Scandinavian societies.

5. Policymaking proceeds through several phases. By the time a policy is implemented it may have undergone substantial change and be in the hands of a bureaucracy that controls how the policy is applied.

6. Policymaking in the United States is characterized by incrementalism, impermanence, dynamism, the use of symbols, complexity, multiple decision makers, and outside influences. The public play a role in policymaking through their elected representatives or, where it is practical, through direct participation as in town meetings. Interest groups and elite groups also have an influence on the policies that are developed.

7. Specialists play a necessary role in policymaking. But the importance of the role is debatable since specialists have been criticized for not fully considering public preferences.

8. The policy process seems a cause for despair when one considers the number of problems that defy solution, the disparities caused by certain policies, and the influence of special interests and organized crime. On the other hand, public policies have in the long run responded to the need for change and provided Americans with a relatively high standard of living.

9. Like the United States, other countries practice policies that may be economically self-defeating. Japan's unequivocal protection of its inefficient rice farmers is an example.

10. A great policy issue that looms on the horizon for many, if not most, of the industrialized democracies is the growing immigration of manual workers from the Third World and from Eastern Europe and the Soviet Union. Governments will have to decide how to best care for and educate large numbers of newcomers.

11. The centralized control of the economy in communist societies was an enforced and mistaken policy that benefited only bureaucrats. Ideology has driven some disastrous policy decisions in China. In former communist systems policies must be created anew to inspire and encourage individual innovation.

12. Authoritarian regimes don't usually offer productive or compassionate policies because the regime is usually solely concerned with policies that keep it in power.

13. New democracies that succeed authoritarian regimes in the Third World often find it difficult to develop policies to alleviate or significantly reduce poverty because of the long-term neglect that characterized the preceding authoritarian regimes.

Terms to Define

Capitalist model	Mixed model
Communist model	Networks
Containment	New world order
Detente	Public policy
Distributive policy	Redistributive policy
Fascist model	Regulatory policy
Foreign aid	Revolving door
Isolationism	Socialist model
Keynesian economics	Supply-side economics
Laissez faire	

Suggested Readings

Anderson, James E. *Public Policymaking*. Boston: Houghton Mifflin, 1990. A brief survey of the policymaking system.

Friedman, Benjamin. *Day of Reckoning*. New York: Random House, 1988. Presents a liberal perspective on what should be done to reduce the deficit.

Hilsman, Roger. *The Politics of Policymaking in Defense and Foreign Affairs*. Englewood Cliffs, N.J.: Prentice-Hall, 1987. Reviews theories about how foreign policy is made.

Leichter, Howard M. *Free to be Foolish: Politics and Health Promotion in the United States and Great Britain.* Princeton: Princeton University Press, 1991. The role of the state in health care is discussed in terms of how far the state can go in a democracy to encourage citizens to behave in ways that will improve or maintain their health.

Murray, Charles. *Losing Ground: American Social Policy, 1950–1980.* New York: Basic Books, 1984. Contends that social welfare policies have failed to improve life for the poor and may have made conditions worse than they should be.

Rosenbaum, Walter A. *Environmental Politics and Policy,* 2nd ed. Washington, D.C.: Congressional Quarterly Press, 1991. Examines policymaking on environmental issues, such as air, water, chemicals, nuclear power, and space.

Schwarz, John E. *America's Hidden Success: A Reassessment of Twenty Years of Public Policy,* 2nd ed. New York: Norton, 1988. Defends the Great Society social welfare programs, contending that they reduced poverty and achieved additionally helpful goals.

Weidenbaum, Murray. *Rendezvous with Reality.* New York: Basic Books, 1988. Offers a conservative perspective on what should be done to reduce the deficit.

Notes

1. *Regents of University of California* v. *Bakke,* 438 U.S. 265 (1978).
2. *Brown* v. *Board of Education,* 347 U.S. 483 (1954).
3. *Alexander* v. *Holmes County Board of Education,* 369 U.S. 19 (1969).
4. Joseph Nye, *Bound to Lead: The Changing Nature of American Power* (New York: Basic Books, 1991).
5. Michael Barone, *Our Country: The Shaping of America from Roosevelt to Reagan* (New York: Free Press, 1990).
6. Henry R. Nau, *The Myth of America's Decline: Leading the World Economy into the 1990s* (New York and Oxford: Oxford University Press, 1990).
7. Ben J. Wattenberg, *The Real America* (New York: G.P. Putnam's Sons, 1974).
8. Bernard Nathanson, *Aborting America* (Garden City, N.Y.: Doubleday, 1979). See also *The Washington Post,* September 27, 1979, p. A23.
9. "On Being a Good Neighbor: The Opportunities for Japan, and the Dangers," *The Economist,* February 24, 1990, p. 12.
10. "Europe's Would-be Westerners," *The Economist,* August 17, 1991, p. 12.
11. *The Economist,* January 23, 1993, pp. 17, 18, 31, 32.
12. "Morning Edition," National Public Radio, February 8, 1993.
13. Craig Forman, "Freedom's Perils: Soviet Economy Holds Potential for Disaster as the Union Weakens," *The Wall Street Journal,* September 4, 1991, A1.
14. Steven Erlanger, "A Typical Town in Russia, Caught in the Market's Web," *The New York Times,* January 5, 1993, pp. A1 and A6.
15. Abol Hassas Bani-Sadr, *My Turn to Speak: Iran, the Revolution & Secret Deals with the U.S.* [Washington: Brassey's (U.S.), Inc., 1991], p. 4.
16. "The forgotten," *The Economist,* August 17, 1991, p. 40.
17. Ibid.
18. Ibid.

THE DECLARATION OF INDEPENDENCE

IN CONGRESS, JULY 4, 1776

When in the Course of human events it becomes necessary for one people to dissolve the political bands which have connected them with another, and to assume among the Powers of the earth, the separate and equal station to which the Laws of Nature and of Nature's God entitle them, a decent respect to the opinions of mankind requires that they should declare the causes which impel them to the separation.

We hold these truths to be self-evident, that all men are created equal, that they are endowed by their Creator with certain unalienable Rights, that among these are Life, Liberty and the pursuit of Happiness. That to secure these rights, Governments are instituted among Men, deriving their just Powers from the consent of the governed. That whenever any Form of Government becomes destructive of these ends, it is the Right of the People to alter or to abolish it, and to institute new Government, laying its foundation on such principles and organizing its Powers in such form, as to them shall seem most likely to effect their Safety and Happiness. Prudence, indeed, will dictate that Governments long established should not be changed for light and transient causes; and accordingly all experience hath shown, that mankind are more disposed to suffer, while evils are sufferable, than to right themselves by abolishing the forms to which they are accustomed. But when a long train of abuses and usurpations, pursuing invariably the same Object evinces a design to reduce them under absolute Despotism, it is their right, it is their duty to throw off such Government, and to provide new Guards for their future security. Such has been the patient sufferance of these Colonies; and such is now the necessity which constrains them to alter their former Systems of Government. The history of the present King of Great Britain is a history of repeated injuries and usurpations, all having in direct object the establishment of an absolute Tyranny over these States. To prove this, let Facts be submitted to a candid world.

He has refused his Assent to Laws, the most wholesome and necessary for the public good.

He has forbidden his Governors to pass Laws of immediate and pressing importance, unless suspended in their operation till his Assent should be obtained; and when so suspended, he has utterly neglected to attend to them.

He has refused to pass other Laws for the accommodation of large districts of people, unless those people would relinquish the right of Representation in the Legislature, a right inestimable to them and formidable to tyrants only.

He has called together legislative bodies at places unusual, uncomfortable, and distant from the depository of their Public Records, for the sole Purpose of fatiguing them into compliance with his measures.

He has dissolved Representative Houses repeatedly, for opposing with manly firmness his invasions on the rights of the People.

He has refused for a long time, after such dissolutions, to cause others to be elected; whereby the Legislative Powers, incapable of Annihilation, have returned to the People at large for their exercise; the State remaining in the mean time exposed to all the dangers of invasion from without, and convulsions within.

He has endeavoured to prevent the Population of these States; for that purpose obstructing the Laws for Naturalization of Foreigners; refusing to pass others to encourage their migrations hither, and raising the conditions of new Appropriations of Lands.

He has obstructed the Administration of Justice, by refusing his Assent to Laws for establishing Judiciary Powers.

He has made Judges dependent on his Will alone, for the tenure of their offices, and the amount and payment of their salaries.

He has erected a multitude of New Offices, and sent hither swarms of Officers to harass our People, and eat out their substance.

He has kept among us, in times of peace, Standing Armies without the consent of our legislatures.

He has affected to render the Military independent of and superior to the Civil Power.

He has combined with others to subject us to a jurisdiction foreign to our constitution, and unacknowledged by our laws; giving his Assent to their Acts of pretended Legislation:

For quartering large bodies of armed troops among us:

For protecting them, by a mock Trial, from Punishment for any Murders which they should commit on the Inhabitants of these States:

For cutting off our Trade with all parts of the world:

For imposing Taxes on us without our Consent:

For depriving us in many cases, of the benefits of Trial by Jury:

For transporting us beyond Seas to be tried for pretended offences:

For abolishing the free System of English Laws in a neighboring Province, establishing therein an Arbitrary government, and enlarging its Boundaries so as to render it at once an example and fit instrument for introducing the same absolute rule into these Colonies:

For taking away our Charters, abolishing our most valuable Laws, and altering fundamentally the Forms of our Governments:

For suspending our own Legislatures, and declaring themselves invested with Power to legislate for us in all cases whatsoever.

He has abdicated Government here, by declaring us out of his Protection, and waging War against us.

He has plundered our seas, ravaged our Coasts, burnt our towns, and destroyed the lives of our people.

He is at this time transporting large armies of foreign mercenaries to compleat the works of death, desolation and tyranny, already begun with circumstances of Cruelty and perfidy scarcely paralleled in the most barbarous ages, and totally unworthy the Head of a civilized nation.

He has constrained our fellow Citizens taken Captive on the high Seas to bear Arms against their Country, to become the executioners of their friends and Brethren, or to fall themselves by their Hands.

He has excited domestic insurrections amongst us, and has endeavoured to bring on the inhabitants of our frontiers, the merciless Indian Savages, whose known rule of warfare, is an undistinguished destruction of all ages, sexes and conditions.

In every stage of these Oppressions We have Petitioned for Redress in the most humble terms: Our repeated Petitions have been answered only by repeated injury. A Prince, whose character is thus marked by every act which may define a Tyrant, is unfit to be the ruler of a free People.

Nor have We been wanting in attentions to our British brethren. We have warned them from time to time of attempts by their legislature to extend an unwarrantable jurisdiction over us. We have reminded them of the circumstances of our emigration and settlement here. We have appealed to their native justice and magnanimity, and we have conjured them by the ties of our common kindred to disavow these usurpations which, would inevitably interrupt our connections and correspondence. They too have been deaf to the voice of justice and of consanguinity. We must, therefore, acquiesce in the necessity, which denounces our Separation, and hold them, as we hold the rest of mankind, Enemies in War, in Peace Friends.

We, therefore, the Representatives of the United States of America, in General Congress, Assembled, appealing to the Supreme Judge of the world for the rectitude of our intentions, do, in the Name, and by Authority of the good People of these Colonies, solemnly publish and declare, That these United Colonies are, and of Right ought to be Free and Independent States; that they are Absolved from all Allegiance to the British Crown, and that all political connection between them and the State of Great Britain, is and ought to be totally dissolved; and that, as Free and

Independent States, they have full Power to levy War, conclude Peace, contract Alliances, establish Commerce, and to do all other Acts and Things which Independent States may of right do. And for the support of this Declaration, with a firm reliance on the protection of Divine Providence, we mutually pledge to each other our Lives, our Fortunes and our sacred Honor.

THE CONSTITUTION OF THE UNITED STATES

WE THE PEOPLE OF THE UNITED STATES, IN ORDER TO FORM A MORE PERFECT UNION, ESTABLISH JUSTICE, INSURE DOMESTIC TRANQUILITY, PROVIDE FOR THE COMMON DEFENSE, PROMOTE THE GENERAL WELFARE, AND SECURE THE BLESSINGS OF LIBERTY TO OURSELVES AND OUR POSTERITY, DO ORDAIN AND ESTABLISH THIS CONSTITUTION FOR THE UNITED STATES OF AMERICA.

ARTICLE I

Section 1. All legislative Powers herein granted shall be vested in a Congress of the United States, which shall consist of a Senate and House of Representatives.

Section 2. The House of Representatives shall be composed of members chosen every second Year by the People of the several States, and the Electors in each State shall have the Qualifications requisite for Electors of the most numerous Branch of the State Legislature.

No person shall be a Representative who shall not have attained to the Age of twenty five Years, and been seven Years a Citizen of the United States, and who shall not, when elected, be an Inhabitant of that State in which he shall be chosen.

Representatives and direct Taxes shall be apportioned among the several States which may be included within this union, according to their respective Numbers, which shall be determined by adding to the whole Number of free Persons, including those bound to Service for a Term of Years, and excluding Indians not taxed, three fifths of all other Persons. The actual Enumeration shall be made within three Years after the first Meeting of the Congress of the United States, and within every subsequent Term of ten Years, in such Manner as they shall by Law direct. The Number of Representatives shall not exceed one for every thirty Thousand, but each State shall have at least one Representative; and until such enumeration shall be made, the State of New Hampshire shall be entitled to chuse three, Massachusetts eight, Rhode Island and Providence Plantations one, Connecticut five, New York six, New Jersey four, Pennsylvania eight, Delaware one; Maryland six, Virginia ten, North Carolina five, South Carolina five, and Georgia three.

When vacancies happen in the Representation from any State, the Executive Authority thereof shall issue Writs of Election to fill such Vacancies.

The House of Representatives shall chuse their Speaker and other Officers; and shall have the sole Power of Impeachment.

Section 3. The Senate of the United States shall be composed of two Senators from each State, chosen by the Legislature thereof, for six Years; and each Senator shall have one Vote.

Immediately after they shall be assembled in Consequence of the first Election, they shall be divided as equally as may be into three Classes. The Seats of the Senators of the first Class shall be vacated at the Expiration of the second Year, of the second Class at the Expiration of the fourth Year, and of the third Class at the Expiration of the sixth Year, so that one third may be chosen every second Year; and if Vacancies happen by Resignation, or otherwise, during the Recess of the Legislature of any State, the Executive thereof may make temporary Appointments until the next Meeting of the Legislature, which shall then fill such Vacancies.

No Person shall be a Senator who shall not have attained to the Age of thirty Years, and been nine Years a Citizen of the United States, and who shall not, when elected, be an Inhabitant of that State for which he shall be chosen.

The Vice President of the United States shall be President of the Senate, but shall have no Vote, unless they be equally divided.

The Senate shall chuse their other Officers, and also a President pro tempore, in the Absence of the Vice President, or when he shall exercise the Office of the President of the United States.

The Senate shall have the sole Power to try all Impeachments. When sitting for that

Purpose, they shall be on Oath or Affirmation. When the President of the United States is tried, the Chief Justice shall preside: And no Person shall be convicted without the Concurrence of two thirds of the Members present.

Judgment in Cases of Impeachment shall not extend further than to removal from Office, and disqualification to hold and enjoy any Office of honor, Trust or Profit under the United States: but the Party convicted shall nevertheless be liable and subject to Indictment, Trial, Judgment and Punishment, according to Law.

Section 4. The Times, Places and Manner of holding Elections for Senators and Representatives, shall be prescribed in each State by the Legislature thereof, but the Congress may at any time by Law make or alter such regulations, except as to the Places of chusing Senators.

The Congress shall assemble at least once in every Year, and such Meeting shall be on the first Monday in December, unless they shall by Law appoint a different Day.

Section 5. Each House shall be the Judge of the Elections, Returns and Qualifications of its own Members, and a Majority of each shall constitute a Quorum to do Business; but a smaller Number may adjourn from day to day, and may be authorized to compel the Attendance of absent Members, in such Manner, and under such Penalties as each House may provide.

Each House may determine the Rules for its Proceedings, punish its Members for disorderly Behaviour, and, with the Concurrence of two thirds, expel a Member.

Each House shall keep a Journal of its Proceedings, and from time to time publish the same, excepting such Parts as may in their Judgment require Secrecy; and the Yeas and Nays of the Members of either House on any question shall, at the Desire of one fifth of those Present, be entered on the Journal.

Neither House, during the Session of Congress, shall, without the Consent of the other, adjourn for more than three days, nor to any other Place than that in which the two Houses shall be sitting.

Section 6. The Senators and Representatives shall receive a Compensation for their Services, to be ascertained by Law, and paid out of the Treasury of the United States. They shall in all Cases, except Treason, Felony and Breach of the Peace, be privileged from Arrest during their Attendance at the Session of their respective Houses, and in going to and returning from the same; and for any Speech or Debate in either House, they shall not be questioned in any other Place.

No Senator or Representative shall, during the Time for which he was elected, be appointed to any civil Office under the Authority of the United States, which shall have been created, or the Emoluments whereof shall have been encreased during such time; and no Person holding any Office under the United States, shall be a Member of either House during his Continuance in Office.

Section 7. All Bills for raising Revenue shall originate in the House of Representatives; but the Senate may propose or concur with Amendments as on other bills.

Every Bill which shall have passed the House of Representatives and the Senate shall, before it become a Law, be presented to the President of the United States; If he approve he shall sign it, but if not he shall return it, with his Objections to that House in which it shall have originated, who shall enter the Objections at large on their Journal, and proceed to reconsider it. If after such Reconsideration two thirds of that House shall agree to pass the Bill, it shall be sent, together with the Objections, to the other House, by which it shall likewise be reconsidered, and if approved by two thirds of that House, it shall become a Law. But in all such Cases the Votes of both Houses shall be determined by Yeas and Nays, and the Names of the Persons voting for and against the Bill shall be entered on the Journal of each House respectively. If any Bill shall not be returned by the President within ten Days (Sundays excepted) after it shall have been presented to him, the Same shall be a Law, in like Manner as if he had signed it, unless the Congress by their Adjournment prevent its Return, in which Case it shall not be a Law.

Every Order, Resolution, or Vote to which the Concurrence of the Senate and House of

Representatives may be necessary (except on a question of Adjournment) shall be presented to the President of the United States; and before the Same shall take Effect, shall be approved by him, or being disapproved by him shall be repassed by two thirds of the Senate and House of Representatives, according to the rules and Limitations prescribed in the Case of a Bill.

Section 8.   The Congress shall have Power To lay and collect Taxes, Duties, Imposts and Excises, to pay the Debts and provide for the common Defence and general Welfare of the United States; but all Duties, Imposts and Excises shall be uniform throughout the United States;

To borrow Money on the credit of the United States;

To regulate Commerce with foreign Nations, and among the several States, and with the Indian Tribes;

To establish an uniform Rule of Naturalization, and uniform Laws on the subject of Bankruptcies throughout the United States;

To coin Money, regulate the Value thereof, and of foreign Coin, and fix the Standard of Weights and Measures;

To provide for the Punishment of counterfeiting the Securities and current Coin of the United States;

To establish Post Offices and post Roads;

To promote the Progress of Science and useful Arts, by securing for limited Times to Authors and Inventors the exclusive Right to their respective Writings and Discoveries;

To constitute Tribunals inferior to the supreme Court;

To define and punish Piracies and Felonies committed on the high Seas, and Offences against the Law of Nations;

To declare War, grant Letters of Marque and Reprisal, and make Rules concerning Captures on Land and Water;

To raise and support Armies, but no Appropriation of Money to that Use shall be for a longer Term than two Years;

To provide and maintain a Navy;

To make Rules for the government and Regulation of the land and naval Forces;

To provide for calling forth the Militia to execute the Laws of the Union, suppress Insurrections and repel Invasions;

To provide for organizing, arming, and disciplining, the Militia, and for governing such Part of them as may be employed in the Service of the United States, reserving to the States respectively, the Appointment of the Officers, and the Authority of training the Militia according to the discipline prescribed by Congress;

To exercise exclusive Legislation in all Cases whatsoever, over such District (not exceeding ten Miles square) as may, by Cession of particular States, and the Acceptance of Congress, become the Seat of the Government of the United States, and to exercise like Authority over all Places purchased by the consent of the Legislature of the State in which the Same shall be, for the Erection of Forts, Magazines, Arsenals, dock-Yards, and other needful Buildings;—And

To make all Laws which shall be necessary and proper for carrying into Execution the foregoing Powers, and all other Powers vested by this Constitution in the Government of the United States, or in any Department or Officer thereof.

Section 9.   The Migration or Importation of such Persons as any of the States now existing shall think proper to admit, shall not be prohibited by the Congress prior to the Year one thousand eight hundred and eight, but a Tax or duty may be imposed on such Importation, not exceeding ten dollars for each Person.

The Privilege of the Writ of Habeas Corpus shall not be suspended, unless when in Cases of Rebellion or Invasion the public Safety may require it.

No Bill of Attainder or ex post facto Law shall be passed.

No Capitation, or other direct, Tax shall be laid, unless in Proportion to the Census or Enumeration herein before directed to be taken.

No Tax or Duty shall be laid on Articles exported from any State.

No Preference shall be given by any Regulation of Commerce or Revenue to the Ports of one State over those of another: nor shall Vessels bound to, or from, one State, be obliged to enter, clear, or pay Duties in another.

No money shall be drawn from the Treasury, but in Consequence of Appropriations made by Law, and a regular Statement and Account of the Receipts and Expenditures of all public Money shall be published from time to time.

No Title of Nobility shall be granted by the United States: And no Person holding any Office of Profit or Trust under them, shall, without the Consent of the Congress, accept of any present, Emolument, Office, or Title, of any kind whatever, from any King, Prince, or foreign States.

Section 10.   No State shall enter into any Treaty, Alliance, or Confederation; grant Letters of Marque and Reprisal; coin Money; emit bills of Credit; make any Thing but gold and silver Coin a Tender in Payment of Debts; pass any Bill of Attainder, ex post facto Law, or Law impairing the Obligation of Contracts, or grant any Title of Nobility.

No state shall, without the Consent of the Congress, lay any Imposts or Duties on Imports or Exports, except what may be absolutely necessary for executing its inspection Laws: and the net Produce of all Duties and Imposts, laid by any State on Imports or Exports, shall be for the Use of the Treasury of the United States; and all such Laws shall be subject to the Revision and Control of the Congress.

No State shall, without the Consent of Congress, lay any Duty of Tonnage, keep Troops, or Ships of War in time of Peace, enter into any Agreement or Compact with another State, or with a foreign Power, or engage in War, unless actually invaded, or in such imminent Danger as will not admit of delay.

ARTICLE II

Section 1.   The executive Power shall be vested in a President of the United States of America. He shall hold his Office during the Term of four Years, and, together with the Vice President, chosen for the same Term, be elected, as follows:

Each State shall appoint, in such Manner as the Legislature thereof may direct, a Number of Electors, equal to the whole Number of Senators and Representatives to which the State may be entitled in the Congress: but no Senator or Representative, or Person holding an Office of Trust or Profit under the United States, shall be appointed an Elector.

The Electors shall meet in their respective States, and vote by Ballot for two Persons, of whom one at least shall not be an Inhabitant of the same State with themselves. And they shall make a List of all the Persons voted for, and of the Number of Votes for each; which List they shall sign and certify, and transmit sealed to the Seat of the Government of the United States, directed to the President of the Senate. The President of the Senate shall, in the Presence of the Senate and House of Representatives, open all the Certificates, and the Votes shall then be counted. The Person having the greatest Number of Votes shall be the President, if such Number be a Majority of the whole Number of Electors appointed; and if there be more than one who have such Majority, and have an equal Number of Votes, then the House of Representatives shall immediately chuse by Ballot one of them for President; and if no Person have a Majority, then from the five highest on the List the said House shall in like Manner chuse the President. But in chusing the President, the Votes shall be taken by States, the Representation from each State having one Vote; A quorum for this Purpose shall consist of a Member or Members from two thirds of the States, and a Majority of all the States shall be necessary to a Choice. In every Case, after the Choice of the President, the Person having the greatest Number of Votes of the Electors shall be the Vice President. But if there should remain two or more who have equal Votes, the Senate shall chuse from them by Ballot the Vice President.

The Congress may determine the Time of chusing the Electors and the Day on which they shall give their Votes; which Day shall be the same throughout the United States.

No Person except a natural born Citizen, or a Citizen of the United States, at the time of the Adoption of this Constitution, shall be eligible to the Office of President; neither shall any person be eligible to that Office who shall not have attained to the Age of thirty five Years, and been fourteen Years a Resident within the United States.

In case of the Removal of the President from Office, or of his Death, Resignation, or Inability to discharge the Powers and Duties of the said Office, the Same shall devolve on the Vice President, and the Congress may by Law provide for the Case of Removal, Death, Resignation or Inability, both of the President and Vice President, declaring what Officer shall then act as President, and such Officer shall act accordingly, until the Disability be removed, or a President shall be elected.

The President shall, at stated Times, receive for his Services, a Compensation, which shall neither be encreased nor diminished during the Period for which he shall have been elected, and he shall not receive within that Period any other Emolument from the United States, or any of them.

Before he enter on the Execution of his Office, he shall take the following Oath or Affirmation:—"I do solemnly swear (or affirm) that I will faithfully execute the Office of President of the United States, and will to the best of my Ability, preserve, protect and defend the Constitution of the United States."

Section 2. The President shall be Commander in Chief of the Army and Navy of the United States, and of the Militia of the several States, when called into the actual Service of the United States; he may require the Opinion, in writing, of the principal Officer in each of the executive Departments, upon any Subject relating to the Duties of their respective Offices, and he shall have Power to grant Reprieves and Pardons for Offences against the United States, except in cases of Impeachment.

He shall have Power, by and with the Advice and Consent of the Senate, to make Treaties, provided two thirds of the Senators present concur; and he shall nominate, and by and with the Advice and Consent of the Senate, shall appoint Ambassadors, other public Ministers and Consuls, Judges of the supreme Court, and all other Officers of the United States, whose Appointments are not herein otherwise provided for, and which shall be established by Law; but the Congress may by Law vest the Appointment of such inferior Officers, as they think proper, in the President alone, in the Courts of Law, or in the Heads of Departments.

The President shall have Power to fill up all Vacancies that may happen during the Recess of the Senate, by granting Commissions which shall expire at the End of their next Session.

Section 3. He shall from time to time give to the Congress Information of the State of the Union, and recommend to their Consideration such Measures as he shall judge necessary and expedient; he may, on extraordinary Occasions, convene both Houses, or either of them, and in Case of Disagreement between them, with respect to the Time of Adjournment, he may adjourn them to such Time as he shall think proper; he shall receive Ambassadors and other public Ministers; he shall take Care that the Laws be faithfully executed, and shall Commission all the Officers of the United States.

Section 4. The President, Vice President and all civil Officers of the United States, shall be removed from Office on Impeachment for, and Conviction of, Treason, Bribery, or other high Crimes and Misdemeanors.

ARTICLE III

Section 1. The judicial Power of the United States, shall be vested in one supreme Court, and in such inferior Courts as the Congress may from time to time ordain and establish. The Judges, both of the supreme and inferior Courts, shall hold their Offices during good Behaviour, and shall, at stated Times, receive for their Services, a Compensation, which shall not be diminished during their Continuance in Office.

Section 2. The judicial Power shall extend to all Cases, in Law and Equity, arising under this Constitution, the Laws of the United States, and Treaties made, or which shall be made, under their Authority;—to all Cases affecting Ambassadors, other public Ministers and Consuls;—

to all Cases of admiralty and maritime Jurisdiction;—to Controversies to which the United States shall be a Party;—to Controversies between two or more States;—between a State and Citizens of another State;—between Citizens of different States;—between Citizens of the same State claiming Lands under Grants of different States, and between a State, or the Citizens thereof, and foreign States, Citizens or Subjects.

In all Cases affecting Ambassadors, other public Ministers and Consols, and those in which a State shall be Party, the supreme Court shall have original Jurisdiction. In all the other Cases before mentioned, the supreme Court shall have appellate Jurisdiction, both as to Law and Fact, with such Exceptions, and under such Regulations as the Congress shall make.

The Trial of all Crimes, except in Cases of Impeachment, shall be by Jury; and such Trial shall be held in the State where the said Crimes shall have been committed; but when not committed within any State, the trial shall be at such Place or Places as the Congress may by Law have directed.

Section 3. Treason against the United States, shall consist only in levying War against them, or in adhering to their Enemies, giving them Aid and Comfort. No Person shall be convicted of Treason unless on the Testimony of two Witnesses to the same overt Act, or on Confession in open Court.

The Congress shall have Power to declare the Punishment of Treason, but no Attainder of Treason shall work Corruption of Blood, or Forfeiture except during the Life of the Person attainted.

ARTICLE IV

Section 1. Full Faith and Credit shall be given in each State to the public Acts, Records, and judicial Proceedings of every State. And the Congress may by general Laws prescribe the Manner in which such Acts, Records and Proceedings shall be proved, and the Effect thereof.

Section 2. The Citizens of each State shall be entitled to all Privileges and Immunities of Citizens in the several States.

A Person charged in any State with Treason, Felony, or other Crime, who shall flee from Justice, and be found in another State, shall on Demand of the executive Authority of the State from which he fled, be delivered up, to be removed to the State having Jurisdiction of the Crime.

No Person held to Service or Labour in one State, under the Laws thereof, escaping into another, shall, in Consequence of any Law or Regulation therein, be discharged from such Service or Labour, but shall be delivered up on Claim of the Party to whom such Service or Labour may be due.

Section 3. New States may be admitted by the Congress into this Union; but no new State shall be formed or erected within the Jursidiction of any other State, nor any State be formed by the Junction of two or more States, or Parts of States, without the Consent of the Legislatures of the States concerned as well as of the Congress.

The Congress shall have Power to dispose of and make all needful Rules and Regulations respecting the Territory or other Property belonging to the United States; and nothing in this Constitution shall be so construed as to Prejudice any Claims of the United States, or of any particular State.

Section 4. The United States shall guarantee to every State in this Union a Republican Form of Government, and shall protect each of them against Invasion; and on Application of the Legislature, or of the Executive (when the Legislature cannot be convened) against domestic Violence.

ARTICLE V

The Congress, whenever two thirds of both Houses shall deem it necessary, shall propose Amendments to this Constitution, or, on the Application of the Legislatures of two thirds of the several States, shall call a Convention for proposing Amendments, which, in either Case, shall be valid to all Intents and Purposes, as Part of this Constitution, when ratified by the Legislatures of three fourths of the several States, or by Conventions in three fourths thereof, as the one or the other Mode of Ratification may be proposed by the Congress; Provided that no Amendment which may be made prior to the Year One thousand eight hundred and eight shall in any Manner affect the first and fourth Clauses in the Ninth Section of the first Article; and that no State, without its Consent, shall be deprived of its equal Suffrage in the Senate.

ARTICLE VI

All Debts contracted and Engagements entered into, before the Adoption of this Constitution, shall be as valid against the United States under this Constitution, as under the Confederation.

This Constitution, and the Laws of the United States which shall be made in Pursuance thereof; and all Treaties made, or which shall be made, under the Authority of the United States, shall be the supreme Law of the Land; and the Judges in every State shall be bound thereby, any Thing in the Constitution of Laws of any State to the Contrary notwithstanding.

The Senators and Representatives before mentioned, and the Members of the several State Legislatures, and all executive and judicial Officers, both of the United States and of the several States, shall be bound by Oath or Affirmation, to support this Constitution; but no religious Test shall ever be required as a Qualification to any Office or public Trust under the United States.

ARTICLE VII

The Ratification of the Conventions of nine States, shall be sufficient for the Establishment of this Constitution between the States so ratifying the Same.

Done in Convention by the Unanimous Consent of the States present the Seventeenth Day of September in the Year of our Lord one thousand seven hundred and Eighty seven and of the Independence of the United States of America the Twelfth. In witness whereof We have hereunto subscribed our Names.

[The first 10 Amendments were ratified December 5, 1791, and form what is known as the Bill of Rights.]

AMENDMENT 1

Congress shall make no law respecting an establishment of religion, or prohibiting the free exercise thereof; or abridging the freedom of speech, or of the press; or the right of the people peaceably to assemble, and to petition the Government for a redress of grievances.

AMENDMENT 2

A well regulated Militia, being necessary to the security of a free State, the right of the people to keep and bear Arms shall not be infringed.

AMENDMENT 3

No Soldier shall, in time of peace, be quartered in any house, without the consent of the Owner, nor in time of war, but in a manner to be prescribed by Law.

AMENDMENT 4

The right of the people to be secure in their persons, houses, papers, and effects, against unreasonable searches and seizures, shall not be violated, and no Warrants shall issue, but upon probable cause, supported by Oath or affirmation, and particularly describing the place to be searched, and the persons or things to be seized.

AMENDMENT 5

No person shall be held to answer for a capital or otherwise infamous crime, unless on a presentment or indictment of a Grand Jury, except in cases arising in the land or naval forces, or in the Militia, when in actual service in time of War or public danger; nor shall any person be subject for the same offence to be twice put in jeopardy of life or limb; nor shall be compelled in any criminal case to be a witness against himself, nor be deprived of life, liberty, or property, without due process of law; nor shall private property be taken for public use, without just compensation.

AMENDMENT 6

In all criminal prosecutions, the accused shall enjoy the right to a speedy and public trial, by an impartial jury of the State and district wherein the crime shall have been committed, which district shall have been previously ascertained by law, and to be informed of the nature and cause of the accusation; to be confronted with the witnesses against him; to have compulsory process for obtaining witnesses in his favor, and to have the Assistance of Counsel for his defense.

AMENDMENT 7

In Suits at common law, where the value in controversy shall exceed twenty dollars, the right of trial by jury shall be preserved, and no fact tried by a jury, shall be otherwise reexamined in any Court of the United States, than according to the rules of the common law.

AMENDMENT 8

Excessive bail shall not be required, nor excessive fines imposed, nor cruel and unusual punishments inflicted.

AMENDMENT 9

The enumeration in the Constitution, of certain rights, shall not be construed to deny or disparage others retained by the people.

AMENDMENT 10

The powers not delegated to the United States by the Constitution; nor prohibited by it to the States, are reserved to the States respectively, or to the people.

AMENDMENT 11 [Ratified February 7, 1795]

The Judicial power of the United States shall not be construed to extend to any suit in law or equity, commenced or prosecuted against one of the United States by Citizens of another State, or by Citizens or Subjects of any Foreign State.

AMENDMENT 12 [Ratified July 27, 1804]

The Electors shall meet in their respective states and vote by ballot for President and Vice-President, one of whom, at least, shall not be an inhabitant of the same state with themselves; they shall name in their ballots the person voted for as President, and in distinct ballots the person voted for as Vice-President, and they shall make distinct lists of all persons voted for as President, and of all persons voted for as Vice-President, and of the number of votes for each, which lists they shall sign and certify, and transmit sealed to the seat of the government of the United States, directed to the President of the Senate;—The President of the Senate shall, in the presence of the Senate and House of Representatives, open all the certificates and the votes shall then be counted;—The person having the greatest number of votes for President, shall be the President, if such number be a majority of the whole number of Electors appointed; and if no person have such majority, then from the persons having the highest numbers not exceeding three on the list of those voted for as President, the House of Representatives shall choose immediately, by ballot, the President. But in choosing the President, the votes shall be taken by states, the representation from each state having one vote; a quorum for this purpose shall consist of a member or members from two-thirds of the states, and a majority of all the states shall be necessary to a choice. And if the House of Representatives shall not choose a President whenever the right of choice shall devolve upon them, before the fourth day of March next following, then the Vice-President shall act as President, as in the case of the death or other constitutional disability of the President.—The person having the greatest number of votes as Vice-President, shall be the Vice-President, if such number be a majority of the whole number of Electors appointed, and if no person have a majority, then from the two highest numbers on the list, the Senate shall choose the Vice-President; a quorum for the purpose shall consist of two-thirds of the whole number of Senators, and a majority of the whole number shall be necessary to a choice. But no person constitutionally ineligible to the office of President shall be eligible to that of Vice-President of the United States.

AMENDMENT 13 [Ratified December 6, 1865]

Section 1.   Neither slavery nor involuntary servitude, except as a punishment for crime whereof the party shall have been duly convicted, shall exist within the United States, or any place subject to their jurisdiction.

Section 2.   Congress shall have power to enforce this article by appropriate legislation.

AMENDMENT 14 [Ratified July 9, 1868]

Section 1.   All persons born or naturalized in the United States, and subject to the jurisdiction thereof, are citizens of the United States and of the State wherein they reside. No State shall make or enforce any law which shall abridge the privileges or immunities of citizens of the United States; nor shall any State deprive any person of life, liberty, or property, without due process of law; nor deny to any person within its jurisdiction the equal protection of the laws.

Section 2. Representatives shall be appointed among the several States according to their respective numbers, counting the whole number of persons in each State, excluding Indians not taxed. But when the right to vote at any election for the choice of electors for President and Vice-President of the United States, Representatives in Congress, the Executive and Judicial officers of a State, or the members of the Legislature thereof, is denied to any of the male inhabitants of such State, being twenty-one years of age, and citizens of the United States, or in any way abridged, except for participation in rebellion, or other crime, the basis of representation therein shall be reduced in the proportion which the number of such male citizens shall bear to the whole number of male citizens twenty-one years of age in such State.

Section 3. No person shall be a Senator or Representative in Congress, or elector of President and Vice-President, or hold any office, civil or military, under the United States, or under any State, who, having previously taken an oath, as a member of Congress, or as an officer of the United States, or as a member of any State legislature, or as an executive or judicial officer of any State, to support the Constitution of the United States, shall have engaged in insurrection or rebellion against the same, or given aid or comfort to the enemies thereof. But Congress may by a vote of two-thirds of each House, remove such disability.

Section 4. The validity of the public debt of the United States, authorized by law, including debts incurred for payment of pensions and bounties for services in suppressing insurrection or rebellion, shall not be questioned. But neither the United States nor any State shall assume or pay any debt or obligation incurred in aid of insurrection or rebellion against the United States, or any claim for the loss or emancipation of any slave; but all such debts, obligations, and claims shall be held illegal and void.

Section 5. The Congress shall have the power to enforce, by appropriate legislation, the provisions of this article.

AMENDMENT 15 [Ratified February 3, 1870]

Section 1. The right of citizens of the United States to vote shall not be denied or abridged by the United States or by any State on account of race, color, or previous condition of servitude.

Section 2. The Congress shall have power to enforce this article by appropriate legislation.

AMENDMENT 16 [Ratified February 3, 1913]

The Congress shall have power to lay and collect taxes on incomes, from whatever source derived, without apportionment among the several States, and without regard to any census or enumeration.

AMENDMENT 17 [Ratified April 8, 1913]

The Senate of the United States shall be composed of two Senators from each State, elected by the people thereof for six years; and each Senator shall have one vote. The electors in each State shall have the qualifications requisite for electors of the most numerous branch of the State legislatures.

When vacancies happen in the representation of any State in the Senate, the executive authority of such State shall issue writs of election to fill such vacancies: *Provided,* That the legislature of any State may empower the executive thereof to make temporary appointments until the people fill the vacancies by election as the legislature may direct.

This amendment shall not be so construed as to affect the election or term of any Senator chosen before it becomes valid as part of the Constitution.

AMENDMENT 18 [Ratified January 16, 1919]

Section 1. After one year from the ratification of this article the manufacture, sale, or transportation of intoxicating liquors within, the importation thereof into, or the exportation thereof from the United States and all territory subject to the jurisdiction thereof for beverage purposes is hereby prohibited.

Section 2. The Congress and the several States shall have concurrent power to enforce this article by appropriate legislation.

Section 3. This article shall be inoperative unless it shall have been ratified as an amendment to the Constitution by the legislatures of the several States, as provided in the Constitution, within seven years from the date of the submission hereof to the States by the Congress.

AMENDMENT 19 [Ratified August 18, 1920]

The right of citizens of the United States to vote shall not be denied or abridged by the United States or by any State on account of sex. Congress shall have power to enforce this article by appropriate legislation.

AMENDMENT 20 [Ratified January 23, 1933]

Section 1. The terms of the President and Vice President shall end at noon on the 20th day of January, and the terms of Senators and Representatives at noon on the 3d day of January, of the years in which such terms would have ended if this article had not been ratified; and the terms of their successors shall then begin.

Section 2. The Congress shall assemble at least once in every year, and such meeting shall begin at noon the 3d day of January, unless they shall by law appoint a different day.

Section 3. If, at the time fixed for the beginning of the term of the President, the President elect shall have died, the Vice President elect shall become President. If a President shall not have been chosen before the time fixed for the beginning of his term, or if the President elect shall have failed to qualify, then the Vice President elect shall act as President until a President shall have qualified; and the Congress may by law provide for the case wherein neither a President elect nor a Vice President elect shall have qualified, declaring who shall then act as President, or the manner in which one who is to act shall be selected, and such person shall act accordingly until a President or Vice President shall have qualified.

Section 4. The Congress may by law provide for the case of the death of any of the persons from whom the House of Representatives may choose a President whenever the right of choice shall have devolved upon them, and for the case of the death of any of the persons from whom the Senate may choose a Vice President whenever the right of choice shall have devolved upon them.

Section 5. Sections 1 and 2 shall take effect on the 15th day of October following the ratification of this article.

Section 6. This article shall be inoperative unless it shall have been ratified as an amendment to the Constitution by the legislatures of three-fourths of the several states within seven years from the date of its submission.

AMENDMENT 21 [Ratified December 5, 1933]

Section 1. The eighteenth article of amendment to the Constitution of the United States is hereby repealed.

Section 2. The transportation or importation into any State, Territory, or possession of the United States for delivery or use therein of intoxicating liquors, in violation of the laws thereof, is hereby prohibited.

Section 3. This article shall be inoperative unless it shall have been ratified as an amendment of the Constitution by conventions in the several States, as provided in the Constitution, within seven years from the date of the submission hereof to the States by the Congress.

AMENDMENT 22 [Ratified February 27, 1951]

Section 1. No person shall be elected to the office of the President more than twice, and no person who has held the office of President, or acted as President, for more than two years of a term to which some other person was elected President shall be elected to the office of the President more than once. But this Article shall not apply to any person holding the office of

President when this Article was proposed by the Congress, and shall not prevent any person who may be holding the office of President, or acting as President, during the term within which this Article becomes operative from holding the office of President or acting as President during the remainder of such term.

Section 2. This article shall be inoperative unless it shall have been ratified as an amendment to the Constitution by the legislatures of three-fourths of the several states within seven years from the date of its submission to the States by the Congress.

AMENDMENT 23 [Ratified March 29, 1961]

Section 1. The district constituting the seat of Government of the United States shall appoint in such manner as the Congress may direct:

A number of electors of President and Vice President equal to the whole number of Senators and Representatives in Congress to which the District would be entitled if it were a State, but in no event more than the least populous State; they shall be in addition to those appointed by the States, but they shall be considered, for the purposes of the election of President and Vice President, to be electors appointed by the State; and they shall meet in the District and perform such duties as provided by the twelfth article of amendment.

Section 2. The Congress shall have power to enforce this article by appropriate legislation.

AMENDMENT 24 [Ratified January 23, 1964]

Section 1. The right of citizens of the United States to vote in any primary or other election for President or Vice President, or for Senator or Representative in Congress, shall not be denied or abridged by the United States or any State by reason of failure to pay any poll tax or other tax.

Section 2. The Congress shall have power to enforce this article by appropriate legislation.

AMENDMENT 25 [Ratified February 10, 1967]

Section 1. In case of the removal of the President from office or of his death or resignation, the Vice President shall become President.

Section 2. Whenever there is a vacancy in the office of the Vice President, the President shall nominate a Vice President who shall take office upon confirmation by a majority vote of both Houses of Congress.

Section 3. Whenever the President transmits to the President pro tempore of the Senate and the Speaker of the House of Representatives his written declaration that he is unable to discharge the powers and duties of his office, and until he transmits to them a written declaration to the contrary, such powers and duties shall be discharged by the Vice President as Acting President.

Section 4. Whenever the Vice President and a majority of either the principal officers of the executive department or of such other body as Congress may by law provide, transmit to the President pro tempore of the Senate and the Speaker of the House of Representatives their written declaration that the President is unable to discharge the powers and duties of his office, the Vice President shall immediately assume the powers and duties of the office of Acting President.

Thereafter, when the President transmits to the President pro tempore of the Senate and the Speaker of the House of Representatives his written declaration that no inability exists, he shall resume the powers and duties of his office unless the Vice President and a majority of either the principal officers of the executive department or of such other body as Congress may by law provide, transmit within four days to the President pro tempore of the Senate and the Speaker of the House of Representatives their written declaration that the President is unable to discharge the powers and duties of his office. Thereupon Congress shall decide the issue, assembling within forty-eight hours for that purpose if not in session. If the Congress, within twenty-one days after receipt of the latter written declaration, or, if Congress is not in session, within twenty-one days after Congress is required to assemble, determines by two-thirds vote of both Houses that the President is unable to discharge the powers and duties of his office, the Vice President shall continue to discharge the same as Acting President; otherwise, the President shall resume the powers and duties of his office.

AMENDMENT 26 [Ratified June 30, 1971]

> **Section 1.** The right of citizens of the United States, who are eighteen years of age or older, to vote shall not be denied or abridged by the United States or by any State on account of age.

> **Section 2.** The Congress shall have power to enforce this article by appropriate legislation.

AMENDMENT 27 [Ratified May 18, 1992]

> No law varying the compensation for the services of the Senators and Representatives shall take effect, until an election of Representatives shall have intervened.

GLOSSARY

Absolutist position test The argument that the First Amendment means exactly what it says and cannot be qualified.

Administrative law Guidelines and rules established by executive branch agencies to implement and enforce acts of Congress.

Adversary journalism A type of journalism that views the government as an enemy to be distrusted.

Adversary process The basis for the American system of justice in which two sides oppose each other on a point of law.

Affirmative action The effort to remedy past discrimination against groups by providing them with legal advantages, thereby enabling them to compete more effectively with previously advantaged groups.

Amicus curiae brief Arguments from a third party in a case, who wishes to influence the decision of a court.

Appellate jurisdiction The right of a higher court to review decisions of lower courts.

Authoritarianism A form of government with an essentially pyramidal structure in which power is filtered down from and is monopolized by a small and privileged elite that permits no political challenge while allowing some individual freedom in nonpolitical activities.

Backgrounder A technique by which government officials provide information to reporters on condition it be published without attribution.

Bail Money posted as a guarantee that a person will appear in court at the proper time in exchange for release from jail.

Balancing of interests test The contention that the First Amendment freedom of speech guarantee should be weighed against the interests of society in maintaining order.

Bicameral legislature A two-house assembly usually including a lower house and an upper house with different forms of representation.

Bill of Rights The first ten amendments to the Constitution, which are explicit protections accorded to the individual citizen against government abuse.

Bills of attainder Legislative acts punishing persons without a trial (forbidden by the Constitution).

Bipartisanship Cooperation between the two major parties in legislative matters and executive actions.

Blanket primary A primary election in which all the candidates of all the parties appear on the same ballot.

Block grants Federal funds that a recipient government uses for any of a variety of purposes that fall under a general heading.

Built-in constituency A grassroots lobbying group that is "built into" the constituency of a member of Congress.

Bureaucracy An administrative system that implements policy pursuant to law, follows standardized procedures, and assigns specialized duties to its employees.

Cabinet An executive-branch group consisting of the vice president, the heads of the several executive departments, and any appointed officials the president chooses to add.

Capitalist model A political and economic system in which all the means of production are in private hands and the government does not normally interfere with economic decision making.

Categorical grant A matching grant that is available for only one category or type of project.

Caucus A relatively small group of active party members who meet to determine party nominees and policy; normally held at the precinct level.

Ceremonial president A head of state who performs basically non-political and symbolic functions.

Checks and balances A cross-checking arrangement by which each of the three branches carefully observes the activities of the others in order to guarantee their constitutionality.

Civil law The body of law pertaining to disputes between individuals or organizations.

Civil liberties Those rights that all citizens have that protect them from arbitrary actions by government.

Civil rights Protections that government is expected to extend to individuals, regardless of their racial, gender, or ethnic characteristics, to ensure that all citizens are treated equally under the laws.

Civil service The system that employs government workers chosen on the basis of ability.

Clean bill A redrafted bill after a congressional committee has radically altered it.

Clear and present danger test The contention that speech loses its constitutional protection if it presents a danger to public welfare.

Clientelism The special relationship between industries and the federal commissions that regulate them.

Closed primary An election in which only registered members of a particular party participate.

Closed rule A rule that prevents any amendment from being offered to a bill on the House floor.

Cloture A means of terminating debate in the Senate if 60 members vote to do so.

Coalition government The control of a government by two or more political parties.

Common law A body of law made by judges as they decide cases.

Communism An economic and political system in which the entire society is coordinated and monitored by a government whose actions are both authorized and justified by the Communist party.

Communist model An economic and political system in which the government owns all farms and industries and rigidly controls all economic decision making.

Comparable worth The requirement that positions with comparable skill levels and responsibilities receive comparable pay.

Competitive federalism A sys-tem under which the states and the federal government compete for political power; characterized the United States prior to the Civil War.

Concurrent powers Those powers that belong to both the national and state governments.

Concurrent resolution A proposal in Congress that requires action of both houses and expresses their opinion.

Concurring opinion Opinion delivered by an individual justice who may agree with a court's majority decision for his or her own reasons.

Confederation A political system in which the central government exists only at the sufferance of the constituent governments, and its powers are limited by the confederated states.

Conference committee A joint committee in Congress appointed to reconcile differences in a bill; usually consisting of ranking members from the House and Senate committees that handled a bill earlier.

Conservative One who favors a more limited government and places a high value on individual liberty.

Constitutional democracy A system in which basic laws allow majority rule while protecting minority rights and individual freedoms and promoting the general interest.

Constitutional law A body of law based on the Constitution and court decisions that interpret and apply it.

Containment The American government's policy to "contain" the spread of Soviet influence in various regions of the world.

Convention A meeting of party delegates who select party nominees and determine policy; can be held at county, state, and national levels.

Cooperative federalism A system under which money and regulations are the domain of the national government while execution and administration are in the hands of state and local governments; characterized the United States from the 1940s to the 1980s.

Countervailing force An interest group that acts as a check on another group's lobbying efforts, such as labor on business (and vice versa).

Criminal law The body of law pertaining to crimes against the government or the public welfare.

Dangerous tendency test The contention that speech loses its constitutional protection if it tends to lead to a substantive evil or danger.

Dealignment A situation that occurs when voters avoid identifying with either major political party.

Delegate A type of legislator who tries to determine what constituents want and votes accordingly.

Democracy A form of government created by and responsible to the people it serves, ensuring equal and universal application of civil liberties, laws, and political leaders chosen through regularly scheduled elections in which adult citizens participate.

Democratization The process of establishing a democratic political culture.

Détente The relaxation of tensions between the United States and the Soviet Union through finding areas of common agreement, such as arms control and disarmament; characterized United States foreign policy in the 1970s.

Deviating election An election in which the minority party wins the presidency on a short-term basis.

Direct democracy A system of government that directly involves all adult citizens in decision making.

Directive public opinion Opinion that plays a large role in the decisions of public officials; can be a consensus for or against an action of government.

Discharge petition A petition that when signed by a majority of House members can bring a bill dead in committee before the full House.

Dissenting opinion An opinion delivered by a justice who disagrees with a court's majority opinion.

Distributive policy Domestic public policy that is used to encourage private citizens and companies to perform or not perform certain functions.

Divided government The situation in which one party controls Congress and the other party controls the presidency.

Divine law The idea that all humans have rights because they are creatures of God and that all human-made or reasoned law must be subscribed to divine precedent in order to be legitimate.

Division of power An arrangement whereby power is divided between the national and state governments in the American federal structure.

Divisive public opinion Active public opinion that is sharply divided on what government should do.

Double jeopardy The situation that occurs when an accused person is tried twice for the same offense (forbidden by the Constitution).

Dual federalism A system in which the states and the central government act separately and independently of each other, within their respective spheres; characterized the United States from the Civil War to 1937.

Due process of law The constitutional protection against arbitrary deprivation of life, liberty, or property.

Economic democracy A system that emphasizes collective or governmental ownership of the means of production and distribution of goods and services.

Elastic clause A phrase in Article I of the Constitution that has been construed to "stretch" national powers.

Electoral college The constitutionally prescribed means by which electors chosen from each state formally elect the winning presidential and vice presidential candidates.

Electronic democracy The means by which issues can be debated and voted on nationwide using communication and media technology.

Elitism The notion that in every society it is inevitable that a small group (usually between 1 and 10 percent of society's members) eventually comes to dominate the power structure.

Emerging interest group A newer lobbying group countering an older group, such as environmentalists versus industrial interests.

Establishment clause Clause in the First Amendment which guarantees that the United States government will not support a particular church or theological doctrine.

Ethno-nationalism The expression of a nationalist identity by a subgroup in an overall political society.

European Economic Community An economic union of European nations created to foster free trade.

Exclusionary rule Legal principle holding that evidence is inadmissible in federal and state criminal trials if it is obtained in an "unreasonable search and seizure."

Executive agreement An understanding between the president and another head of government on policies to be taken by each other's government; has the legal status of a treaty but does not require Senate approval.

Executive Office of the President The staff arm of the presidency that deals with various national problems.

Executive privilege An assertion of the right of the president to withhold information, documents, or testimony from either Congress or the courts in the interest of national security or the proper functioning of the executive branch.

Ex post facto laws Laws that enable the government to punish acts that were legal when committed; such laws are unconstitutional in the United States.

Express powers Those powers specifically enumerated in the Constitution as belonging to the national government.

Fairness doctrine Standards established by the Federal Communications Commission to ensure that broadcasters report fairly all sides of community issues; repealed in 1987.

Fascist model A political system in which the government is politically supreme and does not tolerate dissent, but does allow private ownership in the economic system.

Federalism A system of government in which powers are divided between a central government and constituent governments in a manner that provides each with substantial power and functions.

Filibuster Continuous debate used in the Senate as a device to talk a bill to death.

Foreign aid An American program that offers a variety of economic, social, and educational aid programs intended to assist developing nations in improving their living standards.

Frank The free-mailing privilege enjoyed by members of Congress.

Free exercise clause Clause in the First Amendment that guarantees the right to practice any religious activity (or not to practice any).

General election The election that fills the public office.

Gerrymandering The practice by state legislatures of drawing congressional district lines along party lines in order to favor one political party over another.

Government The formal social instrument through which conflicts that arise among individuals or groups are partially or wholly resolved.

Grandfather clause Laws that were adopted in several states which prevented anyone from voting whose grandfather had not voted before the Civil War.

Habeas corpus A court order directing an official who has a person in custody to bring the prisoner to court and show cause for that person's detention; a protection against arbitrary arrest and imprisonment.

Ideological center The moderate position between the ideological extremes of the left and right.

Impeachment A process by which certain federal officials (including the president) can be removed from office for crimes and misdemeanors: The House of Representatives brings charges and the Senate tries the official.

Imperial presidency The notion that the chief executive is increasingly removed from and is out of touch with the real common problems of the country; can lead to unlawful acts.

Implied powers Those powers of the national government inferred from the "elastic" clause of Article I, Section 8.

Impoundment A procedure by which the president refuses to spend certain funds appropriated by Congress in a given fiscal year.

Incrementalism The process by which a bureaucratic unit requests an increase over the previous year's budget and does so every year.

Independents Voters who do not affiliate with a political party, but support individual candidates on the basis of their views and policies.

Inherent powers Certain powers the national government may exercise by virtue of its position.

Initiative An electoral procedure permitting the public to put propositions on the ballot and vote on them.

Instantaneous democracy Any country whose democratic political institutions did not evolve but were created full-blown and immediately put in place.

Interest group An organized group representing a special segment of society that seeks to influence government policy directly affecting its members.

Interposition A procedure by which a state tries to impede a federal law through interposing its own authority.

Interstate compact An agreement through which two or more states with a common interest or problem establish a legally binding solution.

Investigative reporter A journalist who searches through the activities of public organizations seeking to expose conduct contrary to the public interest.

Iron triangle A close relationship among special interests, congressional committees, and the bureaucracy.

Isolationism The idea that American overseas interests, especially military, are minimal and do not require involvement in foreign affairs.

Issue networks Groups composed of persons inside and outside of government who are interested in the same issues.

Joint committee A congressional committee that includes both House and Senate members.

Joint resolution A proposal passed by both houses of Congress that has the force of law but does not require the president's signature.

Judicial activism A process by which the Supreme Court plays a vigorous role in trying to bring about social change.

Judicial notice The tendency of the Supreme Court to take note of other facts not provided in a case itself while ruling on the case.

Judicial policy-making The practice of setting policy by means of Court decisions.

Judicial restraint The avoidance of the urge to set public policy through Court decisions.

Judicial review The Court's ability to declare acts of the executive and legislative branches of government on both the state and national levels unconstitutional.

Junketing Travel taken ostensibly on government business, but in reality for pleasure at government expense.

Jurisdiction The types of cases that a court may decide.

Justiciable issue An issue that can be decided by the law.

Keynesian economics An economic policy allowing the government to spend and tax in a way that produces deficit budgets in economic bad times and surplus budgets in good times.

Laissez faire The practice of allowing the private sector to function without interference from the government.

Lame duck One who has not been elected to a new term but is still in office during the interregnum between election day and inauguration; also, someone in office who cannot be reelected because of term limitations.

Laws The rules that form the basis of politics.

Legislative veto A procedure used by Congress to "veto" federal administrative regulations that violate congressional intent.

Legitimacy The means by which governments justify their existence and which may be based on ideology, theology, or free elections.

Liberal One who favors a strong and active government and places a high value on equality.

Libertarianism A strong belief in the autonomy of the individual and as small a role as possible for government.

Line item veto A device that allows an executive to eliminate individual items in a bill without having to veto the entire bill.

Literacy test Test requiring citizens to have a minimum knowledge of American government before registering to vote.

Lobbyist A representative of an interest group that seeks to influence government policy.

Loyal opposition The party(ies) out of power in a democratic system whose job it is to be critical of government policies considered to be in error.

Maintaining election An election in which the status quo between the parties continues: The party in power stays in power.

Majority opinion Opinion delivered by the senior justice on the prevailing side of a court case.

Majority party The party in a two-party system with the largest following and votes.

Majority rule A democratic principle whereby the people make their decisions (either on their own or through representatives) based on the wishes of the majority or plurality.

Mass media All the forms of communication that bring messages to the public.

Matching grants Federal funds earmarked for a specific purpose; the state government is required to match certain portions of the federal grant.

Maverick A legislator with unorthodox (but not necessarily unpopular) positions who challenges congressional leadership on important issues.

Merit system The process by which government employees are hired on the basis of merit and protected against arbitrary firing.

Minority opinion Opinion delivered by the senior justice on the losing side of a court case.

Minority party The party in a two-party system with the second-largest following.

Minority rights A democratic principle that allows a minority the

rights to unencumbered and continued existence, expression of its points of view, and the opportunity to become the majority at the next election.

Mixed model A political and economic system that combines both socialist and capitalist elements.

Modified closed rule A rule that allows amendments on only certain portions of a bill debated in the House.

Muckraking The overzealous investigation of public issues, especially in the area of political corruption.

Multimember district An electoral district in which two or more representatives are chosen to represent constituents.

Multinationalism The presence of several national or ethnic communities within a single jurisdiction.

Multiple access points The means by which a citizen can work to influence governmental decisions through a variety of government levels (local, state, national) as well as through the legislative, executive, and judicial branches.

National preemption A political doctrine holding that a national action precludes a state action.

Natural law The idea that humanity possesses absolute rights on which no government can trample and requires all human laws to conform with natural law to be legal; adhered to by those who believe that humans have rights just because they are human and not necessarily because their existence is divinely endorsed.

Neoconservatism A political point of view adhering to democratic social welfare policies but rejecting reduction in military power and excessive emphasis on equal rights.

Nepotism The practice of hiring a near relative on the government payroll.

Network An informal group of people known to one another who communicate on policy ideas of common interest.

New world order The idea that collective policymaking by the nations of the world through the United Nations could maintain peace and enforce standards of human rights in the post-Communist world.

Nullification The procedure by which a state disregards (by declaring null and void) a federal law within its boundaries.

Ombudsman An office established to make the bureaucracy more responsive to average citizens' needs.

Open primary A primary election in which independent voters can participate in either party's primary and Republicans and Democrats can cross over.

Open rule A rule that allows amendments to be offered to a bill on the House floor.

Original jurisdiction The cases that come directly to a court and not as the result of an appeal.

Parliamentary system A democratic form of government in which the executive is recruited from an elected legislature rather than being separate from it.

Partition The division of a territory or already existing state into two or more sovereign parts.

Party boss A strong party leader in a big city.

Party discipline The consistent support of the policies of the party leadership by rank and file party members in a legislature.

Party platform The policy positions on which a candidate or party runs for office.

Party-state A system in which the state functions as the agent of a singe totalitarian party.

Patronage system A system of awarding government positions to the party faithful.

Per curiam decision A decision issued by a court without a written opinion.

Permissive public opinion Uninformed or unaroused opinion on the part of the public that enables government to have a free hand in decision making.

Plea bargaining The procedure by which a plaintiff pleads guilty to a lesser charge in exchange for a reduced sentence.

Plebiscite An electoral procedure used by a government to ask the public to vote yea or nay on a particular issue.

Pluralism The notion that public policy results from compromises made between and among competing groups of people.

Pocket veto A device used by a president to veto a bill by taking no action on it within a ten-day period while Congress is adjourned.

Political action committee (PAC) The financial lobbying arm of an interest group.

Political consensus National agreement on the kind of political institutions a country should have.

Political culture A society's widely shared ideas about how government and politics should function.

Political democracy A political system in which government's primary objective is to ensure the political freedom of individuals through such guarantees as the freedoms of religion, speech, press, and assembly, as well as the right to vote.

Political ideology A society's ideas as to what the political process should accomplish or do.

Political megalomania A form of psychotic madness associated with dictators who become intoxicated with power.

Political party An organization that selects and sponsors candidates for office under the party name.

Political self-righteousness A term used to describe those regimes that refuse to submit their programs to either criticism or to the electorate.

Political socialization The process of public opinion formation beginning in childhood that teaches about the political culture and instills fundamental civic virtues.

Politico A type of legislator who votes as a trustee on some issues and as a delegate on others.

Politics The method by which societies decide how to allocate values and distribute valued resources that are usually in short supply.

Polls Surveys of public opinion.

Poll tax A tax required of registered voters before they may vote.

Populism The belief that average citizens must be aroused to fight for changes in public policies in the face of an unresponsive government.

Pork barrel The practice of loading down legislation with something for most, if not all, members of Congress.

Preferred position test The contention that First Amendment freedoms have the highest priority in the constitutional hierarchy; any restrictions must have some overriding justification.

Presidential preference primary A primary election that records only a preference for a presidential candidate and is not binding on party delegates.

Presumed constitutionality The idea that a law is presumed to be constitutional as long as there is an interpretation by which it can be declared valid.

Primary Election in which all party members are allowed to vote for a nominee for a general election.

Prior restraint The procedure by which government can prevent the publication or broadcast of forbidden material.

Private bill A bill in Congress that concerns the private interests of an individual or corporation, such as a financial claim against the government.

Program budgeting An organizational technique requiring agencies to budget their programs before requesting new programs and appropriations.

Project grants Funds from the national government that bypass state governments and are placed directly on target with local governmental authorities.

Proportional representation An electoral system in which a political party receives a number of legislative seats in proportion to the percentage of popular votes it receives.

Prospective voting The practice of casting a vote on the basis of how well one believes his or her choice will perform in the future.

Public bill A bill in Congress that deals with matters of concern to the general population.

Public interest group An organized group that represents the general public on a wide range of issues and typically has no economic self-interest at stake.

Public opinion Opinion that relates to government and its activities.

Public policy The government's response to a public issue or problem whereby it establishes a goal and makes decisions to achieve that goal.

Random sample A sample of the population being surveyed that is intended to be representative of that population.

Realigning election An election in which the minority party comes to the fore to assume a long-lasting majority position.

Redistributive policy Domestic public policy that is used to help one segment of society at the expense of another.

Referendum An electoral procedure allowing the public to vote on legislative actions.

Regulatory policy Domestic public policy that specifies how private individuals or groups may conduct themselves.

Reinstating election An election in which the majority party returns to its dominant position after short-term losses of the presidency.

Representative democracy A system of government in which the electorate chooses representatives to make its decisions. (Also known as indirect democracy.)

Republic A political system in which representative democracy is the accepted form of government.

Reserved powers Those powers belonging to the states alone, including the right to regulate local governments and to maintain the public health, welfare, safety, and morals.

Retrospective voting The practice of casting a vote on the basis of one's opinion of the candidates' records.

Revenue sharing A flexible form of federal funding that returns a portion of national government revenue to state and local governments for discretionary use.

Reverse discrimination A situation that occurs when the law favors disadvantaged groups, giving them preference over other groups in such matters as employment.

Revolving door The practice of high-level bureaucrats moving in and out of government and the private sector, providing less than objective analysis for policymaking.

Safe seat A congressional district in which the representative has little or no competition for the office.

Secession A process by which a constituent part of a country withdraws in order to establish its own sovereignty.

Secular state A political system in which separation of church and state is scrupulously enforced, and religious and other associations are distinctly submissive to legitimate political authority.

Select committee A congressional committee established to explore a subject of extraordinary interest, such as aging or hunger in America.

Selective incorporation The gradual application of specific portions of the Bill of Rights to the states.

Selective perception The tendency to listen to viewpoints with which one is already in agreement.

Self-incrimination The situation that occurs when an accused person is forced to testify against him- or herself (forbidden by the Constitution).

Senatorial courtesy A custom that allows senators of the president's party to exercise veto power over presidential appointments in their states.

Seniority system A procedure used in Congress by which the committee chair usually goes to the person from the majority party with the greatest continuous service on the committee.

Separate but equal doctrine The notion that segregation of the races is constitutional if the separate public facilities are equal; illegal since 1954.

Separation of powers A political arrangement that makes the three branches of government—legislative, executive, and judicial—co-equal.

Shared powers An arrangement by which the federal and state governments have some powers in common, such as taxation.

Simple resolution A proposal in Congress that requires the action of only one house, does not have the force of law, and simply expresses the opinion of that house.

Single-issue group An interest group that cares only about one issue, such as abortion.

Single-member district An electoral district that allows the election of only one candidate to represent constituents.

Socialist model A political and economic system that attempts to maximize economic security for the individual but also allows both private and public ownership of industries.

Special publics Segments of the public with views about particular questions of public concern.

Split public opinion When public opinion is divided without much middle ground on such controversial issues as abortion.

Standing committee A permanent congressional committee that continues its work from one session to the next.

Stare decisis The principle by which judges render decisions using decisions from earlier similar cases as precedents.

States' rights The point of view that the Constitution provides the national government with very limited authority; any conflict between the national government and the states should be resolved in favor of the latter.

Statutory law Bills passed by a legislature and signed into law.

Suffrage The voting franchise.

Sunset law A law providing for the automatic abolition of a governmental agency after a prescribed time period unless there are good reasons for continuing it.

Supply-side economics An economic policy calling for reduced taxes in order to enable Americans to retain more of their earnings to save and invest, thus stimulating the economy.

Supportive public opinion Active public opinion that upholds the decisions of government officials.

Supremacy clause A clause in Article VI of the Constitution declaring that the Constitution and the laws and treaties adopted pursuant to it are the highest law of the land and take precedence over state laws.

Third party A minor party that has no chance to win national elections but does occasionally win a state or local election.

Ticket-splitting The practice of splitting one's vote among candidates of different political parties for different offices.

Torts Lawsuits in which an injured person attempts to recover money for damages.

Totalitarianism A form of government in which the state controls nearly every aspect of an individual's life.

Trustee A type of legislator who attempts to work out a position through factual analysis and conscience, even though that position

may conflict with constituent interests.

Two-party system A political system in which two major parties can count on regularly winning elections.

Unanimous consent agreement A device used to expedite action in the Senate; leaders agree to procedures for debating and voting on a bill and then request the membership to accept the agreement.

Unicameral legislature A one-house legislature.

Unitary government A form of government in which all political power is placed in the central government; subordinate units have only as much authority as the central government allows.

Universe The community whose views are being sought by pollsters.

Veto Presidential refusal to sign bills passed by the Congress.

Vote of no confidence A vote taken by legislatures in parliamentary systems when the executive can no longer command a majority of legislators to support government policy; results in a new election or selection of a new government by the majority party.

Whistle-blowers Those individuals who try to reveal (and in doing so, risk their livelihoods) an impropriety in a government agency.

White primary A device used by the Democratic party in southern states that declared the party a private club and that only its members could vote in primaries to nominate candidates for office.

Writ of certiorari A request from justices in a higher court to a lower court to send up a case's record for review.

Writ of habeas corpus A requirement that an arresting officer show adequate grounds for jailing or imprisoning a person.

Zero-based budgeting A device that forces an agency to justify the previous year's budget before seeking an increase.

CREDITS

Page 2, Christopher Smith/Impact Visuals; *5*, Tom Wagner/SABA; *7*, Robert Harbison/*The Christian Science Monitor*; *13*, Chester Higgins/NYT Pictures; *15*, Stock Boston; *18*, Reuters/UPI/Bettmann; *28*, Steve Benson for *U.S. News & World Report*; *32*, Chuck Nacke/Picture Group; *38*, Bob Daemmrich/Stock Boston; *41*, Thomas Ames, Jr./f/Stop Pictures, Inc.; *44*, New York Public Library, Astor, Lenox and Tilden Foundations; *47*, Brad Markel/Gamma-Liaison; *49*, UPI/Bettmann; *57*, UPI/Bettmann; *63*, Reuters/UPI/Bettmann; *72*, Michael Geissinger; *77*, Gift of Colonel and Mrs. Edgar W. Garbisch/Virginia Museum of Fine Arts, Richmond; *87 (left)*, Anonymous Collection; *87 (right)*, Culver Pictures; *92*, Walter Neal/Copyrighted, Chicago Tribune Company, all rights reserved; *97*, UPI/Bettmann; *102*, Paul Conklin; *105*, Christine Spengler/Sygma; *110*, Rick Smolan/ Against All Odds; *114*, UPI/Bettmann; *116*, Massachusetts Cammandry Military Order of the Loyal Legion and the U.S. Military History Institute; *123*, Spencer Grant/Stock Boston; *125*, Independence Historical Park Collection/Eastern National Parks and Monuments Association; *132*, Boroff/ TexaStock; *135*, AP/Wide World; *146*, UPI/Bettmann; *149*, Jerry Tomaselli/Copyrighted, Chicago Tribune Company, all rights reserved; *154*, Library of Congress; *158*, Reprinted with permission, Copley News Service; *161*, Cham/SIPA-Press; *166*, Tass/SOVFOTO; *172*, Bob McNeil/JB Pictures Ltd.; *176*, *Santa Barbara News-Press*/Steve Malone; *178*, Shelly Katz/Black Star; *180*, Reprinted by permission: Tribune Media Services; *195*, Reuters/UPI/Bettmann; *197*, *Palm Beach Post*/Don Wright; *203*, Reuters/UPI/Bettmann; *212*, Jerome Friar/Impact Visuals; *215*, Michelle Agins/NYT Pictures; *224*, Reuters/UPI/Bettmann; *226*, UPI/Bettmann; *232*, Patricia Hollander Gross/Stock Boston; *235*, Charles Caratine/Sygma; *238*, World Wildlife Fund; *248*, Paul Conklin; *257*, Bob Daemmrich/ Stock Boston; *264*, Paul Conklin; *270*, Dirck Halstead/Gamma-Liaison; *274*, Paul Hosefros/NYT Pictures; *283*, Albert Facelly/SIPA-Press; *290*, Reuters/UPI/Bettmann; *292*, Moir/*Sydney Morning Herald*; *302*, Larry Downing/Sygma; *308*, Brad Markel/Gamma-Liaison; *314*, AP/Wide World; *325*, Luigi Baldelli/SABA; *338*, The White House/Sygma; *343 (top left)*, Paul Hosefros/NYT Pictures; *343 (top right)*, Agence France-Presse Photo; *343 (bottom left)*, Jose Lopez/NYT Pictures; *343 (bottom right)*, AP/Wide World; *347*, The Franklin D. Roosevelt Library; *353*, Reuters/UPI/Bettmann; *359*, Allan Tannenbaum/Sygma; *362*, Photo by Y. R. Okamoto/Courtesy Lyndon Baines Johnson Library, Austin, TX; *366*, Tiziou/Sygma; *372*, Press Association; *378*, J. Richards/Agence France-Presse Photo; *384*, David Burnett/Contact Press Images; *393*, The Bettmann Archive; *402*, UPI/Bettmann; *405*, Reprinted by permission: Tribune Media Services; *410*, Peter Jordon/Gamma-Liaison; *420*, Sandra Baker/Gamma-Liaison; *425*, AP/Wide World; *441*, Jose Lopez/NYT Pictures; *443*, Courtesy, Office of Senator Paul Simon; *451*, Drawing by Mankoff; © 1992 The New Yorker Magazine, Inc.; *459*, Adam Woolfitt/Woodfin Camp & Associates; *463*, By MOCHALOV in Izvestia (Moscow)/ C&W Syndicate; *478*, Dennis Brack/Black Star; *483*, Paul Conklin; *488*, AP/Wide World; *492*, Susan May Tell/SABA; *499*, Reuters/UPI/Bettmann; *503*, The Bettmann Archive; *508*, James Nubile/JB Pictures Ltd.; *514*, Bryce Flynn/Picture Group; *518*, Michael Geissinger; *522*, Roger Malloch/Magnum Photos; *527*, Jose Lopez/NYT Pictures; *529*, Taylor-Fabricius/Gamma-Liaison; *531*, Carrie Boretz/NYT Pictures; *545*, Diego Goldberg/Sygma; *547*, J. P. Laffont/Sygma; *556*, Dirck Halstead/Gamma-Liaison; *559*, Handelsman for *The Times-Picayune*, New Orleans; *562*, Brown Brothers; *570*, Angel Franco/NYT Pictures; *576*, AP/Wide World; *579*, Ted Soqui/Sygma; and *591*, Alfred Gregory/Camera Press/Globe Photos, Inc.

INDEX